THE BUDDHIST MONASTERY

THE BUDDHIST MONASTERY

A cross-cultural survey

Edited by Pierre Pichard
and François Lagirarde

ÉCOLE FRANÇAISE
D'EXTRÊME-ORIENT

Silkworm Books

ISBN: 978-616-215-068-5

This edition is published by
Silkworm Books
6 Sukkasem Road, T. Suthep
Chiang Mai 50200 Thailand
info@silkwormbooks.com
http://www.silkwormbooks.com

THE EFEO-SILKWORM BOOKS SERIES is an innovative new series of research work on Asia, a collaboration between the École Française d'Extrême-Orient (EFEO) and Silkworm Books to translate French publications for an English-language readership. The Ninth Panchen Lama (1883–1937) is the first publication in the EFEO-Silkworm Books Series.

Printed in Thailand by O. S. Printing House, Bangkok

5 4 3 2 1

CONTENTS

Contributors

Olivier de Bernon
École française d'Extrême-Orient, Phnom Penh

Isabelle Charleux
Centre national de la recherche scientifique, Paris

Ashley De Vos
Architect, Colombo

Louis Gabaude
École française d'Extrême-Orient, Chiang Mai

Vincent Goossaert
Centre national de la recherche scientifique, Paris

Corneille Jest
Centre national de la recherche scientifique, Paris

Hiraoka Jōkai
Tōdaiji, Nara

Karma Wangchuk
Special Commission for Cultural Affairs, Thimphu

Kim Dong-uk
Department of Architecture, Kyonggi University

François Lagirarde
École française d'Extrême-Orient, Bangkok

Michel Lorrillard
École française d'Extrême-Orient, Vientiane

Min Bahadur Shakya
Nagarjuna Institute of Exact Methods, Patan

Pierre Pichard
École française d'Extrême-Orient, Bangkok

Françoise Pommaret
Centre national de la recherche scientifique, Paris

Christophe Pottier
École française d'Extrême-Orient, Siem Reap

François Robinne
Centre national de la recherche scientifique – Irsea, Marseille

Thada Sutthitham
Faculty of Architecture, Khon Kaen University

Wiroj Srisuro
Faculty of Architecture, Khon Kaen University

List of maps

INTRODUCTION

In 1997 a rather ambitious research program was initiated by the Bangkok branch of the École française d'Extrême-Orient: the comparative survey of the Buddhist monastery throughout Asia. The program included field surveys, the compilation of bibliographies, and a workshop. The latter was organized from November 8th to 10th, 1999, at the Princess Maha Chakri Sirindhorn Anthropology Centre in Bangkok. It brought together twenty contributors, including architects, historians, and specialists in Buddhist studies.

The present volume is the outcome of this workshop. The original papers have been thoroughly revised and some new contributions have been added. We have attempted to make this first overview as comprehensive as possible, with contributions ranging India to Japan and from the beginnings of Buddhism to the present. Nonetheless, we regret that there are four conspicuous omissions: the records of Buddhist remains in Afghanistan and Indonesia on one hand, and surveys of monasteries in Mongolia and Vietnam on the other.

Given the constraints of space, the presentation of the monastery in each country is necessarily brief, and may appear rather basic to specialists in the countries in question. We feel, however, that the juxtaposition of studies of monasteries in several Buddhist cultures can generate an appreciation of local developments in broader contexts, and bring into relief parallels and borrowings, constancies and variances.

A tentative framework, sent to participants in advance of the workshop, concentrated on the spatial layout of the monastery and on its architectural configuration, features which were deemed relatively amenable to analysis and comparison. Architects and art historians followed the framework more readily than the other scholars; the contributions of the latter develop a variety of approaches, opening a wider range of perspectives and interests beyond the architectural and archaeological fields. The focus of the contributions varies: several attempt to provide a comprehensive view of the monastery in the country in question, some deal with a specific aspect, or with a modern and sometimes unexpected development.

What is a Buddhist monastery? We might define it as a long-term residence of monastics, whether monks or nuns. But even such a deceptively comprehensive and consistent definition fails to cover the whole Buddhist world. There are ritual centres considered as monasteries where no monks reside, for instance in the Newar community of Nepal, where married Buddhist followers, having received temporary ordination as young boys, live around, but not inside, their monastery, and are collectively in charge of its maintenance, rituals and activities. And it is clear that in all periods and in all countries, the scale of the monastery has varied considerably, from many hectares to a single building, from several hundred monks sharing the great monasteries of China and Japan or the royal monasteries of Bangkok, to the single caretaker monk in some Bhutanese or Singhalese village monasteries.

Several contributions examine the manner in which monasteries were founded, confirming the critical and enduring role of royal or political power. Instances are numerous. Kings like Bimbisāra in India or Devanampiyatissa in Sri Lanka offered royal gardens to the Saṅgha. Buddhist emperors like Houan-ti in China and Shōmu in Japan promoted the spread of Buddhism in their realms; the latter had monasteries set up in each provincial capital. Ever since the reign of Aśoka—the dawn of the Indian historical record—sovereigns have been eager to appear as protectors of the religion; and have also attempted to keep its institutions under their control, especially by organizing (or restricting) the ordination ceremonies.

The Buddhist monastery is primarily a living place for bhikkhus and, depending on historical and social circumstances, for bhikkhuṇīs. (At present there are officially sanctioned institutions for ordained nuns only within the Chinese, Korean, Japanese, and Vietnamese Vinaya lineages. Fully-fledged nuns are not recognized in the Theravādin, Tibetan, and Mongolian traditions.) The monastery is the place where ordained monastics ensure the continuity and purity of their congregations by means of the requisite rituals, the valid "acts for the community" (Sanskrit *saṅghakarma*, Pāli *saṅghakamma*). It is the place where they practise the Dharma and preserve and disseminate the rich heritage of Buddhism, not only the teachings of the Blessed One but also arts, crafts, and skills. Beyond this, monasteries may be viewed as human organizations economically and politically dependent on social environments that welcome and enrich them. In other words, monasteries are products of, and agents within, society, and do not exist in isolation (although isolated hermitages and retreats do exist).

Many monasteries are archaeological sites, some of considerable antiquity. Such monasteries, together with the monuments, artefacts, and documents they keep, constitute primary historical sources which allow us to imagine the cultural life of entire societies. From villagers and village headmen to rulers and wealthy citizens, a monastery can get land, food, goods, equipment, servants, and, ultimately, candidates for monkhood. As a locus for individual and collective ceremonies, the monastery is an accessible meeting place – a forum – where monks, religious teachers, members of the elite and ruling classes, and lay followers in general participate in a variety of activities that express their religious conceptions and aspirations, necessarily impinging upon the political, social, and economic worlds. A fundamental and shared aspiration is the wish to maintain and perpetuate the *Sāsana* within a hospitable lay society. But the manner in which this idealized act of merit is expressed may differ considerably, determined by different cultural heritages, local beliefs, or surviving elements of earlier religious systems.

Within this open social space offered by the monastery, ordained and non-ordained individuals share common devotional and cultural activities that are not strictly defined, since in general they lie outside the scope of the rules prescribed by the Vinaya. Often – but not exclusively – these activities are animated by feelings of devotion towards different images or objects of reverence, which can encode specific religious values or insights or engage an intimate fideistic inclination. Again, let us stress that Buddhist "social" cults are expressed within wide cultural contexts and depend on specific historical and local heritages as much as they depend on doctrinal, textual and scholarly traditions.

Each contributor uses or refers to the local vocabulary of his or her subject area. We have tried as far as possible to use consistent English equivalents, and, with regard to naturalized Sanskrit and Pāli terms – which may be treated as English words – to follow the recommendations of the *Journal of the International Association of Buddhist Studies* (Vol. 5.2, 1982, pp. 141-142). But the task is daunting, and we have been unable to compile a systematic inter-language glossary of monastic terminology – let us hope this will be achieved in the future. Part of the problem is the fact that classical terms are not used consistently throughout the Buddhist world: a single term may be assigned different meanings in different cultures, and usage changes over time. The vocabulary of monasticism includes many Sanskrit and Pāli terms, but the different vernaculars often apply such terms to different architectural elements or assign them new meanings. One example is the word *vihāra*. Even in the early Sanskrit and Pāli literature the term could refer to either a residence (whether individual or collective) or to a monastic complex as a whole. In Thailand '*wihan*' (the same word as pronounced in Thai) designates an assembly hall, while in Cambodia the '*wihian*' (*vihāra* as pronounced in Khmer) is a multifunctional structure – an assembly, recitation and ordination hall. Conversely, the ordination hall in Thailand and Laos is a functionally distinct building and independent structure known as *ubosot* (equivalent to the *uposathaghara* of Sri Lanka) in Thai and as *sim* in Lao.

European terminology can also be confusing. For instance, the familiar English word *pagoda* has many meanings – in Burma it can denote either a temple complex or a stūpa, while in the Far East it refers to a specific architectural form, a multi-tiered tower which is nonetheless a stūpa. In Cambodia or Vietnam the French equivalent *pagode* can mean a tiered tower or a whole monastic complex. Here it is worth remembering that the stūpa, in its many different sizes and shapes, has acquired distinct local names in practically all Buddhist cultures: *dagoba*, *caitya* or *vehera* in Sri Lanka, *zedi* in Burmese, *chedi*, *prang*, *sathup*, or *phra that* in Thai, *that* in Lao, *caitya* or *cibhā* in Newar, *chörten* (*mchod rten*) in Tibetan and Bhutanese, *suburγan* in Mongolian, *ta* in Chinese, *tō* in Japanese... It is this creative diversity that makes the study of the Buddhist monastery both a challenge and a fascination.

Lastly, none of the contributors was a native English speaker. We would like to thank our English speaking colleagues who kindly edited all the papers. We, the editors, assume responsibility for any errors which may remain.

Pierre Pichard and François Lagirarde

INDIAN BUDDHIST MONASTERIES

Pierre Pichard

Except in the Himalayas (in Ladakh and Sikkim most notably) where Buddhist communities following the Tibetan traditions are still active (Handa 1987, Khosla 1979, Rivol 1983), Buddhist monasteries in India are now deserted and survive only as archaeological sites. In addition, many Buddhist sites were deliberately destroyed during the twelfth and thirteenth centuries, possibly during Brahmanical retaliations and certainly after Muslim conquests. Only their foundations remain today, or at best the lowest parts of their walls.

1 – *Monastery 2 at Ratnagiri (Orissa),* ca. *9th century AD, from south-west*
Bases of brick walls delineate the entrance in the foreground, facing the rectangular shrine, and monks' cells around the stone-paved central courtyard.
(photo P. Pichard)

Pierre Pichard

Main historical events of Indian Buddhism

ca. 400 BC*	generally accepted date of Gautama Buddha's Parinirvāṇa
ca. 400 BC*	First Council at Rajagriha
ca. 300 BC*	Second Council at Vaisali – division between Theravādins and Mahāsāṅghikas
ca. 260 to 224 BC	Reign of King Aśoka, spread of Buddhism in India and to Sri Lanka
ca. 242 BC	Third Council at Pataliputra
1st-2nd cent. AD	Reign of Kaniṣka, spread of Buddhism in Gandhāra and Kashmir
1st-2nd cent.	First production of Buddha sculptures in Mathurā and Gandhāra
1st-2nd cent.	Life of Nāgārjuna and development of Mahāyāna doctrines
2nd-3rd cent.	Construction of Buddhist centres at Amaravati and Nagarjunakonda
ca. 350 and after	Development of Tantric Buddhism
460	Destruction of Taxila by the White Huns
5th cent.	Life of Buddhaghosa and Buddhadatta
5th cent.	Foundation of Nalanda Mahāvihāra
*ca.*790	Foundation of Somapura Mahāvihāra (Paharpur)
1197	Destruction of Nalanda Mahāvihāra by Muslim invaders

Studies of Chinese Buddhist pilgrims in India:

402-411	Faxian (Fa-hien)
518-522	Song yun
627-645	Xuanzang (Hsuan-tsang)
673-685	Yijing
751-790	Wukong
964-976	Jiye

General location of monasteries

map 1 opposite page

Sites of former Buddhist monasteries, either rock-cut in cliffs or built on the surface, have been identified all over India, from Kashmir to the south and from Sindh to Bengal. New sites continue to be uncovered through excavations or chance discoveries. They are relatively scarce in the centre of the country and more dense on the periphery, where the main concentrations are historically linked with the patronage of rulers or dynasties, particularly the Mauryas (first of all Aśoka) in the Gangetic plain, the area associated with Buddha's life, the Kushāns and the Śakas in Gandhāra, the Guptas in northern India, the Sātavāhanas and Vākāṭakas in Maharashtra, the Ikshvākus in Andhra, the Pālas and Chandras in Bengal and Orissa.

* 543 BC is the base of the Buddhist Era in Theravāda countries, as the date of the Buddha's Parinirvāṇa at the age of 80, which would situate his birth in 623 BC. For a time, most scholars agreed on the revised Parinirvāṇa date of 486 BC, until recent research concluded that the available evidence does not allow to fix it more accurately than around 400 BC, with a margin on some 20 years on either side (see Bechert, Heinz: *The Dating of the Historical Buddha*, part 1, Göttingen 1991). The first Council is reputed to have been held in the year following the death of Buddha and the second hundred years later.

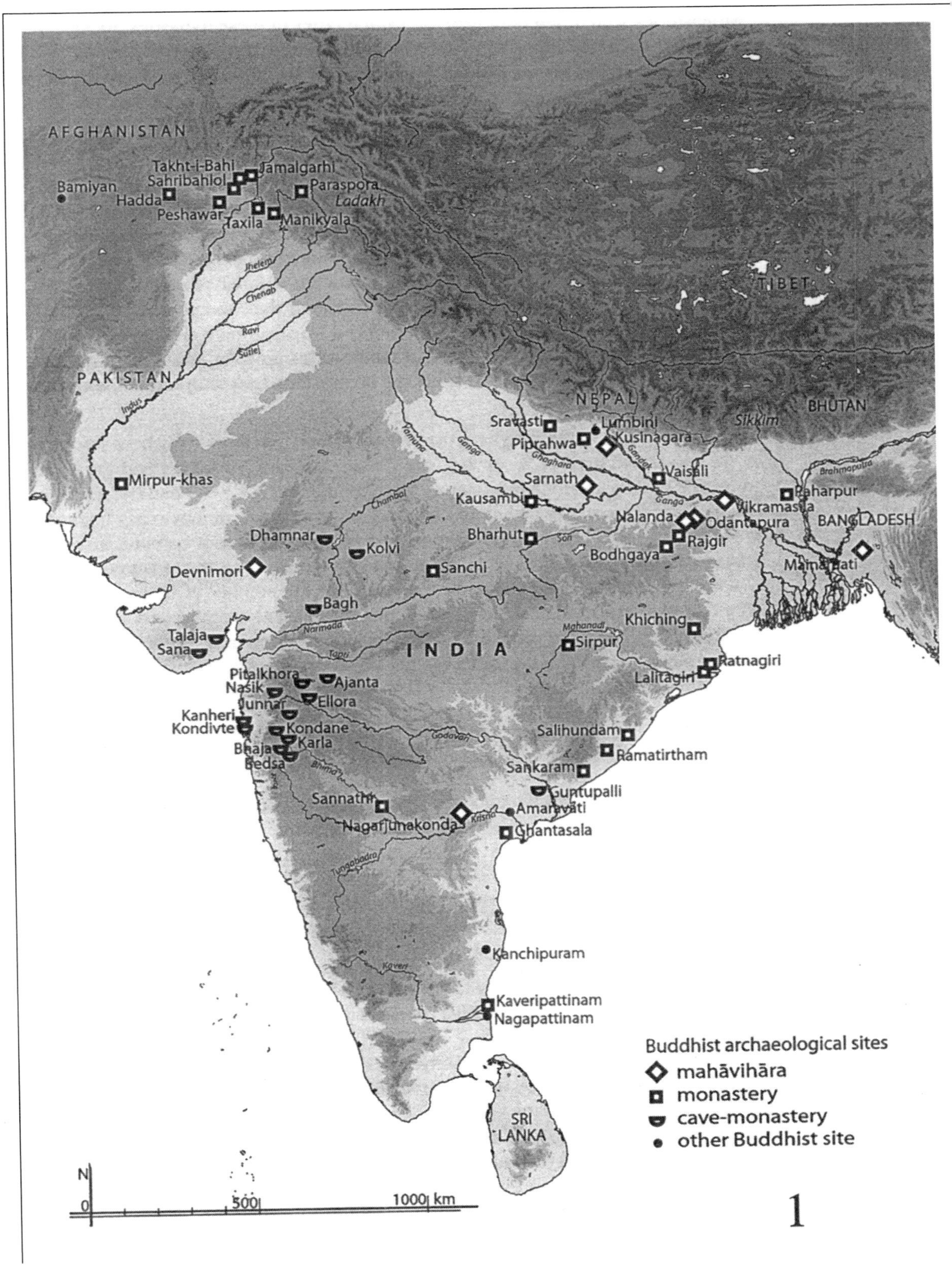
AFGHANISTAN
PAKISTAN
NEPAL
BHUTAN
TIBET
BANGLADESH
INDIA
SRI LANKA
Ladakh
Sikkim
Bamiyan
Hadda
Takht-i-Bahi
Sahribahlol
Jamalgarhi
Peshawar
Taxila
Manikyala
Paraspora
Jhelem
Chenab
Ravi
Sutlej
Indus
Mirpur-khas
Yamuna
Ganga
Ghaghara
Gandak
Chambal
Son
Brahmaputra
Sravasti
Lumbini
Piprahwa
Kusinagara
Sarnath
Vaisali
Kausambi
Paharpur
Vikramasila
Nalanda
Odantapura
Rajgir
Bodhgaya
Mainamati
Bharhut
Dhamnar
Kolvi
Devnimori
Sanchi
Bagh
Narmada
Tapti
Talaja
Sana
Khiching
Mahanadi
Sirpur
Ratnagiri
Lalitagiri
Pitalkhora
Nasik
Ajanta
Ellora
Junnar
Kanheri
Kondivte
Kondane
Karla
Bhaja
Bedsa
Bhima
Godavari
Salihundam
Ramatirtham
Sankaram
Guntupalli
Amaravati
Sannathi
Nagarjunakonda
Krishna
Ghantasala
Tungabadra
Kanchipuram
Kaveri
Kaveripattinam
Nagapattinam
Buddhist archaeological sites
mahāvihāra
monastery
cave-monastery
other Buddhist site
N
0
500
1000 km
1

Monasteries were often built near the capital cities of these dynasties, located at some distance to ensure enough seclusion and to favor peace and meditation, but also not too distant, as the monks needed to rely on the town people for support. The topography of the Taxila region exemplifies how these criteria were applied, distances between monasteries and villages allowing a round trip during the morning hours (Marshall 1951).

By exposing the plan of monasteries, archaeological excavations provide the basis for an overall survey of their relative importance and of the number of their residents, but fail to allow an accurate computation of the Saṅgha at any time, because many monasteries were active during several centuries and were constantly rebuilt or modified, and also because even the foundations of an unknown number of others have been totally erased by subsequent constructions or re-use of their material. In the Tamil country for instance, the cities of Kanchipuram and Nagapattinam are known to have been active Buddhist centres with several monasteries up to at least the thirteenth century, but the only traces are a few stone and bronze Buddhist sculptures now stored in museums (Mitra 1971: 193-7).

map 2 opposite page

A partial account of the Saṅgha in the seventh century can tentatively been inferred from the travel narrative of Xuanzang, the Chinese pilgrim who described the local condition of Buddhism along his itinerary all over India between 627 and 645, though the numbers of monasteries and monks he gives for each place are obviously no more than rough estimates provided by chance informants, and cannot be exhaustive or consistent. For too many sites he seems to base his statistics on the assumption that one monastery housed 100 monks, far too many for the number of individual cells usually found in archaeologically excavated monasteries. The extent concerned is also very uncertain, as the same name may refer to a city, a region or a whole kingdom as well as for the mere surroundings of its capital. Whatever the case, Xuanzang is still our best available source.

Early monasteries

It appears from the ancient literature (the *Vinayapiṭaka* particularly) that two different forms of monastic establishment co-existed in the formative period of the Saṅgha: the *āvāsa*, a cluster of huts built by the monks themselves, and the *ārāma*, an enclosed site with more permanent buildings, offered to the congregation and maintained by the donor. In both cases however, the site was fully inhabited only during *vassa*, the rainy season, as the monks were supposed to wander from place to place during the rest of the year (Dutt 1962).

The description of the necessary facilities given by the *Cullavagga* reflects on the basic needs of monks and nuns: dwelling rooms and cells, service-halls, well, bath and latrines, and a simple hall for the ceremonies – particularly the periodic recitation of the *Pātimokkha*. There is neither mention of anything like a temple, nor of course of Buddha images. Archaeological excavations were conducted at three of the earlier *ārāmas* said to have been founded during the life of Buddha, the Jīvakārāma at Rajagriha in Bihar (*Indian Archaeology* 1954-55), the Jetavanārāma at Sravasti in Uttar Pradesh, and the Ghoshitārāma at Kausambi in Madhya Pradesh (*Indian Archaeology* 1955-56). As the sites were active during more than one thousand years, the unearthed architectural

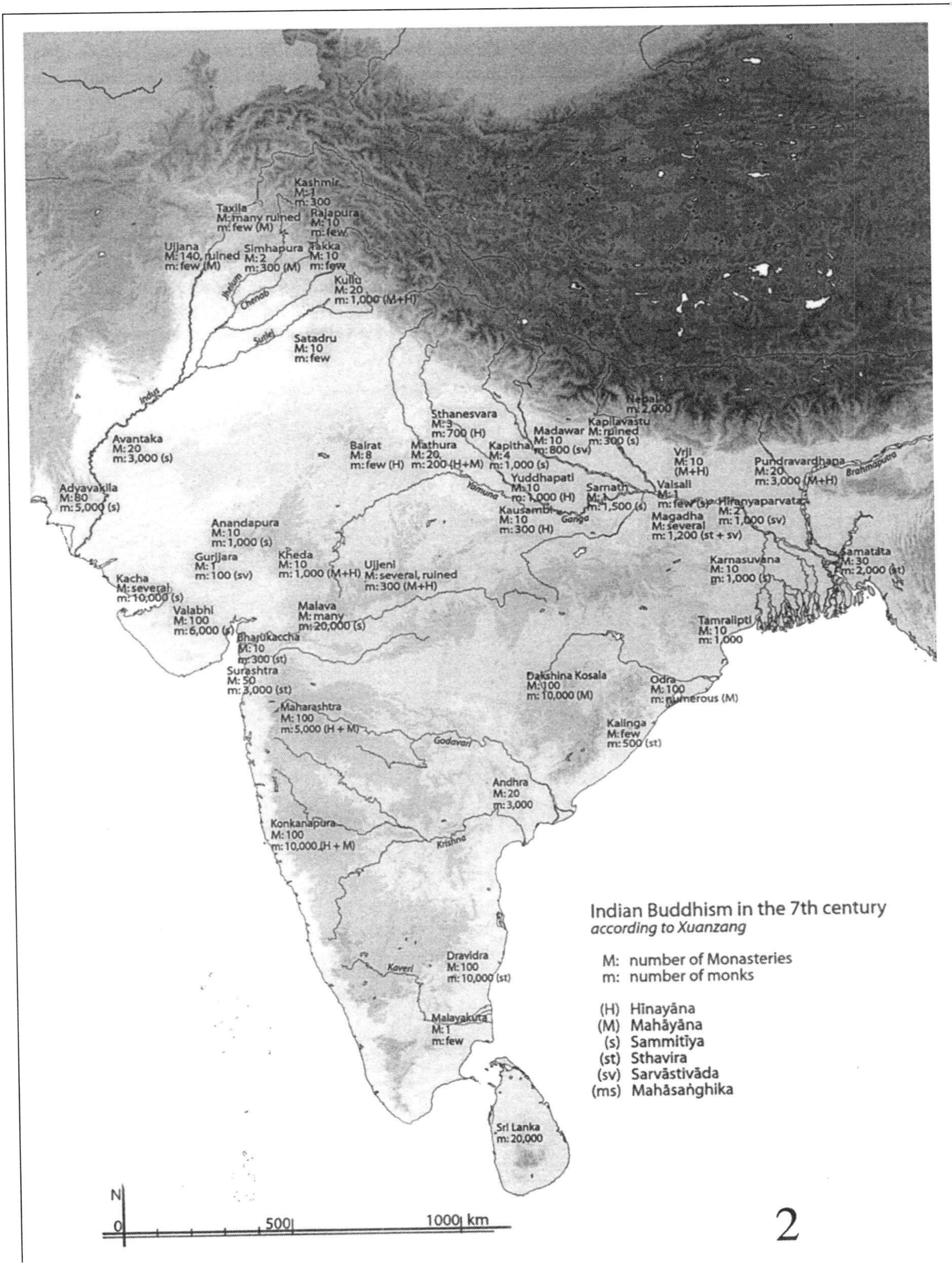
Indian Buddhism in the 7th century
according to Xuanzang
M: number of Monasteries
m: number of monks
(H) Hīnayāna
(M) Mahāyāna
(s) Sammitīya
(st) Sthavira
(sv) Sarvāstivāda
(ms) Mahāsaṅghika
Kashmir
Taxila
Rajapura
Ujjana
Simhapura
Takka
Kullu
Jhelum
Chenab
Sutlej
Satadru M: 10 m: few
Indus
Avantaka M: 20 m: 3,000 (s)
Adyavakila
Sthanesvara
Bairat M: 8 m: few (H)
Mathura
Kapitha
Madawar M: 10
Kapilavastu
Nepal
Vrji M: 10 (M+H)
Pundravardhana
Brahmaputra
Yamuna
Yuddhapati
Kausambi M: 10 m: 300 (H)
Ganga
Sarnath
Valsali
Hiranyaparvata
Magadha M: several m: 1,200 (st + sv)
Anandapura M: 10 m: 1,000 (s)
Gurjjara
Kheda
Ujjeni M: several, ruined m: 300 (M+H)
Kacha
Valabhi M: 100 m: 6,000 (s)
Malava
Bharukaccha
Karnasuvana
Samatata
Tamralipti
Surashtra M: 50 m: 3,000 (st)
Dakshina Kosala M: 100 m: 10,000 (M)
Odra
Maharashtra M: 100 m: 5,000 (H + M)
Kalinga
Godavari
Andhra M: 20 m: 3,000
Konkanapura M: 100 m: 10,000 (H + M)
Krishna
Dravidra M: 100 m: 10,000 (st)
Kaveri
Malayakuta M: 1 m: few
Sri Lanka m: 20,000
N
0
500
1000 km
2

evidence relates mostly to later structures, from the fifth and sixth centuries, though bases of stone walls at the Jīvakārāma reveal a complex of four oblong, double-apsed halls attributed to Buddha's time, but no traces of dwellings: these long buildings may have been used as collective dormitories (Sarkar 1966: 13), or as assembly halls, in which case the monks' quarters may have been wooden huts or houses scattered around.

fig. 2 below

Some three centuries after the Buddha's time, a type of plan was developed which became the common monastic pattern all over India. It consists of a quadrangle of cells around a square open space which could be either a pillared hall or a courtyard, a configuration which was adopted for cave monasteries, excavated from the face of a cliff, as well as for stone or brick structural monasteries built on the ground (the cave monasteries by their very nature and location having been better preserved from ruin and destruction than the structural ones).

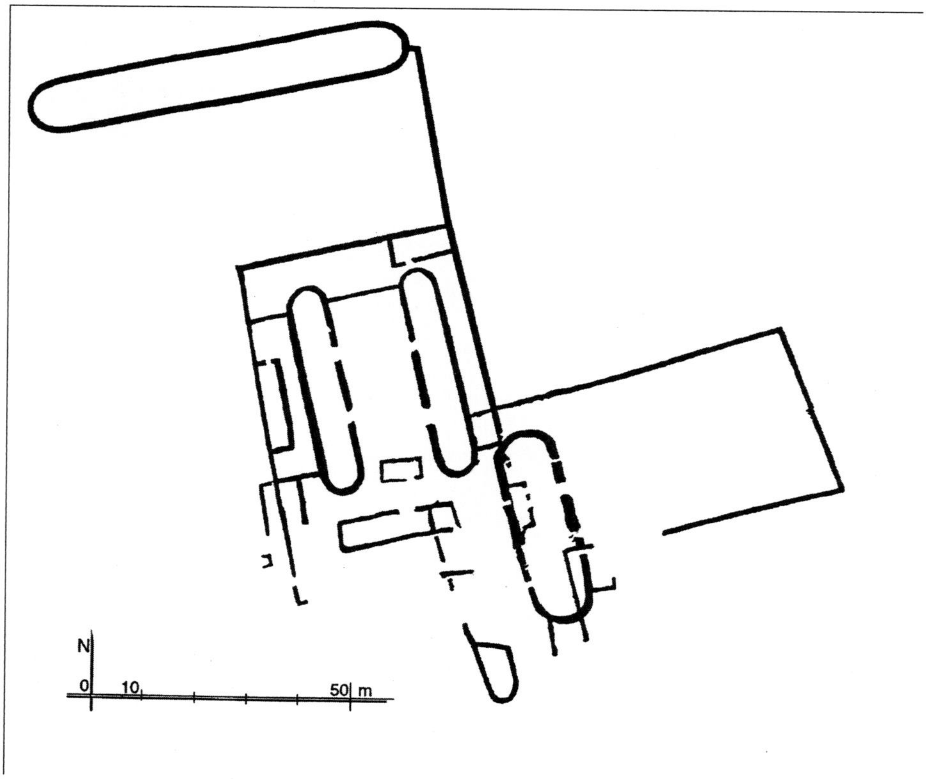

2 – *Jīvakārāma monastery at Rajgir (Bihar), 4th century BC (?)*
Bases of stone walls, excavated in 1950-55 revealing four double-apsed halls.

(P. Pichard, after Mitra 1971: 37)

Layout of the monastery

In most sites, monasteries are closely related to a dominant monument, generally a great stūpa. At Taxila several monasteries were erected at various dates between the first and the sixth centuries around the great Dharmarājikā stūpa, and in the hills around the city the satellite monastic sites (Giri, Mhora Moradu, Jaulian, Bamala, etc.) consist similarly of a stūpa and one or several quadrangles for the monks' cells. Though located close to each other, the monastery and the stūpa are spatially separated, each in its own enclosure: the stūpa in the centre of a courtyard, the monks' cells around another. The monks' quadrangle usually faces the stūpa, with its main or single entrance opening towards it. *fig. 3 below*

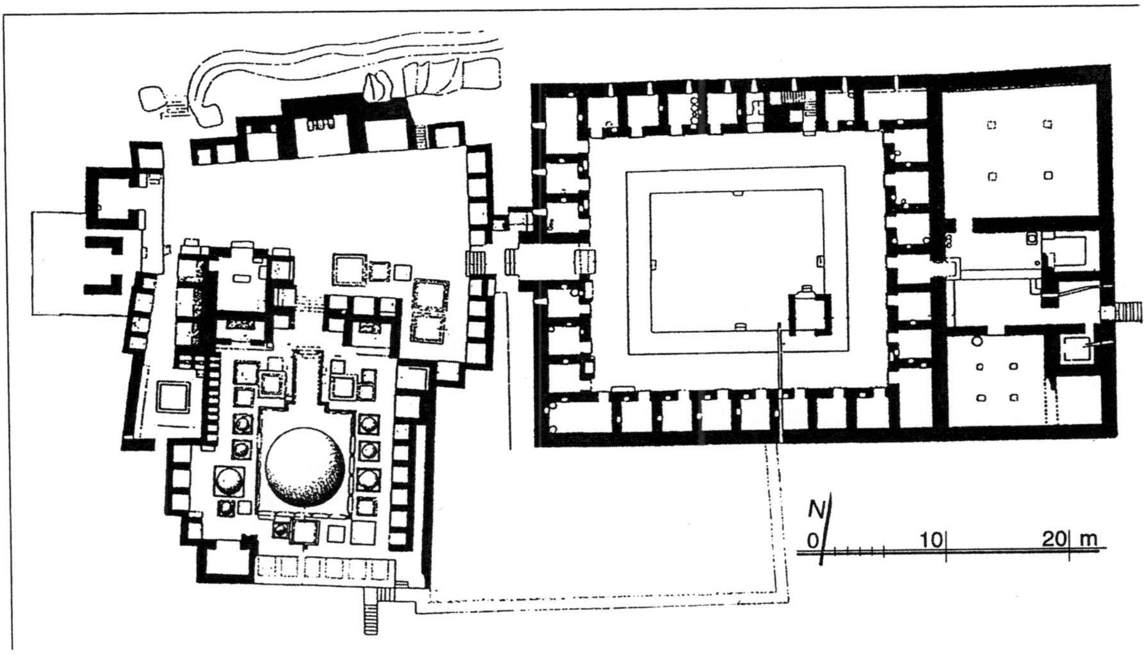

3 – *Stūpa and monastery at Jaulian, near Taxila (Pakistan), built from 2nd to 5th centuries, destroyed by the invading White Huns around 460.*

Entrances from the west, to a lower court surrounded by shrines housing Buddha images. This court is connected by stairways to the upper court on the south and to the monastic cells onto the east.
The main stūpa marks the centre of the upper court, with rows of small stūpas and of shrines forming concentric squares around it.
The quadrangle of cells has its main entrance onto west, towards the stūpa courts. There are 26 cells on the ground floor, all opening under the gallery, the cells of the north side provided with windows. In the north wing, a staircase gave access to a vanished upper floor, probably on the same plan. In the small cell to the west of the staircase were stored clay Buddhist images.
The bathroom (with drain) is located in the south-east corner of the courtyard.
The large square room with four pillars at the north-east corner of the complex is supposed to have been the assembly hall, while the southern part of this extension (probably a later addition) houses a kitchen, a dining hall (also four-pillared), store rooms and toilet.
A service door is also provided in this west part. (P. P., after Marshall 1951, pl. 101 and p. 368-87)

fig. 4 below
fig. 5 opposite page

The cave-monasteries were generally excavated in dense clusters, side by side along the length of a cliff. While some of these caves consist of a single, individual cell entered from a door in the cliff, other have multiple cells around a hall. Alternating with these dwelling caves are *caitya-gṛha*, rock-cut shrines containing a stūpa: a long apsidal hall perpendicular to the face of the cliff, with a small circular stūpa marking the centre of the apse. The most extended of such rock-cut complexes are found in the western part of the Dekkan (Nagaraju 1981), particularly at Junnag (252 caves in 4 groups), Kanheri (101 caves) or Nasik (26 caves), while Ajanta is particularly famous for the exceptional quality of the sculptures and mural paintings, and Ellora for sheltering side by side contemporary Buddhist, Hindu and Jain caves.

fig. 6 opposite page

At the earlier sites, the stūpa either isolated in a courtyard or at the focal point of a shrine, is not included in the dwelling unit. In the latter the central space of the quadrangle is surrounded by aligned cells, on four sides in built quadrangles, on three sides in caves, the fourth one being the entrance from the face of the cliff as illustrated by the cave 2 at Kondane or by caves 4, 6, 7, 9 at Pitalkhora and 12 and 13 at Karle. In the first half of the second century, however, a stūpa is carved in bas-relief between the doors of

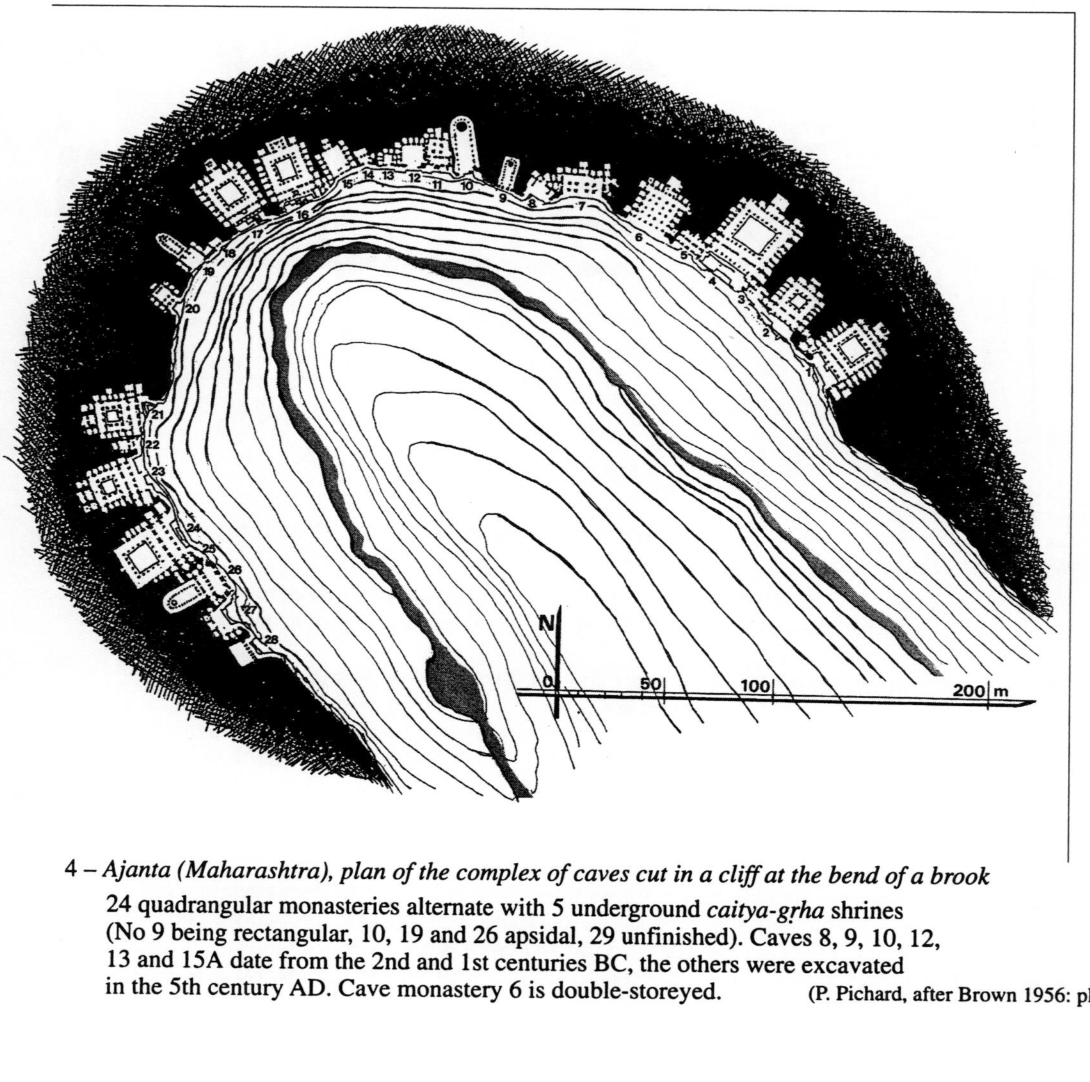

4 – *Ajanta (Maharashtra), plan of the complex of caves cut in a cliff at the bend of a brook*
24 quadrangular monasteries alternate with 5 underground *caitya-gṛha* shrines (No 9 being rectangular, 10, 19 and 26 apsidal, 29 unfinished). Caves 8, 9, 10, 12, 13 and 15A date from the 2nd and 1st centuries BC, the others were excavated in the 5th century AD. Cave monastery 6 is double-storeyed. (P. Pichard, after Brown 1956: pl. XXV)

the two median cells, facing the entrance of caves 3 and 10 at Nasik. This develops into a small shrine at the same place, in the median cell of the side opposed to the entrance, which progressively becomes larger than the others and is entered through a small vestibule. As in the *caitya-gṛha*, this shrine can shelter a small stūpa as in Shelarwadi (cave 8, third century) or Bargh (cave 4, fifth-sixth centuries), but more regularly after the fifth century it contains a Buddha image, for instance at Ajanta (caves 1, 2, 4, 6, 7, 11, 15, 16, 17) and Ellora (caves 2, 3, 4, 6, 8, 11, 12). In some cases the shrine is a late addition to the monastery: cave 20 of Nasik was first hollowed in 179 AD according to an engraved inscription, but a sixth-century inscription refers to the modification of its back part and the addition of its shrine (Nagaraju 1981: 275). *fig. 7 page 26* *fig. 8, cave 1 page 26*

A similar and contemporaneous development can be discerned in the structural monasteries. Already noticed at both ends of the Jivakarama halls, the apsidal end which is common to the *caitya-gṛha* rock-cut shrines is also present in many free-standing temples associated to monasteries. (There is also one example, in Bedsa, where this apsidal configuration was applied to the cell distribution of a cave-monastery.) *fig. 9 page 27*

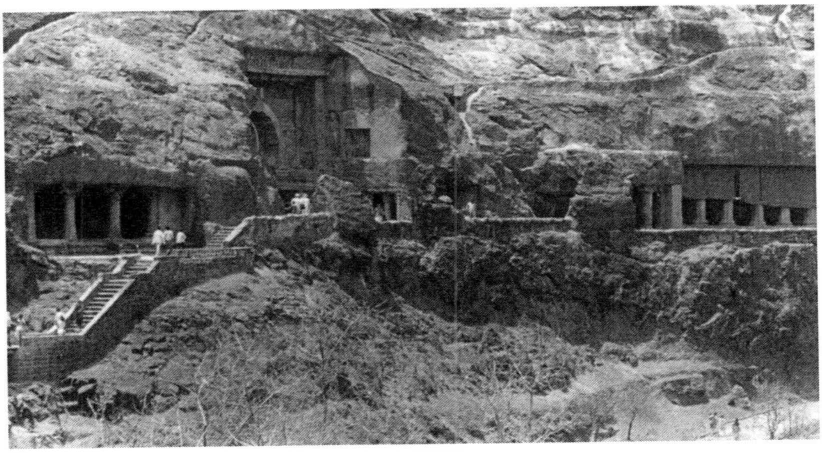

5 – *Ajanta (Maharashtra), central part of the site from south-east, 5th century AD*

Façade of the apsidal shrine 19, with entrances to cave monasteries 20 on one side and to cave monasteries 17 and 16 on the other.
(photo P. Pichard)

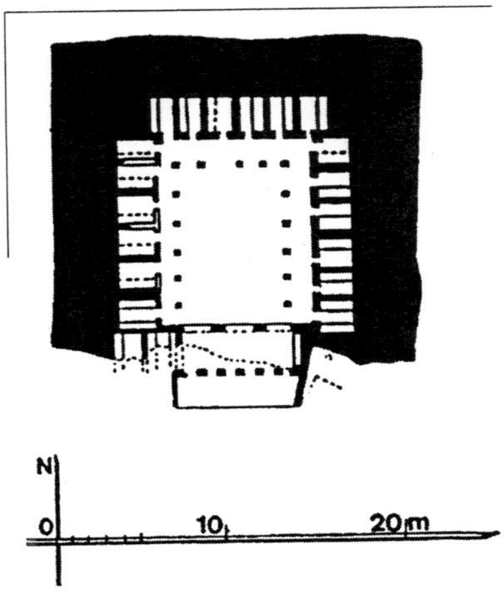

6 – *Cave monastery 2 at Kondane (Maharashtra), 2nd century BC*

A pillared gallery and three wings of six cells each surround the rectangular hall. The two cells near the entry side have two rock-cut beds, the others only one.
(P. Pichard, after Nagaraju 1981: fig. 47)

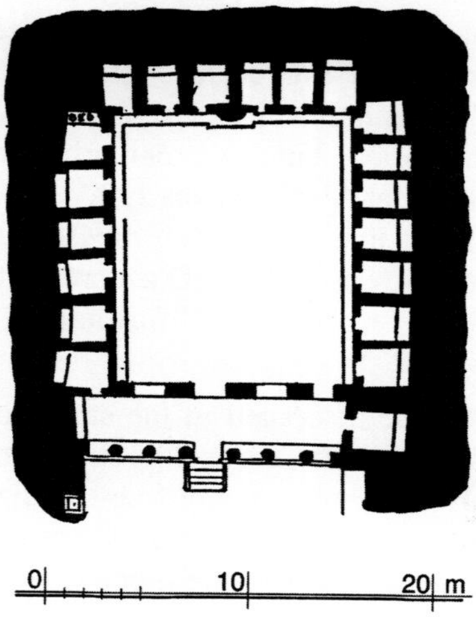

7 – *Cave monastery 3 at Nasik (Maharashtra), 2nd century AD*

The plan is quite similar to fig. 4, except that the central hall has no pillars. A noticeable innovation is however the carving of a stūpa in bas relief, facing the entrance on the central panel of the rear wing.

(P. Pichard, after Mitra 1971: 35)

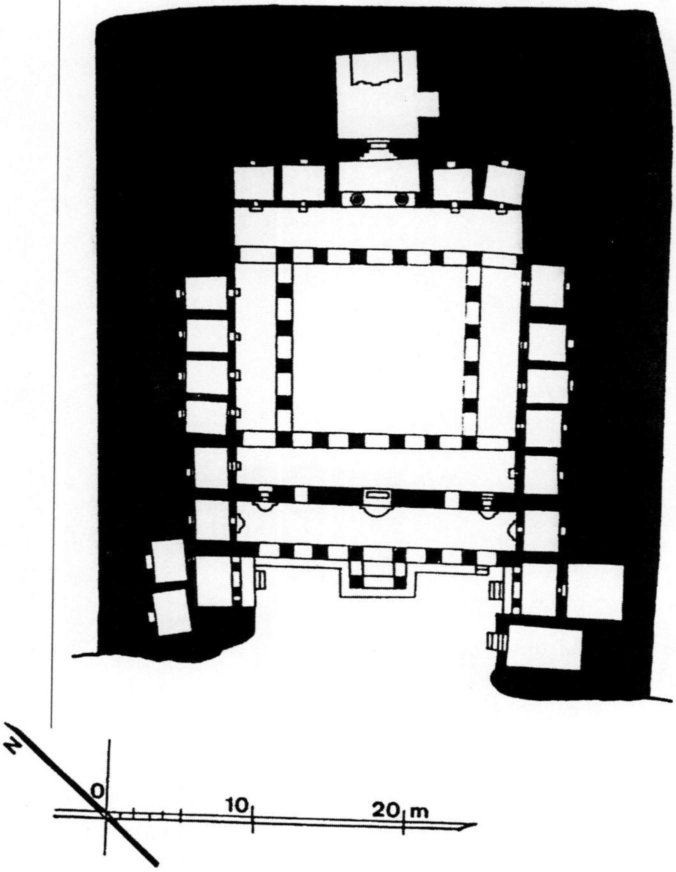

8 – *Cave monastery 1 at Ajanta (Maharashtra), 5th century AD*

Facing the entrance of the monastery, at the middle of the back wing, is a square shrine (housing a sculpture of the seated Buddha) with a vestibule. The whole monastery is lavishly adorned with sculpture and wall paintings.

(P. Pichard, after Michell 1989: 337)

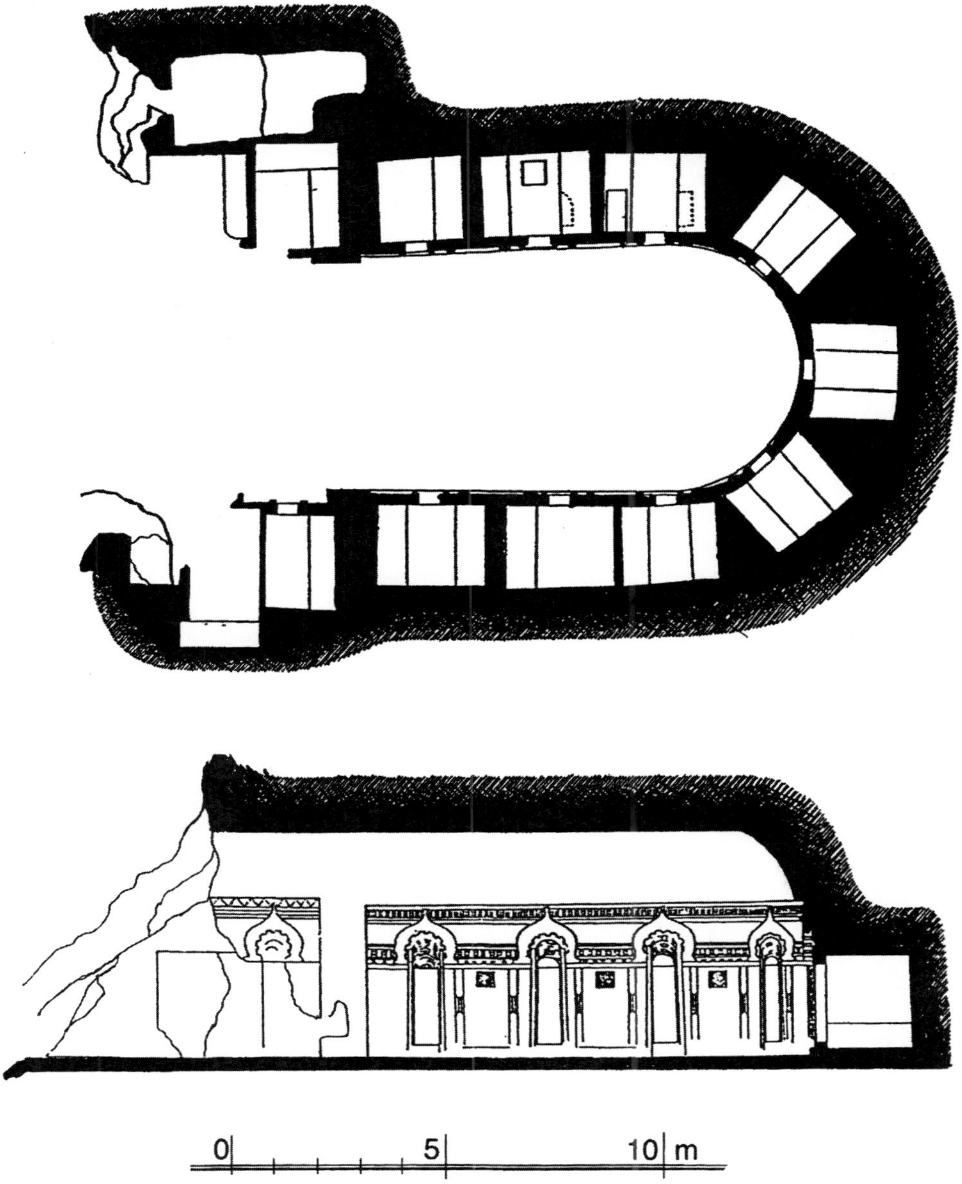

9 – *Cave monastery 11 at Bedsa (Maharashtra), 1st century BC*

A unique apsidal monastery with 11 or 12 cells of 1.8 by 2 m, all with rock-cut beds (8 of them with two).
On the right of the entrance is a water cistern.
The front façade wall, destroyed, could have been a wooden screen.
The ceiling of the axial hall is barrel shaped.

(P. Pichard, plan and section after Mitra 1971: 34)

Nagarjunakonda, in Andhra Pradesh, is an exceptional site where Buddhist and Hindu foundations were simultaneously patronized by the Ikshvaku dynasty during the third and fourth centuries. From 1954 to 1960, prior to the construction of a dam which flooded the site, archaeological excavations revealed some thirty Buddhist establishments on the right bank of the Khrishna River. These monastic complexes were affiliated to various schools belonging to Hinayāna as well as to Mahāyāna, and in the relatively short period of one century, their architectural configuration reflects an evolution of the cult object, from the stūpa to more anthropomorphic representations like the Buddha's footprint and statue, particularly in the monasteries of the Aparamahāvinaseliya sect (Sarkar 1966: 74-96).

The layout of the monastic complexes in Nagarjunakonda connects monasteries, shrines and stūpas in various configurations. The simplest (12 establishments) associate a stūpa with a simple quadrangular monastery, and two of them are linked to the Theravāda school by an inscription (Sarkar 1966: 79). As at Taxila, the main entrance of the quadrangle opens towards the stūpa. In sixteen complexes, one, or more frequently two, shrines facing each other are built between the stūpa and the monastery, and in several cases the shrine was built as an addition to a complex initially planned with only a stūpa and a monastery. In four examples (sites 2, 3, 4 and 23) the shrines are included inside the boundary wall of the quadrangle, flanking the entrance, but there is no case yet of a shrine inserted in the back row of cells, a feature which becomes regular after the fifth century.

fig. 10 below
fig. 11 opposite page
fig. 12 opposite page

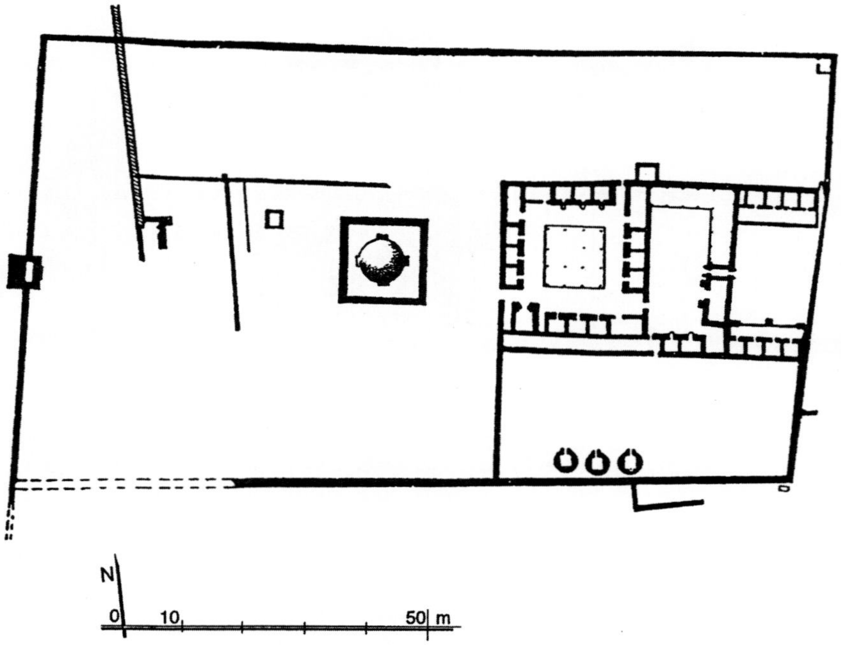

10 – *Site 32A at Nagarjunakonda (Andhra Pradesh), 3rd century*

Built at some distance from the main stūpa, the monastic quadrangle faces it with a single entrance. The two eastern courts are probably later extensions.

(P. Pichard, after Sarkar 1966: pl. XIII)

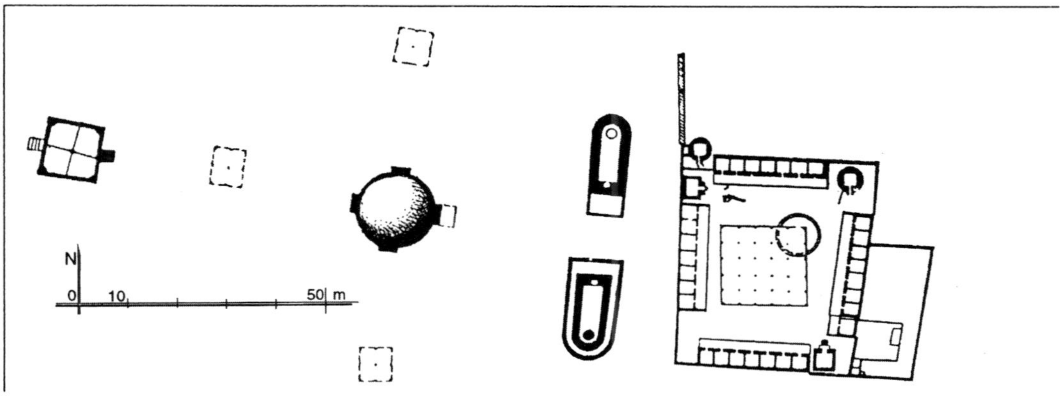

11 – *Site 5 at Nagarjunakonda (Andhra Pradesh), 3rd century.*
Two apsidal shrines frame the open space between the stūpa and the monastery, both with a small stūpa at the focal point of the apse.
At a later stage, a rectangular shrine was built inside the quadrangle.
The function of the two small circular buildings sheltering a square room is not known.
Epigraphic evidence attaches this site to the Bahuśrutīyas, whose doctrine is said to be transitional between Hīnayāna and Mahāyāna (Sarkar 1966: 78).
(P. Pichard, after Sarkar 1966: pl. XIII)

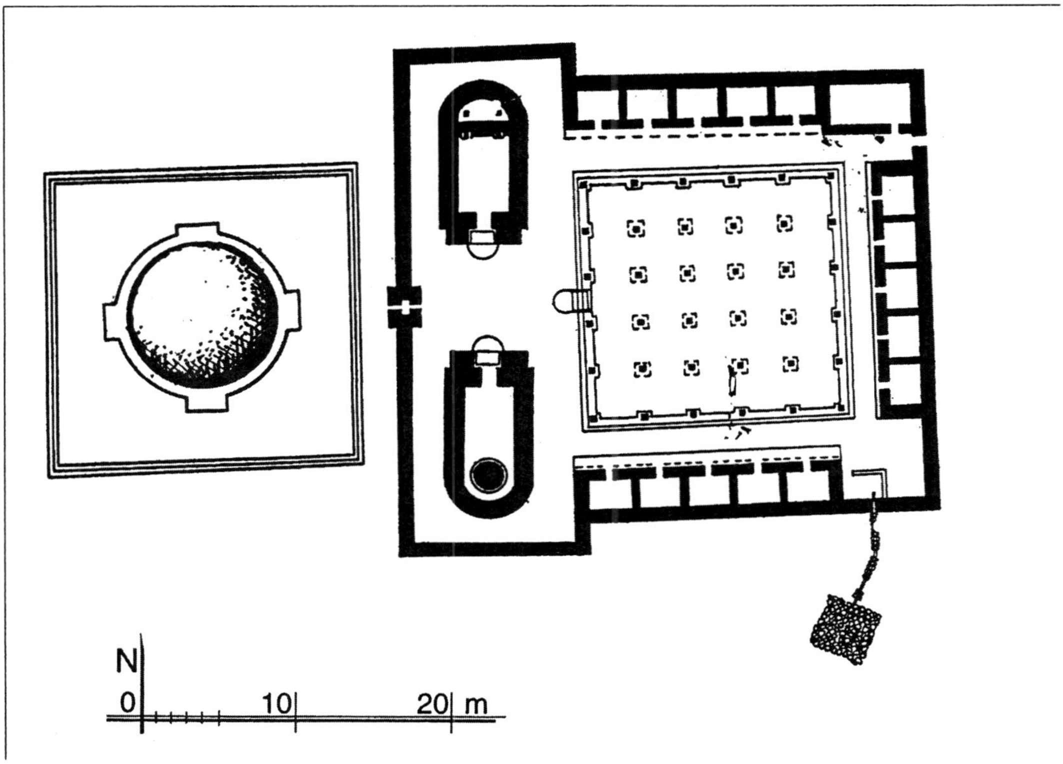

12 – *Site 3 at Nagarjunakonda (Andhra Pradesh), 3rd century*
Facing each other, the two apsidal shrines are now included in the monastic enclosure.
The south one shelters a small stūpa, the north one a Buddha image, a feature shared by 7 other sites.
The square, central space of the quadrangle was a pillared hall. (P. Pichard, after Sarkar 1966: pl. XIII)

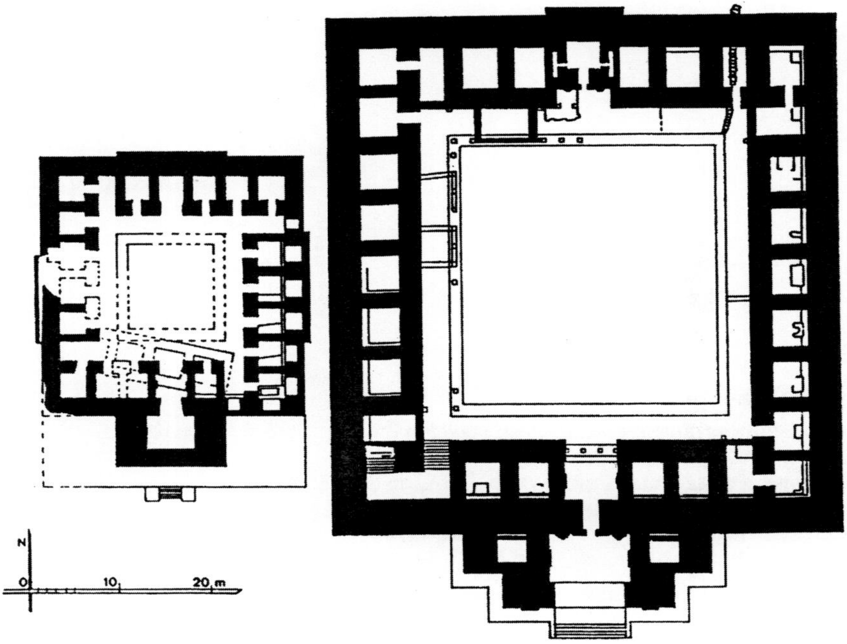

13 – *Monasteries 1 and 2 at Ratnagiri (Orissa), 7th-11th centuries*

The two-storeyed quadrangles of cells have a unique entrance on the south side. Facing it at the middle of the back wing is the shrine. Stairs to the upper floor are located in the south-west corner. The gallery before the cells was covered but the central courtyard was open to sky.
(P. Pichard, after Mitra 1983)

The apsidal shape is then abandoned for a rectangular shrine, axially located in front of the entrance and housing images of the Buddha and of Bodhisattvas, as in the 11 monasteries built side by side in the great Buddhist university of Nalanda, facing a row of rectangular shrines, or in the two monasteries of Ratnagiri, built and several times rebuilt on the same plan between the seventh and eleventh centuries. Both are in brick masonry, stone being used for the delicate carvings at the entrances to monastery 1 and to its shrine, for sculptures of Buddhist images and for special elements like the pillars in the gallery or the window-bars of the cells.

fig. 13 above
fig. 1 p. 17
fig. 14 and 15 opposite page

In a span of some six centuries, the monastic establishment bears witness to the gradual integration of the shrine, as a place of worship sheltering firstly the stūpa and eventually the Buddha image, inside the dwelling quarters. Sarkar (1966) and Mitra (1983) explain this evolution by the increasing inclination towards devotion, possibly under the influence of the *bhakti* movement in Hinduism, starting with the worship of the stūpa with its circumambulatory path and the small shrines and votive stūpas installed around it, but spatially separated from the monastic quadrangle. Together with the adoption of the Buddha image and its multiplication under the Mahayanist schools, this movement induced the monks to locate the shrine inside their quarters, with stūpas and Buddha images of various sizes and in various combinations, complementing each other in different ways. Architecturally, this evolution culminates with the setting of the stūpa or the shrine, at the very centre of the quadrangle, as was attempted as soon as the

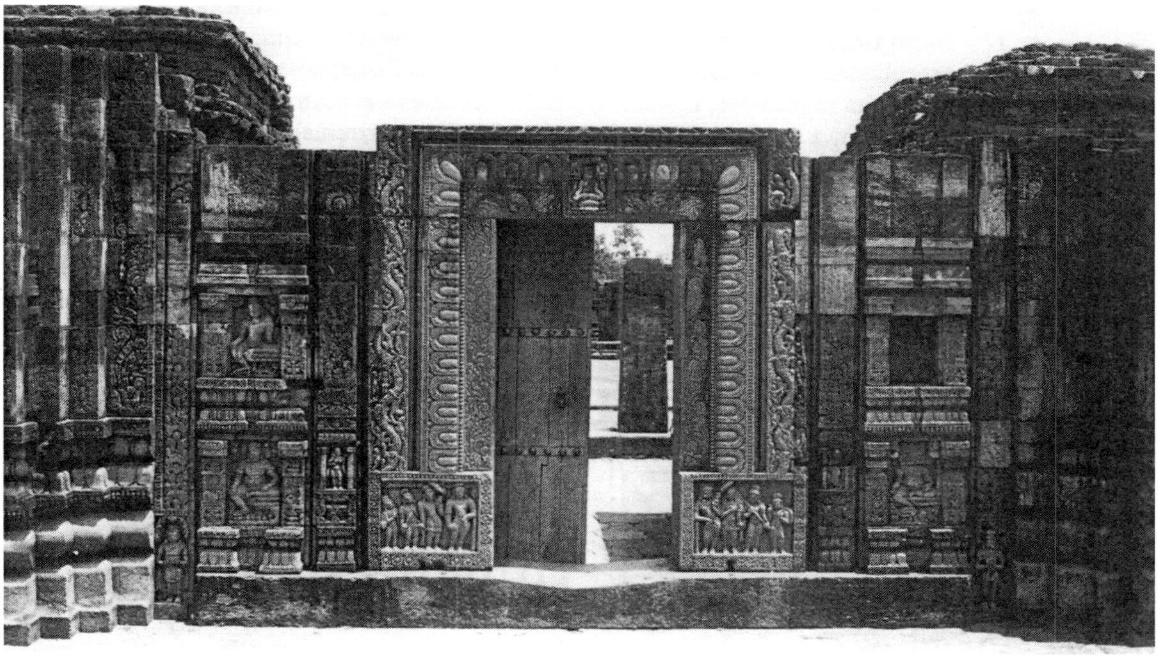

14 – *Stone relief adorning the entrance to monastery 1 at Ratnagiri, 7th-11th centuries, from south* (photo P. Pichard)

15 – *Monk's cell in the northeastern corner of monastery 2 at Ratnagiri,* ca. *ninth century, from southeast), covered by a brick barrel-vault and aerated by a window with sculpted stone bars* (photo P. Pichard)

fig. 16 third century at Sankaram. The location of a stūpa at the centre of monastery 38 at fig. 17 below Nagarjunakonda proceeds from the same trend, which is ultimately illustrated on an exceptionally large scale under the Pāla dynasty at Paharpur (end of the eighth century), where the impressive, cruciform temple occupies the centre of a wide courtyard sur- fig. 18 opposite page rounded by a quadrangle of cells measuring 280 m externally.

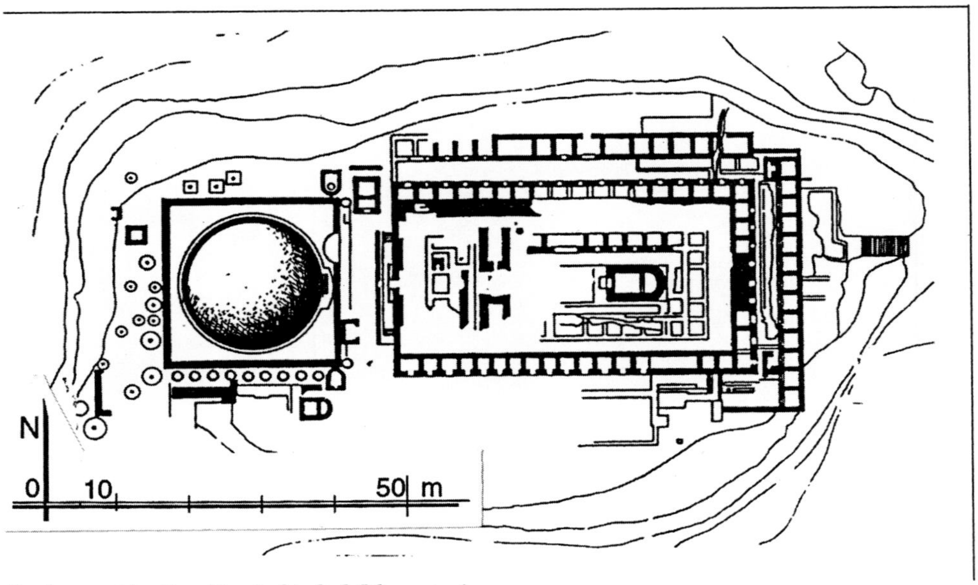

16 – *Sankaram (Andhra Pradesh), 3rd-5th centuries*

On west side, the main stūpa is surrounded by smaller ones, many of them rock-cut. On the east was a wide brick monastery, open on west towards the stūpa, with an apsidal shrine at the centre of its rectangular court and two others facing each other in the front part of the courtyard. Double rows of cells (some of them cut directly in the hill bedrock) constitute the sides of the monastery on north, east and south.

(P. Pichard, after Michell 1989)

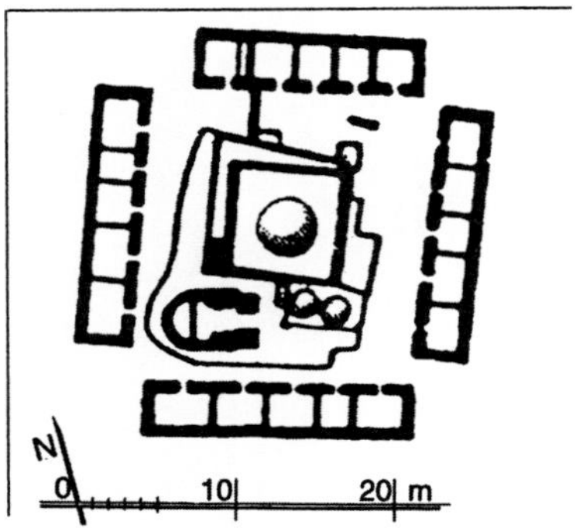

17 – *Site 38 at Nagarjunakonda (Andhra Pradesh), 3rd century*

Epigraphic evidence suggests that the monastery was affiliated to the Theravāda of the Mahāvihāra Singhalese school (Sarkar 1966: 77).
With the stūpa located at the very centre of the small monastic quadrangle, this layout differs widely from the Sri Lankan examples. An apsidal shrine was added at a latter phase.

(P. Pichard, after Sarkar 1966: pl. XIII)

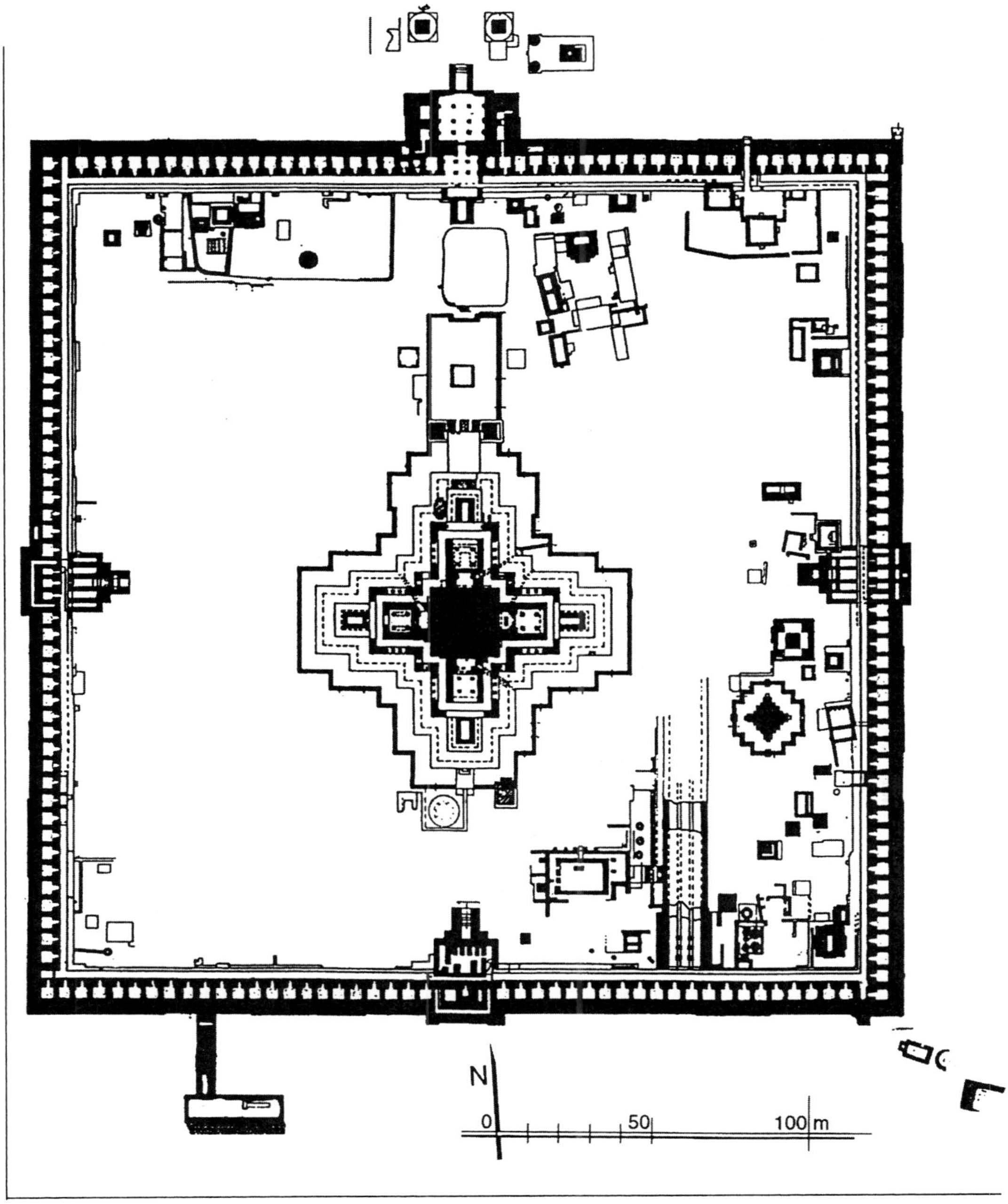

18 – *Somapura monastery at Paharpur (Bangladesh), late 8th century*

A huge, cruciform temple marks the center of the wide courtyard surrounded by 177 cells fronted by a gallery.
In the south-east corner were the kitchen and the long pillared structure of the refectory.

(P. Pichard, after Dikshit 1938)

Elements of the monastery

Religious functions

Stūpa

The stūpa is in most cases the main architectural landmark of the monastery. It must be remembered however that because of their very nature (solid monuments of the most stable shape) the great stūpas were more able to sustain the ravages of time and vandalism than ordinary buildings with walls, ceiling, roofs or vaults: the present appearance of archaeological sites could have been quite different during their lifetime.

From the simple funerary tumulus of its origin, the stūpa has become a sophisticated monument and the repository of elaborate sculptures (Sanchi, Bharut, Amaravati). On later examples, the major innovation was the placing of Buddha's image in niches, as in Ratnagiri. At a much smaller scale, the stūpa figures as the focal point inside a shrine (*caitya-gṛha*).

Shrine

Independent shrines of apsidal shape, either excavated from a cliff or built on the ground, are of varying but comparable size (Sarkar 1966: 35-7): rock-cut *caitya-gṛha*, from 5.36 x 2.54 m Pitalkhora 10) to 37.87 x 13.87 (Karle), structural ones from 4.27 x 2.44 m (Nagarjunakonda 32) to 25.14 to 11.83 m (Sarnath). The cult object, either a stūpa or a Buddha's image, is located at the far end, in front of the entrance. In some complexes at Nagarjunakonda where two identical apsidal shrines face each other at the entrance of the quadrangle, one shelters a stūpa and the other an image. From the *fig. 12 p. 29* fifth century onwards, the rectangular shrine housing Buddha images becomes common, particularly when included into the monastic dwelling quadrangle. Usually larger than the dwelling cells, it is often entered through a more or less developed vestibule in which other images can be installed, specially in Mahayanist centres.

Hall

According to the most ancient canonical texts (*Cullavagga, Mahāvagga*), the periodic recitation of the *pātimokha* was to be held by the assembly of all monks belonging to the monastery. In cave monasteries as well as in built ones, the central space inside the quadrangle was probably used as an assembly hall for this purpose. When this space was an open courtyard, as in most Taxila monasteries, special rooms much larger than the cells could accommodate the recitation.

No evidence has been found of specific halls for ordination ceremonies, nor of boundary stones (*sīmā*) used as markers for a particular building as in Sri Lanka, Cambodia, Laos and Thailand.

Commemorative or funerary functions

In Taxila and other sites, a small stūpa was occasionally found in some of the cells, which were not otherwise distinct from the other ones in the quadrangle. It has been supposed (Marshall 1951) that these stūpas were erected to commemorate the virtues of greatly venerated monks who spent their last years in these cells.

Educational functions

It is well known that several sites generally referred as *Mahāvihāras* (Nalanda, Vikramasila, Nagarjunakonda, Valabhi, Odantapuri) were devoted to advanced studies and learning to the point of being often described as Buddhist universities, attracting scholars and students from all over India and farther. The famous seventh century Chinese pilgrims, Xuanzang and Yijing, spent several months at Nalanda, together with

Tibetan and Korean monks, and an inscription from c. 860 commemorates the building by a Sumatra (?) king of a monastery for visiting monks from his kingdom (Epigraphia Indica XVII: 310). As no building has so far been identified in India as specifically devoted to education, teaching could possibly have been carried out in the same halls as assembly and recitations: cave 5 at Ellora, a long pillared hall (36 by 17 m) where parallel rows of benches suggest study-desks, could represent a class room directly surrounded by scholars' quarters (Mitra 1971: 183-4). *fig. 19 below*

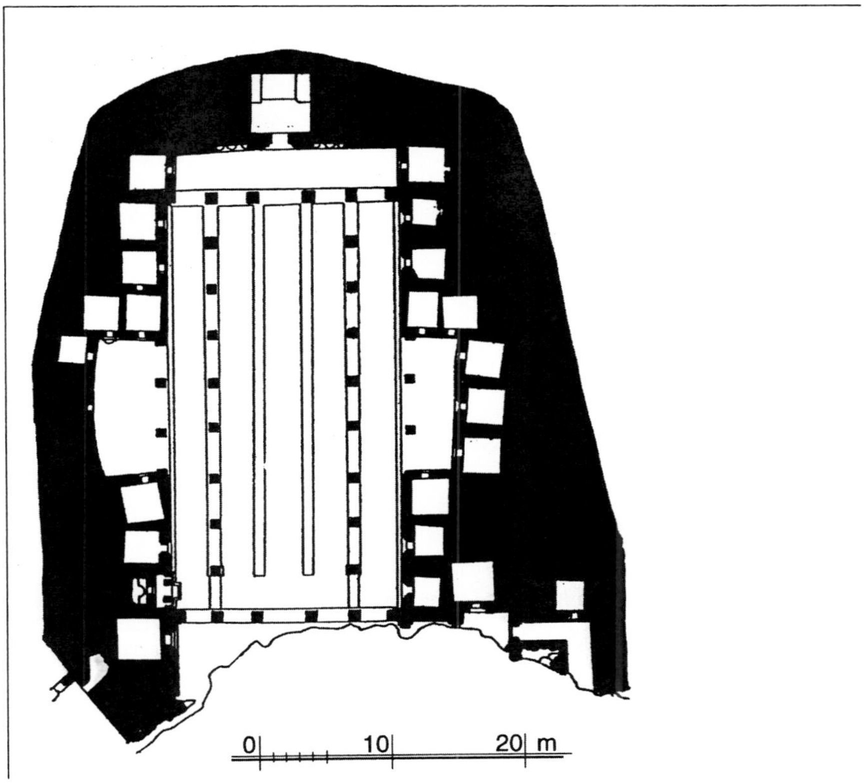

19 – *Cave 5 at Ellora (Maharashtra), 7th century*
A teaching establishment? Surrounded by 17 cells, the spacious central hall is divided by long, rock-cut benches, possibly used as study-desks (Mitra 1971: 183). The shrine at the end houses a Buddha image. (P. Pichard, after Mitra 1971)

Monks quarters

In practically every case, the basic cell, generally intended for a single monk, is a small room, nearly square in plan, its sides measuring between 2.4 m and 3 m, with a single door and sometimes a small window. Many cells have a built-in bench in stone or brick along one side (some have two), to be used as a bed, and a small niche in one wall for the monk's belongings or for his cult articles.

Single independent cells, directly entered from the face of the cliff, occur in rock-cut complexes. Independent rows of two to five cells, aligned behind a gallery shading their entrance, occur in surface monasteries, but the general pattern is the quadrangle of sometimes three and more often four rows, arranged on two storeys around a central square either covered or open to sky, the doors of all cells opening under a gallery surrounding this square. In the quadrangles fully planned with four rows, the number of cells varies greatly, from 12 at Sirkur to exceptionally 177 at Paharpur, 25 to 40 being the average in quadrangles with an external side of 30 to 60 m.

fig. 18 page 33

Ancillary rooms built adjacent to the cell quadrangle and with the same materials are present at Taxila, including kitchen and dinning room, store room, bath and toilets, while these facilities do not appear in later examples, for instance in Nalanda or Ratnagiri, where they could have been extensions less solidly built, possibly in wood, and did not survive.

fig. 3 page 23

In rock-cut complexes, caves with benches for up to 40 or 50 monks and provided with water cisterns seem to have been dining halls used by the monks living in the quadrangles excavated nearby (Mitra 1981: 157).

BIBLIOGRAPHY

BROWN, Percy
1956 – *Indian Architecture,* 2 vol., Bombay, Taraporevala Sons (3rd ed.).

DIKSHIT, K.N.
1938 – *Excavations at Paharpur, Bengal,* New Delhi, Memoir ASI No. 55.

DUTT, Sukumar
1924 – *Early Buddhist Monachism*, London, reprint 1996, New Delhi, Munshiram Manoharlal, 172 p., bibliography, index.

DUTT, Sukumar
1962 – *Buddhist Monks and Monasteries of India, their History and their Contribution to Indian Culture*, London, George Allen and Unwin, 397 p., photographs, maps, drawings, bibliography, index.

FUSSMAN, Gérard
1994 – "Upāya-kauśalya – L'implantation du bouddhisme au Gandhāra", *Bouddhisme et cultures locales – Quelques cas de réciproques adaptations*, Fukui Fimimasa and Gérard Fussman ed., Paris, EFEO, p. 17-51.

HANDA, O.C.
1987 – *Buddhist Monasteries in Himachal Pradesh*, New Delhi, Indus Publishing Co., 216 p., maps, photographs, bibliography, index.

INDIAN ARCHAEOLOGY –
1954-55 – p. 16 + pl. 29, excavation of Jivakamravana (Rajgir), plan, photo.
p. 24-26 + pl. 48-49, excavation at Sirpur (Raipur), plan, photos.

KHOSLA, Romi
1979 – *Buddhist Monasteries in the Western Himalaya*, Kathmandu, Ratna Pustak Bhandar, 147 p., maps, photographs, bibliography.

KURAISHI, Maulvi Muhammad Hamid
1931 – "Nalanda", *List of Ancient Monuments Protected under Act VII of 1904 in the Province of Bihar and Orissa,* Calcutta, ASI, New Imperial Series 51, p. 67-94, plan, photographs

LONGHURST, A.H.
1938 – *The Buddhist Antiquities of Nagarjunakonda, Madras Presidency,* Memoirs 54, New Delhi, Archaeological Survey of India, maps, drawings, photographs.

MARSHALL, John
1951 – *Taxila*, 3 vol., New Delhi, Motilal Banarsidass (reprint 1975), maps, drawings, photographs.

MICHELL, George
1989 – *The Penguin Guide to the Monuments of India – Vol. 1: Buddhist, Jain, Hindu*, London, Penguin Books, 519 p., maps, drawings, photographs, bibliography, glossary, index.

MITRA, Debala
1971 – *Buddhist Monuments*, Calcutta, Sahitya Samsad (reprint 1980), 307 p. maps, drawings, photographs, bibliography.

MITRA, Debala
1983 – *Ratnagiri (1958-61)*, Memoirs 80, 2 vol., New Delhi, Archaeological Survey of India, maps, drawings, photographs.

NAGAO, Gadjin
1980 – "The Architectural Tradition in Buddhist Monasticism", *Studies in the History of Buddhism* (Papers presented at the International Conference on the History of Buddhism at the University of Wisconsin, Madison, August 19-21, 1976), New Delhi, B.R. Publishing Corporation, p. 189-208.

NAGARAJU, S.
1981 – *Buddhist Architecture of Western India (C. 250 B.C.-C. A.D. 300)*, New Delhi, Agam Kala Prakashan, maps, drawings, photographs.

RIVOL, Thierry
1983 – *Shashur Gompa et l'architecture lamaïste*, 2 vol., typewritten dissertation, Grenoble, School of Architecture, maps, drawings, photographs.

SARKAR, H.
1966 – *Studies in Early Buddhist Architecture of India*, New Delhi, Munshiram Manoharlal, 120 p., maps, drawings, photographs.

STONE, Elisabeth Rosen
1994 – *The Buddhist Art of Nagarjunakonda*, New Delhi, Motilal Baharsidass, 143 p. maps, drawings, photographs.

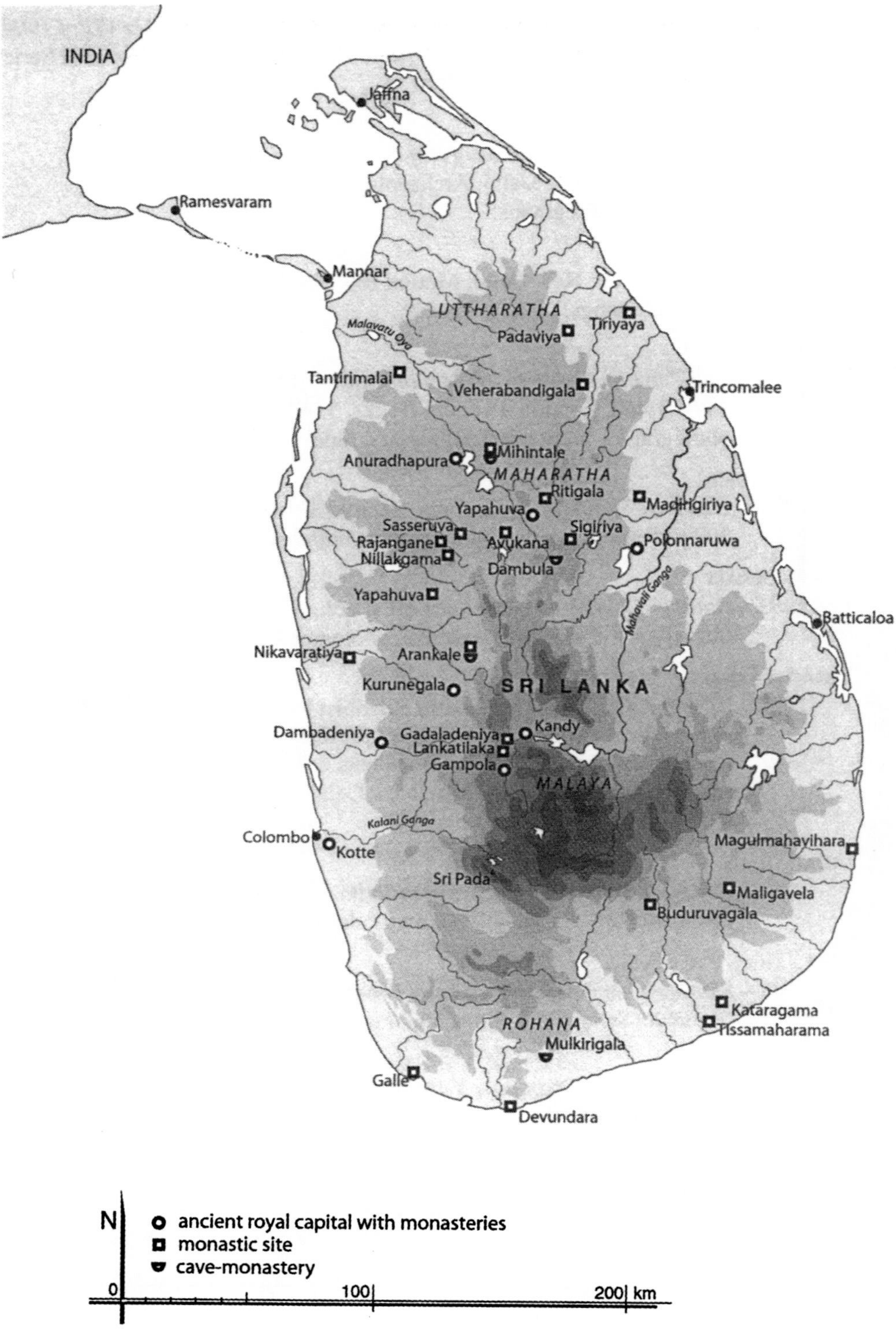
INDIA
Jaffna
Ramesvaram
Mannar
UTTHARATHA
Malavatu Oya
Tiriyaya
Padaviya
Tantirimalai
Veherabandigala
Trincomalee
Anuradhapura
Mihintale
MAHARATHA
Ritigala
Madirigiriya
Yapahuva
Sasseruva
Sigiriya
Rajangane
Avukana
Polonnaruwa
Nillakgama
Dambula
Mahaveli Ganga
Yapahuva
Batticaloa
Nikavaratiya
Arankale
Kurunegala
SRI LANKA
Kandy
Dambadeniya
Gadaladeniya
Lankatilaka
Gampola
MALAYA
Kalani Ganga
Colombo
Kotte
Magulmahavihara
Sri Pada
Maligavela
Buduruvagala
Kataragama
Tissamaharama
ROHANA
Mulkirigala
Galle
Devundara
N
ancient royal capital with monasteries
monastic site
cave-monastery
0
100
200 km

THE BUDDHIST MONASTIC ARCHITECTURAL TRADITION OF SRI LANKA

Ashley de Vos

Historical outline

The history of Sri Lanka is conventionally divided into several periods, named after the capital city pre-eminent at each time:

4th cent. BC to 5th century AD	Early Anuradhapura period
~ 459 to ~ 993	Late Anuradhapura Period
~ 995 to 1072	Chola invasion of Sri Lanka from South India
1065 to 1278	Polonnaruva period
~ 1071	Mission of Burmese monks to Sri Lanka to reform the Saṅgha
1153-1186	Reign of Parakkamabahu I in Polonnaruva
1164-5	Parakkamabahu I reforms the Saṅgha, favouring the Mahāvihāra school against the Abhayagiri and Jetavana schools
13th century	The royal capital shifts from Yapuhuva to Dambadeniya and to Kurunegala
1341-1415	Gompola period
1412-1472	Kotte period
1423	Dhammagambhira, a Siamese monk, receives a new ordination in Sri Lanka and introduces the Mahāvihāra tradition to Thailand
1471-1815	Kandy period
1505	The Portuguese take control of the west coast
1658	The Dutch replace the Portuguese on the west coast
1753	Mission of Siamese monks to Sri Lanka to re-establish the higher ordination – great ordination ceremony at Kandy and foundation of the Siyam Nikāya

The Buddhist Monastery, EFEO, 2003, p. 38-58

1765 A royal decree restricts the ordination ceremony to 2 monasteries in Kandy (later fallen into oblivion)
1796 The British take control of the coastal areas
1802 Foundation of the Amarapura Nikāya
1815 The British enter Kandy and take possession of the whole island
1864 Foundation of the Rāmañña Nikāya
1947 Independence of Sri Lanka

The official conversion to Buddhism of the king of Lanka, Devanampiyatissa (250-210 BC), and of his court,

— gives official credence and establishes Buddhism as the state religion of Lanka;
— opens a new and more reliable historical era of the island;
— implies that the land of King Asoka and Sri Lanka enjoyed a mutually understandable language, an equal social status and a cordial relationship;
— suggests that followers of the Teachings of Buddha existed in the country prior to the event. It is recorded that after the very first sermon, conducted by Arahat Mahinda, forty thousand people, including the king, embraced the Teachings of the Buddha. This is a significant section of the population then residing in the city of Anuradhapura and a considerable number, even though the figure may not be taken at face value;
— and, importantly, records the first gift of a section of the royal pleasure gardens for the use of the Saṅgha. The recent excavations carried out on the site, in Anuradhapura, establishes the existence of ponds and pools below the monastery, at a layer close to the original level of the early park, thereby confirming its origins as a palace garden. The gift of the royal park also formalizes and marks the beginning of royal patronage and of the establishment of the Mahāvihāra, which became the leading monastery in Lanka during the centuries that followed. While the Mahāmeghavana (the royal park) was the location of the Mahāvihāra, the Nandanavana (later renamed the Jotivana or the place from which light emanated, a possible reference to the spot where the Arahat Mahinda preached his first sermons), was the original site of the Jetavana stūpa and monastery. Though originally inspired by early Indian examples, this monastic architecture soon acquired a distinct Lankan character and represents a unique contribution to the architectural tradition of Buddhism.

The stūpa became the chief object of worship from the moment of its introduction to Sri Lanka. The first stūpa to be built at Anuradhapura, the Thuparama, dates back to the third century AD. One is able to picture the enthusiasm of the newly converted and their reaction when the Thuparama was erected to enshrine the right collar-bone relic of the Great Teacher. Though a relatively small stūpa, what was enshrined inside its circular mound, at the symbolical centre of the cosmos, was of immense value.

Originally built by King Devanampiyatissa, the stūpa consisted of a core of precious stones and lumps of clay taken from the bed of the Basvakkulamaveva Tank, with an outer surface of bricks. It was so sacred that it needed to be protected and covered, firstly by a timber structure as a protection and as a mark of respect (a concept similar to the honorific umbrella constructed over the stūpas), of a form similar to the Greek tholos (circular temple). It gave rise to the development of a unique type of building, the *cetiyaghara* or *vaṭadāgē*, reserved only for very special stūpas of which about only ten have been discovered in Lanka. Their early form is today preserved in the circular Hindu temples of South Kerala.

The earliest monasteries probably consisted of a stūpa as the object of worship and of cells for the monks.

1 – *The Jetavana Stūpa, built in the third century in Anuradhapura*

(ph. Pichard 1980)

The concept of having a stūpa within a building as seen in the *caitya-gṛha* of India is also seen in the many caves that had stūpas as their focal point, for meditation. With its circular and centred plan, the stūpa faces no particular direction: it faces all directions at all times. The development of the stūpa as an object of worship silhouetted against the sky exemplifies two basic notions common in the Indian concept of architectural space. The void, such as an area enclosed by a series of walls or balustrades, reinforces the intense concentration of emotion for worship, in contrast to the uncommitted space outside. The solid on the other hand, taking the form of the stūpa, serves as an object of worship. This simple interior space comes to life when animated by the rite of circumambulation (*pradakṣiṇā*), the ingenious age honored practice of translating a path in our world into a religious experience where the pilgrim surrenders to the architectural space once he is on the inside path. The ritual then takes over. This very simple act of circumambulation became a complicated affair in later Buddhism.

The teachings of the Buddha soon attracted a very large number of monks. Faxian, the Chinese monk who visited Anuradhapura and stayed in the Abhayagiri monastery from 412 to 414 AD, recorded the existence of nearly fourteen thousand monks in the monasteries that encircled the citadel. The large royal monasteries of Anuradhapura, the Abhayagirivihāra and the Mirisaveṭivihāra in the first century AD, the Mahāvihāra and the Jetavana in the third century, were set out in concentric circles round the citadel. These were the earliest recorded formal monasteries in Lanka. It is difficult to accept the term "organic" proposed by Bandaranayake (1974: 33-57) as, even though built over a long period of time, they followed a pattern, admittedly not a very strict one, around the stūpa. The Mahāvihāra monastery focused on, and developed around the large Ruwanveli stūpa and similarly, in every one of these early monasteries, the stūpa, centrally located and usually built by a king as an expression of his faith, was the focal point and the first structure to be built. At the collapse of the Roman Empire in the fourth century AD, the three great stūpas of Anuradhapura stood tall: with a height of 100 m and once recorded at 120 m, the Jetavana was the third tallest structure of the known world, next only to the two great pyramids of Gizeh. *fig. 1 above*

The building of such large brick structures consumed a large portion of the material surplus and required heavy investments and special management skills for the manufacture and procurement of materials, the recruitment and supervision of the labour force. The chronicles offer ample proof that man was worthy of his labour. They indicate that bags filled with money were placed at the entrance gates to the city and the workers partaking in the building activity took their dues as they passed through it. This evidence is important as it points to the fact that the labour had a cost and that the royal coffers paid handsomely for it.

The monasteries also set the tone for the spatial planning principles that developed for the city of Anuradhapura, with the villages serving the city and the monasteries forming rings round the citadel. A significant environmental change occurred with the man-made *vevas* or large reservoirs like the Basavakkulam, the Tissaveva and the Nuvaraveva, originally created in proximity to the city to store rain water for the use of the residents and also to irrigate the fields. The demand for good quality bricks for the construction of the stūpas led to the enlargement of these *vevas*, and the large water bodies seen today are directly related to this sudden burst of activity between the second century BC and the third AD.

The development of Anuradhapura was favoured by its central location, only a five-day journey from the western port of Mantota and from the eastern port of Jambukotapotuna of the third century BC, between Thiriyaya and Kuchchuveli (originally referred as the Talakori Emporium by Ptolemy). These ports had an important role to play in the development of Anuradhapura and in Lanka's strategic location at the center of the major sea trade route between Rome and China. Lanka was referred to by the ancient cartographers like Ptolemy (second century AD) as the great Emporium, an indication of the exchanges that took place and the surplus wealth that this trade may have generated. The large hoards of Roman coins found in different parts of the country confirm this fact.

Concurrently with the monasteries of Anuradhapura, cave dwellings were used by monks in other parts of the country. The drip ledges cut deep into the overhangs at the entrance of many caves bear testimony to their special dedication to the Saṅgha. The monasteries that developed on hill slopes, like at Mihintale and Vessagiriya, had their origins in these early caves that were used as resting places by the monks. With the increase in ritual and formalization of the teaching, new types of buildings were progressively added, as was common elsewhere. Therefore these cave monasteries cannot be categorized as a special type, but as a step in the evolution from the earliest caves.

The monastic layout

Early Monasteries of Anuradhapura

Buddhism, the state religion from the third century AD, tempered and regulated the lives of the Sri Lankan people and their artistic expression. The influence of the teachings of the Buddha in its pure form was far-reaching, to the extent that the self-discipline between the individual buildings of a monastery complex was stronger within than without. The monastic community, living according to the prescriptions of the *Vinaya*, determined the nature and form of this early monastic architecture.

fig. 2 and 3 opposite page

The Jetavanavihāra forms a wide monastic complex, on an area of some 80 hectares. The residences of the monks surround the central Jetavana Stūpa, but not under a strict formal layout except for the fact that all entrances face it. A number of residential groups, or colleges (*pañcāyatana*) have been exposed in the recent excavations at which

2 – *Seen from the top of the Jetavana Stūpa, behind the entrance pavilion to the stūpa platform in the foreground, the central monastic quinconx of a* pañcāyatana *college on the west side of the stūpa*
(ph. P. Pichard 1981)

3 – *Plan of the ruined monasteries surrounding the Jetavana Stūpa*

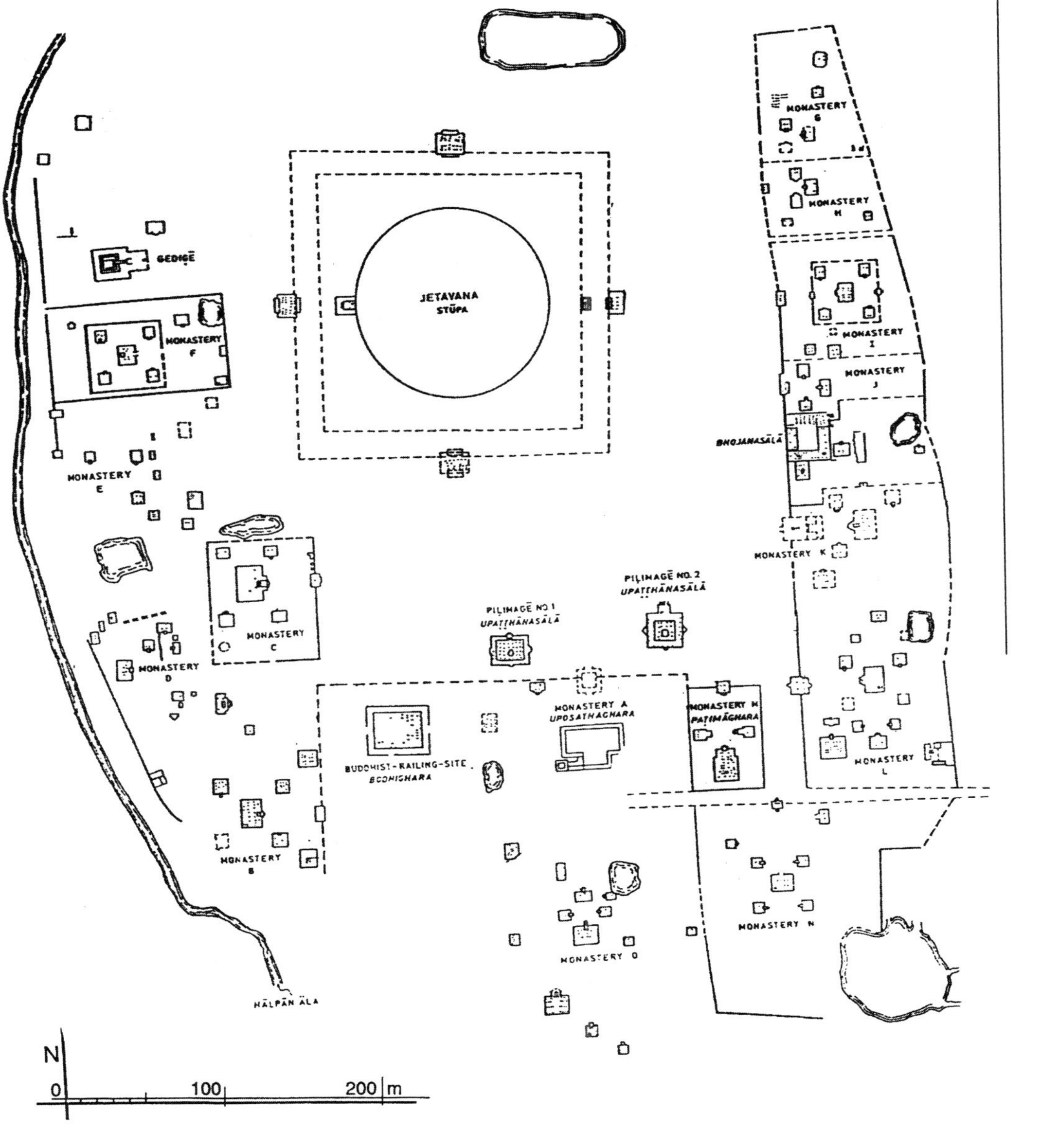

4 – *Monastic buildings on the west side of Jetavana Stūpa, with their platform and the base of their stone pillars* (ph. P. Pichard 1981)

the author was privileged to be an early participant. All these buildings remain today as mere stone-faced basements, on which in many cases rest the base of walls and some of the stone pillars which supported the roof. *fig. 4 above*

One enters a typical college through a gate house (*vāhalkaḍa*), set into a high fortress-like enclosure wall (*prākāra*). The *Vinaya* permits the use of brick, stone, or a wooden fence for such purposes. The walls in Anuradhapura were either in brick or stone, or at times, a combination of both. Even though very little evidence exists of the use of timber fences, it is probable that timber was used in the earliest phase of development of the monastery. These *prākāra* walls were wide at the base with tapering side panels, capped off at the top with a heavy stone coping. The average height of the cloister wall was such that it prevented anyone from outside looking in, or someone from inside looking out. The excessive thickness of the wall, sometimes faced with stone on either side, was a structural requirement, but it also facilitated the creation of two *sīmās*, one inner and one outer, if it became necessary. The *prākāra* wall provided security from wild animals in the more remote locations. In the area immediately within and adjacent to the gate, but recessed into the ground, were placed wash rooms, bath-houses with hot water and attached halls, store rooms, toilets, closets, etc.

The residential unit (*pañcāyatana*) in the college was set further back from the entrance area and was encircled by an equally high *prākāra* wall. In its fully developed state it consisted of a quincunx of five units: a central oblong building (*pāsāda*) and four smaller and square ones (*kuṭi*) at the corners. *fig. 5 opposite page* From the presence of pedestals and stone reliquaries (*yantragala*) in some *pāsādas*, scholars have questioned the actual function of the building, either devotional or residential (Bandaranayake 1974: 86-94). It seems more logical to suppose the central building was reserved for the chief monk or professor, while his pupils were distributed in the four remaining buildings. The monks lived separately, but also joined in the workings of the larger complex. They used the common facilities of the larger monastery, but at times carried their food from the refectory to be consumed within their individual complexes.

As rightly pointed out by Bandaranayake, the *pañcāyatana* is the most common monastic type in the early historic period. In our opinion, each of these colleges was headed by a senior monk who was an expert in a different aspect of Buddhist philosophy and teachings. They in turn professed to the pupils who spent periods of tutelage

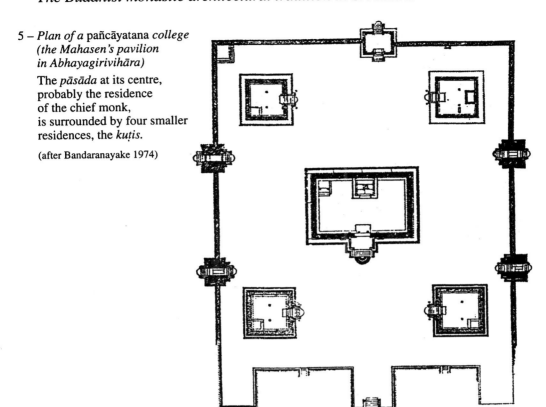

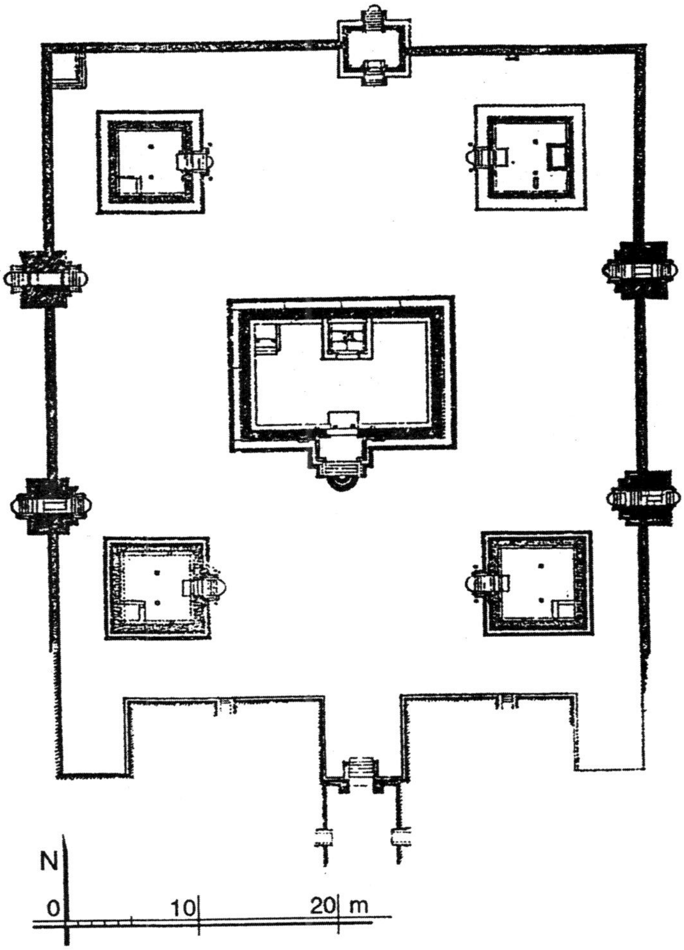

5 – *Plan of a* pañcāyatana *college (the Mahasen's pavilion in Abhayagirivihāra)*
The *pāsāda* at its centre, probably the residence of the chief monk, is surrounded by four smaller residences, the *kuṭis.*
(after Bandaranayake 1974)

attached to a particular college. On completion of their studies they moved on to study a different aspect under an expert in another college. That is to say, early monasteries were universities.

This concept would also fall in line with the *Vinaya* chapter on the settlement of disputes, where separate lodging places were to be found for monks who were studying different aspects of the teachings, so that they would not disturb each other. This may also help to explain the presence of conflicting and unusual objects like books written on gold plate, Bodhisattva statues, statues of Hindu deities, etc., in the different colleges. The objects were probably kept by the different experts in their individual colleges, for study or for purposes of worship. The strictly disciplined and almost formal layout, contained within the boundary, of the individual colleges, is not seen in the overall layout of the main monastic complex. This could stem from the Buddhist requirement to discipline oneself from within and/or from the fact that all residential complexes were not built at the same time.

Over a period of time, a number of distinct forms of monastic architecture have evolved, but our knowledge today is limited, due to a lack of serious in-depth study. Complementary structures in the monastery like the stūpa, the image house, (*paṭimāghara* or *piḷimagē*), the bodhi-tree shrine (*bodhighara*), the refectory, (*bhojanasālā* or *dānasālā*), the chapter house (*upposathagara*), the bath-house (*jantāghara*), were used as common property by all the residents in the monastery. Evidence also points to the fact that many of these buildings are part of the formalization of the monastery complexes and were added as the concept developed. It is therefore, probable that the early monks living in the monasteries did not have meals prepared in the individual monasteries, but were either offered *dāna* by the lay population, or came to the refectory specially constructed for the purpose in the King's palace, within the citadel.

The pabbata vihāra

The *pabbata vihāra* is an interesting type of monastery with a very formally planned layout, belonging to the late Anuradhapura period and found in the outskirts of the city (Prematilleke and Silva 1968; Bandaranayake 1974: 58-85). Some twelve examples have been identified, six around Anuradhapura and six in provincial sites (Bandaranayake 1974: 73).

In these *pabbata* or mountain monasteries, a confusing term as they were constructed on relatively flat ground, the terracing of the site surrounded by an open moat produces a hierarchy of building forms. The artificially raised site may be a clue to the allusion to the mountain in an architectural sense, different levels being used to enhance the focal space, a raised terrace.

fig. 6 opposite page

see Burma p. 65

The predominant architectural feature is a large rectangular sacred terrace at the centre, accessed by a single stair entrance or by four entrances orientated to the cardinal points, on which are distributed the four major ritual buildings, the stūpa, the bodhi-tree shrine (*bodhigara*), the image house (*paṭimāghara*) and the chapter house (*uposathaghara*), each in its quadrant: no building was placed at the precise centre of the compound in order to avoid giving predominance to any one of them, a concept similarly applied in Pagan in the 13th and 14th centuries). The residences of the monks are small square cells (*kuṭis*), usually facing inwards and arranged in single or double row around the central terrace. The whole was secured within a moated and walled area, outside of which could be located a shrine complex, at the end of an avenue.

The padhānaghara pariveṇa

The first monasteries of this type discovered in Anuradhapura were on the western part of the city, a sparsely populated area devoted to funerary ceremonies.

fig. 7 opposite page

fig. 8 opposite page

Constructed entirely in stone, the central area rests on two platforms connected by a stone bridge. The design is such that the platforms could be encircled by water, creating an area of total seclusion. The front building was an open platform or at times roofed with a timber pillared structure, where the eaves met in a hollowed out timber gutter carved on two carved stone columns. The rear building, usually a *pāsāda,* had stone pillars to carry a permanent roof. The whole complex is encircled by high *prākāra* wall and its entrance is through a secured gate house. Within the walled enclosure is a *caṅkamana* pathway, used for walking meditation. The absence of the usual ritual buildings like stūpa, bodhi-tree or image house suggests that these edifices were constructed for ascetics. Many more examples of this type have been discovered, and most interestingly about fifty examples have been found in the Ritigala forest which is known to have been a meditation place possibly belonging to the Paṁsukūlika sect. The use of water seems to have some significance as great care has been devoted to landscaping in the Ritigala forest. Water carried up using gravity to different levels is sent into the streams over rock outcrops in a series of spouts. Except for a recent cursory study, very little is known of the use of water as a vehicle.

These forest meditation monasteries are exceptional examples of a Lankan contribution to architecture. The edifice referred to as a Queen's Palace at Ratuboko in Java, is a monastery of the same type.

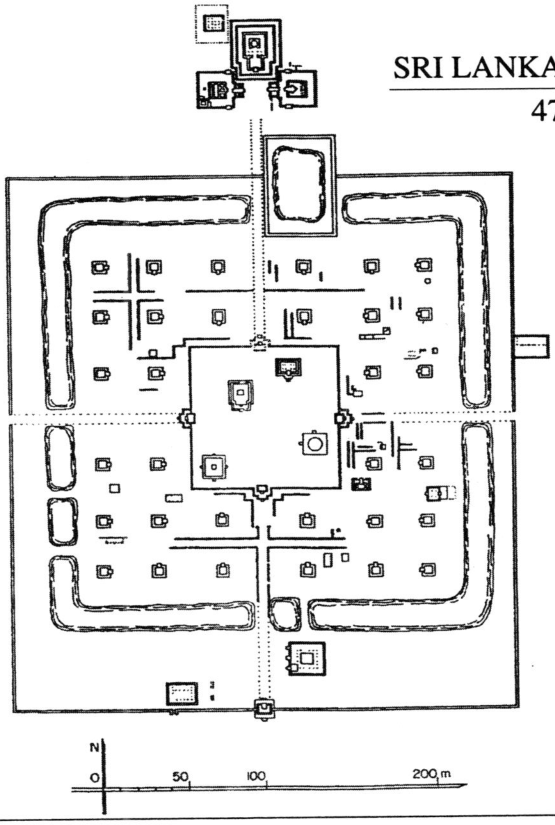

6 – *Plan of Puliyamkulam monastery, a strictly planned* pabbata vihāra *built in the 9th or 10th century on the north-west of Anuradhapura*

At the centre of the wide enclosure (300 by 330 m), the four major ritual buildings occupy the raised terrace: stūpa on south-east, bodhi-tree on south-west, image house on north-west and chapter house on north-east. Residential cells form the two peripheral rows in the enclosure, while an exterior shrine complex is on the north side, at the end of the axial walkway.

(after Bandaranayake 1974)

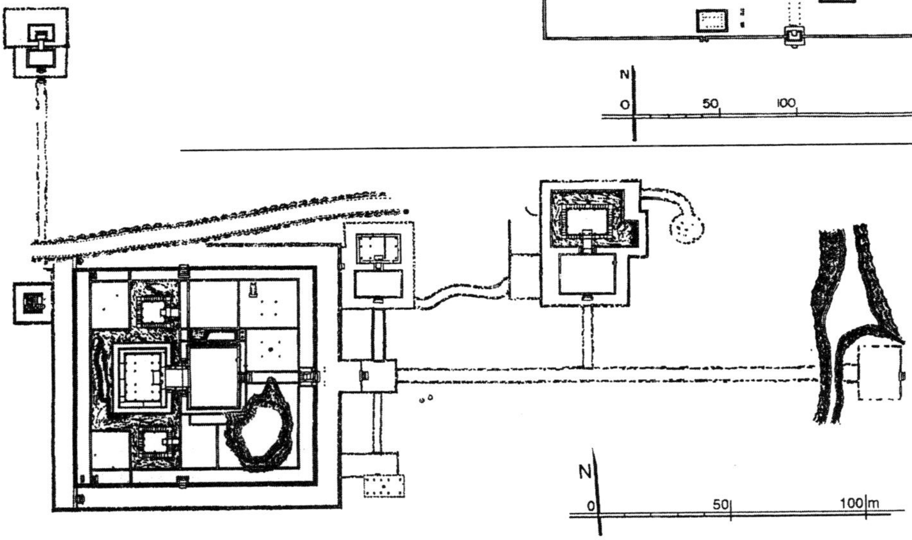

7 – *Plan of Monastery I, a particularly elaborate* padhānaghara pariveṇa *built in the eighth century in the west of Anuradhapura*

The central *pāsāda* on the western platform is flanked by two *kuṭis*, each on its own platform. The double-platform pattern of the central group is systematically repeated at a smaller scale on three satellite structures in the north side. (after Bandaranayake 1974)

8 – *The* padhānaghara pariveṇa *Monastery I from north, with its northern lateral gate in the foreground*

The stone bridge in the centre of the picture connects the eastern open platform, on the left, to the western one with the stone pillars of its *pāsāda*, on the right.

(ph. P. Pichard 1980)

The Courtyard Monastery

Another type seen in Anuradhapura and possibly belonging to the earlier period is the courtyard monastery. Similar to the early Indian examples, this type of monastery, of which there are only a few, is made up of a number of small cells placed around a courtyard to form a single building.

The walkway is located on the inside, facing the courtyard. In the centre of the courtyard is a single building which may have been a shrine. The whole complex is encircled by a *prākāra* wall and entrance is by a secured gate, while toilets and ancillary facilities are placed between the *prākāra* wall and the building.

As a building form, construction is easy and it is probable that it was built within a short period of time, unlike the other monasteries that had elaborate prefabricated plinths, the construction of which would have taken up a considerable period of time. Could these buildings then, have been built for visitors from India, who had to be hosted and accorded the highest honour? The one in Mihintale has been designated as an hospital, as stated in the inscription. But was this a later conversion? As a building tradition, it was not copied or duplicated in the later years.

Contemporary monasteries

Except for a short period during the sixteenth and seventeenth centuries AD, when the coastal belt of the Island saw destructions and a reduction in the building activity of villages, monastic building has been a prolific pastime. Today almost every village, a total of about 4000, boasts of a monastery or a temple. Some, like the family temples built by important people in the village, are now into hard times. Evidence of royal patronage from Thailand endowed some of the southern monasteries, like the Thuvakkakanda in Galle.

The compound contains the important ritual buildings, the stūpa, the image house, the bodhi-tree and the chapter-house (*uposathaghara* or *poyage*), the *dharmasālā* used for preaching and for conducting the Sunday school, the library (*pusthakala*), the residence of the monks (*pansālā*) and the refectory (*bhojanasālā*). The buildings, commonly in masonry with a tiled roof, are small on quite compact sites. The stūpa is raised on a high multi-ringed *pēsāva* and sometimes protected by a roof, not unlike the ancient *cetiyaghara* but at a smaller scale. Though the study to assess whether they conform to a *silpaśāstra* has not been conclusive, it seems however that a kind of basic rule has been followed.

fig. 9 below

9 – *A small stūpa under a tiled roof at Gadaladeniya*
(ph. P. Pichard 1981)

The architectural elements of the monastery

The stūpa

As the first expression of a Buddhist architectural tradition to be constructed, some Sri Lankan stūpas are amongst the largest examples in the world. The stūpa occupied the central location in the early monasteries, a position to be challenged in later examples. Hundreds of stūpas of varying sizes were built and many studies shows that new elements were introduced, superseding the early examples to arrive at the stūpas that are built today.

The stūpa in its basic form consisted of a *maḷuva* or platform, a *pēsāva* or plinth, and a dome, with its relic chamber. The dome was crowned by a *satarākoṭuva* or square box, derived from the square railing placed at the top of the early stūpas, and a *kota*, which is divided into the *devatā-koṭuva*, the cylindrical enclosure for the gods, the *chattrāvalī* or spine and the *kota* or finial with gem or crystal. The *kota* replaced the *yūpa* or cosmic pillar, the *yaṣṭi* or stem and the *chattra* or honorific umbrella of the early examples. Facing the four entrances to the *maḷuva* and adjacent to the *pēsāva*, were four *āyaka* projections.

Early ritual required the pilgrims to circumambulate the stūpa at the level of the *pēsāva* and the steps and railings as at Sanchi, allowed access to the upper level. With the introduction of the *āyaka*, the size of the steps were substantially reduced but the steps still existed and were seen between the *āyaka* and the *pēsāva*.

However , with the substantial increase in the numbers of pilgrims, the function of the *pēsāva* or basal terraces changed and the large groups of pilgrims were accommodated on an elevated *maḷuva* which was paved in stone. At first, like at Ruwanvelisaya stūpa, the *maḷuva* was a circular attachment to the stūpa, soon to be increased to a large square *maḷuva* capable of accommodating the ever increasing numbers that visited the stūpa. The *pēsāva* which was now ornamental changed from a single ring to three, and to the multiple *pēsāvas* of today.

The larger stūpas had multiple *maḷuvas* or terraces with formal *vāhalkaḍas*, or entrance gates and steps that faced the cardinal points. The outer *maḷuva*, at times referred to as the *velimaḷuva* or sand terrace, used for processions and similar activities, was surrounded by a wide *prākāra* wall that cleared the floor level of the elevated *vāhalkaḍas*. The raised inner terrace with its sides lined with an impressive *hastivedi*

fig. 10 below

10 – *The north entrance pavilion (*vāhalkaḍa*) of the Jetavana Stūpa after its restoration*
(ph. P. Pichard 1984)

or rows of elephants was accessed by climbing up wide steps to the level of the stone-paved terrace. The stūpa impressively rose up out of the stone terrace to stand high on the *pēsāvas*. As the stūpa evolved through time, so did the symbolism.

The bodhi-tree

A sapling grown from a branch of the tree at Bodhgaya, under which the Great Teacher attained enlightenment, was brought to Lanka in the reign of King Devanampiyatissa (250-210 BC) by Samghamitta Theri, the sister of Arahat Mahinda. It was planted in Anuradhapura and after 2500 years is the oldest historical tree in existence. Since its introduction in the third century BC, the bodhi-tree has been accepted as a basic requirement of every monastery.

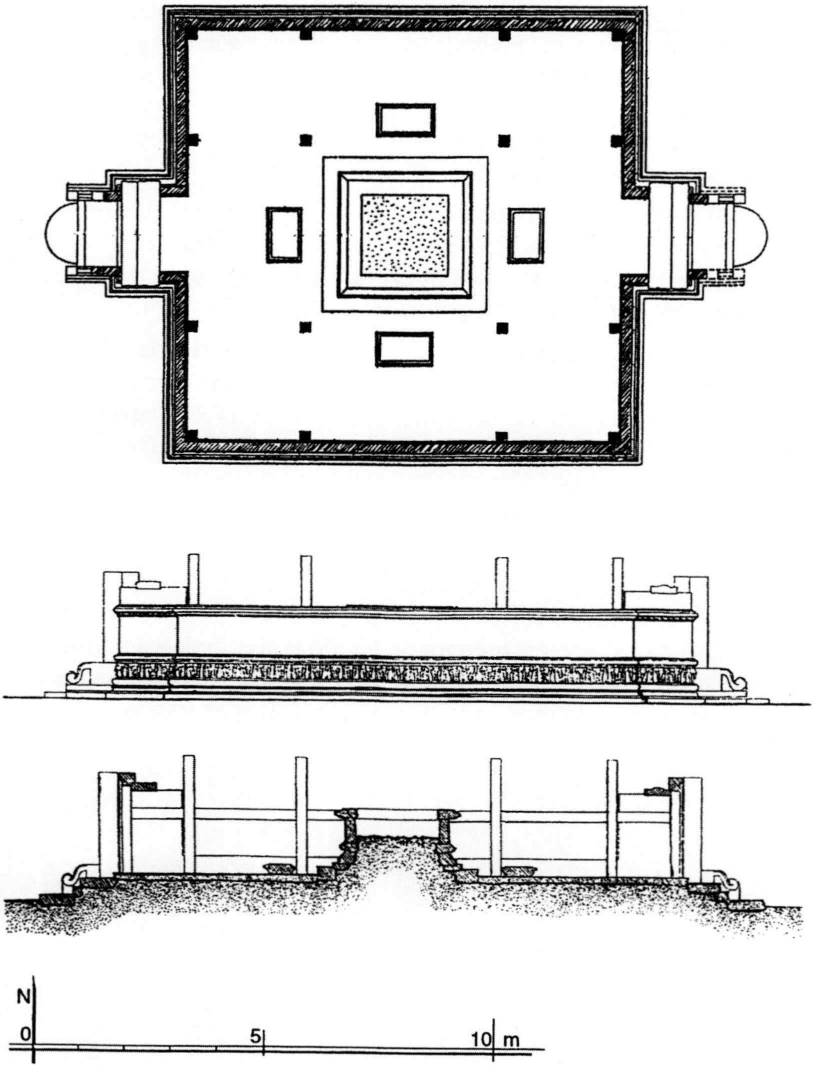

11 – *The* bodhighara *of Nillakgama (8th-9th century)*

Numerous tiles found when clearing the building indicate that the stone pillars supported a roof over the paved platform, around the open central square where was planted the Boddhi tree. (after Bandaranayake 1974)

It must be recorded that the introduction of the bodhi-tree to the monastic concept gave rise to two distinct architectural types, the *bodhimalaka* or *bomaḷuva*, a bodhi-tree surrounded by a wall or railing, and the *bodhighara*, an enclosure with a roof to protect the other sacred objects placed around the tree. It is probable that many *bodhigharas* started off as *bomaḷuvas* and only at a later period were converted to *bodhigharas*. The encircling of an object with a fence will not only protect it, but also enhance its sacred character.

As the ritual evolved, *āsanas* or raised platforms, introduced at the cardinal points with pyramidal roofs supported first on timber and later on stone columns, gave adequate protection to the objects placed on it. Later examples saw the roof encircle the tree giving protection to the circumambulatory path and meditation area. At times Buddha images were placed on the covered *āsanas* and the simple *bomaḷuva* had evolved into the *bodhigara* or bodhi-tree shrine. The more complex examples have full encircling walls with entrances surrounding the tree. The ritual watering of the bodhi-trees and the removal of excess water needed special care. Excavations have shown that some of these bodhi-trees were planted in restricted spaces, pointing to the fact that a deliberate attempt had been made to control and restrict their growth to almost a semi bonsai, to protect the *bodhigara*, whereas in the *bomaḷuvas* the trees were permitted unlimited and natural growth.

fig. 11 opposite page

The chapter house

The chapter house (*uposathaghara* or *poyage*), where religious observances are conducted, is specifically the building where the *uposatha* ceremony, the recitation of the *Pātimokha* and the listed offenses against the *Vinaya* rules, is held by the assembly of monks. It was a most important building in a monastic complex.

As the *uposatha* required that, on the new and full moon days, all monks from one residence should be present, the limits of the monastery had to be demarcated. It was also necessary to allocate a specific building for this ceremony within the compound. *Sīmās* were demarcated with due consideration to practical requirements. If for reasons of overcrowding, the *uposathaghara* was unable to accommodate all members of the assembly, the introduction of a second *sīmā* outside the first was considered to be in order (examples of this have been found). *Sīmāmalakas* constructed on water were also in use.

The *uposathaghara* was also used for other acts of the Saṅgha which had to be performed in the presence of all monks, like the Katihina ceremony. A study by Silva identifies four types of buildings used for this purpose:

1 – the single-storey building on land;
2 – the single-storey building in water;
3 – the double-storey building;
4 – the multi-storey building.

The multi-storeyed examples like the Lohaprasada of the Mahāvihāra in Anuradhapura were attached to the larger monasteries and served many purposes which included those for living and others for the administration of the community. Bandaranaiyake believes that it was also the abode of the abbot of the monastery and that its dual function differed from that of the *poyage* in contemporary monasteries. He also observes that the *uposathaghara* as a religious building was in vogue from the third century BC to the thirteenth AD, became rare between the fourteenth and the seventeenth centuries, while the eighteenth century saw a revival.

The image house or temple

Together with the stūpa and the Bodhighara, the *paṭimāghara* or image house was an important ritual monument. It had its origin in the mid-Anuradhapura period. The formal acceptance of the image as a separate object of worship requiring separate edifices had a long gestation period. Barrett refers to the first appearance of the Buddha image in the *āyakas* at Amaravati as only in the last two decades of the second century AD. However, since the third quarter of the first century AD, the artists of North India had already sculpted the Buddha image in the round.

Devotion to the Buddha image within the privacy of a cloistered unit is noticed at several sites from an earlier period as seen in the small niches for lamps and other articles in some of the early cells. So while some monks started to worship the image, there were others who persisted in venerating only the relics within a stūpa. Dutt refers to double shrines, one for a stūpa and another for the image, which existed in several monasteries at Nagarajunakonda.

see India p. 17-38

In Lanka, the chronicles refer to an image being made by Devanampiyatissa (250-210 BC) and a second by Dutthagamini (161-137 BC). But the first independent image house can be attributed to the reign of Jettliatissa (266-277 AD) even though examples of Buddha images placed in the *āyakas* or *bodhigharas* have been recorded.

The second *paṭimāghara* is attributed to Upatissa (368-410 AD) but as it was constructed within the palace, it may have been a private shrine of the king. The earliest noteworthy evolution of the *paṭimāghara* in Lanka, according to Silva, took place in the Abhayagiri monastery, and the acceptance of the design encountered considerable opposition from the Mahāvihāra until about the fifth century. After the fifth century AD, the activity of erecting Buddha images increased in popularity. Silva also records that a developed school of sculptors, capable of producing stone, jade, ivory and bronze images existed about the same time and some of the exports to China included images. The earliest examples had a square sanctum with a projecting gathering space in front. The circumambulation path around the statue was a later development. The seated, standing, or reclining image was placed on a raised lotus pedestal, which in turn stood on a relic chamber.

The development of the image house in Lanka gathered momentum with the royal patronage ushered in by Dhatusena (459-477 AD), who is recorded to have been responsible for more than thirty-six monasteries. The Mahāyāna influence in Lanka was predominant about the ninth or tenth century AD, and this period saw the sculpting of many colossal images. The timber and stone structures of the early period gave rise to large brick edifices of great proportions, notably the *gediges*. The construction of brick *paṭimāgharas* came to a halt in the tenth and eleventh centuries AD, with the Chola invasions and the complete sacking of Anuradhapura.

The Polonnaruva period is noted for its variety of *paṭimāghara*, from the three and four storeyed edifices in the city to the simple one storey and two storey examples. The brick and stucco type of construction was abandoned in the later period. Many image houses attributed to later periods had in fact earlier beginnings, as considerable changes are known to have taken place and obliterated the original features beyond recognition.

fig. 12 opposite page

The *paṭimāgharas* built after the thirteenth century reflect a return to the practice of the Anuradhapura period. Their timber, wattle and daub structure was supported on stone columns. Appearing later in the tradition than the stūpa and the bodhighara, their evolution as an architectural form is associated with the development of image worship.

Most of the image houses had by now become an integral part of the monastery and were constructed for seated, standing or recumbent images. Some were a combination of the different types and contained sculptures of the Buddha, of Bodhisattvas, kings and even interior stūpas.

2 – *Plan of the Hatadage, an image house built around 1190 in the Daladamaluva complex at Polonnaruva* (after Nakagawa 1991)

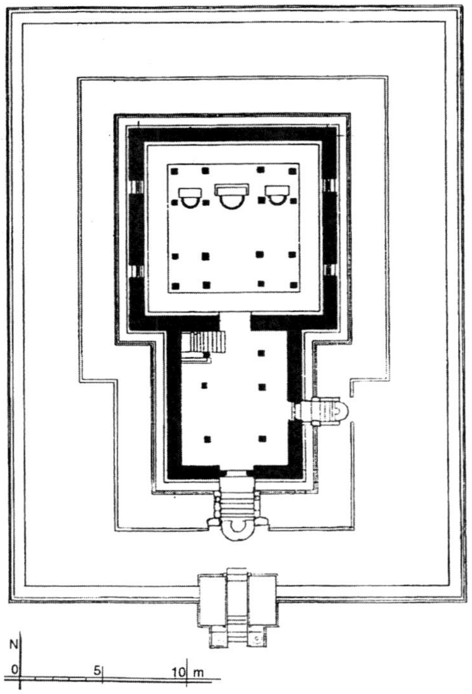

13 – *Plan of a residential cell (*kuṭi*) at Toluvila monastery, Anuradhapura*

It seems that three monks shared the pillared square room (with an interior side around 5 m).
As the stone base in one corner could be the landing of a staircase, these buildings were supposedly storeyed.
(after Bandaranayake 1974)

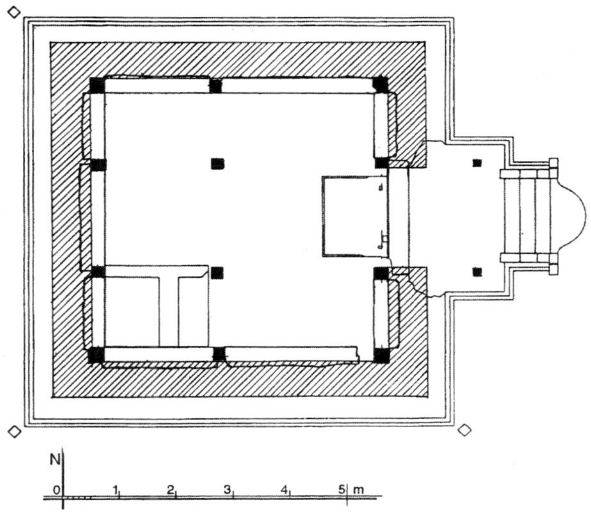

Residential Buildings

The residential buildings are not large in scale. They have rectangular plans similar to the *Vinaya* proportions of seven to twelve. A few stone steps flanked by balustrades and guard stones or *dvārapālas* lead one up into the building which is raised on a high stone plinth, a concept used even today in rural housing in Sri Lanka, where the raised plinth integrates it with the ground and protects the building on which it is raised, a simple but necessary method to protect the building from the monsoon floods, rising damp and the numerous creeping insects and reptiles commonly associated with the region. *fig. 13 above*

As an added precaution the area falling within the boundaries of the residential *sīmās* was laid out devoid of grass, as a sand terrace, the surface of which was combed every morning into a coconut leaf pattern.

The entrance threshold was a large flat slab of granite, with its center hollowed out as a shallow, rectangular, recessed, water container or trough with an outlet, in which one stood for washing his feet, pouring water with one hand from the container placed nearby and washing with the other prior to entering the dwelling unit. The *Vinaya* also refers to the use of door-mats and rugs converted from discarded robes.

The vertical members of the stone doorpost were fixed by dowels in a horizontal base slab also of granite. The door, made of a solid piece of wood with projecting dovel type pivot hinges to revolve on, was held vertically in mortises hollowed out in the granite inner threshold slab and the projecting top lintel that completed the stone door. The wisdom in the use of a slab of granite as a threshold is evident from the scrape marks left by the constant opening and closing of the door. These doors were lockable and had bolts and keys of bronze, hardwood or horn.

Construction techniques

An examination of the debris of the walling system above the plinth indicates the use of a limited amount of brick work. A more detailed investigation of the collapsed sections reveals that the brick wall on the stone plinth which formed the outer enclosure was a purely infill and did not exceed a height of half a meter, a height only adequate to protect the section of the wall most vulnerable to wear and tear due to physical leaning while sitting on the floor, and changes in the weather. The bricks were bonded using a fine butter-clay like mortar (*navanītha*). The fine silty sand and small brick fragments in the rest of the debris point to an earth type of construction more akin to the wattle and daub. This is logical, as many monks in the monasteries came from the surrounding villages where the same wattle and daub techniques were used. The walls were plastered inside and out using a mud plaster, which was first roughened using a small ball of paddy husk, after which lime mixed with tree-resins was applied as a finishing coat.

Most structures did not have actual foundations. The walls were founded a couple of inches below the finished ground level. In individual buildings, the vertical sections of the plinth, were made up of flat stone slabs and uniformly spaced header-stones which acted as countreforts to stabilize the wall and prevent collapse. In boundary walls, stability was achieved by increased width at the base.

The super-structure of the building was supported on carefully chiseled stone columns with their lower sections encased in brick and buried deep in the ground, thereby freeing the walls of the stresses of any direct roof loads. It is again a methodology, conceptually typical of the wattle and daub technique, where the timber frame carrying the roof transferred the loads direct to the ground. The original timber columns were merely replaced by stone in the later variations of this basic type. All the elements that went into fabricate a building were quarried and chiseled to size before being fitted together scientifically to produce the eventual building. These buildings that were prefabricated were the earliest examples of this type of construction known.

When the structures had a second floor, the adze-prepared heavy timber subframe of beams and thick planks of the flooring system were carried on the stone columns, giving rise to the taller version of a temple built on piles. A steep timber ladder providing access rested in two recesses hollowed out in a horizontal base slab of granite to protect the stair from termite attack, and also to absorb and resist the shock of the impact of a person landing on the ground on descending or ascending the stairway. The appropriateness of the use of hard wearing granite slabs was appreciated, but used only for special purposes, because the rest of the floor was made up of small pieces of a mixed matrix, of rubble, tile and brick fragments rammed into the floor to form a solid consolidated base, prior to leveling and finishing it off, using clay extracted from termite mounds mixed with cow dung. This again was a renewable technique commonly used in the village.

The *Vinaya* required the walls of the residences to be whitewashed externally and painted inside in a red or reddish brown colour. The floors were required to be black. The only wall ornamentation permitted at the time of the Buddha was drawings of flowering vines and creepers. It is interesting to note that this strict requirement for uniformity of colour influenced the whole of the traditions of later temple-painting. The priest painters continued to use the colour of the tradition and adorned the walls of their image houses with the themes of *jātaka* stories laid out in narrow strips of continuous visual narration painted on backgrounds of varying shades of red.

Most buildings in the monastery did not have windows with lockable sashes as it was felt that the gloom was detrimental to the eyes and encouraged a musty odour. Instead windows with permanent openings using security screens of railings, lattices of horizontal and vertical slats of wood were installed to maintain constant ventilation through the space. These openings at times had cloth blinds or curtains to keep out the squirrels and bats which were frequent visitors.

Roof forms

The roof in Sri Lankan architecture is the most significant and noticeable in the landscape. This architecture of roofs was a direct by-product of the climate. The high rainfall experienced at certain times of the year dictated its final shape and form. In the traditional village, the roofs were covered in straw thatch. They were steep to quickly shed off the rainwater and had wide and low eaves to protect the mud walls from erosion and to keep out the strong winds. The use of straw suited an agricultural people who re-thatched the roofs and re-rendered and re-plastered the floor and walls after every harvest.

A close examination of the few examples of religious architecture from the historic period reveals that two distinct roof forms have survived to this day. Both are of the hipped roof-type with the basic difference however, being in the shape and slope of the roof. It is obvious that the double-sloped roof, presently referred to as the "Kandyan roof" is a much later development probably brought about by:

(a) a need to use shorter timbers because of the lack of long straight timber trees in the hill country. Soft woods were not used for temple construction, only hardwood timbers like milla, satin, na, etc. The difficulty of carrying long, individual pieces of heavy timber up steep slopes;

(b) the reduced scale of the buildings amid the requirement for a visual impact of the roof when seen at close quarters on the hill sides. A single sloped-roof looks flat when viewed from a close proximity and from a lower level - hence the need to exaggerate its form;

(c) the later addition of an ambulatory around to protect the smaller inner building usually constructed in mud;

(d) a concept introduced by monks returning from a visit abroad.

The converse is true of buildings in the flat plains of Lanka. Large long straight timbers were available and a single pitched roof had sufficient impact when viewed from any distance. An accentuation of the visual character of the architecture was enhanced by the transition through a series of level changes as one moved through the architectural spaces. As this was usually not possible in the hill country, visual impact was achieved only by the exaggeration of the roof form. It is, therefore, logical to infer that the original roof of the Anuradhapura period was a steep, single sloped, hipped roof constructed using large long straight timbers that were available in abundance in the surrounding jungles.

A unique occurrence, the monastic architecture of Sri Lanka is a unique achievement, as it saw a continuous development for over 2500 years. Buddhism tempered every aspect of life and the heritage it generated exemplifies the whole evolution of the Sri Lankan architecture. We are all proud to be part of it. As the many scholars working on these subjects, cloistered in tight compartments and jealously guarding their findings, are unable to even agree on a common definition, a more correct interdisciplinary approach is necessary and should be encouraged.

BIBLIOGRAPHY

BANDARANAYAKE, Senake
1974 – *Sinhalese Monastic Architecture*, Leiden, E.J. Brill, 404 p.

BAREAU, André
1957 – *La vie et l'organisation des communautés bouddhiques modernes de Ceylan*, Pondichéry, PIFI 10, 90 p.

CASPARIS, J.G. de
1961 – "Cultural Relations between Java and Ceylon in Ancient Times", *Artibus Asiae* Vol XXIV.

DUTT, Sukumar
1962 – *Buddhist Monks and Monasteries of India, their History and their Contribution to Indian Culture*, London, George Allen and Unwin, 397 p.

EVERS, Hans-Dieter,
1967 – "Kinship and Property Rights in a Buddhist Monastery in Central Ceylon", *American Anthropologist* 69-6, p. 707-711.

EVERS, Hans-Dieter
1969 – "Monastic Landlordism in Ceylon", *Journal of Asian Studies* 28-4, p. 685-692.

GOMBRICH, Richard F.
1971 – *Buddhist Precept and Practice*, London, reprint 1991, New Delhi, Motilal Banarsidass, 427 p.
1988 – *Theravada Buddhism – A Social History from Ancient Benares to Modern Colombo*, London, Routledge & Kegan Paul, 237 p.

GUNAWARDANA, R.A.L.H.
1979 – *Robe and Plough. Monasticism and Economic Interest in Early Medieval Sri Lanka*, Tucson.

HOCART, A.M.
1924 -26 – *Memoirs of the Archaeological Survey of Ceylon*, vol. I & II, Colombo.

HORNER, B.
1940-52 – *The Book of Discipline*, Sacred Books of the Buddhists, London.

JAYASURIYA, M.H.F; PREMATILLEKE, Leelananda; SILVA, Roland
1995 – *Mañjuśri Vāstuvidyāśāstra*, Archaeology Survey of Sri Lanka, Colombo

NAGAO, Gadjin
1980 – "The Architectural Tradition in Buddhist Monasticism", *Studies in the History of Buddhism* (Papers presented at the International Conference on the History of Buddhism at the University of Wisconsin, Madison, August 19-21, 1976), New Delhi, B.R. Publishing Corporation, p. 189-208.

NAKAGAWA, Takeshi (ed.)
1991 – *Ancient Architecture of Sri Lanka, Studies in Planning and Restoration of Temple Architecture in the Late Anuradhapura and Polonnaruva Period*, Tokyo, Waseda University, 294 p.

PARANAVITANA, Senarat
1946 – *The Stūpa in Ceylon*, Memoirs of the Archaeological Survey of Ceylon V, Colombo, 105 p.

PREMATILLEKE, Leelananda; SILVA, Roland
1968 – "A Buddhist Monastery Type of Ancient Ceylon Showing Mahayanist Influence", *Artibus Asiae* 30, p. 61-84.

PREMATILLEKE, Leelananda
1996 – "Ancient Monastic Hospital System in Sri Lanka", *Ancient Trades and Cultural Contacts in Southern Asia*, Bangkok, National Culture Commission, p. 115-126.

NICHOLAS, C.W.
1963 – "Historical Topography of Ancient and Mediaeval Ceylon", *JRAS*, vol. VI, Colombo.

RAHULA, W.
1956 – *History of Buddhism in Ceylon; the Anuradhapura Period, 3rd Century BC – 10th Century AD*, Colombo.

SILVA, Roland
1988 – *Religious Architecture of Ancient and Mediaeval Sri Lanka*, Leiden.

VOS, Ashley de
1988/89 – "A Typology for a Monastery Building from Anuradhapura", *JRAS* vol. XXXIII, Colombo.

WIJESEKERA, Dr. N.
1990 – Volume Three, *Architecture, ADC*, Colombo

WIJESURIYA, G.S.
1998 – "Buddhist Meditation Monasteries of Ancient Sri Lanka", *Memoirs of the Archaeological Survey of Ceylon*, vol. 10, Colombo.

ANCIENT BURMESE MONASTERIES

Pierre Pichard

The earliest monastic building in Burma appears to be a brick structure attributed to the fourth century AD, excavated in 1959 in the Pyu city of Beikthano and known as KKG2 (Aung Thaw 1968). The Pyu, whose language has only been partially deciphered, had established several cities in Burma before the arrival of the Burmese and could have adopted Buddhism since the second or third century. By its plan, KKG2 seems very akin to the simplest Indian monastery: a single row of eight cells of 3,05 by 2.90 m, entered from a common corridor connected with a small entrance hall on the east side. The building is associated with a ruined stūpa located some 30 metres away in front of it, and with a square structure, possibly a shrine. In the absence of any epigraphic or iconographic confirmation however, the Buddhist dedication of these three buildings has been inferred only from their similarity with Indian Buddhist monasteries and stūpas, particularly those at Nagarjunakonda. It is only in the other Pyu city of Sriksetra, 130 kilometres south of Beikthano, that Buddhism can be unquestionably ascertained through sculptures, stūpas and inscriptions dated from sixth to ninth centuries, but no monastery has so far been identified there.

fig. 1 following page

see map p. 73 for sites mentioned in this article

Buddhism was introduced around the same time to the Môn country of lower Burma, around Thaton and Pegu, but there again no ancient monastic remains have been discovered, with the possible exception of sculptured slabs which could have been used as *sīmā* boundary stones (Luce 1969: 252-3; Krairiksh 1974).

1 – *Plan of monastery KKG2 (4th century) in Beikhtano, with the associated stūpa and shrine, showing a similarity with the plan of Indian monasteries of the same period, particularly at Nagarjunakonda (fig. 11 p. 29 or 17 p. 32 in this volume; see also Aung Thaw 1968, fig. 86)*

(P. Pichard, after Aung Thaw 1968)

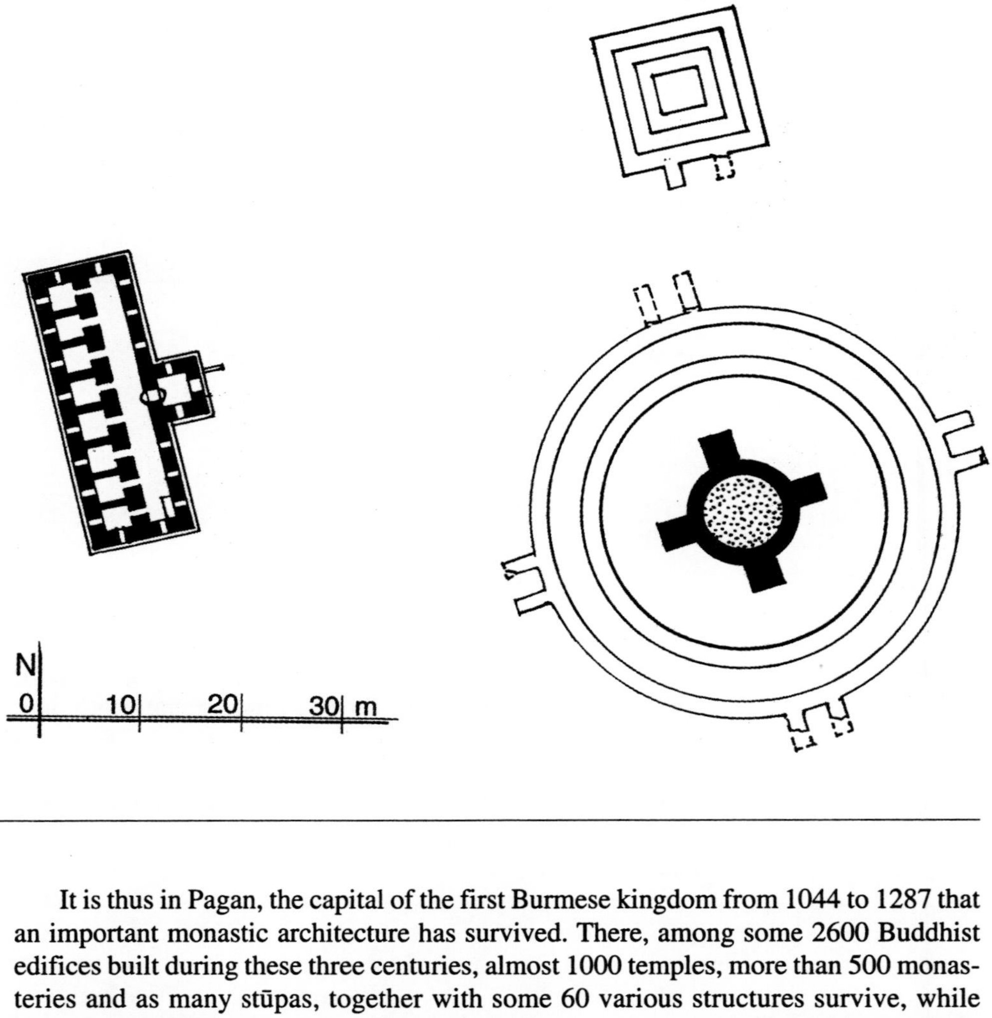

It is thus in Pagan, the capital of the first Burmese kingdom from 1044 to 1287 that an important monastic architecture has survived. There, among some 2600 Buddhist edifices built during these three centuries, almost 1000 temples, more than 500 monasteries and as many stūpas, together with some 60 various structures survive, while 400 brick mounds represent collapsed buildings (since 1993, many of these mounds have been cleared by the authorities and conjecturally rebuilt on the basis of their foundations). Monasteries therefore, easily distinguished from the other monuments by their specific features, amount for approximately a quarter of all the buildings of the site. Just like the other structures, only few of them (the largest ones and usually founded by the crown) can be securely dated by dedicatory stone inscriptions.

fig. 2, No. 1147
fig. 3, No. 1371
opposite page and Ratnagiri p. 30-31

Together with some of the earliest monuments of Pagan, in the area along the Irrawaddy bank and around the village of Myinkaba, two of these monasteries (Inventory Nos 1147 and 1371) show a strong similarity with the Indian monastic quadrangle, and specially with the monasteries of Ratnagiri, except that they are entered from east

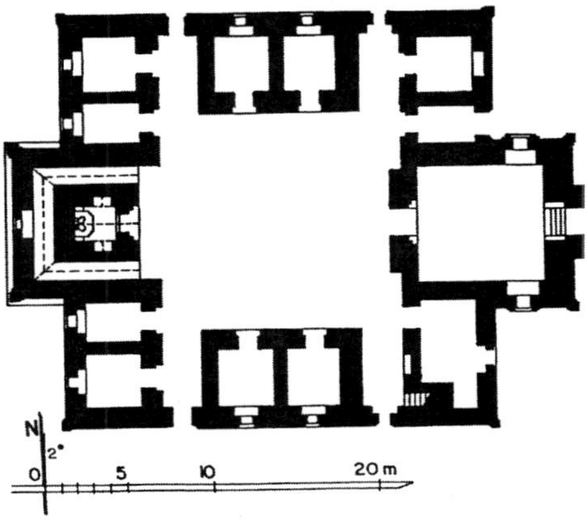

2 – *Plan of Somingyi monastery 1147, Pagan (12th century?)* (P. Pichard)

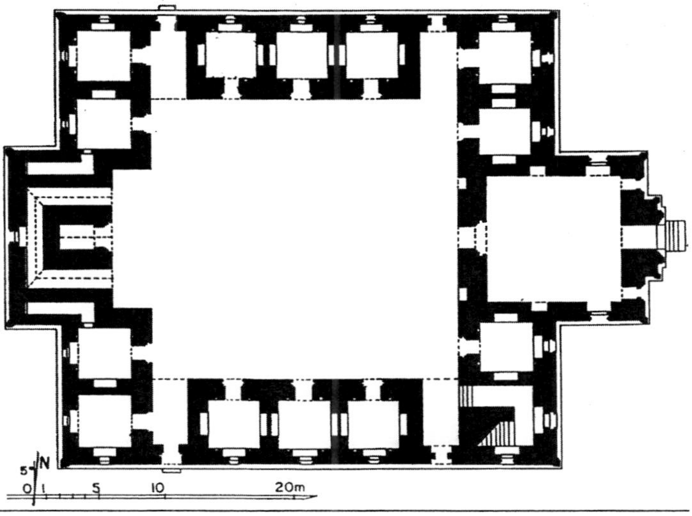

3 – *Plan of monastery 1371, Pagan (12th century?)* (P. Pichard)

instead of south. Their cells are slightly larger and less numerous, 10 for monastery No. 1147 and 13 for No. 1371, and seem to had opened directly on the central courtyard (or was there a wooden gallery?). At present, walls remain at the ground floor only, but a staircase in the southeast corner (that is, in the left hand corner after entering the quadrangle, exactly as in monastery 1 of Rajagiri) suggest an upper storey. In the middle of the east side is a square entrance hall, as in Beikthano but much larger. While the hall and cells of KKG2 were approximately of same size, the halls in Pagan reach 7.09 by 7.62 m (in No. 1147) and 9.95 by 10.12 m (in No. 1371). Such large rooms, which would have been difficult to cover without the support of interior wooden pillars, could have been used as meeting places for the monastic ceremonies, and probably also, given their location directly at the entrance, for sermon readings and other gatherings between monks and lay people. Besides this large meeting hall replacing the simple porch, two passages open on each lateral side of the quadrangle offer a direct access to the courtyard, another feature not seen in India. It appears that both monasteries were less closed to the outside world than their Indian counterparts.

Conversely, the shrine facing the main entrance is directly related to the Indian model. But here an addition appears, a corridor open from the courtyard by two doors and allowing one to circumbulate the shrine and its image (much later, the very same configuration can be found again in Nepalese monasteries).

see Nepal p. 219-244

Besides these two examples and a few multi-cell monasteries also derived from the Indian prototype, particularly in the Thamathi group, the architects of Pagan devised an original model and built it by the hundreds in the thirteenth and fourteenth centuries. In its simplest form, it consisted of a single-room brick building, nearly cubical, with an axial niche between two doors on its main face and one more door on each lateral side. To this main face, most often the eastern one, was attached a large open hall consisting

fig. 4 below
fig. 5 below

4 – *Plan of monastery 1394, Pagan (13th century)*
The simplest type of brick monastery, built in large numbers all over the site (P. Pichard)

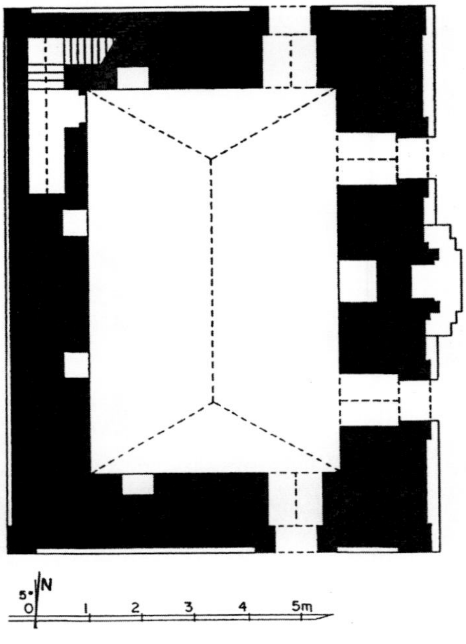

5 – *Monastery 526, Pagan (13th century), from N.-E.*
On the main eastern face, traces from the tiered roof of the former timber hall appear over the axial niche flanked by two doors (photo P. Pichard)

6 – *Reconstructed sketch of monastery 449 (Pagan, 13th century, in the immer courtyard of the Le-myet-hna monastic complex) with its former timber pavilion attached on the east side of the brick building* (P. Pichard)

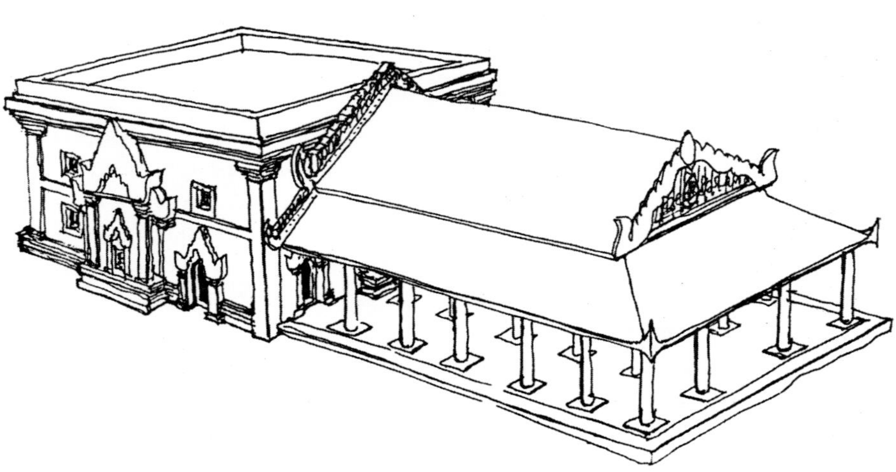

of a tiled roof supported by wooden pillars. This hall has today disappeared but can be precisely reconstructed on several instances by the trace of its roof on the masonry wall, the stone plinth around its floor and the stone sockets on which rested the pillars. *fig. 6 opposite page*

A Buddha image, probably of wood, was installed in the axial niche, at the precise centre of the wall separating the timber hall from the monastic brick building The monks could circumambulate it through the two doors of the front wall, reminiscent of the ones which framed the shrine entrance in monasteries 1147 and 1371. The sharp contrast of the two adjacent structures is a clear expression of their relative functions: a closed brick cube for the monks, an open pavilion where the surrounding lay community could assemble and be preached, under the Buddha image presiding in its niche. The whole design appears as a simple and sensible solution to shape the relationship between monks and laity while preserving the formers' privacy.

On this common pattern, the numerous monasteries built in Pagan vary on size, complexity and decoration.The single vaulted room of the simplest monasteries measures usually a little more than five metres by four. When more developped, partition walls create two or more interior rooms. Some monasteries had two full storeys and other a single mezzanine under their vault, some had a small central cell (possibly used to keep their manuscripts, a copy of *Tripiṭaka* being one of the most costly gift mentioned in inscriptions) surrounded by a wide corridor, occasionally with a projection in the middle of the lateral and back walls. While most monasteries have a flat roof supported by the brick vault and accessible through an interior staircase, the most elaborate have an additional shrine at the upper floor, crowned by a tiered tower, the brick version of the square wooden spire (*pyathat*). *fig. 7 below* *fig. 6 opposite* *fig. 4 opposite* *fig. 8 below*

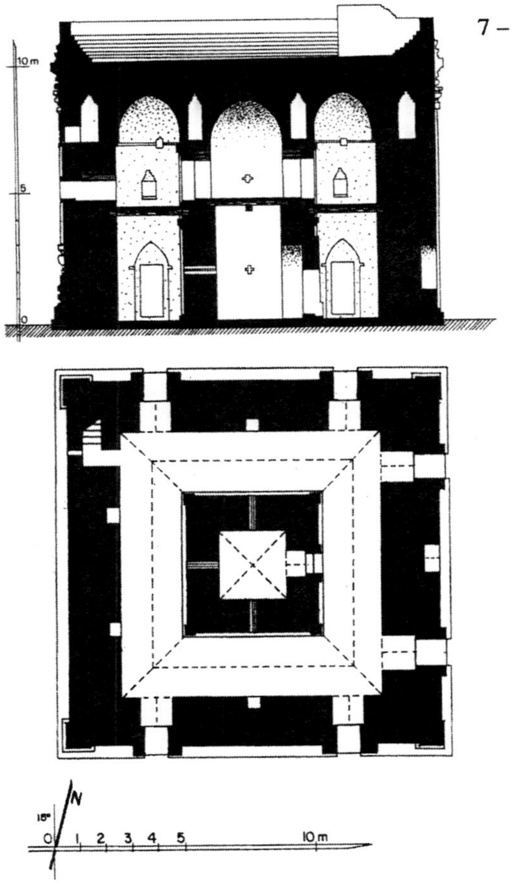

7 – *Plan and section of Shin-bo-me monastery 291, Pagan (13th century)*
Central cell and corridor, two doors on three sides but the axial niche exists only on the east face, on which was attached the timber hall; upper storey on the same plan, with a timber floor (P. Pichard)

8 – *East face of Swe-daw-gu monastery 73, Pagan (13th century)*
Upper storey crowned by a brick *pyathat*

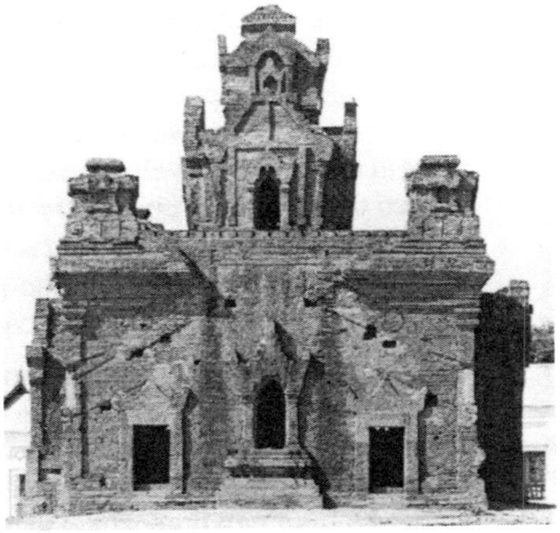

(photo P. Pichard)

Several underground monasteries were also excavated in a few sectors of Pagan, sometimes reflecting the quadrangular plan of the Indian model: from a central courtyard, dug down in the soil and open to the sky, tunnels give access to several small cells. The only feature above the ground is the entrance gate, from which a staircase goes down to the courtyard.

fig. 9 below

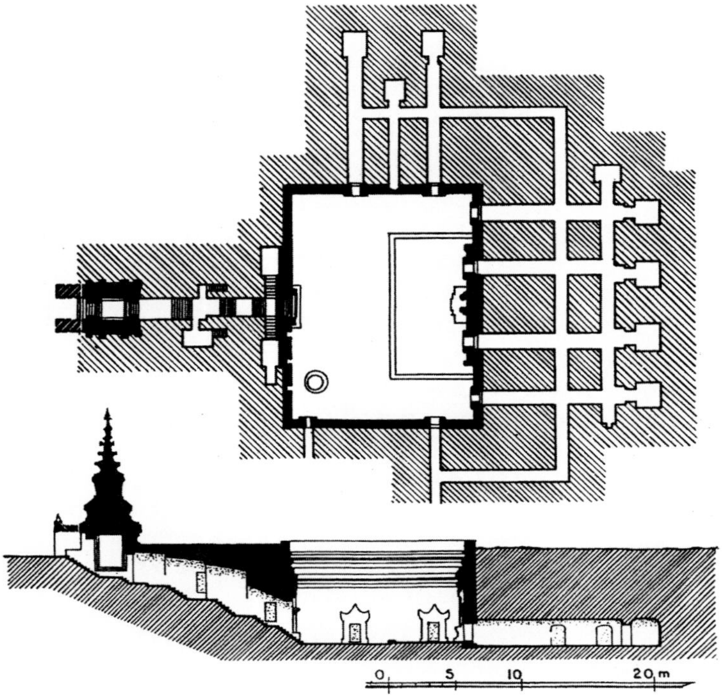

9 – *Plan and section of Taung-Kyanzittha Umin underground monastery 297, Pagan (14th century?)*
From the central courtyard open to the sky, tunnels and cells were cut out of solid soil.

On a very compact size, the typical brick building of the Pagan period and its attached wooden hall combined all the basic elements of a monastery: the dwelling place for monks, the space for assemblies and the Buddha image at their junction. At Pagan, effectively, several such monasteries are located quite away from other monuments and seem to represent a whole, single monastic foundation (at least today, but they could have been originally surrounded by ancillary buildings in wood or bamboo). More numerous however are monasteries of exactly the same type, but spatially linked with a main centre of devotion: they surround the great stūpas and temples of Pagan, either inside their enclosure but on a side or in a corner, or outside the boundary wall and close to it.

In three large monastic complexes founded in Pagan during the 13th century, the same structure becomes a mere element of a regularly planned layout, consisting of a double rectangular enclosure on a total area of more than six hectares each. In the inner courtyard were located the major buildings: either a temple or a stūpa, a large monastery with its front pavilion, which was probably the residence of the abbot, an ordination hall

fig. 10 and 11 opposite page

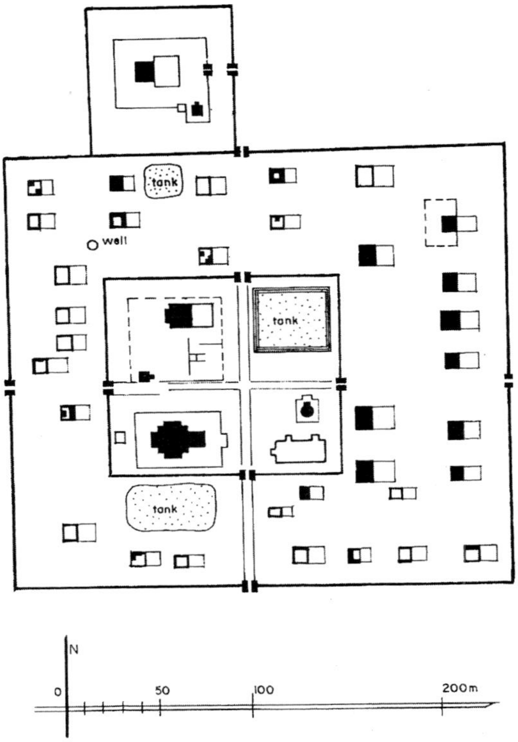

10 – *Plan of the Hsin-byu-shin monastic complex (Pagan, 13-14th centuries)*
Five major buildings occupied the quadrants of the inner central courtyard, measuring 109 by 124 m: the Hsin-byu-shin temple 697 in south-west, the abbot's residence in north-west, a tank in north-east, an ordination hall in the south-east corner together with the small circular temple 684. In the outer enclosure of 237 by 264 m were 35 monasteries, each with its wooden extension on the east side. (P. Pichard)

11 – *Reconstructed sketch of the Hsin-byu-shin monastic complex (Pagan, 13-14th centuries), from south-east* (P. Pichard)

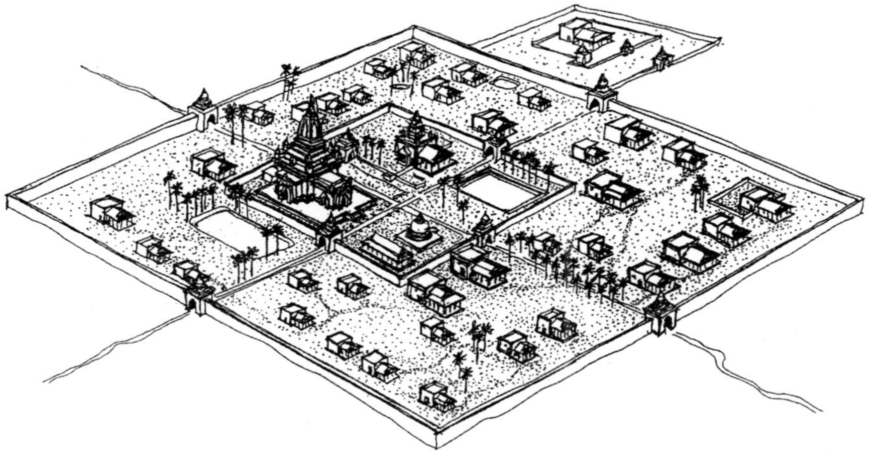

built as an open pavilion surrounded by *sīmā* boundary stones, and in two cases a school building. The two axes of the rectangular compound, clearly marked by the alignments of gates in the two boundary walls, divide this inner enclosure into four quadrants, amongst which the buildings are distributed. There is no structure at the very centre, a specific characteristic shared with the Sri Lankan monasteries known as *Pabbata Vihāra* built between the eighth and eleventh centuries in Anuradhapura. *see Sri Lanka p. 46*

In the outer enclosure around this central courtyard, several monasteries of the common type were aligned in rows, each with its attached wooden pavilion. The number of monks is not mentioned in inscriptions, which concentrate on recording donations and dedications (including lands, rice fields and servants). Each building, clearly larger than an individual cell, could have been intended for four or five occupants such as a senior monk and his followers, either younger monks or disciples. It has been proposed (Frasch 1996: 311-2) that each of these three monastic complexes could have been occupied by some 40 to 50 titular monks and 80 to 100 novices, disciples and lay servants.

Still in Pagan but in the early fifteenth century (that is, after the fall of the city), a development of the typical monastery can be followed in the Tain-hsaung kyaung (Inv. 299), built in 1408 (and now in ruined condition). The usual two-storey brick building was surrounded by a first boundary wall, on the east side of which the axial *fig. 12 below* niche and its image were replicated, and the roof of the wooden pavilion covered also the passage now created between the building and the new front wall. A second, lower boundary wall enclosed the whole complex in a rectangle of 80 by 38 metres. It can be supposed that this arrangement, creating an intermediate space between the monastic quarters and the public hall, was designed to allow the lay people to circumambulate the image in the front niche without entering the monks' quarters.

12 – *Plan of Tain-hsaung monastery 299, Pagan (1408 CE)* (P. Pichard)

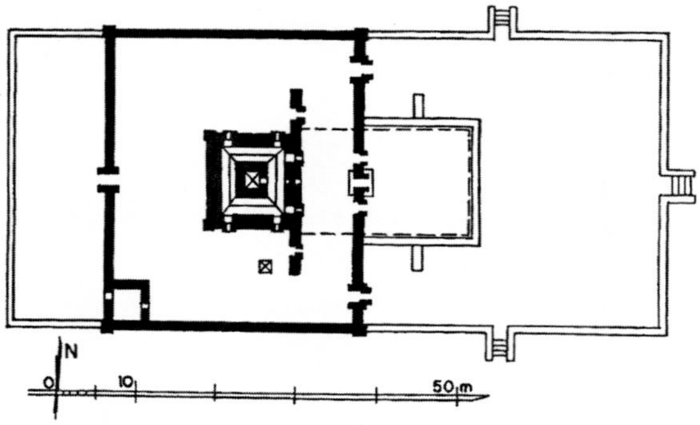

13 – *Patama Taik monastery, Sagu, built 1920 and today a Pāli teaching centre, from south-east*
Three contiguous elements, clearly distinghished by their roof configuration:
from east to west, *phyathat saung*, *sanu saung* and *marabin saung* (photo P. Pichard)

The linear composition, from East to West, will become more systematic in the large wooden monasteries built during the Konbaung period (18th and 19th centuries) in the last capital-cities of Burma, Amarapura and Mandalay, as well as on several provincial *fig. 13 above* sites. Several survive in various conditions and some are still occupied by theSaṅgha. In addition, a few monasteries in brick masonry reproduce the general configuration of their wooden model, like the Ananda Ok-kyaung built in Pagan in 1756 and famous for its mural paintings, or the Aung-mye-bon-zan Ok-kyaung in Ava, built in 1818.

They consist of three or four structures, each with its own roofing configuration, aligned on a common platform supported by rows of pillars and accessible by several masonry stairways. The whole structure as well as the floor, walls and partitions are in *fig. 14 below*

14 – *Plan, section and elevation of Shwei-in-bin monastery, Mandalay, built 1895*
On a linear plan, the distinct elements of the monastery are linked
by a common wooden platform, 55 by 24 m, supported by 167 teak pillars
(P. Pichard, after Myo Myint Sein 1970)

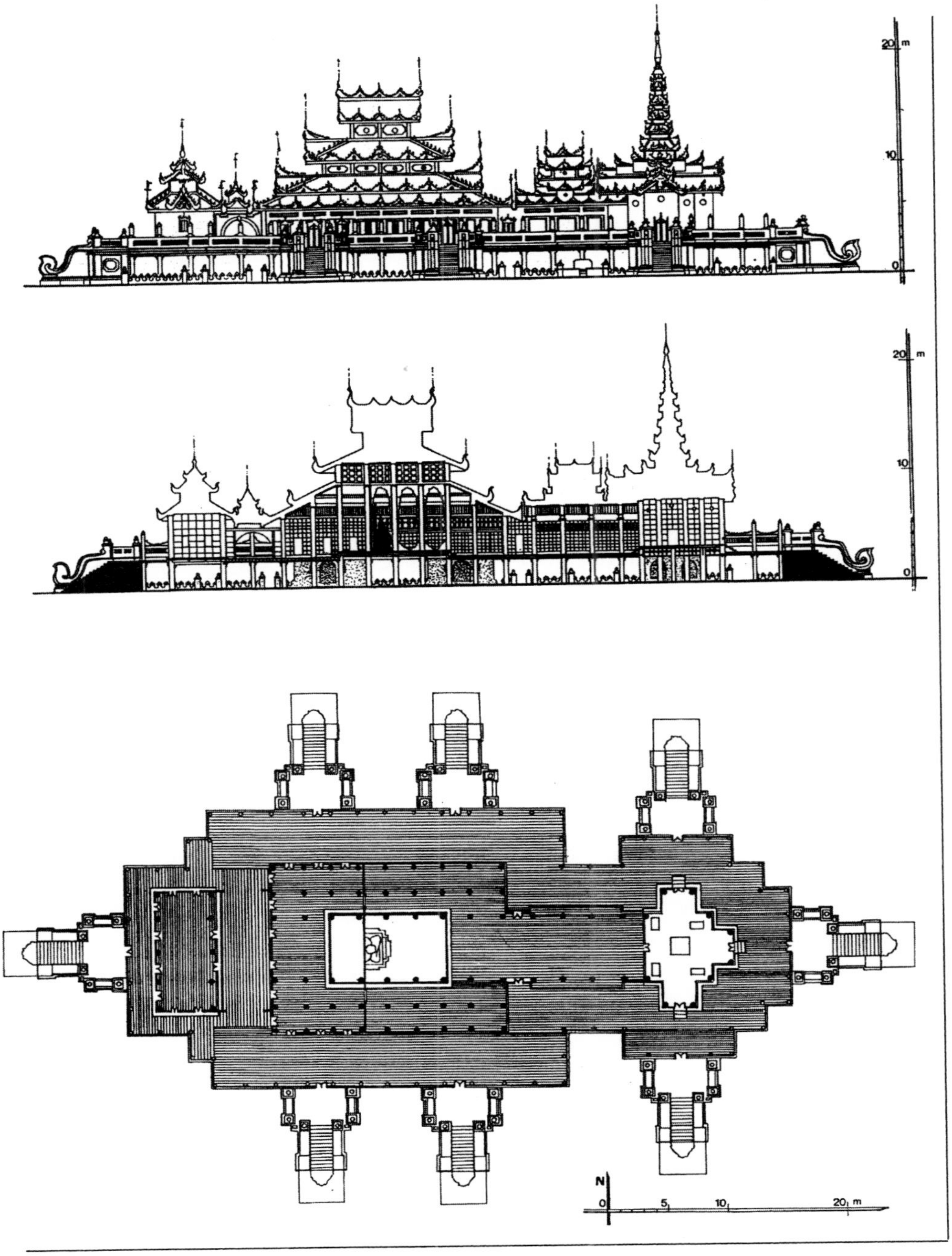

15 – *Detail of woodcarving on the balustrade of the platform of Hman-khin Yok-son monastery, Sagu, built around 1886*
See also detail in the same monastery p. 59 (photos P. Pichard)

wood, which was also used for roofing where it is now commonly replaced by corrugated iron sheets. Finely decorative wood-carvings adorn window frames, doors and roof eaves, and depict lively scenes on the balustrades, featuring human beings, animals and mythical creatures on intricate floral patterns, illustrating the *jātakas* and other Buddhist legends.

fig. 15 above and fig. 16 opposite page

fig. 17 opposite page

At the eastern end of the platform is a small square pavilion, the *pyathat saung*, crowned by a tiered spire (*pyathat*) and sheltering Buddha images or in some cases a collection of sacred manuscripts. Next is the *sanu saung*, a transitionnal space sometimes used by the abbot as reception room or as his residence. The core of the monastery is the next and central building, a rectangular hall under a high tiered roof supported by the tallest teak pillars, divided in two rooms by a transverse partition called *marabin*. At the western end of the line, the last structure is used as a storeroom or kitchen.

fig. 18 opposite page

Another image in the central hall, generally a seated Buddha facing east with its back against the partition, dominates the eastern part of the *marabin* where sermons and teaching are delivered, while the monks' quarters occupy the western part. In the partition, important enough to give its name to the whole central structure (*marabin saung*), two doors, one of each side of the statue, connect the two halves of the building. This symmetrical pattern at right angle to the main axis, identified by a statue on a pedestal (or in a niche) between two doors, appears as a notable invariant throughout the evolution of the Burmese monastery. In Thailand similarly, from the fourteenth century onwards, the entrance to monastic halls is more often through two stairs or two doors than by a single axial one, a feature that seems to have been closely associated with the monastic context, in sharp contrast with the Indian and Khmer model of the shrine always entered by a single, axial door, directly located in front of the image.

see Thailand p. 105

16 – *Corner figure at the Kyaung Thit-Lyaung monastery, built in 1870 at Sale*
(photo P. Pichard)

Fig. 17 – *Stairway and* pyathat *of Shwei-in-bin monastery, Mandalay, from south*

Massive brick stairways give access to all sides of the platform, and act as buttresses to limit the displacement of the flexible timber framework, a clever technical solution for an earthquake-prone country like Burma.
(photo P. Pichard)

18 – *Exposed structure of Taungbi monastery, (19th century), Pagan, from east*

Under renovation in 1991. Rows of huge teak pillars of various heigh support the tiered roof.
The platform will be reinstalled at the level of the lower horizontal beams.
(photo P. Pichard)

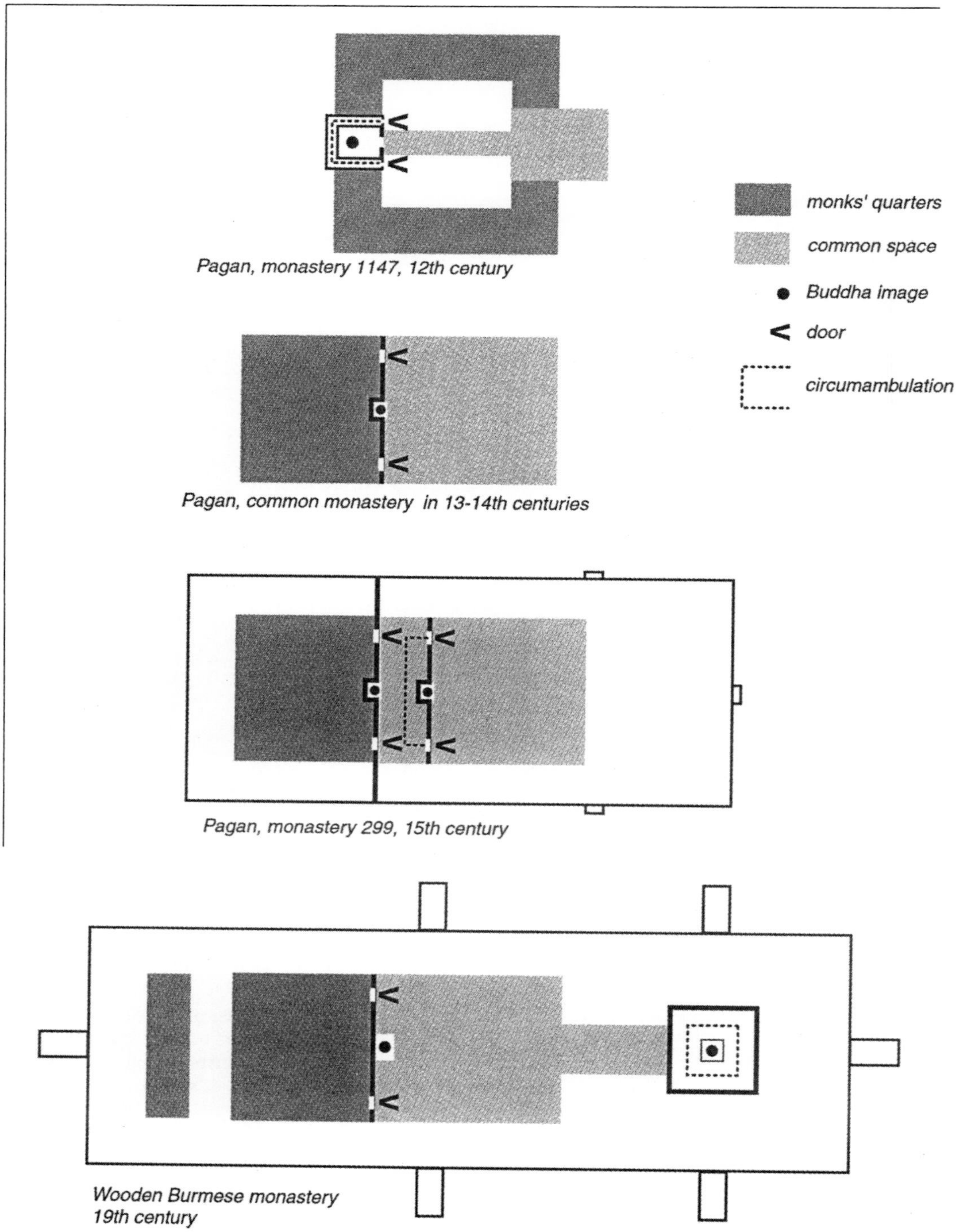

19 – *Evolution of the Burmese monastery* (P. Pichard)

From the quadrangular plan of monasteries 1147 and 1371 in Pagan to the linear configuration of the eighteenth and nineteenth-century royal monasteries, architectural elements have slid frontwards or backwards along the main axis: the cells, originally located between the entrance and the shrine, became a single monastic space behind the main image, who moved frontwards and was duplicated to allow its circumambulation by the lay devotees. The main hall, used by monks and lay people for rituals, ceremonies and sermons as well as by individuals paying respect to the Buddha, has moved from the entrance to a central position in front of the image. Through this development, the brick of the earlier monasteries was replaced by wood as the main construction material. In a country like Burma, where everybody live in wooden or bamboo houses raised on posts above the ground, it appears that using the ground floor of masonry buildings during the Pyu and Pagan periods was a deliberate appropriation of the Indian model, which was progressively superseded by the indigenous dwelling practice. (The traces of a former timber upper floor, partial or complete, in many brick monasteries of Pagan, attest probably a first step under the same process.)

fig. 19 opposite page

All over its evolution, the layout of the Burmese monastery tends to form a single but complex building. Its elements can have different shapes or materials, but are either contiguous, as in Pagan, or linked by the long common platform on which they rest, as in the Konbaung period. On a smaller scale and with a less regular layout, the village monastery is still a single building sheltering a lecture hall, a shrine and the monks' quarters (see the next contribution). Besides some ancillary facilities like *zayats* (shelters for pilgrims) or toilets, the main separated element is the ordination hall (*thein*), present in few monasteries only and then shared by the others in the vicinity. It is commonly a small structure, built away from the main building and even outside the enclosure in many cases.

Bibliographical references

Aung Thaw
1968 – *Report on the Excavations at Beikthano*, Rangoon, Ministry of Union Culture, 220 p.

Ferguson, John P.
1976 – *The Symbolic Dimension of the Burmese Sangha*, PhD, Cornell University, Ithaka, New York, 298 p.

Frasch, Tilman
1996 – *Pagan: Stadt und Staat*, Stuttgart, Franz Steiner Verlag, 365 p.

Fraser-Lu, Sylvia
2001 – *Splendour in Wood: The Buddhist Monasteries of Burma*, Bangkok, Orchid Press, 344 p.

Htun Hmat Win
1986 – *The Initiation of Novicehood and the Ordination of Monkhood in the Burmese Buddhist Culture*, Rangoon, Dept. of Religious Affairs, 172 p.

KRAIRIKSH, Piriya
1974 – "Semas with scenes from the Mahanipata-Jatakas in the National Museum at Khon Kaen", *Art and Archaeology in Thailand*, Bangkok, p. 35-65.

LEHMAN, F.K.
1987 – "Monasteries, Palaces and Ambiguities: Burmese Sacred and Secular Space" *Contributions to Indian Sociology* 21-1, p.169-186.

LUCE, G.H.
1969 – *Old Burma-Early Pagan*, 3 volumes, Artibus Asiae, Ascona and Locust Valley.

MENDELSON, E. Michael
1975 – *Sangha and State in Burma: a Study of Monastic Sectarianism and Leadership*, Ithaka, New York, London, Cornell University Press, 400 p.

MYO MYINT SEIN et al.
1970 – "Konbaung hkit hnaung phongyi kyaung mya" [Monasteries of the Late Konbaung Period], *Journal of Rangoon University* 5-3, p. 269-292.

PE MAUNG TIN
1936 – "Buddhism in the Inscriptions of Pagan", *JBRS* XXVI-I, p. 52-70, reprinted in *JBRS-50/2,* p.423-441 (Le-myet-hna inscription, p. 426-427).

PICHARD, Pierre
1992-2001 – *Inventory of Monuments at Pagan - Inventaire des Monuments*, 8 volumes, Paris, Unesco-Efeo-Kiscadale, maps, drawings, photographs, index.
1998 – "Entre Ajanta et Mandalay, l'architecture monastique de Pagan", *Études birmanes*, Paris, EFEO, p. 147-167, maps, drawings.

SINCLAIR, W.B.
1920 – "The monasteries of Pagan", *JBRS* X-I, p. 1-10, reprinted in *JBRS-50/2*, 1960, p. 505-515.

SPIRO, Melford E.
1970 – *Buddhism and Society: a Great Tradition and its Burmese Vicissitudes*, Berkeley, Los Angeles, London, University of California Press, 2nd ed.: 1980, 510 p.

STARGARDT, Janice
1990 – *The Ancient Pyu of Burma - 1: Early Pyu Cities in a Man-made Landscape*, Cambridge, Pacsea, 416 p.

TAW SEIN KO
1915 – "The Sangyaung Monasteries of Amarapura", *Annual Report* 1914-15, Archaeological Survey of India, p. 56-65, pl. XXXVI-XLVII.

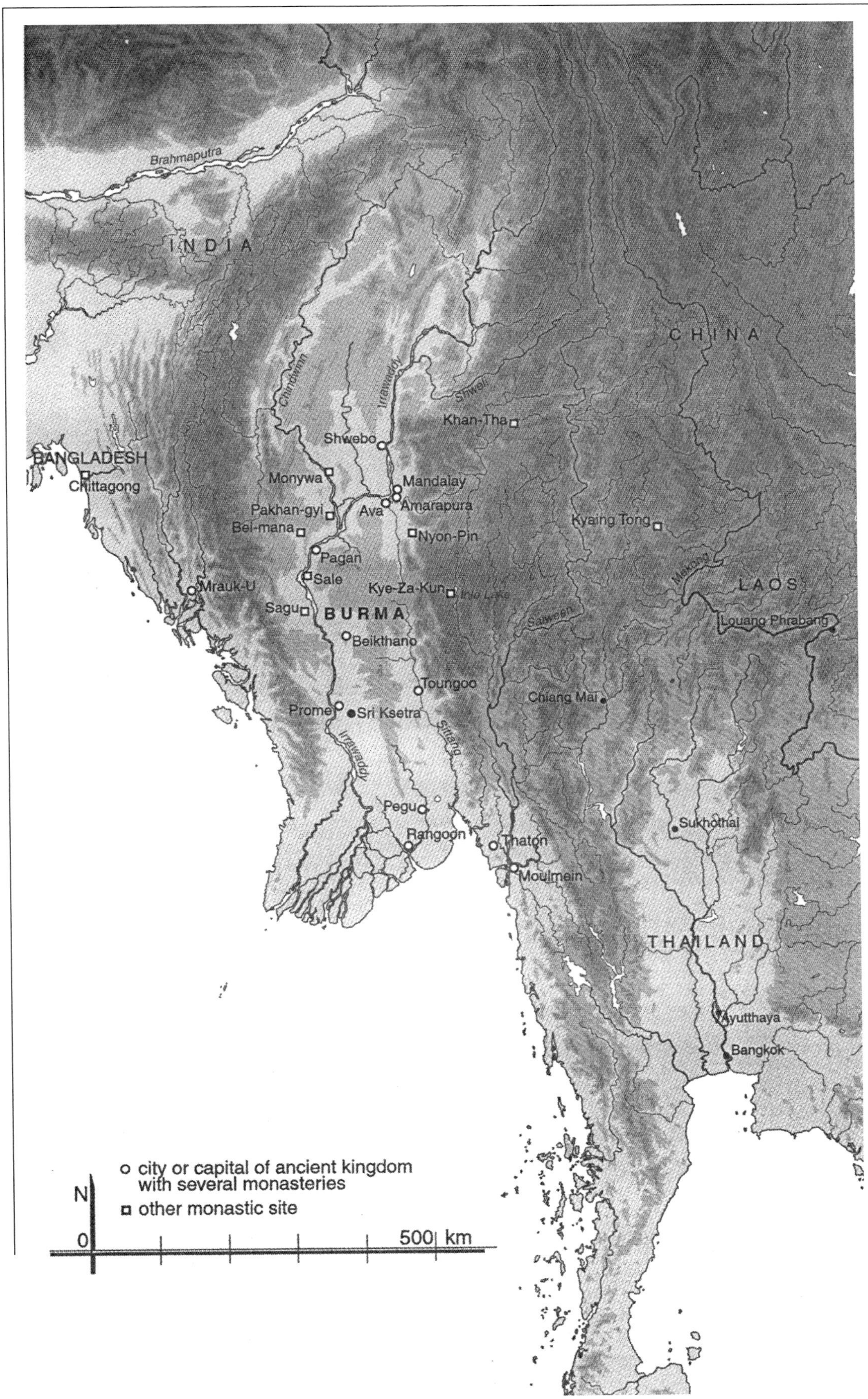
Brahmaputra
INDIA
CHINA
BANGLADESH
Chittagong
Chindwin
Irrawaddy
Shweli
Khan-Tha
Shwebo
Monywa
Mandalay
Amarapura
Ava
Pakhan-gyi
Bei-mana
Nyon-Pin
Pagan
Sale
Mrauk-U
Kye-Za-Kun
Inle Lake
Kyaing Tong
Mekong
LAOS
Louang Phrabang
Salween
Sagu
BURMA
Beikthano
Toungoo
Chiang Mai
Prome
Sri Ksetra
Sittang
Irrawaddy
Pegu
Rangoon
Thaton
Moulmein
Sukhothai
THAILAND
Ayutthaya
Bangkok
city or capital of ancient kingdom with several monasteries
other monastic site
N
0
500 km

THE MONASTIC UNITY
A contemporary Burmese artefact?

François Robinne

In the village context, most of the wooden monasteries of contemporary Burma constitute a "unit" by themselves, a single building sheltering the Buddha images in a wide hall, together with the monk cells, more often with no stūpa (*zedi*) or ordination hall (*thein*) within the precinct and, when there is one ordination hall it is a small building relegated behind the monastery or in a corner of the courtyard (Pichard 2000: 126). This was not the conception of Sadler, when semantically discussing the Burmese term for a monastery:

> In Burmese there is no word for monastic enclosure as a whole, as a *gestalt*. There is consequently [...] no conception of a unified whole, of a monastic compound as a unit. (Sadler 1970: 287, quoted by Richard O'Connor 1985: 4)

This problem thus stated, plus the reflections conveyed by the different contributors during the workshop and the following discussions as well, led me to revise my paper originally entitled "Buddhist monasteries of Burma as operator of transethnicity". Compared more especially to the Thai *wat,* which is a monastic complex generally consisting of a shrine (*wihan*), an ordination hall (*ubosot*), a stūpa (*chedi*) and monks quarters (*kuti*), the Burmese building, *kyaung,* makes up a whole by itself at least for a great majority of the wooden village monasteries.

The fieldwork mainly focused on three monasteries:

1 – the Burmese monastery of Nyun-Pin in Central Burma;
2 – the Shan monastery of Kan-Tha in the old site of Thibaw in the Northern Shan State;
3 – the Intha monastery of Kye-Za-Kun and other villages of the Inle Lake in the Southern Shan State;

in any case, it will be referred to neighbourhood monasteries.

See map of Burma page 73

Notwithstanding their effective spatial and cultural diversity,[1] these selected monasteries have in common the fact that they are all located in a region which was under a Shan influence after the fall of Pagan at the end of the 13th century, and which is nowadays under the growing influence of a burmanization process. All these wooden monasteries are more or less restored, but were originally built at the end of the 19th century. This study does not include the urban monasteries.[2]

Number and density of monasteries in the concerned areas

The census of the High Authority of the Buddhist Sects, published in 1985,[3] records the total number of monasteries, together with a more controversial number for the Saṅgha community members, in each administrative region all over the country. The estimated numbers for the three concerned areas show as follows:

	Number of monasteries	Number of monks	Number of novices
Kyaukse District Central Burma	256	557	1205
Nyaung-Shwe District Southern Shan State	179	571	
Thibaw District Northern Shan State	218	566	1938

As a rule, each village would have its own monastery. Such was the case for most of the Intha villages around the Inle lake in the Southern Shan State as well as for those situated on the Shan high plateau and in the surrounding Palaung mountains of the Northern Shan State; such is also the case of Nyun-Pin and the neighbouring villages in Central Burma: one monastery for one village figuring the ideal situation.

In fact, villages without their own monastery are numerous and their number is more and more increasing. According to the above-mentioned census there are only 179 monasteries for a total of 451 villages in the whole Nyaung-Shwe district, let the ratio be of 1 monastery for 2,5 villages. Some reasons can explain this lack of balance between the number of monasteries and that of villages. It may be due to accidents. For example, a few years ago, in the lake-village of Khan, the head monk was killed when a home-made rocket, ritually launched by the Taungyo during the full moon of April-May, unfortunately fell on his holy skull while he was going out of his monastery. The fatal crash was understood as a supernatural warning intervention owing to a wrong

1. The Intha – and the Taungyo whom we shall refer to – belong to the Tibeto-Burmese linguistic family; the Shan or Taï belong to the Thaï-Kadaï family; cited below: the Palaung and the Danaw are Austro-Asiatic while the Pao are Karen.

2. For an introduction to some monasteries in Mandalay, *cf.* Elizabeth Moore 1996, 304-327. Mostly for the quality of the iconography, we can refer also to Irene Moilanen and Sergey S. Ozhegov 1999. For a compilation of the vernacular architectural words, see Gilles Garachon 1983.

3. Refered to in the bibliography as "High Authority…".

spatial organisation. The monastery was demolished and part of the villagers followed a widow to search for and select a new place of settlement where they rebuilt their houses and, thereafter, a new monastery. The ones who remained in the previous village had to wait for years before getting a new monastery. Violent death, epidemic, fire, accident, etc., all inauspicious events of any kind are interpreted as an inadequate combination between the social and the cosmic orders.

The demographic growth, going together with the ever-increasing number of villages, may also – or mostly – account for the lack of monastery in some villages, or in other words, it may explain that only one monastery can be serving a group of two, three, four and even more villages. Such is the case, for example, around the lake where five Intha villages named "Top Yua-Kyi", "Low Yua-Kyi", "Lay-Khye", "Middle Lay-Kye" and "Pway-Kun" share one single monastery; the same applies to the neighbouring villages and far beyond. In any case, with regard to the roundup of the villages the presence of a monastery prevails by far over any administrative division. On both sides of the lake, a group of eight Pao villages and another one of three Taungyo villages are, each of the two groups, dependent on one central monastery despite their official belonging to different townships, despite also the presence, in one case, of an Intha village and in the other case of a Danaw village (Robinne 2000: 144-46).

Whatever the administrative or ethnic references may be, three main types of monasteries – including the Palaung's monasteries built in bricks – can be singled out from their architectural features.

Architectural features

The Pāli-Burmese commentaries of the Culawaga (*Cullavagga*) – the first of the three divisions of the Piṭaka and the fourth of the five books of the *Vinaya* – give a list of five different types of monasteries derived from architectural criteria:[4]

Vihāra
The generic pāli term for "monastery", defined in the Buddhist texts as a monastery with a two- or four-sided roof according to the pāli or the Burmese version. The latter mentions the word *ca kyo,* spelled *ca kro* in the Judson's dictionary (1960: 346) and described as a "four-sided roof ".

Amu yoga
According to the Pāli-Burmese text, it is defined as "a one-sided roof of a bamboo monastery".

Pāsāda
Pāli term also spelled *prasād* or *prāsād.* Monastery with a multitiered roof with three up to seven tiers.

Hāmmiya
Pāli term for a monastery with a multitiered roof topped by an umbrella.

Gūham
Monastery having the shape of a cave when it is not a natural cave. It is also called *umaṅ lhuiṅ gu kyoṅ:*, with *umaṅ* and *gū* which designate a cave or an artificial grotto.

4. Two volumes have been consulted and discussed with the head monk of Nyun-Pin in Central Burma: a pāli-burmese version published in 1936 and a burmese translation published in 1958.

If the pāli terminology refers to a comparatively accurate architectural typology based on the roof shape, no one among the monks we interviewed was really able to name the type of his monastery after this list, even with the text in hands. This is certainly because each monastery possesses other specific characteristics and the variations are numerous from one wooden monastery to another. Nevertheless, among the three main types of monasteries emerging from this diversity, two of them can be distinguished by their roof shape and arrangement: those with contiguous roofs, and those with cross-shaped roofs.

Monasteries with contiguous roofs

figure 1 (a, b, c) opposite page

The monastery of Kan-Tha in the Northern Shan State is an example of this type. The following is the translation of a pāli-burmese inscription commemorating the donation of this monastery:

> Wish you everything auspicious in this world South of Mount Meru. In *Kambojā* [5] there are mountains, forests, rivers with seasonal flows from right to left. The new city of Thibaw is surrounded by moats. [...] Five relics of *rahandas* have been placed in the middle of the *zedi*. The donator has built nine *zedi*. His Kudaw is well-known in every region of the reincarnation cycle. The donators[6] of this monastery are the governor *amat krī:* U Myat Mwun Myat Zan and his wife Ma Khe Yu [...]. They founded this monastery by being full of the three noble wishes of charity (*puppā cetanā*), honesty (*munca cetanā*) and altruism (*para cetanā*). They expected to be free from the affairs of this world, from anger, from ignorance and from stupidity (*loka-dosa-moha-awijjā*). The foundations (*panak*) of this monastery were dug on the 15th day of the waxing moon of the month of Tasaungmun in the year 1237 ME[7] (1875 AD). According to the Buddhist precepts, a ceremony of pouring water (*re cak khya*) has been performed in order to share the good actions with others. We have offered this foundation to the head monk. [...]

The structure of this monastery is divided outside and inside into three parts: to the three groups of parallel multitiered roofs correspond the three different levels of the floor. On the highest level stand the Buddha images, the medium one being reserved for the monks and the lowest one for the donators (lay people).

Such a pattern is common, whatever the region or the linguistic origins may be, at least for the village monasteries built from the middle of the 19th century and afterwards. Of course, many variations can be noted in space and time. Some are material: in the Kan-Tha monastery, the space built behind the shrine is used as a dining room for the monks. But the symbolic is never very far: by the addition of such a building behind the altar the images were shifted from against a gable towards a central position; this trend to move the sacred images to the centre follows a more general evolution engaged earlier in Pagan (Pierre Pichard: 1998 and *supra* in this book).

5. *Kambojā* is a former name of the Shan State.

6. *Kyoṅ: takā*, a burmese-pāli term made up of *Kyoṅ:* "monastery" and *takā*, short for *dāyakā* "donators", meaning every Buddhist. In Adoniram Judson's days the expression was used also for a respectable old man (1966: 223).

7. ME for "Myanmar Era", different from BE or "Buddhist Era".

1 | *Kan-Tha Monastery, Northern Shan State*

(drawings Guy Robinne)

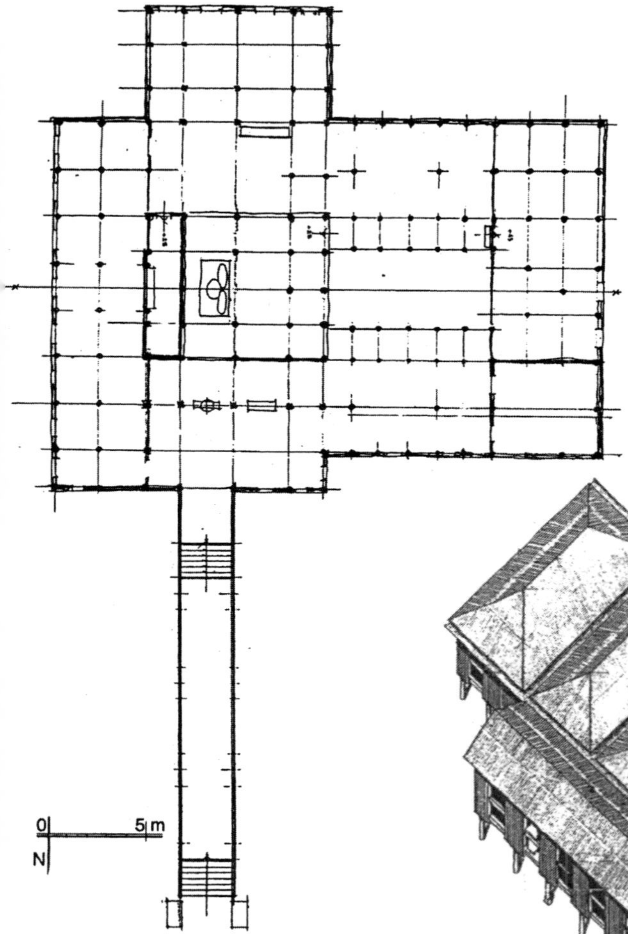

1a – *Plan*

1b – *Perspective, view from above*

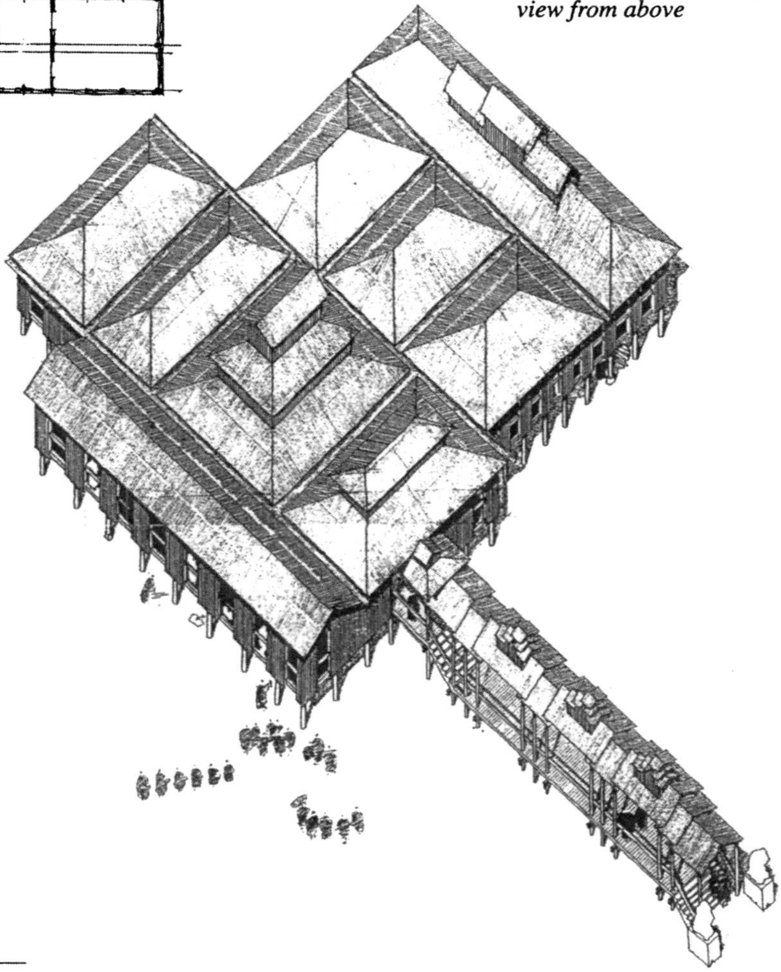

1c – *Section*

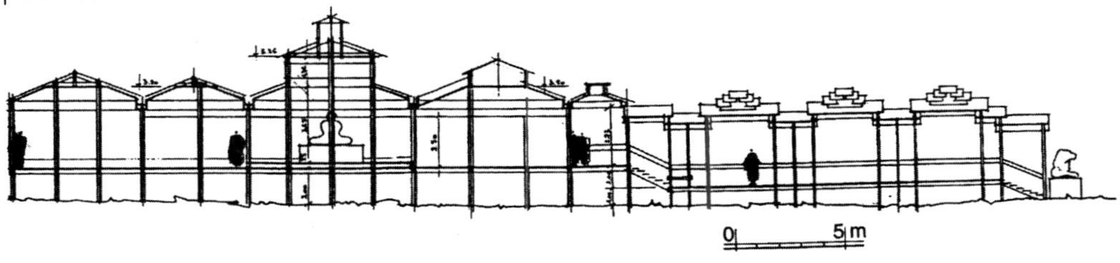

Monasteries with cross-shaped roofs

Two main ridges intersect perpendicularly, giving a crosswise plan to the roof and therefore to the whole building.

figure 2 (a – e) pages 81-3

Built on posts, according to such a plan, the Nyun-Pin Monastery, in Central Burma, stands in the south part of a large religious complex. The upper floor shelters the Buddha images on a raised platform in the eastern part of the cross; monk and novice quarters are in the southern part, the space for the meals in the western one and the storerooms in the northern branch. Between the posts, the ground floor is used for storage, water supply, rest beds and for a school for lay pupils and novices. A roofed stairway leads up to the upper-floor entrance, right in the middle of the west wall of the southern wing of the building.

The successive steps of the monastery construction, together with the enumeration of the different owners,[8] are recorded in a book belonging to the head monk of Nyun-Pin:

> The 8th day of the waxing moon of the month of Tasaungmun in the year 1294 ME (1932 AD), the great donators U Naing and his wife Daw Hle, inhabitants of Nyun-Pin village, offered 750 kyats to the carpenter in order to build a monastery at the head of the village. The whole cost was 10,000 kyats.
>
> The 8th day of the waning moon of the month of Wazaw in the year 1311 ME (1949 AD), the donator U Naing made offerings to repair the monastery which suffered of the assaults of impermanence.
>
> The head monk named U Nemeindaka gave the monastery to the monk U Laba. When the latter died, the monastery became U Thun Aung's property. U Thun Aung offered the monastery to the monk U Azera. When he died, the monastery became one more time the property of U Thun Aung. He offered it to the last monk disciple U Kukla in 1305 ME (1943 AD).

The same document points out in what way the initial dimensions were drawn up for each one of the five parts constituting the building:

> U Thun Ka, chief of the village drew the general form of the monastery with a bamboo having a man height, and then he prescribed the measures to the carpenter in charge of the task : 4 x 4 bamboo lengt hs for the place intended for the Buddha shrine on east, 4 x 3 bamboo lengths for the place assigned to the monks, novices and students on south, 4 x 4 bamboo lengths for the refectory, on west, 3 x 4 bamboo lengths for the storeroom on north, 6 x 5 bamboo lengths for the central part.

An old wooden house designed on such a cross-shaped plan still exists in Nyun-Pin village. According to the owners, whose grandparents were U Thun Ka's first cousins, this house was built sixty or so years ago, just after or before the monastery construction in 1294 ME (1932 AD). The same crosswise plan characterises also the monastery of East Phwazaw village in Pagan, but these typical features are far from being limited to Central Burma. What seems to be derived from a colonial influence can be also noticed in some houses and monasteries in Mandalay and Rangoon.

---

8. Melford E. Spiro (1970: 313) and E. Michael Mendelson (1975: 124-127) discussed the monastery ownership systems in Burma, distinguishing between the individual property (*poggalika*) and the Saṅgha community property (*sangghika*). The lay owners of the two monasteries considered here are natives – at least inhabitants – of the corresponding village. On the other hand, the origins of the monks and the students living in a monastery are much more diversified.

2 | *Nyun-Pin Monastery*
Central Burma

2a – *The monastic complex, site plan*
(schema F. Robinne)

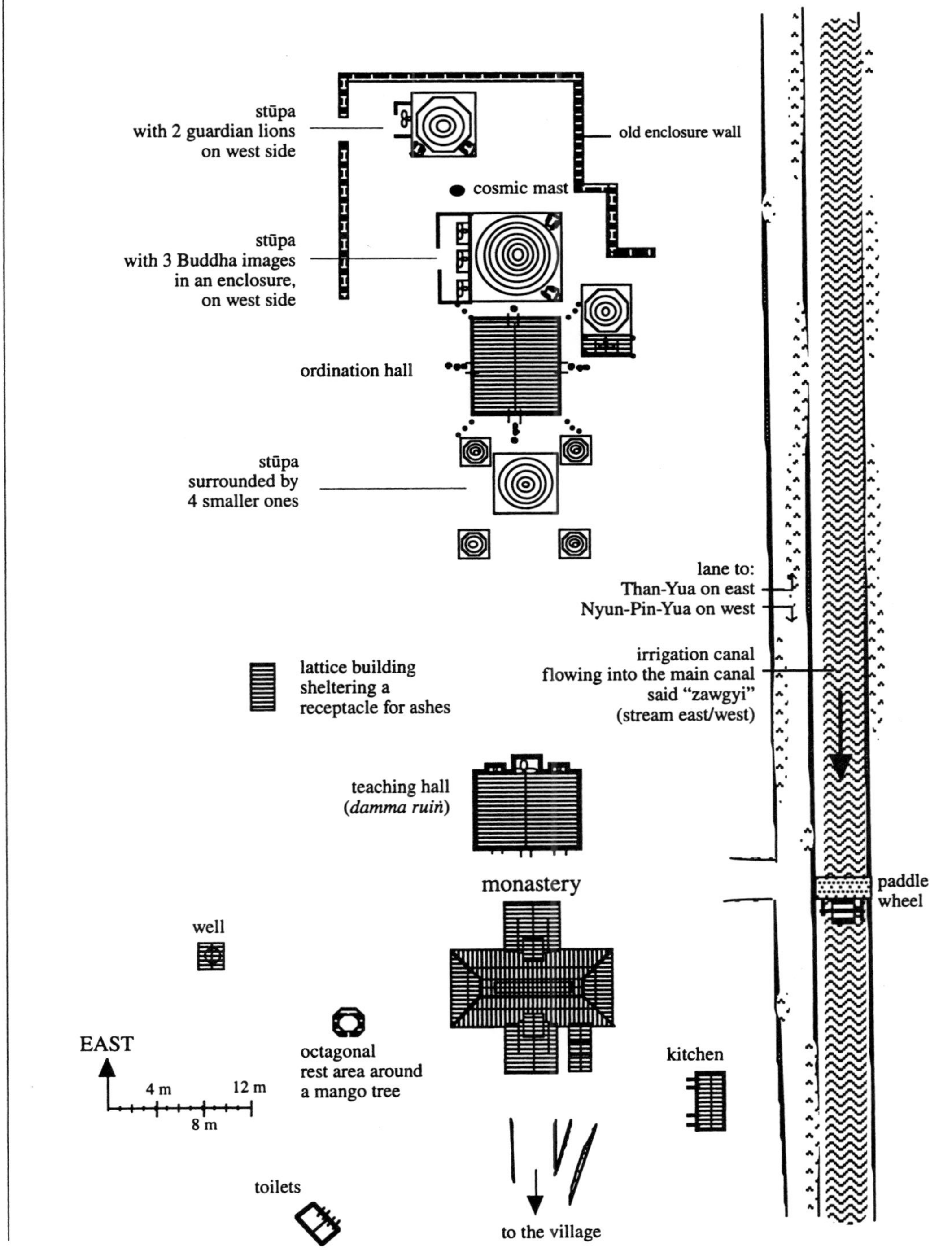

François Robinne

2 | *Nyun-Pin Monastery, Central Burma*

(continued)

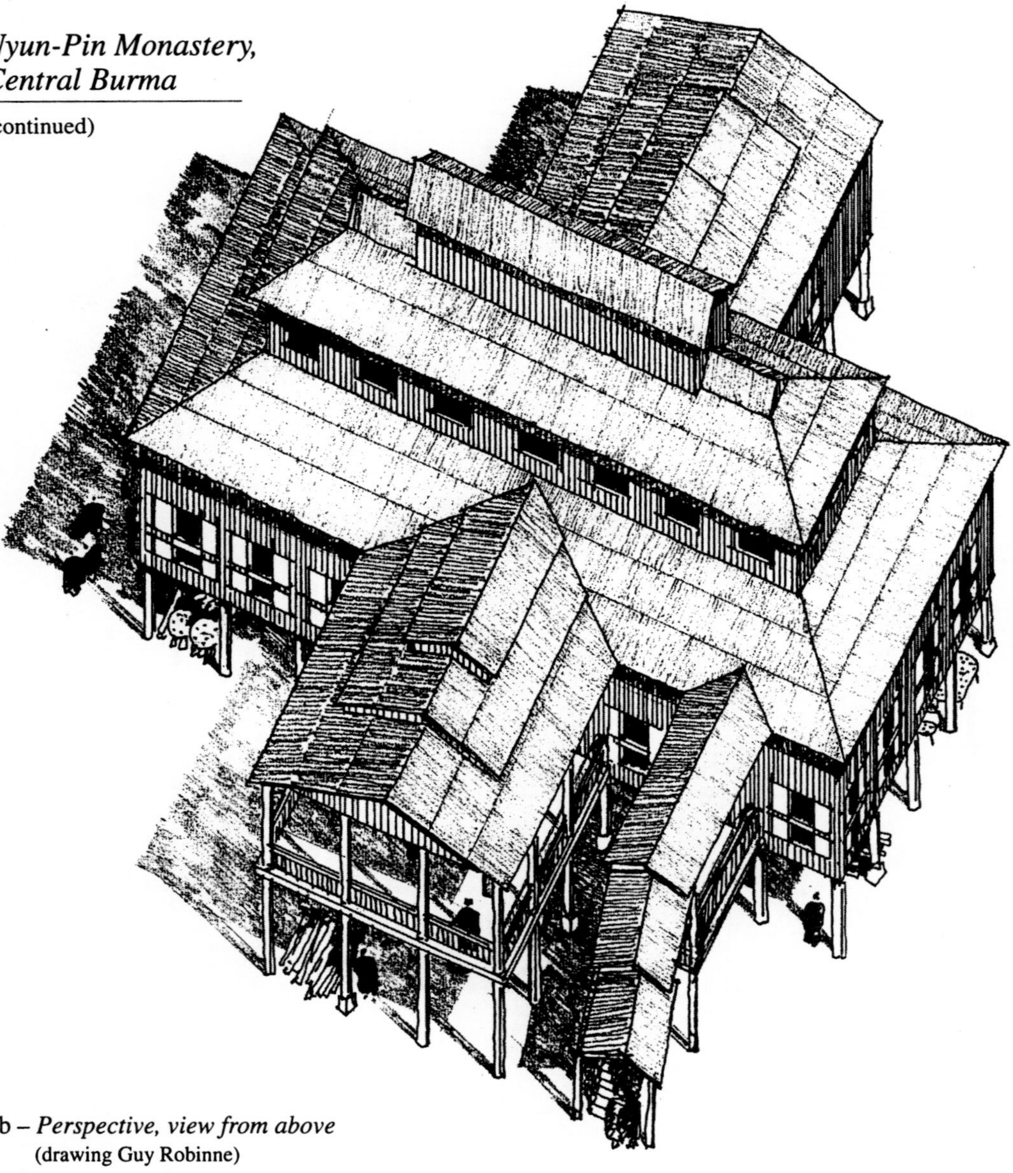

2b – *Perspective, view from above*
(drawing Guy Robinne)

2c – *Section*
(drawing Guy Robinne)

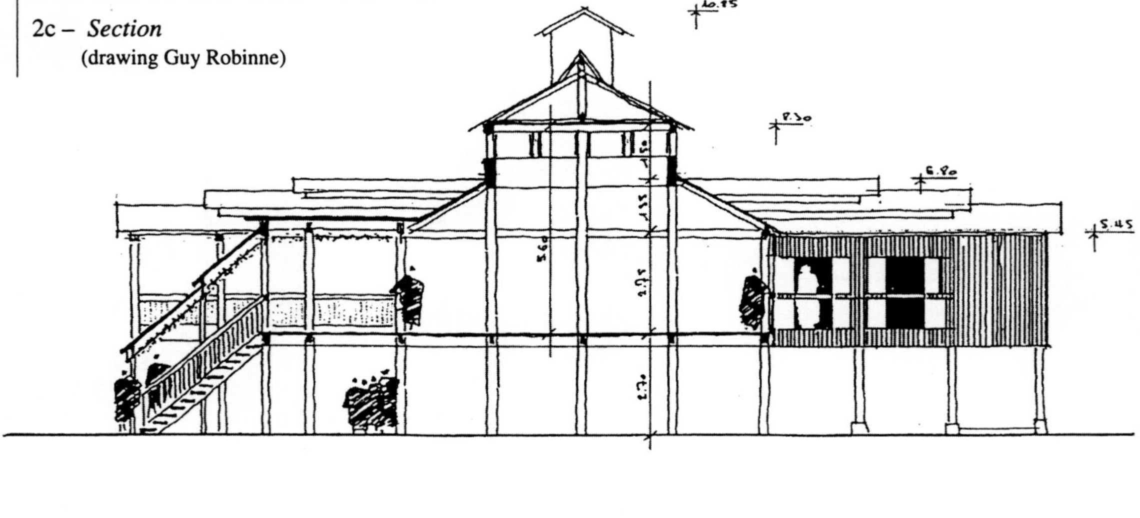

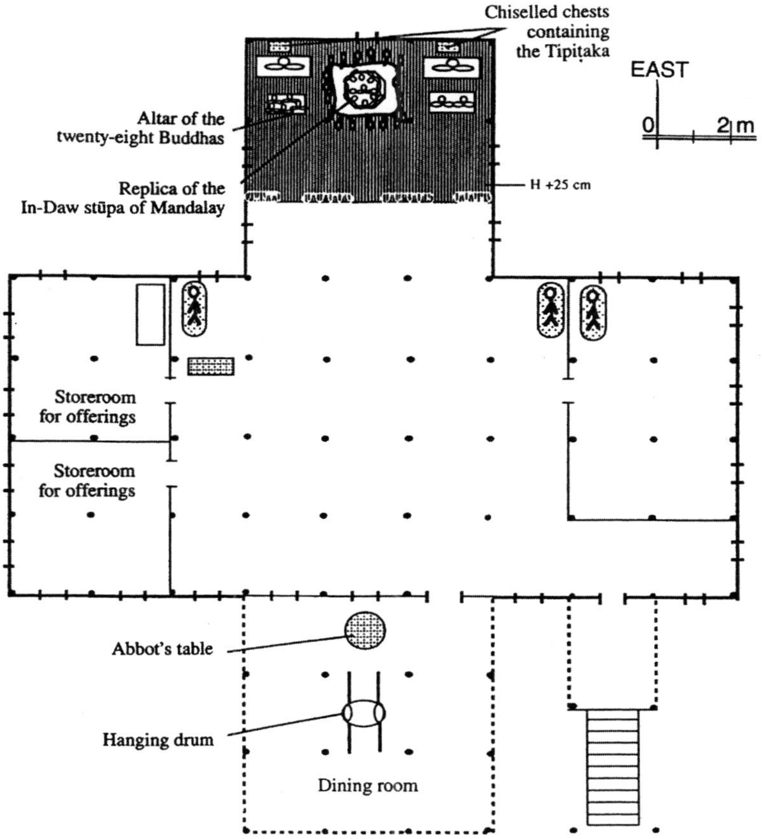

2e – *Upper floor*
(schema F. Robinne)

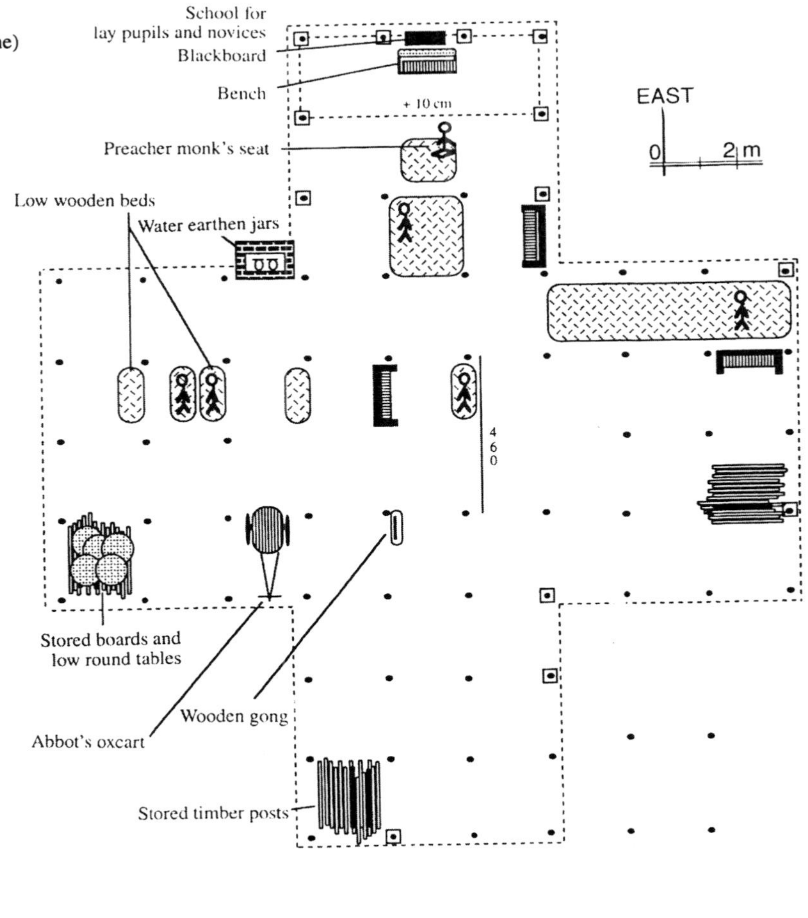

2d – *Ground floor*
(schema F. Robinne)

Staging monasteries and staging halls

Besides the two types of monasteries defined above a third model is to be found in the Nyaung-Shwe district of the Southern Shan State, characterised by the inner space organisation of the buildings due to the specific purpose they fulfil: they are staging monasteries and staging halls destined to shelter the so called Phaung-Daw-U Buddha images, settled for one night upon their central altar, during the time of an annual processional ceremony all around the Inle Lake.

In the Phaung-Daw-U hall, at the lake centre, stands a very sacred group of five Buddha images – so venerated that they are completely misshapen by layers and layers of gold leaves continuously stuck as offering by the pilgrims. Every year, on the new moon of *sītaṅ: kywat* (September-October) four of the five images are taken aboard a sacred barge to perform, in successive stages, a large circumnavigation around the lake. At the end of the 19th century the procession stopped off at seven villages and lasted for five days. Later on, this processional ceremony expanded steadily, both in space and in length of time, up to stop off nowadays at twenty-one villages and to last for twenty-six days.

In the staging monasteries or the staging halls the inner space organisation, with a central altar, mirrors the original centred configuration formed by the arrangement of the Buddha images upon the Phaung-Daw-U altar, that is four images surrounding the fifth one. This trend towards an axial configuration partakes of a more general level of elaboration: since the 12th century AD, in the course of time, the five Buddha images were moved step by step from the Pao or Taungyo mountains towards the banks and up to the middle of the lake where they now stand inside the Phaung-Daw-U hall, in the care of the Intha trustees (Robinne 2000: 262-300).

The specific halting places meant to shelter the Phaung-Daw-U Buddha images during the procession are of two sorts: either the inner space of the very village monastery is adapted to the end or an independent hall is purpose-built.

On the one hand, when an ordinary monastery has to be converted into a staging monastery its inside plan must be reorganised according to an axial pattern, shifting the images stand from its customary outlying position to the appropriate central one.

On the other hand, where the village is rich enough and the collected donations permit it, a completely new hall is erected, built on a square or an octagonal plan with brick walls and a multitiered roof.

The staging monasteries keep their daily monastic life going the whole year round and remain a place for the villagers to gather in any occasion, whereas the staging halls open their doors only once a year for the Phaung-Daw-U Buddha images to stop off during one night.

The vernacular terminology gives an imperfect account of the distinction between the both sorts of buildings. The staging hall used once a year is called *kyoṅ: tō*, the "holy monastery"; the staging monastery is called *bhum:krī: kyo*ṅ:, literally "monk + monastery", the ordinary appellation for any monastery. The terms "staging hall" and "staging monastery" are used here in order to avoid any confusion.

Both of them have a holy pavilion in their centre. Its appellation comes from the Burmese word *caṁ,* the semantic value of which is very extensive. In its nominal form, it means "standard", "model", from which are issued the expressions *caṁ kyo*ṅ:, "model + school, monastery" and *caṁ tō*, "model + sacred royal". In its verb form *caṁ* means

3 – *Nga-Phay (Intha)*
Staging monastery
(photo F. Robinne)

4 – *Yua-Ma (Intha)*
Staging monastery
(photo F. Robinne)

5 – *Wa-Kyi-Myaung (Taungyo)*
Staging monastery
(photo F. Robinne)

6 – *Nyaung-Shwe*
Staging hall
(photo F. Robinne)

"to enjoy", "to take delight", "to live" or "to sojourn" when speaking of a king or of a Buddha and his representations; in that sense the verbal expression *caṁ pay* is used when the Buddha images arrive somewhere on the occasion of a processional ceremony. The richly ornamented golden pavilion shelters an octagonal altar called *pallaṅ*, from the pāli *pallaṅka*; this term also names a throne as well as the holy preaching-chair for a monk to sit when giving a sermon.

Not many of the Lake Inle villages can afford to possess an independent staging hall. Out of the twenty-one villages where the processional ceremony stops off, eight of them own a staging hall, the remaining thirteen villages having a staging monastery. Three of these monasteries offer the distinctive feature of having two altars standing side by side right in their centre: one is supporting the monastery permanent large image(s) while the other is devoted to receive once a year the movable small-sized Phaung-Daw-U images during their peregrination.

Nevertheless, even in the Lake area, such an axial composition remains exceptional and out of the 179 monasteries situated in the Nyaung-Shwe District only those 21 staging monasteries and halls show those specific features.

In any case, whatever their axial or outlying inner pattern may be, the different types of monasteries above described cannot be dissociated from a more extended scope, that is the combination between a social order and the cosmic order.

Varying cardinal directions

Let us consider the Nyun-Pin monastery in Central Burma. Originally its structure included a stairway lined up both on the Buddha images and on the main village entrance. The monastery abbot U Sunndara would not accept such an alignment arguing that stairways and tile-roofs offer easy passageways – he said "a crocodile way" – to the roaming spirits in search of a support and that the houses and the monastery should not therefore be built on the same axis. Well known as a skilled astrologer, the monk determined the most auspicious day – which by chance coincided with the date of his induction as the monastery Superior – to shift the stairway from its primitive axial position to an outlying one in relation to the Buddha images and the village axis as well.

For the same purpose, that is to prevent and veer off course the possible wandering spirits attacks, the stairway roof must fit perpendicularly together with the monastery roof. Such an appropriate lay out can be found in the Kan-Tha monastery located on the western bank of the Inle Lake, where the entrance gallery arrives perpendicular to the monastery side wall leading into the shrine sideways to the main Buddha image. When the entrance faces the Buddha images, the axial door is avoided, and there are usually two parallel stairways and two doors. That is why, in the Intha monastery of Kye-Za-Kun and the Pao-Karen monastery of Lway-Kho in the Southern Shan State, as well as in the Shan monastery of Matteya in the Northern Shan State, one, sometimes two or four, lateral stairways give access to the building.

It is more difficult to infer any symbolic justification from the variations as regard to the different floor levels and the related roof levels. Sometimes the platform reserved for the monks runs all along one side between the front wall and the rear wall: such is the case in the Intha and the Taungyo monasteries of the Southern Shan State. In the Shan monasteries of Thibaw, the platform stands against the front wall, the monks happening then to be seated face to face with the Buddha images. The Palaung tea planters, in the same part of the Northern Shan State, build their monasteries with a two-level floor, the Buddha images and the monks sharing the higher level.

Not going further into particulars let us only point out that the traditional rural houses features are not necessarily the corollary of the monasteries architectural structure. A three-level floor characterises both the Burmese monasteries and the houses; but the Intha lake-houses have a continuous one-level floor, whereas the floors of the monasteries are laid out in two or three levels (Bernot 1982; Robinne 1999).

None of these variants happens to be the prerogative of any specific ethnolinguistic community, which they transcend. The same remark could be made concerning the general orientations. On the Inle lake, a monastery is preferably built facing east but this is more a trend than a fixed norm. Referring to the village, the Intha monastery of Aw-Kun faces north, while the monasteries of Sa-Lay and of Nam-Hu are facing south. In the nearby Taungyo mountains, an old monastery was first located on the north-east side of Kun-Pun village, while a new one was later built at the intersection of the three villages of Wa-Kyi-Myaung.

Technical or symbolical, whichever they may be, the variants occur according to a cosmogony framework materialised by the so called "square of directions", made up of the eight cardinal points at the periphery, their related day subdivided and arranged according to the lunar and the solar systems, the whole pattern being organised around the *kit* central square.

The fact that many architectural types can be observed among the monasteries and that the occurring variants cannot be exclusively linked to one type or to one cultural sphere, demonstrates the universally confirmed theorem stating that different forms can ensue from a same norm, and that inversely many norms can result in a same form. The monasteries of Central Burma and Shan State bring us back to this evidence.

For these Buddhist populations who share a same cosmology, the only constraint is to refrain from breaking, or from acting against, the harmonious relationship between social and cosmic orders. Even if Buddhism is imposing few interdicts while offering a large range of possibilities, some unsuitable combinations can nevertheless occur. Extraordinary manifestations may reveal that the social and cosmic orders are not organised into a hard-and-fast – or at least appropriate – coherence. Why did the Phaung-Daw-U images, five images at the time, fall down and drown into the lake water during one of the annual Intha processional ceremony? Why did one ritual home-made rocket kill the head monk on his way out of his monastery? In both examples, the causes of such accidents could be identified. In the Phaung-Daw-U case it was realised that one of the five images was not supposed to leave the sanctuary and had to be kept in its proper place onto the altar during the twenty-six procession days (Robinne 2000: 263). In the case of the lethal rocket it turned out that the monastery orientation was not appropriate in relation to the village houses disposition (Robinne 2000: 143).

Through these few examples one can understand that a Burmese Buddhist monastery is not just an independent holy place where the sacred images stand and the Saṅgha community members live, together under the same roof; if a monastery constitute one structural unit, it is not socially an autonomous one. The monastery life and the village life are necessarily interdependent, the monastery being the point of convergence for more than one activity of the village community and being, moreover, a median pole between the village and the temple. The monastery gets its full meaning out of this dynamic dimension.

Village, monastery and stūpa

The monastery as a point of convergence

The monasteries here considered, except for one, constitute independent units built separately both from the village and from a more complete Buddhist complex. In any case, the monastery represent a median pole between the village and the temple, whatever its distance from them may be; as such it cannot be dissociated from these two other components of a definite space organisation. These three poles and their respective constitutive parts are settled and oriented in relation to each other according to a strict combination principle.

Nowadays in Burma, several villages can be tied to one single monastery as well as several monasteries can be attached to the same stūpa. The stūpa may sometimes be very far from the monastery, but the Richard O'Connor's assertion that "conceptually and physically the Burmese separate monasteries or *kyaung* from pagodas [stūpas]" (1985: 3) needs to be qualified, this fact representing more a trend than an absolute rule. One of the most complete monastic complex I have seen is situated at Nyun-Pin, including a teaching hall (*damma ruiṅ*), an ordination hall (*thein*), three main stūpas (*zedi*) surrounded with smaller ones at the corners, a cosmic mast (*tam khwan tuiṅ*)[9]. Although the ordination hall, with its indispensable boundary-stones, forms the subject of the greatest number of treatises (Main Khain Seyadaw 1966), this building is far from being omnipresent. The existence of monasteries with no ordination halls is also attested in Northern Thailand. In his *Forest Monks and the Nation State* J. L. Taylor (1993: 228) has stressed upon the fact that "most forest monasteries were not sanctioned to carry out ordinations under national Saṅgha regulations as they had no officially consecrated area (*sīmā*)". As pointed out by this author (*ibid.*: 242), the lack of an ordination hall does not mean that there were no ordination at all but that only simple ceremonies for novices (Burmese: *shinbyu*) could be performed and in no case an "higher ordination" (Pāli: *upasampada*): "Previously, interested candidates for higher ordination had to go either to Norngkhaai or Beungkaan some 80 kilometres away" (*ibid.*); this represents the extant situation for many village monasteries – and not necessarily the most remote ones – of contemporary Buddhist Burma.

figure 2a page 81

A stūpa is not a *sine qua non* condition prevailing for the erection of a monastery. The presence of a cosmic mast should also be discussed: if it does not exist in the Intha monastery yards, it is around such a mast that Palaung boys and girls perform a ritual dance two times a year; the cosmic mast, richly carved, topped by a mythical bird or snake, with spirits standing towards the four cardinal points is present in the Burmese context; on the other hand, they are two big bamboo trees which raise their beautiful simplicity in front of the Taungyo pagoda on the hill which overhangs the village of Wa-Kyi-Myaung. And we should speak of the Shan specific bamboo structure as well: built in the middle of a village, it consists of a three-step platform of sand protected by sharp bamboo sticks, with a main pillar erected in the centre.

Actually, very few village monasteries interact directly with such a large holy complex, but all of them are always tied to a village – even when they are isolated hermitages. The monastery position – based on astrological reckoning – becomes

9. "Cosmic mast" is a tentative rendering of the burmese word translitered *tam khwan tuiṅ* which means literally "long piece" + "handled ax" + "pile", the bisyllab *tam khwan* meaning a streamer, an oriflamme.

integrated into an harmonizing configuration, together with the houses, the graveyard, the spirit altars on the one hand, and with the ordination hall, the stūpas and the cosmic mast on the other hand. In fact, the monastery/village pair represents the only constant, considerably overriding the monastery/stūpa pair. The statement, based on our field-work, that not every monastery is systematically a part of a larger religious complex is not historically attested. This was neither the case at the time of "Early-Burma" (see Pierre Pichard's contribution) nor in Thailand from ancient times up to nowadays (see the related contributions).

The monastery as the centre of a social network

A short survey of the different functions of a monastery will put in evidence the structural interactions linking the monastic community to the village one. At least in Burma, the Buddhist monastery is a school. The Burmese terminology expresses this reality, attested everyday and everywhere: the Burmese expressions *bhum:krī: kyoṅ:*, and *ca taṅ kyoṅ:* mean respectively a "Buddhist centre" and a "teaching centre"; the word *kyoṅ:* is a generic term which applies to any pedagogical institution, be it lay or confessional, a state school or a monastery[10]. The monosyllable *kyoṅ:* is sometimes followed by *tuik*, a generic term for "construction". Melford Spiro (1971: 312) introduced

7 – *Nyun-Pin Monastery Ground floor, lay children and novices at school* (see figure 2d p. 83)

(photo F. Robinne)

10. The connotation of the burmese terminology bears witness to the literacy high level among the Buddhist societies.

a distinction between the teaching monastic complex (*kyaung:taik*) and the village monastery (*ywa caung:*). In the same way, Michael Mendelson (1975: 129) seems to distinguish the *Kyaungtaik* from the *kyaung* when associating only the first term to a centre with an educational authority.

I do agree with Richard O'Connor (1985: 4) when he writes that "*kyaung* is not clearly distinguished from school"; and, if it is exact too that "a *kyaung* can have a single monk in a single building" (*ibid.*), I would add that a monastery may also welcome hundred or thousand monks for a few days on specific occasions: a temple ceremony, an initiation ceremony, the ceremony of the first rice, etc.

The terminology does not establish clear distinctions between meditation centre, village and social organisation centre, or teaching centre because each of these functions is an integral part of the monastery role. Besides the spiritual observances, teaching is one of the Saṅgha members main duties; moreover the monasteries are all more or less important economic centres (Himanshu P. Ray 1996): a village market may be an autonomous institution, but no Buddhist celebration can take place without a busy temporary market, the stalls being sometimes put up inside the monastery courtyard itself. Some monasteries specialise as medical centres, according to an ancient tradition which is attested in some archaeological sites of Sri Lanka (Leelanada Prematilleke, 1996) where they can be still observed, as well as in Thailand and Burma. Let us just mention also the political function of a monastery: it is there that any important decision is debated and, in the case of an interethnic situation like in the Shan State, it is first and foremost the place where a comprehensive multilingual dialogue can be instituted. Concerning the border areas of Thailand, Taylor (1993) has, all along his demonstration, insisted upon the predominant place held by the monks and the monasteries at the various levels of relationship: between the disciples and the abbots on the one hand and, on the other hand, between the Saṅgha community and the local political sponsors and at last between the "frontiersmen and the State". In an extreme form of the networks formed by and around the monasteries, Martin Smith has pointed out the "vital role" of the monasteries in the ethnic insurgencies in Burma (Smith 1999: 182, 310).

By way of conclusion, let us just say that this preliminary note elaborates more especially upon the architectural features of the monastery and its situation in the social space, nowadays in Burma. In no case, the architectural structures of the monasteries can be associated to a defined function. A more anthropological research, including studies about monks biographies, monks networks and about the origin of the pilgrims as well, would point out the social dimension of the Buddhist monastery as the focus of so many activities. The study of the exact functions of a monastery, beyond – or combined with – that of its spiritual dimension, should be further developed. Such a systematic analysis would without a doubt demonstrate the role played by the monastery both in the social organisation and, in the case of an interethnic intricacy, in the construction of identities.

REFERENCES

BA U (U)
1974 – *Histoire de Nyaung-Shwé*, Mandalay, History Department, Arts and science University, Thesis for M.A. degree, 133p. multigr. (en birman).

BERNOT, Denise
1978-92 – *Dictionnaire birman-français*, Paris, Selaf/Editions Peeters, 15 volumes.

BERNOT, Lucien
1982 – "The Two-door House: the Intha Example from Burma", *The House in East and Southeast Asia: Anthropological and Architectural Aspects*, K.G. Izikowitz & P. Sorensen eds., Scandinavian Institute of Asian Studies, Monograph Series n°30, Curzon Press, p. 41-48.

CHARPENTIER, Sophie et CLÉMENT, Pierre
1990 – *L'habitation lao*, Paris, Peeters, 2 volumes.

GARACHON, Gilles
1983 – *Lexique de l'architecture birmane traditionnelle en matériaux légers*, Thèse de doctorat, Paris III, 242 p. multigr. (print now forthcoming).

JUDSON, Adonira
1966 – *A Burmese-English Dictionary*, Rangoon, Baptist Board of Publications, 1120 p. (1st ed. 1852).

KHIN GYI, Saw
1973 – *History of the CIS-Salween Shan States (1886-1900)*, Mandalay, History Department, Arts and science University, Thesis for M.A. degree, xvi + 115 p. multigr. (with a map of the Shwe-Yan-Pye monastery).

MAIN KHAIN SEYADAW
1328 ME [1966] – [*Voie intérieure du soleil – divisions de l'univers – voies du surpassement – formes des halls d'ordination*], Rangoon, ratana wadi pitaka editions, 188 p. [in Burmese].

MENDELSON, E. Michael
1975 – *Sangha and State in Burma. A study of monastic sectarism and leadership*, Ithaca and London, Cornell University Press, 400 p.

MOILANEN, Irene and OZHEGOV, Sergey S.
1999 – *Mirrored in Wood. Burmese Art and Architecture*, Bangkok, White Lotus, vi + 178 p.

MOORE, Elizabeth
1996 – "Monasteries of Mandalay: Variations in Architecture and Patronage", *Traditions in Current Perspective*, Yangon, Universities Historical Research Centre, p. 304-327.

O'CONNOR, Richard A.
1985 – "Centers of sanctifies, regions and religions: variety of Tai Buddhism", Annual Meeting of the American Anthropological Association, Washington D.C., 26 p. multigr.

High Authority...
2529 BE, 1347 ME, 1985 AD – [*Amendement to the Procedures and the Foundations of the Buddhist Community Organizations*], Rangoon, Buddhist Sects Committee, 139 p. (in Burmese).

PICHARD, Pierre
1998 – "Entre Ajanta et Mandalay, l'architecture monastique de Pagan", *Études birmanes en hommage à Denise Bernot,* P. Pichard et F. Robinne éds., Paris, EFEO, p. 147-167.
2000 – " Le hall d'ordination dans le monastère thaï", *BEFEO* 87-1, p. 125-149.

PREMATILLEKE, Leelanada
1996 – "Ancient monastic Hospital System in Sri Lanka", *Ancient trades and cultural contacts in Southeast Asia*, Bangkok, The Office of the National Culture Commission, p. 115-126.

RAY, Himanshu Prabha
1996 – "Early trans-oceanic contacts between South and Southeast Asia", *Ancient trades and cultural contacts in Southeast Asia*, Bangkok, The Office of the National Culture Commission, p. 43-56.

ROBINNE, François
1992 – "Habitat et parenté. Essai d'analyse combinatoire entre différentes pratiques sociales des Birmans", *Techniques et culture*, 19, p. 103-137.
1999 – "Formes architecturales et normes cosmiques en Birmanie", *Habitat, source d'interprétation de l'organisation et de la complexité sociale en archéologie*, F. Braemer, S. Cleuziou, A. Coudart éds., Antibes, Editions APDCA, p. 27-51.
2000 – *Fils et maîtres du lac. Relations interethniques dans l'État Shan de Birmanie*, Paris, CNRS-MSH, Collection "Chemins de l'ethnologie", 364 p.

SCOTT, J. George and HARDIMAN, J. P.
1901 – *Gazetteer of Upper Burma and the Shan States*, Rangoon, Government printing, 5 volumes.

SMITH, Martin
1999 – *Burma. Insurgency and the Politics of Ethnicity,* Bangkok, White Lotus, xxi + 521 p. (1st ed. 1991, London, Zed).

SPIRO, Melford E.
1970 – *Buddhism and society. A great tradition and its Burmese vicissitudes,* London, George Allen & Unwin Ltd., xiv+510 p.

TAMBIAH, Stanley Jeyaraja,
1984 – *The Buddhist saints of the forests and the cult of amulets*, Cambridge University Press, xi + 417 p.

TAYLOR, J. L.
1996 – *Forest Monks and the Nation State. An Anthropological and Historical Study in Northeastern Thailand*, Singapore, Institute of Southeast Asian Studies, ix + 377 p. (1st ed. 1993).

THE THAI MONASTERY

Pierre Pichard

Buddhism was certainly present amongst the Mon population of central Thailand in the 6th to 8th centuries AD, as proved by Buddhist inscriptions in Pāli pertaining to the Theravādin tradition (Skilling 1997), and by the architecture and iconography of the Dvāravatī Culture. Up to the 13th century, this Môn culture spread to the north and northeast regions of Thailand, concurrently with the Mahayanist influences from Burma and Yunnan, as well as from Sri Vijaya (centered in Sumatra), and of the Angkor Empire, where Buddhism and Brahmanism co-existed.

Thai kingdoms appeared in Sukhothai (around 1250), Chiang Mai (around 1295) and Ayutthaya (1350), ruling over variable confederations of small principalities. Official sources, mainly chronicles and inscriptions, state that they professed the Theravāda Buddhism of the Mahāvihāra obedience from Sri Lanka, though other Buddhist traditions were most probably present at the same time, of which records have not survived or have been suppressed. The southern town of Nakhon Si Thammarat, with its Wat Mahathat (a large monastery centred on a huge stūpa) seems to have been a focal point in the relationship between the Sri Lankan Mahāvihāra school and the Siamese Saṅgha.

In the Ayutthaya Kingdom, and still more after the foundation of Bangkok (Rattanakosin) in 1782, the progressive construction of a modern, centralised state has induced several reforms of the Saṅgha, promoting a unified Buddhist orthodoxy in the Kingdom and tending to suppress regional variants. This policy did not however deter the recurrent rise of various Buddhist reformers and promoters of new schools.

The Buddhist Monastery, EFEO, 2003, p. 93-118

1. Main historical events of Buddhism in Thailand

5-6th c.	Earliest archaeological evidences of Buddhism in southern Thailand.
6-13th c.	Môn Dvāravatī culture (south and central Thailand).
8-13th c.	Theravāda Buddhism in the Môn Kingdom of Haripunjaya (now Lamphun in North Thailand).
c 1240-1438	Thai Kingdom of Sukhothai
1369	The Venerable Sumana, from Sukhothai, reforms the ordination ritual in Lamphun and Chiang Mai on the line of Sri Lankan Mahāvihāra.
1351-1767	Thai Kingdom of Ayutthaya
1420	Monks from Wat Suan Dok (Chiang Mai) return from Sri Lanka, where their ordination was not accepted as valid at the Anuradhapura Thuparama. Dhammagambhira then goes to Sri Lanka (1423), where he receives a new ordination. Back in Sukhothai and Chiang Mai, he teaches the new ordination but meets with a strong opposition, particularly in Ayutthaya.
1452	A council in Chiang Mai fails to settle the differences.
1475	Council in Chiang Mai for revising the Pāli scriptures.
1750	Monks from Ayutthaya establish the Syamanikaya (Siamese Sect) in Sri Lanka.
1788	"Ninth Council" in Bangkok for revising the Buddhist Cannon.
1829	Foundation of the Thammayut Sect, relying on Môn tradition, by the future King Mongkut (Rama IV)
1898	Involvement of the Saṅgha in the Thai primary education program.
1902	First Saṅgha Act (administrative organization of the Saṅgha)
1941	Second Saṅgha Act (ecclesiastical assembly, cabinet and courts)
1962	Third Saṅgha Act (direct administration under the Supreme Patriarch and a Council of Elders)

2. General location and density of monasteries in the country

2.1 Ancient monasteries

Stūpas are known in Dvāravatī-period archaeological sites, but no monastery has been identified with certainty. In northeastern Thailand (Chi Valley) few rectangular brick platforms surrounded by boundary stones (*sīmā*), found at Mueng Fa Daed and other archaeological sites of northeastern Thailand and dated from the 7th to 9th century (Krairiksh 1974), are supposed to mark the former location of ordination ceremonies.

Two early monasteries, though their precise foundation date is uncertain, are still now very active, attracting numerous Thai pilgrims: Wat Phra Mahathat in Nakhon Sri Thammarat (South Thailand) and Phra Pathom Chedi in Nakhon Pathom (Central Thailand). Both centred on a high stūpa sheltering sacred relics, they have seen several restorations and additions through the centuries.

The Thai Monastery

From the 13th century onwards, there is reliable archaeological evidence of numerous Buddhist monasteries in the three ancient sister-cities of Sukhothai, Si Satchanalai and Kamphaeng Phet. Several large monasteries were located inside these cities, and others, usually smaller, a few kilometres outside: they are considered as "forest monasteries" where "monks residing in forest" (*arannavasin*) used to live. At present, they are deserted and are maintained as archaeological sites.

As the city of Ayutthaya was destroyed by the Burmese invasion of 1767, most of the numerous monasteries which were inside and outside the city are also deserted and preserved as archaeological ruins, though a few still function. In the countryside, several monasteries founded during the Ayutthaya period are still active: some of their ancient buildings are present in various states of preservation, while more recent ones have been reconstructed or added in the compound for the needs of the monks and of the villagers. Such examples can be seen in Wat Lai (Lopburi province), Phetchaburi (Wat Yai Suwannaram, Wat Ko Kaeo Suttharam, Wat Mahathat) or even in Bangkok (Wat Mai Thep Nimit, Wat Bhumarin).

Ancient structures survive also in numerous monasteries of Lan Na (north Thailand), particularly in Chiang Mai, Lamphun, Lampang, Chiang Rai or Nan provinces.

Monasteries were generally built in the main cities (or these cities grew around those monasteries), located near the major rivers of the country. In the central plain in particular, monasteries were mainly established along rivers and canals, which were the most important communication routes before the modern road system. Local materials were preferred: for walls, timber in the north, laterite and brick around Sukhothai, brick mostly in Ayutthaya and Bangkok. The large tiled roofs with woodcarved gables, on a timber frame, were supported by walls and pillars, either in wood or brick. Plastering was made with lime mortar or stucco, elaborately moulded outside since the Sukhothai period, while inside, mural paintings or lacquer adorned walls, pillars and ceilings.

fig. 1 below and fig. 9 p. 104

1 – *Phetchaburi,*
Wat Ko Kaeo Suttharam
The landing gate on the river bank
See also fig. 9 page 104
(photo P. Pichard)

2.2 Present situation

See maps in Appendix p. 112 to 117

At present there are (1997 statistics) 30,377 monasteries in Thailand, housing 270,540 monks during the rainy season (*phansa*) and 164,661 in the rest of the year, since many men become monks only temporarily during the Buddhist Lent. For the whole country, there is an average of 6 monasteries for every 100 square kilometres, which means that the theoretical mean distance between two monasteries is no more that 4.4 km, or one hour walk. There are however wide regional variations, for instance the number of monasteries in 100 square kilometres decreases from 28 to 30 in and around Bangkok to only 1 in the mountainous province of Mae Hong Son and in the southern part of Thailand, which is predominantly Muslim. Similarly, the number of monks for 10,000 people, averaging 44 (during *phansa*) for the whole country, varies from more than 100 in two provinces of the central plain (Suphanburi and Kanchanaburi) to 10 or less in the south, and 25 for Bangkok. It should also be noted that this ratio has decreased steadily during the 20th century, though the total number of monks did increase, but not in proportion to the extremely high population growth, from 8,266,000 in 1911 to more than 60 million today:

	population	number of monks (during *phansa*)	number of monks for 10,000 people (during *phansa*)	number of monasteries
1905	7,741,000			
1910	8,087,000			
1927	11,046,000	129,696	117	16,503
1937	14,464,105	149,146	103	17,592
1951	20,155,000	169,628	84	
1958	25,000,000	156,111	63	21,380
1966	31,847,000	175,266	55	24,105
1989	55,888,393	294,040	53	
1994	59,095,419	279,790	47	
1997	60,816,227	270,540	44	30,377
1999	61,661,701			

(sources: Tambiah 1976; Gabaude 1996; Annual Report 1997, 2000)

From this table we may observe that about half of the monasteries existing today in Thailand were founded and constructed in the twentieth century, at a yearly rate of nearly 200 during the last 70 years. In 1997 for instance, the Office of Religious Affairs recorded that 95 monasteries were constructed (out of which 55 in the North-east), 81 founded, 107 newly registered and that 367 had the *sīmā* of their ordination hall consecrated.

In every Thai city there are several monasteries, some of large size, and, except in the sparsely populated regions or in the Muslim south, a dense network of monasteries is scattered amongst the rural villages all over the country.

The Bangkok region, where 13% of the country population is now concentrated, is clearly a particular case: it has at the same time the largest number of monasteries per square kilometre, the greatest number of monks per monastery, and the smallest number of monasteries relative to the population (less than 1 monastery for 10,000 people while this figure is as high as 9 in the Northeast and 5 for the whole country). The recent expansion of the urban area has drastically changed the surroundings of most monasteries, previously located along rivers and canals and depending on rural settlements, now immersed in populous suburbs. Many of these monasteries have seen their access inverted, as they were initially entered from the waterways and have now their main entrance on the opposite side, from the new motor roads.

The number of monks in a monastery is another important feature. The great and famous monasteries in Bangkok can accommodate more than 100 monks (even out of *phansa*), many coming from provincial monasteries, particularly from the Northeast, to achieve more advanced studies (Tambiah 1976). In 1997, the average number of monks per monastery in the country was 8 during *phansa* and 5 out of *phansa*, but again this number varies considerably: out of *phansa*, that is during three quarters of the year, there was an average of 2 monks per monastery in northern regions, against 21 in Bangkok.

2.3. *Classes of monasteries*

Since the 19th century, two Buddhist obediences exist in Thailand, the Mahanikaya and the Thammayutnikaya. In addition, the Chinese and Vietnamese affiliations are also recognised, but account countrywide to only 8 monasteries for the Chinese and 11 for the Vietnamese (1997 official figures). Quantitatively, the Mahanikaya is largely predominant, with 92% of the monks and 95% of the monasteries. Because of its royal origin, its elitist reputation and its relative importance in the capital, the Thammayutnikaya has however a larger influence in the Saṅgha than its size would suggest.

The Thai official classification refers to the foundation process and divides the monasteries (*wat*) in two main classes: royal and common.

1 – Royal monasteries (*phra aram luang*), founded or renovated by a King, Queen, Viceroy or Crown Prince, or founded or renovated by other people to be presented to the King. There are presently 251 royal monasteries in the country, out of which 85 are in Bangkok (Annual Report 1997).

They are further categorised in three grades:

– 1st grade: very important monastery, where ashes of royal family may be kept, and which may receive highest honours (only 4 wats, all in Bangkok: Wat Mahathat, Wat Po, Wat Suthat, Wat Arun)

– 2nd grade: important monastery, which may receive high honours.

– 3rd grade: locally important monastery.

In each grade are four sub-categories:

– *Rachaworamahawihan*, great monastery with large buildings, founded by a King, Queen, Viceroy or Crown Prince to be dedicated to themselves.

– *Rachaworawihan*, monastery founded by a King, Queen, Viceroy or Crown Prince to be dedicated to themselves.

– *Woramahawihan*, great monastery with large buildings, founded by a King, Queen, Viceroy or Crown Prince to be dedicated to someone else.

– *Worawihan*, monastery founded by a King, Queen, Viceroy or Crown Prince to be dedicated to someone else.

2 – Common Monasteries (*aram rat*), numbering 30,107 for the whole country.
   – *Wat ratsadon*: founded or renovated by a commoner, and possessing an ordination hall (*ubosot*).

Two other categories are:

3 – Monastic residences (*samnak song*): without ordination hall and depending upon another monastery for ordinations.

4 – Deserted Monasteries (*wat rang*): no more used by monks (usually an archaeological site).

3. The monastery layout

The Thai monastery groups several distinct buildings, answering to specific functions, in a large compound enclosed by a boundary wall or a fence. Its evolution can be summarized according to the conventional periods of Thai history, identified by the names of the successive royal capitals.

3.1 Sukhothai period (1238-1438)

The most ancient monasteries of which the layout can be studied are in the three sister-cities of the Sukhothai kingdom, Sukhothai, Si Satchanalai and Kamphaeng Phet. Only the hard masonry, either in bricks or laterite, has survived. This means that only the bases of the main buildings can be assessed today, without their roofs but often with parts of their walls and of their supporting pillars, while we cannot know the location, size and shape of the certainly numerous wooden buildings which completed the complexes, for instance the pavilions, monks quarters or refectories.

The three cities are some 50 kilometres apart. In Sukhothai, 109 religious complexes were recorded, most of them monasteries, 30 located inside the city and 79 outside, including 9 "forest monasteries" on the slope of the hill 3 kilometres west of the city. Together with the monasteries of Si Satchanalai and Kamphaeng Phet, also located both inside and outside the city walls, they constitute a wide corpus from the 13th to the 15th century AD.

fig. 2 opposite page

The compound sizes vary from 5.7 hectares (260 x 220 m) for Wat Mahathat in Sukhothai to less than one hectare. The rectangular boundary is usually a laterite wall, or in some cases a water moat. In the later monasteries, like Wat Phra Non in Kamphaeng Phet, the enclosure is double: an inner wall around the main buildings (stūpa and halls) and an outer enclosure wall around the whole complex, leaving a surrounding courtyard where were probably located the monks' quarters and ancillary buildings.

fig. 3 opposite page

In the larger monasteries, a high stūpa (*chedi*) commonly occupies the centre of the compound, and large, rectangular pillared halls housing a Buddha image are strictly aligned on a major axis, most often from east to west (approximately) in Sukhothai and Kamphaeng Phet, while in Si Satchanalai the axis of the major foundations in the centre of the city is south-east to north-west, parallel to the river. This is in contrast with monasteries of later times, for instance in Bangkok where the main buildings are generally facing the river at right angles. The ordination hall, another pillared hall but a smaller one, is located on one side of the compound in the earliest monasteries, but tends to become larger at the end of the period and to occupy a more conspicuous place, though not the central one.

Smaller monasteries, particularly the outer ones built on the hills, have a much less organised plan, but the various buildings and structures generally keep a common orientation.

2 - *Sukhothai, plan of Wat Mahathat (founded 13th century, with later additions).*

The main *chedi*, with four *prangs* on its sides and four secondary *chedis* on its corners, marks the centre of the monastery. The main *wihans* are aligned eastwards on the major axis while the *ubosot* is located on the north sector, between two ponds.

(P. Pichard after a FAD survey and Aasen 1998)

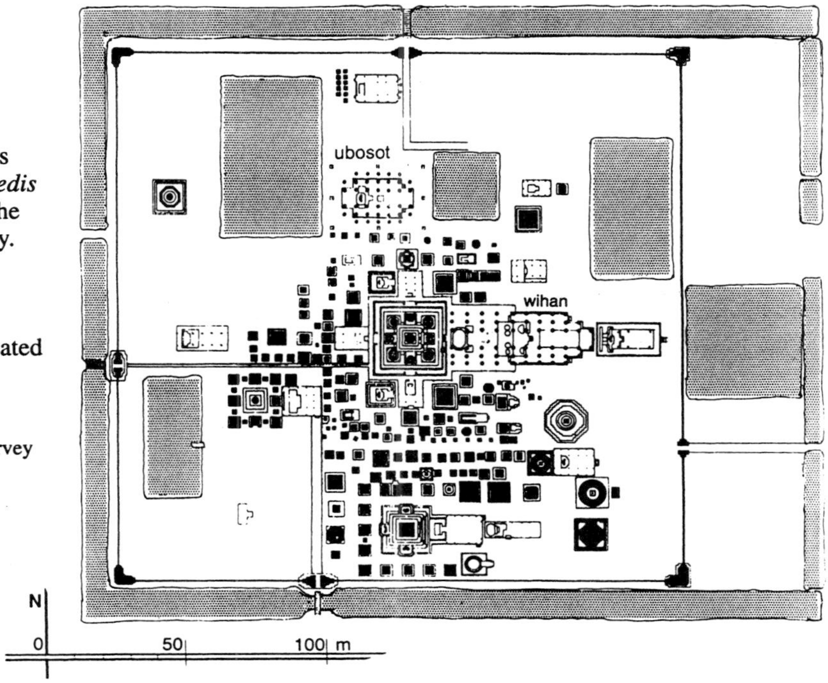

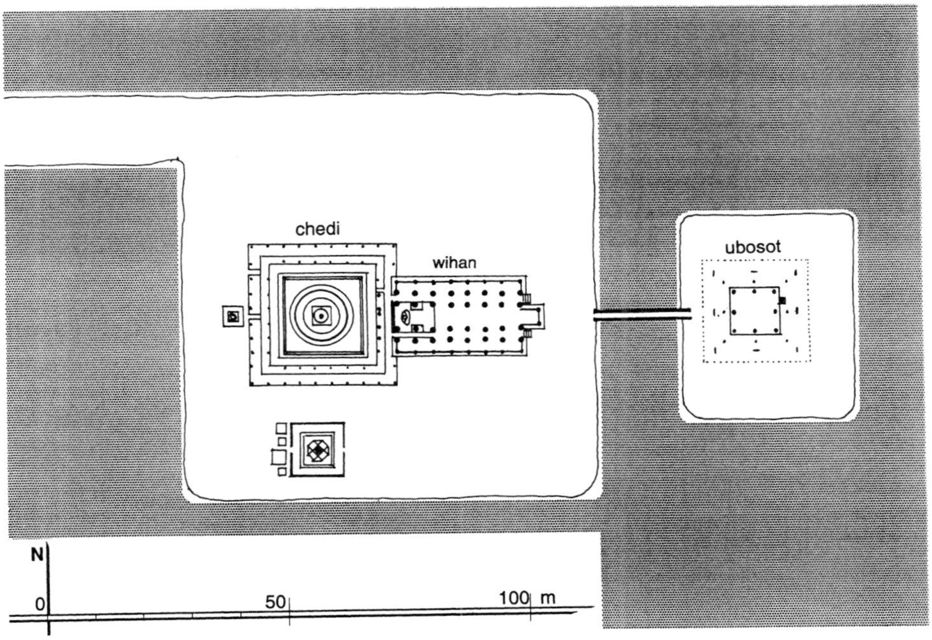

3 – *Sukhothai, plan of Wat Sra Si (14th century)*

The main *chedi*, the *wihan* and the *ubosot* are aligned on an east-west axis, but while the *wihan* is attached to the *chedi*, the *ubosot* is separated on a small island.

(P. Pichard after a FAD survey and Aasen 1998)

3.2 Ayutthaya period (1350-1767)

fig. 4 below

Most of the large monastic compounds in the royal capital-city retained the linear or centred plans of the Sukhothai period, but developed it into a wider, monumental composition. In the most important foundations, the central buildings (usually of the stūpa type, *chedi* or *prang*) were surrounded by a roofed gallery (*rabiang*), possibly inspired by the Angkorian temples. The pillared halls (*wihan*) have a common orientation and are either attached to the gallery or isolated in the compound, and the ordination hall can be on the main axis, but at the other end (western usually) of the line.

fig. 5 opposite page

As in all periods however, the layout varies widely from monastery to monastery, and though it is possible to define typological trends, there is not a single, common pattern. In Wat Phra Si Samphet, one the most important of the city and attached to the Royal Palace, the centre is occupied by a row of six buildings of alternate shapes, three *chedis* and three *mondops*, surrounded first by a gallery, at each end of which a great hall is attached, and again by smaller halls and stūpas inside an outer enclosure. The ordination hall is located in the southeast corner.

fig. 6 opposite page

Out of the capital city, the layout was again less regular, with stūpas and halls more freely scattered in a wide compound.

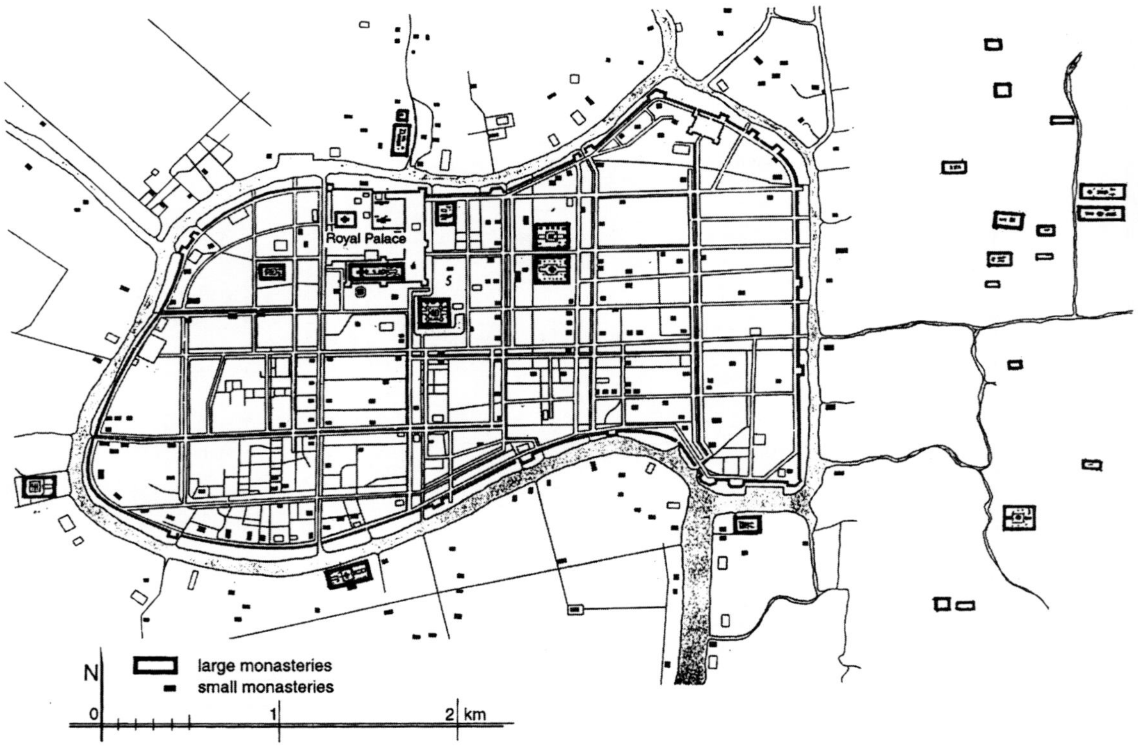

4 – T*he Thai capital of Ayutthaya in the 18th century*

The royal palace and its gardens, together with several of the most important monasteries, occupied the sacred island wich forms the walled centre of the city, while the majority of the population was living in the surrounding territory, on the banks of rivers and canals.

(P. Pichard after Sumet 1970 and Aasen 1998)

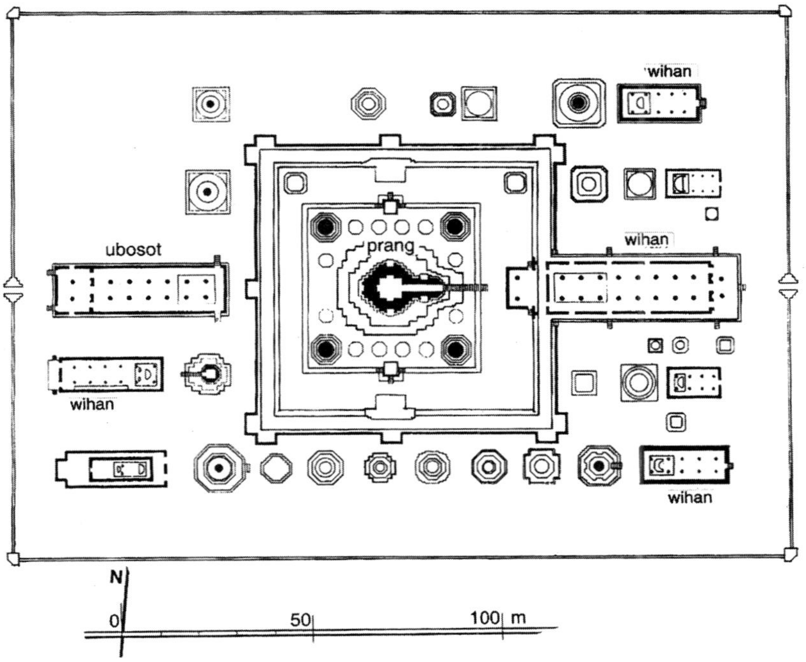

5 – *Ayutthaya, plan of Wat Ratchaburana*

A high *prang* marks the centre of the inner courtyard enclosed in a roofed gallery directly linked to the main *wihan*. The *ubosot* is also axially located, but on the west side and separated from the gallery. Smaller *wihans* and *chedis* surround these central buildings.

(P. Pichard after a FAD survey and Aasen 1998)

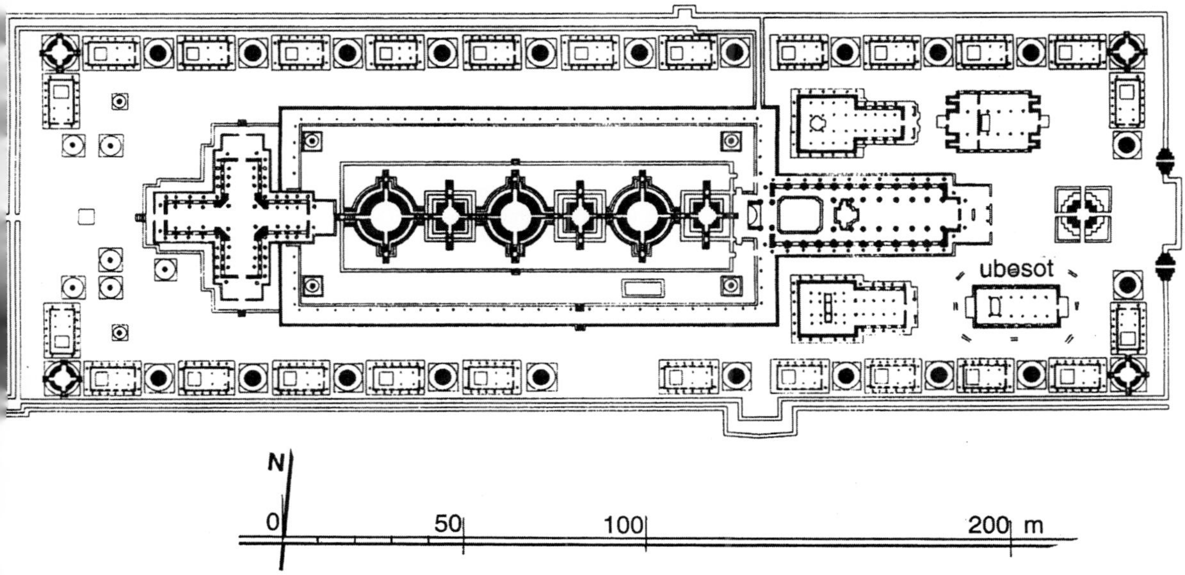

6 – *Ayutthaya, plan of Wat Phra Si Samphet*

A very formal plan for this monastery, attached to the royal palace and used for ordinations of royal family members, but in which no monks resided. The axial alignment of three *chedis* and three *mondops* was enclosed by a roofed gallery, to which the main *wihan* was attached on the east side. The *ubosot* was located in the south-east corner.

(P. Pichard after a FAD survey and Aasen 1998)

3.3 Bangkok period (since 1782)

Numerous large monasteries were built in the new capital during the 19th and 20th centuries, either as new, royal foundations or through a more or less complete rebuilding of previously founded ones.

fig. 8 opposite page

The division into two main parts becomes more systematic: an inner enclosure, which can be either a wall or a roofed gallery, surrounds the cult area, called the *Buddhāvāsa* with the ordination and congregation halls and occasionally one or several stūpas, while in the *Saṅghāvāsa,* an outer area added on one or several sides, are located the monks' quarters, the library and other buildings for sermon reading and teaching activities. An outer boundary wall encloses the whole compound, with landing pavilions (*ta nam*) when on the bank of a canal or a river and gateways on other sides. The main buildings are generally at right angles to the nearest waterway.

fig. 10 p. 105
fig. 7 below

In many modern or recently renovated monasteries, the higher and larger building, and the most elaborately decorated, tends to be the ordination hall, which can also occupy the central point of the complex, sometimes alone inside a cloistered courtyard (and because of this primary importance given to the ordination hall and its Buddha image, these monasteries are often referred as temples). The ordination hall (*ubosot*) and the assembly hall (*wihan*) can also be very similar, their only difference then being the boundary stones (*bai sīmā*) which distinguish the ordination hall. In some cases (examples in Bangkok are Wat Krüa Wan or Wat Mahannapharam), these two buildings are even located side by side and are identical in size, shape and distribution of doors and windows; they differ only in ornamental details and in interior layout.

7 – Bangkok, Wat Krüa Wan (built before 1840 on the west bank of the river)

The *wihan* and the *ubosot*, identical in size and shape, flank three aligned *chedis*. On the south side, the monks' quarters have been recently rebuilt.

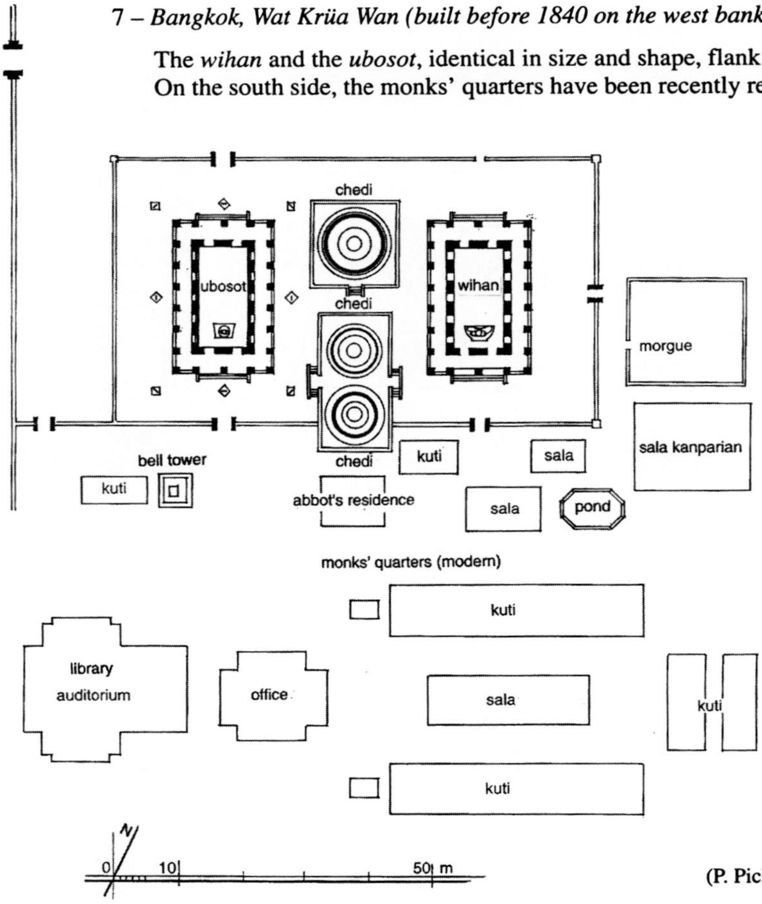

(P. Pichard after a FAD survey)

A few foundations have still their centre marked by an important stūpa, for instance Wat Bowornivet and Wat Ratchabopit with a *chedi*, Wat Arun with a very high *prang*, or Wat Kreua Wan with a row of three *chedis*. Still, when asked "what is the most sacred place in your *wat*?", monks in 35 Bangkok monasteries answered "the Buddha image" (generally the one in the ordination hall) and only in 2 monasteries "the stūpa" (O'Connor 1985).

fig. 7 opposite page

There is however no formal uniformity and different configurations are attested, such as centered, linear, parallel or scattered, in compounds of various sizes from more than 7 hectares (Wat Pho, 300 x 260 m) to less than 0.5 hectare (Wat Ratchapradit, 77 x 64 m).

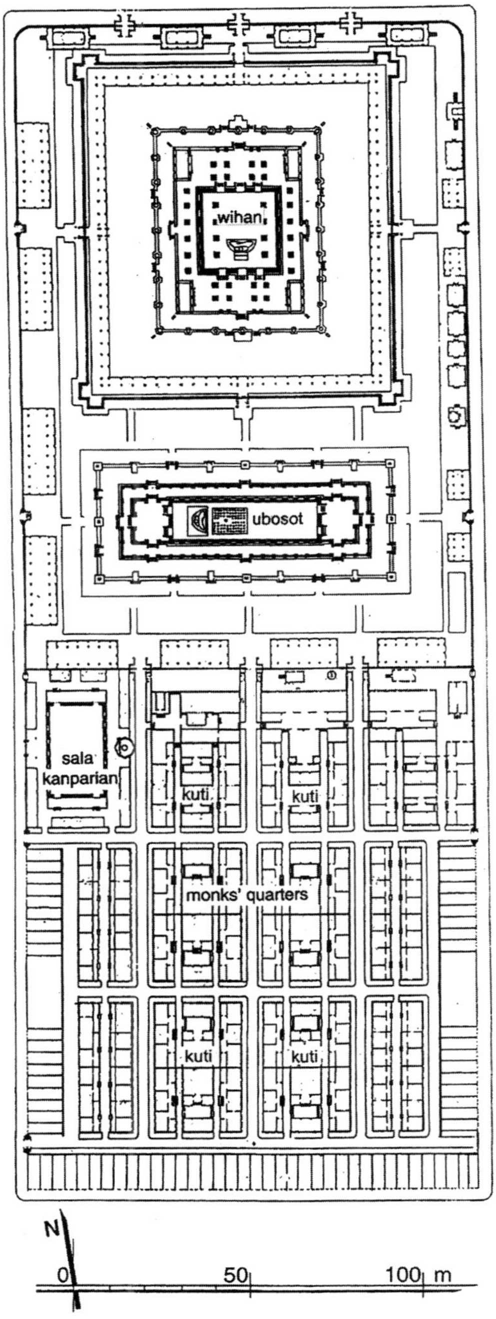

8 – *Bangkok, Wat Sutthat*

Built from 1807 to 1843 at the centre of the artificial island of Ratanakosin (the historical nucleus of Bangkok), the Royal Monastery of Wat Sutthat has a very symmetrical and regular layout.

The centrally located *ubosot* separates the *wihan* and its courtyard from the monastic quarters, designed to accommodate 300 monks.

(P. Pichard, after a FAD survey)

3.4 Country monasteries

fig. 9 below

Away from the royal capitals, monasteries were and still are much less systematically planned. They were often built by the villagers according to the availability of funds, usually starting as *samnak song*, with a simple wooden building to house one or two monks, around which *sala* and *wihan* were added when possible. Only after the formal permission is granted (in the name of the King), can the *ubosot* be erected, which will give the monastery its full statute by allowing ordinations to be performed. In small monasteries, particularly in villages, the inner enclosure separating the *Buddhāvāsa* and the *Saṅghāvāsa* is seldom materialised, though always symbolically present.

See articles: on Northeastern Thailand p. 119-130 Isan Sims p. 131-148

There were important regional variations throughout the country, for instance in the north (Lan Na) the ordination hall is usually smaller than the assembly hall, while in the north-east (Isan) the *ubosot* was only present in few monasteries, the others consisting of a *kuti* (monk quarters) and a *sala* (preaching hall, a roof on pillars often without walls). In recent times, the Bangkok tendency to shift the major accent on the ordination hall has spread nation-wide: new *ubosots*, high and richly decorated through popular donations, are built all over the country in village monasteries, either as new additions or alongside old ones which then become disused. National models are promoted countrywide, with a central office in Bangkok providing standardized drawings for ordination hall, crematorium or meeting hall to the villagers when enough funds have been collected to undertake the building of a new monastery or the renovation of an old one.

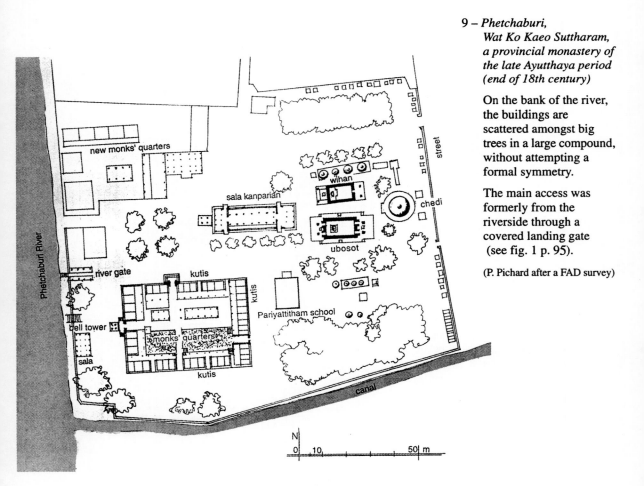

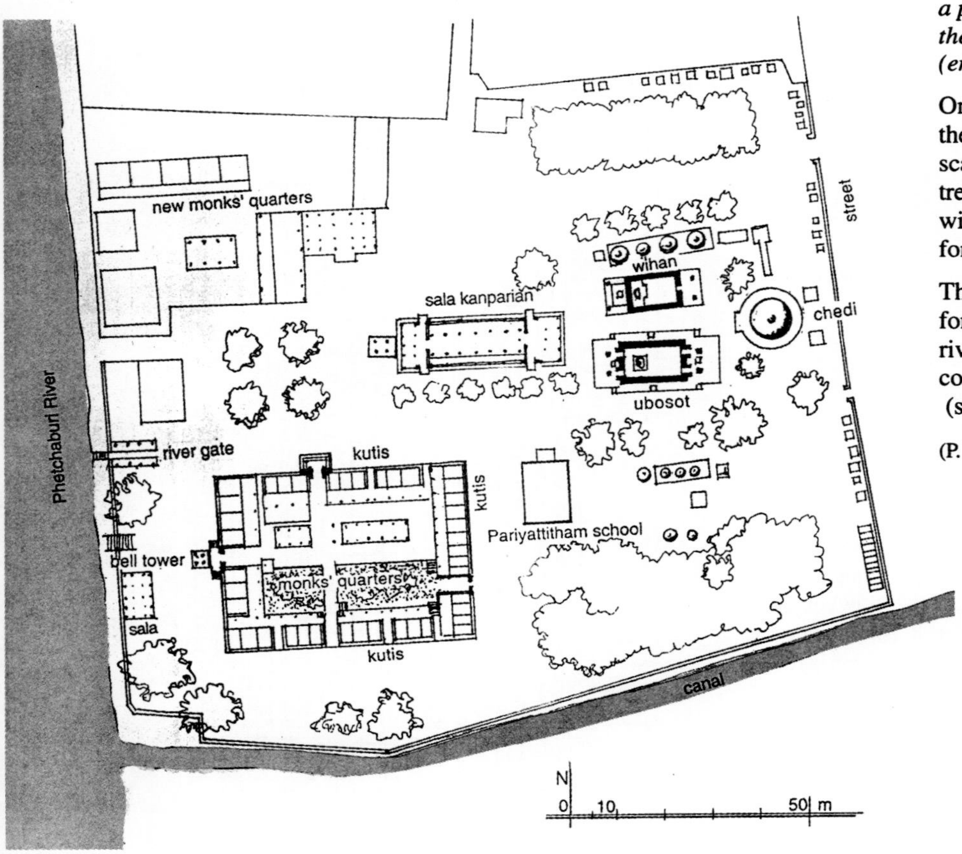

9 – *Phetchaburi, Wat Ko Kaeo Suttharam, a provincial monastery of the late Ayutthaya period (end of 18th century)*

On the bank of the river, the buildings are scattered amongst big trees in a large compound, without attempting a formal symmetry.

The main access was formerly from the riverside through a covered landing gate (see fig. 1 p. 95).

(P. Pichard after a FAD survey)

4. The elements of the monastery

4.1 In the Buddhāvāsa (cult area)

The assembly hall and shrine *(wihan)*

fig. 11 p. 106

- a rectangular building with entrance on one or both ends (often through 2 doors, also 1 or 3).

2 doors: seeBurma p. 62-63, 69

- the Buddha image faces the main entrance (east generally).
- in northern Thailand, several ancient pillared *wihans* are open on three sides and walled only at their end, around the main Buddha image

use: morning and evening ceremonies by monks, lay people admitted (when there is no *wihan*, these functions can take place in the ubosot).

The ordination hall and shrine *(ubosot, bosot, bot; sim* in Northeast Thailand)

fig. 10 below

- a rectangular building with entrance on one or both ends (often 2 doors, also 1 or 3), Buddha image facing the main entrance (east generally), may be accompanied by statues of disciples (8 or more - 80 in Wat Suthat), a raised platform for monks and the seat of the Abbot.
- surrounded by *bai sīmā* boundary stones, usually 8 stones at the cardinal and intermediate points and a ninth one buried under the centre of the hall.

fig. 10 below

- the area delimited by the *sīmā* stones was officially and irrevocably devoted to the Saṅgha by the king; today official (royal) permission is necessary to build a new *ubosot*.
- traditionally, the *ubosot* can also be surrounded by water, in which case there is no need for *sīmā* stones. One of these *bot nam* still exists at Wat Puttha En in

10 – *The* ubosot *in Wat Suwannaram, Bangkok, 19th century*

As an ordination hall, the building is surrounded by its eight boundary stones (*bai sīmā*), each under a small pavilion, on its two axes and its two diagonals. (photo P. Pichard)

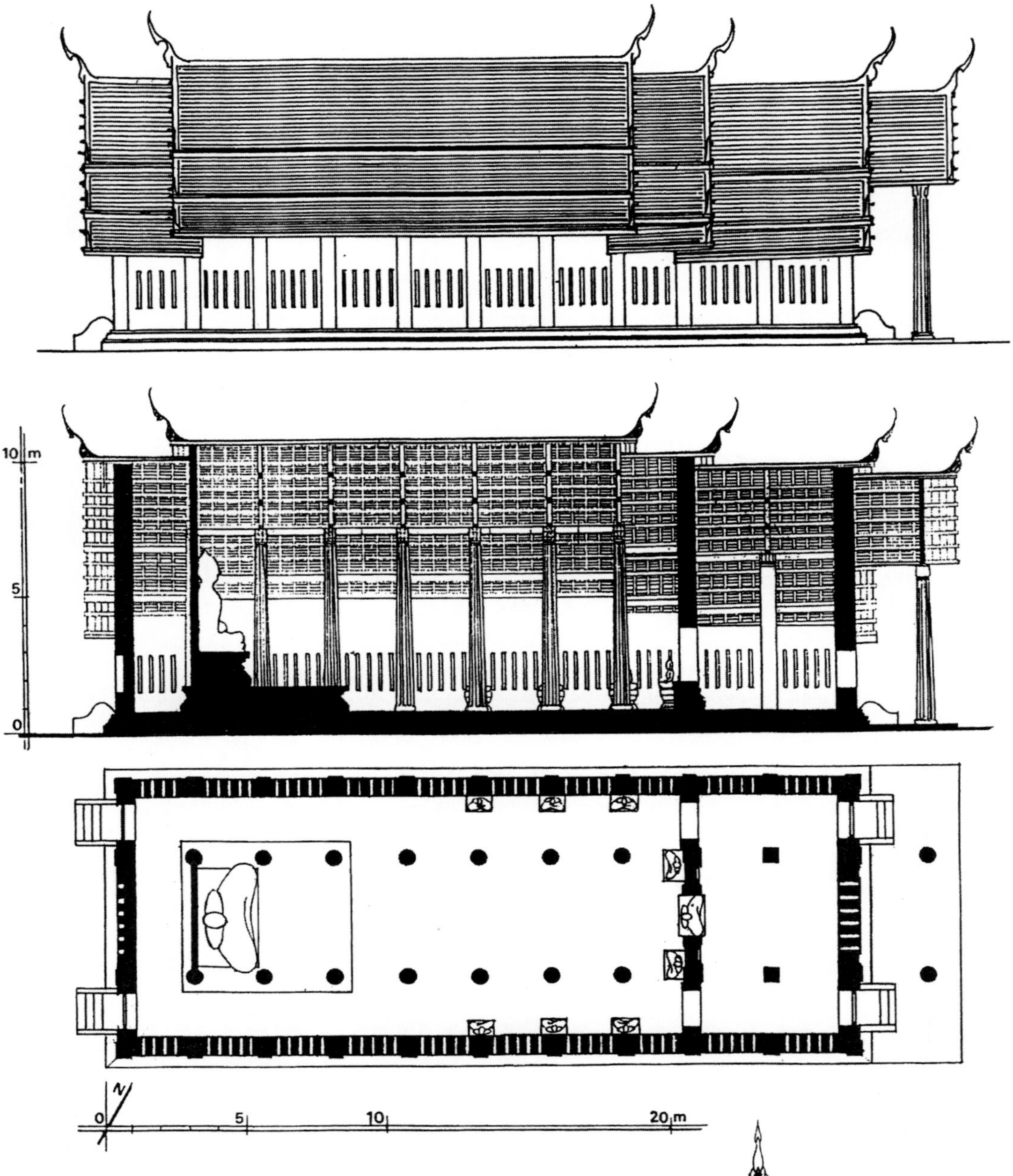

11 – *The* wihan *of Wat Lai (Lopburi province), Ayutthaya period, 18th century*

Walls and interior pillars in brick,
tiled roof on a timber framework.
Two doors on front and rear walls.

(P. Pichard after a FAD survey)

12 – *The main* chedi *in Wat Sra Si, Sukhothai, 14th century* (photos P. Pichard)

13 – *The central* prang *in Wat Ratchaburana, Ayutthaya, 15th century*

Mae Chaem (Chiang Mai province). Ordination can also take place in a temporary floating *ubosot*, for instance the re-ordination of Prince Mongkut (the future King Rama IV), performed on a raft.

use: – ordinations (should be large enough to accommodate 25 monks).
– *pātimokkha* recitations (lay people not admitted) twice a lunar month.
– when no *wihan*, morning and evening ceremonies by monks (lay people admitted).
– in North Thailand, entrance into ubosot may be forbidden to lay people, particularly women.

Wihan and *ubosot* are commonly built on the same model: from outside, the most conspicuous feature is the large roof divided in several superposed tiers, with high gables at both ends, and crowned by a curvilinear finial. On the two longer sides of the rectangle, masonry walls (occasionally wooden pillars or walls in North Thailand) have windows for light and ventilation. Ancient buildings have usually a single porch, at one end of the rectangle, and the number and shape of roof-tiers emphasise the location of the inner main Buddha image at the other end. Since the early eighteenth century, this pattern tends to be replaced by non-directional buildings with a porch on both ends and a symmetrical roofing configuration. *fig. 11 opposite page*

Inside, the main Buddha image on a pedestal faces the entrance, from the other end of the single hall. Depending on the size of the building, the roof may span the whole space between the lateral walls or be supported by two (exceptionally four) lines of internal pillars. Mural paintings on the walls illustrate the Buddhist cosmology (Mount Meru and the many levels of the universe), the main scenes of Buddha's life, or his most famous previous lives (*jātakas*).

The stūpa *(chedi* or *prang)*

- occasionally, one or several large *chedi* (a bell-shaped stūpa) built over relics, or a *prang* (a square tower on the model of the Khmer sanctuary) sometimes with a small shrine inside, may be in the very centre of the monastery. *fig. 12 above* *fig. 13 above and 14 p. 109*
- numerous small *chedis* or *prangs* may be added along the boundary walls, containing ashes of abbots, of monks or of lay persons, either in the *Buddhāvāsa* or in the *Saṅghāvāsa*.
- as in Laos, stūpas are called *that* in north-eastern Thailand.

The image house *(mondop* – infrequent*)*

– a square building housing an image or a footprint.

The gallery *(rabiang)*

fig. 14 – a surrounding portico around a rectangular or square courtyard, with a tiled roof supported by a wall outsideand on one or two files of pillars inwards. A gateway is generally located in the middle of each side. A major building occupies the centre of the courtyard, most often the main *prang* during the Ayutthaya period, and usually the *ubosot* during the Bangkok period.

4.2 In the Saṅghāvāsa *(monks' area)*

The meeting and preaching hall *(sālā kanparian)*

– can be located in the *Buddhāvāsa* as well as in the *Saṅghāvāsa.*

fig. 15 – rectangular pillared hall with or without walls, can be in wood and very large or in masonry and similar to a *wihan.*

– inside, seat of the preacher and a lateral platform for the monks.

use: sermon readings, large meetings between monks and lay people.

The pavilion(s) *(sālā)*

fig. 16 – an open building in wood or masonry, for various uses (meeting place, shelter, etc.).

The library *(ho trai)*

– a small building to shelter manuscript chests.

fig. 17 – generally in wood, sometimes on posts in the middle of a pond to protect its manuscripts from insects and rodents (see Northeastern monasteries p. 128) or above a masonry base.

The monks quarters *(kuti)*

fig. 7 p. 102 – sometimes (especially in Bangkok) in a special enclosure adjacent to the main one, often on the south side (theoretically, on the right side of the Buddha's main image).

fig. 18 – either built in wood, on posts, or in masonry.

– in large monasteries, may be grouped in units of 5-7 monk cells *(khana)* under a senior monk *(chao khana).*

– may come with an open dinning room *(ho chan)* and a kitchen.

fig. 9 p. 104 – in central Thailand, the monk cells are frequently grouped in two parallel lines on both sides of a long and narrow platform, sometimes roofed and used as a dinning place.

– *khana theo*: a building with several cells for a *khana.*

– *khana kuti*: an individual house or cell.

– in a village, *kutis* are often the first building of a new monastery.

The abbot's residence

– either grouped with the *kutis*, or a separate, larger house.

The bell tower *(ho rakhang)*

fig. 18 – a small construction on high posts.

use: announcing morning recitation.

The drum tower *(ho klonk)*

– a small construction on high posts.

use: announcing lunch time at 11.00 am.

14 – *Roofed gallery (19th century) around the inner courtyard of Wat Dusitaram, Bangkok*
East wing with its median gateway.
A small *prang* is located in each corner of the courtyard, while the ordination hall is at its centre.

15 – *Preaching hall (19th century) in Wat Yai Suwannaram, Phetchaburi*

16 – *A small sālā in Wat Ko Kaeo Suttharam, Phetchaburi*

17 – *Library (19th century) in Wat Hua Khuang, Nan*

18 – *Monks quarters (19th century) in Wat Ko Kaeo Suttharam, Phetchaburi, north face and main entrance*
(6 photos P. Pichard)

19 – *Bell tower (19th century) in Wat Ko Kaeo Suttharam, Phetchaburi*

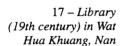

The crematorium *(men)*

- a crematorium with a high chimney surrounded by pavilions where the deceased is kept in a coffin and rites are performed.
- traditionally, cremations were not performed in the monasteries of northern Thailand, and not inside the city walls of Bangkok.
- today, the crematorium can be right inside the monastery (normally in the outer courtyard) or in a separate compound nearby.

use: funeral.

School buildings

- up to the nineteenth century, education of village boys currently provided by the Saṅgha in the monasteries did not seem to have required specific buildings, as teaching took place in *salas* or in the veranda around the *kutis*.
- today, many governmental primary schools are located in a separate part of the monastery compound (primarily because it was there that space was available).
- in addition, *pariyattitham* schools have been set up in some monasteries to teach Pāli to young monks. They are located inside the compound, usually in modern buildings with classrooms, library and auditorium, at least for the most developed.

Appendix: maps

BIBLIOGRAPHICAL REFERENCES

Annual Report:
Annual Report on Religious Activities, Department of Religious Affairs, Bangkok [in Thai].

AASEN, Clarence
1998 – *Architecture of Siam - A Cultural History Interpretation*, Kuala Lumpur, OUP, 291 p., glossary, bibliography, index, drawings, photographs, maps.

BIZOT, François
1993 – *Le bouddhisme des Thaïs – Brève histoire de ses mouvements et de ses idées des origines à nos jours*, Bangkok, Cahiers de France, 114 p.

DÖHRING, Karl
1920 – *Buddhistische Tempelanglagen in Siam.* English translation 2000, White Lotus, Bangkok: *Buddhist Temples of Thailand*, 353 p.

GABAUDE, Louis
1996 – "La triple crise du bouddhisme en Thaïlande", *BEFEO* 83, p. 241-257.

ISHII, Yoneo
1986 – *Sangha, State, and Society: Thai Buddhism in History*, Kyoto, Center for Southeast Asian Studies, 193 p.

SUMET, Jumsai
1970 – "The Reconstruction of the City Plan of Ayudhyā", *In Memoriam Phya Anuman Rajadhon*, Siam Society, Bangkok, p. 301-314.

KALYANAMITR, Choti
1993 – *Dictionary of Thai Architecture*, Bangkok, Office of the National Culture Commission, 150 p.

KRAIRIKSH, Piriya
1974 – "Semas with scenes from the Mahanipata-Jatakas in the National Museum at Khon Kaen", *Art and Archaeology in Thailand*, Bangkok, p. 35-65.

O'CONNOR, Richard A.
1985 – "Centers of Sanctities, Regions and Religion: Varieties of Tai Buddhism", communication at the Annual Meeting of the American Anthropological Association, Washington D.C., 26 p.

SKILLING, Peter
1997 – "The Advent of Theravada Buddhism to Mainland South-east Asia", *Journal of the International Association of Buddhist Studies* 20.1, p. 93-107.

TAMBIAH, S.J.
1976 – *World Conqueror and World Renouncer*, Cambridge University Press, 557 p.

WELLS, Kenneth E.
1939 – *Thai Buddhism, its Rites and Activities*, Bangkok, Suriyabun Publishers (3rd edition, 1975), 331 p.

CHINA
BURMA
Phongsali
Kyaing Tong
Chiang Saen
Chiang Khong
Chiang Rai
Louang Phrabang
Chiang Kham
Xiang Khoang
Chiang Mai
Lamphun
Lanna
Nan
LAOS
Lampang
Phrae
Vieng Kham
Mekong
Uttaradit
Vientiane
Phon Phisay
Si Chiang Mai
Chiang Khan
Tha Bo
Vieng Khuk
Si Satchanalai
Suvanna Khuha
Sukhothai
Phitsanulok
Kamphaeng Phet
That Phanom
That In Hang
Savannakhet
Mae Nam Ping
Mae Nam Chi
Isan
VIETNAM
THAILAND
Mae Nam Mun
Ubon Ratchathani
Nakhon Ratchasima
Lopburi
Ang Thong
Phra Phuttapat
Suphan Buri
Ayutthaya
Champasak
Kanchanaburi
Bangkok
Angkor
Siem Reap
Phetchaburi
Battambang
Cha-am
Pursat
Kompong Thom
Kompong Chhnang
Mekong
CAMBODIA
Kompong Cham
Udong
Phnom Penh
Prey Veng
Takeo
Chaiya
Nakhon Si Thammarat
Phatthalung
Songkhla
MALAYSIA
N
(former) royal capital with monasteries
other city or monastic site
0
100
500
km

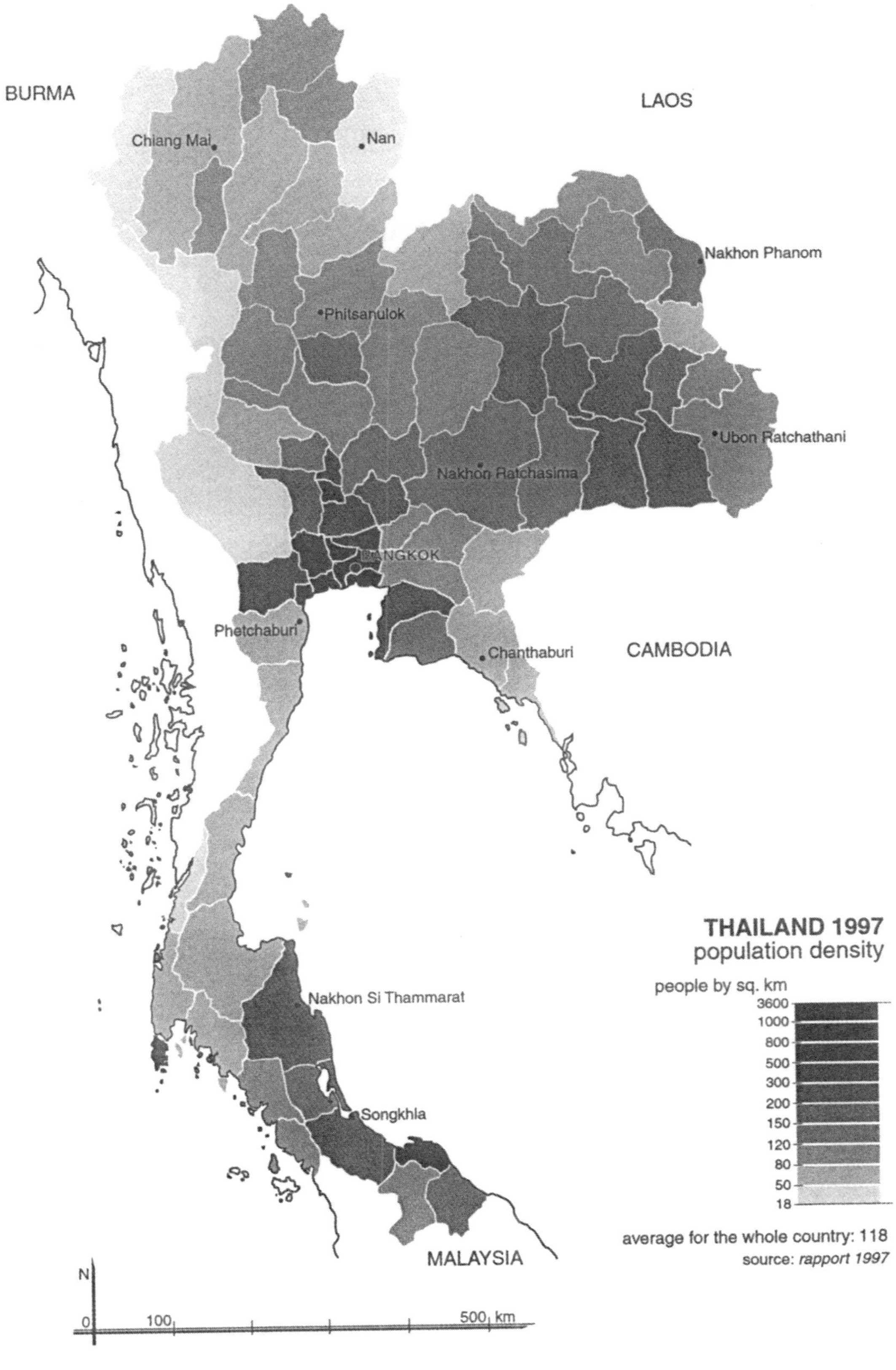
BURMA
LAOS
Chiang Mai
Nan
Nakhon Phanom
Phitsanulok
Ubon Ratchathani
Nakhon Ratchasima
BANGKOK
Phetchaburi
Chanthaburi
CAMBODIA
THAILAND 1997
population density
people by sq. km
3600
1000
800
500
300
200
150
120
80
50
18
Nakhon Si Thammarat
Songkhla
average for the whole country: 118
source: rapport 1997
MALAYSIA
N
0
100
500 km

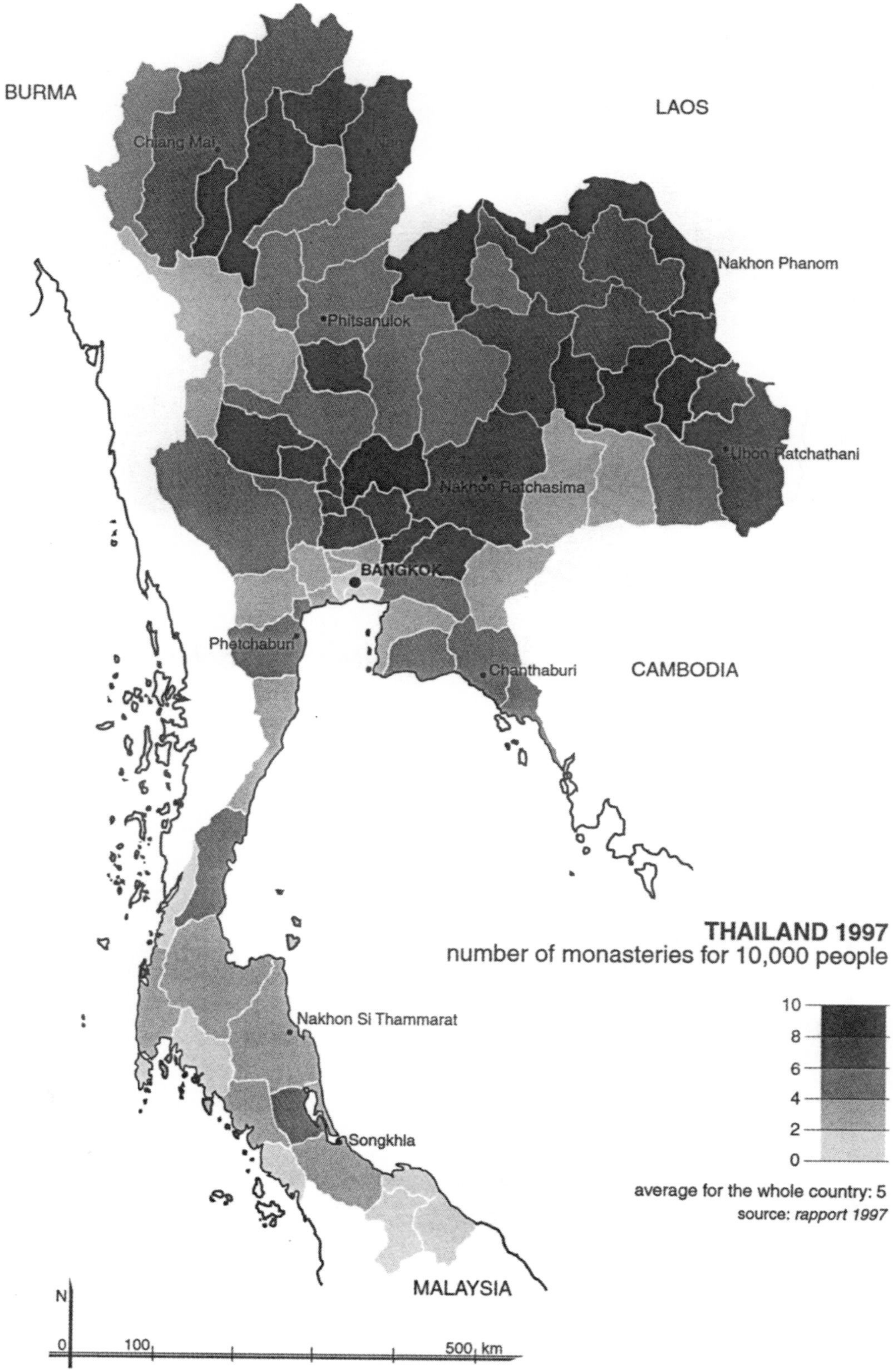
BURMA
LAOS
Chiang Mai
Nan
Nakhon Phanom
Phitsanulok
Ubon Ratchathani
Nakhon Ratchasima
BANGKOK
Phetchaburi
Chanthaburi
CAMBODIA
THAILAND 1997
number of monasteries for 10,000 people
10
8
6
4
2
0
average for the whole country: 5
source: rapport 1997
Nakhon Si Thammarat
Songkhla
MALAYSIA
N
0
100
500 km

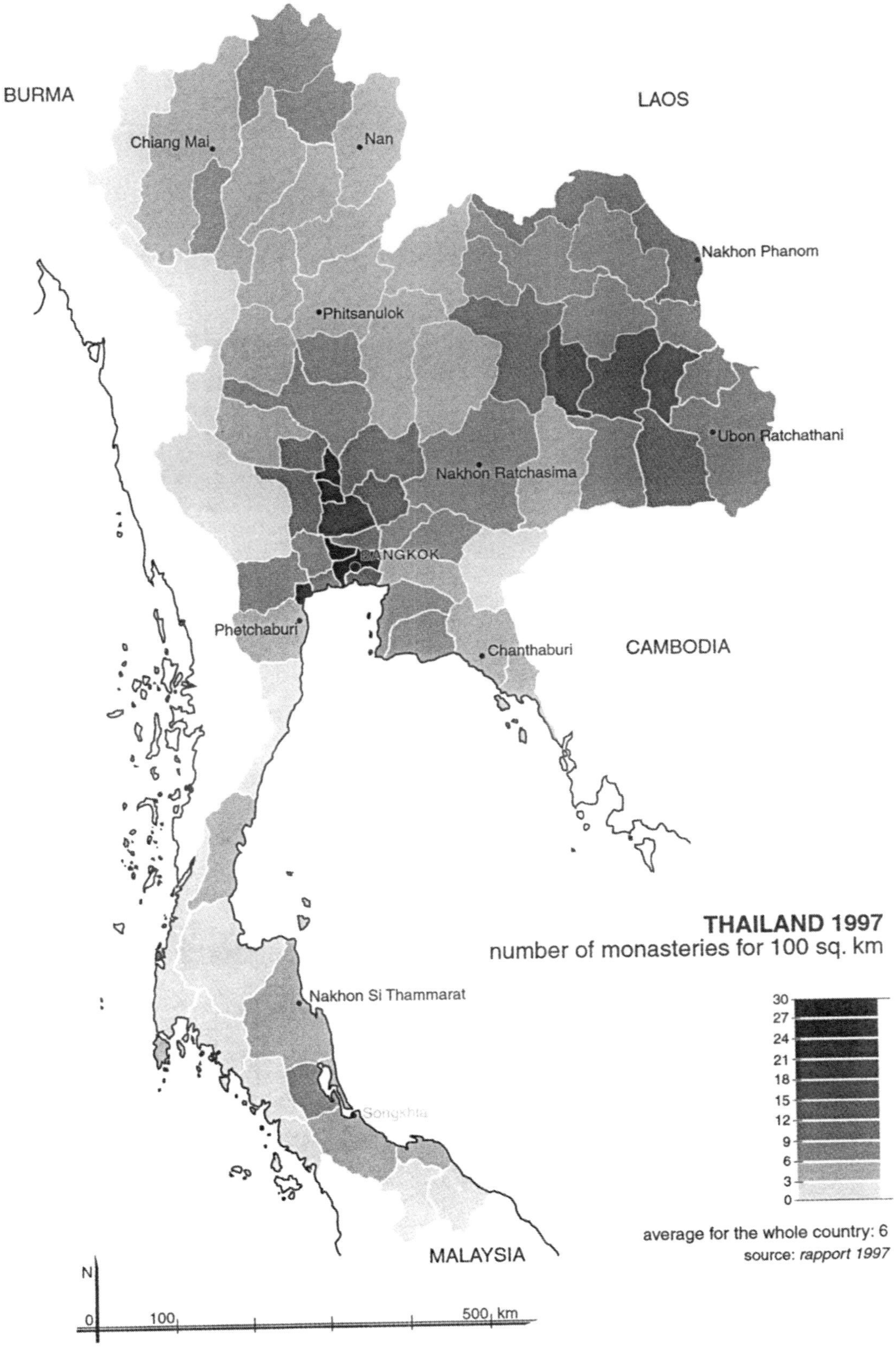
BURMA
LAOS
Chiang Mai
Nan
Nakhon Phanom
Phitsanulok
Ubon Ratchathani
Nakhon Ratchasima
BANGKOK
Phetchaburi
Chanthaburi
CAMBODIA
THAILAND 1997
number of monasteries for 100 sq. km
30
27
24
21
18
15
12
9
6
3
0
Nakhon Si Thammarat
average for the whole country: 6
source: rapport 1997
MALAYSIA
N
0
100
500 km

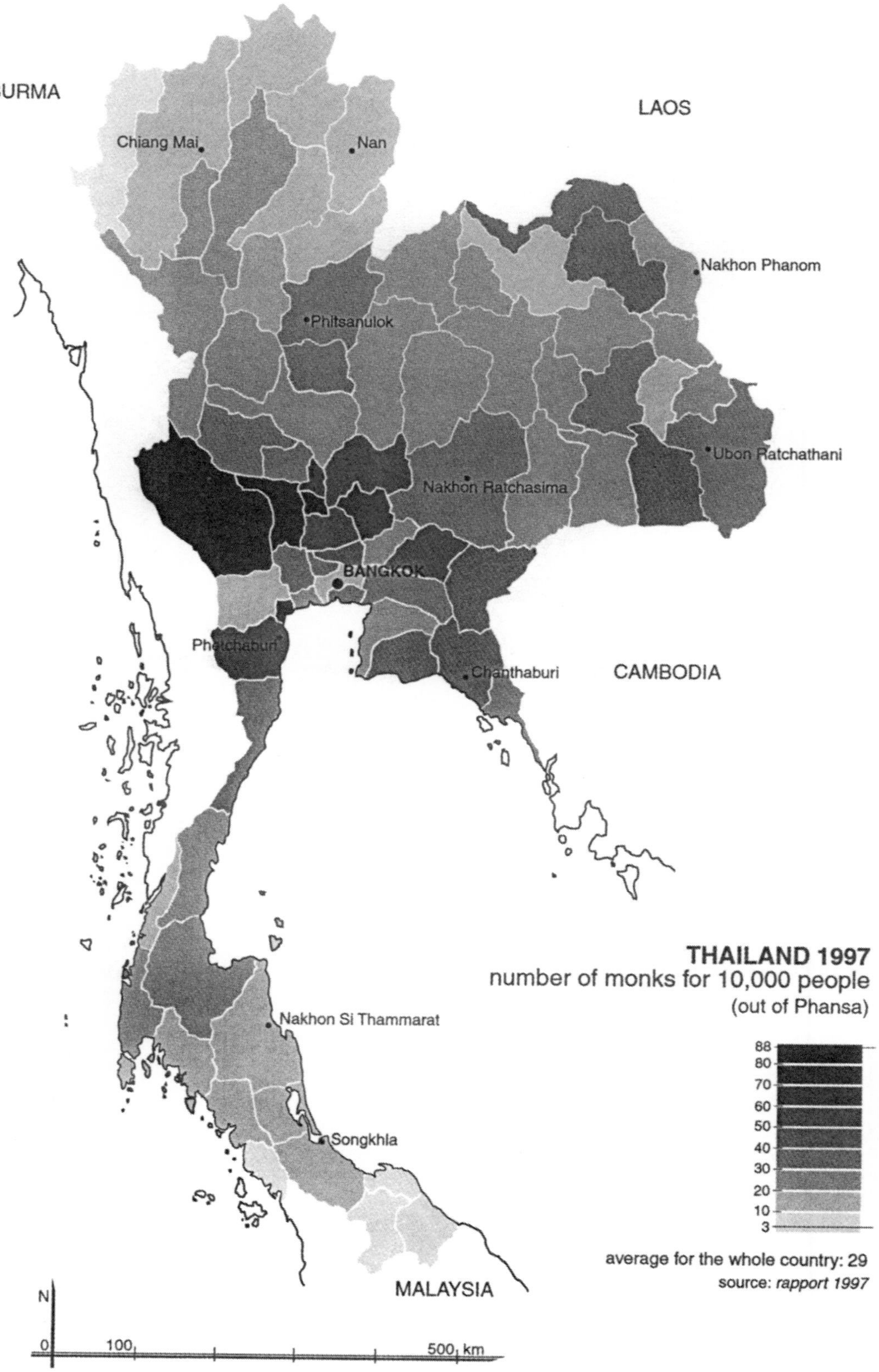
BURMA
LAOS
CAMBODIA
MALAYSIA
Chiang Mai
Nan
Nakhon Phanom
Phitsanulok
Ubon Ratchathani
Nakhon Ratchasima
BANGKOK
Phetchaburi
Chanthaburi
Nakhon Si Thammarat
Songkhla
THAILAND 1997
number of monks for 10,000 people
(out of Phansa)
88
80
70
60
50
40
30
20
10
3
average for the whole country: 29
source: rapport 1997
N
0
100
500 km

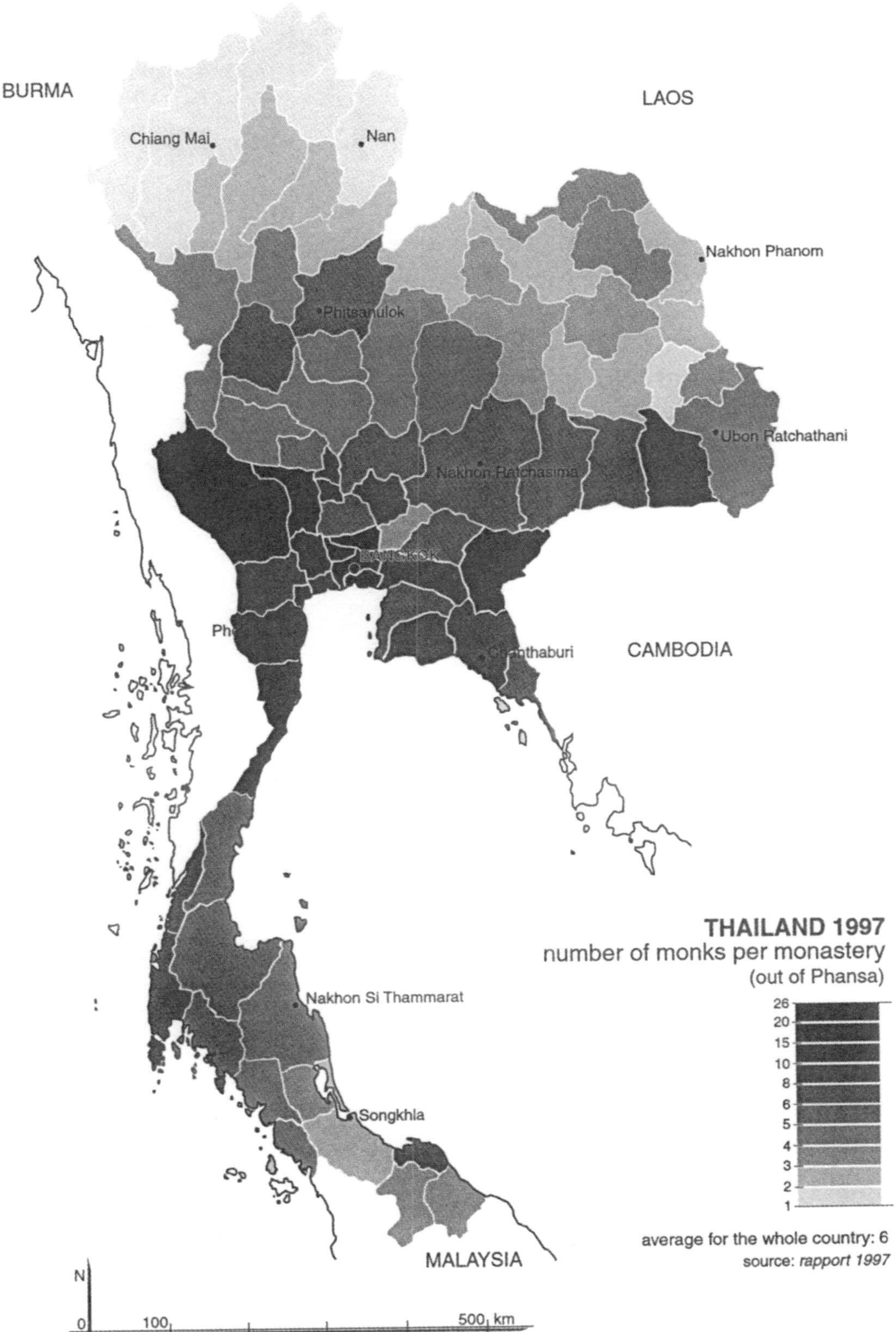
BURMA
LAOS
Chiang Mai
Nan
Nakhon Phanom
Phitsanulok
Ubon Ratchathani
Nakhon Ratchasima
BANGKOK
CAMBODIA
Nakhon Si Thammarat
Songkhla
MALAYSIA
THAILAND 1997
number of monks per monastery
(out of Phansa)
26
20
15
10
8
6
5
4
3
2
1
average for the whole country: 6
source: rapport 1997
N
0
100
500 km

MONASTIC ARCHITECTURE IN NORTHEASTERN THAILAND

Thada Sutthitham

The Northeast, or Isan, is the largest region in Thailand covering an area about the one-third of the country. The region is well known for its prehistoric sites (2 000 BC to the seventh century) and its ancient architecture belonging to the Môn (seventh to eleventh centuries) and the Khmer (seventh to thirteenth centuries) civilizations. Theravāda Buddhism had been flourishing during the Môn period and declined during the Hindu's Khmer Empire. Mahāyāna Buddhism was revered by a Khmer king during the thirteenth century and declined afterwards. However, Hinduism and both Theravāda and Mahāyāna Buddhism have been the foundation of Thai religious architecture.

From the fifteenth to the seventeenth century, the Northeast was isolated from major centres. The area was occupied by two new kingdoms: the smaller and lower part by the Ayutthaya (Thai) Kingdom and the rest by the Lanchang (Lao) Kingdom. In the eighteenth century Lao and Tai people migrated from Laos to settle in the region (especially after 1778 AD because of wars between Laos and Thais) and established their communities, generally over more ancient settlements. From the nineteenth century the whole region has been fully incorporated into the Thai Kingdom (Bangkok/ Rattanakosin). During his reign, King Chulalongkorn (Rama V, 1868-1910 AD) promoted the national unity through administrative reforms all over the country, and the Northeast integrated the modern national model. Since then many villages have grown into district towns and provincial cities.

As the main ancestors of Isan people are Lao and Tai, two beliefs have strong influences on their culture: spirit-worship (*phī* /spirit) on the one hand and Theravāda Buddhism inherited from Lanchang and Thai Kingdoms on the other hand. The establishment and construction of Isan monasteries and architecture follow these kingdoms' cultures. Nevertheless, Isan people have gradually created their own architectural designs and their monasteries have unique characteristics.

The Buddhist Monastery, EFEO, 2003, p. 119-130

Isan monasteries can be classified into 2 types:

1 – The village monastery
This type of monastery plays an important role in the village communities. They have been constructed since the establishment of Isan settlements, from the eighteenth century up to the present time. This article will concentrate on the monasteries belonging to this type because they are historically important and their architecture is especially significant.

2 – The forest monastery
This type has spread out since King Mongkut (Rama IV, 1851-1868) founded a new Buddhist sect called *Dhammayutikanikāya*, a reform of the existing *Mahānikāya* sect with emphasis on stricter interpretation of monastic discipline and seclusion. Numerous such monasteries have been built in Isan, outside the cities and at least theoretically "in the forests".

see map p. 112 for sites mentioned in this article

Commemorative architecture: in addition, a small number of monasteries in Isan acquire a special status from the presence of architectural or landscaped references, such as "*The seven revered commemorative symbols of Buddha (Sattamahasathan)*" at Wat Phra That Bang Puan, Nong Kai; "*The Dhamma Garden*" landmarked by Nadoon Stūpa in Mahasarakam; "*the Golden Mount*" on top of some mountains.

Northeastern village monasteries

The village and its monastery are closely related in Isan culture. The Chronicle of Wat Klang monastery at Ban Khok Kor village, Yang Talad district, Kalasin province, tells us the significance of the monastery for the villagers and the order of architectural construction in the monastery compound:

> When this village was established, a monastery was built immediately, in 1792. The monks' residence and the preaching hall (*ho chek*) were built first. The ordination hall (*sim*) was constructed later, in 1820, when the village was well established.

Location

Monastery or temple in Thai language are called *wat*. When an Isan community was settled, a monastery would be built near the centre or at the perimeter of the village. A small village has a monastery usually named *Wat Pho Sri* or *Wat Pho Chai* (both mean an auspicious bhodi tree monastery). When the community grows larger, a second and later a third monastery will be built in the south or the north side of the village. These three monasteries will be then called *Wat Klang, Wat Nüa,* and *Wat Tai* (central, north, and south monasteries) instead of using their auspicious or official names, related to Buddhism beliefs or important structures in the monastery such as *Wat Phon Chai* (the monastery of good deeds), *Wat Sri Mongkol* (the monastery of auspicious mound), *Wat Phra That* (the stūpa monastery), etc.

Monastery land and land uses

Community monasteries are usually built on an area of 5 to 20 *rais* (8,000 to 32,000 sqm). The shape of the land is often rectangular, corresponding to the grid plan of the village where the monastery occupies one plot.

Land uses can be classified into 3 types:

1 – Green area: fruit trees (e.g. mango, sugar palm, coconut, jack fruit) are usually planted along the monastery boundaries. If there is a bodhi tree, it will be planted near the centre of the land, but this location is not strict.

1 – *A Isan rural village in Sakon Nakhon province, with its modest monastery*
*In the common ground (*lan wat*) stand a preaching hall (*ho chek*) and small monks' residences (*kutis*)*

2 – *Common location of a monastery near a town (Nakhon Ratchasima province)*
The main Isan monastic architecture features are there (ordination hall, preaching hall, monks' residences) but the common ground area is less used than in village monasteries. Thus, the empty ground is less prominent and shows a tendency to shrink because there are less communal activities.

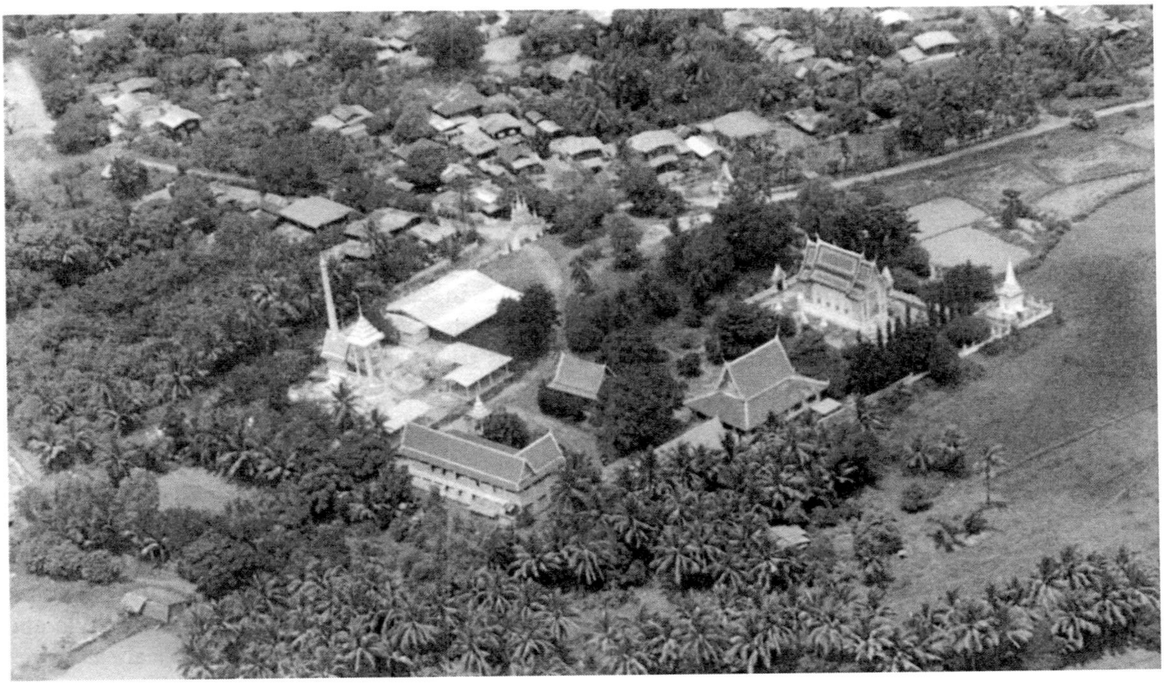

2 – *Common ground area (lan wat)*: as the monastery land is not very large, most of the ground will be kept clean of vegetation. This common ground area, characteristic of Thai monasteries, is essential as a place for people to gather outdoor. For the monastery, it is the area to perform many important festivals and ceremonies such as watering Buddha images and monks during the New Year Festival (*Songkran* festival in April), the sand stūpa construction during the New Year Festival, parades of people and elephants during the Kathin ceremony that takes place annually at the end of the Rain Retreat for the monks. Under the tropical climate, this outdoor space is also needed for many activities not related to Buddhism: it is commonly used as a market place, daily or occasionally, for musical performances and dancing, for villager gatherings and debates, and as a playground for children under the monastery's day-care centre.

3 – *Built area*: the buildings are scattered within the precincts of the monastery as described in the next section.

It is essential to note that in the Northeast monasteries, there is no separation between the public zone (*Buddhāvāsa*) and the monks' residential zone (*Saṅghāvāsa*) unlike in those of Bangkok and of the provinces in the Middle Plain Region of Thailand or in Sukhothai monasteries as well.

Northeastern Monastic Architecture

Although many buildings are constructed following the same Buddhism belief, Isan monastery architecture has its unique own design, whose main characteristics can be conclusively described as follows:

Stūpa

There are two main types of stūpa in Isan: a) a stūpa built over relics of Buddha and his disciples, and b) a stūpa to keep the ashes of monks or commoners.

*a – Reliquary stūpa (*phra that*)*

The square lotus shape is the specific shape of an Isan reliquary stūpa. Important stūpas are made of bricks, plastered with lime mortar and adorned with stucco mouldings or brick carving, such as at Phra That Phnom at Nakhon Phanom, Phra Mahathat (That Phra Ananda) at Roi Et, Phra Sri Song Rak at Loei or Phra That Kam Kaen near Khon Kaen. The reliquary stūpa is usually situated at the centre of the monastery ground.

*b – Stūpa for monks and commoners (*that*)*

They can be found in most monasteries. They are built of wood or brick, and presently of moulded cement. They are small in scale, usually not higher then 2.5 metres and are located along one or two sides of the monastery compound wall. At present, as a need of place to keep ancestors' ashes has arisen, many monasteries provide niches in their enclosure walls for this purpose.

*Ordination hall (*sim*)*

Not every monastery has an ordination hall. In the past, several villages shared the ordination hall of a nearby monastery. At present, almost all village monasteries try to build an ordination hall at the centre of the monastery, in front of the reliquary stūpa, as a symbol of modern development following the Bangkok tendency. In the past, Isan ordination halls were either built of wood or brick, with proportions, roof style and decoration different from other regions of Thailand. Some with open walls are a distinct

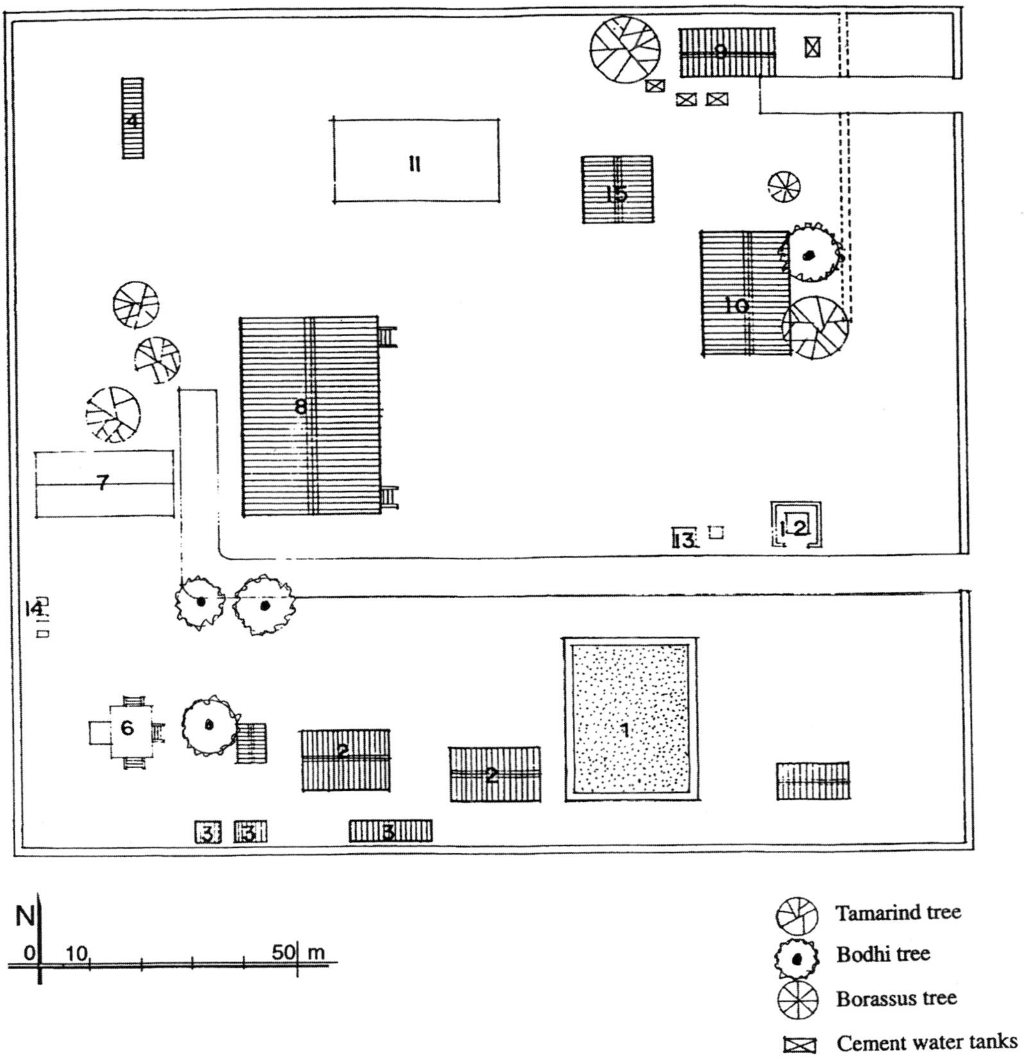

3 – *Wat Klang Khok Kho, Kalasin province*
(Srisuro 1993, page 85)

1. Pink lotus pond
2. Monks' residences, *kutis*
3. Bathrooms – toilets
4. New bathroom in masonry
5. Old bathroom in corrugated iron
6. Crematorium
7. Funerary hall
8. Two-storey preaching hall, *ho chek*
9. Two-storey *kuti* in wood, with walled ground floor
10. Two-storey *kuti* in wood, with open ground floor
11. Base for a new ordination hall
12. Bell tower, *ho rakhang*
13. Two stūpas, *thats*
14. New funerary stūpas, *thats*
15. Ordination hall, *sim*

Isan feature. Mural paintings on the outside are also characteristic of Isan, and together with the iconography of woodcarvings and sculptures, they refer to the Buddhist Dhamma and other stories according to a local interpretation and imagination.

*Preaching hall (*ho chek*)*

The *ho chek* is an important building for monastic and community functions and exists in every monastery. Even when the monastery has an ordination hall, the *ho chek* can be also located at the centre of the monastery ground, which is its more common location. Most villagers come everyday to listen to preaching and offer food to the monks, and monthly to attend the 12-month ceremonies. Since it is the only communal building in the village, assemblies and meetings take also place there. There is usually no Buddha image in the *ho chek*, unlike in monasteries of northern Thailand where people come to the *wihan* which, while housing one or several Buddha images, is also a preaching hall. Originally made of wood, the *ho chek* is a single-story building, with the floor raised on posts about 1 to 1.5 m above the ground. About 60 years ago, under the influence of colonial buildings of Laos, some preaching halls were built of brick, and many old ones are nowadays replaced by concrete buildings in the style of the Bangkok congregation hall (*sala kanparien*), with usually two storeys. Gable roofs with lifted tiers are common to Isan Buddhist buildings.

*Library House (*ho trai*)*

Buildings to house palm-leaf manuscripts were constructed only in those monasteries where monks were educated enough to copy the Scriptures and write other texts which accumulated year after year. Most Isan libraries were made of wood and located in the middle of a pond to be protected from termites and ants, dangerous eaters of palm leaves. Multiple-tiered roofs are the important character of the Isan *ho trai*.

*Monks' residence (*kuti*)*

The head monk's residence is usually larger than the ones of the monks. There are individual cells as well as rooms for groups of monks. They have been constructed in different styles belonging to different periods. Monks' residences are usually located along any sidewall of the monastery. While in the past people in the Central Plain donated their houses for monks' residences, in Isan villagers cooperated to construct the monks' residence when establishing a monastery. First to be built in a new Isan monastery, the monks' residences differ from ordinary people's houses. While in the past the *kutis* were mostly built of wood and later more commonly of brick, they are nowadays built with reinforced concrete and cement blocks.

*Wooden bell (*pong*), metal bell and drum tower*

In the past, the *pong*, a wooden bell commonly hung under the monks' residence or under the preaching hall, was rang to assemble the monastic community members. Recently the metal bell and the drum in use in the Central Plain were introduced in Isan and nowadays, if the old *pong* can be still in place, a metal bell and/or a drum are hung up in a newly built tower.

Other Buildings

– *Buddha Foot Print pavilion*: In some rare monasteries, a pavilion was built to house a Buddha footprint such as at Wat Ban Nong Kung at Khon Kaen and Wat Lattikawan at Mukdahan.

4 – *That Renu, Nakhon Phanom*

5 – *That Ananda, Wat Mahathat, Yasothon*

6 – *Prathat Kam Kaen, Khon Kaen*

7 – *Wooden* that, *Wat Sra Thong, Khon Kaen*

8 – *Small brick* that, *Yasothon*

9 – *The older style of Isan* sim, *ordination hall, Wat Klan Khok Kho, Kalasin province*

10 – *An old* sim *with a new one next to it, Wat Pho Sri, Khon Kaen province*

12 – *Wood carving, north-west corner of the* sim, *Wat Sri Than, Roi Et province*

11 – *Mural paintings on the outside face of the* sim walls, *Wat Sra Thong, Khon Kaen province*

13 – *Preaching hall,* ho chek
Section
Wat Sri Monta,
Mukdahan

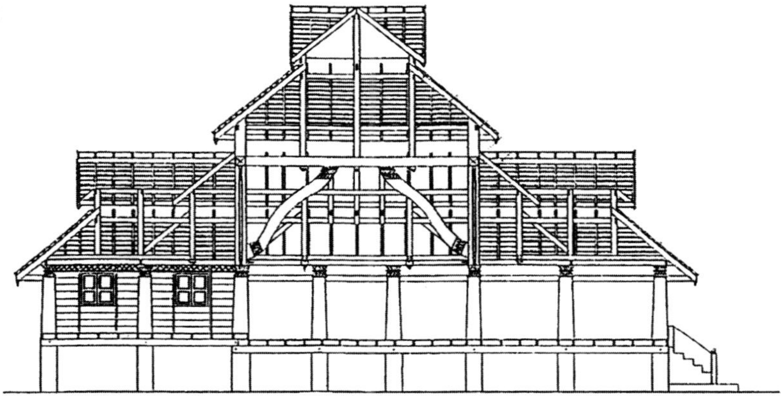

14 – *The preaching hall,* ho chek,
Wat Sri Monta, Mukdahan

15 – *Preaching hall,* ho chek,
Wat Huey Nari, Roi Et

16 – *The pulpit inside the preaching hall,*
Wat Huey Nari, Roi Et

17 – *A library,* ho trai,
in the middle of a natural pond,
Nong Kulu, Ubon Rachathani

18 – *Library,* ho trai,
in the middle of a small monastery pond
Wat Tungsrimuang, Ubon Ratchathani

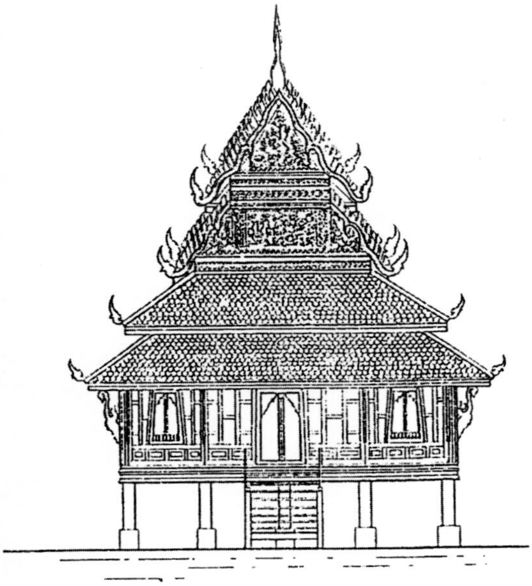

19 – *Front elevation of the library,* ho trai,
Wat Tungsrimuang, Ubon Ratchathani

20 – *Monks' residence,* kuti,
and bell-tower,
Wat Nong Chabok,
Nakhon Ratchasima

21 – *Front elevation*
of the monks' residence, kuti,
Wat Sri Monta, Mukdahan

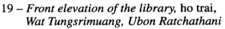

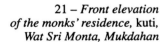

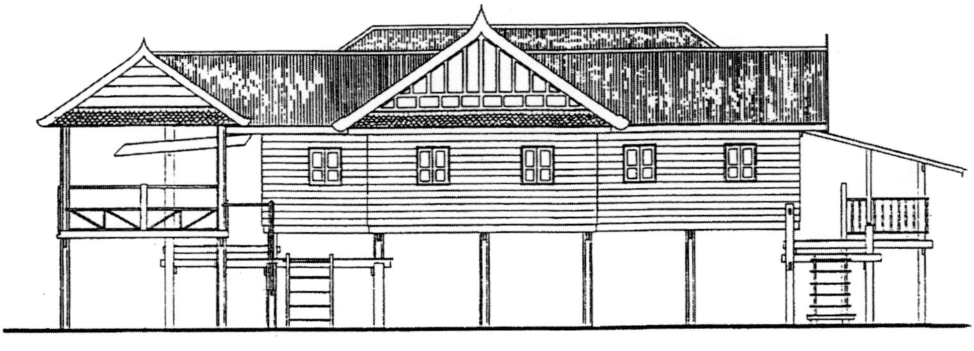

– *Buddha image pavilion or* wihan*:* a building to house a Buddha image, is commonly built in Laos and in the Northern and Middle Region. Some *wihan* can be found in Isan monasteries near Vientiane, in Mukdahan and Nong Khai provinces.

– *Sacred Pond:* it can be found only in rare monasteries such as Wat Phra That Bung Puan at Nong Khai and Wat Lattikawan at Mukdahan.

– *Crematorium:* in the past, dead bodies were cremated in a communal forest, but the trend nowadays is to build a crematorium inside the monastery compounds, especially when they are situated downtown or near cities.

Northeastern monasteries have shown a development closely linked to the needs of the villager communities. The monastery is the very heart of the Isan village which cannot function without it. This is the one place for village life and culture, where all community activities are performed.

Isan monasteries and their architecture possess characteristic features of their own. Although they may seem humble in scale and decoration if compared with the architecture of other regions of Thailand, they mirror the deep religious belief of the Isan people and display interpretations of Buddhist symbols and stories through imaginative and creative architectural solutions and decoration.

REFERENCES

Wiroj SRISURO
1993 – *Isan Sim: Northeast Buddhist Holy Temples* [in Thai], Bangkok, Toyota Foundation, Maeka Press.

Thada SUTTHITHAM, *et al.*
1999 – *Suksa a-deed [the Study of Old Isan Architecture* [in Thai], booklet, Khon Kaen, Pim Patana.
1999 – Ho chek *(preaching hall) in the Northeast* [in Thai], research report, Khon Kaen, Faculty of Architecture.

ISAN *SIMS*

ORDINATION HALLS IN NORTHEAST THAILAND

Wiroj Srisuro

The *sim* is a very significant element of Buddhist architecture for the people of Isan, the northeastern region of the country. It is the building mainly devoted to monk ordinations, called *ubosot* or *bot* in the central Thai plain. Isan people consider *sim* as the second holy structure, just after *Phra That* or reliquary stūpa, and do not allow women to enter it.

The word *sim* comes from *sīmā*, which means a sacred boundary for the ordination area. Isan *sims* are small buildings not used for the laity but reserved to monks' ceremonies, unlike the *ho chek* or preaching hall, which is built on a larger scale and open for lay public.

Sims *can be classified into 2 types:*

Water *sim* or *udakukkhepasīmā*, located in the middle of water if a place needed for ordination is too far away from any village and monastery. The early water *sim* was a boat or a raft. The *Vinaya* (the Book of Discipline) specifies that the water boundary must be either:

- *nadī* or river;
- *samudda* or ocean;
- *chata-sra* or natural waterbody.

A boat or a raft used as a water *sim* cannot be moved, thus it must be anchored or tied to a post, and distant from the bank more than a splash of water. A water *sim* can also be a special building entirely surrounded by water. However water *sims* are relatively rare in Isan.

Land *sim* or *kaṇḍasīmā*, built on land. The land *sim* must have a specify boundary which is called *sīmā*, of which there are two types, *baddhasīmā* or tied boundary and *abaddhasīmā* or untied boundary.

The land *sims* of Isan can be architecturally categorized as follows:

A – The open *Sim,* without outer walls

The building plan is rectangular and 2 or 4 bay long. Only the rear wall, at the back of the Buddha image, is constructed up to the roof. The walls on the three other sides are partially constructed, raising with steps on the two lateral sides and forming a parapet on the front side. The entrance is just an opening on the front lower parapet, without any door. The base of the building is commonly elevated and moulded. The gable roof, sometimes on two tiers with a surrounding lean-to, was originally made of shingles which in most cases have been replaced later by galvanized metal sheets. The roof is adorned by finials, acroterions at all corners, bargeboards and an axial crest spire. There is no *khan tuey (*bracket*)*. Pediments are decorated with sun ray patterns.

fig. 1 below

1 – *Architectural components of the open* sim

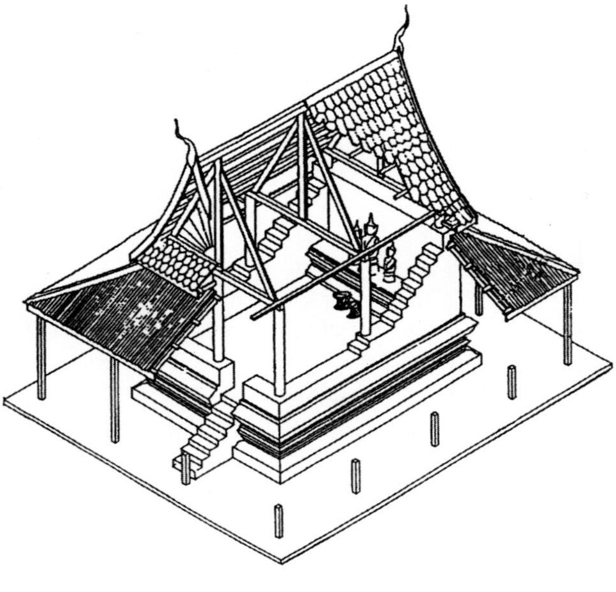

Different open *sim* can be found:

A 1 – Pure local style of two types

A 1.1: without gallery. Examples are:

- Wat Lattikawan, Ban Chanot, Whan Yai district, Mukdahan province; *fig. 2 opposite*
- Wat Srichairaj, Ban Nonpueng, Kanthararom district, Sisaket province. *fig. 3 p. 134*

A 1.2: with gallery. Examples are:

- Wat Klang Khok Kor, Ban Khok Kor, Yang Talat district, Kalasin province. *fig. 4 p. 135*
- Wat Tungsawang Pako, Ban Pako, Kumphawapi dist., Udon Thani province. *fig. 5 p. 136*

A 2 – Imported style modified by local people in later periods

An example is:

- Wat Sri Suk, Ban Koi Yai, Muang Suang district, Roi Et province.

2 – *Wat Lattikawan, Ban Chanot,*
*Whan Yai district, Mukdahan province** A 1.1

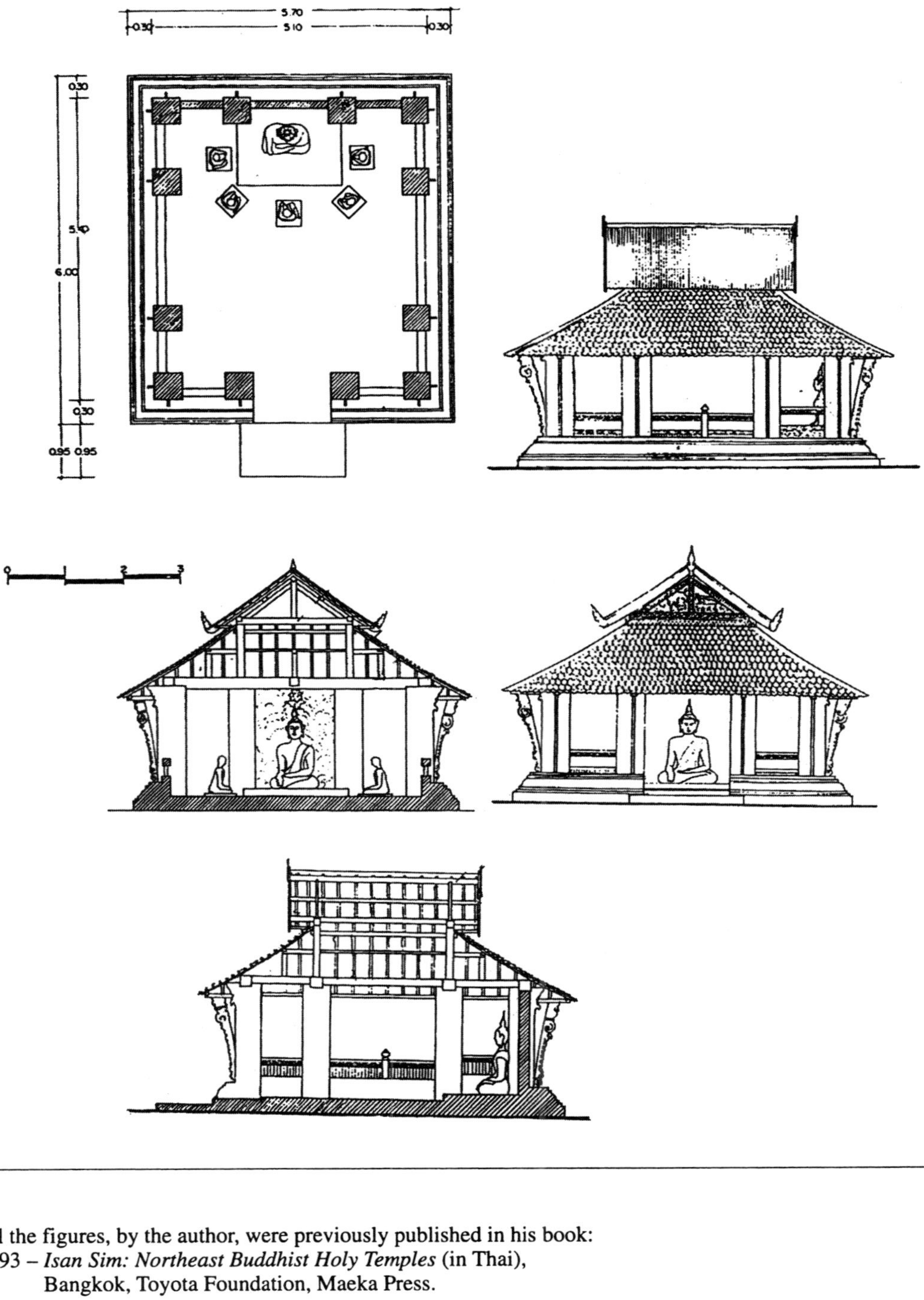

* All the figures, by the author, were previously published in his book:
1993 – *Isan Sim: Northeast Buddhist Holy Temples* (in Thai), Bangkok, Toyota Foundation, Maeka Press.

3 – *Wat Srichairaj, Ban Nonpueng,*
Kanthararom district, Sisaket province

A 1.1

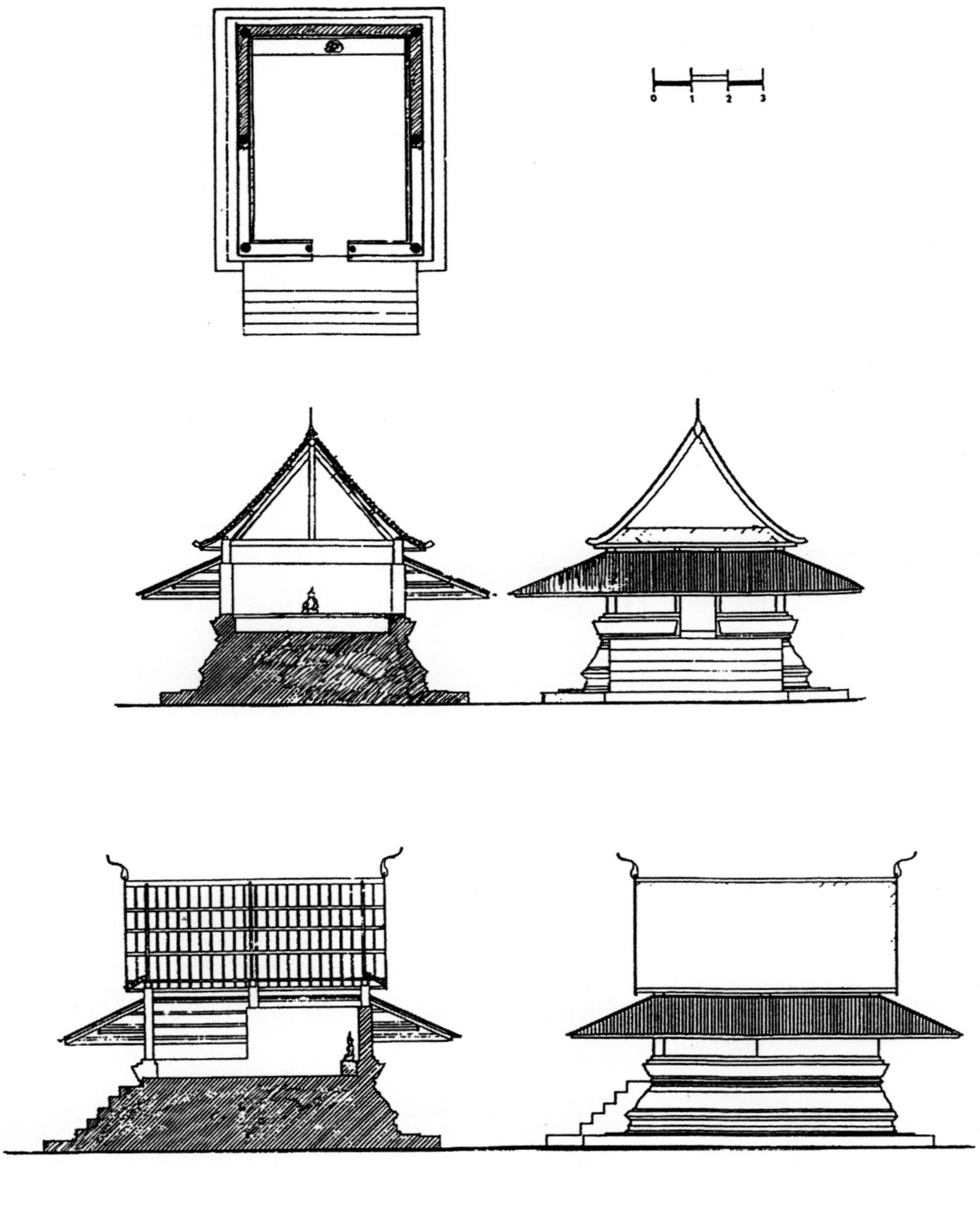

4 – *Wat Klang Khok Kor, Ban Khok Kor,*
Yang Talat district, Kalasin province

A 1.2

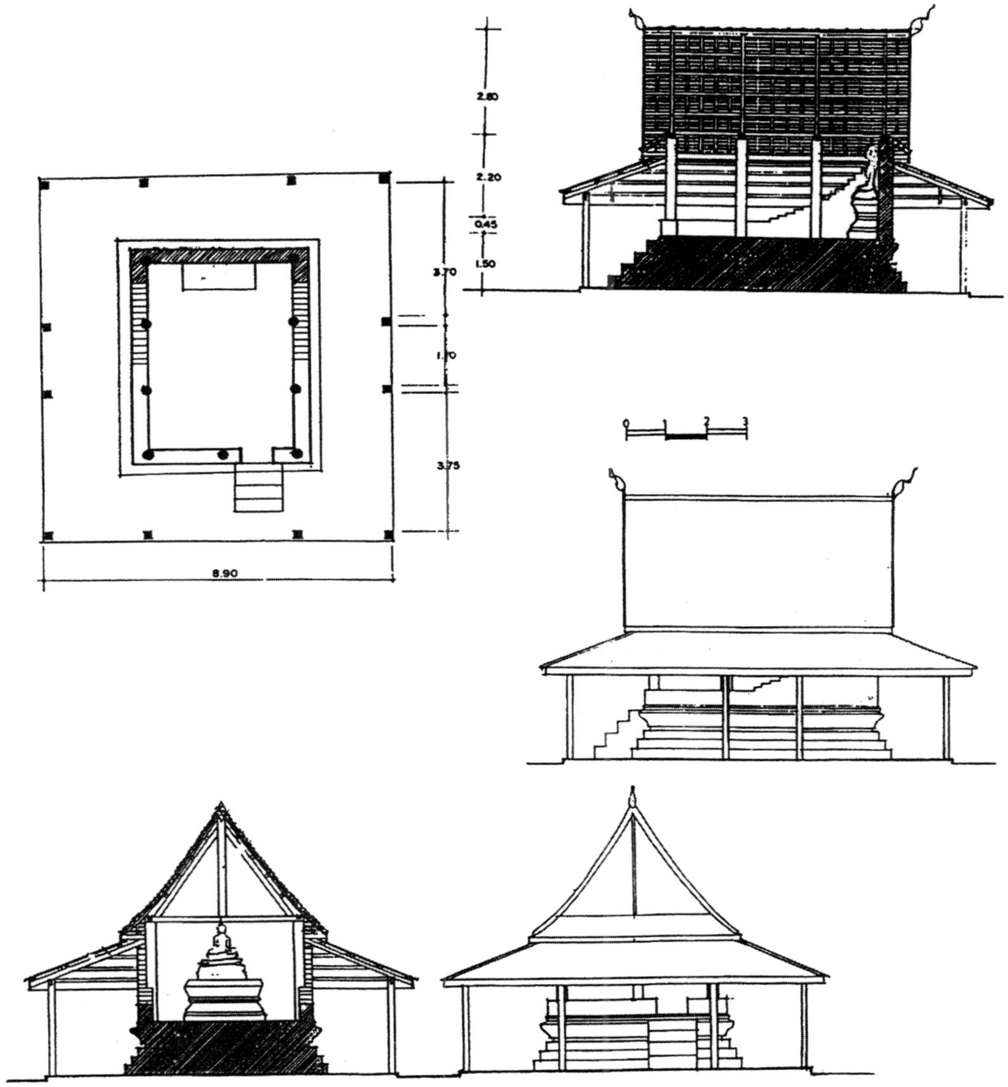

Wiroj Srisuro

5 – *Wat Tungsawang Pako, Ban Pako, Kumphawapi district, Udon Thani province*

A 1.2

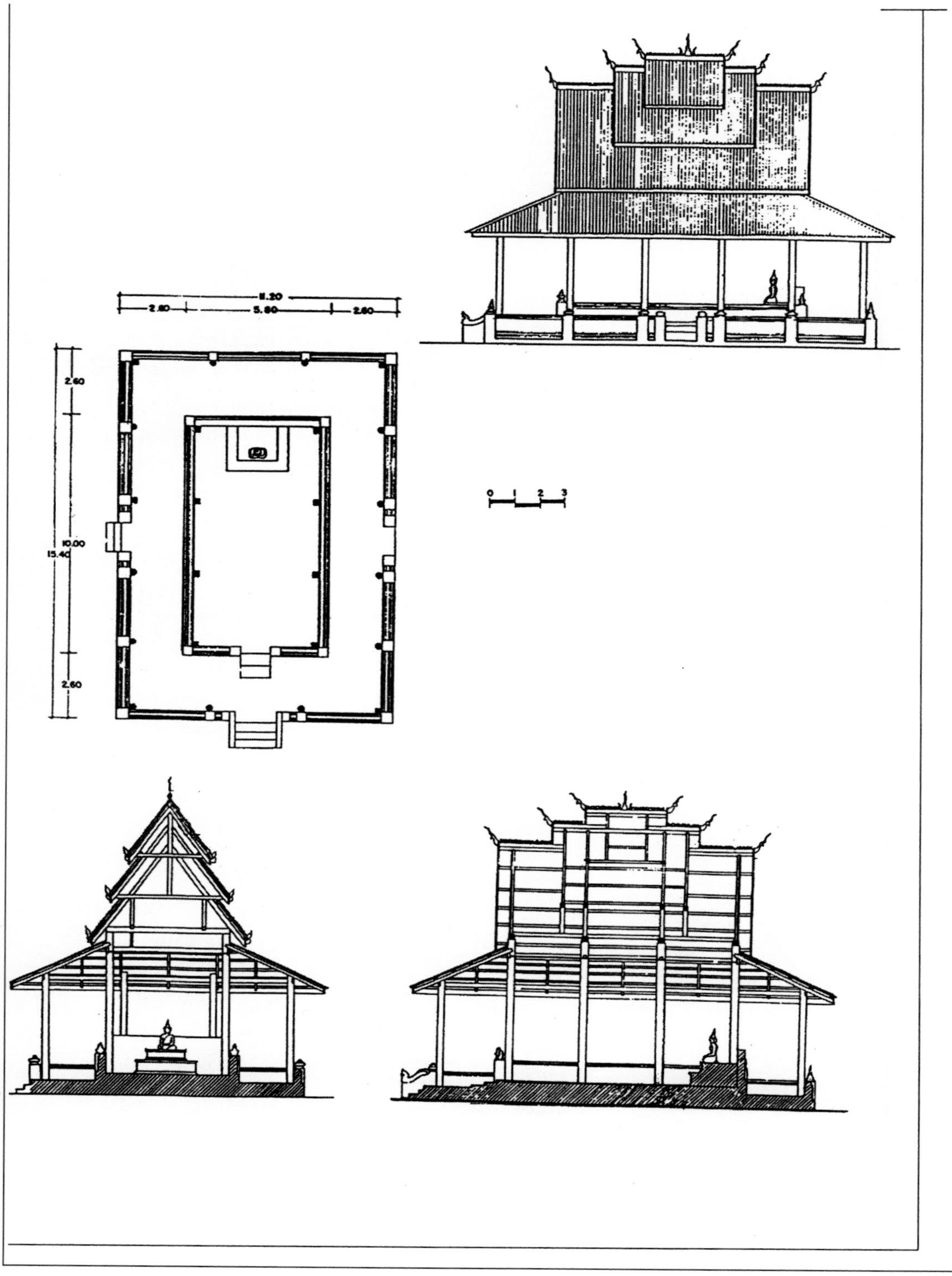

B – The closed *sim*

It is enclosed by four walls made either of wood or bricks. There is generally a single entrance door at the front. The building plan is rectangular and 2 or 4 bay long. The single- or three-tiered gable roof has a side lean-to. Shingles were commonly used. There are more roof decorations than on open *sims*. Additional decorations are *hung pung* (woodcarving pieces under the gable ends) and *khan tuey* (carved wood brackets). Building bases are moulded with a locally made lime plaster called *cha caye*. *figure 6 below*

6 – *Architectural components of the closed* sim

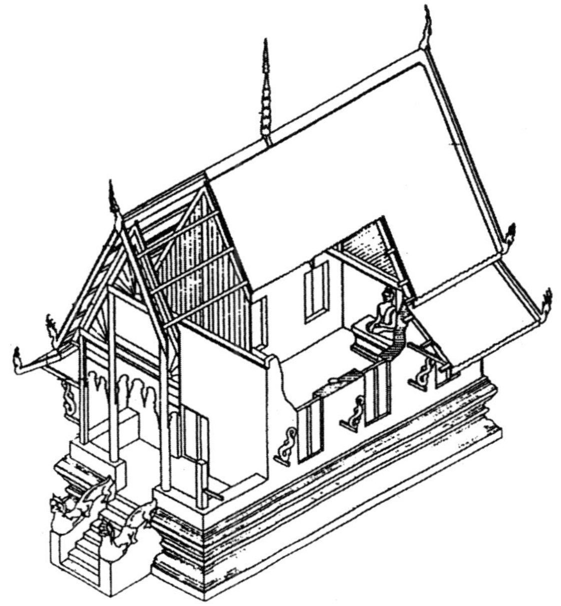

The typology is as follows:

B 1: Pure local style, of two types:

B 1.1: made of wood. Examples are:

- Wat Dan Muang Kam, Ban Dan Muang Kam, Khok Si Suphan district, Sakon Nakhon province. *figure 7 p. 138*
- Wat Pratum Thamachat, Ban Kae Yai, Muang district, Surin province. *figure 8 p. 139*

B 1.2: made of brick, with two sub-styles:

B 1.2.1: without gallery and projecting front. Examples are:

- Wat Sitan, Ban Nad, Thawatchaburi district, Roi Et province. *figure 9 p. 140*
- Wat Nong Nangtum, Ban Nong Etum, Muang district, Yasothon province. *figure 1 p. 141*

B 1.2.2: with gallery and without projecting front. Examples are:

- Wat Chakrawan Phumpinit, Ban Nong Muantan, At Samat district, Roi-ed province.
- Wat Chaeng, Muang district, Ubon Ratchathani province. *figure 1 p. 142*

B 1.2.3: with gallery, as:

- Wat Siphochai, Ban Saengpa, Na Haeo district, Loei province. *figure 1 p. 143*

7 – Wat Dan Muang Kam, Ban Dan Muang Kam, Khok Si Suphan district, Sakon Nakhon province

B 1.1

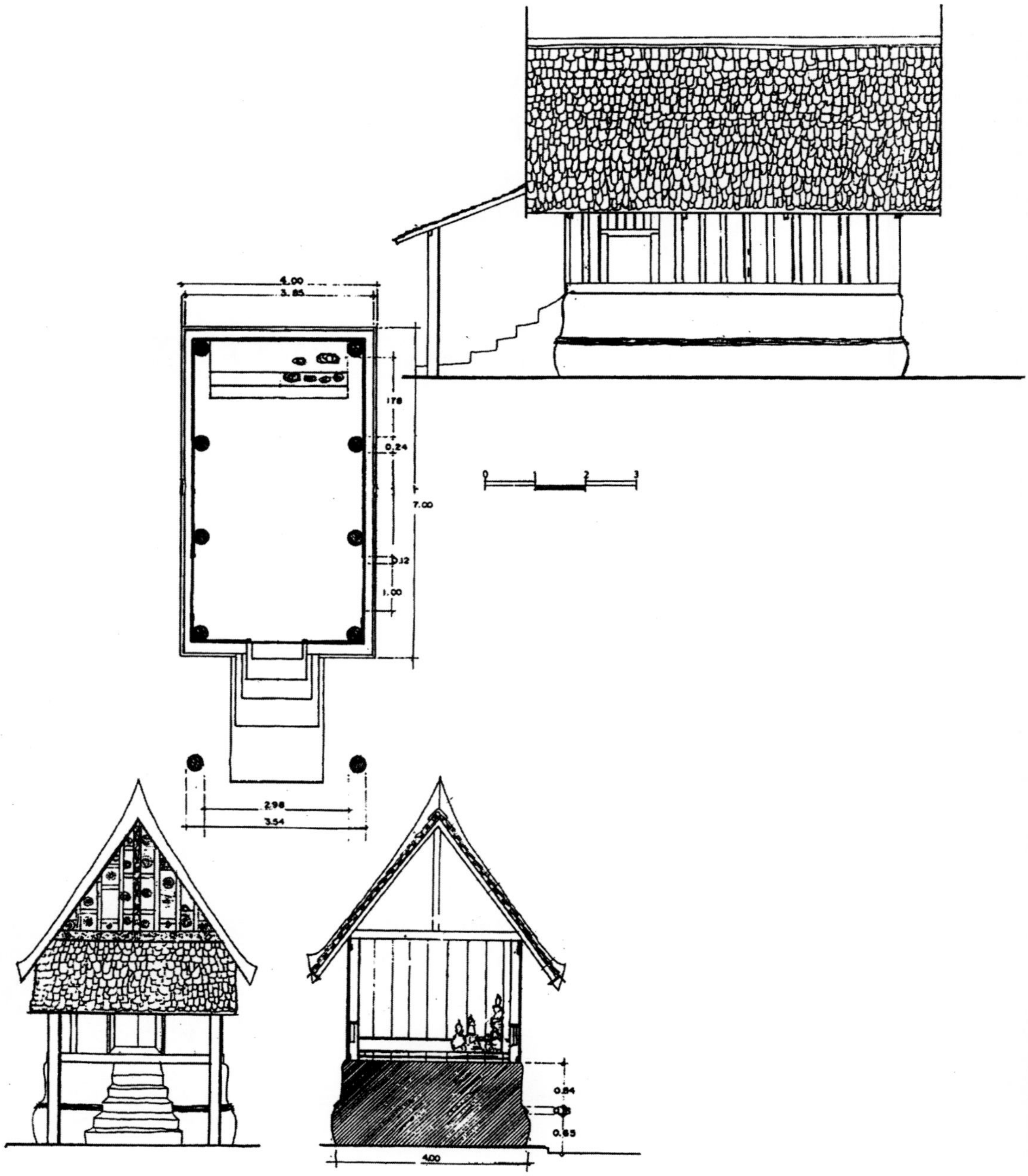

8 – *Wat Pratum Thamachat, Ban Kae Yai,*
Muang district, Surin province

B 1.1

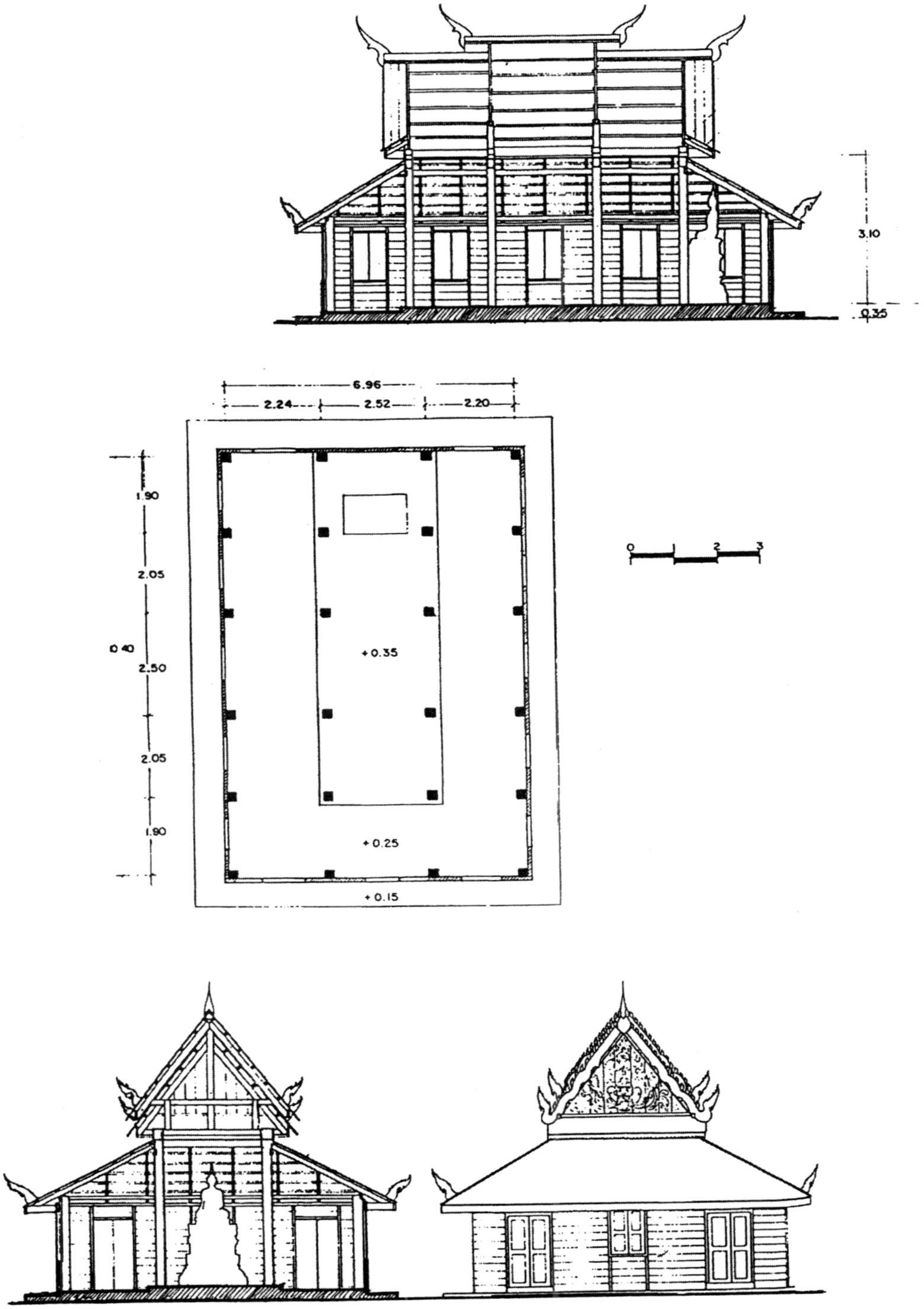

9 – *Wat Sitan, Ban Nad,*
Thawatchaburi district, Roi Et province

B 1.2.1

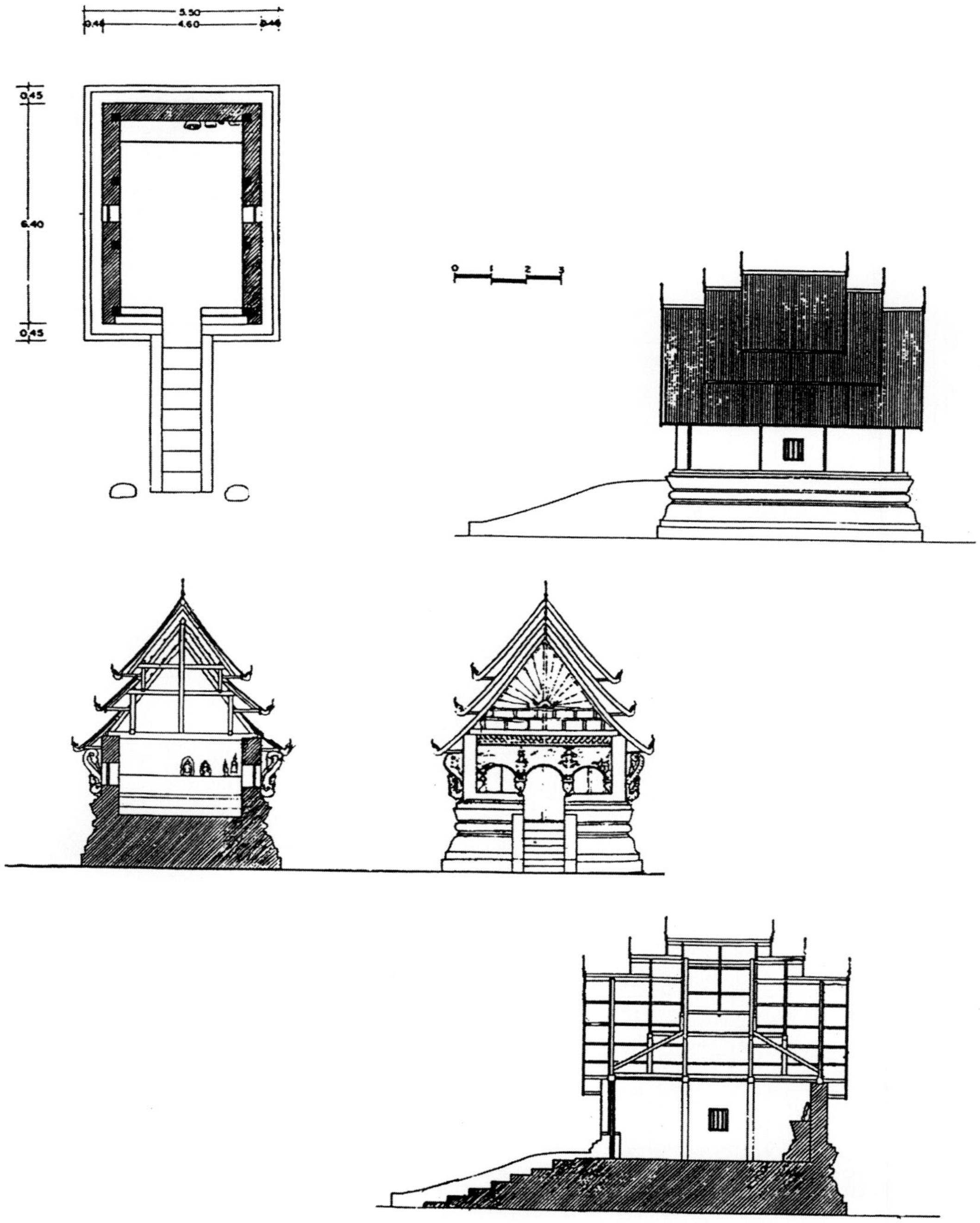

10 – *Wat Nong Nangtum, Ban Nong Etum, Muang district, Yasothon province*

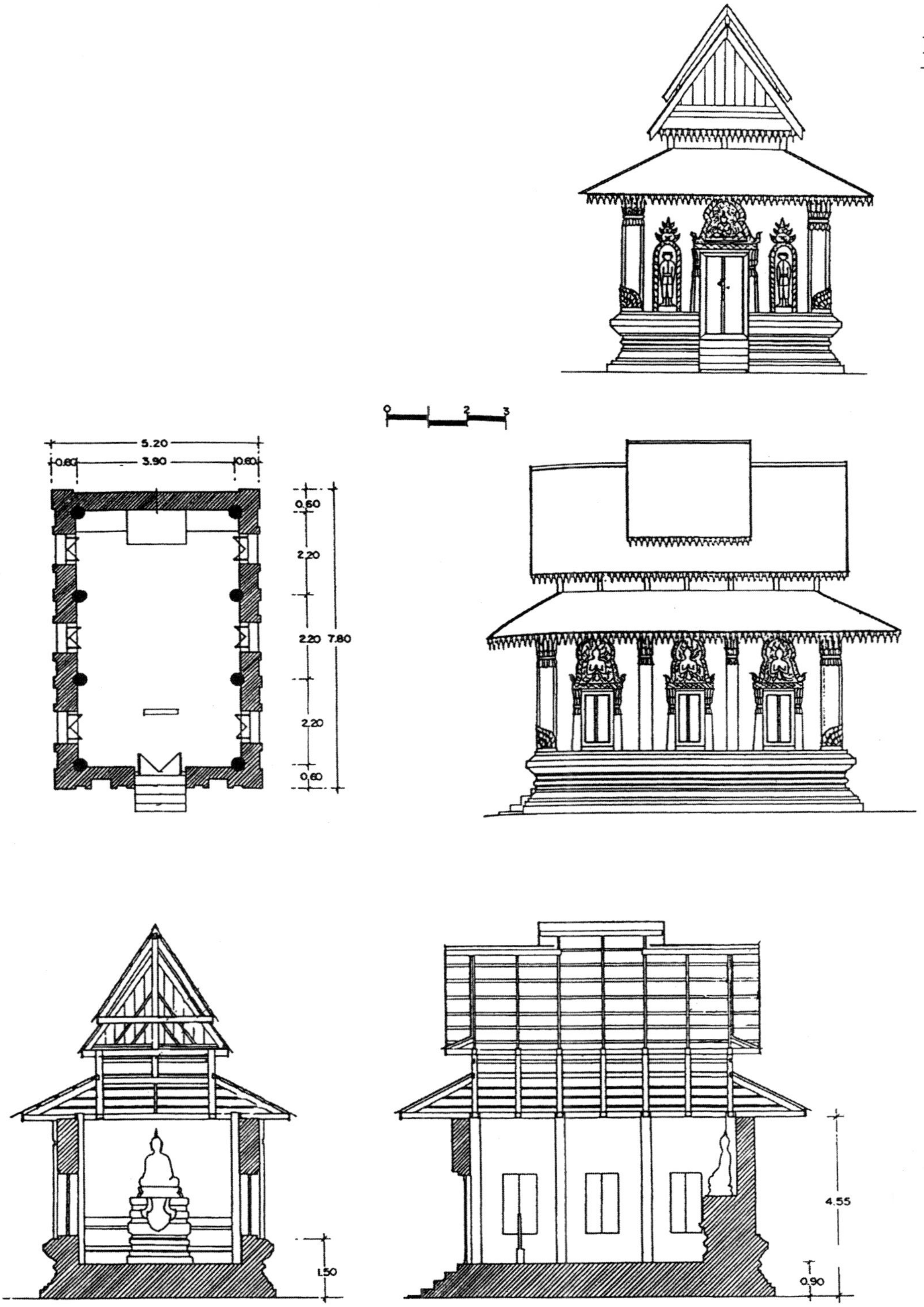

11 – *Wat Chaeng, Muang district,*
Ubon Ratchathani province

B 1.2.2

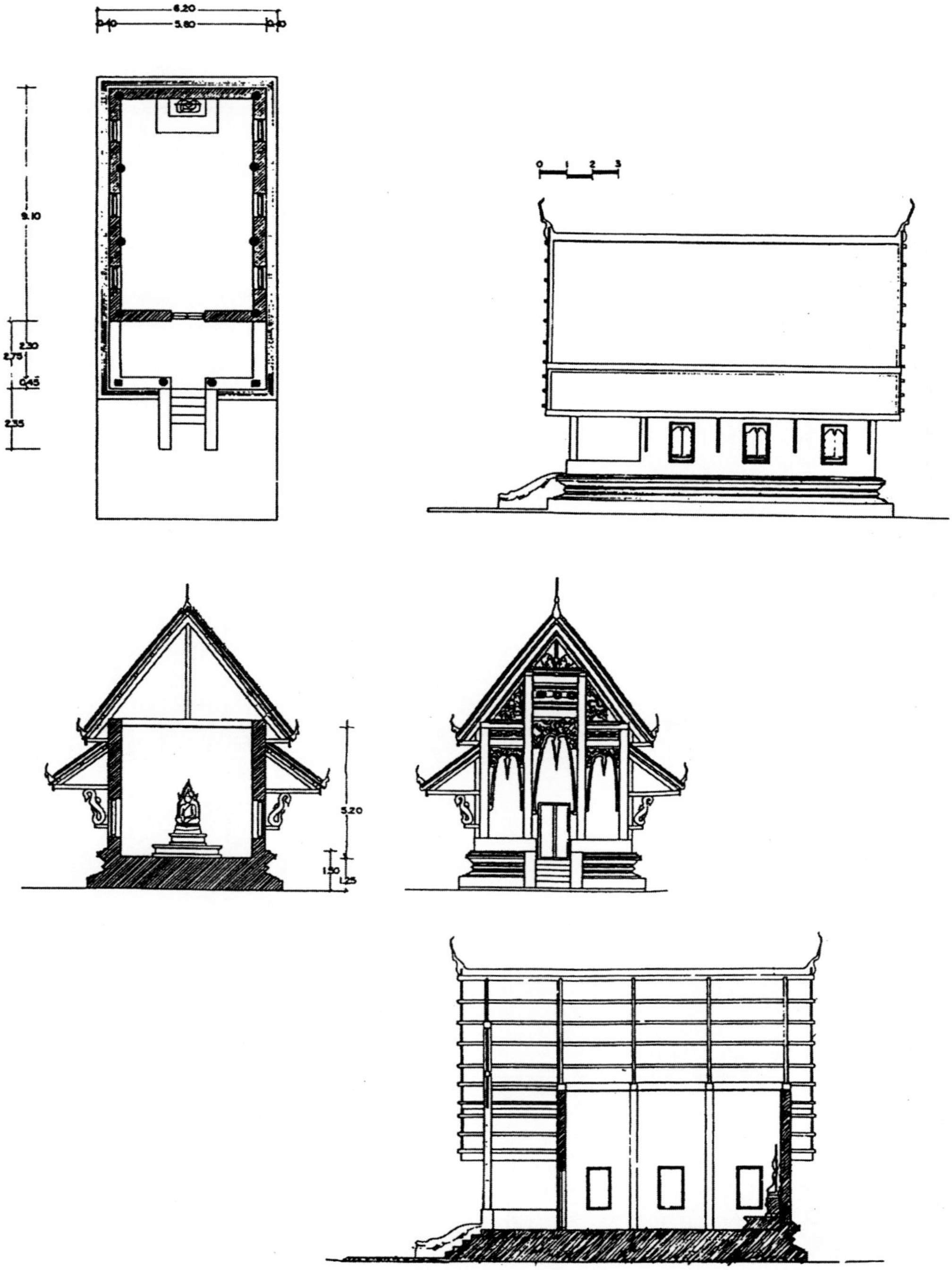

12 – *Wat Siphochai, Ban Saengpa,*
Na Haeo district, Loei province

B 1.2.3

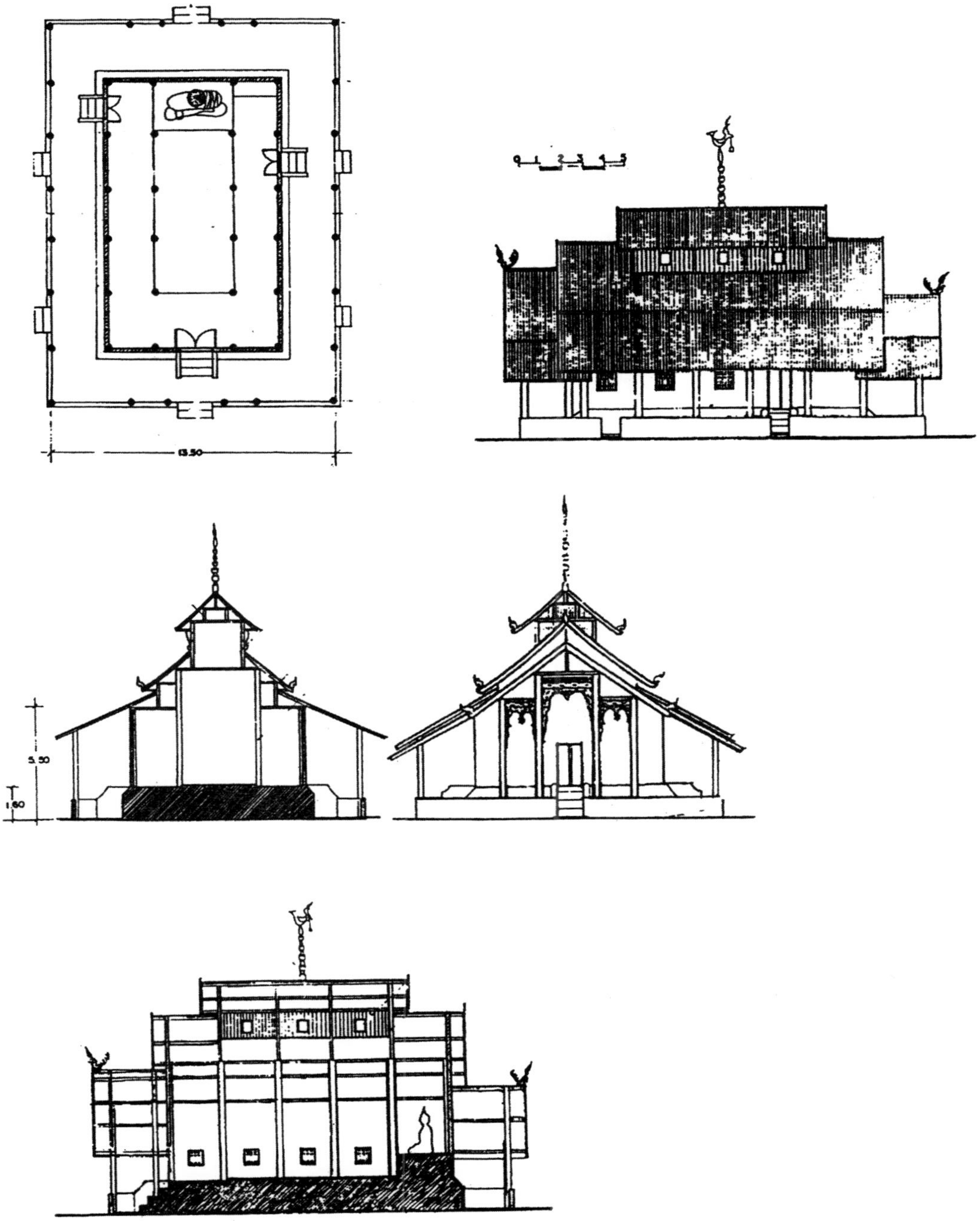

B 2: Imported style modified by local people (in later periods)

B 2.1: built by Thai-Isan craftsmen. Example:

- Wat Ban Na Kwai, Muang district, Ubon Ratchathani province.

B 2.2: built by Vietnamese craftsmen or under their influence.
This type has four sub-styles:

B 2.2.1: without projecting front. An example is:

fig. 13 below
- Wat Phra That Chengchum, Muang district, Sakon Nakhon province.

B 2.2.2: with projecting front. Examples are:

fig. 14 opposite
- Wat Klang, Tha Uthen district, Nakhon Phanom province.

fig. 15 p. 146
- Wat Phra That Simongkon, Ban That, Warichaphum district, Sakon Nakhon province.

B 2.2.3: with projections on front and back. An example is:

- Wat Ketsamakom, Kamalasai district, Kalasin province (*demolished in 1998*).

B 2.2.4: with a surrounding gallery, as:

fig. 16 p. 147
- Wat Machimavat (Wat Klang), Don Tan district, Mukdahan province.

13 – *Wat Phra That Chengchum,*
Muang district, Sakon Nakhon province

B 2.2.1

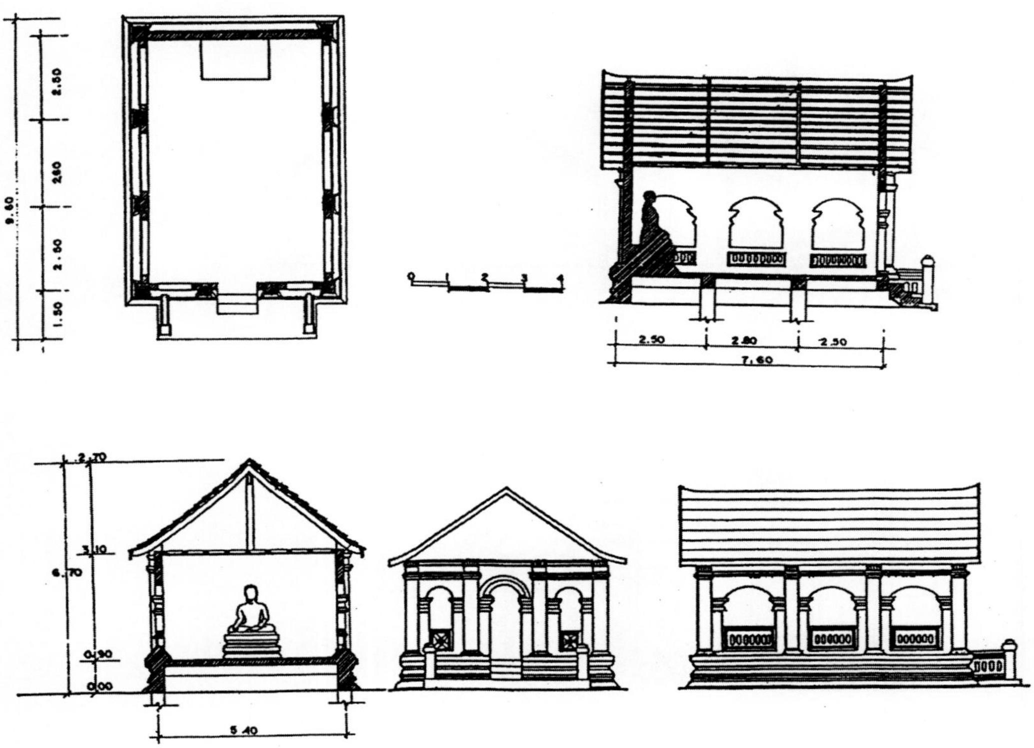

Isan Sims*: Ordination Halls in Northeastern Thailand*

14 – *Wat Klang, Tha Uthen district,*
Nakhon Phanom province

B 2.2.2

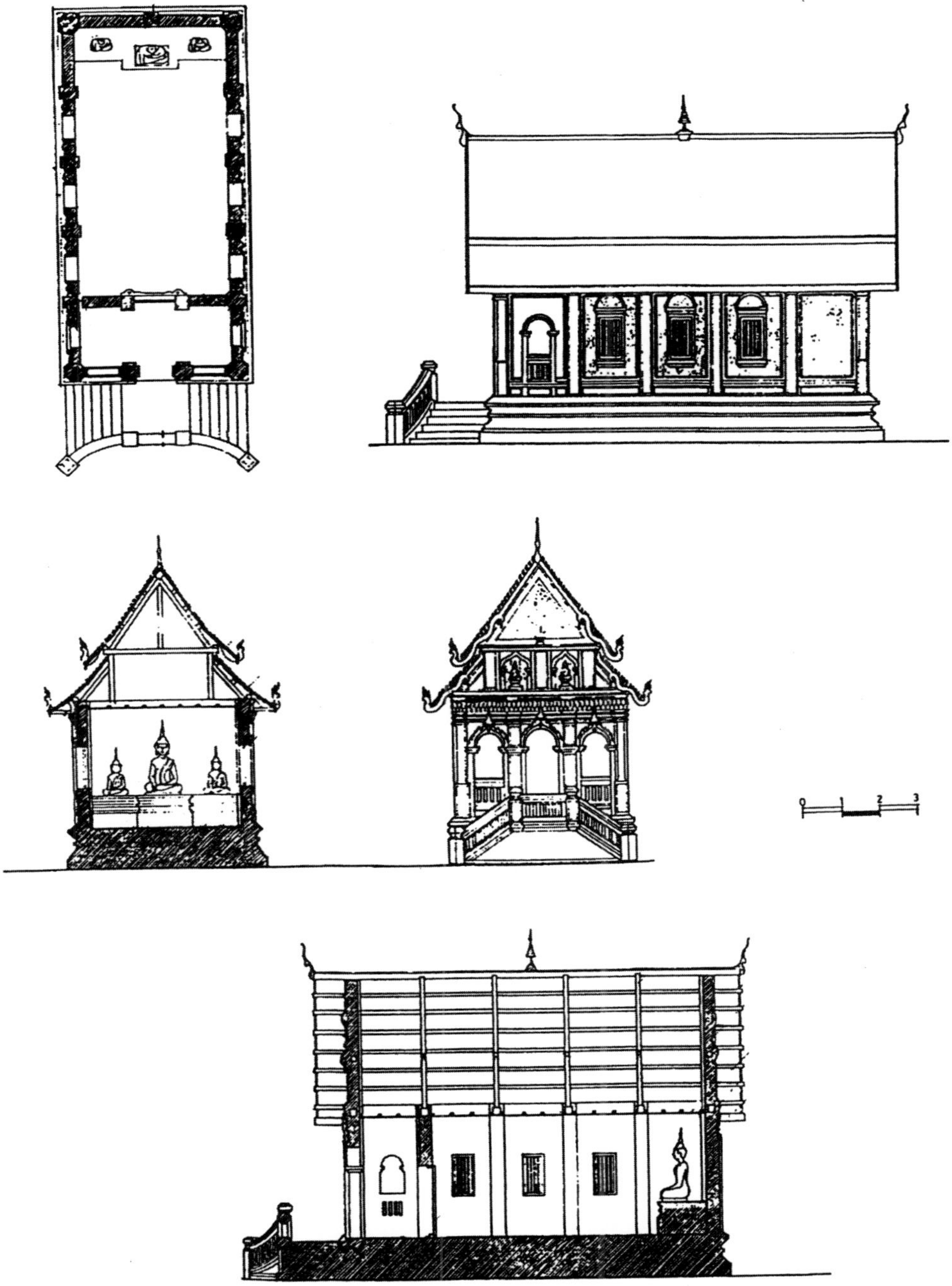

15 – *Wat Phra That Simongkon, Ban That, Warichaphum district, Sakon Nakhon province*

B 2.2.2

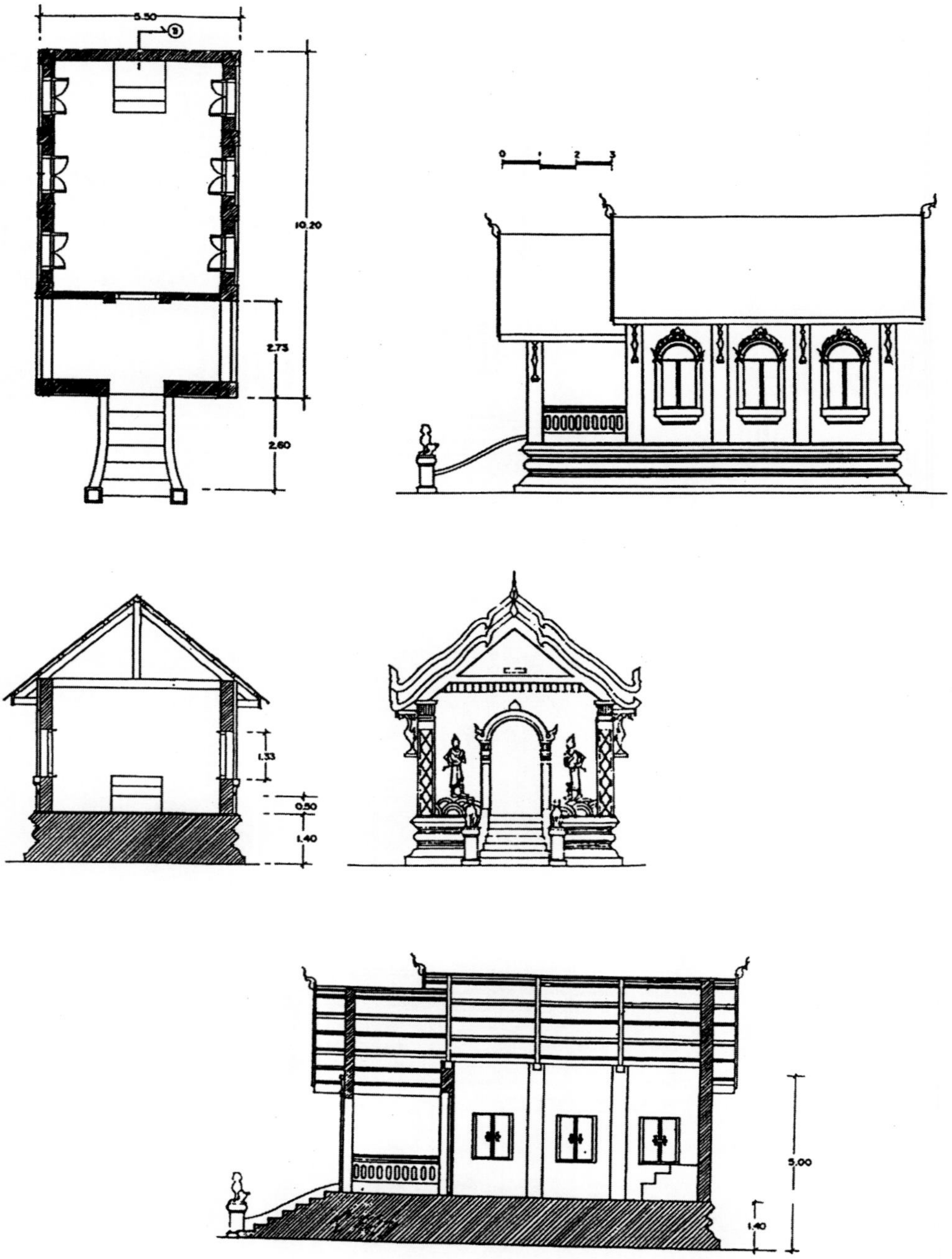

16 – *Wat Machimavat (Wat Klang),*
Don Tan district, Mukdahan province

B 2.2.4

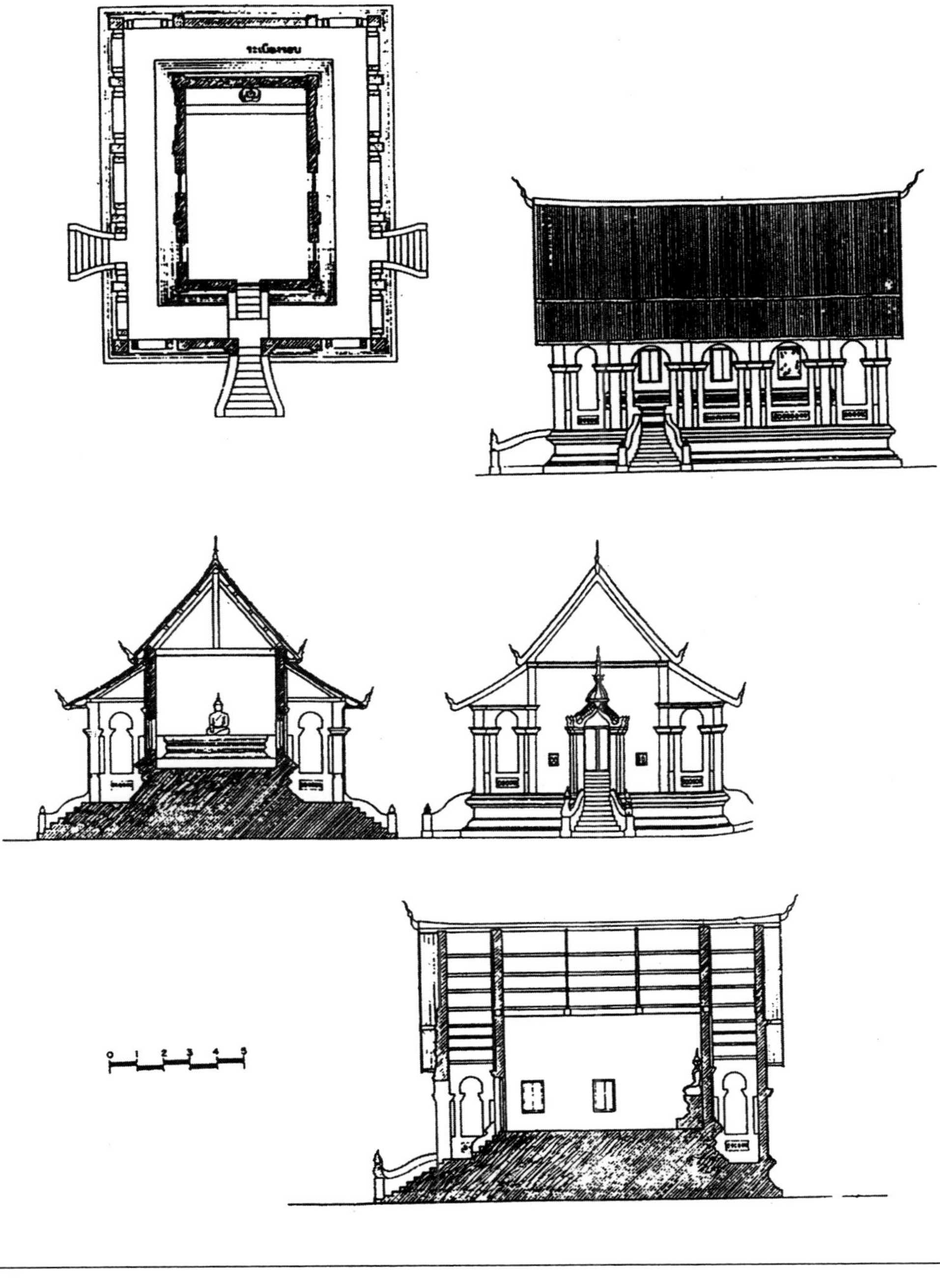

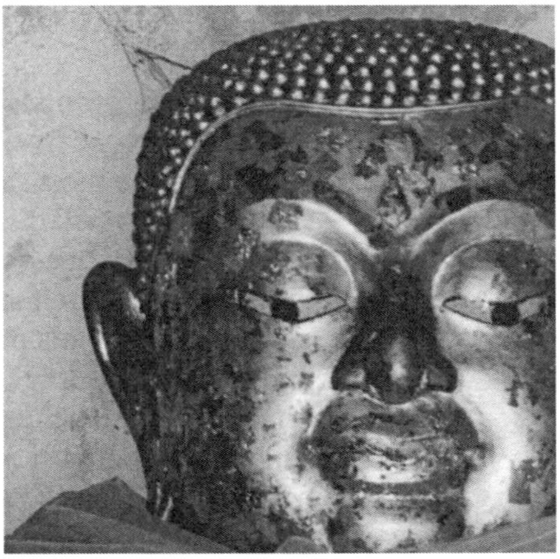

DEVOTIONAL DIVERSIFICATION IN THAI MONASTERIES

THE WORSHIP OF THE FAT MONK

François Lagirarde

Worship within the Thai monastery means essentially devotion to Buddha images and above all to the historical Buddha, Gotama. The true nature of this devotion – shared by monks and laymen – is variable and worshippers remain free to feel more than the minimal respect and calmness expected when meeting with such an object of recollection. Besides, all statues are not considered equal: the most venerated bears the equivalent of a personal name and are regarded as possessing qualities or powers of their own (*saksit*, *śăktisiddhi*) especially if they contain inside their body a holy relic of the Buddha or a revered saint (*arahant*). For the devotees this relic is considered "active" enough to challenge the idea of a total extinction. But, beside this formal, essential, and eventually supernatural presence of the Buddha in any monastery, it is impossible not to notice that a significant part of the veneration also goes to non-Buddha images. Often closely associated to the Buddha, his teachings or his hagiography, they are sometimes unknown to mainstream Buddhism. They may appear quite heterogeneous and even divergent from a standard understanding when our perception of Buddhism is limited to a theoretical frame frequently considered as the heritage of Theravāda and the dominant tradition represented by the Mahāvihāra from Sri Lanka. Most monasteries in Thailand shelter numerous images of historical or legendary figures such as previous kings, nobility or famous warriors, local *arahants* (former revered monks), hermits, saints and disciples or "Great Hearers" of the Buddha (*Mahāsāvaka*).

The later group is the most visible. The disciples are generally represented by subgroups of two, of five, of eight, or of eighty and every disciple in a group is sculpturally identical. The most striking example can be seen in the ordination hall of Wat Suthat in Bangkok where 80 disciples' images of human size are displayed around an image of the Buddha[1]. Only one disciple, considered as a direct disciple of the Buddha, is regularly displayed by himself and is highly individualized. This is a very fat *bhikkhu* immediately recognizable by his protuberant belly and his rather unsightly facial traits. This monk has been called Sangkachai (Săṅkăccāyana) since the beginning of the Ratanakosin era (end of the 18th century) from the name of a peculiar image of Kaccāyana found in the ruins of a Thonburi monastery (Fine Arts Department, 2510). This name became so popular that many images of a Fat Monk have been named after it since this discovery. The Fat Monk's cult – using then this partly new identity of Sangkachai – has continually gained in prestige and images of small size (including amulets) have been reproduced by the thousands. In the monasteries one will notice a clear tendency to position the images above the other "regular" disciples.

ph. 1 opposite page

ph. 2 opposite page

Medium-sized statues of the Fat Monk are to be found especially in the monasteries of Thailand, but they are also found in the Shan States of Burma, in Laos and Cambodia. This article will show that they can be installed virtually anywhere in the monastic compound, but most remarkably in special *vihāras* dedicated specifically to his honor. Such places of worship – giving to the Fat Monk a superior status – should be considered as one important feature of the Thai monastery[2].

The "Fat Monk", Gavampati, Kaccāyana and Sangkachai

The first collection of images of a fat *bhikkhu* in a meditative posture has been examined by Gordon Luce, after field discoveries partly made by Charles Duroiselle. This collection comes from Burma where the images have been found in different Mon and Burmese archaeological sites. Professor Luce actually coined this appellation ("Fat Monk") but came to the conclusion that he was an image of Gavampati (considered as "the patron saint of the Mons") whose cult had been flourishing up to the Pagan period (Luce 1969, I. 208).

Luce proposes to date the oldest image of the Fat Monk to the 7th century AD. It was discovered in a relic chamber, probably in a Mon site called Dé-ap (Bo-ta-htaung), near the riverbank in East Rangoon (Luce 1970, II.75). It is very interesting to note (since we are in a way trying to give a status to this image) that the Monk was found with a gold image of the Buddha "within a miniature stone stūpa." This association with the highest religious symbols is revealing of the eminent position given to the Monk. Other images were found in a rather abundant quantity in and around Pagan. They are now kept in the Pagan Museum but little information is provided concerning their origin and possible dating.

1. In fact, if the artists could easily cast eighty painted images (some having for an unknown reason a darker complexion) there was some problem giving them names: the brief inscriptions at their back cannot provide a total of 80 different names; many are given twice, like Gavampati, Asita, Assaji, etc.

2. This article is mainly based on one chapter of my doctoral dissertation entitled "La place du Moine Ventripotent (braḥ Săṅkăccāy) dans les monastères du pays thaï" (Lagirarde 2001, 207-245).

1 – *Some of the 80 disciples or "Hearers of the Buddha" shown in the ordination hall (*uposatha*) of Wat Suthat in Bangkok* (photo F. Lagirarde, 1998)

2 – *The Fat Monk (Sangkachai) installed above other monks or disciples in a veneration posture Inner gallery of Wat Khanikaphon, Bangkok* (photo F. Lagirarde, 1999)

According to inscriptions, images of Gavampati were installed in Pagan monasteries and even one of them was bearing his name (Shorto 1970, 22). After 1239 AD no more inscriptions mentioning this saint can be found. It seems then that the official cult of Gavampati disappeared from Burma, probably because it was seen unorthodox from the point of view of the dominant congregation of monks ordained in the tradition of the Mahāvihāra from Sri Lanka. Today no historical or official name has been preserved for the image of the Fat Monk. So far no textual tradition has been found giving a connection between the Fat Monk, Gavampati and Kaccāyana. Professor Shorto remained reluctant to associate Gavampati, who received a state cult in Pagan, with the images of the Fat Monk and other amulets called Gawam still used in what he called black magic.

In sharp contrast, the Thai tradition is still very alive, even if we may think that some control on the development of the Fat Monk cult has been exercised. Statues of the Fat Monk are easily visible in Thai monasteries, including those belonging to the reformed congregation (Dhammayutikanikāya) supposed to be stricter in terms of iconolatry. Far from having no name for the Monk, the Thais give him different names for different attitudes, a custom that is still echoed by texts in Pāli, Siamese and Lao connecting, if not explaining, the themes (monkhood, arahantship, obesity or deformity, *parinibbāna*) associated with his personality.[3] These texts – *Gavampati Sutta*, *Gavampati nibbāna* or *Kaccāyana nibbāna* – belong to a collection known as *Sāvakanibbāna*. They do not, however, totally explain the "conflation of Kaccāyana, Kaccāna, Mahākaccāyana and Gavampati".[4] Outside the monasteries, the lay cult of the Fat Monk is represented by small statues placed on private altars and in amulets collected to be worn on the body. Like in Burma, amulets of a fat monk covering at least his eyes (then every "door" [p. *dvāra*, th. *thavār*] of the body) are easy to find. This monk is called Phra Pit Ta ("the monk closing his eyes") but he is also known as Phra Khawam (Gavam[pati]). His images have been and continue to be cast or molded by the thousands by revered living monks. Big size images of Phra Khawam are exceptional and seem to be quite recent. A monumental one can be seen in the Wat Nerancharарама on the coastal city of Cha-am.

ph. 3 opposite page

The conflation between these different personages is even more confusing since images of the Chinese laughing monk Qici (or Budai considered as Maitreya) have been installed in Theravādin monasteries under the Thai name of Sangkachai. In return, the Chinese in Thailand sometimes use this Thai name for their own images of Budai, as if "Sangkachai" was a mere translation, as for instance in the Taoist temple of an Hakka foundation dedicated to Ludongbin in Bangkok's Chinatown. This association is a modern tendency even observable in the biggest monastery of Thailand, Wat Pho (or Wat Jethuphon) in Bangkok, where the pavilions sheltering Sangkachai and Budai are facing each other. But if we admit that pre-Pagan Mon Buddhism invented the Fat Monk the possible influence of this representation of Maitreya on the local Fat Monk should be ruled out. Besides, since the Sukhothai period the typical representation of the laughing Budai was well known by local artists and clearly differentiated from our Monk.

Art historians define the image of the Southeast Asian – or "Theravādin" – Fat Monk by one obvious feature, the unusual size of his stomach. The Monk is seen variously as pot-bellied or totally obese. Most of these historians have noticed the curious and rather ugly shape of the head, enormous and flat with the long ears as a sign of eminence. He is

3. On the textual tradition see my article (Lagirarde 2000, 57-78).

4. This expression has been proposed by Peter Skilling in an article ("Sāvakanibbāna") to be published in *Fragile Palm Leaves Newsletter* n°7.

3 – *This six-metre statue of Phra Khawam (braḥ Gavam[pati]) or Phra Pit Thawan welcomes the visitor at the entrance of Wat Nerancharama in Cha-am*

Three pairs of arms allow him to close the nine orifices of his fat body.

(photo F. Lagirarde, 2002)

4, 5 – *Kaccāyana or Sangkachai, wooden statue kept in the Phimai Museum (h. 63 cm) dated from the late 18th century by Piriya Krairiksh*

The precise origin of this remarkable piece is unknown. Viewed from the side the deformity of the Monk is even more obvious.

(photos P. Pichard, 2001)

mostly found sitting in *vīrāsana* or *vajrāsana,* the hands together in *samādhi* (only when it is possible since the size of the belly will often prevent him from achieving this position). Very rarely is he seen in another posture, but the National Museum in Bangkok has on display one Fat Monk – here called Subhūti – with his hand raised in an attitude presented as "calling the rain." Since most images of the Fat Monk have been cast independently from any other pictorial context, it is difficult to have a clear idea of his physical proportions. However a few images (for instance when represented in a group of five disciples) show clearly that the Fat Monk is not only an obese person, but also a dwarf and a hunchback. This vision is consistent with the descriptions made in the Thai manuscripts that depict him as a deformed person: a self-made freak.

ph. 4 and 5 above

The history of the development of the Fat Monk image has not yet been written[5] and the subject awaits further investigation. So far we can generally stress that between the Mon and Burmese images and the numerous Thai images belonging the Ayutthaya period appears a considerable gap. On the one hand, if we can imagine how the transmission from the Mons to the Burmese in Pagan happened, on the other, we do not know how the Thais received this image. If useful information has been presented by collectors in local publications, unfortunately the images offered to public appreciation are mostly considered out of any context and their claims for authenticity or age cannot be verified anymore. For instance, collectors assert the existence of images of the Fat Monk dating from the Khmer Bayon period and from the Sukhothai period. Moreover, even when found in context, small images may be or may not be contemporary with the monument that has kept them, a fact Dupont suggested about one image of Sangkachai found when excavating the Dvaravati site of Chula Pathon Chedi in Nakhon Pathom (Dupont, 1954, 87).

Places of worship in the Thai monasteries

a – In the vihāra *(th.:* wihan*)*

As the main and often the only open building in a Thai monastery, the *vihāra* is a dedicated place of worship. Images of the Fat Monk are sometimes installed on the main altar in a frontal position (facing west in theory) or even on a row of images before the main altar. In this situation they share the general devotion granted to the Buddha images since like them they face any individual or congregation inside the *vihāra.*

ph. 6 opposite page

The best example of this arrangement can be observed in the northwest *vihāra* of the Wat Sangkrachai in Thonburi. At the feet of the main Buddhas and on the same axis is seated the Fat Monk, a medium size bronze with a massive square body, wider than taller, with a very flat upper head and almost no forehead and no neck. The Monk looks hunchbacked. He is obviously here the focal point of interest and receives more offerings, mainly gold leaves, than any other image.

This peculiar statue was unearthed when it was decided, during the reign of Rama the First, to construct a new monastery on the site of a previous one dating from the time of the Ayutthaya kingdom. The image was found with a conch (th. *saṅ*, p. *saṅkha*) which seems to explain the name of the Monk (Sang + Kachai). But another story tells us that "Sang" was a layman who helped in the reconstruction of the monastery and whose name was added to the extraordinary discovery they made (Sangkachai would then mean the Kachai of Mr Sang). Both stories are interesting since they confirm that the image of the Fat Monk was buried in the time of Ayutthaya (before 1767) and unearthed in the first reign, that is to say between 1782 and 1809. The previous name of the Monk was then simply Kaccāy, a fact that is confirmed in the Thai literature.[6]

ph. 7 opposite page

A similar Fat Monk, in front of a Buddha, well centered, can also be seen in Wat Phlaphlachai (Bangkok) in a room next to the ordination hall (*uposatha*) where are kept ashes of lay people. However, this spectacular disposition of the Fat Monk is not so common in the main *vihāras* of the Thai monasteries. It may suggest a hierarchy unknown in mainstream Buddhism where the top disciples are certainly not *bhikkhus*

---

5. We feel that the Monk has suffered a great deal of disdain from the academic circles.

6. The Kaccāy of Lamphun is mentioned in the *Khlong Nirat Hariphunchai*, a Northern Thai poem rewritten in Ayutthaya in the 17th century. This poem relates a pilgrimage that possibly took place from Chiang Mai to Lamphun in 1517.

7. But it may suggest, as developed in our previous article (Lagirarde, 2000), that the Fat Monk is represented as one of the first five *arahants* coming from a pure lay background. In this case the monk is Gavampati.

called Kaccāyana or Gavampati[7]. Besides, such an installation should have received the agreement of the Lord Abbot and be justified by the importance locally given to the image. In contrast, in the special *vihāras* exclusively dedicated to the Fat Monk, images of the Buddha are even sometimes disposed at his feet in a dramatic inversion of rank. Often it will be small images placed on front altars like in Lamphun (Sangkachai's *vihāra* in Wat Hariphunchai). But we can find sometimes a more radical reversal when big images of the Buddha appear at the feet of a Fat Monk deliberately installed in a higher position. A good example can be seen in Wat Saen Muang Ma in Chiang Kham. *ph. 8 below*

7 – *Sangkachai at the feet of a Buddha image in a special room next to the ordination hall of Wat Phlaphlachai in Bangkok*
(photo F. Lagirarde, 1999)

6 – *The first image of the Fat Monk known as Sangkachai, installed in the northwest* vihāra *of Wat Sangkrachai in Thonburi*
(photo P. Pichard, 1999)

8 – *A Buddha image installed below Sangkachai in a special* vihāra *for the Monk in Wat Saen Muang Ma, Chiang Kham*
(photo F. Lagirarde, 2001)

When on the altar of a main *vihāra*, the Monk is usually placed to the side of the main Buddha image in the sometimes large grouping of other smaller images of Gotama, possibly joined by images of Metteya or even a local master considered as an *arahant*. This situation is very common in Thai monasteries, including Lanna, and also in Chiang Tung (Keng Tung) in the Shan Sates of Burma.

Sometimes another non-permanent altar is installed in front of the main altar of the *vihāra*. It is made of a set of different little tables (*tŏḥ pūjaḥ* [*to pucha*]) standing in the vacant space where worshippers are free to come and go. This installation makes more obvious the destination of the offerings. This is the case at Wat Mahanoparam in Bangkok were the Monk can easily receive offerings. Sometimes statues are installed for a limited period, then "rented" to lay people or moved to a monk's residence.[8] We witnessed this fact when three statues of the Fat Monk were removed in 1999 from the *vihāra* of Wat Chiang Man in Chiang Mai where they had been previously exposed. According to the monks interviewed, they were rented to a generous donor who would benefit from the power accumulated to these images after months of public veneration.[9]

Sometimes, when the altar around the main Buddha image allows circumambulation, images of the Monk can be disposed on the sides or even in the back facing west. There is a strange case visible in the hall of Wat Chayasongkhram in Bangkok. The Monk (a hybrid of the ordinary Sangkachai and Budai) is on the back of the monumental statue of the Buddha, stuck in its huge pedestal. He is facing the west wall in a narrow passage almost two metres above the ground.

But all these installations – even those challenging the status of the other disciples – do not show that the monk is an essential feature: place is rather taken for him rather than pre-arranged. Only in his special *vihāras* will the Monk obtain the predominance over any other image.

b – The special vihāra *(also called* sālā *or* sālā kuṭi*)*

In Thai monasteries, as already mentioned, the Fat Monk is sometimes residing in a special *vihāra* that is reserved to his exclusive worship. These *vihāras* vary in size: from basic open shelters (one to four square metres) to large pavilions (up to seventy square metres) where people can enter in groups and worship his image. One refers also to *sālā kuṭi* for the small sized pavilions (*sālā*) where the devotees have to pay homage outside (a *kuṭi* was originally a hut for the residence of one monk; it means nowadays a dwelling place normally limited in size).

See map p. 112 for sites mentioned in this article

In Thailand, three principal places of worship should draw our attention. They are located in Lamphun, Chiang Mai and Nakhon Sri Thammarat. But we will also mention some other ones, less famous, in the Central and Northern regions. These *vihāras* might represent a modern phenomena : the biggest one in Lamphun has been constructed in the second part of the 20th century over an existing statue.[10] But in other cases the building or part of it seems quite ancient.

8. In Thai a Buddhist image is never sold or given: one is expected to use the verb *chao* (to rent) in order to express any transaction.

9. It was a set of three almost entirely identical bronze images. But the first Monk had a short *saṅghāṭi*, the second one a medium size *saṅghāṭi* and the third one a *saṅghāṭi* reaching his hands.

10. For an old photograph of the Fat Monk of Wat Phra That Hariphunchai before the construction of the present *vihāra* see Lamoon (1989)

Lamphun

The most spectacular statue of the Fat Monk kept indoors can be found in a special *vihāra* in the northwest quarter of the *saṅghavāsa* (monks community area) of Wat Phra That Hariphunchai. Sitting in *vīrāsana,* the Monk welcomes the visitor from a low platform. His huge mass is made of bricks and his image sculpted in plaster or stucco. He was covered with red lacquer, then entirely gilded. The image is wider than higher and his enormous folded legs are four metres wide. From the feet to the top of the head the statue is three metres high. *ph. 9 and 10 below*

The Monk wears his robe with the right shoulder uncovered even when a real piece of cloth is offered by the devotees. The *saṅghāṭi* goes down between his joined fingers and his chest is crossed with a meditation belt neatly knotted. From the side and back – since the image can easily be circumambulated – it is obvious that his body is hunched. The Monk is extremely fat and his belly goes down on the block of the legs. The top of the head is rather flat and the round smiling face is very wide with painted eyes. The Monk looks clever. No wonder if he is known locally under the name of Phra Chao Pum Phanya (*braḥ* cau_2 pum_4 *phaḥñā*$_4$): the wise pot-bellied master.

9 – *The special* vihāra *of the Fat Monk in Wat Phra That Hariphunchai, Lamphun*
(photo F. Lagirarde, 2001)

10 – *The Fat Monk of Wat Phra That Hariphunchai inside his special* vihāra
(photo L. Gabaude, 2001)

The Wat Phra That Hariphunchai was built around a famous stūpa (*haripuñjaya mahādhātu cetiya*) that was designed to receive a Buddha relic found by a certain king Ādicca, who reigned between the 11th and the 12th century. This stūpa has certainly been a religious centre in Hariphunchai since this period, which means before the arrival of the Thais and the beginning of the Lanna period. Buddhism in Lanna would eventually develop with its roots deeply grounded in local Môn Buddhism at the end of the 13th century. We know, according to the *Khlong Nirat Hariphunchai* that an image (this image?) of the Fat Monk (Kaccāy) was installed at the time of the pilgrimage described (between 1411 and 1517) on the perimeter of the stūpa. It seems that his cult was then a well-established custom. It is then possible to put forward the hypothesis that such a cult was transmitted by the Mons of Hariphunchai to the Thais, probably on the model of what had been common in Pagan and in the other Mon kingdoms. This site in Hariphunchai could represent one link between the Burmese-Mon cult of the Fat Monk and the others images found in Lanna for instance.

Today the Monk is sheltered by a new *vihāra* always open to visitors. He receives candles, flowers, incense, robes and money. In return one can get a prediction about the future by throwing sticks on the floor (this is called *siem si*). Every stick bears a number that will correspond to a leaflet kept in an adjacent cabinet. Every leaflet contains a kind of riddle supposed to deliver a horoscope (*duang chata*).

Chiang Mai

Wat Chedi Luang, located within the old walls of the city of Chiang Mai, keeps an extraordinary statue of the Monk inside a *vihāra* next to the famous stūpa whose construction started in 1391. The *vihāra* is a new building (10 x 3 m) open upon request. *ph. 11 opposite page* The statue inside, made of bricks, is 3.70 m high and 3.28 m wide. The original stucco has been apparently restored with concrete and covered with a golden paint. The Monk is sitting in the same position as the one in Lamphun but his proportions are different. Here his head is more detached from the torso and he looks less deformed. He is also sitting on the ground without a pedestal, on a low platform.

The Monk receives the same kind of worship mentioned above, but one will notice that no small Buddha images can be seen at his feet (a restriction that may be explained by the fact that Wat Chedi Luang belongs to the Thammayut congregation). A *gāthā* in mixed Pāli often found in the Monk *vihāras* is leaning at the base. The text is difficult to read but it can be understood that the worshipper is taking refuge in the Community of the Hearers, in the Older Kaccāyana who has great power, and in the Buddha (or as a Buddha?) who brings wealth and possesses Perfection and supernatural power [as if] he were alive.[11]

A short history of the monastery has been written by a senior monk called Phra Dhammadilok (no date) where it is explained that the statue of the Monk is a very venerated image that is considered as old as the monastery itself. But so far no more precise data are known on the topic. Another more recent Fat Monk can be seen in the same monastery. The Monk in installed outside next to the *vihāra* of the so-called "sleeping Buddha".

11. The original says: *iminā săkkărenaḥ sāvaḥkaḥsăṅgho kăccāyanathero mahātejavănto buddha bhogāvaḥho pārimitāro iddhiṛddhi titaḥ maḥṇaḥ tăṅ saḥraṇăṅ găcchāmi*. The difficult reading of these verses was proposed by Peter Skilling.

11 – *The second largest historical Fat Monk of Lanna in his* vihāra *of Wat Chedi Luang, Chiang Mai* (photo L. Gabaude 2001)

If we consider the Lamphun's Fat Monk site as an older or original one, many questions thus remain. Is this type of installation in Wat Chedi Luang a replica? Was it adopted to express the continuity of a characteristic feature of Mon Buddhism?

Unfortunately no chronicle or inscription, so far, has been found mentioning one of the names of the Fat Monk in a ritualistic context. However, the Wat Pa Deng Chronicle from Chiang Tung (Mangrai, 1981, 135) tells us that an image of Phagawam (braḥ Gavam[pati]) was an object of dispute between different groups of bhikkhus. This image is said to have been in the possession of the monk Nyanakhamphira[12] (Ñāṇagambhīra) and can be related to events around the year 1430. Could we then draw a line between the 15th and the 16th century showing that the name Gawampati disappeared around this time to be replaced by Kaccāy, thus perpetuating a cult deeply rooted in ancient Mon Buddhism?

Nakhon Si Thammarat

In Wat Mahathat (Nakhon Si Thammarat, southern Thailand), a special *vihāra* shelters another statue of the Fat Monk who is locally known as Phra Aet (*braḥ èT*), *ph. 12 page 161* although he looks like the ordinary image of Sangkachai: same position, same attitude and same features, including obesity and deformity. Phra Aet is also a large image, albeit less imposing than the ones in Chiang Mai and Lamphun. Seated, it is 1.80 m tall, on a base of 1.95 m.

Wat Mahathat, just like the monasteries mentioned above, is one of the most ancient Buddhist sites of Thailand. Its foundation goes back to the 7th or 8th century and belongs to the culture of Srivijaya. But no image of the Fat Monk has ever been found in archaeological sites related to Srivijaya. Phra Aet resembles other images of the Ayutthaya period, but no information is known of the time of his installation. We know however that he has been moved within the monastery three times in one hundred years (Sathaban., 2529, 6, 2412-2415).

---

12. This monk – reordained in Sri Lanka in 1424 – was the leader of the Siṅhalapakkha, the Singhalese faction, established in Chiang Mai in 1430. He is also known as Dhammagambhīra.

Phra Aet inside his *vihāra* is protected by a window panel with a wooden structure that allows the devotees to deposit photographs at his feet level (their pictures or pictures of relatives). At the ground level a set of small tables supports images of the Buddha and other saints. A little bit lower on a ground-level platform one can find images of Nang Kwak (*nāṅ kvăk*), photographs again, vases and the usual offerings (incense, candles, flowers, etc.).

Phra Aet is obviously a very venerated personality and two reasons are given locally for his fame. He is firstly supposed to bring relief for people suffering from back pain and spinal problems, hence the pictures of people seeking relief or healing. Secondly he is supposed to be able to bring rain. The first gift is somehow consonant with the idea that the Fat Monk (according to the story told in the *Gavampati Sutta* or the *Kaccāyana Nibbāna* mentioned above) has been able to modify his body from beauty to abnormality and could provide help the other way. In any case, there might be some local explanation of this very precise power. The second gift is more problematic. It is true that Gavampati has always been associated with power connected with water,[13] but this is also the case of Subhūti, sometimes represented with a protuberant belly.[14]

The *Encyclopedia of Southern Thailand* mentions the fact that the Chinese community in Nakhon Si Thammarat was eager to obtain some modification of the Phra Aet. It was suggested that his eyes should be wider and that the whole image should look more rotund. Probably it was a way to transform him into Budai or Metteya. Changing the shape of this image would not have been a problem since it is also made of bricks and plaster. But was it ever really reshaped?

To top this list of enigmas we should first acknowledge that the name "Aet" is far from being clearly explained. According to the *Encyclopedia* it could come from the expression *năṅ₁ ete* that is used to describe a person sitting in samādhi who relaxes too much his back and will look stooped. Another interpretation argues that *èT* comes from the Sanskrit or Pāli root *edh* found in a Pāli verb like *edhati* (to gain or succeed). The first explanation relates back to the deformity of the Fat Monk, while the second one presents him as a bringer of prosperity, something closer to what is expected from Budai in Chinese popular cults. Phra Aet meaning "the hunchback" is certainly the most accurate name. It describes the Monk well, indicates a possible know-ledge of the textual tradition mentioned above, and fits in the historical context we have briefly presented.

Other sites

In the Northern province of Chiang Rai, two more remarkable special *vihāras* deserve to be mentioned. They are both located in the little town of Chiang Khong on the bank of the Mekong river.

The first one belongs to the Wat Luang. The *vihāra* is well above the ground and accessible through a little staircase. The building has been heavily restored with concrete but parts of it still show remnants of the ancient structure made of bricks and cob. The *vihāra*, on the flank of the main *vihāra* of the monastery and in the same East-West axis, is of a small size and allows only two or three visitors. The statue cannot be circumambulated. The image of the Monk looks rather awkward since the artist never tried to

ph. 13 opposite page

13. The power of Gavampati is suggested in the *Theragāthā* (Norman, 1997, 6) and explained in the commentary.

14. Small images of Subhūti as a Fat Monk can be seen in the National Museum in Bangkok in the Ayutthaya section.

12 – *Phra Aet*
inside his glass cabinet,
Wat Mahathat,
Nakhon Si Thammarat
(photo P. Pichard, 1999)

13 – *The Fat Monk,*
under restoration,
in his vihāra *of Wat Luang*
in Chiang Khong
(photo F. Lagirarde 2001)

be realistic, even considering the fact that the Monk should definitely look monstrous. Here his monstrosity is partially the result of clumsiness. He is made of bricks and stucco (his head underwent restoration in 2001) and was lacquered and gilded but time (and bad weather because the roof might have been leaking) has washed it out. Just as in many other statues of the Monk, he is wearing a meditation belt that, in this case, seems to separate the upper part of his body, which is normal, with the lower one, completely inflated.

The second *vihāra* of the Fat Monk in Chiang Khong is inside Wat Phra Keo. This bigger but open building is oriented north-south. The statue is about two meters high and has been totally restored recently and repainted (instead of gilded) with a rather brownish color. This Monk is very venerated. He receives the usual offerings together with discarded images of Buddha that shows his power against evil fate.[15] The same *gāthā* as the one found in Wat Chedi Luang has been placed at his feet for the devotees to read.

Many other "private" *vihāras* of the Fat Monk can be observed all over Thailand. For instance in Wat Phra Fang in Uttaradit, the Fat Monk stands in a monastic complex largely ruined and deserted, serving as an incentive to revive the monastery. But these recent avatars of the Fat Monk who benefits greatly from his adoption by the Sino-Thai community, should not mask the fact that his installation is ancient, especially inside prominant monasteries founded at the beginning of the first historical Thai period (14th-16th century). It is also clear that some ancient images of the Fat Monk were probably put aside or hidden during the 20th century, perhaps because of a conceivable rejection from influential members in the Community of monks. For example, in Wat Luang of Chiang Kham we found images looking very old in a brand new environment, as if the situation permitted a residence for an image possibly abandoned. Also, in Wat Phra That Chae Haeng in Nan, another odd image of the Fat Monk is sheltered in a brand new structure in the middle of the monastery surrounded by walls.

In Phitsanulok, the very famous Wat Phra Si Ratana Mahathat had originally one small *sālā kuṭi* sheltering an image of the Fat Monk. The Monk (about 1.5 m) was made of bricks and mortar and was another example of the ordinary images of the Ayutthaya period. But another image – this time of Metteyya as Budai – was installed (in the 20th century) just in front of him probably with the idea of reduplicating his image. This new situation lead to the construction of a bigger *sālā* above the primary structure.

There is no monumental historical image of the Fat Monk in Bangkok. Monasteries built in the early Ratanakosin period generally possess an image of medium size, still moveable, that is generally to be found near the main images of the Buddha next to an altar. For instance, in Wat Suthat a very fine bronze statue of the Monk is seated on the northern side of the main *vihāra* close to the well-known Dvāravatī bas-relief depicting two supernatural episodes of the life of the Buddha. One can also see an interesting image of the Fat Monk in Wat Nang Nong in Thonburi. The statue bears an inscription that gives the name of the donor (a *bhikkhu* called Nuy) and the date of 1913 AD. The Monk is seated in a *vihāra* of an unknown date of construction, possibly older than the statue. This *vihāra* is located in the very middle of the *Buddhavāsa* next to the stūpa and between the two main twin *vihāras* dating from the third reign of the Ratanakosin period (1824-1851), facing a canal. Since the Wat was customarily visited by boat, this special *vihāra* and the Fat Monk inside were the first religious items to be met by the devotees. This bronze image of the Fat Monk (two meters including the pedestal) represents high quality craftsmanship. The usual sketchy molding of the hands is here replaced by very precise and realistic work. On the forehead of his round chubby face the artist has drawn the *uṇṇā* (or *ūrṇā*), a tuft of curly hair that is supposed to be the mark of a great being like the Buddha. The length of his ears is also a mark of elevation.

ph. 14 and 15 opposite page

15. In Thailand a broken or damaged image of Buddha or any other saint or divinity will not be kept in its ordinary place (altars in a monastery or private altars). It will be considered as a bad omen. Since it cannot be simply thrown away it has to be kept near a refuge that is usually a Bodhi tree, a big image of the Buddha, a stūpa, etc.

14 – *The* vihāra *of the Fat Monk next to the stūpa of Wat Nang Nong in Thonburi*
Because of frequent flooding the ground has been elevated and the base of the building is partially buried.

15 – *The Monk inside the* vihāra, *Wat Nang Nong, Thonburi*
(photos F. Lagirarde, 2001)

c. The ordination hall (p. uposatha, *th.* ubosot*)*

In a Thai monastery the *uposatha* is the place where the official acts of the Community are carried out. These acts concern exclusively monks and novices and lay people can only witness them or be used possibly as auxiliaries.[16] An *uposatha* is not usually a place as open to the laity as a *vihāra*. It is often locked up awaiting a ceremony while the *vihāra* is generally open and freely accessible during the daytime. In Lanna (Northern Thailand) for instance, women are not permitted to enter the *uposatha,* a building generally smaller that the *vihāra*. Besides, some monasteries do not have an *uposatha*. In brief, this building is under a stricter control of the authority of the monastery with regional or local characteristics in its management. It is not perceived as a place where general devotion can be expressed. Often the *uposatha* is less decorated than the *vihāra* and the altar more tidy, although they are many exceptions.

For all these reasons this field study was not able to determine the status of the Fat Monk in this context. The problem was indeed to find out if the presence of the Monk was forbidden or avoided, one way or the other, in terms of modern monastic Theravāda Buddhism. So far this question – maybe not relevant – cannot be satisfactorily answered. If we did find some images of the Fat Monk in *uposathas*, they were mostly

16. Very often, former learned monks will help the candidate to monkhood during an ordination ceremony, especially assisting in the recitation of the Pali formulas.

there by accident. For instance, the image mentioned in Wat Chayasongkhram is sheltered by the only building of the monastery: it is both an *uposatha* and a *vihāra*. The *uposatha*, considered as a safe place, can be used to protect valuable items. This is, or has been, the case with the original statue of Sangkachai kept in the *uposatha* of Wat Sangkrachai. The only clear installation of an image of the Monk on the altar can be seen in the ancient *uposatha* of Wat Sawetchat in Bangkok.

d. Outdoor images

Monumental images of the Fat Monk are being built more and more frequently in the open, partly at the imitation of the huge images of Buddha sometimes found at the flank of a cliff or at the top of a hill where they can be visible from miles away. So far these images of the Monk are always inside a monastery on a terrace. They are made of bricks heavily cemented with concrete, then painted. They are becoming part of a way to advertise for a monastery that could offer the biggest Fat Monk of Thailand. They can easily be over six metres high including the pedestal. Often they are as much the work of a construction company as the work of a real artist and the result is often clumsy. For instance, the Fat Monk installed in Wat Chaiyo (Angthong, in the central plain) received a huge body but a surprisingly little head.

On the contrary, Wat Chedi Luang offers a well proportioned image on the west side of the chedi that was constructed thirty years ago, possibly to allow the relocating or dismantling of the original Fat Monk that we have described above. But this more elegant substitute never gained in popularity.

Another interesting monumental Monk can be found in Wat Mung Muang in Chiang Rai. He is installed on a terrace on stilts three metres high and rising four more metres from this base upon a busy central road. He is in the attitude of *vitarka mūdra* reserved for Buddhas (especially the images from the Dvaravati period). He is also wearing a string of wooden beads which is rather an attribute for yogis or non-bhikkhu ascetics. These details add to the dual characteristic of the Monk, both naïve and esoteric.

In Wat Phra That Pha Ngao in Chiang Sen (a forest monastery) a five meter modern statue of the monk has been installed among luxuriant vegetation. He is presented in the attitude given to very recent images of the Monk known as *prathanaphon* (*Praḥdānabara*) which means benediction for prosperity or gift. On his forehead he has been endowed with an *uṇṇā*. No doubt this image reveals the influence of the cult of Budai considered as the bringer of prosperity and wealth. The most curious detail about this statue can be observed at its back. A small door has been opened at the lowest part of the body that literally allows people to stuff the Fat Monk with other discarded images. His body is therefore considered a safe and ultimate haven.

ph. 16 and 17 opposite page

Smaller images of the Monk (less than a metre high) are sometimes installed in important places of worship of great dimensions in such a way to allow the devotees to focus on a peculiar figure. For instance, in Wat Phra That Changkham Worawihan in Nan, the devotee is expected to circumambulate the *chedi.* On its eastern side he may stop under a tent where an image of the Fat Monk is sitting on a pedestal topping a set of worshipping tables. Each table is bearing an image of the seven Buddhas of the week and seven alms bowls are awaiting a small donation.

e. Miscellaneous places

Since he is mostly considered as performing samādhi, the Monk is often to be found in what is called a meditation cell (*kuṭi*), a one-person shelter. The best example is provided by Wat Putthabat (Buddhapāda), a well-known pilgrimage centre outside the city of Lopburi where two powerful images are venerated. The first one is Saccabandha, the yogi type hermit who is supposed to have discovered the footprint of

16 – *A modern image of the Fat Monk installed in the natural park of Wat Phra That Pha Ngao in Chiang Saen*
(photos F. Lagirarde, 2001)

17 – *The opening in the back of the Fat Monk at Wat Phra That Pha Ngao in Chiang Saen*
It contains damaged images of the Buddha and of the Fat Monk himself.

the Buddha. The second one is the Fat Monk. They both are installed in *kuṭis* that could have been built in the first part of the 17th century (Luang Boribal, 2525). Although not dated, the image of the Monk (a human size bronze) seems fairly old. He has already a grotesque pear shape but continuous veneration by sticking gold leaves on his body has added to his deformity. Many other little sanctuaries of this *kuṭi* type can be found in the most important monasteries of Thailand, for instance Wat Na Phra Men in Ayutthaya and Wat Pho in Bangkok where the Monk is facing his *alter ego*, Budai. Sometimes this shelter is a simple niche (*sum* [*Jum*$_2$]) leaning against a bigger structure like a stūpa or *chedi* (*cetiya*) as can be seen in Wat Phra That Chom Cheng in Phrae.

In the imaginary situation of the Monk, his meditation could indeed be performed also in the wild in the same manner as real monks have chosen to retreat in forests and remote places. Hence the possible installation of the Monk in caves. Those caves (mostly artificial in the monastery but not always) are part of the monastery landscape. They are sometimes made of empty jars piled up by the hundreds, recovered with concrete then rearranged, opened and decorated. Their base will be transformed in a small garden that will accept images of yogis and animals. It is also usual to leave ashes of the deceased in this "natural" environment under miniature cetiyas. In the Wat Chakravan, in Bangkok, a well molded bronze of the Monk has been installed in the artificial caves "assembled" at the end of the 20th century. But the image was the property of the monastery long before. It is a well-known image that receives offerings and robes.

The contemporary urban monastery has become more and more a place for funerals. Bodies are kept before the incineration in a morgue and cremated with more and more modern installations. Then the ashes are collected, put in a small urn and eventually deposed in a funerary case set up in an appropriate place inside the monastery that becomes *de facto* also a *funerarium.* Remains of the deceased are "buried" in all kinds of places like special rooms, galleries, outside gardens with mini stūpas or *chedis,* etc. There is often left behind a small square marble slab with an inscription bearing at least the name of the dead. Depending on his size, the Fat Monk can be used as a general guardian of a funerary room or a private guardian for one. In the Thai context it is customary to put ashes in the pedestal of the statue when it is cast or molded, and in a way, the fact of dedicating one image on one box used as a base for a statue reduplicates this action.

ph. 7 page 155
ph. 2 page 151

Sometimes the Fat Monk has just been installed at the door of a monastic building where he will be visited and venerated – or rather forgotten – according to the importance of the building itself. The first case is visible at the entrance of the *vihāra* of Wat Phananchoeng in Ayutthaya. This *vihāra* is one of the most visited in Thailand because of its ancestry, because of the legends associated with its history, and because it has been raised above one of the biggest statues of the Buddha (19 m). The monastery itself was founded in 1324, twenty-six years before the founding of the Siamese capital, as it is explained in the Royal Chronicles of Ayutthaya. Moreover the Chinese community always supported this monastery[17] which seems to have been wealthy through the ages. A Chinese touch then is added here and there. For instance, just on the side of the Fat Monk, one will find an image of Chikong, an eccentric figure well known in the Chinese pantheon. The Fat Monk, made of bronze, is supported by a simple platform. He belongs to the most monstrous category, totally obese and hunched but without any features of Budai. No robe or *saṅghāti* is visible as is often the case with many ancient images of the Monk. He continuously receives incense, garlands, candles and gold leaves in the greatest quantity and a regular cleansing is therefore indispensable.

Very different indeed is the situation of the Fat Monk of Wat Bowoniwet in Bangkok, See of the Supreme Patriarch of Thailand and headquarters of the reformed congregation, the Thammayut. The Monk is made of bricks and stucco (about 0.7 m) and has been installed on a low wall next to the entrance of the traditional library in which are kept the manuscripts belonging to the monastery. This building is almost always locked and no ordinary visitors are allowed. Therefore the Monk is a little bit secluded. However it seems that faithful supporters are taking great care of him. Here the cleanest and most complete set of utensils for worship (*khrüang bucha* [*grīoṅ₁ pūjā*]) can be found: flowers, vases, garlands, clear water, little cups for tea, incense, matches, candles and betel nuts. If made discreet, the cult of the Fat Monk is nevertheless well represented in this monastery where ordinary forms of "superstitious" and "un-Thai" Buddhism are systematically banned.

---

17. It is said that the Chinese admiral Zheng He visited Ayutthaya in the very beginning of the 15th century. Many people associate the Phananchoeng Buddha and the Chinese warrior, using one name for both, Sam Po.

Oratories reserved for modern revered monks or saints (*ho phra* or *ho luang pho* [*hà braḥ, hà hluaṅ bà₁*] have been built in the 20th century inside the monasteries. They are dedicated to great historical figures like, for instance, Khruba Siwichai who became very famous as an activist for Lanna Buddhism and who lead in 1934 thousands of Chiang Mai people to build the Doi Suthep monastery. These new buildings are generally shared: the oratory of Khruba Siwichai in Wat Chiang Man also provides a good accommodation for the Monk. This is a fine bronze image in the attitude of giving (*thanaphon*) and wearing the *uṇṇā*, seated on the left of Khruba Siwichai.

Many atypical installations of the Monk can actually reveal the great deal of freedom that monks and laymen had in dealing with this image. For instance, the moveable Fat Monk (on casters) of Wat Khanikapon in Bangkok usually stays in a gallery around the *vihāra* but will be placed at the gate of the monastery to welcome the devotees on "holy" days (*uposatha* days or *wan phra*). Furthermore, when a monastery is abandoned and turns into an archaeological field or a ruined area, devotees might install a statue of the Monk where there used to be images of the Buddha. In the decrepit part of Wat Chulamani (Phitsanulok), a destroyed *vihāra* is now housing a Fat Monk painted in red (the *vihāra* is then known as the Vihāra Luang Phra Deng, or *vihāra* of the red holy Monk).

This paper results from a general survey carried out in the framework of the Monastery project (EFEO and Sirindhorn Anthropolgy Centre) between 1997 and 2001. It gave us the opportunity to visit more than one hundred monasteries selected because of their importance in history at large or because of their fame in religious matters. We found that about a third of them – usually the most prestigious – sheltered an image of the Fat Monk. This provided an answer to our first factual question: was the cult of the Fat Monk an isolated practice or a general phenomenon? This survey shows at least that the cult of the Fat Monk – devotion to whom can be performed anywhere in a monastery – is a definitive characteristic of Thai Buddhism and not only a facet of the urban centered modern Buddhism, since we have noted also its deeply rooted provincial identity. This cult has certainly been transmitted by the Mon community that shared it before with the Burmese in Pagan. Additionally, the Monk does not represent a form of "popular" or "degenerate" Buddhism. As shown above, he belongs to the biggest Buddhist foundations, mostly monasteries that have been active and learned Buddhist centers since the foundation of the first Thai domains (*müang*).

Today, this bearer of an evanescent identity (isn't he a symbol of anamorphosis?) is known as Sangkachai in Thailand: he is a normal figure in both Mahānikāya and Dhammayutikanikāya monasteries. No other image shares his status. It is true that more and more a new tendency is observable. Urban Sino-Thai worshippers tend to reappropriate his image and associate the *arahant* with a bodhisatta (when confusing him with Budai, a manifestation of Metteyya). However this issue is not clear. Will Budai be disciplined into a chief saint and a strict monk or will the already complex Gavampati-Kaccāyana be transformed into a Buddha to be?

* * *
*

BIBLIOGRAPHY

AUNG KYAING (U)
1985 – "Pot Belly Images", *Nyan Lin Dharma Padesa*, Rangoon, loc. not known, in Burmese.

Damrong RAJANUBHAB (Prince)
1973 – *Monuments of the Buddha in Siam*, second edition (revised) Bangkok, The Siam Society.

DUPONT, Pierre
1959 – *L'archéologie mône de Dvāravatī,* Paris, École française d'Extrême Orient.

Fine Arts Department
[2510] (1967) – *Prawat wat sangkrachai* [History of Wat Sangkracai], Bangkok, Krom Silapakorn.

LAGIRARDE, François
2000 – "Gavampati et la tradition des quatre-vingts disciples du Buddha: textes et iconographie du Laos et de Thaïlande", *BEFEO* 87-1, p. 57-78.
2001 – *Gavampati-Kaccāyana: le culte et la légende du disciple ventripotent dans le bouddhisme des Thaïs,* Doctoral dissertation presented the 14th May 2001 at the École Pratique des Hautes Études, La Sorbonne, Paris.

Lamoon JANHOM
[2532] (1989) – Khlong Nirat Hariphunchai *kanvinichai ton chabap* [Klong Niras Hariphunchai: *a text critical study*], thesis submitted for the degree of Master of Art, department of Lanna Language and Literature, Chiang Mai University.

Luang Boribal BURIBHAND
[2525] (1955) – *The Buddha's Footprint in Saraburi Province*, translated by Dr. Luang Suriyabongs, for distribution to the public who donated funds to the footprint, 2498, reprinted B.E. 2525.

LUCE, Gordon H.
1969-1970 – "Old Burmȧ-Early Pagán", *Artibus Asiae*, 3 volumes, New York: J. J. Augustin.

Prasert NA NAGARA
[2516] (1973) – *Khlong Nirat Hariphunchai*, modern Thai edition and translation by Prasert na Nagara, Bangkok, 3rd edition, from the manuscripts kept in Chiang Mai and in the National Library in Bangkok.

Sathaban thaksin khadi süksa [Institute of Southern Studies]
[2529] (1986) – *Saranukrom watannatham phak tai 10 lem* [Encyclopedia of Southern Thai culture, 10 vol.] Songkhla: Mulnithi Toyota [Songkhla, Toyota Fondation].

SHORTO, H. L.
1970 – "The Gavampati Tradition in Burma" , *R.C. Majumdar Felicitation Volume*, ed. Himansu Bhusan Sarkar, Calcutta, K.L. Mukhopadhyay, p. 15-30.

A NEW PHENOMENON IN THAI MONASTERIES: THE STŪPA-MUSEUM

Louis Gabaude

Among the broad spectrum of Buddhist monasteries found in Asia, new architectural forms have appeared from time to time at periods which may be difficult to identify with any accuracy. We have the opportunity to witness the rather intense production of a new kind of structure: the museum for a saint, with a strong tendency to associate the concept of a museum to that of a stūpa. Up to now, many Buddhist temples offered museums featuring local crafts, or local archaeological finds, *curiosa* collected by the abbot, or collections of Buddha images or amulets.One might see an oratory or chapel dedicated to a disciple of the Buddha such as Upagupta (Strong 1992) in the North or Kaccāyana (Lagirarde 2001). In the last fifteen years, the Thai bastion of Theravāda Buddhism has allowed chapels to Kuan-yin to compete with Kaccāyana as a way to enrich anybody and the monastery. But never in our wildest dreams could we imagine venerating a saint's toothpick or admiring his spittoon. This is now possible for Thai Buddhist saints, as seen in the selection of photographs taken from a survey of twenty-five Buddhist sites throughout the north and the north-east of Thailand[1].

1. The survey was completed in May 1998. Another paper on this subject was published as "Where Ascetics Get Comfort and Recluses Go Public: Museums for Buddhist Saints in Thailand" (Gabaude 2003).

The common feature of these sites is one or more structures (building and/or monument) dedicated to the memory of a famous monk who is considered to be a saint.[2] Before presenting this new architectural form, I will briefly review the main types of historical development of monasteries so that this contemporary phenomenon can be put into perspective. The thread of my brief reflections here will be that while the common meaning of "monastery" in English is a place where monks dwell together, many other purposes have contributed to the conception of *wat* in Thailand which is also a place for the dead and their cultic veneration by the living.

Historical rationale for Buddhist monasteries

Throughout the course of history, monasteries were built and patronized for many reasons, but there is one deep and abiding one that encapsulates them all: merit-making to ensure a positive retribution in good rebirths. At the upper end of the society, for example, a king may wish to leave a sign of his victories at war by skilfully transforming his killings and spoils of war as a marvellous expression of his benevolence and generosity; at a lower end, a courtesan may want to use her carnal earnings for a supramundane and eternal benefit. In such cases as in a multitude of others, monastery-building for the benefit of the community of monks (Saṅgha) is an ingenious process for recycling shady karma.

If we look now at the incidental reasons why a monastery may be built, we discover two main rationales, a common one, and a miraculous one.

The common rationale is the most obvious one: a monastery is established to provide a decent abode for a community of monks. If villagers invite a wandering monk[3] to settle down in their midst, the first structure built to mark the place as a future monastery is not any grand building but a simple wooden or bamboo shelter consisting of a tiny cell, a *kuṭi* for the monk. No stūpa, no preaching hall yet, just some open place called *sālā* which may be located in front of the cell at the beginning but later moved under a different roof, where devotees come, to prostrate, make offerings, sit, chat, and chant. At this stage of development, the administration of the country does not call the place a "monastery" or a *wat*, only a "Centre for Monks", or *samnak song*. Later, as patrons increase and money flow in, more permanent structures will appear successively, and, provided that the community is not considered as heterodox, in time the Saṅgha administration and the Thai state will acknowledge the site as a fully-fledged monastery – a *wat* – with the structures now associated with the image of a Buddhist temple,

---

2. I use the word "saint" to indicate a revered person—in this case a monk—considered as *Phra ariya*. "*Ariya*" here refers to the technical classification of *ariya puggala* but the popular calling reflected or created by the media is no guarantee of supernatural truth. According to the books, the *ariya puggala* is someone who has realized the last stages of holiness. In brief, there are 4 levels of sainthood: *sotāpanna*, *sakadāgāmi*, *anāgāmi*, and *arahatta* or *arahant*. The *arahant* who will never be reborn again is considered by Hinayana Buddhism to be the ideal and highest type of "man perfected" (See Horner, 1979).

3. In Thai, these wandering monks are called *phrathudong*, literally "monks who practice austerities or *dhutaṅga*". In the Theravāda world, the standard number of austerities is thirteen (Nyanatiloka 1961, p. 69-71; 1997, p. 59-60; for a broader perspective: Ray 1994, p. 293-323). In contemporary Thailand, some of these austerities – most of them conditioned by wandering – informed the nucleus of a brand of asceticism first practiced or taught by Man Bhuridatto (1870-1949), continued by his disciples. Now, a fraction of the Saṅgha practice them during the dry season. On Man's tradition, see Taylor 1993 and Kamala 1997.

the number, size and style dependent upon political, economical and regional factors. In the end, from its beginning as a residence for an ascetic and a solitary monk, the *wat* will have become the centre of the village social life and the symbol – the proof – of its economic prosperity.

In contrast, the miraculous reason for *wat* buildings departs from such prosaic beginnings. We find in the written or oral chronicles (*tamnan*) that many sites and temples link the *wat* to the Buddha himself: He is supposed to have come to a particular site during his lifetime, uttered such and such a prediction, or left some relic here in the form of a hair, there in the form of a bowl, or a footprint. In another type of story, a corporeal relic of the Buddha is hidden or brought there by a saint or a deity in the past until the secret is unveiled to a meritorious person in the present. In all these cases, the founding of the monastery belongs to a well defined process that demonstrates a kind of control of the land by the Buddha, the sacredness of a certain site the Buddha visited as well as the protection it enjoys from above. The relic is often linked by the chronicles to the foundation of a city before even mentioning the stūpa or the monastery to be built, which will protect it[4]. Finally, one can regard the monastery as a kind of by-product of the relic. When a relic is considered as especially auspicious or powerful, it is often called a *mahathat* (*mahā dhātu*) or a "Great Relic", generally linked to a local or a national ruler who as patron must maintain the monastery built around the relic. Thus, the power of the relic and that of the ruler become interdependent.[5]

A Great Relic is generally enshrined in a monument known as a stūpa.[6] However, in Thai, the word corresponding to stūpa – *sathup* – is not commonly used. While the corporeal relic itself is technically called a *dhātu-cetiya*, the monument which contains it is called a *chedi* in central Thailand a *that* in northern and northeastern Thailand as well as in Laos.[7]

In addition to the literary genres mentioned above, Prince Damrong Rajanuphab has given his own catalogue or reasons why monasteries have been built which may reveal something both very Buddhist and very Thai. According to him, one of the first

---

4. See for example the case of the relic of Haripunchai or Lamphun in Notton 1930, p. 5.

5. Examples of these links can be found in local or temple chronicles. See Notton 1926, 1930; for a general analysis of this relationship in northern Thailand, see Swearer and Sommai 1978. The stūpas, like all the other reminders of the Buddha, were protected by law: see Skilling 2003.

6. It may be kept elsewhere too. InWat Phra That Si Jom Thong, Chom Thong, Chiang Mai Province, it is kept in a special reliquary, a *ku*, which stands at the very place where normally is a big Buddha image.

7. In Thailand, the standard classification of *cetiya* is fourfold:
1. "*Dhātu-cetiya*" refers to "any object containing [corporeal] relics, such as teeth or fragments of bone left over after the Buddha's cremation." In practice, it refers to a reliquary and by extension to the monument built upon the reliquary, *i.e.*, the stūpa;
2. "*Paribhoka-cetiya*" refers to "a 'reminder by association,' such as a bodhi tree [...], the sites of the Eight Great Events [...], the 'Seven Stations' where [the Buddha] spent the seven weeks following the Enlightenment, the seats he sat on, and the footprints he stamped" throughout Asia;
3. "*Dhamma-cetiya*" refers to"a 'doctrinal reminder' such as the Pāli Canon, or a commentary on it, or an extract from the Canon inscribed on stone, brick or metal";
4. "*Uddesika-cetiya*" refers to "an 'indicative reminder,' *i.e.*, any object that the general opinion accepts as a suitable reminder of the Buddha". (Quotations above taken from Griswold 1973, p. vi).
In standard Thai, *chedi* (from *cetiya*) refers now only to *dhātu-cetiya* and is therefore a "monument containing a corporeal relic of the Buddha". On the contrary, Lao dialects have retained only the first part of the compound, *dhātu-cetiya*, and call a stūpa *that*.

monasteries to be built in Thailand is Wat Phra Pathom Chedi in Nakhon Pathom.[8] With this Thai example and others from India, he shows that the establishment of permanent monasteries resulted as a by-product of the cult of relics enshrined in stūpas, (Damrong 1935: 11-12) while the first *ārāma* or park-like abodes offered to the Buddha were temporary ones for use during the rainy season.

Prince Damrong regards two kinds of stūpas or *cetiyas* as the origin for the first monasteries in Thailand:

1) the Buddha-*cetiyas* containing a corporeal relic of the Buddha, and

2) the memorials containing the bones of a local celebrity – monk or ruler – all having the shape of a stūpa, or *chedi*. This observation would account for the multiplication of monasteries around Nakhon Pathom which he divides accordingly into "monasteries as Buddha-*cetiya*" or *Wat Phutthachedi* for the first model, and "Monasteries as memorial" [of some famous local] or *Wat Anusawari* for the second (Damrong 1935: 21). In short, some monasteries were built exclusively for the cult of the Buddha while others were built for the veneration of particular rulers, monks, or ancestors.

Prince Damrong connects the advent and spread of Theravāda Buddhism during the Sukhothai Period (13th-14th c.) to a renewal of interest and devotion to the corporeal Buddha relics enshrined in stūpas. But his distinction between "Monasteries as Buddha-*cetiya*" and "Monasteries as memorial" [of a famous local] remains valid for the Sukkhothai period. He cites as proof the obvious role played by local chiefs and princes in building monasteries where their cremated bones would be kept in the stūpa(s).[9] Whereas at the beginning, the stūpa was the primary central structure of the monasteries,[10] the creation and multiplication of Buddha images, the need for a preaching hall and for ritual shelters led to the creation of chapels and halls (called *wihan* from *vihāra*). And the concern for authenticity of lineages joined to the ordination of a growing number of monks generated the building of *uposatha* halls (Damrong 1935: 27).

For the Ayutthaya Period (14th-18th c.), Prince Damrong recalls the saying that in properous times rich families would found monasteries "as a play-ground for their children and grand-children", meaning these children would play in the monastery compound whenever the family would come and pay hommage to the ancestors whose ashes were kept in the stūpas of "their" temple (1935: 30). At the same time, the social importance of the monastery increased through its role in the education of young boys.

For the Rattanakosin or Bangkok Period (1782 to the present), Prince Damrong believes that his distinction between "Monasteries as a Buddha-cetiya" and "Monasteries as a memorial" [of some famous local] is still valid because some monasteries were

8. Damrong Rajanuphab 1935, p. 6, 17-19. The author takes for granted the Buddhist chronicle according to which two of Aśoka's envoys came and spread Buddhism in what is now central Thailand. The best assessment to date of the period alluded to here is Brown 1996.

9. Damrong 1935: 26, 28. On p. 31, the author adds that the bones were enshrined in the main stūpa of the monastery, whereas in the later Ayutthaya period rich families built separate stūpas for each family member.

10. Prince Damrong cites the case of Sawankhalok-Sri Satchanalai in Sukhothai Province, where of five Royal temples (*wat*), only one had residences for monks: *ibid.*, p. 29. If we accept the early preeminence of the stūpa as a well-known fact, I would hesitate to infer that this always meant no residences for monks as any wooden structure would have completely disintegrated after centuries of ruin.

first built for the Buddha and others as a memorial for some dignitary. However, even in the first case – the monastery as a Buddha-*cetiya* –, the importance of the stūpa and of the great hall or *wihan* decreases, perhaps "because they think that so many stūpas have already been built that we cannot even look properly after them" and "that large teaching halls (*sala kanparian*) are now used instead of the *wihan* for the ceremonies." However, stūpas for the deceased were still being built, albeit in fewer numbers because more and more frequently bones were kept at home (Damrong 1935: 35).

This brief look at the rationale behind the foundations of Buddhist monasteries in Thailand reveals two main kinds of concerns. The first concern is for the living: the monks and the laity who support them, the community who uses the temple grounds for social purposes, and the ruler who may have built it or patronizes it. The second concern is for the dead: for the Buddha first of all since stūpas enshrining his corporeal relics were often the reason why a community of monks was attached to it, which in turn led to the building of a monastery. After the concern for the dead Buddha made present through his relics, came the concern for the dead rulers or other notables whose bones and ashes were enshrined either in the main stūpa or in separate ones. One could say that the history of a Buddhist monastery is *essentially* woven from the threads of life and the threads of death reflected in its built structures.

I will now look at what is a new thread of life and death, the building of stūpa-museums for saints.

The museum for saints

In the 20th century, Thailand has seen the emergence of a monastical movement initiated by the Venerable Man Bhuridatto (1870-1949) that extends from the deep forests of Thailand to quite different forests in New Zealand, England, and the U.S. Because Man himself was exclusively interested in solitary asceticism and meditation, he was criticized by his intellectual and urban brothers within his own congregation, the Thammayut.[11] However, after his demise, his belonging to this "royal" congregation facilitated finally – for his closest disciples – attention and funding from the upper classes of Thai society, at a time of great prosperity.[12] His radical way of life and practice of strict mental discipline miles away from merit-making or protective rituals, in a pristine, natural environment appealed to westerners who found there a genuine and original way of practice beyond religion, and a monastic tradition previously unknown to them.

Man died in 1949. After his cremation, his disciples who had kept some of his bones and ashes opened their caskets and discovered that the bones and ashes had changed into a kind of crystalline and glossy grains, evidence that their spiritual master was an

11. When still a monk, the future King Mongkut (r. 1851-1868) gathered a group of monks concerned with a stricter observance of the rules (*vinaya*). This group – called here in short form "Thammayut" – eventually parted from the other monks who have been called from then on *mahanikai*, the "big nikai" or the "big congregation". These groups are usually defined as "sects", I prefer and use the word "congregation" instead because they do not differ in doctrine but only in their observations of the minor rules (*vinaya*).

12. On this movement, see Tambiah 1984; Taylor 1993; Kamala 1997.

arahant who would never be reborn[13]. Later, whenever one of his immediate disciples passed away, the same "miracle" occured again and again.[14]

Genuine attachment to and admiration for these masters coupled with easily obtainable relics and patron's monetary support led to the creation of a new kind of structure which now is found in many Thai Buddhist monastery compounds under a variety of names.Their primary purpose is to keep alive the memory of a monk considered to be exemplary and more importantly a source of merit.

During the 1998 survey, I visited twenty-five sites containing these memorials. Some had two different structures dedicated to the same saint, putting the total number of buildings at thirty-two.[15] I will introduce here to their main features:

A. Types of structures; B. Corporeal relics; C. Images of the saint; D. Belongings; E. Amulets; F. Published work; G. Honorific Fans and Titles.

A. Types of structures

See map and list for location of sites in Annex p. 182-83

There is no uniformity either in the type or in the names of the structures. These are the names I found with some comments following: Museum, *Cetiya*, *Cetiya*-Museum, Memorial, *Maṇḍapa*, *Maṇḍapa*-Museum, *Prāsāda*, *Meru*.

a – A "Museum"(*Phiphitthaphan*) was found on thirteen sites."Museum" refers to a structure which does not look like a stūpa but more like an ordinary building, although it may not be a square one: octagonal at Wat Tham Pha Pu for Khamdi Pabhaso, or at Wat Pa Wang Loeng for Bunmi Siritharo; irregular at Wat Pa Sutthawat for Man Bhuridatto or at Wat Burapharam for Dun Atulo. Square or rectangular "museums" can be found at Wat Pa Khok Mon for Chop Thanasamo, at Wat Tham Khlong Phle for Khao Analayo, and at Wat Nong Pa Phong for Cha Subhaddo.

ph. 1 opposite page

b – A *Cetiya* (*chedi*) was found at nine sites. *Cetiya* refers to a structure which looks generally like a stūpa from afar. Normally, Buddhist stūpas are massive and solid structures with an invisible chamber at its core and sometimes small niches on the outside or at the most a narrow access to the center. The stūpas/*cetiyas* for saints, on the contrary, have one or several doors opening onto a central exhibition room with windows or showcases along the walls, and sometimes a statue of the saint and/or his relics at the center.

---

13. Thai devotees have always tried to appreciate *post mortem* the degree of holiness of their monks. In the north at least, for the cremation of a dignified monk a piece of cloth, called "ceiling" (*phedan* or *phidan*) is fixed to and stretched between four very long bamboo poles as a canopy in such a way that the cloth is precisely above the fire. According to my own informations, the less the cloth is burnt, the purer was the monk, or the more he has merit (*bun*). The more the cloth is burnt, the more the monk will have to be reborn in lower states of life. However, Charles F. Keyes (2000, p. 130-134) reports an opposite interpretation. Whatever it is, this popular test, to my knowledge, did not establish that the monk was an *arahant* because the common belief, until Man Bhuridatto, was that there were no more *arahants* in this world anyway. All that was hoped for a "pure" monk or a monk with much merit was a rebirth in some highest heaven. Since Man, the crystallization of bones is a much more straightforward and "sure"proof of arahantship which is exposed at length in the Thai Buddhist magazines.

14. The general topic and problem of relics is beyond the scope of this paper. *Relics of the Buddha* by John S. Strong, forthcoming at Princeton University Press, will present a state of the question. For a discussion of Man Bhuridatto and others' relics, see Tambiah 1984, p. 109-110; Taylor 1993, p.175-180.

15. I found: one *cetiya* with one museum (on two sites), one *cetiya* with one *meru*, one museum with one *meru*, one *maṇḍapa* with one *cetiya*-museum, one *prāsāda* with one museum, one memorial with one museum. See the brief presentation of these buildings below.

The base of the stūpa/cetiya may have various forms: round at Wat Pa Sutthawat for Lui Candasaro; octagonal at Wat Tham Pha Pu for Khamdi Pabhaso, at at Wat Hin Mak Peng for Thet Desarangsi, or at Wat Phu Thok for Chuan Kulajeṭṭho; cross-shaped at Wat Tham Khlong Phle, for Khao Analayo. *ph. 2 below* *ph. 3 below*

1 – *Museum of Chop Thanasamo, Wat Pa Khok Mon* (photo L. Gabaude)

2 – Cetiya *of Lui Candasāro, Wat Pa Sutthawat* (photo L. Gabaude)

3 – Cetiya *of Khao Anālayo, Wat Tham Khlong Phle* (photo L. Gabaude)

4 – *Stūpa-Museum of Wan Uttamo, Wat Pa Udomsomphon* (photo L. Gabaude)

5 – *Stūpa of Waen Sucinno inside the Maṇḍapa-Museum, Wat Doi Mae Pang* (photo L. Gabaude)

c – A *Cetiya*-Museum (*chedi-phiphitthaphan*) was found on three sites. All is said: here we have a *cetiya*, stūpa shaped, which contains a museum. Actually, all the *cetiyas* mentioned above in paragraph *b* could as well be called *cetiya*-museum, and for us stūpa-museum. Of the latter, one is cross-shaped at Wat Pa Aphai Damrong Tham for Wan Uttamo and two are octagonal: at Wat Pa Dong Khu for Kim Dipathammo, and at the Samnak Song Tham Pha Plong for Sim Buddhacaro.

ph. 4 above

d – A Memorial or a monument(*anusawari*) was found on one site, under construction at the time of the survey.

e – A *Maṇḍapa* (*mondop*) was found on one site at Samnak Song Tham Pha Plong for Sim Buddhacaro. A *maṇḍapa* is a small building with a square roof and often exquisite decorations. In this case, since the same site also has a stūpa-museum, the *maṇḍapa* provides shelter only to a statue of the saint.

f – A *Maṇḍapa*-Museum (*mondop-phiphitthaphan*) was found on one site at Wat Doi Mae Pang for Waen Sucinno. The *mondop* here actually contains a smaller stūpa encasing the ashes of the saint.

ph. 5 above

g – A *Prāsāda* (*prasat*)[16] was found on one site at Wat Ban Pang for Khruba Siwichai. This site also has a separate museum and this prasat, like in Waen Sucinno's site, shelters the stūpa of the saint.

16. Normally, a *Prāsāda* (*prasat*) is a provisional wooden structure built around and upon the coffin as a pyre.

6 – *Reliquary of Cha Subhaddo, Wat Non Pa Phong* (photo L. Gabaude)

7 – *Corporeal relics of Wan Uttamo with magnifying lenses, Wat Pa Udomsomphon* (photo L. Gabaude)

h – A *Meru* was found at three sites.[17] In two of our cases, the *meru* was a permanent structure made of concrete and cement, specially built for the cremation and kept afterwards, one at Wat Hin Mak Peng for Thet Desarangsi, and the other at Wat Nong Pa Phong for Cha Subhaddo. In the latter case, this *meru* has become an open stūpa with the crystallized relics of the saint exhibited at the center of a very modern and luxurious building. At Wat Hin Mak Peng, the *meru* has become a shelter for a statue of the saint.

B. Corporeal relics:

There are of two kinds of corporeal relics: those collected during the life of the saint and those kept from his ashes. Hair, nails, teeth, have been collected by the immediate disciples who have reduplicated for their master what is supposed to have been traditional for the Buddha. But the main purpose and the focal point of these memorials seems to be the exhibition of the small pieces of bones, often crystallized, kept after the cremation. In somes cases, like for Cha Subhaddo, the fine design of the structure, the quality of the materials used, the play of light, produce a striking and emotional effect on the visitor. *ph. 6 and 7 above*

17. A *meru* is a reference to the Mt Meru and a provisional wooden structure built for the cremation and put above the coffin or the urn. For royals and famous monks, the *meru* or funeral pyre may be a very intricate piece of art.

C. Images of the saint

ph. 8 below, 9 and 10 opposite page

The tradition of casting images of monks is a relatively recent one in Thailand, dating back to the nineteenth century. But the economic bubble of the 1990s has led to a multiplication of statues of famous monks who seem to have problems resisting the devotion of their disciples. This occured at a time where new techniques allowed the production of incredibly look-alike resin statues. These images can be found not only in a special museum near Bangkok[18], but also in temples throughout the country where the model is still alive, and, of course, in the saint's museum where he remains present in his most familiar mood and attitude.

ph. 11 opposite page

Imagery concerning the saints is not limited to the cast and resin statues. Photography is well represented, betraying sometimes the conscious fabrication of images, when a spiritual "rhinoceros" strikes a pose in the wilderness to show his love of solitude. The saint's imagery may also be expanded through his bio-hagiography told in pictures, as is the case with baked-clay low-reliefs for Fan Ācāro at Wat Pa at Wat Pa Udomsomphon, of Chuan Kulajeṭṭho at Wat Phu Thok.

See photo p. 169: footprint of Cha Subhaddho

Sometimes, in a striking parallel with the Buddha's footprint tradition, the museums exhibit footprints or handprints of the saint either on cloth or on plaster.

8 – *Cast image of Man Bhuridatto, Wat Sutthawat* (photo L. Gabaude)

18. The "Thai Human Imagery Museum" is located at 43/1 Mool, Thanon Pinklao-Nakhonchaisi Tambon Khun Kaeo, Amphoe Nakhonchaisi, Nakhon Pathom Province. It exhibits several resin and look-alike images of the most revered monks of Thailand.

9 – *Resin image and relics of Lui Candasāro, Wat Pa Sutthawat* (photo L. Gabaude)

10 – *Resin image of Cha Subhaddo, Wat Non Pa Phong* (photo L. Gabaude)

11 – *Hagiography on the walls of the Museum of Fan Ācāro, Wat Pa Udomsomphon* (photo L. Gabaude)

D. Belongings

ph. 12 and 13 below

The saint's most familiar objects are exhibited under glass or in the open, depending on their size. To name a few: abacus, adjustable wrench, alarm clock, armchair, bag, bamboo for ablutions, bathroom scale, belt, betelnut set, bill-hook, binoculars, blanket, bowl, can, cardigan, clothes line, dentures, diary, drill, ear cleaner, electric heater, fan, fly swatter, fork, glasses, handsaw, hat, kettle, knife, lamp, magnifying glass, matches, medicines, metal tumbler, mortar, mosquito net, nail clippers, needles, paper knife, pen, pillow, pipe, plate, radiator, razor, robes, scissors, sheets, shoes, socks, spectacles, spittoon, spoon, stick, string, teapot, tensiometer, thermometer, thermos, thread, tissue box, toothbrush, toothpicks, towels, umbrella, universal pliers, urinal, watch, water filter, wheel-chair, whistle, yardstick, etc...

12 – *Showcase in the Museum of Bunmi Siritharo, Wat PaWang Loeng* (photo L. Gabaude)

13 – *Personal belongings in the museum of Khao Anālayo, Wat Tham Khlong Phle* (photo L. Gabaude)

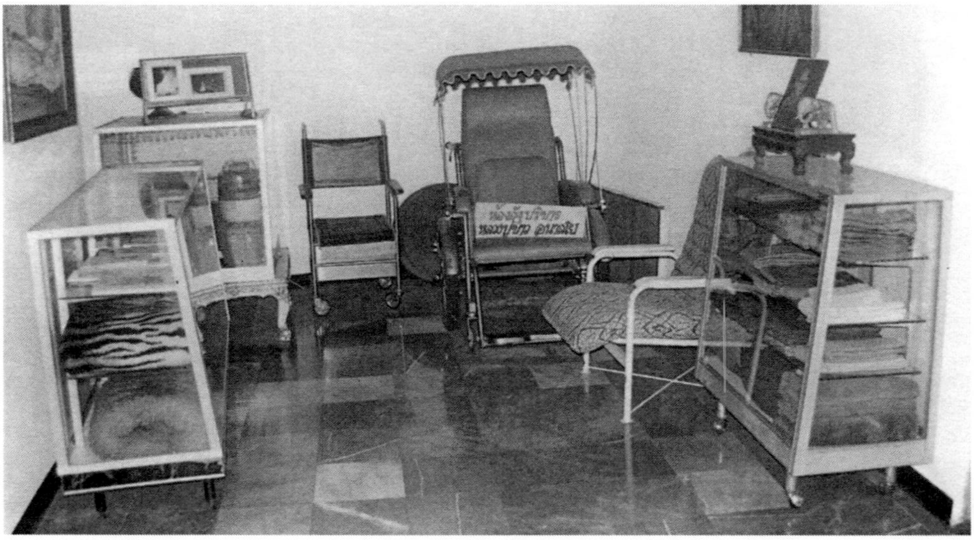

E. Amulets

The production of amulets is problematic for Thammayut monks whose congregation is supposed to frown upon magic. However, some of the museums exhibit various models of amulets produced and/or consecrated by the saint, or in his name.

F. Published works

The majority of these saints have been forest monks mainly interested in mental and ascetic practices transmitted by word of mouth. They were not naturally inclined to publish their teachings. Their living far from towns did not help for that matter also. However, after the 1960s, when Buddhadasa Bhikkhu had been a forerunner in that domain, there has been a demand for Buddhist books never seen before. Moreover, the western disciples of some of these saints have translated and published their sermons in English and other languages. This has become a supplementary asset to establish their reputation of a saint.

G. Honorific Fans and Titles

Even though Man Bhuridatto, the Master of the modern forest tradition, had no fondness for Bangkok-given charges and honors, his disciples have been gratified with honorific fans and titles, have received royal visits, and have given royal instructions. All this is listed and illustrated in the museums, either with photographs or clippings from newspapers.

The saints' museums are an expression of a traditional pattern in a modern setting. The thread of death pulled out by Damrong in the history of Thai monasteries is still valid but with a new function: it does not link the devotee directly to the Buddha like a Buddha's relic could and can do. It does not link either the devotee to his/her ancestors whose ashes are buried in the family stūpa. It does link the devotee to the contemporary spiritual master he/she may have known personally, and who is regarded by that person like the Buddha. While apparently neglecting the model for his imitators, the stūpa-museum actually pulls the Buddha back into the present, back into life by exhibiting the life of one who has succeeded on the same battlefield as the Buddha's, and who is now like the Buddha himself, completely liberated. The stūpa-museum shows Buddhahood in action, Buddhahood here and now, Buddhahood visible, as solid as crystal.

The corporeal crystalline relics of these contemporary saints have appeal not only for those with a traditional faith but to a modern mind as well. The contemporary devotee sees these saints as a material proof that spiritual achievement is possible for anybody who has the will. The relics are regarded as a concretion, a crystallization of flesh and spirit, matter and mind, at the crossing point of spirituality and science. This may explain why western disciples – most of them with Jewish or protestant roots and convictions – may not dismiss this cult of Buddhist relics, even when their denial was at the root of their own former heritage.

We can give credit to the Thais forgiving a new expression to the traditional veneration of relics which had been so important in the development of Buddhism throughout Asia.[19] Today, the saints' museums can also claim the land, just like the ancient chronicles wherein the Great Relics and the footprints of the Buddha claimed the land. However,

19. See, for example, Schopen 1997; Trainor 1997.

there is a big difference, especially in the eyes of the monks belonging to the Mahanikai congregation: most of the sites visited – 22 out of 25 – were showcases for Thammayut monks who represent only 8% of the Thai Saṅgha. While most of the Mahanikai monks remain mute in public about their brothers, in private some question the authenticity of these relics as well as the accompanying cult to acquire material advantages. But to the external observer the presence of relics, the sale – euphemistically called "renting" – of amulets, the casting of images, the building of showcases years before one's death have

Annex

List of sites visited

	PROVINCE	DISTRICT	SITE	MONK
1.	Loei	Loei	Wat Tham Pha Pu	Khamdi Pabhaso
2.	Loei	Loei	Wat Si Sutthawat	Sijan Vaṇṇabho
3.	Loei	Wang Saphung	Wat Pa Khok	Chop Thanasamo
4.	Loei	Wang Saphung	Wat Nong Sawang	Sijan Vaṇṇabho
5.	Nongkhai	Sichiangmai	Wat Hin Mak Peng	Thet Desarangsī
6.	Nongkhai	Sichiangmai	Wat Si-arannyabanphot	Rian Varalābho
7.	Nongkhai	Siwilai	Wat Phu Thok	Chuan Kulajeṭṭho
8.	Sakonnakhon	Song Dao	Wat Pa Aphai Damrong Tham	Wan Uttamo
9.	Sakonnakhon	Phannanikhom	Wat Pa Udomsomphon	Fan Ācāro
10.	Sakonnakhon	Sakonnakhon	Wat Pa Sutthawat	Man Bhuridatto
11.	Sakonnakhon	Sakonnakhon	Wat Pa Sutthawat	Lui Candasāro
12.	Mahasarakham	Kanthrawichai	Wat Pa Wang Loeng	Bunmi Siritharo
13.	Roi Et	Nong Phok	Wat Tham Pha Nam Yoi	Si Mahāvīro
14.	Mukdahan	Nong Sung	Wat Banphotkhiri (Phu Jo Ko)	La Khamapatto
15.	Ubonratchathani	Warinchamrap	Wat Nong Pa Phong	Cha Subhaddo
16.	Surin	Surin	Wat Burapharam	Dun Atulo
17.	Surin	Lamduan	Wat Pa Dong Khu	Kim Dīpathammo
18.	Surin	Surin	Wat Pa Traiwiwek	Sam Akiñcano
19.	Surin	Surin	Phanom Sawai Park	Dun Atulo
20.	Udonthani	Udonthani	Wat Pa Ban Tat	Bua Ñāṇasampanno
21.	Nong Bua Lamphu	Nong Bua Lamphu	Wat Tham Khlong Phle	Khao Anālayo
22.	Chiang Mai	Phrao	Wat Doi Mae Pang	Waen Suciṇṇo
23.	Chiang Mai	Chiang Dao	S. S. Tham Pha Plong	Sim Buddhacāro
24.	Lamphun	Li	Wat Ban Pang	Khruba Siwichai
25.	Lamphun	Li	Wat Phrabat Huai Tom	Chaiyawong Phatthana

* Site No. 20, for Bua Ñāṇasampanno in Udonthani had neither stūpa nor museum but only a simple structure for the cremation of the abbot when he passes away, a reaction against the luxurious rites arranged for other famous monks.

come to be regarded as all too familiar tools whether Thammayut or Mahanikai. The Thammayut have just been more successful building these museums, whereas the Mahanikai have focussed on the amulets.

How do we regard a Buddhist monastery? As a place for the living? As a place for the dead? As a playground for children? It is also a battlefield where the dead are regarded as a weapon in the battle for Dharma.

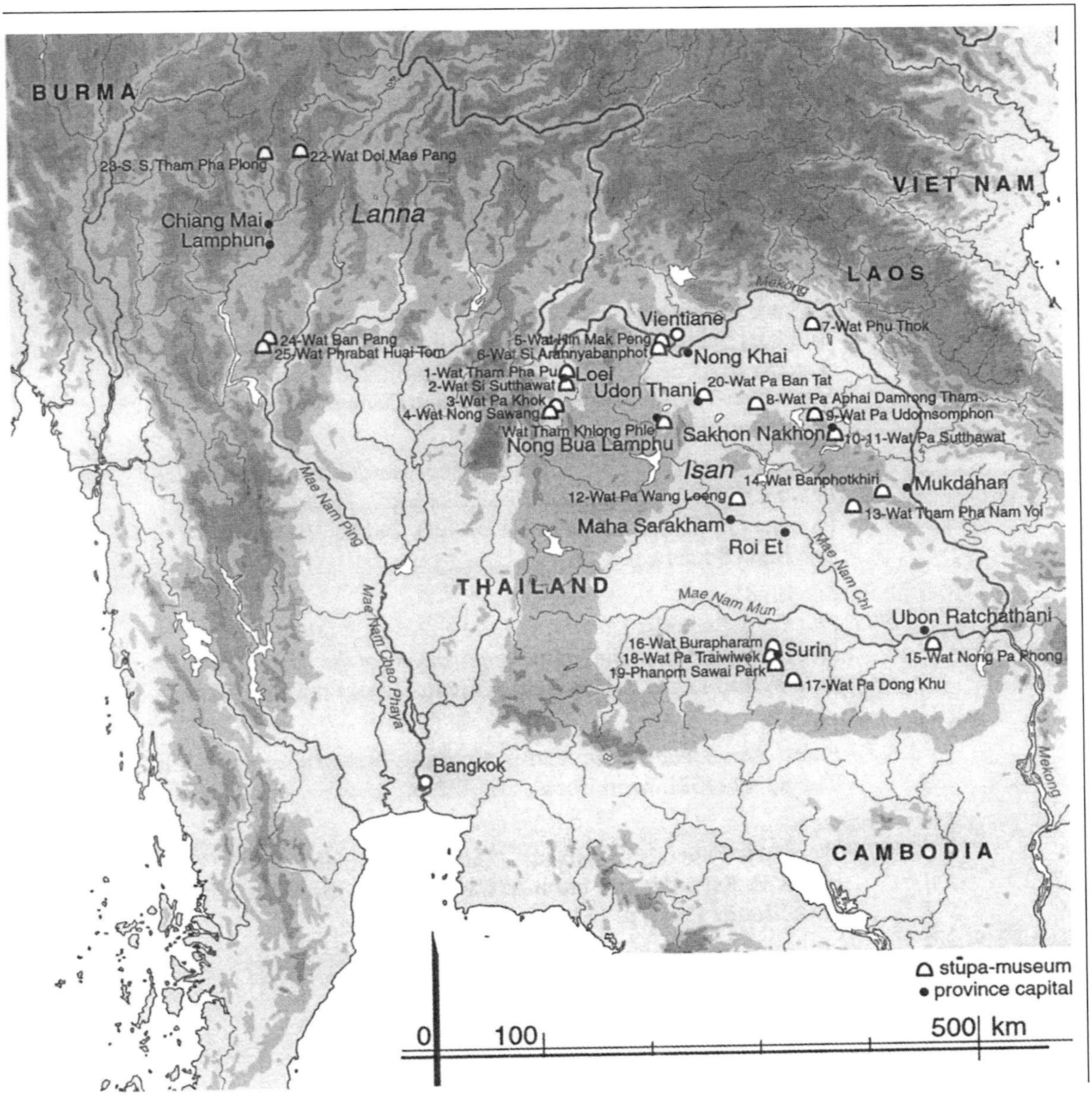

BIBLIOGRAPHY

BROWN, Robert T.
1996 – *The Dvāravatī Wheels of the Law and the Indianization of Southeast Asia*, Leiden, E.J. Brill, XXXII+237 p., 11 phot. h.-t.

Damrong RAJANUPHAP
1935 – *Munhethaeng kansang wat nai prathet sayam – Somdet Phrajaoborommawongthoe KromPhraya Damrongratchanuphap song sadaeng pen pathakatha thi samakkhayajansamakhom müa wan thi 24 singhakhom pho so 2471*, Phim jaek nai ngan plong sop Nang Hun Phlaeng-akkhane na Wat Noi Nopphakhun Bansü Phanakhon müa wan thi 24 phrütsajikayon pho so 2478, [4]+45 p.
1973 – *Monuments of the Buddha in Siam* (Translated by Sulak Sivaraksa and A.B. Griswold with footnotes by Prince Subhadradis Diskul), 2nd ed., Bangkok,The Siam Society, ix+60 p.

GABAUDE, Louis
2003 – "Where Ascetics Get Comfort and Recluses Go Public: Museums for Buddhist Saints in Thailand", *Pilgrims, Patrons, and Place: Localizing Sanctity in Asian Religions* (Phyllis Granoff and Koichi Shinohara, eds.), Vancouver-Toronto, University of British Columbia Press, p. 108-123

GRISWOLD, A. B.
1973 – "Introduction" in Damrong Rajanuphap, *Monuments of the Buddha in Siam* (Translated by Sulak Sivaraksa and A.B. Griswold with footnotes by Prince Subhadradis Diskul), 2nd ed., Bangkok, The Siam Society, p. v-ix.

HORNER, Isaline Blue
1979 – *The Early Buddhist Theory of Man Perfected: A Study of the Arahan Concept and of the Implications of the Aim to Perfection in Religious Life* [...], NewDelhi, Oriental Books reprint, 328 p.

Kamala TIYAVANICH
1997 – *Forest Recollections: Wandering Monks in Twentieth-century Thailand*, Chiang Mai, Silkworm Books, xiii+410 p.

KEYES, Charles F.
2000 – "Monastic Funerals (Thailand)", *The Life of Buddhism* (Frank E. Reynolds and Jason A. Carbine, eds.), Berkeley, University of California Press, p. 123-135.

LAGIRARDE, François
2001 – *Gavampati-Kaccāyana: Le culte et la légende du disciple ventripotent dans le bouddhisme des Thaïs*, Tome I et II, Thèse de doctorat en histoire des religions et des systèmes de pensée, École Pratique des Hautes Études, Section des sciences religieuses, 580 p.

NOTTON, Camille
1926 – *Annales du Siam, Première Partie, Chroniques de: Suvanna Khamdëng, Suvanna K'ôm Kham, Sinhanavati*, Paris, Charles-Lavauzelle, xxvii+216 p.
1930 – *Annales du Siam, IIe vol., Chronique de La:p'un, Histoire de la Dynastie Chamt'evi*, Paris, Charles-Lavauzelle, [16]+68 p.

NYANATILOKA, Thera
1961 – *Vocabulaire bouddhique de termes et doctrines du canon pāli*, Paris, xviii, 336 p.
1997 – *Buddhist Dictionary. Manual of Buddhist Terms and Doctrines* (Nyanaponika,Thera: ed.), 4th rev. ed., Kandy, Buddhist Publication Society, 258 p.

PHITPHITHAK
1994 – *Phrathat prasat hin prang chedi*, Bangkok, Samnakphim
2537 Hosamutklang 09, 192 p.

RAY, Reginald A.
1994 – *Buddhist Saints in India: A Study in Buddhist Values and Orientations*, New York and Oxford, Oxford University Press, xviii, 508 p.

RINGIS, Rita
1990 – *Thai temples and Temple Murals*, Singapore, Oxford University Press, xxix+163 p.

Royal Institute
1982 – *Romanization Guide*, Bangkok, Royal Institute, 26 p.

Sathüan SUPHASOPHON
1994 – *Tamnan Phraborommasaririkathat 1*,
2537 Bangkok, Phon Lok, 127 p.
1994 – *Tamnan Phraborommasaririkathat 2*,
2537 Bangkok, Phon Lok, 127 p.

SCHOPEN, Gregory
1997 – *Bones, Stones, and Buddhist Monks: Collected papers on the Archaeology, Epigraphy, and Texts of Monastic Buddhism in India*, Honolulu, University of Hawaii Press, xvii+297 p.

SKILLING, Peter
2003 – "Ideology and Law: The Three Seals Code on Crimes related to Relics, Images, and Bodhi-trees", *Sichamaiyajan: phiphitniphon choetchukiat sastrajan Dr. Prasert Na Nagara – sastrajan Visut Butsyakun nüang nai okat mi ayu 84 pi nai pho. so.2545* (Vinai Phongsiphian, bannathikan), Bangkok, Ministry of Culture, p. 287-307.

STRONG, John S.
1992 – *The Legend and Cult of Upagupta: Sanskrit Buddhism in North India and Southeast Asia*, Princeton, NJ, Princeton University Press, xviii+390 p.
2002 – *Relics of Buddha* [Manuscript. Publication expected in 2004]

SWEARER, Donald K.; Sommai PREMCHIT
1978 – "The Relationship Between the Religious and Political Orders in Northern Thailand (14th-16th Centuries), *Religion and Legitimation of Power in Thailand, Laos, and Burma* (Bardwell L. Smith, ed.), Chambersburg, Anima Books, 231 p.

TAYLOR, Jim L.
1993 – *Forest Monks and the Nation-State: An Anthropological and Historical Study in Northeastern Thailand*, Singapore, Institute of Southeast Asian Studies (ISEAS), xi+377 p.

Thanaphan METHAPHITHAK
1994 – *Prawat lae khwampenma wat rüan thai*,
2537 Bangkok, Samnakphim Hosamutklang 09, 207 p.

TRAINOR, Kevin
1997 – *Relics, Ritual, and Representation in Buddhism: Rematerializing the Sri Lankan Theravāda tradition*, Cambridge, Cambridge University Press, xiv+223 p.

THE EARLIEST LAO BUDDHIST MONASTERIES

ACCORDING TO PHILOLOGICAL AND EPIGRAPHIC SOURCES

Michel Lorrillard

The first Lao Buddhist monasteries left no architectural remains, apart from a few stūpas modified over the centuries.[1] The chronicles and the inscriptions constitute therefore our only source of information on the environment and way of life of the ancient monastic communities. These documents, although they hardly consider material, technical and visual aspects of construction, do however offer essential data about the spread of Buddhism in territories inhabited by Lao peoples. It is therefore important to take them into consideration.

1. The only work available on the subject is that of Henri Parmentier, *L'art du Laos*, 2 vol. (text and iconography), EFEO-Hanoi, 1954 (edition revised by M. Giteau, PEFEO, Paris, 1988). The studies were made from 1911, when a number of ruins were still in existence. According to the architect, the most ancient of the Lao pagodas did not appear to be more than two hundred years old (p. 1, *op. cit.*). This is in sharp contrast to the robust architecture of the Khmer monuments of Vat Phu (southern Laos).

The Buddhist Monastery, EFEO, 2003, p. 187-198

The chronicles

The most ancient chronicles were written from the end of the 15th century and originate in Luang Prabang.[2] They tell us among other things of the adoption of the Buddhist religion and the appearance of the first Buddhist monasteries in the former Laotian kingdom of Lan Xang.[3] The informations they give us can be summarized as follows:[4]

– Even if there is a vague reference to a former Buddhist religion in Vientiane and in the north-eastern region of Thailand, the true appearance of Buddhism in Laos took place during the reign of Fa Ngum (1353-1373/74), in 1363.

– It was the Khmer king who, on the request of his daughter and his son-in-law (Fa Ngum), sent a Buddhist religious mission to the newly formed kingdom of Lan Xang so that Buddhism would flourish there.

– Apart from monks, amongst whom some were said to be from Laṅka (Sri Lanka), the religious mission included a large entourage composed of craftsmen, astronomers and laymen whose duty was to feed and assist the monks.

See map p. 112 for sites mentioned in this article

– The first monastery was established at Luang Prabang, the royal capital.

One of the oldest chronicles[5] gives us interesting information about this first monastery. To build it, the religious mission chose a site on the banks of the Mekong, at Sop Hop, which is at the mouth of the river Hop. The first thing the monks did to bless the site was to plant a Ficus tree (*ton pho* or *phothi*) from a cutting which was said to come from Sri Lanka. Therefore, the tree appears here as a central element of the sacred ground. After that, the mission built a stūpa, inside which they placed a phalanx from Buddha's right hand. It is only following these first acts that the king built the monastery which he named Vat Pasaman, after the name of the leader of the Cambodian religious mission.

For the subsequent monastery, known as Vat Kaeo, new characteristics appear. First of all there was a place of asylum, where criminals could find refuge. Many donations are also mentioned. Among them, paddy fields, families of servants with their land to provide for the monks, families of servants to maintain the pagoda and supply materials for worship, as well as an important area of land.[6]

Afterwards monasteries were built during practically every reign. Here we have some interesting points:

– First of all, the chronicles tell us that, in many cases, the monasteries were built in order to preserve the ashes of a deceased member of the Royal family. The constructions of stūpas are sometimes mentioned. These appear therefore to be funeral monuments.

---

2. For a description of these chronicles and all the informations related to them contained in this paper, see Michel Lorrillard, *Les chroniques royales du Laos (1316-1887)*, PhD dissertation, Paris, 1995 and Michel Lorrillard, "Quelques données relatives à l'historiographie lao", *BEFEO* 86, 1999, p. 219-232.

3. The unified kingdom of Lan Xang ($l\bar{a}n_2\ j\bar{a}\dot{n}_2$) lasted from the mid 14th century to the end of the 17th century. It's territories covered important parts of present day Laos as well as certain regions of north-eastern Thailand.

4. These informations must be considered with extreme caution since they are not supported by any historical evidence. It seems obvious that literary traditions had a certain influence on the memories of the historiographers. In the last part of this study, a possible interpretation of the references made to the Cambodian mission will be given.

5. The "bôṅsāvatān hlvṅ braḥ pāṅ" in *bôṅsāvatān hēṅ$_1$ Padet lāv*, Hanoi, 1926/27, p. 18.

6. *Cf.* the *nidān khun porôm* (Ministry of the Cults, Vientiane, 1967, p. 80) and the "Charte en faveur du Vat Kèo" (L. Finot, "Recherches sur la littérature laotienne", in *BEFEO* 1917, p. 169).

- The following monasteries were no longer to be found only at Luang Prabang, but were more widespread. By the end of the 15th century they spread over a vast area but always on the banks of the Mekong. At Vientiane, the establishment of Vat Pasak (on the mouth of the River Pasak), Vat Sihom and Vat Tai are mentioned. Further downstream, it seems that the present region of Phon Phisay is designated because there is a reference of the Vat Sop, at the mouth of the Huay Luang, otherwise known as Vat Sop Phraya Pak.[7] Between Vientiane and Luang Prabang, we also learn of the construction of a monastery called Vat Sop Sieng Khan at Sieng Khan (Chiang Khan).[8] Moreover we find that the term *sop* is an ambiguous one, it means both mortal remains – in fact the monastery houses the remains of a Lord or King – and mouth of a river, as is found at Phon Phisay and near Chiang Khan.
- Third point. Even if the chronicles are slightly contradictory about the date and the true founders of the monasteries, it seems that the constructions mainly began around the second half of the 15th century, during the reign of Chakkaphat Phaen Phaeo (~1438-1479). Here, it is important to note that he was the first Laotian monarch to have a Buddhist name. The term *chakkaphat* is a modified Thai/Lao version of the Pāli word *cakkavattin* (Skt. *cakravartin*), which means "universal, ideal monarch". At the end of his reign, Chakkhaphat Phaen Phaeo received aid from the kingdom of Lan Na – where Buddhism was flourishing – to repel a Vietnamese invasion, which all sources mention.

Concerning the actual building we can only look to the tradition about the foundation of Vat Visun in 1512 for some details. For the construction of the *vihān* (p. *vihāra*) 70 carpenters and craftsmen were needed. The work took three years and seven months to complete. We are told that the roof was supported by exactly twelve pillars, each measuring 27 meters high (which seems a little exaggerated), with each one coming from a different forest.[9] It appears that the building was made entirely of wood, which was probably the case for all of the ancient monasteries. For several centuries it was the home of the famous Phra Bang statue.

The first monasteries are always presented as having been established by Royalty. The people seem to have been involved only when requisitioned to serve the Three Jewels. The monks of highest standing similarly owed their positions and titles to the Royal will. Among the titles we note with interest *mahā sāmī*, which in the chronicles only appears during the period prior to the half of the 16th century. This title can be found often in the oldest Lan Na inscriptions.[10] It is also mentioned in those of Sukhothai.[11] In Laos it can be found on some of the oldest inscriptions on Buddha statues, dated from 1538 and 1541, the true origin of which is unknown.[12]

7. *Cf.* the *nidān khun porôm* (*op. cit.*, p. 104).

8. *Cf.* the *nidān khun porôm* (*op.cit.*, p. 101), *bôṅsāvatān müaṅ hlvṅ braḥ pāṅ* (manuscript) and *bôṅsāvatān hlvṅ braḥ pāṅ* (*op. cit.*, p. 24).

9. *Cf.* in particular the *Pavat sāṅ$_2$ vat vijun*, for which a manuscript is conserved in Luang Prabang.

10. *Cf.* for instance *Prajum cārük müaṅ bayau*, Bangkok, 1995, pp. 198, 254.

11. *Cf.* *tarrjanī gon$_2$ gāṃ nai cārük sukhoday* (*A Glossarial Index of the Sukhothai Inscriptions*), Bangkok, 1989, p. 151.

12. *Cf.* P.M. Gagneux, *Contribution à la connaissance de la civilisation laotienne d'après l'épigraphie du royaume de Vientiane (XVe-XIXe siècles)*, PhD dissertation, EHESS, 1975, pp. 86-89.

Among the rituals which surround the founding of a monastery is that of pouring sacred water on the ground to call the earth goddess, Nang Thorani, to witness different undertakings. These undertakings are recorded. In a text[13] dealing with the founding of Vat Visun, at the beginning of the 16th century, it is written that

> the names and dimensions of land given will be inscribed on a sheet of gold. The names of servants, so that they cannot leave the service to undertake any other work, will be inscribed on a sheet of silver.

The inscriptions on stone are hardly mentioned in the chronicles. For Luang Prabang, where most of our texts have come from, it is true that few ancient inscriptions have been found.

Religious practices must certainly have experienced important changes under the reign of Phothisarat (1520-1547), who married a princess from Chiang Mai. If first of all we refer to an important ancient Pāli chronicle from Lan Na – the *Jinakālamālī* – we learn that the sovereign of Chiang Mai sent in 1523 to the sovereign of Luang Prabang the Thera Thevamangala with a train of monks and a *Tipiṭaka* in sixty volumes.[14] In 1527, according to the Laotian annals called *phongsāvadān* (*bôṅsāvatān*), Phothisarat made a decree forbidding animism and built Vat Sangkhalok on the same place where the principal among the spirits was worshipped. Here is an important fact: the most ancient stele of Lan Xang – which dates back precisely to 1527 – is that of Vat Sangkhalok.[15] The partly spoiled text has not been published. However we know that it refers to the founding of a monastery, to the purification of the site and to a collection of donations including villages.[16] In an inscription close to Vientiane which was written eight years later, an undertaking led by Phothisarat to preserve order in the monasteries is also referred to.[17]

The inscriptions

Above all we will take into account inscriptions on steles as they are hardly likely to be moved. The inscriptions on Buddha statues also prove the presence of a monastery where the image must have been placed. However it is not certain that the statue originated in the place where it was found. Testimonies of Buddha images being moved from place to place are frequent; sometimes they were transported over long distances. The presence of a dated image in a monastery, unless the image is monumental, therefore cannot be considered as evidence when dating the monastery. The inscriptions on the steles give a better guarantee on this subject, especially those which concern the foundations.

13. "Histoire du pays de Lan-Chang Hom Khao", *Mission Pavie: Études diverses II*, Paris, 1898, p. 59. This is a French translation of a version of the *nidān khun porôm*.

14. *Cf.* G. Cœdès, "Documents sur l'histoire politique et religieuse du Laos occidental", *BEFEO* t. XXV, 1925, p. 139 (for a French translation); N.A. Jayawickrama, *The Sheaf of Garlands of the Epochs of the Conqueror*, London, 1968, p. 183 (for an English translation).

15. Putting aside the stele of Ban Huay Say, which today seems to be preserved in Hanoi, and the stele originating from Chiang Khong, which is part of the Vat Visun collections. They date respectively from 1458 and 1530 but are in fact related to the kingdom of Lan Na both politically and culturally.

16. It is probable that the writers of the *phongsāvadān* were directly inspired by the text of the inscription.

17. Inscription n°2 of Vat Daen Muang, Phon Phisay (*cf. śilā cārük īsān*, p. 236-240; *cārük nai Pradeś daiy,* lem_1 5, p. 327-330).

At present, very little work on Laotian epigraphy exists. Nevertheless those that have been written do cover ancient political and cultural centres. Here we base our study on the extensive inventories made in the province of Vientiane[18] and Northeast Thailand,[19] plus on an inventory which covers the area of Luang Prabang.[20] It appears that there were not many steles at Sieng Khuang. Henri Parmentier, who studied a large number of monasteries in Laos from 1911, did not cite a single one from this region, although he mentioned them elsewhere, especially those from Luang Prabang and Vientiane.[21] No really ancient Lao inscriptions on steles have been mentioned for the south of Laos.[22]

If we base our studies on paleographic facts and on the study of the chronology of the whole of the inscriptions from the T'ai world, it appears certain that Laotian epigraphy – or we could say Lan Xang epigraphy – is directly related to the Lan Na epigraphy which preceded it. Lan Xang inherited two scripts from Lan Na: *tham* (< p. *dhamma*) script which seems most likely to have been derived from Mon script, plus the script known as *fak khām* in Thai, which is close to Sukhothai script and gave us the present day Laotian script. The two types of writing must have arrived in Lan Xang at practically the same time, in the second half of the 15th century. Here we note without doubt a strong link between the diffusion of the scripts and that of the scriptures – that is to say the religion itself. The use of *tham* letters, which were above all for writing Pāli, is enough to prove this link.

The first true Laotian stele (not including certain steles found in Laos but which originated from Lan Na), is the aforementioned Vat Sangkhalok stele at Luang Prabang. The second one is at Vat Daen Muang downstream from Vientiane, which dates back to 1530[23]. Inscriptions on some Buddha images are from a slightly earlier date but it is not certain that the oldest images are actually Lao. At Luang Prabang, two Buddha inscriptions, found at Vat Sangkhalok, date back to 1487 and 1494, and at Vientiane one inscribed Buddha dates back to 1491.

Archeological evidence agrees here with the chronicles showing that Buddhism in Laos developed first at Luang Prabang prior to Vientiane. However Vientiane, where the royal capital was transferred in the mid 16th century, quickly became the flourishing centre of the religion. It is certainly there that the most important monasteries were founded, due to the proximity of the king. Leaving aside a few inscriptions found at Luang Prabang (in the 16th and 17th centuries steles number only nine, plus another tenth downstream on an island on the Mekong river), we will concentrate mainly on the greater number found on the land under Vientiane influence, on both the left bank (in present day Laos) and on the right bank (in present day Thailand).

---

18. *Cf.* P.M. Gagneux, *Contribution... (op.cit.)*.

19. *Cf.* Thawat Punnothok, *śilā cārük īsān*, Ram Khamhaeng University.

20. *Cf. Recueil des inscriptions du Laos*, Service des Monuments Historiques, Vientiane, 1977.

21. *L'art du Laos (op. cit.)*

22. The *Recueil des inscriptions du Laos* (*op. cit.*) only quotes two inscriptions in Lao language for southern Laos, all of them posterior to the 16th century. However it seems that extensive research for this region has not been conducted.

23. Inscription of Vat Daen Muang n°1, Phon Phisay (*cf. śilā cārük īsān*, p. 230-235; *cārük nai Pradeś daiy,* lem$_1$ 5, p. 322-326).

An extremely interesting fact to note here is: when the inventories were written in detail by Pierre-Marie Gagneux for the whole of Vientiane province, and by Thawat Punnothok for all the Northeastern provinces of Thailand - we actually realised that the first Lao inscriptions dating back to the 16th and 17th centuries were from a quite restricted area, close to Vientiane and grouped around precise points. The area concerned covers the present day provinces of Vientiane (Laos), Nongkhai (Thailand) and Udon Thani (Thailand) in the most northern part. The nearby Thai provinces of Loei, Sakon Nakhon and Nakhon Phanom also give us inscriptions but in very small number. In all cases the inscriptions, and therefore the sites they refer to, are situated on the banks of the Mekong or a tributary. In many cases they are even situated on the confluence with the Mekong river. The sites correspond with the localities which the chronicles describe as important political, military and commercial centres from the 14th century. If we use the Mekong as an axis, from upstream to downstream, we have the present day sites of Vientiane (left bank), Si Chiang Mai, Tha Bo and Vieng Khuk (right bank), Say Fong (left bank) and Phon Phisay (right bank). Further back, but still close to the tributaries of the Mekong we also have the sites of Suvanna Khuha (right bank) and Vieng Khaṃ (left bank). For the whole region, related to the 16th and 17th centuries, we have found fifty-nine inscriptions on steles in the inventories. Thirty-eight were initiated by Royalty, the others by lords, locals or monks. The nearby provinces of Loei, Sakon Nakhon and Nakhon Phanom offer us six inscriptions on steles, two of which were of royal origin. All of the inscriptions on steles, with the exception of one which commemorates a treaty of allegiance between Lan Xang and the kingdom of Ayuthya, concern the monasteries; particularly their foundation, donations of land, servants and goods.

If we look exclusively at inscriptions, the first sovereign founder of a monastery or donator of land, seems to have been Visun (1501-1520), cited retrospectively on a stele in the Luang Prabang region that dates back to 1577, which would be fifty years after his death.[24] The second of the steles at Vat Daen Muang gives us further interesting information; dating back to 1535, therefore during the reign of Phothisarat, it refers to an important person in the past named Say Muy, who conceded goods to the monastery, by sacred act of pouring of water on the earth. Then, if we refer to the chronicles, we learn that a certain Say Muy, son of the governor of Pak Huay Luang (precisely where the stele of Vat Daen Muang was found), was governor of Vientiane at the beginning of the reign of Chakkaphat Phaen Phaeo (mid 15th), first king of Lan Xang who we are certain was Buddhist.[25]

If we put aside the inscriptions of the lords and locals, the contents of which are short and simple, it is interesting to note that the royal orders are all stereotyped. They generally begin with the date, written in *cūḷa* era and showing the day and month, contain an introduction which is generally *subham astu* (a persistent Sanskrit formula which means "let happiness reign"), give an explicit royal order (*braḥ rāja ājñā*), and the name of the sovereign making the decree. They go on to mention the monastery, the guarantors and witnesses, both religious and laymen. They relate to accorded goods and they forbid the lords from taking possession of them. They then finish with an

---

24. Inscription of Don Ron (*cf.* L. Finot, "Les inscriptions du Musée de Hanoi" in *BEFEO* XV-2, pp. 36-38).

25. *nidān khun porôm* (*op. cit.*, p. 92), "Histoire du pays de Lan-Chhang Hom Khao" (*op. cit.*, p. 46), Maha Sila Viravong, *bôṅsāvatān lāv*, Vientiane, 1973, p. 47).

imprecatory formula threatening hell and damnation to anyone who does not conform to the royal order. It appears that the style of these orders was fixed under Phothisarat and hardly changed afterwards. In the royal acts of the 19th century, we still find the same style. The initial model was no doubt taken from Lan Na, where numerous inscriptions, similar in their rhetoric, have been found for the whole of the 15th century.[26] Compared to the Lan Na inscriptions, whose contents seem quite diverse, the Lan Xang inscriptions offer less information.

The terminology about the monastery is relatively limited. The word *vat* is often mentioned and it apparently refers to the whole of the monastic complex, as does the term *ārāma* (original meaning in pāli: "park, garden"), which appears several times. There is also reference to a *phihān* (or *vihān*, p. *vihāra*), that undoubtedly indicates the building of worship, but in certain cases could have a wider meaning. On one occasion, in an ancient stele, unfortunately not dated with certainty,[27] there is a reference to a *rong upposot*, an *uposatha* room also known in Thailand as *bot*.[28] This leads us to believe that two distinct buildings of worship existed, as this is the case in Lan Na. In 1601, we can find a reference to a *sim* which is now the sole building of worship for the entire region of Vientiane and many places in North-East Thailand.[29] In fact the question of what kind of buildings are designated by the terms *vihān*, *bot* and *sim* and the respective purpose they served still needs to be clarified. The question of the boundaries or *semā* also seems complex. In the inscriptions the distinction is still made between the *phutthakhet*, which designates the domain of the Buddha and therefore the actual terrain of the monastery, and the *khamakhet* which designates the domain of the village (p. *gāma*) destined to provide for the monks. In one particular case, that of a forest monk, only a *Khamakhet* is mentioned.[30] To our knowledge there is no reference in the first inscriptions to a library or *ho tai*. However the presence of several stūpas is mentioned, the most important of which is That Luang at Vientiane founded (or maybe enlarged) in 1566.

The objective of the inscriptions was most frequently to commemorate the donation of land to the monastery. Logically, the demarcations were clearly noted. The unity of length is mainly the *vā* which measured 1,80 m, provided that the measurement has not changed. It seems that there were two methods of measuring land. The first one consisted of taking a central point – almost always the *phothi* or Ficus tree, the sacred importance of which has already been mentioned (noted in other T'ai inscriptions as well as those from Sukhothai). From the tree the distance to the four cardinal points was fixed. To determine the length and width of the land it was only necessary to join on one side the eastern point to the western point, on the other side to join the southern point to the northern point. The other method of demarcation of the land consisted of using, for example, a river bank as a limit. Then the length of the bank was decided and the width was determined by drawing perpendiculars at each extremity. The surface appears to have been quite variable. The largest seems to be that which is mentioned by an inscription

---

25. *Cf.* in particular *cārük lān₂ nā₂*, bhāk 1, Bangkok, 1991; *Prajum cārük müaṅ bayau*, (*op. cit.*).

27. Inscription n°1 of Vat Phra Ngam Nam Mong, Tha Bo (*cf. śilā cārük īsān*, *op. cit.*, p. 229). The

28. The "*bot*" is reserved for specific practices, such as the bimonthly recital of the *Pāṭimokkha* or the ordination.

29. Inscription of Vat Manikhot, Phon Phisay (*cf. śilā cārük īsān*, *op. cit.* p. 295-299).

30. Inscription n°2 of Vat Phadung Sukh (*cf. śilā cārük īsān*, *op. cit.* p. 267-269).

linked to That Luang.[31] It gives for a first plot of land a length of 1000 *vā* (1800 m) and a width of 500 *vā* (900 m), and for a second one 1000 *vā* for both length and width. In the second stele of Vat Suvanna Khuha forested lands are mentioned, the four sides of which also measured one thousand *vā* (1800 m).[32] According to a chronicle, that is still half the size of a plot of land given to one of the first monasteries of Lan Xang, the Vat Kaeo[33].

In total the number of monasteries constructed in the 16th century was still fairly modest. For Vientiane we are sure about Vat Phya Vat, Vat Kang (at the latter, no stele has been found, but it is cited several times in other inscriptions) and Vat Sieng Yeun, all three situated on the same line on the banks of the Mekong. They are perhaps prior to the arrival of Setthathirat in Vientiane (mid 16th). Five other steles from the 16th century, preserved in Vientiane, are linked to monasteries which unfortunately have not been identified. Perhaps at the site of the present day Vat Phon Savan a monastery known in 1582 under the name of Vat Hmeun Sang could have been found. We have no archeological proof that Vat Ho Phra Keo, the most famous Vientiane monastery, was founded under the reign of Setthathirat (1547-1571/72) as mentioned in a specific chronicle. On the other hand, just outside of the town are the remains of the foundation steles of That Luang – dated 1566 and 1593. It is difficult to study them due to the state of the stone. However it seems certain that future work can develop this point: one of the original names of That Luang was "Phra Maha That Chao Chiang Mai". This establishes a direct link with the capital of Lan Na where Setthathirat governed for some time. Still on the left bank of the Mekong we have two other foundations from the 16th century, that of Vat Vieng Kham on the banks of the Nam Ngeum, a tributary of the Mekong at about fifty kilometres north of Vientiane, plus Vat Kang of Say Fong, opposite Vieng Khuk. On the right bank in present day Thailand we have proof of the existence of a number of monasteries already important in the 16th century. In the current township of Si Chiang Mai – which faced Vientiane – Vat Phan Phao was found. Further downstream at the mouth of the Nam Mong was Vat Nikhot, of which the foundations go back to Phothisarat. The river Nam Mong permitted access to the interior grounds, in a rocky site where forest monks lived. There, a monastery called Vat Suvanna Khuha seemed to have been of great importance as Setthathirat and his direct successors accorded it their blessing. Once again on the Mekong but even further downstream opposite Say Fong was the territory of Vieng Khuk, which was a place of commercial importance. Several seemingly ancient stūpas are dispersed over the area, among them That Bang Phuan, cited in an inscription dating back to 1566.[34] Not far away is Nongkhay, a relatively new town where today several 16th century inscriptions are preserved. They are no doubt from the region of Vieng Khuk. These inscriptions seem to refer to the presence of four monasteries. Continuing down the Mekong, we arrive next at a rivermouth where Pak Huay Luang (now called Phon Phisay) is situated, and for which several ancient sources underline both its political and commercial importance. It is there where the two most ancient steles of the Vientiane region are to be found: the first and second inscriptions of Vat Daen Muang dated 1530 and 1535 (reign of Phothisarat).

see ph. (detail) page 187

31. Inscription of Vat Nong Bone, Vientiane, (*Cf. Contribution ..., op. cit.*, p. 121-126).

32. *Cf. śilā cārük īsān, op. cit.* p. 270-273.

33. "Charte en faveur ...", *op. cit.*, p. 169.

34. Inscription of Vat Sri Muang, Nongkhay (*śilā cārük īsān, op. cit.* p. 261-264).

At Pak Huay Luang there are eight inscriptions from the 16th century referring to three monasteries and a site in the forest inhabited by a monk. In the present region of Thakhek/Nakhon Phanom, much further down the Mekong River, was Lakhon, an important location where one of the most powerful lords of Lan Xang resided. The oldest inscription found in this region (apart from a Buddha of unknown origin dating back to 1503), only dates back to 1614 .[35] It is linked to the undisputedly ancient That Phanom, which was often rebuilt and is difficult to date.

Archaeological research, especially during the last thirty years, has shown that in the Northeast of Thailand and in the plain of Vientiane Buddhist remains existed which were considerably older than the Thai-Laotian period. They belong to two civilizations: the Mon civilization, attested to between the 6th and 10th centuries, after which the Khmer civilization left its important monuments between the 10th century and the beginning of the 13th century. It is strange to find a total hiatus, from the beginning of the 13th century to the end of the 15th century, as all traces of Buddhism come to a halt. Geographically speaking, this break is even more obvious. In fact in the North-East of Thailand the religious sites founded by the Mons were mainly located on the Korat plateau, where Lao inscriptions only appeared from the 18th century. Some minor relics have also been found in Loei province. In the Vientiane plain, according to Pierre-Marie Gagneux, if it is certain that Buddhism was introduced by the Mons from at least the 7th century, no Mon relics of town or urban life, such as those found in Thailand, had been identified by 1977.[36] This remains the case since until now no extensive aerial survey has been made. However certain rocky sites which show visible organization of the land have been identified, as well as an important cultural centre which Pierre-Marie Gagneux places in the Phone Hong-Thurakhom region, close to the Nam Cheng, Nam Ngeum and Nam Lik rivers.[37] We therefore find ourselves at the northern extremities of the Vientiane plain, at a place untouched by the Lao royal inscriptions. Among the typical Mon relics exhumed in this region – many can also be found on the Korat plateau – we can observe anepigraphical (bearing no inscription) sandstone steles, on which an image in low-relief of a tall, fine stūpa is carved. Some steles of this type have been listed at Vientiane, among the cultural materials of the monasteries. It is however highly probable that they were imported. The chronicles also provide numerous examples about the discovery of an ancient image, which was transported to an important centre and worshipped. In at least one case, an anepigraphical stele bearing the Mon image of the stūpa was even reused, a text in Lao language and writing being clumsily carved on it.[38]

Similarly, the Khmer relics are mainly found in the southern area of the North-East of Thailand.[39] At least five centuries passed before Lao people put up steles as foundations for monasteries in this region. A Cambodian settlement in the Vientiane region has long been thought to have existed, due to the discovery of a hospital stele of Jayavarman VII at

35. Inscription n°2 of Vat Phra That Phanom, (*Cf. śilā cārük īsān, op. cit.* p. 304-307).

36. *Cf. Les sites anciens de la plaine de Vientiane (VIIe-XIe siècles) – Rapport préliminaire* (non published), 1977.

37. *Ibid.*

38. Inscription of Vat Sisaket, National Museum of Khon Kaen.

39. The only example, it seems, of monasteries situated above the plateau of Korat is the Prasat Naray Chieng Veng, in the province of Sakon Nakhon.

Say Fong. Several other relics have been found, particularly images of Buddha. The sandstone of which they are often made however, is fine and cannot be found in the region. It is therefore probable that pieces were imported. No true Khmer monument has been found. Certain clues could lead us into thinking that a *prāsāt* (skt. *prāsāda*), later covered over, stood on the present site of That Luang. But as yet, no specialist has come to confirm this hypotheses.[40] These remarks concerning the Khmer relics also apply to Luang Prabang.[41]

To our knowledge, at this point, there is still a total break, both chronological and geographical, between the Buddhist Mon and Khmer civilizations (from the Angkorian empire) and the Lao Buddhist civilization as it developed from the 15th century. In any case it is obvious that the religious forms practiced were very different. The coexistence in Lao monasteries of "new" Buddhist material with pieces coming from several cen-turies before, could partly explain the preservation of the memory (especially in the literary tradition) of "Khrom" culture. The word "Khrom" designates both the Khmer and Mon civilizations. The episode of the introduction of Buddhism under Fa Ngum could be related to this fact.

Concerning strictly the banks and surrounding areas of the Central Mekong (the part which flows through Laos), if we cannot exclude the hypothesis of an ancient presence (and maybe of the persistence) of forms of Buddhism which were linked to the Mon or/and the Khmer from the Angkorian Empire, we can however establish with certitude, at a time between the second half of the 14th century and the second half of the 15th century, the emergence of a new religious phenomenon. This resulted in a political change and territorial expansion of a Lao dynasty. It is also possible that Cambodia (in the 14th century) and Sukhothai may have had a small influence on the development of Lao Buddhism. But, at any rate, it was completely overwhelmed by Lan Na influence, which appears dominant from the 15th and 16th centuries onwards. Lao Buddhism was certainly not a religion for the masses in its early days. For a long time it was subject to the King's wishes and served his purposes. It was around the King that the monasteries – places of elaborate culture – were created. An extremely rich period as far as the founding of monasteries is concerned, was the mid-16th century, taking into account the large number of inscriptions found from this time. Here we must look at the effect of the short reign (around 1545) of Setthathirat in Chiang Mai. The sovereigns of Lan Xang, however, did not have the same means at their disposal as their T'ai counterparts in the South (Sukhothai, Ayutthya) and in the West (Lan Na). It is also necessary to put the spread of Lao Buddhism into context during its most ancient period. In fact everything shows that only certain precise places, often close together, were actually involved.

---

40. In a personal communication, C. Pottier tells us of an aerial photograph of Vientiane showing the form of a *baray*. The presence of artificial lakes close to That Luang had also been suggested by P.M. Gagneux.

41. P. Lévy ("Les traces de l'introduction du bouddhisme à Luang Prabang", *BEFEO* t. XL, 1940, p. 411-424) does not establish a formal link between the Lao art of Luang Prabang and the Khmer style sculptures, dated 11th and 12th centuries, found in this town. The majority of the latter were obviously imported.

BIBLIOGRAPHY

CŒDÈS, George
1925 – "Documents sur l'histoire politique et religieuse du Laos occidental" *BEFEO* XXV, 1-2, Hanoi, p. 1-200.

Collectif
1986 – *cārük nai Pradeś daiy, lem$_1$ 5* (Inscriptions of Thaïland, vol. 5), National Library, Bangkok.

Collectif
1989 – *tarrjanī gon$_2$ gāṃ nai cārük sukhoday* (A Glossarial Index of the Sukhothai Inscriptions), Amarin Publication, Bangkok.

Collectif
1991 – *Prajum śilā cārük, bhāk 7* (Corpus of Thai Inscriptions, Instalment VII), Bangkok.

Collectif
1991 – *cārük lān$_2$ nā$_2$, bhāk 1* (Lanna Inscriptions, Part 1), 2 vol. (texts and plates), Amarin Printing Group, Bangkok.

Collectif
1995 – *Prajum cārük müaṅ bayau* (Inscriptional History of Phayao), Bangkok.

FINOT, Louis
1915 – "Les inscriptions du Musée d'Hanoi", *BEFEO* XV-2, p. 28-36.
1917 – "Recherches sur la littérature laotienne", *BEFEO* XVII-5, p. 1-218.

GAGNEUX, Pierre-Marie
1975 – *Contribution à la connaissance de la civilisation laotienne d'après l'épigraphie du royaume de Vientiane (XVe-XIXe siècles),* thèse de 3e cycle, EHESS, Paris.
1977 – *Recueil des inscriptions du Laos*, Service des Monuments Historiques, Vientiane (ronéotypé).
1977 – *Les sites anciens de la plaine de Vientiane: rapport préliminaire*, Vientiane (ronéotypé).

JAYAWICKRAMA, N.A.
1968 – *The Sheaf of Garlands of the Epochs of the Conqueror*, London.

LÉVI, Paul
1940 – "Les traces de l'introduction du bouddhisme à Luang Prabang", *BEFEO*, t. XL-2, Hanoi, p. 411-424.

LORRILLARD, Michel
1995 – *Les chroniques royales du Laos: essai d'une chronologie des règnes des souverains lao (1316-1887)*, thèse de doctorat de l'EPHE, Paris.
1999 – "Quelques données relatives à l'historiographie lao", *BEFEO* 86, Paris, p. 219-232.

PARMENTIER, Henri
1954 – *L'art du Laos,* PEFEO XXXV, T. 1: texte, T. 2: iconographie, Paris-Hanoi.
1988 – *L'art du Laos,* 2e édition mise à jour par Madeleine Giteau, PEFEO XXXV, T. 1: texte, T. 2: iconographie, Paris.

PAVIE, Auguste
1898 – *Mission Pavie Indochine – Études diverses II: Recherches sur l'histoire du Cambodge, du Laos et du Siam*, Ernest Leroux éd., Paris.

PUNNOTHOK, Thawat,
s. d. – *śilā cārük īsān* (Inscriptions of Isan), Ramkhamhaeng University Bangkok.

Main chronicles used (in Lao language)
– *bônsāvatān hēṅ$_1$ Padet lāv (hlvṅ braḥ pāṅ, vyṅ can, müaṅ bvn lēḥ cāṃPāsak)*, Hanoi, 1926/27.
– *bônsāvatān müaṅ hlvṅ braḥ pāṅ*, National Library, Vientiane, 1969.
– *bônsāvatān müaṅ hlvṅ braḥ pāṅ*, (manuscript, private collection).
– *nidān khun porôm*, Ministry of the Cults, Vientiane, 1967.
– *Pavat sāṅ$_2$ vat vijun* (manuscript, collections of the Museum, Luang Prabang).

YAŚOVARMAN'S BUDDHIST *ĀŚRAMA* IN ANGKOR

Christophe Pottier

Epigraphic and archaeological evidence indicate the presence of Mahāyāna Buddhism in Cambodia as early as the pre-Angkorean period (Cœdès 1908a, 207). It is often considered to have been a religion of secondary importance, following Brahmanism, in particular, Saivism. This was apparently the situation until the reign of Jayavarman VII, at the end of the twelfth century, wherein it was promoted as the "state religion" for a short period. In the thirteenth century a strong Brahmanist reaction against Mahāyāna Buddhism occurred, although only at Angkor, and Brahmanism reasserted itself briefly before the decline of Angkor in the fifteenth century. It appears that a real syncretism characterizes religion in the Angkorean period. Cœdès arrived at these conclusions mainly from data contained in the epigraphic corpus (Cœdès 1964). It is quite difficult, however, to confirm these with architectural or archaeological data since we face two main problems.

The first of these is the fact that the Angkorean civilization, as a perfect example of a *civilisation du vegetal*, left little evidence of buildings other than its temples and its shrines dedicated to sheltering divinities. Indeed, except for very rare particular structures, only shrines were built in lasting materials such as brick and stone (mainly laterite and sandstone). Any other buildings – royal residences, houses or possibly monastic habitations – were erected in wood with tiled roofs. In light of this, speaking of monasteries at Angkor runs the risk of error.

The second problem is that even when epigraphic or iconographic evidence points to a Buddhist dedication for a temple, such kind of building does not differ markedly from a Brahmanic sanctuary. Stūpas appear in Angkor during the late period, if not during the post-Angkorean period, and they remain at any rate very rare, most of them built with re-used Angkorean blocks (Marchal 1954). The case of Bat Chum, for instance, shows clearly that a Buddhist settlement follows exactly the same architectural pattern as others dedicated to Śiva or Viṣṇu. Inaugurated in 953, Bat Chum was a private foundation of Kavīndrārimathana, a Buddhist who was also minister, war chief, and architect of the king Rajendravarman, in the second half of the tenth century (Cœdès 1908c, and Jacques, unpublished translation of Bat Chum inscriptions). We observe here not only that a king worshipping Siva had a Buddhist among his highest-ranking dignitaries, but that he also employed him as his principal architect – and, I believe, as urban planner, as he conceived the most important buildings of the reign. These buildings included the East Mebon in the East Baray, the royal palace (which may have been located south-west of the centre of the capital at that time), and probably the 'temple-mountain' itself, Pre Rup, as well as the first stage of the Sra Srang (Pottier 1999: 183-199). Thereafter, Kavīndrārimathana erected in Bat Chum three very "classical" towers on a common platform, dedicated to a Buddhist triad. Inscriptions (especially K. 267, central tower, st. XXXIII, XXXVI, and XXXVII; Cœdès 1908c: 246-247) carved on doorframes clearly indicate the existence of a residential area for *bhikṣus* (monks) close to the temple, under the shadow of trees. But today nothing remains on the surrounding surface and no excavation has ever been carried out there.

If we can not identify any Buddhist monastery in Angkor during the Angkorean period, we do find evidence of an early tenth-century Buddhist *āśrama* (usually translated as "hermitage") established by Yasovarman, of which the foundation decree and rules have been preserved on stele K. 290 (Cœdès 1908a). This stele was found in the nineteenth century, standing on the terrace in front of the large seated Buddha of Tep Pranam (RCA 01/1908, 04/1912, and 07/1918), a late Buddhist monastery of which only various basement elements and two monumental statues remain, along with a new monastery since the 1980's. However, as Cœdès noted (1932: 267 and n. 1), this stele was not in its original location in Tep Pranam and clearly had been moved there far later than the tenth century.[1]

Stele K. 290 was examined by Cœdès, once in 1908, then again in the 1930's (Cœdès 1932), after research conducted by Goloubew had identified the Phnom Bakheng with the problematic centre of Yaśovarman's capital, the first Yaśodharapura mentioned in several inscriptions (Goloubew 1933).[2] This identification of Yaśodharapura raised the issue of the similarly problematic Yaśodharāśrama, believed at that time to be one single and prestigious creation by Yaśovarman. After a fruitful collaboration in the field with Trouvé, Cœdès proposed to understand Yaśodharasrama as a general term designating any of the *hundred āśramas* erected by that king (Cœdès 1932: 268). More precisely, Cœdès considered the Saugatāśrama, the Buddhist *āśrama* described in stele K. 290, to correspond possibly with 394 Prasat Ong Mong. Also important is the comparison he made with two other very similar steles: K. 209 and K. 701, coming respectively from 720 Prasat Prei and 747 Prasat Kâmnâp. In the same way that K. 290 reproduces a royal decree about the foundation and rules of a Buddhist *āśrama,* K. 209 presents a *Brāhmaṇāśrama* at 720 Prasat Prei, and K. 701 a *Vaiṣṇavāśrama* at 747 Prasat Kâmnâp. Each of these three sites (394 Prasat Ong Mong, 720 Prasat Prei and 747 Prasat Kâmnâp) shows a very singular laterite pavilion erected in order to shelter the stele (Trouvé 1932: 122). These pavilions are similar to the ones which contained other Yasovarman stele located at each angle of the Yaśodharataṭāka, the East Baray, a huge seven kilometre-long water storage reservoir also built by Yaśovarman.

fig. 1 opposite page

1. It is difficult to propose any precise date for Tep Pranam monastery. However, as some parts of the neighbouring Prah Palilay and many sculpted blocks from the northern staircase of the Leper King's terrace (late twelfth to late thirteenth century at least) were re-used in its erection, Tep Pranam monastery can only date from an later period.

2. We can now seriously doubt the urban pattern of the capital proposed by Goloubew, the so-called *Goloupura*, a city inside a large double walled moat 4 by 4 km (Pottier 1999: 164-69). But the identification of Phnom Bakheng as the main shrine of Yaśodharapura seems well established.

1 – *Map of the East Baray and its surroundings, black dots indicate the stele pavilions* (Christophe Pottier)

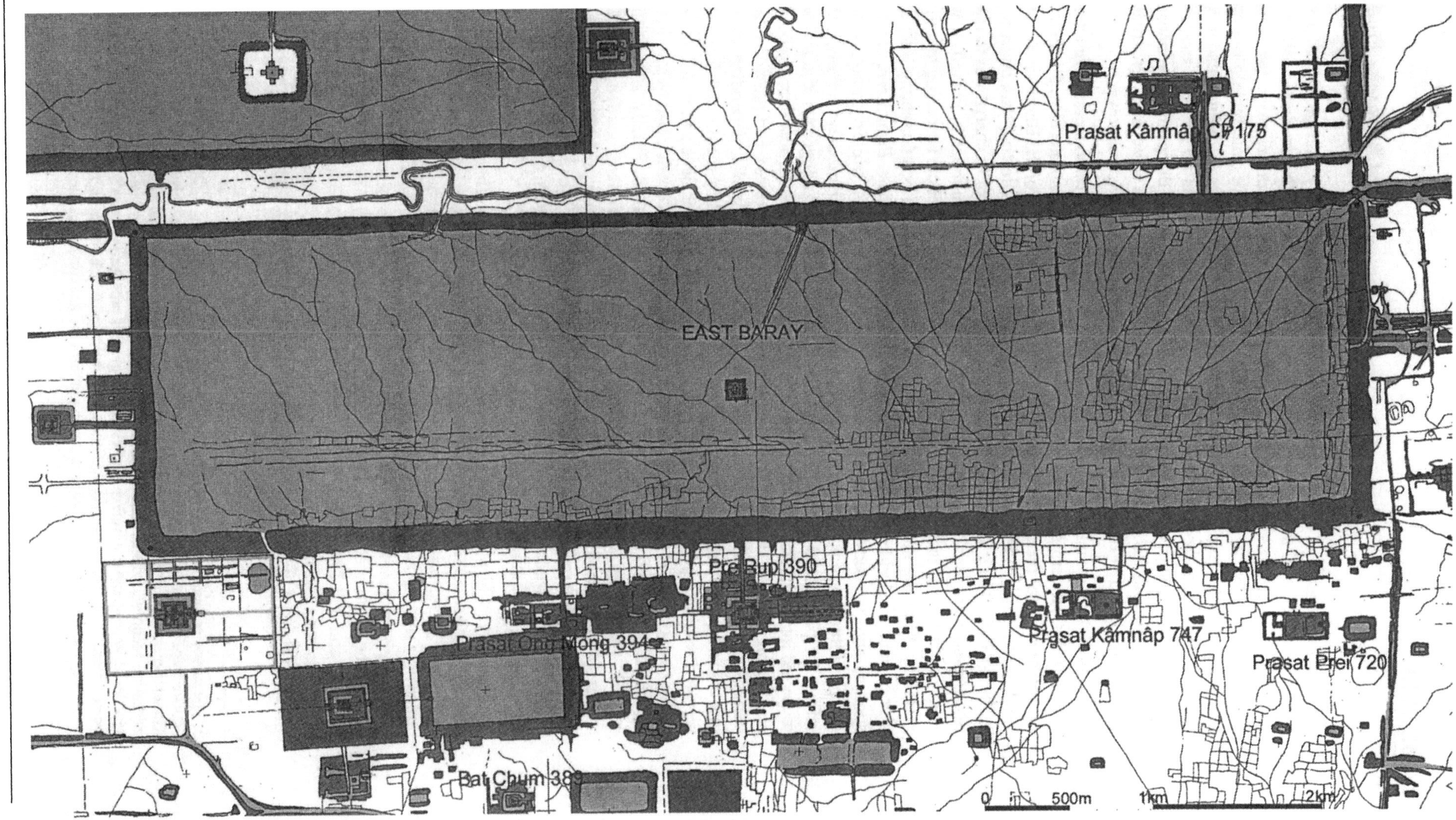

The investigations by Cœdès and Trouvé also indicate a very interesting settlement pattern for the royal *āśramas* of Yaśovarman in his capital. This is characterized by three sites marked by similar pavilions and steles (even though inscriptions distinguish themselves relative to each religious affiliation) nearly, but not exactly, laid out on a *fig. 1 p. 201* line parallel to the south bank of the *baray*. This research, however, did not lead to any tangible precision about the composition of these *āśramas*, as no physical evidence other than the stele pavilions testifies to their existence. Trouvé discovered one unusual linear building in 720 Prasat Prei close to a pavilion, but in spite of a remarkable architectural study (Trouvé 1932: 113-122), its function remains unknown.

This lack of remains is especially frustrating because the three steles give exceptional details concerning the operation of each *āśrama*, their common rules, procedures, as well as some of their differences. Focusing today on the rules of the Buddhist *āśrama*, I will summarize, following Cœdès' translation, some of the interesting data taken from K. 290 (Cœdès 1932: 253-261). The responsibility of the superior in charge was to make his *āśrama* grow wealthy and to protect its personnel as its number increased. It was requisite to provide temporary hospitality to various kinds of people according to a strict hierarchy, from the king and his queens down to the common people, young, old, and sick or lonely individuals, and even to animals such as black cows. Princesses, old king spouses, and "women of good" were welcome (except in the cells) while common women and prostitutes were not, "even if they ask for hospitality". The *āśrama* was an inviolable refuge for persecuted innocents, and animal life – except for dangerous kinds – was respected inside the *āśrama* and around the Yaśodharataṭāka. The *āśrama* accommodated any hermit or monk devoted to studies (but rejected ignorant ones), and provided daily various quantities of food, betel leaves, firewood, and toothpicks, depending on the individual's age. Some extra food for special ceremonies was duly mentioned. Residents received writing equipment once every four months, and a couch once a year. All *āśrama* properties (objects in gold, silver, or other materials, and alms bowls), had to stay in the *āśrama* except when monks went out temporarily to collect alms. Finally, at least fifty servants (including scribes, keepers for the "royal cell", librarians, gardeners, cooks, etc.) were in attached to the facility, plus ten more for the "main professor" and twenty (one female, nine males, and ten cultivators) for the superior. It can be seen from these details that the *āśramas*, far from being simple hermitages, were in fact monastic schools with a significant number of resident monks and lay people.

Recently, while conducting research on territorial planning in the Angkorean period,[3] I investigated the area south of the East Baray and those sites already surveyed by Trouvé. To reiterate briefly, nothing really new comes to light from ground surveys, but remote sensing has provided useful information (Pottier 1999: 176-182). An analysis of aerial photos reveals that the three *āśrama* sites known by their steles and pavilions *fig. 2 opposite page* present the same specific and unique spatial environment. 720 Prasat Prei, 747 Prasat Kâmnâp and 394 Prasat Ong Mong are each located inside a small dyke delimiting a rectangular area, 375 metres east-west by 150 metres north-south. These dykes, 15 kilometres wide, are flanked by two depressions of equal size. In this rectangular compound, some

3. The survey covered a region of 600 square kilometres, and through the production of a new archaeological map, I proposed some modifications to the presently accepted history and development of Khmer settlements in this area (Pottier 1999). This map has been realized by combining existing documentation accumulated since the beginning of the century, systematic remote sensing analysis from a new aerial photographic coverage and extensive ground prospecting over five years. This new map locates more than 530 archaeological sites, two-thirds of which are new. It also adds new data on previously known sites, especially concerning environmental conditions they generated.

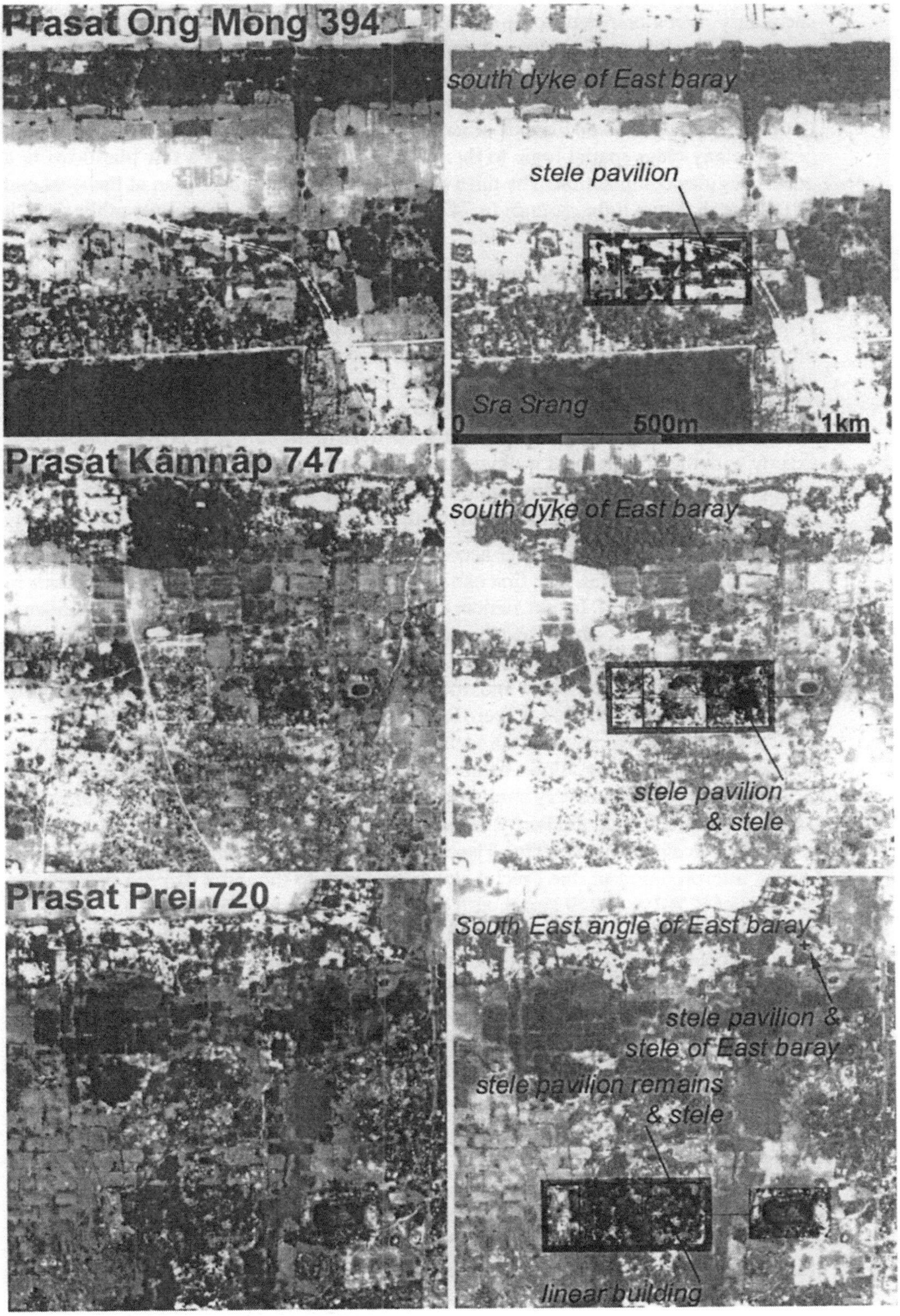

2 – *Details and localisation of* āśrama *enclosure and architectural remains: Prasat 394 Ong Mong, 747 Kâmnap and 720 Prei* (Aerial photo Finmap, 1992)

secondary dykes oriented north-south divide the space into three parts: two square ones and a smaller, rectangular one on the west side. The first square part, on the east, is a light platform where, located in the centre in near-identical fashion in all three instances, are the laterite stele pavilions (and the linear building in 720 Prasat Prei). Ground checking showed various other light topographic anthropic elements without, however, any clear spatial logic to them. The middle square has a few platforms in a quite irregular composition. The third part, on the double-square plan at the west end of the site, has two light mounds in 747 Prasat Kâmnâp only; in the two other sites, it consists only of low lying rice fields.

fig. 2 p. 203

The configurations of the surroundings differ slightly from one site to another: the eastern axial walkway of 720 Prasat Prei leads after 140 m to the axis of a large pond (Trapping Tap Bagna CP 391, 110 by 55 m), while that of 747 Prasat Prei joins after 40 m the south dyke of a smaller pond (60 by 30 m), and no pond is located east of 394 Prasat Ong Mong. At 747 Prasat Kâmnâp and 394 Prasat Ong Mong (more hypothetically at 720 Prasat Prei), a flat dyke 10 m wide and running north-south links the north-eastem corner of the rectangular enclosure to the south dyke of the *baray*. This dyke corresponds exactly with the processional walkway used during the special rituals mentioned by inscriptions, and involved offerings on the banks of thę *baray* (Cœdès 1932: 255). These hermitages were then related physically to the *baray*.

Finally, to conclude this brief account, it is noteworthy that environmental observations raise a few issues. The first concerns the complex chronology of settlements in the Angkor region itself. In fact, remote sensing investigation shows us a similar *āśrama*-type site located just north of Yaśodharataṭāka, near its northeastern comer. Surprisingly, this site is also called Prasat Kâmnâp (CP175) and Trouvé, who discovered and briefly cleared it more than sixty years ago, found a linear building basement quite similar in shape to the one in 720 Prasat Prei (RCC 06/1932). He did not find any remains of pavilions or steles and gave up the idea that it could have been a hermitage site. Now however, remote sensing allows us to confirm his initial hunch: the physical layout of CP 175 Prasat Kâmnâp is very similar to that of 747 Prasat Kâmnâp. We then have four *āśramas* located around the *baray*. Cœdès maintained that only three *āśramas* existed, one each dedicated to the Buddha, Viṣṇu, and Śiva. However, Jacques recently corrected Cœdès interpretation of one crucial stanza common to the three *āśrama* inscriptions (st. XCIV of K 701 & K 279 and st. XCII of K 290). Understood by Cœdès as "the chiefs of the four *orders* must unite to protect Yaśodharataṭāka" (1932: 260), Jacques proposed instead to read "the chiefs of the four *āśramas* must unite to protect the Yaśodharataṭāka" (1989: 149). Thus, the problematic term *Brāhmaṇāśrama*, which Cœdès – with many reservations – suggested was the name for a Saivite establishment (1932:262-263), could be reinterpreted as a specific reference to Brahmā. Then, one could surmise that there was a total of four *āśramas*, dedicated to Buddha, Viṣṇu, Brahmā, and Śiva, the last one being probably the CP 175 Prasat Kâmnâp.

fig. 1 p. 201

fig. 3 opposite page

The configuration of these four sites is somewhat perplexing, but here again remote sensing offers an interpretation: a fifth site could match the *āśrama* pattern, at least in its general form, dimensions, and characteristics. Aerial photos show traces of such a rectangular compound just east of Pre Rup, at a place where a strict spatial and geometric logic would have located the "missing" *āśrama*. Other convergent evidence leads us to assume that the temple of Pre Rup, built sixty years after Yaśovarman's *āśrama*, was established close to the location of the ancient Siva *āśrama*, but not exactly on the spot as Jacques suggested (1990: 56, 75). This *āśrama* then would have

fig. 1 p. 201 and fig. 3 opposite page

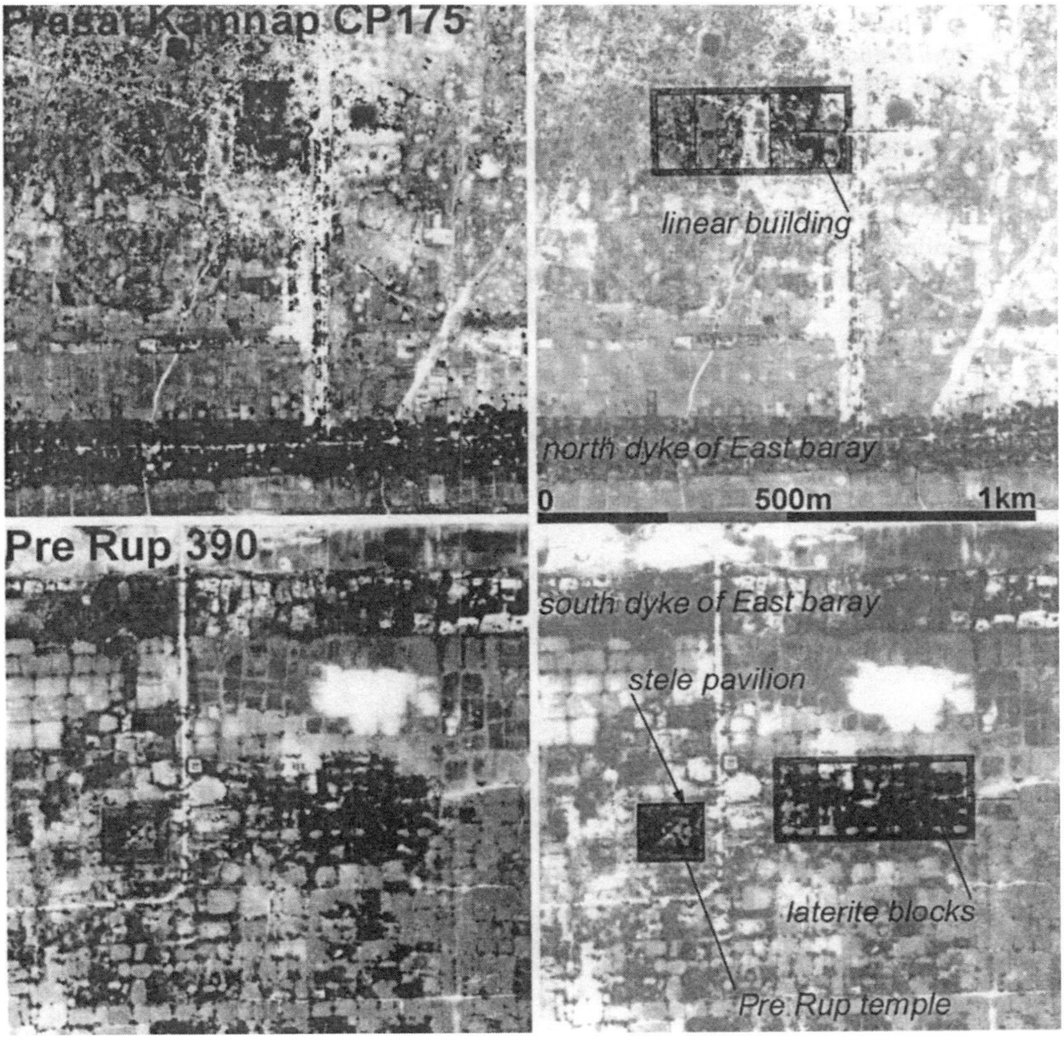

3 – *Details and localisation of* āśrama *enclosure and architectural remains: Prasat CP175 Kâmnâp and east of 390 Pre Rup* (Aerial photo Finmap 1992)

been moved away[4] to its present location – to the northeast – at CP175 Prasat Kâmnâp. Finally, we recognize for Yasovarman's time a clearly organized settlement of four *āśramas* south of the associated *baray*. In the middle was the Siva *āśrama* (the most important despite a strong syncretism?), followed to the east by those dedicated to Viṣṇu and Brahma, and then to the west, the Buddhist *āśrama*.

The second issue is that of the potential for further archaeological research among these five sites, wherein we have a unique opportunity to compare the information drawn from the inscriptions with evidence from archaeological excavations.

4. This hypothesis could for instance explain the problematic presence of the stele pavilion located at the north-east corner of the first enclosure of the Pre Rup temple.

Finally, in the area I studied, (from Angkor and its *baray* to the Tonle Sap, and from Rolûos to Puok), no other similar environmental configuration has been noticed, while Yaśovarman is known to have founded a *hundred āśramas* in his large empire (Cœdès 1964: 212). Twelve of these have been identified by the presence of an identical (except for the name of the main divinity) digraphic inscription, found at each site. In light of this, it could prove interesting to investigate by means of remote sensing whether the areas where such inscriptions were found also feature a similar layout pattern. If this were the case, it could support the idea of the appearance of a strong royal "ready-made *āśrama* kit", designed to be sent around the empire as were, some 300 years later, the famous "hospital chapels" and *dharmaśālās* of Jayavarman VII.

BIBLIOGRAPHIC REFERENCES

Abbreviations

AA Arts Asiatiques, Paris.
BEFEO Bulletin de l'École française d'Extrême-Orient, Paris.
EFEO École française d'Extrême-Orient, Paris.
JA Journal Asiatique, Paris.
RCA Rapports de la Conservation d'Angkor, unpublished, EFEO Paris archives.
RCC Rapports de la Conservation du Cambodge et de la Cochinchine, unpublished, National Museum of Phnom Penh archives.

CŒDÈS, George
1908 a – "La stèle de Tép Pranam", *JA 10 (11)*, Paris, p. 203-225.
1908 b – "La stèle de Tép Pranam, (Note additionnelle)", *JA 10 (12)*, Paris, p. 253-254.
1908 c – "Les inscriptions de Bat Cum (Cambodge)", *JA 10 (12)*, Paris, p. 213- 254.
1932 – "À la recherche du Yaśodharāśrama", *BEFEO 32 (1)*, Hanoi, p. 71-112 (Rééd. 1989, in *Articles sur le Pays Khmer*, vol. 1, Réimpressions de l'EFEO, textes réunis par Claude Jacques, Paris, p. 240-268).
1964 – *Les états hindouisés d'Indochine et d'Indonésie*, Histoire du Monde, vol. VII, Paris (Rééd. 1989, Ed. de Brocard, Paris, 494 p.).

JACQUES, Claude
1989 – "Epigraphie de l'Inde et de l'Asie du Sud-Est. Rapport 1987-1988", *Livret de la IVe Section de l'Ecole pratique des Hautes Etudes, 5*, Paris, p. 149-150.
1990 – *Angkor*, Bordas, Paris, 200 p.

GOLOUBEW, Victor
1933 – "Le Phnom Bakhèn et la ville de Yaçovarman", *BEFEO 33 (1)*, Hanoi, p. 319-344.

MARCHAL, Henri
1954 – "Note sur la forme du stupa au Cambodge", *BEFEO 44*, Paris, p. 581-590.

POTTIER, Christophe
1999 – *Carte archéologique de la région d'Angkor – Zone Sud*, Université de Paris III, Thèse de Doctorat dactylographiée, Paris, 3 vol., 382 p., 41 cartes.

TROUVÉ, Georges
1932 – "Étude sur le Prei Prasat, le Prasat Komnap et l'édicule qui abritait la cinquième stèle inscrite du Baray Oriental", *BEFEO 32 (1)*, Hanoi, p. 113-126.

ABOUT KHMER MONASTERIES: *Organization and Symbolism*

Olivier de Bernon

How far is it possible to say anything general about Khmer Buddhist monasteries[1] since, although Buddhist influence has reached the lands inhabited by the Khmers most probably around the 3rd century AD, no monastic buildings which predate the 19th century can be seen in Cambodia?

First, it must be stressed that, in Khmer dominated areas, we know nothing precise about Buddhist monastic life, even about school affiliation, before the 14th, or even the 15th century. For lack of written documents, all that we may assume about the early history of Buddhism in Cambodia is derived from archaeology, which gives no precise clue to discern clearly how much this early history owes to ancient Hīnayāna sects – the Mahāsaṅghika and the Mūlasarvāstivāda – (3rd to 7th centuries), to early forms of Mahāyana (mid. 6th century to 10th century), to Môn Theravādin influences (7th to 10th centuries), or to Indonesian Vajrayāna or Cham Vajrayāna (mid. 8th century to 13th century). And if one knows more about Singhalese Theravādin influence from the 14th century onward, it is essentially derived from Siamese sources, that is through the ideological prism of Siamese Theravādin tradition, developed under the firm political control of the State upon the religious administration during the last period of Ayutthaya and since the foundation of Bangkok (16th to 19th centuries).

1. The word "monastery", as employed here, is conventional. It is used without any ideological implication, as if opposed to "abbey", "convent", "priory", or even "pagoda", or any other word. It only renders, in a neutral way, the word *vatt* used in Khmer, or the more precise term *vatt ārām,* the proper meaning of which could be "a place to perform rules in order to attain exaltation."

If we begin the investigation backward, from present day to earlier times, the picture is again obscured by the trauma endured by the whole of Khmer society from 1970 to 1979, and even during the following years, but also by the lack of documentation concerning the history of Cambodia in pre-colonial times. Due to four centuries of protracted civil war, the subsequent weakness of political power during these centuries, the central power of this kingdom, if there was any, seems to have never been able, or willing, to set up a strong religious organization, installed in durable and dignified buildings; at least, there is no record of a powerful king, resolute to implement a strong religious reformation, as happened in neighbouring countries.

Even the French colonial administration, for both altruistic and political purposes, interfered in the development of Buddhist practices in Cambodia, by promoting scholarly education for the monks, by favouring the printing of religious books, by setting safety regulations for the construction of public buildings, including the sanctuaries (*vihāras*), etc. The effects of this influence were, nevertheless, mostly visible around the capital city of Phnom Penh and in some provincial capitals, and, even there, it did not extend to all the monasteries.

With all these restrictions, it is still possible to point out consistent and characteristic features in traditional Khmer monasteries, at least since Theravāda definitely dominated Cambodia after the 14th century. The most important of these features was the double function of the sanctuary (*vihāra*), devoted both to the gathering of the lay community for hearing sermons and to the restrictive gathering of the chapter of monks for their constitutive rituals (*saṅghakamma*) such as the lower and the higher ordinations (*pabbajjā* and *upasampadā*). In Thailand, these two functions have normally a dedicated building: the rather large *vihāra*, for the gatherings of the whole Buddhist community (monks and lay people) and the smaller *uposatha*[2] or *bot* – surrounded by height boundary markers (*sīmā*) – for the chapter of monks. Indeed, the stone boundary markers (*sīmā*) found around the many "Buddhist terraces" in Angkor Thom, supposed to date back to the 13th century, are always implanted around the principal and unique ruined structures of the old *vihāras*. Since then, all the inscriptions relating the foundation of a new monastery would refer to the laying of such *sīmā* around a *vihāra*. It might then be possible, considering the consistency and the ancientness of this peculiar feature, to extend this consistency and this ancientness to other observed features of modern Khmer monasteries, and to assume both their historic and general accuracy for all traditional monasteries. Such a traditional Khmer monastery would then be:

a) an inhabited place;
b) a carefully delimited and oriented space;
c) a set of specific buildings.

Finally, it seems that these basic elements have given birth, in Cambodia, to different sophisticated layers of symbolic interpretation, not necessarily inter-related, which turn the monastery into a symbolic space, and a representation of the universe.

---

2. The technical word *uposatha* would not occur in Khmer to designate a type of building (*uposatha* for *uposathāgāra*), but only with its original meaning of an "obligation performed by the monastic community" (*uposathakamma*). The only, generally unnoticed, exception would be the official name of the chapel of the Royal Palace in Phnom Penh, *uposuth braḥ kèv mārakaṭṭh*, usually call by the Khmers *vatt braḥ kèv marakaṭṭh*, and by the foreigners "Silver Pagoda", after its pavement made of silver tiles. Actually, the royal chapel is not, properly speaking, a monastery, being inhabited by no monk, and its construction has been deeply influenced by Thai conceptions recently imported to Cambodia by kings educated in Bangkok.

The monastery considered as an inhabited place

Basically, a monastery would exist as soon as a "fully ordained monk" (*bhikkhu*) has set up his regular quarters in a durable abode. Even before the completion of the *vihāra* – the hall built to house the statue of the Buddha – a monastery, in a primitive and temporary form, can be articulated around the lodgings of a monk (*kuṭi*).

The usual inhabitants of Khmer monasteries are, the "abbot" (*adhikār*), the fully ordained *bhikkhus*, aged at least 21 years, who follow the 227 obligations of the monastic rule (*pāṭimokkha*), the novices (*sāmaṇera*), of which the youngest may be less than twelve years old, and who follow only the "ten rules" (*dasasīla*), and the "students of the monk" (*kūn siss lok*) who are not ordained in any way, who do not wear the robe and have no other obligation than to obey the elders. In addition, the monastery can house few devout laymen (*tā jī*), mostly old men leaving a recluse life in their own small cell (*tūp*), usually wearing the white shirt (*puos sa*) of people practising meditation.

Most of the time, especially in Phnom Penh, a monastery can also be a shelter for penniless male students with no obligation regarding the monastery and its religious community, provided they are permitted to stay by the abbot, provided they behave decently, and provided they do not allow women in their rooms.

There are no ordained women in Cambodia, and the many old devout ladies (*ṭūn jī*), bearing white robes and shaving their hair, are just ordinary laywomen, and their cells should not, normally, be built in the precinct of the monastery, though it often is.

In ancient Cambodia, both Hindu temples and Buddhist monasteries, possessed lands and slaves, the *bal braḥ* (i.e. strength [to serve] the Lord), to cultivate these lands. This feature lasted, in some respects, as late as the 19th century, and disappeared with the abolition of slavery by the Protectorate. Nowadays, Buddhist institutions live only with the occasional or regular donations (*pragen*) presented by lay people to the monks. The use to be made of large donations would be decided by the "lay members of council of the monastery" (*gaṇăkammakār vatt*). Besides, both the *sāmaṇeras* and the *bhikkhus*, except for the abbot himself, would go "alms begging" (*piṇḍapāta*) every morning to collect their food.

The monastery as a delimited and oriented place

Even though the some 3800 monasteries of Cambodia may be located in quite different surroundings, even if they may be the result of the recent foundation by a king, a prince, a wealthy person or a pious community, or even if they may occupy the previous foundation of an old sanctuary not necessarily devoted to the Buddhist cult, they all have in common their structure of a space delimited by two sets of enclosures, one containing the other.

The larger enclosure (*mahāsīmā*) is the delimitation inside of which all the different buildings of the monastery are constructed, each of them generally oriented East-West.

It generally forms a quadrangular space, depending on the configuration of the land, often enclosed with a wall or a fence (*kampeṅ vatt*), or even delimited by pathways or roads. It could as well be only virtual and marked by a few poles (*kol*). This enclosure is open to the outside world with four monumental gates (*kloṅ dvār*), sometimes only *ph. 1 page 213* formally, one at each of the four cardinal points.

Though it has sometimes the function of a protective fence for the monastery, the great enclosure is, before all, devised to mark the limits inside of which the monks and the novices must stay, except for their morning alms begging, during the three lunar months of the yearly "retreat of the rainy season" (*vassa*). It marks also the limits inside of which they are allowed, all year round, to be at ease in not wearing or carrying folded on the shoulder their "upper mantle" (*saṅghāṭī*).

ph. 2 opposite page

The smaller enclosure (*badhasīmā*) is marked by eight stone-markers (*sīmā*), each formed with a "root" (*ṛ sīmā*), i.e. a big round stone buried in the soil, under a "leaf" (*slik sīmā*), formed with a vertical stone slab, often ornate with sculpted motifs. These eight markers are placed around the *vihāra*, respectively in each the four cardinal and intermediate directions. A ninth root, called the great marker (*sīmā kil*), is buried in the floor, inside of the *vihāra*, in front of the main Buddha statue, marking, theoretically, the direction of both the nadir and the zenith. The festival during which the nine roots are buried is of the greatest importance for the community: it marks the day after which the monastery has its own autonomy; only then is the *vihāra* fit to house the most important ceremonies in the regular life of both *sāmaṇera* and *bhikkhus*, principally the performing of their ordination, which would be considered to be invalid if the *sīmā* were improperly laid.

In some traditional monasteries, nowadays very rarely, the ritualistic importance of the *sīmā* is stressed by its association with a complex set of notions and sacred figures, like, for instance, a vowel, itself being a symbol for a denoted "precept" (*sila*), a special direction, the name of a buddha, and the name of a "great auditor [of the Buddha]" (*aggasavāka*), etc., forming all together a closed and complex *maṇḍala*.

ph. 3 opposite page

Following the old Khmer tradition, each day, before a monk or layperson would enter a *vihāra*, holding nine sticks of incense, he would first bow near the *sīmā* of the east and plant one incense stick at its base. Pronouncing the vowel "A", he would pay respect to the *aggasavāka* Aññāttakoṇḍaña Thera. He would then perform the same act toward the *sīmā* of the south-east, paying respect to Mahākassapa Thera, intoning the vowel "Ā". Toward the south he would honor Sāriputta Thera with the vowel "Ī"; to the south-west Mahā Upāli Thera, pronouncing "I" , to the west Mahā Ānanda Thera with "U", to the north-west Gavampati Thera with "Ū" , to the north Moggalāna Thera with "E", and finally to the northeast, to honor Rāhula Thera with "Ao". Only then he would enter the *vihāra* and prostrate himself near the emplacement of the great *sīmā*, to pronounce the sacred formula (*gāthā*) "ARAHAṂ".[3]

Ū North-West *(bāyabya)* Medhaṅkara GAVAMPATI	E North *(Uttara)* Samaṇagotama MOGALLĀNA	Ao North-East *(īśāna)* Saraṇaṅkara RĀHULAKUMĀRA
U West *(pascima)* Sikhī ĀNANDA		A East *(pūṛba)* Padumuttara AÑÑAṬṬAKOṆḌAÑÑA
I South-West *(niratī)* Sumaṅgala UPĀLI	Ī South *(daksiṇa)* Kassapa SĀRĪPUTTA	Ā South-East *(āgneya)* Revata KASSAPA

3. Following different texts, the nature and the order of the eight vowels may be different.

1 – *Vatt Saravaṇṇ, Phnom Penh*
Eastern gate
(photo O. de Bernon)

2 – *Vatt Kien Kléang, Phnom Penh*
*Stone-marker (*sīmā*)*
sheltered under a pavilion
(photo O. de Bernon)

3 – *Vatt Saravaṇṇ, Phnom Penh*
Vihāra *north-west corner,*
sīmā *in a niche*
(photo O. de Bernon)

According to a Khmer metaphor, the sanctuary (*vihāra*) is taken as the "boat of crystal" (*saṃbau kèv*). The whole space of the monastery is the "great ocean" (*mahā samudr*). The statue of the Buddha is the "captain" (*thau kè*). The roots of the stone bound markers (*ṛ sīmā*) are the "raw blocks" (*jöṅ cev*), the leaves of the stone bound markers (*slik sīmā*) are the "oars", and the eight *aggasavāka* are the "oarsmen". Altogether, the crystal boat and the freight on board are the "meritorious deeds" (*kusala*) and the "fruits of these meritorious deeds" (*phala*) with the merits (*puṇya*) acquired by all the living creatures from the beginning of the five thousand years of the age of [the teaching of] this Buddha, up to the time when the crystal boat having unfolded its "sails" (*ktoṅ*), goes through the ocean and reaches the "The immortal city of the Saint Nibbāna" (*nagar amṛiddh purī srī mahā nibvān*).

The monastery as a collection of specific buildings

There is no "treatise" (*kpuon*) specifically for the construction of a monastery and, even if the variety of forms and styles is wide, enriched by the wildest fantasy or attached to the most repetitive stereotype, people who build the monastery have the deep consciousness to follow traditional models, to "do as it has always been done" (*dhvö tām ge*). Being a collective deed, such a construction of a monastery is, in the course of time, generally conducted without a master plan; only the members of the council of the *gaṇăkammakār vatt*, who, more than the monks, have a word regarding the material life of the monastery, agree together to follow unwritten rules, supposed to be known by all, for the construction or the transformation of the different parts of the monastery.

4 – *Vatt Saravaṇṇ, Phnom Penh*
The vihāra *from south-west* (photo O. de Bernon)

5 – *Vatt Kien Kléang, Phnom Penh*
The vihāra *eastern gable,*
double roof and jahvās
(photo O. de Bernon)

6 – *Vatt Kien Kléang, Phnom Penh*
*From north-east: the flag poles (*taṅ daṅ'*),*
the eastern gate and the north-east sīmā
under a pavilion
(photo O. de Bernon)

The largest building of any monastery is the sanctuary (*vihāra*) in which is housed the main statue of the Lord Buddha (*braḥ jī*). Traditionally built in wood, or even in palm leaves during the periods of misfortune, since the end of the 19th century the *vihāra* has, most often, been built in masonry, and nowadays in concrete, projecting the double slope of its roof, prolonged by the elegantly arched horns of the *jahvā*, always higher toward the sky. Their characteristic silhouette, itself dominated by the "sacred geese" (*haṅsa*) adorning the top of the two flag poles (*ṭaṅ daṅ'*) planted in front of the eastern façade,[4] signals the presence of a village.

ph. 4 opposite page

ph. 5 and 6 above

---

4. There is only one such flag pole in the khmer monasteries of South Vietnam (Kampuchea Krom) and it is not crowned by a *haṅsa*.

The supremacy of the "Sacred Law [taught by the Lord Buddha]" (*dharma*) over the world is symbolized by the position of eight small altars of the divinities (*rān devatā*), oriented inwards, toward the *braḥ jī*, often simple poles planted in the soil outside of the *vihāra* in all the cardinal direction, sometimes elaborate pavilions built in masonry.

The real core of the monastery is the "hall of merits" (*sālā puṇya*). It is the place where the pious lay people recite the formulas to answer the chanting of the monks during the daily rituals of offerings (*puṇy pragen*), or during the rituals for requesting the precepts (*puṇy suṃ sil*) performed during the days of the full or of the new moon. In most of the monasteries, this hall is also used as a dining hall for the monks. Spacious and wide open, its roof is always lower than the roof of the *vihāra*; in a typically Khmer symbolic metaphor, the *sālā puṇya* would be called "the father" (*pitā*) in the monastery, when the *vihāra* would be considered as the "mother" (*mātā*):

> In the sanctuary *(vihāra)*, men should sit on the right section (the southern section) of the floor. The reason why is that when "the children of the spirit" *(cittakumārā cittakumārī)* come to "take birth" *(paṭisandhi)* as a baby boy, they enter through the right nostril of his mother; it means, otherwise, that the virtues *(guṇa)* of his father are placed in the right part of the body.[5]
>
> Women should sit on the left section (the northern section) of the floor. The reason why is that when "the children of the spirit" *(cittakumārā cittakumārī)* come to "take birth" *(paṭisandhi)* as a baby girl, they enter through the left nostril of her mother, or it means otherwise that the virtues *(guṇa)* of her mother are placed in the left part of the body.
>
> The reason why, when accomplishing a ritual ambulation (*pradakṣina*), one walks three times first around the "hall of merits" *(sāla puṇy)*, [i.e. the "father"] is, following what the elders say, because when the children of the spirit *(cittakumārā cittakumārī)* come down to become a human being, they first reach the father and move him to unite with the mother. Only afterwards do they enter the mother's womb. That is why making a *pradakṣina*, one should enter the *vihāra* [i.e. the "mother"] only afterward.
>
> The central stone marker *(sīmā kil)* is considered as the mother's navel; the statue of the Buddha on his throne is considered as the "embryo" *(dārak)* in his mother's womb staying in the supramundane "plane of existence" *(ṭhān lokuttara)*.[6]

The *vihāra*, the *sālā puṇya*, and the lodging of the Abbot (*kuṭi dhaṃ*), together with the sharp pyramids of the *cetya*, devised to deposit the ashes of the deceased, are often the only buildings in an ordinary monastery. Wealthier, larger or more prestigious monasteries would also possess a dining hall (*sālā chān'*) separated from the *sālā puṇya*,

---

5. On this topic see F. Bizot (1976).

6. Testimony received in Vatt Kien Khléang *(kīen ghlāṃṅ)*, in the district of Russey Kéo *(ṛssī kèv)* of Phnom Penh:

> *nau knuṅ braḥ vihār pö manuss prus trūv aṅguy phnèk khāṅ stāṃ (khāṅ tpūṅ) gī pān năy thā kāl cittakumārā cittakumārī mak cāp' paṭisandhi manus prus gī cūl mak tām randh cramuḥ khāṅ stāṃ rapas' mātā . ṛ năy muoy dīet thā guṁ pitā ṭhit nau phnèk khāṅ stāṃ . pö manuss srī trūv aṅguy phnèk khāṅ chveṅ (khāṅ jöṅ) gī pān ăy thā kāl cittakumārā cittakumārī mak cāp' paṭisandhi manus srī gī cūl mak tām randh cramuḥ khāṅ chveṅ rapas' mātā . ṛ năy muoy dīet thā guṁ pitā ṭhit nau phnèk khāṅ chveṅ . hetu ṭèl hè pradaksiṇ 3 juṃ sālā puṇy jā mun noḥ broḥ bāky purāṁ thā nau bel ṭèl cittakumārā cittakumārī mak cūl cāp' paṭisandhi mun ṭampūṅ pān cūl dau pitā jā mun döp ṭās' pitā Aoy raḷk ruoc höy pitā ka ruom prabaiṇī niṅ mātā döp cittakumārā cittakumārī cūl nau cap' paṭisandhi nau phdai mātā jā kroy. ṭūcneḥ höy döp mān bidhī ṭaṅhè cūl knuṅ braḥ vihār jā kroy ṭūcneḥ . sīmā kil duk jā phjit rapas' mātā braḥ buddh rūp gaṅ' nau lö pallăṅg ṭūc jā dārak knuṅ phdai mātā ṭèl nau knuṅ ṭhan lokuttara.*

few or many lodgings of the [ordinary] monks (*kuṭi tũc*), a repository for the sacred scriptures (*ho trai*), more rarely a specific hall for the learning or the copying of the sacred texts (*sālā dhammasabhā*), and a pavilion for cremations (*sālā pūjā sab*). Only in modern monasteries would one find a library (*paṇṇalăy*) instead of a *ho trai*, or a pāli school (*sālā pālī*) instead of a *sālā dhammasabhā*. Finally, in quite a great number of monasteries built alongside a river or on the shores of the Great Lake, one can find a long boat shed (*roṅ dũk*) in which a pirogue lays upside down on blocks, waiting till the next race organized for the water festival.

The building of a monastery is a pious deed, supposed to be part of the general eschatological economy of accumulation of merits (*puṇya*). These merits, earned by each member of the community, following his rank as a royal protector, a patron, a worker or a simple follower, are personally fixed upon himself during the "rituals of completion" (*puṇy chlaṅ*) organized after every important step of the general undertaking.

If there is no written rule for the construction of the different parts of the monastery, this eschatological economy is abundantly and precisely expressed in the various "[books of the] advantages" (*ānisaṅsa*) read during these rituals of completion: there are as many of these texts as there are different parts in a monastery. There is, for instance, an *ānisaṅs vihāra* exposing the benefits or "advantages" that can be expected when one builds a sanctuary; an *ānisaṅs braḥ*, for those who erect a statue of the Buddha; an *ānisaṅs sālā* for the construction of a hall of merit or a refectory hall; an *ānisaṅs ṭaṅ daṅ'* for the erection of flag poles; an *ānisaṅs ṭöm bodhi* for the planting of a *ficus* tree; an *ānisaṅs sraḥ* for those who dig a pool for the monks to bathe; an *ānisaṅs paṅgan'* when one builds toilets, etc.

Much could be added regarding the social function of Khmer monasteries, such as their use as schools for the poor, hospices for the elderly, homes for the lost children, as places for all important festivals in village life, or places for conciliatory meetings. But this would much exceed the scope of this paper.

SELECTED BIBLIOGRAPHY

BERNON, Olivier de
1997 – Les Vatt du Cambodge, *Phnom Penh, développement urbain et patrimoine*, Paris, Ministère de la Culture, Atelier parisien d'Urbanisme, pp. 78-83.

BIZOT, François
1988 – *Le figuier à cinq branches: Recherche sur le Bouddhisme Khmer*, Publications de l'École française d'Extrême-Orient, vol. CVII, Paris, 164 pages + iv + 15 pictures.

GITEAU, Madeleine
1969 – *Le bornage rituel des temples bouddhiques au Cambodge*, Publications de l'École française d'Extrême-Orient, vol. LXVIII, Paris, 152 pages + xiv carts + 39 pictures.

LECLÈRE, Adhémard
1899 – *Le Bouddhisme au Cambodge*, Paris, Ernest Leroux, 535 pages.
1916 – *Cambodge, Fêtes civiles et religieuses*, Paris, Imprimerie Nationale, xii + 669 pages.

PORÉE, Guy et MASPERO, Éveline
1938 – *Mœurs et coutumes des Khmers, Origine, histoire, religions, croyances, rites*, Paris, Payot, 271 pages.

PORÉE-MASPERO, Éveline
1962-1969 – *Études sur les rites agraires des Cambodgiens*, La Haye, Paris, Mouton & Co, 3 volumes (continued pagination), xix + 988 pages + 4 maps.

HIRAṆYAVARṆA MAHĀVIHĀRA
A unique Newar Buddhist Monastery

Min Bahadur Shakya

This paper looks at the architecture, iconography, history, legends, rituals and other features of a Newar Buddhist Monastery, Hiraṇyavarṇa Mahāvihāra, a center of Vajrayāna Buddhism in Lalitpur/Patan in the Kathmandu Valley of Nepal.

The Historical Setting

The religion of the Kathmandu Valley has five main components. The first is animism, the worship of the spirits. The second, and the most widespread, is worship of the Eight Mother Goddesses and Devī. The third is worship of the Great God Śiva. The fourth is worship of Viṣṇu and the fifth is Vajrayāna Buddhism.

Buddhism during the lifetime of the Buddha

Although the Lord Buddha is believed to have taught the dharma in his home city, Kapilavastu and both the *Swayambhū Purāṇa* and *Vaṃṣāvalis* claim that his teachings reached the valley in his lifetime and even that the Buddha himself came to Kathmandu, we have no evidence for this. But his legacy is to be seen everywhere.

The *Mūlasarvāstivāda Vinayavastu,* a sanskrit Vinaya translated into Chinese by I-tsing in AD 700, mentions, in an episode relating to the transport of wool, a group of *bhikṣus* who set off for Nepal (Ni-po-lo) when the Buddha was residing in Śrāvasti. The same text relates that Ānanda, Buddha's cousin, went to the Kathmandu valley.

Concerning the early introduction of Buddhism to Nepal, Dr. John K. Locke, has written:

> Given the proximity of the valley of Nepal to Lumbini, Kapilavastu and areas of North Bihar, where Buddhism spread rapidly even during the time of the Buddha, it is quite possible that the Dharma found its way to the valley during the lifetime of the Buddha himself. (Locke 1989: 97)

Buddhism in the time of Aśoka

Emperor Aśoka is believed to have visited Kapilavastu and Lumbini where he erected a pillar stating that Buddha was born here. He also visited all the other places believed to have been the scenes of the principal events in the Buddha's life. According to Nepalese chronicles, Emperor Aśoka visited Kathmandu with his royal preceptor Upagupta. He erected many *caityas* and offered his daughter Cārumati to a local prince called Devapāla. Later Cārumati erected a *vihāra* in her own name and spent the rest of her life as Bhikṣuṇi. The *vihāra* erected by queen Cārumati still exists today and is now called Cābahil. However we cannot confirm that Cārumati ever visited Kathmandu because none of the Aśokan inscriptions mention that he had a daughter by this name.

In Lalitpur/Patan there are four great stūpas located in the four cardinal directions. Nepalese tradition asserts that they were erected by Aśoka himself since the structure of these stūpas resembles ancient stūpas raised by Aśoka.

Professor David Snellgrove writes:

> Such was Aśoka's fame as the greatest of all benefactors of Buddhism, that his name was readily associated with missionary activities that far exceeded their considerable historical range. If Khotan in the remotest part of Central Asia can preserve traditions concerning its founding as a city state by an imaginary son of Aśoka, named Kustana, it is by no means surprising to learn that Aśoka personally visited the Nepal Valley, where he founded the royal city of Patan together with its great stūpas, each to one of four cardinal points. (Snellgrove 1987: 365)

Again he writes:

> this city is certainly the early Buddhist city of Nepal, but there is nothing surviving above ground to suggest a date earlier than the fourth century AD.

John Locke writes:

> It is not impossible that the emperor Aśoka visited the valley, but there is no contemporary evidence of such a visit, either from Nepal or from Buddhist sources in India. Unlike India, where the ancient Buddhist sites are abandoned ruins, the ancient sites in Nepal are still active shrines. (Locke 1989: 97)

So although a visit by Aśoka is a possibility it is by no means certain.

Buddhism in the Licchavi period: 400-880 AD

The first documentary evidence of the presence of Buddhism in the valley comes from the inscriptions of Cāṃgunārāyaṇa and Jayadeva II ranging from 464 to the eight century AD. Vṛṣadeva (387-412) was a Buddhist monarch who renovated the *caitya* of Dharmadatta and in addition several *vihāras* to serve as lodging for monks. He is also credited with having founded a monastery at the great Swayaṃbhū Mahācaitya.

The Tyāgal inscription of Aṃśuvarmā (605-621) mentions deities such as Amitābha, Akṣobhya, Śākyamuni, Samantakusum and Mañjuśrī indicating that the cult of Mahāyāna in its developed form was present at that date. Other inscriptions also testify to the growth of Mahāyāna Buddhism. Again, in that same century King Srong btsan Gampo of Tibet married the Nepalese princess Bhṛkuṭī Devi. Indeed she is the one to be credited with playing a major role in the introduction of Buddhism to Tibet. Although her marriage was not recorded in texts outside Tibet, not only did Bhṛkuṭī Devi propagate Buddha Dharma in her adopted home but also she ordered the construction of temples in both Tibet and Bhutan including the great Jokhang temple in Lhasa.

Transitional Period: 880-1200

Buddhism appears to have reached its zenith during the transitional period. Patan became essentially a Buddhist university center, not unlike the celebrated sites of Bihar and Bengal such as Odantapurī, Nālandā and Vikramaśila. Nepalese Buddhists went to India to study and Indians came north to Nepal.

Nāropā (1016-1100) had seven disciples who like him taught the Mahāyāna sūtras and Vajrayāna tantras, two of whom were Lord Maitrīpā (of Kapilavastu), and sPhyi-therpā who was also from Nepal. In addition, Nāropā had fifty-four Nepalese yogis. Of Patan, Snellgrove has written, "Patan must have been a kind of vast university-city, differing little in its way of life from similar towns in medieval Europe". In fact its building, its traditions and its way of life must have been modeled on the great monastic universities of Central India. Again, he writes, "This city was once a place of sanctity and learning, where monks and paṇḍits were glad to come and visit. Some came from India to teach, others from Tibet to learn." This is borne out by the 1230 AD inscription, which is inscribed on the statue of Dīpaṃkara Buddha in Guita Vihāra.

It runs thus:

> *Vikhyātā lalitapuriti nagaridikṣu sarvasvapy vidyābhyām*
> Lalitpur is famous in all directions for its practice of academic life.

The great translator Marpa stayed in Patan and Kathmandu for three years to study *anuttara yoga tantra* under famous Nepalese Gurus like Paindapā and sPhyi-therpā.

Again, the great translator Rwā Lotsāva studied Vajrabhairava under Bhāro Vajrācārya in the eleventh century.

To quote Mary Slusser:

> From the hands of the Nepalese monks there was a vast outpouring of manuscripts. Most of the extant works of the Transitional Period date from eleventh century on, are written in Sanskrit, employ diverse scripts, and are sometimes illuminated. (Slusser 1998; 281)

The Malla Period: 1200-1768

By the end of the twelfth century, a profound change had come about in Nepalese Buddhist practice. Celibate monasticism came to an end following the introduction of tantric ritual practices associated with the female principal *prajñā*. With the rise of *vajrayāna* practice, especially *anuttara yoga tantra*, *karmamudrā* was regarded as essential for speedy enlightenment. The formerly celibate monks married and, calling themselves "Śākya" and "Vajrācārya", took their place at the head of a caste hierarchy which over centuries was being imposed upon the Buddhist community by a Śaivite monarchy. Hundreds of monastery complexes containing living space for these now married monks, temples, libraries and educational facilities were built during this period, a time when Newar Buddhism reached its full flowering. These complexes, dating from the Malla period, survive today as residential quarters – not for celibate monks but for married householders, among whom Śākyas are temple priests and Vajrācārya are family priests.

Decline of the Celibate Buddhist Monastic Community in Nepal

Now the question must be asked, why did Newar Buddhists choose to be Gṛhastha Bhikṣu rather than celibate monks? Both historians and local Buddhists maintain that celibate monasticism hardly survived the reign of King Jayasthiti Malla in the fifteenth century. I am convinced however that Jayasthitimalla alone – an aggressively orthodox Hindu who is thought to have completed the imposition of a caste system on the Buddhist community – could not have destroyed celibate monasticism. Rather the decline of celibate monasticism started long before he ascended the throne of Nepal. Although Jayasthiti Malla may have sounded its death knell, the institution seems already to have been weakened by the time of Atiśa's arrival in Kathmandu in 1041 AD.

Newar Buddhism as a lay Bodhisattva Practice

Indeed there had long been a provision for lay Buddhist monkhood, and by the arrival of Jayasthiti Malla it was already very popular in the valley of Kathmandu. The antiquity and strength of this tradition is evidenced by the eighth century compendium *Śikṣāsamuccaya* of Ācārya Śāntideva. It runs thus:

> *Pūnar aparam kulaputra bhaviṣyanti anāgata adhvāni gṛhastha pravajita ādikārmika bodhisattva.*

With regard to Ādikārmika Bodhisattva, Ācārya Anupamavajra is prominent. His works had a great impact on the Newar Buddhist tradition. Indeed, *Āḍdikārmika Pradīpa* which was composed in 1098 AD by Anupamavajra is a part of the daily practice of many Newar Buddhists today.[1]

According to Newar Buddhist tradition, after the disrobing ceremony of Cūdākarma, Śākyas and Vajrācāryas do not cease to be bhikṣus or Buddhist monks, but rather, they pass from the state of celibate bhikṣus to that of Gṛhasthia bhikṣus.

In the disrobing ceremony the following lines describe a bhikṣu:

> You have gone through *Śrāvakayāna* and now come to *Mahāyāna,* the greatest of the Buddhist *Yānas*. You have participated in some *Vajrayāna* rituals and after going through some higher ordinations you will know what *Cakrasaṃvara* is. (Allen 1973)

That Buddhism survived in the Kathmandu valley to the end of Malla period is largely due to the benign influence of Tibetan Buddhism. When King Pratāp Malla (1641-1674) encouraged closer trade relation between the two countries Newar traders began to travel to and from Lhasa regularly. They not only amassed wealth in Tibet but brought back Buddhist values to Nepal, along with the paraphernalia of their faith such as statues and *paubhās* thereby revitalizing the Buddhist tradition of Kathmandu. There are many accounts of Nepalese sojourning in Tibetan monasteries, especially at Tashi Lhunpo in Shigatshe. In 1667 AD a monk, one Padmadhvaja by name, returned from Tashi Lhunpo, and established a *vihāra* in Bhaktapur. He donated an image of Dipaṃkara Buddha and an endowment of guthi lands "with the approval of his wife, daughter, and son". Tibetan Buddhism was gradually favored by the Nepalese merchants and artisans domiciled in Tibet. Furthermore, it was possible for these people to be ordained as monks in Tibet, which was impossible in Nepal.

In the meantime, Nepal had assumed the role of holy land for Tibetans and at certain seasons of the year Tibetan pilgrims would make their way to the great shrines of Baudhanāth, Swayaṃbhū and Namobuddha.

---

1. To state briefly, it deals with the following practices of Newar Buddhists:
    1. Taking refuge in the Triple Gem;
    2. Reciting Nāmasangīti;
    3. To recite Bhadracaryā Praṇidhāna;
    4. To offer Preta bali;
    5. To circumambulate *caityas*, Buddha statues, etc.;
    6. To perform the Gurumaṃḍala rite;
    7. To meditate on the tutelary deity;
    8. To recite Prajñāpāramitā and other Mahāyāna sūtras;
    9. To recite Dānagāthā;
    10. To perform Bodhisattva practices joyfully;
    11. To study Buddhist scriptures;
    12. To offer food to the Triple Gem and the tutelary deity before eating;
    13. To offer fivefold prostration to the Buddhas of the ten directions;
    14. To sleep in a lion's posture after meditating on Deity Yoga.

Buddhism in the Shah Period: 1768-present

The stature and financial health of Buddhist monasteries greatly declined after the invasion of the Hindu Gorkhālis in 1768 AD when most of the property of the Guṭhis, the organizations that supported the monasteries, were usurped by the new government. The Newars have been subject since that time to the political control of Gorkhās and between 1846 and 1950 they were subject also to the rule of the autocratic Rana family.

It is fashionable, especially among Theravāda Buddhists who since the end of Rana rule have been a vibrant presence in the valley, to say that Newar Buddhism is corrupt form of Buddhism. This charge reflects an important reality, namely that Newar Vajrayāna Buddhism assimilated most of the Hindu pantheon as well as many Hindu practices such as domestic sacrifices and so forth. It is true that after Jayasthiti Malla forced the Vajrācārya priests and Śākya monks into the straightjacket of the caste system, Buddhism became a closed, exclusive community in which initiation was transmitted through the patriline. The monasteries became the home of married monks and the Buddhism they practised became highly ritualistic; they abandoned the path of purification (meditation); and meanwhile the Buddhas and Bodhisattvas were worshipped as gods. Nevertheless with its medieval Indian form otherwise largely unchanged, Newar Buddhism continued to provide a source of spiritual comfort and support to the common people.

Although in the minds of most Newars, there is little to distinguish Buddhism from Hinduism, from the viewpoint of Brāhmin orthodoxy, the Buddhists are heretics. But in reality there is immense tolerance for diverse practices. Within a single Newar family, members may worship both Buddhist and Hindu gods. At festival time all the inhabitants of each city are united in worship of their major deities who may have both Buddhist and Hindu identities.

On the other hand, Tibetans continued to support Buddhist monuments such as Baudhanāth, Swayambhū and Namobuddha at frequent intervals. Nepal became the holy land for the Tibetans. Tibetan pilgrims have frequented the Kathmandu valley since the early Malla period down to this day.

General location and density of monasteries in the Kathmandu Valley

The Buddhist shrine of Kwābahā, popularly known as Golden Temple, is one of Nepal's most beautiful monasteries. It is situated north of Patan's Darbar Square on the road leading to Kumbheśvara. Although it is more commonly known in Patan as Kwābahā its Sanskrit name is Hiraṇyavarṇa Mahāvihāra.

Today the city of Lalitpur alone contains more than one hundred and sixty monasteries (*bahās* and *bahīs*) and Kathmandu more than one hundred. The monasteries began as living quarters for celibate monks, but with the development of Tantric Buddhism they evolved into communes of married *yogīs* and *yoginīs*.

Almost all the *bahās* and *bahīs* enshrine Śākyamuni Buddha or Avalokiteśvara and a secret tantric deity (*āgam*) who is the principal focus of esoteric worship.

At present there are eighteen main *bahās* in Patan, with numerous branches, and twenty-five *bahīs*.[2]

2. But Hem Raj Shakya suggests thirty-two *bahīs* in total.

Layout of the Newar Monastery

In the Kathmandu Valley there are two distinct types of *vihāra*: *bahās* and *bahīs*. Their architectural features include the following:

1. All *bahās* and *bahīs* are square and have square courtyards;
2. The ground floor is open for visitors;
3. The platform surrounds the courtyard on four sides;
4. A separate shrine room is for the main deity;
5. The entrance door faces the main shrine;
6. A door to the garden is on the right or the left side of the courtyard;
7. Buildings are only of two storeys;
8. In the *bahī* the main shrine can be circumambulated by a passage way;
9. Generally in the *bahī* a flight of steps leads from the street level up to the main entrance whereas the entrance to the *bahā* is usually at street level.
10. The shrine of the tantric deity (*āgam*) is located directly above the *kwāpādya*.

The basic design is undoubtedly ancient. For example, in Sārnāth, Lumbini, Śrāvastī and Jetavana all the archaeological sites are square. The square-shaped enclosed space is paved with brick tiles or stone slabs (Newari: *cikaṇ appā)*. This style of paving has kept the interior courtyard free of moss and fungus. The brick, tiled or stone paved courtyard is mostly used by the community for listening to Buddhist teachings or *strotra, dhāraṇī*, and *nāmasaṇgīti* recitations.

A Dharmadhātu *caitya*, miniature votive *caitya* or a separate shrine in the middle of courtyard is normative in most *bahās* and *bahīs*. Examples are the Bungadeva shrine in Tabahā, Cakvādya shrine in Jeṣṭhavarṇa Mahāvihāra, Swayaṃbhū caitya in Hiraṇyavarṇa Mahāvihāra, Janabahā shrine in Kanakacaitya Mahāvihāra and so forth. In most of the *bahās* and *bahīs* there is a separate shrine for the main deity Kwābāju. This represents the Mūlagandhakuṭī of Buddha's time.

One universal feature of the Newar *bahā* and *bahī* is that no one is allowed to enter this Gandhakuṭī except the god guardian and the boys who have been properly ordained during *Cūdākarma* ceremony. Sometimes a miniature of Vajradhara is placed in front of Buddha Śākyamuni.

Most *bahās* and *bahīs* are of only two storeys. The first floor of the main shrine is fronted by a triple-window (*tikijhyā*), which inclines forward. This triple-window represents the triple jewel while a five-framed window symbolizes the five Buddhas.

The platform surrounding the courtyard is used for *cankramaṇa* in case of *bahīs*. One can circumambulate the main deity of a *bahī* shrine on this platform.

In addition to features listed above, the following are normative in *bahā* or *bahī* shrines.

1. Two metallic or stone lions flank the main entrance door (for example in Hiraṇyavarṇa or Rudravarṇa Mahāvihāra);
2. The door of the main shrine consists of a *toraṇa* symbolizing three jewels or five Buddhas or else the deity inside the shrine;
3. Images of Gaṇesh and Mahākāla as protector deities are at the main entrance;
4. Beyond the main entrance are two open platforms (*phalechā*), which are central to the religious life of the community; here devotees recite *strotras,* play religious musical instruments and sing *dapha bhajan* or *gyānamāla bhajan*, and during the month of Guṃla, Buddhist deities are exhibited here.

5. At the apex of the main shrine is a *caitya*;
6. To the rear of the main shrine is a garden or open space;
7. A well is located behind the complex;
8. The main deity of the *bahā / bahī* is either a Buddha or a Bodhisattva.

The Chronicle of Hiraṇyavarṇa Mahāvihāra
(unpublished version)

A lady was married and gave birth to a baby. At that time Lord Buddha had just passed into Great Parinirvāṇa and as yet no Buddha statue had been erected anywhere. The lady lost her husband only one year after she gave birth to her son and so it was she who, by and by, taught the boy the skills of sculptor. When the boy was ten years old, his mother told him to make a Buddha statue. The boy asked his mother how it should be made. That night in a dream the lady saw Lord Buddha's body endowed with the thirty-two major and the heighty minor marks. The next day, she told her son all the details she had seen in her dream and the boy began to prepare a mold for the Buddha statue. He sculpted one, which was about 6 ft.9 inches high. When his mother had inspected the statue very carefully she pronounced it to be just about perfect. But it still lacked four qualities.[3] His mother thanked him for creating a most beautiful Buddha statue.

In the mean time, Lord Indra, the king of gods, came to know of the statue and, having stolen it, placed it in his heavenly garden in which, they say, it remains to this day. The unfortunate mother and son could do nothing but gaze at the empty spot where the Buddha statue had once been. After a while, the lady asked her son to make another statue and he did so. She inspected the new statue and she saw that it was as well made as its predecessor. Many people learned of this statue; they paid homage and with great devotion offered the Buddha statue whatever they had. News of it spread as rapidly as fire even as far as Lhasa, whereupon some Tibetans came from Lhasa and, perceiving the uniqueness and beauty of the statue, stole it. So again the poor lady and her sculptor son suffered the loss of their cherished statue.

They decided to make another statue but this time they would keep it a secret. The statue was made perfectly as before out of eight kinds of precious metals. The mother was very happy and satisfied with her son's superb workmanship. After a time, she passed away and was reborn in Sukhūvatī heaven. Her son married a lady and begot a son. His descendents were all devotees of the Buddha while he himself became renowned as an emanation of Great Viśvakarma.

In that degenerate age people developed great ignorance and delusion rather than faith. A great earthquake occurred and many people perished. The house in which the Buddha statue was kept cracked, split and its fragment was buried. People forgot the statue's whereabouts.

---

3. They were:
Lord Buddha uses to walk;
He preaches the Dharma;
On either side monks follow him;
He has an aura of lights (130 ft) on either side.

Once all of a sudden when they were in the field harvesting the crops they heard a bell ring but when they went to the place from which the sound seemed to be coming, they found nothing. So they put up a marker and next day they returned to dig in that spot. It was then that they discovered the Buddha statue. They cleared away the earth and cleaned it off and many people came to pray and worship.

At that time, Bhāskara Deva (1045-48 AD), a Ṭhakurī king was ruling in Lalitpur city. Someone informed him about the discovery of the Buddha statue. That night, the king saw the Buddha statue in a dream. The statue told him to send his royal priest Vajrācārya Kūlapāda to bring it to the palace. The next day, the king sent for Vajrācārya Kūlapāda who appeared in his presence. The king asked the Vajrācārya to name an auspicious time at which to fetch the Buddha statue.

Vajrācārya Kūlapāda with his disciple Cailaka Bhikṣu set off for the place where the Buddha statue had been found. When they arrived there, Vajrācārya Kūlapāda made offerings to and worshipped the Buddha statue throughout the night and consecrated it with *vajrayāna* ritual. Using his binding mantra (Skt: *ākarṣana mantra*) he brought the consciousness-principle of the Buddha statue to Śaṃkhamūla, Patan. Then, he informed the king who, accompanied by many courtiers and musicians, came out to receive the Buddha statue.

After crossing the Śaṃkhamūla Tīrtha, the procession headed towards Patan. The goddess Mahālakṣmī of Lagankhel transformed herself into an eagle and snatched away the *vajra* held by Vajrācārya Kūlapāda and flew up into the sky. At that point, the Buddha statue became rooted to the spot, which is known today as " Swoṃtha".

However Guru Kūlapāda immediately brought Mahālakṣmī back with his tantric power and threatened to kill her. Mahālakṣmī, appearing in her divine form, told him that she was very much pleased with his tantric power and explained to him that she had intervened merely to express her displeasure at his not informing her about such a meritorious project. The Buddha statue, which could now proceed, was brought to the center of Nyākhāchowk Square and erected there.

The next morning Vajrācārya Kūlapāda having bathed and purified himself, worshipped the Buddha with prostrations, offerings, prayers and by 108 recitations of *Aparamitā Dhāraṇī.* Thenceforth this became his daily routine. After two months King Bhāskar Deva began to build a new *vihāra* to house the Buddha statue and once it was completed he summoned the Vajrācārya to perform the consecration. Kūlapāda told the king that it would be difficult for the king to attend to the Buddha statue as his duties would involve continuous devotional exercises, purification ritual, and recitations; but the king did not heed the guru's warning.

He had the Buddha statue installed in the new *vihāra* and he himself attended it. But shortly after the consecration, the Lord Buddha appeared to the king in a dream and told him to build another *vihāra.* This *vihāra* should be in a place where there was:

a – a mouse called Hiraṇyaka bathed daily in Kumbha Tīrtha,
b – a pond which had not dried up since Mañjuśrī cut the gorge at Cobhār,
c – a jeweled *caitya* in the centre of the pond,
d – two Nāgas called Varuṇa and Varuṇāvatī, and
e – a mouse who chases away a cat.

The king consulted many learned Vajrācāryas who invoked Nāgas and Nāginīs dwelling in the pond filled in and a *vihāra,* with a jeweled *caitya* in the courtyard built on the spot on Thirteen Bodhisattva levels which was the traditional style. The *vihāra* was named Hiraṇyavarṇa Mahāvihāra after the Hiraṇyaka mouse. At the outset, the *saṃgha* had six hundred members. To this day, the daily ritual practice includes the purification by bathing, recitation of Aparimitā Dhāraṇī, Strotras, offering Āratī lamps, striking wooden rod at specified times and so forth.

Historical Documents

The earliest information we have about Hiraṇyavarṇa Mahāvihāra are two manuscript references. The first is in the colophon of a palm leaf manuscript copy of the *Vajravalī* written in NS 202 (1082 AD) by one Candra of the Turaharṇavarṇa Mahāvihāra in Manigalake (Locke 1989: 39).

The second reference is in the colophon of a manuscript copy of the *Pratisṭhāloka* written during the time of Guṇakāmadeva. There were two kings by the name of Guṇakāmadeva during the Ṭhakūri period; one ruled from about NS 107 to 110 and the other from about NS 303 to 316. There is only one Bhāskaradeva in this period. He ruled from at least NS 165 to 167. Hence if he is indeed the founder of the *vihāra,* the second reference must date from the reign of the second Guṇakāmadeva, *circa* NS 303-16 (Locke 1989: 39).

Today there are thirty-eight copper plate inscriptions and seventeen stone inscriptions located in the *bahā*:

1 – Of these, a copper plate inscription dated NS 529 (1409 AD) affixed to a beam at the northern-end of the court of the main temple seems to be the most ancient and important inscription inside the *bahā* premises.[4]

2 – Two copper-plate inscriptions, dated NS 653, and 762 (donated by Sri Ujotadeva of Dolakhā).

3 – Of the inscriptions (102 in number) in the alms bowl *(piṇḍapātra)* the oldest is dated 645 NS (1525 AD).[5]

4. This inscription reads as follows:

Śubha śrayastu saṃvat 529 māgha kṛṣna navamyāmra tithau hasta nakṣatra harṣana śukravara sare śrī uttara vihāradhipati śrī yogamvara gesthita śrī Hiraṇyavarṇa Mahāvihāra gaṇa madhyasthita śrī śrī caitya bhattārakasyālaya tatraiva Vajrācārya śrī davyajanaya pāsya śrī Meghārāma thavara pāsana bhāryā dharmapatni Jayalakṣmī bhari sahitana kanakalaśa dhvajā varohana yangādina juro// śubham//

In Saṃvat 529 on the dark fortnight of Māgha at the time of Śrī Davyajana Vajrācārya, head of the *bahā*, Āju megharām with his wife Jayalakṣmī donated a pinnacle to Śrī Yogāṃvara of the north side of the *vihāra* and a golden pinnacle Kalaśa dhvaja to the *caitya* in the middle of the Hiraṇyavarṇa Mahāvihāra.

5. The inscription reads as follows:

śreyo astu/ saṃvat 645 śrāvaṇa śukla aṣṭamyaya tithau/ vaiśākha nakṣatre śukla prabramha yoge jatha karna muhurte brihaspativasare idamadivase śrī Nyākhācoka vihāravasthita śrī harshasiṃhasya bhāryā herasmi putra putrī saheta śrī mat śrī 3 dipaṃkara tathāgatebhya sarva sangha piṇḍapatra udghosita ānena dānena sukha sampadam bhavatuh// śubha//

In NS 645 (1525 AD) on the eighth day of the bright fortnight of Śravana on Thursday, Śrī Harshasiṃha's wife Herasmi together with her sons and daughter who hailed from Nyākhācok vihāra offered this alms bowl to Dīpaṃkara Tathāgata and Sarva Saṃgha and wished for happiness and prosperity from the merits of this generosity.

4 – The large bell in Hiraṇyavarṇa Mahāvihāra (Kwābahā) has the following inscription: *Śrī manigardhipati śrī śrī jaya śiva siṃhadeva prabhu Thakulsa, putra śrī śrī hariharasiṃha.* The date is Āśvin of 728 NS (1600 AD).[6]

5 – A copperplate inscription describes the organization of a large *guṭhi* of *bahā* members to oversee repairs and to donate a new gilt roof to the central shrine. Siddhī Narsiṃha is reigning at the time Māgha 757. A stone inscription of the same date describes a large *guṭhi* of Bhawas (Jyāpus) which was organized to donate new Gajuris to the Vihāra. The king is mentioned as being Narsiṃha. A second date is also inscribed: Phalguṇa 762.

6 – A new *toraṇa* was donated to Hiraṇyavarṇa Mahāvihāra in Jesṭha NS 800 by a Vajrācārya. Śrī Nivāśa and Yoganarendra were joint rulers at that date.

Mahārājādhirājasya śrī 3 jaya Nivāśamalla prabhu, putra śrī 3 joganaladra malla prabhu thakura ubhaya vijaye rajyes (Regmi 1966: 307).

7 – A group of Vajrācāryas donated new windows and *toraṇa* to Hiraṇyavarṇa Mahāvihāra in Mangsir 822 during the reign of Yoga Narendra.

8 – The wooden frame inside the small central temple in Hiraṇyavarṇa Mahāvihāra was replaced and four Buddha images were donated by a group of *bahāl* members in Chaitra 831 (1711 AD) Vīra Mahindra ruled at that date (Regmi 1966 IV: 265-266). He is also mentioned as being king in a stele of Baisākha 831 (1711 AD) (*ibid*: 250-252).

9 – A *bhikṣu* of Nakabahil sent an invitation to king Mahendra Singha (NS 837-843) to attend a special feast, *samyek*, at Hiraṇyavarṇa Mahāvihāra in Māgha 839 NS.

Description of the monastery

See plan opposite page

This monastery has a beauty of its own. It is multi-storied and heavily decorated with gilt ornaments. At the centre of the inner courtyard a freestanding shrine is dedicated to Swayaṃbhū Caitya. In this paved court, numerous bronze sculptures, oil lamps and prayer-wheel railings are displayed. A raised circumambulatory walkway gives access to the main shrine and to the enclosing buildings containing halls that house sculptures and whose artistry and philosophical symbolism are well-known both in Nepal and abroad.

Entrance Setting

ph. 1 and 2 p. 230

Two black stone lions guard the monastery gate known as Bhairava Gate on which Bhairava's eyes are painted. After entering the gate and walking along a short narrow passage we reach a second stone gate with a *toraṇa-dvāra* displaying various tantric form of five transcendental Buddhas. Images of Nārāyaṇa and Śiva are installed on both sides of the door as guardians.

On the right side of the passage is the platform where a counter was recently established from which tickets are sold to tourists. Ticket sales bring substantial revenues to cover daily rituals and monastery maintenance.

6. Mentioned in *Itihāsa Saṃśodhana ko* p. 287; Regmi p. 48.

Inside the door is the reception office where a paid staff takes care of daily upkeep and deals with the god-guardians' problems and complaints. From here one enters the raised walkway that leads round the main courtyard of the temple. The doorway opening into the main courtyard from the entry passageway is mounted by a large bronze *toraṇa* similar to the one over the main shrine.

One may descend to the courtyard and circumambulate the central shrine of Swayaṃbhū. To do so one must remove leather shoes, first picking plastic slippers from the ticket counter.

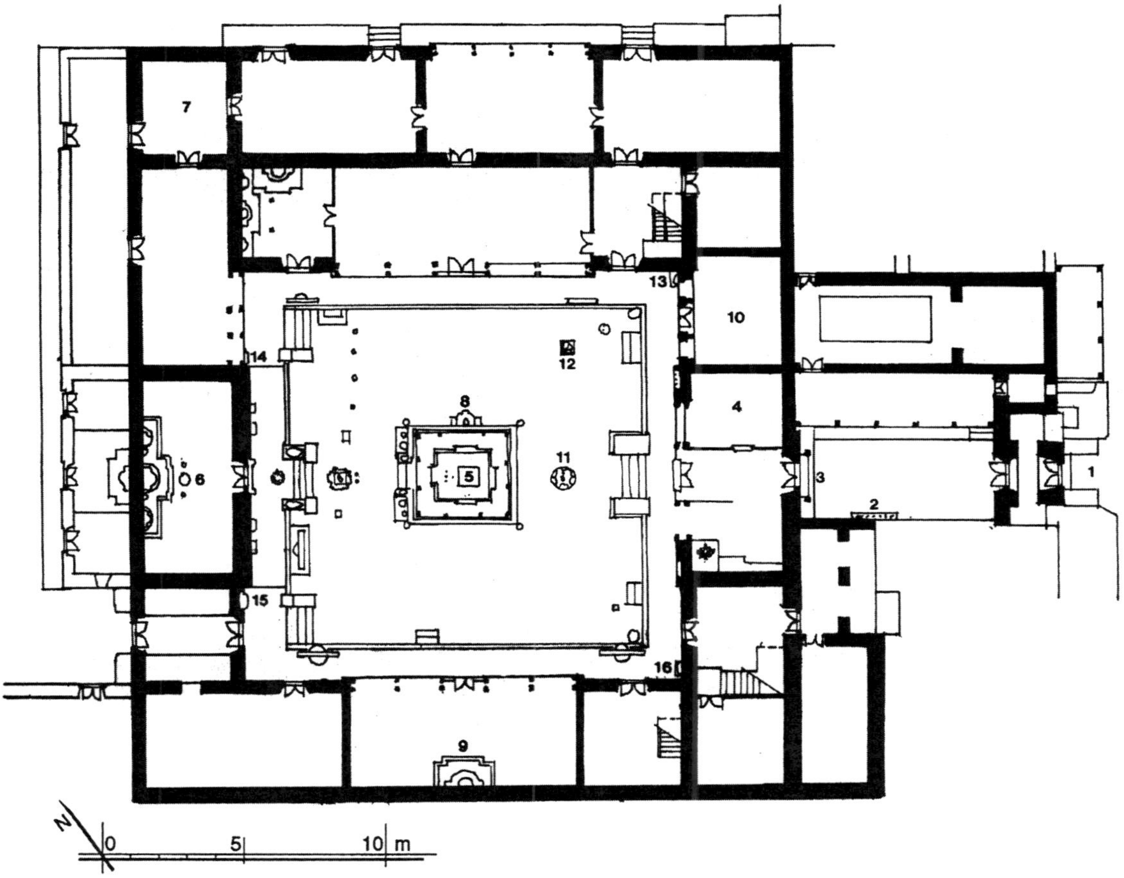

Hiraṇyavarṇa Mahāvihāra Monastery (Kwābahā or Golden temple), Patan

Ground-floor plan

1. Main gate
2. Water tank
3. Inner door
4. Reception office
5. Central Shrine, Swayaṃbhū Caitya
6. Main Shrine, Kwābāju, Śākyamuni image
7. Vajrasattva Shrine
8. Stone representing Vasuki Nāgarāja
9. Tārā Shrine
10. Nāmasaṃgīti Shrine
11. Dharmadhātu
12. Stone-carved lions
13. Image of Padmāpani
14. Image of Padmāpani
15. Image of Padmāpani
16. Image of Mañjuśrī

1 – Main entrance gate with two stone lions
[1] on the plan p. 229

2 – Inner door with a magnificent toraṇa-dvāra
[3] on the plan p. 229

3 – *Top vue of the Monastery, from north-east, showing the three-storied Main Shrine and the pinnacle of the Swayaṃbhū Caitya Shrine* respectively [6] and [5] on the plan p. 229

The Main Shrine: Śākyamuni Buddha

The main shrine where Lord Buddha Śākyamuni is venerated is a three-storied structure with all three of its roofs gilded. The pinnacle of the main temple consists of thirteen smaller stūpas with three umbrellas (Skt: *chatra*) topping the three central stūpas. The first and second roofs are supported by numerous struts (*toṇāl*) bearing multi-armed deities. Four gilded banners fly down from the roof pinnacle. The small faces at the ridges of the roofs are said to be Mahāsiddhas of this Jambudvīpa. Just below the ridge are a series of metal bells which tinkle in the breeze. *ph. 3 above*

The curved roof corners are mounted by miniature birds holding leaves in their beaks; four metal plates embossed with the four guardian kings (Skt: *caturmahārājas*) are below.

As is the case with most Newar monasteries, the main deity is Śākyamuni Buddha in the earth-touching gesture, in the shrine opposite the entrance door. He wears a serene expression.

Unlike Buddha images of the Theravāda tradition, this Vajrayāna Buddha is richly ornamented. He wears a diadem, ornaments, necklaces; his crown is embedded with emeralds and his forehead with a diamond known as *Urṇakoṣa*. Like most Buddha images seen in Newar monasteries, he wears a yellow robe and makes the *bhūmisparśa mudrā*, i.e., earth-touching gesture. He has *Uṣṇiṣa*, on the crown of the head and *Urṇakoṣa* between the eyebrows. He has long lobed ears. Golden in color, he bears the thirty-two major and heighty minor marks of a *Sambhogakāya* Buddha. He is seen with *piṇḍapātra* (alms bowl) in his left hand which rests on his lap and he is flanked by his chief disciples Śāriputra and Maudgalyāyāna wearing monastic dress.

Before the Buddha two bells used in daily worship (newari: *dékhe chāyéké*) hang from the ceiling of the shrine.

In front of him is the Buddha Vajradhara. Although in the view of some this is Balbhadra, a Hindu god, in this instance the image is clearly the Buddhist deity Vajradhara making the *Vajrahuṃkāra-mudrā.*

Over the doorway into the main deity's shrine is a solid silver *toraṇa.* The central figure is Buddha Akṣobhya identified with Buddha Śākyamuni making the *bhūmisparśa mudrā.* On either side of him stand his chief disciples Śāriputra and Maudgalyāyana, backed by the remaining four of the five Buddhas. At the top of the *toraṇa* is a figure of Buddha Vajrasattva. A second identical silver *toraṇa* stands above the first.

At the base of the shrine a platform standing 2 feet above the courtyard is considered to be even more sacred than the courtyard itself. No one except the currently officiating god guardian, his family and helpers, may set foot onto this platform; however on certain ceremonial occasions caretaker committee members and officiating Vajrācārya priests may also step on it.

On the wall a series of repoussé scenes depict the life of Buddha according to *Lalitavistara Sūtra.* The scenes on the left side are of the Buddha being born from his mother's hip; seeing the three signs – a dead man, an sick man, and an old man – which motivate him to renounce his princely life; his shooting an arrow through seven trees; his leaving the palace on horseback, cutting his own hair (*cūḍākarma*) and attaining enlightenment. On the right side he is saluted by all the gods as he proceeds triumphantly on a holy serpent (*nāga*) to Lumbini.

Four three-feet tall Lokeśvara images together with the Buddha's two chief disciples Śāriputra and Maudgalyāyana, are seen on either side of the main entrance. Above the *toraṇa* of the main shrine there are seven seated images, depicting Prajñāpāramitā the five transcendental Buddhas and six-syllabled Avalokiteśvara who signifies the Triple Gem in the Mahāyāna Buddhist pantheon. Four large bronze oil lamps are suspended from the roof by chains. On both sides of the entrance to the main shrine there are large bronze lions of excellent artistry on the back of which stand two Siṃhanāda Lokeśvaras in *lalita* attitude. Besides that a big bell dated 1608 AD hangs on the left of the main shrine gate (also dated 1608 AD).

Swayaṃbhū Caitya

Legend suggests that the Swayaṃbhū Caitya shrine, standing at the centre of the courtyard and in which is enshrined the lineage deity of the Kwābahā members, including myself, pre-dates the monastery.

It is attended by ten elders (*daśapāramitā ājus*) of the Kwābahā Saṃgha who serve for a period of a month. Once each year (in April/May) all members of Kwābahā Saṃgha should come to the lineage shrine to celebrate Digu Pūjā. The monastery has the largest initiated membership of any Newar monastery in the valley. Some of them who live in other parts of Nepal, such as Dolakhā, Tānsen, in the west and Bhojpur, Chainpur, in the east make a point of returning to Lalitpur for the ceremony.

4 – *Swayaṃbhū Caitya, facing the Main Shrine at the centre of the courtyard, with a huge vajra in front of its door*
[5] on the plan p. 229

This shrine which has some extraordinary metal work is dazzling in appearance. The roof is entirely covered with gold. The pinnacle consists of four serpent deities (*nāgas*) with their curved tails raised to hold seven-tiered umbrella (*chatra*) over the bell-shaped dome. Four metal banners attached to the pinnacle hang down, one over each side of the shrine. This shrine is adorned with twelve fine statues of Lokeśvara,[7] the images of the five transcendental Buddhas and a rare image of Mañjudeva with his two consorts Varadā and Mokṣadā. *ph. 3 page 231*

The two donors sculpted in bronze which face the main shrine were installed by Rājendra Siṃha and his wife in 1804 AD. The headdress of the donors is in the Rājput style of that period. By contrast, two donors sculpted in stone on the other side dated 1608 AD are depicted in old Newar style. *ph. 4 above*

Of all the bronze images, the largest and fiercest are four five-foot tall celestial beings at the four corners of the shrine. They have long pointed teeth, sharp curled claws, and curved snouts and stand on their hind legs.

---

7. They are: Ṣaḍakṣari Lokeśvara, Halahal, Khaṣarpaṇa, Siṃhanāda, Padmanṛtya, Harihariharivāhan, Trailokyavasaṅkari, Rakta, Nīlakanṭha, Māyājālakrama, and Kāraṇḍavyūha.

Vajrasattva shrine

In the northwest corner of the courtyard is the shrine of Vajrasattva, regarded as Ādi-Buddha by Nepalese Buddhists. Vajrasattva is depicted in his father-mother aspect. However, this form is not publicly exhibited but is shown only to those who are initiated in Highest Yoga Tantra.

Vajrasattva is a very popular tutelary deity for Nepalese Vajrācāryas: all the Vajrācāryas of Kwābahā (numbering approximately 300) are obligated to attend the shrine, each for a period of two weeks. The shrine houses in addition other important deities such as the Buddha Vairocana, Vasudharā, Mañjuśrī, and Karuṇāmaya. Some forty years ago this shrine was also closed to visitors.

Tārā Shrine

On the south side of the courtyard is the shrine of Tārā, established in 1958 AD. The shrine is mostly frequented by the devotional song group named Jñānamālā Bhajan Saṃgha which has 80 members. The shrine houses other images including Mañjuśrī. The members of Jñānamālā group must each attend the shrine for a period of two weeks.

Tārā represents the enlightened deeds of all the Buddhas and hence she is called the mother of the Buddhas of three times. A *sūtra* recalls how Avalokiteśvara Bodhisattva saved and ferried over countless suffering beings from the sea of birth and death. One day when Avalokiteśvara beheld the misery of the world, he shed tears out of great compassion. His tears turned into a lotus flower from which appeared a white and a green Tārā who said to him: "Please do not be sad. We will assist you in liberating living beings, Although they are countless in number, the power of our vow is immeasurable".

ph. 5 opposite page

Since that time the two Tārās have been liberating countless sentient living beings everyday. There are twenty-one forms of Tārā (the Saviouress). In reality, they are all the transformed bodies of Avalokiteśvara, the Buddha of compassion.

Green Tārā appears as beautiful young maiden. Her body is green. She has one face and two arms. She wears a crown ornamented with five Buddha images as well as all kinds of Bodhisattva ornaments studded with jewels and many-colored celestial garments. She sits on a lotus throne in the *lalita* attitude and in the half lotus posture. Her left hand shows the gesture of giving refuge and her right hand the *varadā-mudrā*, indicating that she is quick to respond to the petitions of those who seek her aid. Through the cultivation of Tārā Sādhanā all demonic and karmic obstacles may be eliminated, disasters avoided and one's life lengthened.

Mañjuśrī Nāmasaṃgīti Shrine

In the northeast corner of the courtyard is the shrine of Nāmasaṃgīti founded in 1985 by the fifteen-member Nāmasaṃgīti recitation group. To Nāmasaṃgīti's left is Maitreya, to his right is Tārā.

Members must each attend the shrine for a period of one month. They are required to attend the morning ceremony at which they recite the Nāmasaṃgīti text and other hymns between 3.30 am and 5.30 am It is here that the god guardian spends the night.

Mañjuśrī Nāmasaṃgīti is one of the most important manifestations of Mañjuśrī, the embodiment of wisdom of all the Buddhas. It is said that though he had already been enlightened countless aeons before, in Śākyamuni's time he appeared as one of

5 – *Image of Ārya Tārā with offerings of flowers and alm bowl*
(Shrine [9] on the plan p. 229)

the Buddha's eight chief Bodhisattva disciples. Since countless Buddhas of the ten directions have been his disciple, he is called Ādi-Buddha Mañjuśrī. The deity Nāmasaṃgītiis very popular in the valley and the text which bears his name is of spiritual significance to many of the local people.

Amitābha Buddha with his two bodhisattvas

In the first floor of the southern side building is the Amitābha Shrine flanked by two Bodhisattvas. Amitābha in Sanskrit means immeasurable light. He resides in the western land of unlimited bliss (Skt. Sukhāvatī). Two bodhisattvas, Avalokiteśvara and Mahāsthāmaprāpta, assist him.

When he was still a Bodhisattva he was called Bhikṣu Dharmākara. He made forty-eight vows to establish a land of unlimited bliss, and to ferry over to it sentient beings who recite his name. Any sentient being who has faith, makes vows and practices diligently will be received by this Buddha and reborn in the pure land.

Amitābha Buddha presides over the *Bhadrakalpa*, the Fortunate Aeon. He is always depicted making the *dhyāna mudrā* and can be recognized by the symbol of the lotus to whose family he belongs. The recitation of the name of Amitābha Buddha is a common practice in China and Japan. In Tibet too, devotees very frequently recite the prayer asking to be reborn in land of Amitābha Buddha.

Recently, the *vihāra* reform committee commissioned a series of frescoes on the theme of Sukhāvatī heaven, Akṣobhya heaven, the Confession Buddhas, the Five Protectress Deities, the Five Buddhas and the Four Heavenly Kings.

Amoghapāśa Lokeśvara shrine

The hall on the first floor of the north side of the building contains an excellent image of Amoghapāśa Lokeśvara as well as a very large prayer wheel. The walls of this hall are decorated with frescoes containing members of the Tibetan Buddhist pantheon such as Guru Padmasambhava, the Eight Great Bodhisattvas, the one-thousand-armed Lokeśvara, Vajradhara, Buddha Aparimitā, the Medicine Buddha, the Two Herukas, the Wheel of Life, the Four Heavenly Kings, the Tārās and innumerable Bodhisattvas and Gurus. Kept in the *gompa* is a set of *Tibetan Tripitaka-Kanjur*, Narthang edition and also a set of *Serphyin*, namely the Perfection of Wisdom in Eight Thousand lines Sūtra.

Learned Tibetan Buddhist Masters often come here to give initiations and teachings on the dharma. Indeed, for Newar lay people, Kwābahā is the centre of Tibetan Buddhism. Here Newar laity performs the fasting ritual known as Nyungné, Aṣṭamīvrata and Daśamīpūjā and so forth. At present there is no resident monk in this *gompa* but Newar monks who follow the Tibetan tradition come regularly to give *upoṣadha* vows and the five precepts, or eight precepts to the laity.

Amoghapāśa Lokeśvara is a multi-armed form of Avalokiteśvara that seems to have been popular in Nepal since the Middle Ages. The name suggests that he is the lord of world who possesses an infallible noose by which he leads suffering beings to enlightenment.

According to the *Amoghapāśa Hṛdaya Dhāraṇī Sūtra*, ninety-one aeons ago, Avalokiteśvara received the transmission of this Dhāraṇī from Lokeśvararājā Tathāgata. Since then he used that *dhāraṇī* to teach uncountable sentient beings. Since Avalokiteśvara manifests the transformed body *(nirmāṇakāya)* of the Buddha and uses this *dhāraṇī* to ferry over sentient beings, he may be addressed as Amoghapāśa. Amoghapāśa is popular not only in Nepal but also in all countries where Mahāyāna Buddhism has spread.

The image of Amoghapāśa in its earliest known form can be found in the *Ārya Amoghapāśa Sūtra* preserved in the Keshar Library, Kathmandu.

Mahākāla

Mahākāla is worshipped by both Hindu and Buddhists and can be seen in the entrance of every Buddhist monastery of the Kathmandu valley. He is said to be the protector of the dharma of Buddha Śākyamuni. There are many forms of Mahākāla, the two-armed, four-armed, six-armed and sixteen-armed being the most popular. In the Newar Buddhist tradition the two-armed form of Mahākāla sculpted in stones is widely found.

It is said that Mahākāla is the manifestation of Bodhisattva Avalokiteśvara (Shakya 1994: 69). Mahākāla has remained as the Protector of the Dharma in all the Buddha fields in most of the *mahāvihāras* and *bahīs* in Nepal.

Prajñāpāramitā Scripture

A widely renowned and venerated text called *Ārya Aṣṭasahasrikā Prajñāpāramitā sūtra* written in gold Raṃjana script has been preserved in the main shrine for generations. No one is allowed to enter this shrine aside from the two priests who are currently attending the deity and small boys who have just been ordained monks in their *Baré chuyégu* ceremony; however it is brought out of the shrine almost daily by the two *bāphācās* of god guardian assistants to be recited by Buddhist *vajrācāryas* who are bound by strict rules and regulations. Since the text consists of profound wisdom teachings of Lord Buddha, the recitation of this *sūtra* brings blessings to the devotees who have commissioned the reading of the text as well as to sentient beings. The manuscript dates back to NS 345 (1215 AD) and was copied by Bhikṣu Ānanda of Kapitanagar during the reign of Abhaya Malla (1217-1255). The manuscript contains several coloured illustrations of the birth of Siddhārtha and so forth.

Four Metal Statues

At the four corners of the monastery are four forms of Avalokiteśvara. Fearful of theft, the Monastery Reform Committee has installed thick metal belt around their midriff. Art historians believe three of the images are of Padmapāṇi Lokeśvara: the one in the north-east corner is 12th-century, that of the north-west corner, 10th-century, and of the south-west corner, 14th-century; in the south-east corner is Mañjuśrī as a child (14th century).

Yogāṃvara Shrine

The Tantric shrine of Yogāṃvara is located on the first floor in the building on eastern side of the courtyard. No outsider, and certainly no foreigner, may enter it. Only, the Cakreśvara, the most senior Vajrācārya member of the monastery, may enter the shrine of Yogāṃvara, a highest yoga tantra deity. Most of ceremonies related to *cūḍākarma, ācārya abhiṣeka, gaṇacakra, caryāgīta* and so forth are performed here. The Daśapārāmitā elders have special seating arrangements during tantric performances. Members of Kwābahā Saṃgha gather here for annual Deopūjā (April/May) ceremonies when they hold ritual feasts.

Cakrasaṃvara Shrine

Passing out of the back gate of Kwābahā, in the southwest corner, one enters the residential courtyard called Ilānani. Here is the second tantric shrine of Kwābahā dedicated to tantric deity Cakrasaṃvara.

This too is closed to outsiders. Twenty elders hold regular meetings and *pūjās* such as *amāipūjā, aṣṭamivrata*, and others in this shrine. Once a year (October/November) the open space in front of this shrine is used for a feast called Saṃgha bhojan in which all initiated members of *saṃgha* community participate.

Cakrasaṃvara is a deity of Highest Yoga Tantra. He is one of the most popular tutelary deities among Newar Buddhists. Almost all the Śākyas and the Vajrācāryas of Patan and Kathmandu regard Cakrasaṃvara as their tutelary deity. Vajrācāryas follow the ancient practice of Cakrasaṃvara, a highly developed technique of contemplation to realize the Clear Light and Emptiness aspect of the mind. A special tantra called Cakraṣamvaramūla tantra is dedicated to this Iṣṭadevatā.

On the ground floor is a small shrine dedicated to the deity Śaṃkatā the eliminator of distress, obstacles and adverse circumstances. The shrine is surrounded by miniature images of Great Eight Mahāsiddhas. This is the reason why visitors to this shrine are more numerous than to other shrines. One can see visitors, confident that worship of this tantric god will bring efficacious results, lining up at his shrine.

Rituals at the Main Shrine

Here is an account of the routine I followed each day during the month in which I fulfilled the responsibility of god guardian (*devapālaka*), a term which all members of Kwābahā must undertake once in their lives.

In other *vihāras* the turn of god guardianship passes down the roster of members from the most senior to the most junior for a week, a fortnight, or a month at a time. Depending on the number of members and length of service, one's turn may occur once a year, once every few years, or at even longer intervals. In the case of Kwābahā, whose membership is very large, one's turn comes only once in a lifetime. (Saṃgha is restricted to male Śākyas and Vajrācāryas.) As I was ordained (Newari: *baréchuyégu* ceremony) in 1956, my turn fell forty-three years later, in the month of May/June, 1999.

At the outset, I appointed two boys (called *bāphāchā* senior and *bāphāchā* junior aged 8 and 22 years respectively) to assist me in attending to the main shrine, and also a young lady, known as *nikulimha* to cook food to be offered to Kwābāju and also for the two *bāphāchās.* I registered my appointments in the evening (usually 8 or 9 pm) in front of Yogaṃvara Shrine along with traditional ritual offering substances. A Guru maṇḍala rite was performed by the senior-most Vajrācārya, the Cakreśvara-Āju, whose responsibility is to attend to the Yogaṃvara shrine. Only he is permitted to see the main deity of the shrine. After performing a *pūjā* at Yogṃvara shrine, Vajrācāryā blessed and gave *prasāda* to the *bāphāchās* after which they were not allowed to eat anything until they became full-fledged temple priest.

Next day, both *bāphāchās* went to bathe in the Bāgmati River, shaved their heads, and donned the white garments of a temple priest. It is a monastery rule that the two *bāphāchās* must wear the same white garments for the whole month; they are forbidden to wash them, however dirty they might get.

Around 1 pm they came back from the river to Kwābahā and rested in the Swayaṃbhū shrine until the moment that all the paraphernalia and ornaments of the main deity were handed over in the presence of members of Kwābahā Saṃgha.

At 3 pm, the new temple priests entered the main shrine and offered betel nuts, coins with rice grains in 37 different places within the main shrine, and offered lamps to the deities. The outgoing priests instructed the new priests about how to conduct the daily rituals. The outgoing priests then left the shrine carrying yellow sandalwood paste and flowers.

The Bétāju, the chief ritual officer, checks off each item on the roster. If some items are missing, the god guardian has to pay for the loss or replace what is lost with new articles. The god guardian is burdened by the fear of losing articles during his guardianship, by the lack of manpower and by the expenditure of the substantial sums of money involved in attending to the shrine for one whole month.

After all the items have been checked, the list is handed over to the new god guardian and both outgoing and incoming god guardian must offer refreshments to the elders and their family members and to people who have been invited to observe this ritual event.

Now the new *bāphāchās* take up the position of temple priests inside the main shrine.

It is they who perform the rituals whereas the god guardian oversees and coordinates but rarely directly participates.

First Watch

At about 3 am, the recital group comes to Kwābahā to read the *Nāmasaṃgīti*. After they have read for about twenty minutes, the senior *bāphāchā* who has slept the night on a mat near the Vajrasattva shrine, gets up and takes a bath. He goes into the shrine of Kwābāju and bows to Śākyamuni Buddha. He sweeps the floor clean inside the shrine and lights the wicks. He removes the clothes of Kwābāju, takes a waterpot located inside the shrine, and goes to fetch water from the well. He puts the pot of pure water down at the shrine door and goes out to wash his face. Then he takes it inside, bows to the Buddha again, rinses the Worship Plate (*pūjābhaḥ*), water pot, and silver plate (*babhu*), and places them all in front of Balabhadra. He pours half of the pure water into the flask (*kalaśa*), and then grinds yellow powder (*mhāsu sinhaḥ)*. As soon as he has finished this, he lights a ghee lamp.

By this time the recitation of *Nāmasaṃgīti* will have reached the half-way; the coordinator of the *Nāmasaṃgīti* recital group asks the *devapālaka* to wake up the junior *bāphāchā* whereupon the younger priest gets up, hastily washes his face and comes into the shrine and bows down to the deities inside the main shrine.

The senior priest comes out to light the wicks along the balcony and goes inside again. Then, while the junior priest rings a bell, the senior priest pours water from the flask into the silver plate, takes the small flask which stands on it, and washes the faces of Kwābāju, and of Vajradharā.

After this, he makes offerings to the deities while the junior priest holds up a mirror to the Buddha. Standing at the door, he holds up the mirror to Svayaṃbhū; the junior priest sprinkles pure water on Svayaṃbhū and over the waiting devotees. Meanwhile, the junior priest comes out with rice and flask in his hand, and puts rice and water in a circle on the *maṇḍala* below the balcony. Next, the two priests come outside to strike the wooden gong 108 times. Meanwhile the devotees, who by now are reciting the concluding verses of *Nāmasaṃgīti*, watch the ritual with rapt attention.

Usually, on receipt of small amounts of money from the devotees, the *Nāmasaṃgīti* Recital group also recites *Aparimitā Dhāraṇī* for long life, *Bhaisajya Buddha Dhāraṇī* for patients and *Tārā Dhāraṇī* for the sake of overcoming obstacles.

During my guardianship three foreigners were invited to witness this beautiful morning ceremony and each of them contributed for Dhāraṇī Recitation and made Thai flowers offerings to Śākyamuni Buddha in the main shrine.

On the completion of this ritual, the junior priest rings the bell, and the readers come up onto the balcony below the shrine of Kwābāju and read the *Buddham trailokyanātham*. When this is over, the senior priest takes the yak-tail whisk and the juinor priest takes the silver whisk with peacock feathers, and the two of them ring bells while the recitation of *Dānabalena* is underway. Then, the two priests put yellow powder paste on their foreheads, and give yellow paste and flowers to the devotees waiting in the courtyard outside. Other devotees continue coming to the monastery for worship until about 8 or 9 am, and, on important days (full moon, *saṃkrānti/sanhu*, eighth, and new moon day), until later.

Second Watch

At this time, the lady who prepares the priests' food arrives; she is known as *nikulimha*. She goes into the kitchen and removes the clothes she has come in and puts on pure clothes. She fetches pure water, and then smears cow dung on the floor inside and makes the cooking area neat and clean. She next comes to the door of the main shrine, and the senior priest passes her the worship plate with a ghee lamp, wicks and a small water pot on it. She takes these back to the kitchen, lights the ghee lamp, and cooks the priests' pure food meal (*palan*).

At 9 a.m., the junior priest goes off ringing his bell to *Nhu Bahāḥ, Nyākhācok*, (my ancestral home), *Tāpā Hitī, Nāg Bahā, Ilā Nanī, SaraśvatīNanī,* and returns through the main door of Kwābahā. He stands at the door of the shrine and puts down the things he has been carrying. The senior priest sprinkles him with holy water (*jal*) and hangs up the paraphernalia. The junior priest washes his face, goes into the main shrine and bows to the deities. The two priests again beat the gong 108 times, and while the junior priest rings the bell, the *Buddham trailokyanātham* is read. Once again, they bow to the gods.

After a short while, the junior priest takes the silver food carrier to the kitchen and places it outside the door. The cook washes it, puts food on three worship plates, places them in the silver carrier, and puts it outside. The junior priest puts one plate before Kwābāju, one before Balabhadra, and the other he scatters to left and right for the mice. Then, the junior *bāphāchā* goes to eat; after a little while, the senior *bāphāchā* does the same. All food, other than milk, rice green lentils, ghee, molasses, and ginger, is forbidden.

After this, the priests may take a rest and if they are sleepy, lie down for an hour and a half, until noon.

Third Watch

The priests must wash again, and may not touch anyone. At 3 pm, they enter into the shrine and bow to the gods. The junior *bāphāchā* puts on the shoulder piece (*cīvara*) and comes out wearing the monastic sandals (*kwāpālakān*). The senior *bāphāchā* takes the large wooden gong outside, and again they beat it 108 times. The junior *bāphāchā* goes inside and rings the bell while the *Buddham trailokyanātham* is recited outside. At 4 pm, the cook goes into the kitchen, changes into a set of pure clothes, and goes to fetch pure water. Then, she puts out beaten rice, molasses, cakes, fruit, and yoghurt for the priests. She calls them, and they come to eat.

ph. 6 opposite page

Fourth Watch

After eating, they take a short rest, and at 5.30 pm they wash again. The senior *bāphāchā* goes with two water pots to the well to bring pure water. He puts water down outside the shrine and goes to wash his face. Then he goes in and bows to the deities. The junior *bāphāchā* likewise washes his face, sweeps the balcony, goes into the shrine, brings the flask outside, and pours water on the *maṇḍala* there. The elder priest takes out the wooden gong and rests it on the junior *bāphāchā's* shoulder. The junior *bāphāchā* beats it 108 times again.

After a while as before the junior priest goes off ringing the bell. Meanwhile the cook comes to offer wick lamps to the various deities as specified. By this time the junior *bāphāchā* has returned from his tour. He takes off the shoulder piece and bell, and comes out of the shrine. The senior *bāphāchā* stays inside for those who come to read in the evening.

ph. 7 opposite page

6 – *Third Watch:*
The senior and the junior bāphāchās *performing the afternoon ritual of beating the wooden gong at 3 pm*

7 – *Fourth Watch:*
The senior bāphāchā *stays inside the Main Shrine for those who come to read in the evening*

At 7 pm, the junior *bāphāchā* washes his face and goes into the shrine. The readers come and take out the hymn book, and the younger priest rings the bell while they read the *Buddham trailokyanātham.* When the reading is finished the priests stand by the both sides of Kwābāju and ring bells and wave whisks, while the *Dānabalena* is read. When this is over, they light the *dip jwālā* lamp, and ringing the bell they wave it around. Both the *bāphāchās* then take light, and so do those who have read. Then they read more verses, while the younger priest rings the bell and elder priest waves the lamp (*āratī*)

When the reading is over, the *āratī* is put down, and the senior *bāphāchā* takes the worship plate, worships Kwābāju with rice, applies yellow paste to his forehead, and then to Balabhadra's forehead and to other deities around him. Then the junior *bāphāchā* takes yellow powder paste for himself and the senior *bāphāchā* does likewise. Then they give paste to the readers outside in the courtyard.

When everyone has placed a spot of paste on his or her forehead the paste bowl is passed back inside. The senior *bāphāchā* then covers Kwābāju with a special cloth. The junior *bāphācā* comes out with the key. The senior *bāphāchā* puts the flask and silver plate in front of Balabhadra, and then puts out rice for the mice. He puts three piles on the silver plate, and three at the legs of the flask's tripod. Then he uncovers the pure waterpot, bows to Kwābāju, and comes out. He locks the shrine door with an old key, and checks to make sure that the shutters and doors are closed up. By 9.30 pm their daily duties are over and they go to rest.

Festivals at Golden Temple

There are several religious festivals carried out in this monastery, among them the following are most popular

a – Samyaka Festival

The monastery management committee organizes the Samyaka festival once every four years with colorful rituals in which giant-sized bronze Buddha images, among them, one of Dīpaṃkara Buddha, are honored and worshipped.

b – Pañcadāna Festival

In Patan every year this festival takes places during the month of July/August in which Śākyas and Vajrācāryas are honored as Buddhist monks and devotees offers *pañcadāna.*

c – Saṃgha Feast Festival

This is an annual event in which the main Buddha image is carried in procession through adjacent neighbourhoods. Devotees sing devotional hymns accompanied by musical instruments. After completing the tour, initiated members of the Kwābahā Saṃgha gather for a feast behind the Kwābahā shrine.

d – Dīpaṃkhā Festival

This festival is carried out once every twelve years or at even longer intervals depending on when astrologers calculate the auspicious date for the event. Devotees make a twenty-hour pilgrimage on foot of sacred places in the Kathmandu valley worshipping Buddhas, Lokeśvaras, Tārās, and other deities.

SELECTED BIBLIOGRAPHY

ALLEN, Michael
1973 – "Buddhism without monks: the Vajrayāna religion of the Newars of the Kathmandu Valley", *South Asia 3*, p. 1-10.

BERNIER, Ronald M.
1979 – *The Nepalese Pagoda,* New Delhi, S.Chand and Co. Ltd.

BHISHU, Sudarshan
1994 – *Nepāyā Bahā Bahī yā viśeṣatā* [in Newari], Patan, Nepal, Bauddha Pariyati Sikṣa.

GELLNER, David
1991 – "A Newar Buddhist Liturgy: Śrāvakayānist Ritual in Kwābahā", *Journal of the International Association of Buddhist Studies,* Vol 14,No.2, Lalitpur, Nepal.
1992 – *Monk, Householder, and Tantric Priest: Newar Buddhism and its hierarchy of ritual*, Cambridge, Great Britain, Cambridge University Press.

HUTT Michael
1994 – *Nepal: A Guide to the Art and Architecture of the Kathmandu Valley,* Gartmore, Scotland, Kiscadale Publications.

LA VALLÉE POUSSIN, L. de
? – "Ādikarmapradīpa", *Étude et Matériaux – Bouddhisme,* Partie II, p. 162-232.

LOCKE, John K.
1985 – *Buddhist Monasteries of Nepal*, Kathmandu, Nepal, Sahayogi Press PVT. Ltd.
1989 – "The Unique Features of Nepalese Buddhism", *The Buddhist Heritage*, Tring, U.K., The Institute of Buddhist Studies, p. 71-116.

SHAKYA, Min Bahadur
1984 – *A short history of Buddhism in Nepal,* Patan, Nepal, Young Buddhist Publication (15th WFB and 6th WFBY Conference, Kathmandu).
1986 – *Introduction of Buddhist Monasteries of Kathmandu Valley,* Lalitpur, Nepal, YMBA publication (published on the occasion of the 15th WFB Conference in Kathmandu).
1994 – *Iconography of Nepalese Buddhism,* Kathmandu, Nepal, Handicraft Association of Nepal.
1997 – *Nepalese Princess Bhrikuti Devi,* New Delhi, Book Faith India.

SLUSSER, Mary Shepherd
1998 – *Nepal Mandala: A Cultural Study of the Kathmandu Valley,* (reprint), Kathmandu, Nepal, Mandala Book Point (1st edition: 1982, Princeton University Press).

SNELLGROVE, David L.
1987 – *Indo-Tibetan Buddhism*, Inc. Boston, USA, Shambala Publications.

THE MONASTERIES IN DOLPO, NORTH-WEST NEPAL

From the Monastery to the Village Temple: a historical perspective

Corneille Jest

The interdisciplinary approach undertaken in this contribution is a rather broad one as it encompasses several aspects which cannot be dissociated, namely the history and religious history of a Tibetan speaking population, its way of life, both from the economical and religious point of view, and the "monastery" as a religious unit, its past and present functions in the community.[1]

Methodology

Our sources of information are contained in historical records *karchag (dkar-chag)* and biographies of revered lamas,[2] *namthar (rnam-thar)*. The archaeological remains (which up to now have not been systematically studied), mural paintings and religious objects complement these sources.[3]

1. To complement this presentation we would like to suggest to the reader to consult the book written by Roberto Vitali, *Records of Tho.ling. A literary and visual reconstruction of the "Mother" monastery in Gu.ge*, Dharamsala, High Asia/Amnye Machen Institute, 1999.
R. Vitali presents a detailed analysis of one of the oldest temple complexes in Tibet. It includes the historical background, a study of the buildings composing the Tho.ling complex and inventories based on both textual and oral evidence (illustrated).

2. For the Tibetan words, in italics, we use a simplified phonetic rendering; in brackets transliteration in classical Tibetan.
lama: in a popular sense, one who is capable of reciting the liturgies and performing ceremonies; a title given to a learned religious person.

3. A survey of the religious and historical monuments of the northern regions of Nepal was undertaken in 1978-1981 by the Department of Archaeology, Government of Nepal, and Unesco. The reports of the field surveys are published in the journal *Ancient Nepal*, Department of Archaeology, Nepal.
In 1996-1998 a survey and preliminary investigation of the shrines and temples have been undertaken in the upper valley of the Kali Gandaki in Central Nepal by the "Nepal-German High Mountain Archaeology Project".

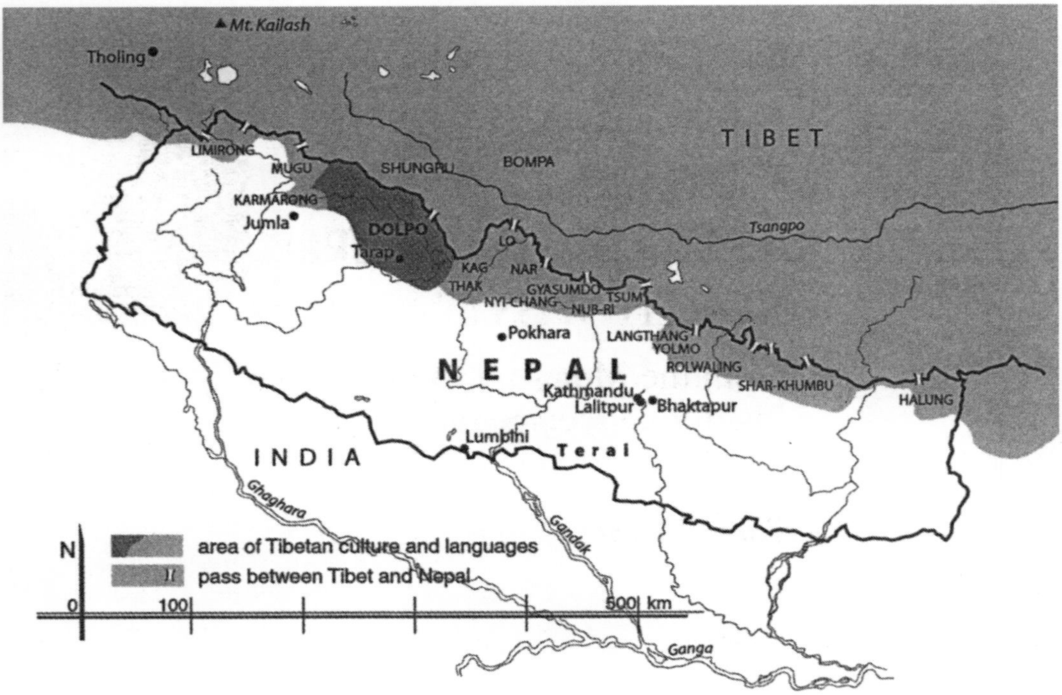

1 – *Map of Nepal: areas where populations of Tibetan language and culture are dominant in the northern part of Nepal*

Geography of Dolpo

Dolpo, which is sometimes called by the inhabitants *bè yül* (*sbas-yul*),[4] the "hidden country", is located on the southern side of the great Himalayan divide, in Nepal; however it is completely isolated from the southern Himalayan valleys (28° 50'-29°40' north latitude, 82°-83°30' east longitude).

Dolpo is part of the present State of Nepal

Population and settlements

According to the tradition, the inhabitants of Dolpo were originally pastoralists Drog-pa, living on the Tibetan Plateau. Looking for better pastures they settled in valleys located on the southern slopes of secondary ridges of the great Himalayas.

Their origin explains the ongoing contacts which they have maintained with the pastoralist groups living to the north, in what is called "Western Tibet", and with which they are in close contact.

At present they are about five thousand, living in the four main valleys of Dolpo. The settlements are located at an average altitude of 4000 metres, allowing the cultivation of barley, the only crop which grows at this altitude and the rearing of yaks, sheep, goats and horses.

4. This term refers to a kind of unspoiled territory, where human beings have never resided since it is the abode of deities.

2 – *In spring, the villagers take the sacred books in procession around the inhabited and cultivated area to pray for the protection and blessing of their crops* (photo C. Jest)

A harsh climate as well as calamities such as epidemics affected the population which sometimes abandoned a site because of the lack of water supply or the curse of the deities.

1. Buddhism in Dolpo, links with Tibet

The expansion of Buddhism in Dolpo.

The Dolpo-pa are Mahāyāna Buddhists. The presence of Buddhism can be traced back to the 12th century. Dolpo is close to the western Tibetan province of Ngnari Korsum, the sacred mountain Mount Kailas (Gang Tise), and the trail linking Central Tibet to Western Tibet and Ladakh; this road was an active axis for the propagation of Buddhism.

Dolpo has a rich historical and religious past, with a number of sacred sites, caves and summits.

This remote region was converted to Buddhism by the *Ka-gyü-pa* order[5] and revered lamas have participated periodically in the revival of the faith.

5. The order of the *Ka-gyü-pa*, "Order of the Transmitted Word", was established in Tibet by Marpa (1012-1097), a great collector and translator of texts.

In Dolpo, monasteries belong to a specific religious order. This can be reflected sometimes in the building structure but mostly in the choice of the paintings that adorn the walls.[6]

A series of biographies of lamas, *namthar*, historical records, *karchag*, of temples and descriptions of pilgrimage places, *neyig,* are the primary sources of our information.

Lama Pema Tondrol, head lama of the valley of Tarap distinguished three phases in the development of Buddhism in Dolpo:[7]

> a) a phase of monasticism during which a group of monks lived in a community, belonging to an order which encouraged monastic life (such as the *Ka-gyu-pa* or *Sa-kya-pa*),
> b) a phase during which the monastery was used for temporary gatherings, meditation and retreats of celibate lamas, the ceremonies being sponsored by the lay community,
> c) the present phase in which only the assembly hall of the monastery is in function for ceremonies, the lamas, mostly married, living outside the monastery. This later phase is related to the expansion of the *Nying-ma-pa* order. In the previous phases the monks' livelihood depended directly on their own family.

An analysis of the biographies of lamas indicate that "Masters" were very often on the move, called by villagers or donors, to teach, perform ceremonies and build shrines and temples, the most prestigious act of merit.

Each valley can be considered as an entity with its clusters of houses, with its own shrines and major temples (former monasteries).

The practice of religion in Dolpo today

The priests, called lamas, belong to the *Nying ma pa*, the "Old Order".[8] Only a certain number of a particular lineage of the upper social strata can engage in religious activities (Jest 1975).

A boy, at the age of thirteen, will be instructed by his father or a senior lama, in reading, learning texts, participating in the ceremonies and be "ordained" at the end of a three year period of retreat. Once a year he will spend some weeks in "meditation" in a monastery or in a village temple.

The lama marries and has a layman's life as a farmer and herder, engaged in trade with Tibet and the lower valleys of Nepal. He does not dress in the monastic red robe like the monks of the other orders, but wears the usual layman's red home spun; for the religious ceremonies he wears a red robe, *chuba,* and a white raw silk shawl with a red band. The lama does not cut his hair which is twisted in turban shape, similar to the ones of the Indian ascetics.

---

6. Many of the monasteries were *Sa-kya-pa* foundations, but nowadays they have become *Nying-ma-pa* in practice.
For example in a *Nying-ma-pa* shrine, Padmasambhava, "Lotus Born", is regarded as the supreme manifestation of the Buddha essence.

7. In the neighbouring region of Lo-Manthang, the monastic life is still in existence, the monks belong to the *Sa-kya-pa* order.

8. The worship of the *Nying-ma-pa* order centres around the "Lotus-Born", Padmasambhava, a historical figure who developed Buddhism in Tibet and the Himalayan region in the 8th century. In Dolpo the "Lotus Born" is popularly considered as the founder of Tibetan Buddhism.

3 – *Lama printing protective charms to be put in amulets* (photo C. Jest)

2. The monastery: generalities

Lama Pema Tondrol gave the following definition of a monastery, called *gompa* (*dgon-pa*)[9] in Dolpo:

– the temple enshrines a principal deity, most often Sakyamuni to whom the site is dedicated;
– the layout pattern of the temple should follow precise rules of construction;
– space or room should be devoted to the collection of sacred texts;
– a closed room is necessary to keep the secret tantric deity, protector of the site.

The foundation

Once one has decided to build a monastery, the founder, a monk or a community, has to go through a certain number of steps. One has to find an ideal site, as defined by a religious text.[10] The final choice will be made by a lama astrologer, instructed in geomancy. Whenever possible the main facade should face east, "the great white way leading to the rising sun". To the south the site will be bounded by a river, identified

9. *gompa, dgon-pa*, lit. solitary place, hermitage, monastery.

10. In Dolpo one refers to a canonical work, the Rinchenterdzö (*rin-chen gter-mdzod*) of the *Nyingma-pa* order.

with the "turquoise dragon". To the west, the back of the temple should be set against a mountain, corresponding to the "red bird". To the north, another mountain with the shape of a turtle should delimit the sacred precinct.

A series of rituals will follow to propitiate the deities of the soil. Other ones will take place when the first pillar is erected, the entrance door put into place and the roof completed.

A consecration ceremony concludes the series of rituals after completion of the work (Thubten Legshay Gyatsho1979; Jest 1981).

A name will be given to the monastery, for example *sgrol-lung*: "place of salvation".

The construction

The monastic complex is very often located on a terrace above the settlements, in a realm which is considered pure.

The lama, head of the community, has knowledge concerning the proportions of the buildings which have to be adjusted to the available space. In Dolpo there is no direct reference to a specific text giving the instructions for the building process. The lama and the master craftsman will decide on the final proportions depending on the site.

The size of the temple, which is one component of the monastic complex, is defined by the number of pillars and beams which support the ceiling, for example one would say *ka shi gdung gye,* "a temple with four pillars and eight beams".

The external walls are built of stones or compacted earth on a stone plinth, up too one metre in thickness. The building is constructed upon a grid of pillars, which support heavy brackets and beams. Over the beams smaller ceiling joists are closely spaced. The roof over the entire structure is flat and has a clay covering. The roof is slightly sloped, the rainwater being diverted away from the building through gutters.

Materials used are local except the timber, mostly pine, which has to be bought and transported from the lower valleys.

The shrine

The altar is the most important place in the temple, considered as sacred; the statues of the main divinities are set up on a plinth above the altar.

The walls are covered with paintings representing divinities in a specific order. Beams, pillars, lintels are painted with definite colours in a standard fashion.

In Dolpo, where the communities are very poor, the construction of a temple is considered as an outstanding act of high merit.

Organization and maintenance

Each household is represented in an assembly responsible for the organization of rituals, festivals and the general maintenance. Four householders take the responsibility in a yearly turn.

The repairs are made by the members of the community under the guidance of a skilled craftsman.

The wall paintings, when in bad condition, are repainted most of the time. (This is an issue for the conservation of the old paintings as some of them are of very important aesthetic and historical value).

4 – *Dolpo, monastery of Sharing in the valley of Tarap, at an altitude of 4,200 metres* (photo C. Jest)

5 – *Assembly hall, monastery of Dzong, Baragaon* (photo C. Jest)

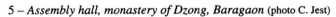

3. An example of a monastic complex in Dolpo: the monastery of Yangtsher and the hermitage of Margom.

The monastery of Yangtsher and the hermitage of Margom are situated in the northern part of Dolpo on the slopes overlooking the Panzang-chu and Namgung chu, at an altitude of 4,200 metres.

The reason of the choice of the location was, according to the tradition, its barren environment and wilderness. The site is remarkable for its isolation, thus it has become one of the most important places of pilgrimage in Dolpo and possesses a special sacred power for the Dolpo-pa. Yangtsher and Margom are part of a sacred geography marked by famous temples relics and marvellous revelations of deities. The pilgrims come at regular intervals to obtain blessings and avert calamities, perform penance, ask for heirs or recovery and pray for good health.

Wildlife is preserved all along the itinerary of pilgrimage; wild sheep are in plenty and protected.

Yangtsher gompa

Yangtsher gompa (a local name which refers to its location, meaning "the right side settlement" *(gyas-mtsher)*; the religious name is (*byang-chub-gling*) "Island of Enlightenment") can be considered a typical monastic settlement in Dolpo. It has a very ancient history and is still used as a temple and semi-permanent residence of lamas (a detailed description is given in Snellgrove 196I, 85-92 for the year 1956).

Built five to six hundred years ago, the monastery is mentioned in the biography of venerable Lama Chögyab Palzang (*chos-skyabs dpal-bzang*) "Religious Protector, Glorious and Good".[11] It is a *sa-kya* foundation, as reflected in the choice of the paintings that adorn the walls.

The monastery stands on a terrace about 150 metres above the narrow gorge of the Panzang chu, next to its confluence with the Namgung chu, on its right bank, facing south-east. The trail which leads to it from the valley of Namgung crosses two torrents and climbs up to the religious settlements.

A boundary wall c*hagri* (*lcags-ri*), made of big rocks surrounds a compound of buildings of different sizes and functions.

On the eastern side, an entrance-chörten, *kani chörten*, gives access to the courtyard which extends from east to west (approximately 30 by 60 metres), on the northern side of the complex.[12]

Around the courtyard stand different edifices:

fig. 6a, 6b opposite page

The first one [1] is a rectangular hall containing a row of eight large *chörten* and a circumambulatory pathway. The walls are covered with old frescoes of very fine craftsmanship, in *sa-kya-pa* style, in particular three famous *sa-kya* lamas of the thirteenth and fourteenth centuries, Buddhas and Bodhisattvas.

---

11. See biography in Snellgrove 1967: 125-182. Lama Chögyab Palzang, "Religious Protector Glorious and Good", (1476-1565), was abbot of Margom and Yangtsher.

12. *chörten* (*mchod-rten*) "support for worship", is the typical Buddhist monument, derived from Indian models. It can be a shrine in which relics are enclosed, or just an expression of faith, built by a donor.

6a – *Monastery of Yangtsher, from east* (photo C. Jest)

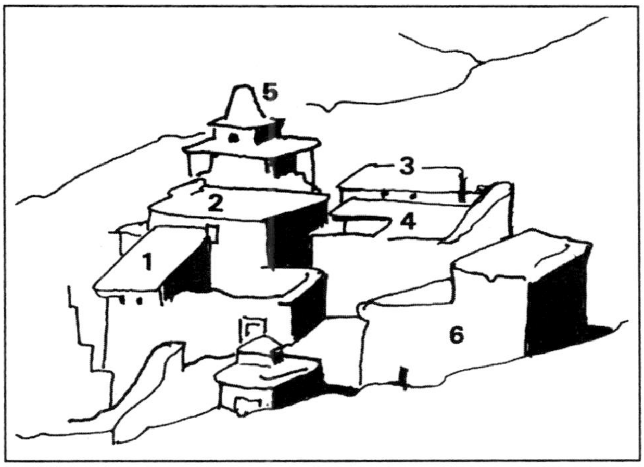

6b – *Monastery of Yangtsher*

1 – Hall
2 – *tsuglakhang*
3 – *serkhang*
4 – *lama'i zimchung*
5 – *chörten*
6 – *jomo lakhang*

The second building [2], called *tsuglakhang*, (*gtsug-lag-khang*) an assembly hall, is square; the walls have been repainted in *nying-ma-pa* style.

The third edifice [3] called *serkhang* (*gser-khang*) is square with four pillars surmounted by extended capitals which support the beams. It is decorated in *nying-ma-pa* style. Against the northern wall, facing the entrance, is placed the main altar. At one time there were several statues. Alas all these statues have disappeared in recent times. The central image represents Padmasambhava, the "Lotus Born". The *serkhang* is used for the regular ceremonies and can be a dormitory for the devotees on special occasions. The upper floor is occupied by a library containing the religious texts.

The lama caretaker lives in a building, the *lama'i zimchung* (*bla-ma'i gzim-chung*) [4], which contains a chapel.

In the far end of the courtyard stands a *chörten* [5], containing the remains of Lama Chögyab Palzang, who is considered the founder of the monastery.

At the entrance of the courtyard, to the right, stands a small two-storey building, the *jomo lhakhang*, the chapel of the nuns [6].

All the external walls are painted red, sign of the religious function of the buildings.

Between this group of buildings and a row of nine *chörten*, which flank the southern side and are said to have been built in less than one year, there is a stony area lined with rows of prayer-walls and heaps of stone slabs engraved with the formula *Om mani padme hum*, quotations from texts or refuge formulas.

At short distance above the monastery is a shrine, cubic in shape, for the local god *shibdag* (*gzhi-bdag*). He is considered the protector of the site and receives regularly a share of the offerings.

The lamas attached to Yangtsher, all married, live either in small houses close to the monastery on the eastern side or in the neighbouring villages. The present head lama is Gelong Dawa Tenzing.

They perform a ceremony which regularly takes place on the 10th day of every lunar month. An important festival is held in midsummer with the participation of the villagers of the Panzang Valley.

The hermitage of Margom

See Annex: drawing and comments, p. 260-61

The hermitage of Margom (*dmar-sgom*) is part of the religious entity of Yangthser; it is a retreat and place of meditation, hidden above Yangtsher between cliffs, big rock falls and bare grey brown slopes. It is only accessible after a difficult climb along a rocky track.The first hermit lived in a cave, partly closed by a wall. Later on, another construction was added.

The hermitage, abandoned for a long time, has been renovated in 1996 at the initiative of Tsering Tashi, a local lama.[13] From 1996 to 1998, under his direction, the villagers have been able to build four shrines.

The hermitage consists of small buildings, the rock used as the back wall, from top to bottom, they are:

– at the highest level, where the first hermitage and cave temple existed, a chapel with a statue of Öpame; it is also the residence of the lama;
– at the second level: a chapel with the statues of the three Protectors;
– at the third level: a chapel with a statue of Guru Rimpoche measuring eight cubits;
– at the lowest level, a chapel of the tantric protective divinities, Gombo Maning and Dorji Phurwa; a small kitchen is attached to this chapel.

Near the original hermitage water is collected in a small cavity in the rock which provides water for daily use and rituals.

Close by, a grove of juniper shrubs, *shug-pa,* the only patch of vegetation in this barren landscape, is protected; no wood can be cut or collected.

The shrine of the Pho-lha Meme Bala, the local protective divinity, is located above this grove.

---

13. Tsering Tashi, born in 1947 in Namgung, has been educated in Dolpo. He belongs to the *nyingma-pa* order. He visited several places of pilgrimage in Nepal and India; in 1993 he spent one year in Taiwan, invited by a Buddhist community. With the generous donations given by Chinese devotees he printed several religious texts which he donated to different monasteries and rehabilitated temples in Dolpo. Margom is his favourite place for meditation.

The rehabilitation of such sites is very common in the Tibetan tradition.

The most sacred spot is on the summit of the mountain ridge dominating the valley of Panzang; it culminates with a *chörten*, receptacle of the ashes of Lama Sonam Lotrö abbot of Margom,[14] particularly venerated in Northern Dolpo.

The community in charge of maintenance and worship ofthe complex consists of families living in several small groups of houses located on both sides of the Panzang chu. Villagers visit the temple of the monastery to seek blessings and avert calamities. They circumambulate the prayer-walls and *chörten,* offer butter lamps on auspicious days. During the winter months, when there is no work in the fields they assemble in the temple for a short period of fasting, recite prayers and read Buddhist texts.

The monastery receives land and cattle as endowments from villagers.

4. Present usage of monasteries, shrines and temples in Dolpo

There is very little information as to the functioning and management of a monastery in Dolpo in the remote past. In former times the monks, living in community were bound by a very strict code of rules.

Today the lamas called locally *chöpa* (*chos-pa*, lit."of the doctrine") marry and live a householder's life, work in the fields or are engaged in trade and barter with Tibet and the valleys of Nepal. As priests, after a period of initiation and an ordination, they perform daily a regular worship in their private chapel.

7 – ***Private chapel in the lama's house at Tagar, Baragaon***
(photo C. Jest)

14. Lama Sonam Lotrö (*bsod-nams blo-gros*)"Merit Intellect" (1456-1521) was abbot of Margom.

In the monasteries only the assembly hall is used for the major ceremonies of the religious calendar. The lamas meet when performing ceremonies which regularly take place on the 10th day of the lunar month with a liturgy of a specific divinity, during major festivals such as the *yartön* (*dbyar-ston* lit. "the summer festival") usually from the 10th to the 15th day (full moon) of the 5th lunar month, and the general offerings *mangja* (*mang-ja* lit. "collective tea") offered by a benefactor after a wish.

As a result of this change in the lamas' way of life, the monastery has lost most of its institutional functions and only the temple/assembly-hall remains in use during the major ceremonies and festivals.

8 – *Midsummer religious festival at Tarap*
The community assembled around the entrance of the main temple (photo C. Jest)

9 – *Monastery of Trangmar*
Ceremony performed by the lamas for the welfare of the community (photo C. Jest)

10 – *Lama of the* nying-ma-pa *order performing a regular ritual* (photo C. Jest)

11 – *In winter the villagers gather in the assembly hall for prayers and periods of fasting* (photo C. Jest)

12 – *Kathmandu: a new monastery under construction.*
The Lama founder, Sangsang Tulku, of the ka-gyu-pa *order, is Tibetan and most of the donors are merchants of Tibetan origin settled in Nepal* (photo C. Jest)

5. Tibetan monasteries in the Kathmandu valley

Though it is not the purpose of our presentation, one cannot omit to mention the existence of the monasteries built in recent years in the Kathmandu valley. It is to these monasteries that the young boys from Dolpo are now sent by their fathers, lamas, for a better religious education. However that does not mean that they will become monks or return to their remote villages as village priests!

The Kathmandu valley has been for centuries a place of worship and pilgrimage for the Tibetans and Buddhists of Central Asia.[15] One must recall that in 1959 there were only three small monasteries in the valley of Kathmandu (Jest 1989). In 1999 one counts more than sixty monasteries, religious centres and schools. These new monasteries are built by patrons with the support of the Tibetan community living in Nepal.

The new buildings, are all of very large size, inspired by the plans of the monasteries built in Northern India during the first period of Buddhist expansion (the builders of new assembly halls/temples in Katmandu refer to the plan of the monastery of Odantapuri).

6. Conservation of the Heritage

Let us also mention the present state of the monasteries and temples in Dolpo. Most of them are old and need repair. The population of Dolpo has suffered from the political unrest in Tibet after 1959 and its economical consequences on the trade between Tibet and Nepal. More young people migrate towards the urban centres of Central Nepal and the maintenance of the religious buildings is no more a priority.

Tibetan Buddhism has elaborated in the course of more than ten centuries very complex structures over a vast area (more than two thousand kilometres, from east to west). The region described in this paper is on the edge of the Tibetan cultural area where specific traditions have been preserved and have not been submitted to the unifying pressure which developed elsewhere in Central Tibet. Thus the monastery in Dolpo cannot be considered as a "centre of excellence" as it was in Central Tibet.

However, as important for an adequate sense of the place as its physical description is an appreciation that the monastery is a sacred realm, an entrance to a sacred world especially appropriate for an ascetic effort.

Dolpo is now in contact with the modern world where new types of Buddhism have arisen which might require neither monasticism nor monasteries... In the same way the current popular religiosity is in a transition from a "medieval" to a modern stage of development.

One can fear that, because the young boys are now sent for religious education to the monasteries in the Kathmandu valley, the lamas of the remote regions will be soon too few in number for their traditions to survive the shock of the modern world.

---

15. For the Tibetan Buddhists, Kathmandu is one of the major pilgrimage sites, visited during the Tibetan year of the Bird.

ANNEX

Drawing representing the mountain of Margom by Kungya, painter from Tarap, Dolpo.

The numbers correspond to specific monuments and sites on the Yangtsher-Margom slope.

1. *Doro zam chung*, "the small bridge on the confluent" on the Saldang chu;
2. *Kani chörten* an entrance *chörten* built near the confluence of two streams to protect the environment;
3. *Doro zam chen*, "the big bridge on the confluent" on the Namgung chu and the Panzang chu;
4. Monastery of Yangtsher;
5. Changchub semba gompa (owner Lama Jigme Trogyal);
6. Two *chörten*, built recently;
7. Chapel dedicated to the protective divinities Dorji Phurwa, Gombo Maning and at the same level a small kitchen;
8. Chapel dedicated to Guru Rimpoche/ Padmasambhava, (statue);
9. Chapel dedicated to the protectors of the three families: Chenresi/Avalokitesvara, Jampeyang/Manjusri, Chanagdorji/Vajrapani.
10. The old hermitage and dwelling of the present lama, statue of Öpame/Amitabha;
11. Grove of juniper shrubs;
12. Dead juniper tree, considered sacred, used to prepare incense;
13. *Chu lensa*, small spring, the only source for water on the slope;
14. *Gyaltsen tsemo*, mast with printed banner;
15. Pholha Meme Bala, shrine of the local deity;
16. Juniper grove;
17. Flat stone where the cremation of lama Sonam Lotrö took place;
18. *Tsamkhang*, small meditation cave;
19. Cave where the body of Lama Sonam Lotrö rested before the cremation;
20. *Kudung chörten (sku-gdung mchod-rten)*, reliquary *chörten* containing the remains of Lama Sonam Lotrö and a *darchog*, prayer flag.

To each monument or site are associated a series of events, historical facts or legends which are part of the "memory" of the area.

The *kani chörten* which was built near the confluence of the Namgung and Panzang streams was perceived by the villagers as the residence of a harmful spirit and as a result animals died in great numbers. A revered lama staying close by in meditation found out the reason; he threw a stone with his sling hitting a crow, *cha kyunka*, which was sitting on the top of the *chörten*; the crow flew away and the evil forces disappeared. A prayer wall was built later near by as an other measure of protection.

When Lama Sonam Lotrö died, his disciples wanted to move his body but could not do it. Finally his closest disciple was called and he carried alone the body towards the cremation ground. He put the body in a cave close to the crest of the ridge the face turned towards the west. The next morning the face of the dead lama was turned towards the east. The reason of this miracle was that the lama was also the abbot of the monastery of Shimen, in the eastern direction.

The local deity, Meme Bala, is very helpful when properly worshipped; twice a year offerings are made by the community. People spend some time close to the shrine and the deity visits them in their dreams.

Lama Tsering Tashi while restoring and expanding the hermitage, intended to materialize in the layout the three-fold expression of Buddhist faith, therefore he built in a vertical succession three chapels each one dedicated to one of the three expressions *chos, lung, sprul gsum*:

– Öpame representing *chos*, the Buddhist religion;

– the three Protectors, representing *lung*, the spiritual precepts;

– Guru Rimpoche/Padmasambhava, representing *sprul,* the emanation of Faith.

BIBLIOGRAPHICAL REFERENCES.

JEST, C.
1975 – *Communautés de langue tibétaine du Nord du Népal*, Paris, CNRS.
1981 – *Monuments of Northern Nepal*, Paris, Unesco.
1989 – "Le Bouddhisme, son expression tibétaine dans la vallée de Kathmandu, Népal. Aspects sociologiques et économiques d'une expansion hors du Tibet, 1959-1984", *Acta Orientalia Academiae Scientiarum Hungariae*, XLIII, (2-3), p. 431-444.

MEYER, F. et JEST, C.
1987 – "Architecture: fonctions techniques, sociales, symboliques et religieuses", p. 52-68,
"Milieux, matériaux et techniques", p. 135-167,
Demeures des Hommes, Sanctuaires des Dieux. Sources, développement et rayonnement de l'architecture tibétaine, (P. Mortari Vergara, Gilles Beguin éds.), Roma, Il Bagatto.

SNELLGROVE, D.L.
1959 – *Buddhist Himalaya. Travels and Studies in quest of the origins and nature of Tibetan Religion*, Oxford, Bruno Cassirer.
1961 – *Himalayan Pilgrimage*, Oxford, Bruno Cassirer.
1967 – *Four Lamas of Dolpo, Tibetan Biographies,* Oxford, Bruno Cassirer (2 volumes).

SNELLGROVE D.L. et RICHARDSON, H.E.
1968 – *A Cultural History of Tibet*, London, Weidenfeld and Nicolson.

THUBTEN LEGSHAY GYATSHO
1979 – *Gateway to the Temple. Manual of Tibetan Monastic Customs, Art, Building and Celebrations,* (translation by D. Jackson), Kathmandu, Ratna Pustak Bhandar, (Bibliotheca Himalayica Series III, Vol 12).

13 – *Activity of the lamas:*
painting scrolls representing deities and life stories of revered teachers (photo C. Jest)

14 – *Pilgrims circumambulating the sacred mountain of Shey, in Dolpo* (photo C. Jest)

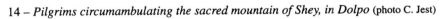

DZONGS AND *GOMPAS* IN BHUTAN

Karma Wangchuk

Bhutan, the only Buddhist kingdom of the peaceful Thunder Dragon, lies in the eastern Himalayas between India and China, two of the largest and most populous countries in the world.

Bhutan was cut off from the rest of the world for centuries. It was opened to the outside world only three decades ago. Its varied population, right up to the present day, have lived in valleys isolated from one another by formidable mountain passes. As such, Bhutan has a rich mosaic of different cultures, traditions, lifestyles, ethnic groups, languages and belief systems. It is astounding that a country with a population of 650,000 speaks as many as nineteen different dialects and four major languages. Diverse as it may seem, yet the Bhutanese socio-cultural fabric is well interlaced and harmonized mainly due to the common threads of simple Buddhist values shared by the people.

Bhutan has an area of 46,500 square kilometres, 72% of which being under forest cover that shelters numerous species of flora and funa. Bhutan is home to one of the world's richest natural environment. Because of its rich and untouched natural heritage, Bhutan has been declared by scientists as one of the ten global "Hot Spots".

At the same time, Bhutan's rich culture, pristine scenery and relative remoteness, combine to surround it with a unique mystique, making it a strong attraction to the outside world. Social and religious customs, *dzongs* (fortified monasteries) and *gompas* (monasteries), buildings and landscape still remain in a form which evolved centuries ago. The intrusions of modernity do not, up to now, disrupt the ancient equilibrium of a hierarchical, well ordered, agricultural and pastoral society under which evolve a way of life, an architecture and an art firmly routed in the philosophy of Buddhism and exceptionally well related to its natural surroundings.

The Buddhist Monastery, EFEO, 2001, p. 265-282

History

Many historians connect the arrival of Buddhism in Bhutan to the construction of two of the oldest existing Buddhist temples in the country. The King of Tibet, Songtsen Gampo, is said to have built these two temples – the Kyichu Lhakhang in Paro in western Bhutan and the Jampa Lhakahng in Bumthang in central Bhutan – in the 7th century AD.

However, it is now believed that newly discovered information on some of our ancient temples may prove that Buddhism may have already been introduced to Bhutan from India as early as the 2nd century AD. Beside this, old sites and documents suggest that Bhutan's association with Buddhism might date back to several hundred years BC. See map p. 271 There are sites in Punakha (western Bhutan) and Trongsa (central Bhutan) that are connected with the lengendary story of King Drime Kunden (which concerns one previous life of the Buddha), and that might be an indication of an old connection to Buddhism. Buddhism that prevails now in Bhutan is the Mahāyāna tradition, introduced during later centuries from Tibet, and is now the main form of Buddhism practiced in Bhutan. In fact, today, Bhutan is the only nation that practices the Tantric form of Mahāyāna Buddhism as its state religion.

The actual establishment of Buddhism in Bhutan is credited to the Indian Buddhist saint, Padmasabhava, popularly known as Guru Rinpoche "Precious Teacher", who arrived in Bhutan in the 8th century AD. He was the founder of the Nyingmapa "old school" of Himalayan Buddhism and is actually considered as the second Buddha. As in Tibet, Guru Rimpoche introduced in Bhutan, the tantric form of Buddhism, which is a highly esoteric and mystical form of the Mahāyāna Buddhism, incorporating many of the existing local spiritual beliefs and rituals.

All the places that Guru Rimpoche is said to have visited in the 8th century in Bhutan are now sacred places of pilgrimage. Many of the most important monasteries in Bhutan have been built around the places he visited or where he meditated.

Buddhism further flourished in the 11th century in Bhutan by the activity of *tertons* mainly in the main districts of Paro (western Bhutan) and Bumthang (central Bhutan). The *tertons* were believed to be pre-destined discoverers of religious treasures. The treasures were sacred religious texts and objects which Guru Rimpoche and other saints had concealed so that they could be discovered at favorable times for the spread of Buddhism.

From the period between the 11th century to the 17th century numerous famous religious figures from Tibet and India came to Bhutan and established various schools of Buddhism. The most famous Nyingmapa saint in Bhutan, other than Guru Rimpoche, is Pema Lingpa (1450-1521) who was born in Bumthang (central Bhutan). He is worshipped as one the most famous "tertons" in the Himalayan world. He founded the famous monasteries of Petsheling, Kunzangdra and Tamshing that still play an active religious role. The Nyingmapa School was further strengthened by his descendants. The famous Annex fig. 7 (a to f) p. 276-77 Nyingmapa monastery of Dramitse in eastern Bhutan was founded by one of them. Pema Thinley, his grandson, established Gangtey monastery, another famous Nyingmapa monastery in the Black Mountains where western Bhutan and central Bhutan meet. The Royal family of Bhutan descends from Pema Lingpa.

1 – *Tango Monastery, from above*
(photo P. Pichard)

The 13th century marked the establishment of the Drukpa Kagyupa school by Phajo Drugom Shigpo in the western part of Bhutan with the foundation of Phajoding and Tango monasteries. *fig. 1 above*

Although the Drukpa school was politically and religiously strong, from the 13th to the 17th century, Tibetan Buddhist teachers from other schools also came to western Bhutan. One of the most famous is Thangtong Gyelpo who established the "chagzams" (iron-chains bridges). Besides many iron bridges and other structures, he built the temple-stūpa of Dungtse in Paro in the first half of the fifteen century in order to subdue an evil spirit. This stūpa is unique: it is the only stūpa that doubles as a temple that was built in Bhutan before the 20th century.

However, no one has had a greater impact on the religious history of Bhutan than the Shabdrung Ngawang Namgyel (1594-1651), popularly known as Shabdrung Rinpoche. He was a hierarch of the Drukpa Kagyupa school, and came to Bhutan from Tibet in the early 17th century. The Shabdrung Ngawang Namgyel was not only a great spiritual personality but also a statesman and leader of exceptional ability. He not only successfully repelled several Tibetan invasions, but unified Bhutan under a theocracy with a dual system: a religious leader called the "Je Khenpo" alongside a temporal leader called the "Desi".

He also constructed a chain of sturdy monastery-fortresses called *dzongs* in most of the important valleys of Bhutan. These *dzongs* became centres of both religion and administration. They housed many shrines and residential areas for the monks as well as space for administrative and governmental functions. Today, they are still functioning in the same manner.

fig. 2, 3, 4 below and opposite page

The first state monastic community in Bhutan was instituted, in 1620 AD, by the Shabdrung Rinpoche with only 30 monks, when he completed the first monastic centre at Cheri Dorjiden about 14 kilometers north of Thimphu, the present capital of Bhutan, under the Chief Abbot Pekar Jungney (the 1st Je Khenpo). He then established other monastic communities in the *dzongs* that he built. Nowadays, the most famous ones are the Punakha and the Thimphu *dzongs* which are respectively the winter and summer residences of the central monastic body of Bhutan which is still run under the direct leadership of the Chief Abbot of Bhutan, the Je Khenpo, as it was in the 17th century.

After the establishment of the monarchy in 1907, Mahāyāna Buddhism was adopted as the state religion with the Drukpa Kagyupa as the main school. However, the Nyingmapa School is widely practised in eastern and central Bhutan.

2 – *Rinchenpung Dzong in Paro, from above* (photo P. Pichard)

Built in 1645 and restored after the fire of 1907.
The five-storey central tower (*utse*) is surrounded by the monastic and administrative quarters.

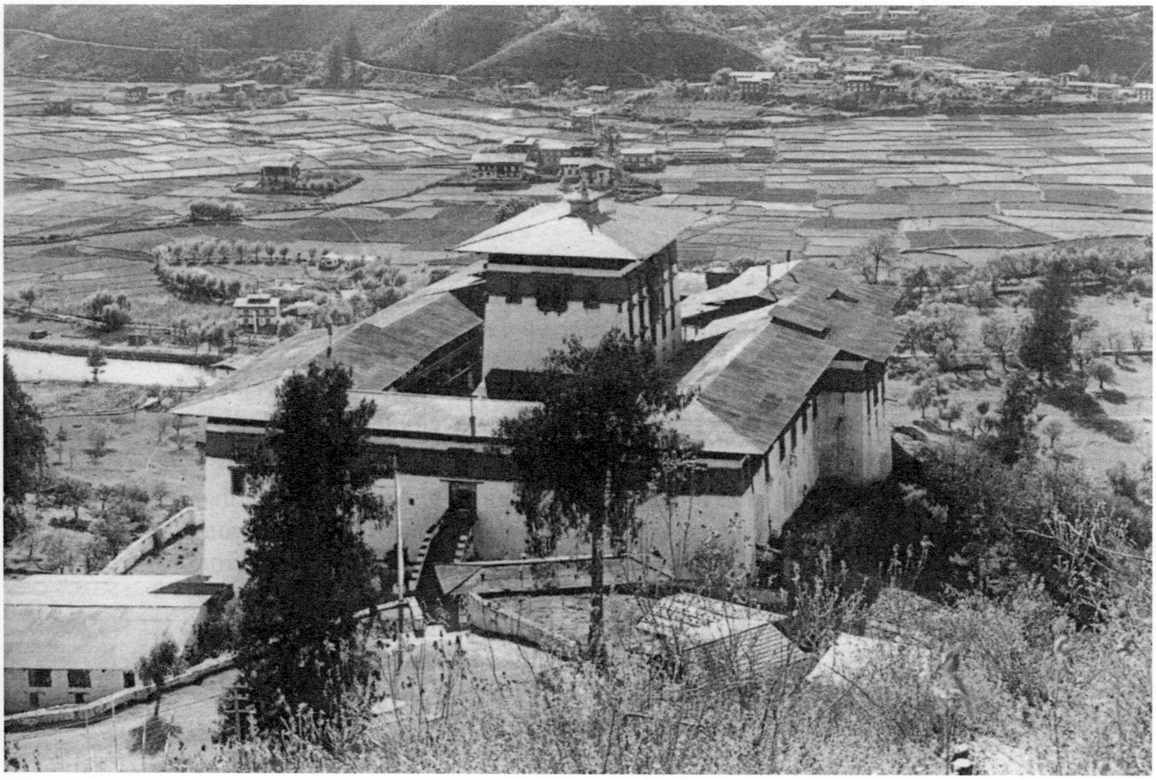

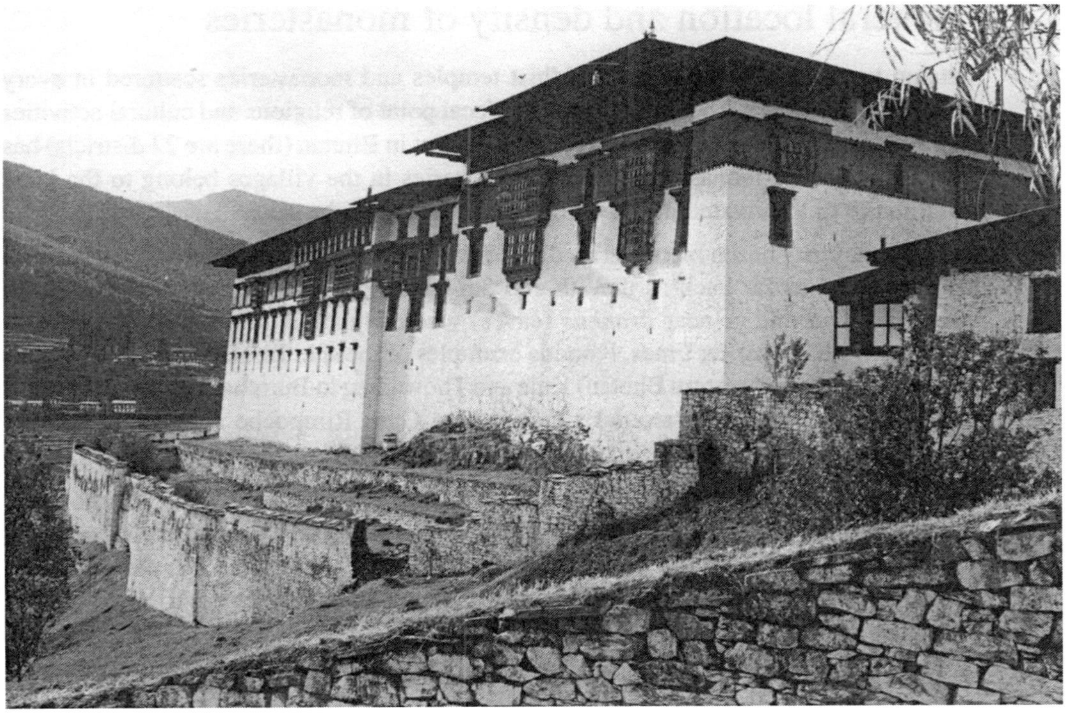

3 – *Rinchenpung Dzong, from south-west*
(photo P. Pichard)

4 – *Rinchenpung Dzong*
View inside the courtyard
(photo P. Pichard)

General location and density of monasteries

Bhutan has over two thousand Buddhist temples and monasteries scattered in every corner of the country. The monastery is the focal point of religious and cultural activities in a Bhutanese village. At an average, each district in Bhutan (there are 22 districts) has around a hundred monasteries. Many monasteries in the villages belong to the local community or to private familes while others belong to the state.

The majority of the monasteries date back to the 17th and 18th century but several were founded as far back as the 7th and 8th century. Most of the monasteries were constructed around or near *draphus* (caves) where Buddhist saints were believed to have meditated in earlier times. Famous examples of these in Bhutan are the Taktshang monastery in Paro, (western Bhutan) Kuje and Thowadrag in Bumthang (central Bhutan). All of these are centered around a cave where Guru Rimpoche is believed to have meditated in the 8th century.

Some monasteries are located on ancient trade routes. This type of location was selected mainly as a mean of getting rid of powerful evil spirits who harmed the people taking that route during old days. Likewise on every pass in the mountains, we find *chörtens* (Skt. *stūpas)*, surrounded by prayers flags. Their function is to ward off evil spirits and spread the message of Dharma.

Many monasteries were also built in locations high up in the mountains where access was difficult, so that the monks could meditate in peace without disturbance from local villagers. There are no stone monuments as such, but large amounts of local stones are used for the foundations upon which structures made almost entirely of rammed earth and wood are erected. Strictly speaking the use of different kind of stones as single medium of structures is rarely found, except in few modern religious constructions. The use of finer stones like marble and slates in the construction is a recent introduction and is purely domestic and commercial. Natural decaying due to climatic conditions, earthquakes, fire and floods are the main problems for the conservation of the monuments but the environment being free of atmospheric pollution, measures against this scourge are not needed.

Present situation

Two thousand temples and monasteries are scattered all over the country with different status: some belong to the state, some to the local communities and some to private owners. Besides monasteries, there are a total of 15 registered monastic centres with 19 Primary-cum-Junior High Schools attached to them, 13 Buddhist Colleges (*Shedras*), 24 Meditation Centres (*Drubdras*), 206 *Upasaka* Centres (*Gomdeys*) and 10 Nunneries throughout Bhutan.

In fact, there is no record of any architectural and civil engineering designs and drawings of all the *dzongs* and monasteries because there were neither architects nor civil engineers in the past. It was the master carpenter who was the "maître d'œuvre" and all his skill was based on the memory of the ancestral knowledge. No drawings and no material specifications were put down on paper as late as 1964, when the present *fig. 5 page 272* massive Trashichho Dzong, the Central Capital Secretariat of Bhutan, was renovated and rebuilt on traditional lines.

Dzongs *and* Gompas *in Bhutan*

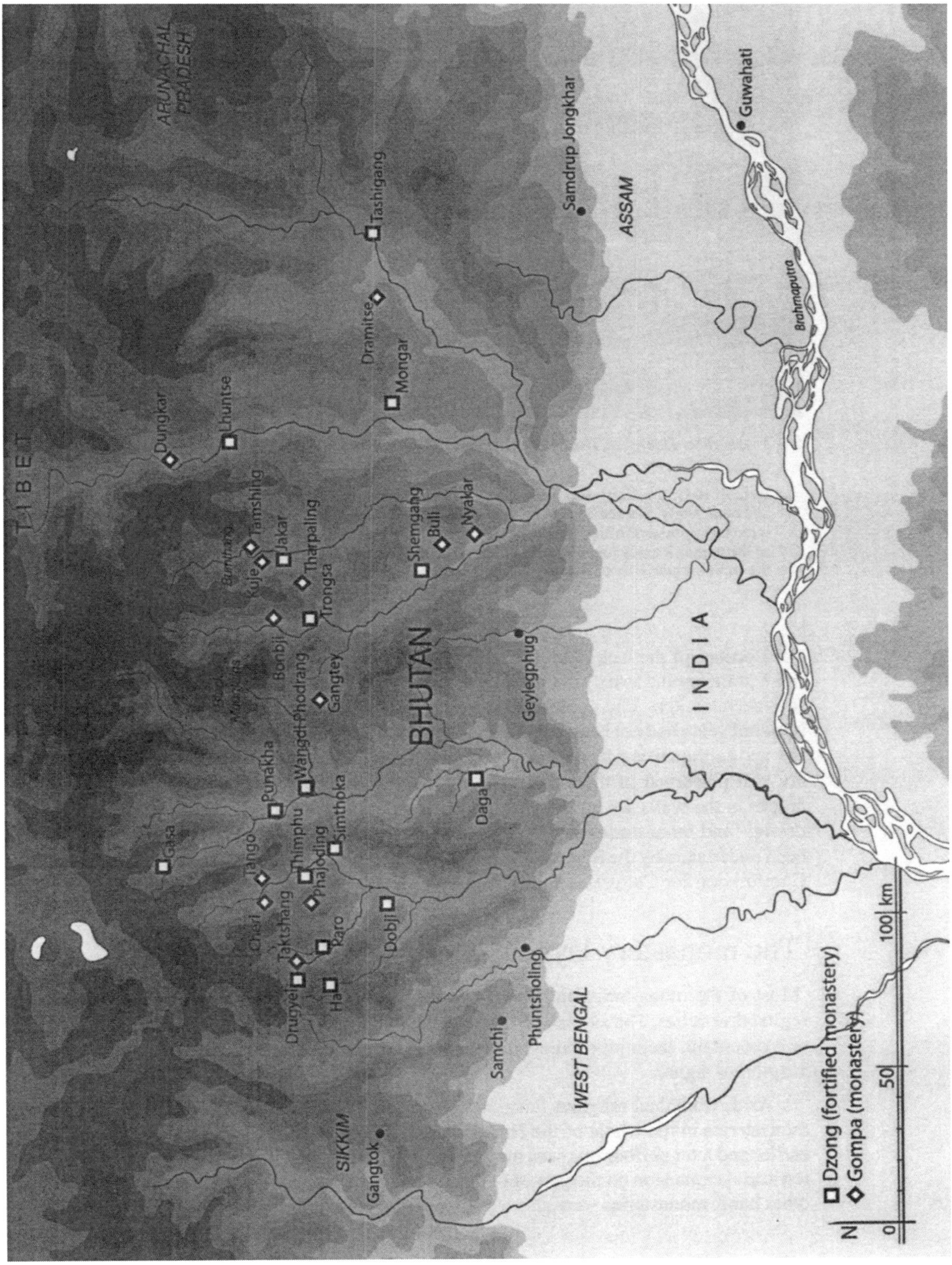

5 – *Trashichho Dzong in Thimphu, the present capital of Bhutan, from north-west*
(photo P. Pichard)

Built in 1641, the dzong was reconstructed after a destructive fire in 1772, and completely restored and enlarged from 1962 to 1969 to house the Royal Government, including ministers' offices and the National Assembly, as well as the central administration of the monastic body together with the summer residence of the Je Khenpo, the supreme patriarch of Bhutan.

Because of the lack of systematic records, dates for the renovation works done on most of the monasteries are difficult to find, except for those which were carried out a few decades ago. The conservation of *dzongs* and monasteries over the last three hundred years had not been a problem in the country. Except for the damages by floods, fire and earthquakes which entailed punctual renovation works, *dzongs* and monasteries are still preserved in their original state. However, in recent times, water leakages, cracks in the walls are observed. In view of the importance of the maintenance of the *dzongs* and monasteries and of their function, surveys and works of renovation have been undertaken by the Restoration and Archaelogical Division set up under the National Commission for Cultural Affairs.

The monastery layout

Most of the monasteries and *dzongs* were built according to a common plan, with regional varieties. The site selected was usually a commanding place, on a cliff, a ridge, or a mountain, facing the valley, or near a sacred stream. The site selected had to bear auspicious signs.

Aside from their religious functions, one of the most important aspects of the earlier monasteries in the whole of the Himalayan region was their political role. In both the earlier and later periods one sees the development of monasteries as part of a process of territorial expansion on the part of both the secular and the religious authorities. On the other hand, monasteries were also a residence and meditation place for the great lamas.

Planned monasteries

These were normally built by powerful religious leaders with political powers.

The *dzongs* are the best examples and were built on the order of the Shabdrung Ngawang Namgyel who was the religious and political leader of Bhutan in the 17th century and they command each major valley in Bhutan.

They all follow a regular common layout with certain basic features. Most consisted of buildings arranged around a single or several courtyards.

Annex fig. 8 to 12 p. 278-281

The main temple was usually set up in the centre of the courtyard with the other buildings containing domestic spaces, classrooms for monks, and administrative spaces, surrounding the courtyard to create an enclosure. Deviations from this pattern were generally due to physical characteristics of the site.

Organic monasteries

These were normally built by local communities or by religious saints, and grew according to circumstances and donations. They were sometimes built like *dzongs* but on a lesser scale with a main temple in the courtyard, surrounded by other dwellings. The alternative pattern was a series of small shrines and residential quarters built alongside the main temple and controlled by the layout of the site. The Taktshang monastery, which consists of a series of shrines, scattered along the slope of the ridge is one of the most interesting examples. Phajoding monastery (13th -18th century) and Cheri monastery (17th centruy) are meditation centres with a main temple and other shrines and hermitages scattered along the mountainside. Some monasteries built by the local communities consisted of just a main temple structure with a small residence for the monks built on one side.

Elements of the Bhutanese Buddhist Monastery

The various different elements of a Bhutanese Buddhist monastery normally served specific functions.

Lhakhang *(shrine)*

The main building called *utse* is situated normally at the centre of the courtyard with a paved path around it for circumambulation. Small prayer-wheels can be fixed in a long row around the lower part of the *utse*, and are turned by the faithful in order to gain religious merit as the building is circumambulated. This central building, can house one or several shrines. The main hall with its major shrines, is used for all important ceremonies and also sometimes for educational activities. The square or oblong building comprises three main components. The inner space is used for the main shrine, while the outer one is used for the gathering of monks who face the shrine when performing religious ceremonies. The third component is the *gonkhang*, a small shrine dedicated to the guardian deity of the monastery, though in some monasteries it can be a separate sanctuary by itself.

Kunrey *(assembly hall)*

This hall, where monks gather several times a day, may form a part of the structure enclosing the courtyard or be a separate building. The *kunrey* is a large hall with one or more smaller shrines. In this hall, the monks receive ordination, perform morning and evening prayers and may also use it as dining hall and dormitory.

Dasha *(monks' quarters)*

The *dashas* are buildings surrounding the main temple and enclosing the courtyard. They are used by the monks for sleeping, eating, cooking and form general domestic spaces. Classes may also be held there when the space in Kunre is not available.

Dochhen *(courtyard)*

In the courtyard, also an important part of the monastery, the annual religious festival takes place. Great ceremonies and masked dances narrating various religious stories and teachings are performed for the public by the monks.

6 – *Simtokha Dzong*
Courtyard north-west corner
and monks' living quarters
Annex, figure 8 (a-c) p. 278-79
(photo P. Pichard)

Gonkhang *(shrine for protective deities)*

The *gonkhang* is a special place designated or devoted to the protective and terrifying deities. In some monasteries, the *gonkhang* will be a separate sanctuary while in other cases it is a small shrine in the main building.

Thapsang *(kitchen)*

In the kitchen, situated in a separate building and normally attached to a store room, large-sized earth stoves are fueled by wood. There is no exhaust system and the smoke goes out of the kitchen through craks and windows. However, some monasteries are now provided with modern iron smokeless stoves fitted with cooking pots, and water facilities.

Phu *(store)*

The store room is usually attached to the kitchen; food grains and other food items are kept there under lock, the key being with the chief cook.

Chapsa *and* thrukhang *(toilets and bathrooms)*

Many of the monasteries have now modern sanitary facilities, except for those in remote places. Toilets and bathrooms are constructed separately or in some cases a few metres away from the monastery. In summer, however, monks often wash their clothes and take bath in a nearby river as they used to do it until the 1970s. An ancient common toilet system existed in many monasteries and all *dzongs* .

In Bhutan, the National Commission for Cultural Affairs is responsible for the protection and promotion of Buddhism, so very central to Bhutan's existence and identity. As such, the National Commission for Cultural affairs works with the central Monastic Body and the local ecclesiastical institutions in educating the monks, especially in the fields of conservation and sanitation. Workshops are regularly organised for the monks as well as the local caretakers.

Preservation of historic sites and excavation of buried cultural properties are given higher prority. As such, an inventory and documentation of monasteries throughout the country by the National Commission for Cultural Affairs is underway.

Today, with the introduction of modern concepts of engineering and architecture plus the availability of new materials, more and more houses in the villages and towns are being built with concrete hollow blocks and reinforced concrete. The government in its effort to preserve the unique architectural designs and forms developed in this country over centuries is discouraging any external influences in the architectural style of public and private buildings and structures of importance.

The current problem facing the country is the preservation and continued practice of the very art and architecture carried on over centuries as well as the conservation of monuments. The current policies of the Royal Government aim at ensuring a balanced economy growth and at preserving the country's rich cultural and spiritual heritage of Bhutan.

ANNEX

7 | *Dramitse Monastery*

(Survey: National Commission for Cultural Affairs)

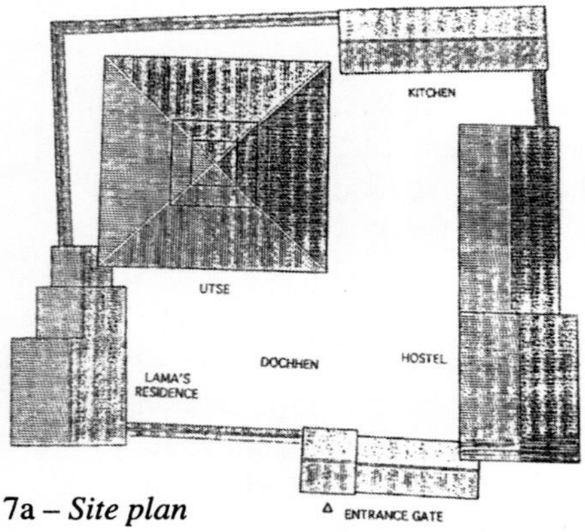

7a – *Site plan*

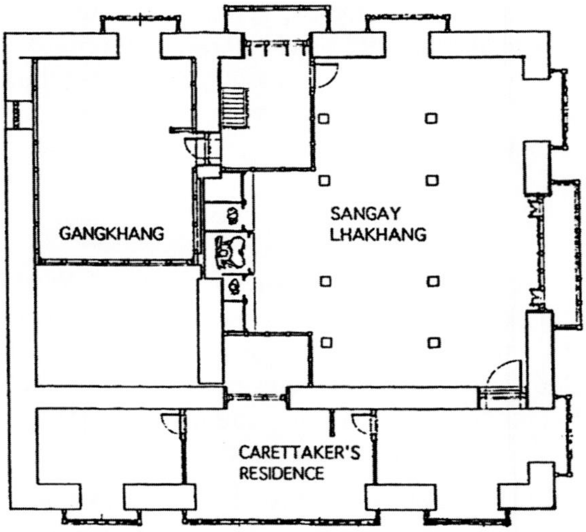

7d – Utse, *second-storey plan*

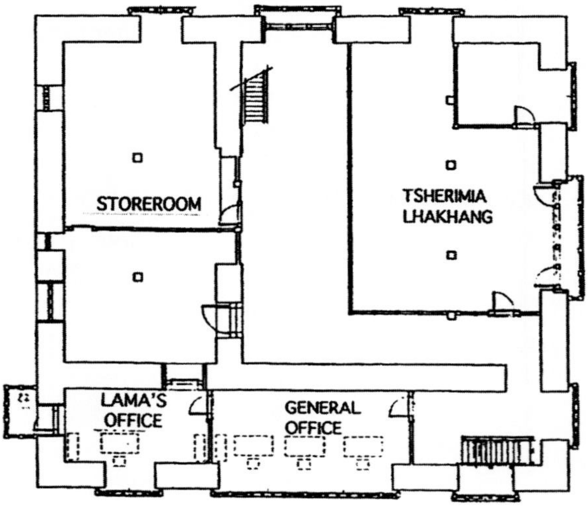

7c – Utse, *first-storey plan*

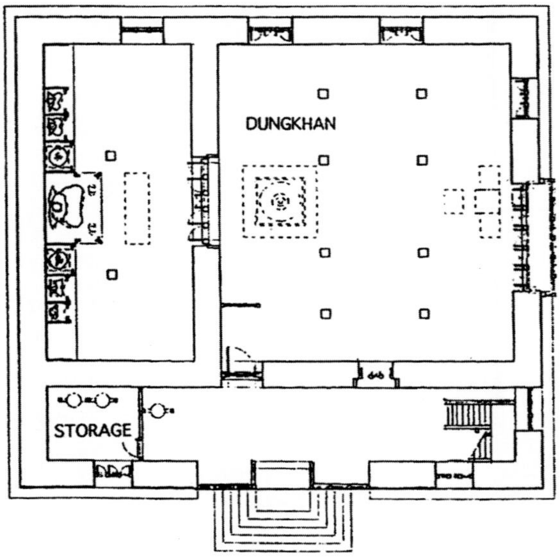

7b – *Utse, ground-floor plan*

7e – Utse, *section*

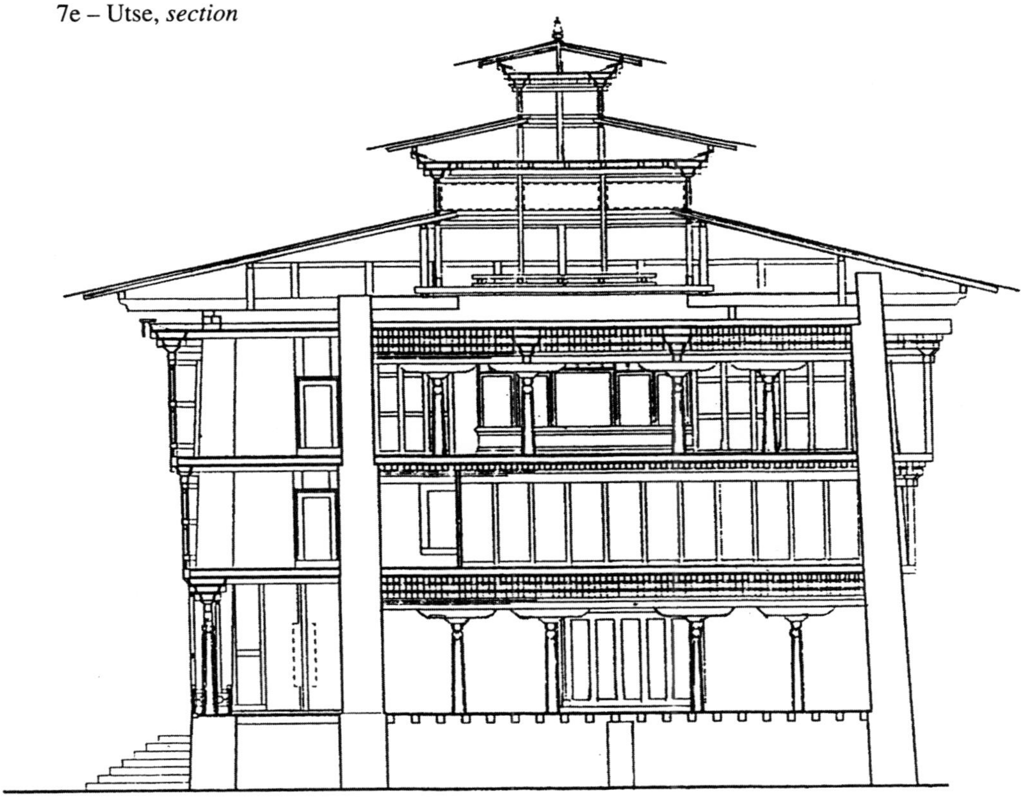

7f – Utse, *south elevation*

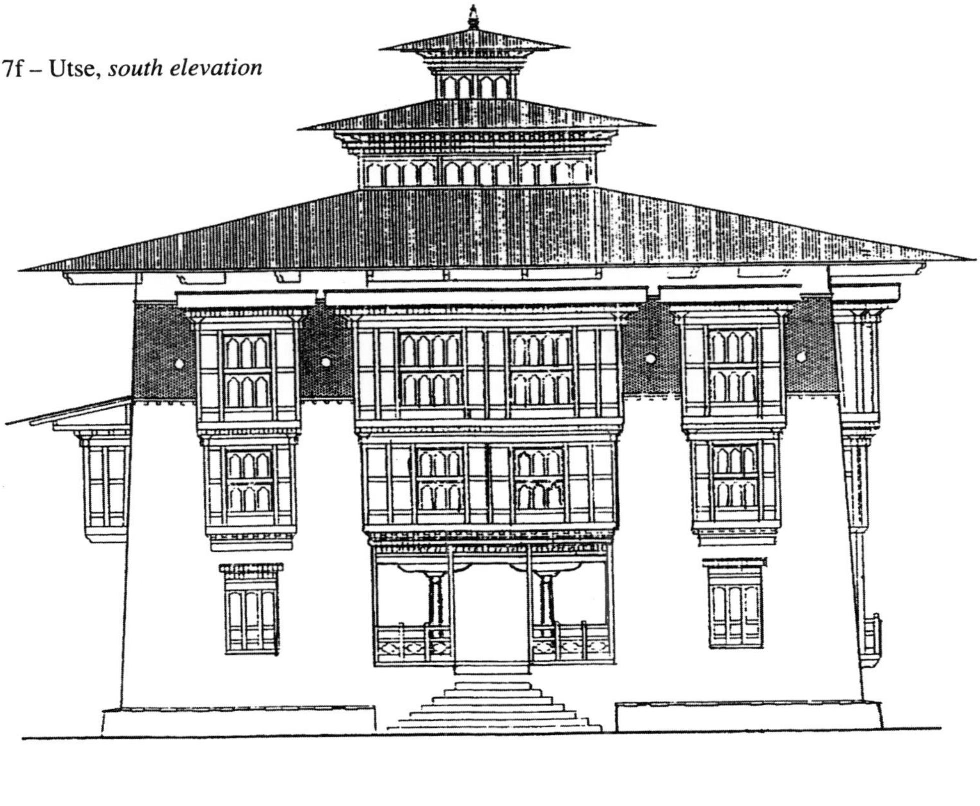

8 | *Simtokha Dzong*

(Survey Pierre Pichard)

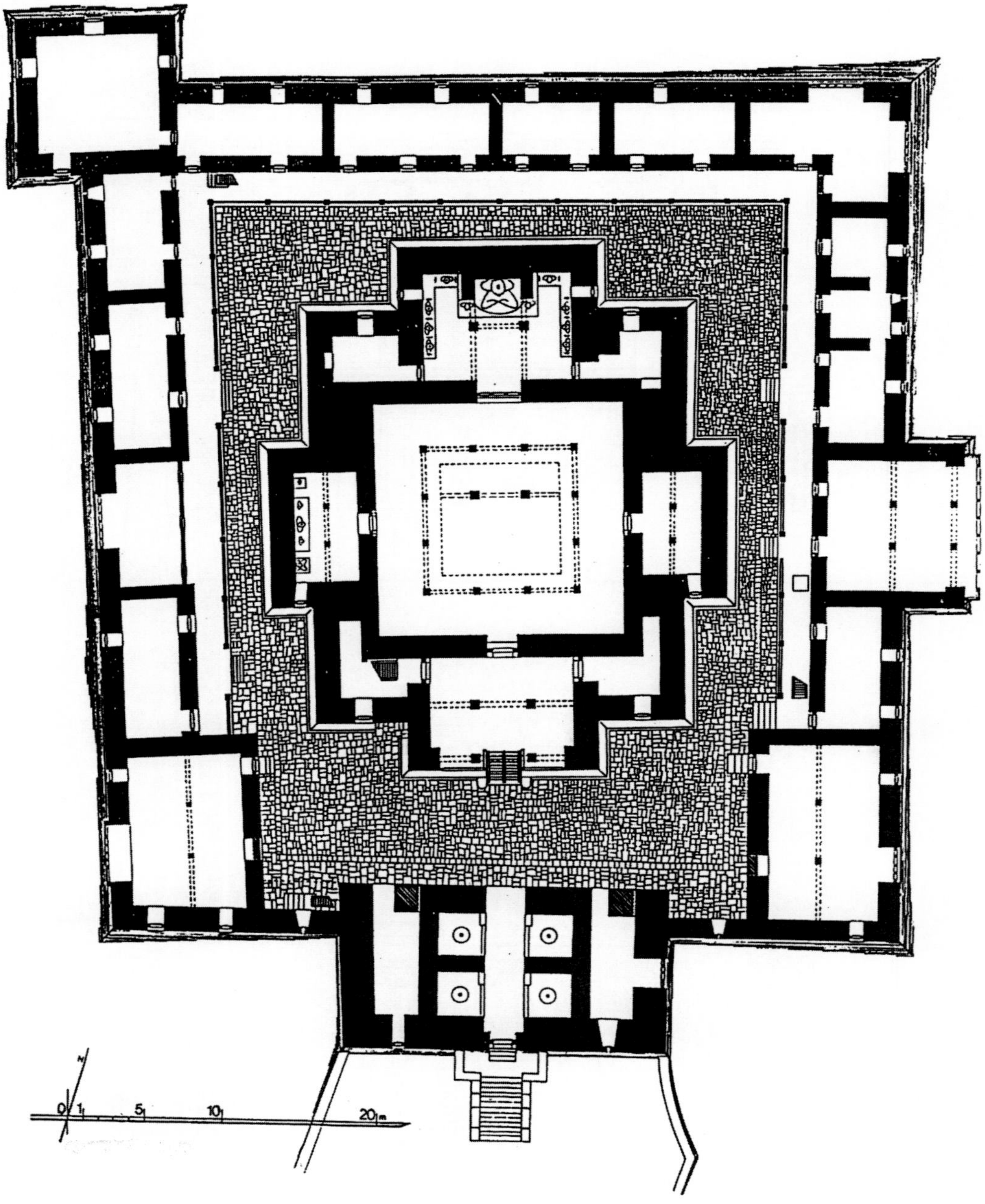

8a – *Simtokha Dzong, plan*

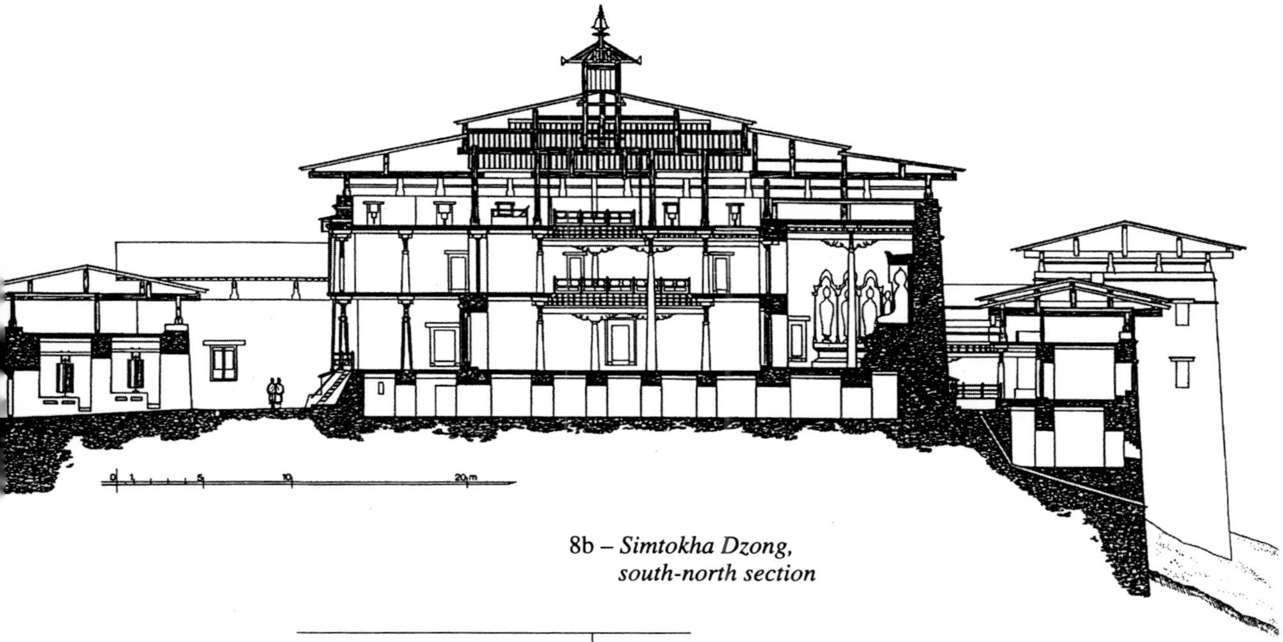

8b – *Simtokha Dzong, south-north section*

8c – *Simtokha Dzong Courtyard, west gallery and* utse, *south-west corner, from south*

Built in 1629, Simtokha is the most ancient *dzong* in Bhutan, and its historical significance is still increased by the fact that it has conserved its original design up to today, while most of the larger *dzongs* have been altered by repeated additions.

The whole complex forms a rectangle of 70 by 60 m located upon an outcrop of the mountain, with steep slopes going down on three sides. The single entrance, on the fourth and southern side towards the mountain, gives access to the interior courtyard.

As in other *dzongs*, the main structure is a central towering building, the *utse*, housing the shrines. Above a basement, whose floor is only slightly below the pavement of the courtyard, its main floor is reached by nine wooden steps facing the entrance of the dzong. A vestibule and a large, square hall provide access to the main shrine, axially located and very high, since its ceiling is level with the floor of the third storey, and to the two lateral shrines. All these rooms have mural paintings on their walls, a total painted area around 560 m^2, and most of the woodwork is finely enhanced by polychromy.

Trongsa Dzong

(Drawing and photos P. Pichard)

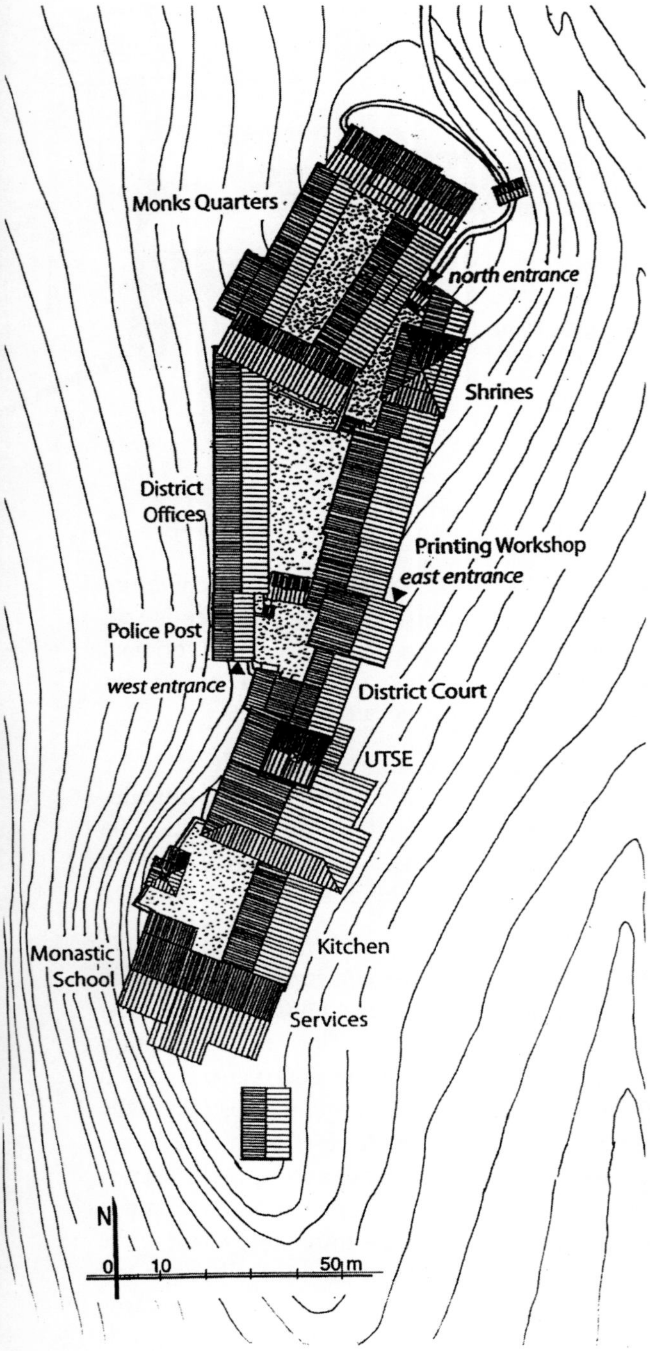

9 – *Trongsa Dzong*
Site plan

Commanding an important confluence of valleys, the whole complex of Trongsa Dzong has been built in successive phases along the centuries, on a rocky ridge running 240 m from north to south. Founded in 1543, the dzong was enlarged in 1650 and 1652. The two lower floors of its main tower, the utse, were built in 1667, with the two upper floors added in1767. Various additions were built up to 1927, while amenities such as kitchen and toilets were added or renovated in the recent years. The dzong was damaged by the 1897 Assam earthquake and repaired soon after.

It forms today a huge complex of courtyards and buildings linked at various levels by passages and galleries. At its southern end, the floors of Monastic School suround the Chorten Lhakhang which, constructed in 1543, is the most ancient part of the Dzong and contains valuable wall paintings. The small middle courtyard, accessible by entrances on the east and west sides, was used as a check point to travellers on their way up from the bottom of the valley to passes in the western mountains.

In addition to his monastic and educational areas (multiple shrines, religious offices, class rooms, printing workshop, monk cells, student dormitories) the dzong today is still used as the administrative and judicial centre of the valley (district office, tribunal and police post).

10 – *Trongsa Dzong*
View from above
(east side)

11 – *Trongsa Dzong*
East side with lateral entrance
from north-east

12 – *Trongsa Dzong*
Lower north courtyard
and utse, from north

SELECTED BIBLIOGRAPHY

ARIS, Michael
1988 – "The Temple-palace of gTam-zhing as Described by its Founder", *Arts Asiatiques* 43, Paris, p. 33-39.

Departments of Works, Housing and Roads
1993 – *An Introduction to Traditional Architecture of Bhutan*, Thimphu, 259 p., photographs, drawings, maps, bibliography.

IMAEDA, Yoshiro; POMMARET, Françoise
1987 – "Le monastère de gTam zhing (Tamshing) au Bhoutan central", *Arts Asiatiques* 42, Paris, p. 19-30, maps, drawings, photographs.

Ministry of Home Affairs
1987 – *Dzongs in Bhutan - Conservation of Bhutan's Endangered Heritage*, Thimphu, 62 p., photographs, drawings.

PICHARD, Pierre
1988 – *Conservation of Simtokha Dzong*, Paris, UNESCO, 17 p. drawings, photographs.
2000 – "Dechenphug: destin d'un monastère bhoutanais", *Arts Asiatiques* 55, p. 21-31.

POMMARET, Françoise; IMAEDA, Yoshiro
1984 – *Bhoutan – Un royaume de l'Himalaya*, Geneva and Paris, Olizane and Vilo, 175 p., map, photographs, bibliography

13 – *Simtokha Dzong, entrance, south prayer wheel*
(photo P. Pichard)

BUDDHIST MONASTERIES IN TIBET

Françoise Pommaret

When considering a preliminary study of Buddhist monasteries in Tibet, several factors have to be taken into consideration: the exact definition of "Tibet"; the sheer size of the area; the diversity of socio-ecological patterns; historical periods; the different religious schools; the absence of an overall scientific survey; and finally, the massive destruction that took place between 1950 and 1976.

As Meyer and Jest have written:

> *Le milieu naturel influence l'architecture par le biais de plusieurs facteurs: les conditions climatiques (amplitude thermique, vent, précipitations...), la disponibilité des matériaux aptes à la construction, le mode de production économique qu'il conditionne et les représentations culturelles le concernant, partagées par les hommes qui l'habitent.* (Meyer et Jest 1987: 146)

A monastery cannot be conceived and built at an elevation of 4,000 m. like a monastery at sea-level; this remark, though it may sound trivial, is necessary as architecture is often studied *per se* and unfortunately dissociated from its milieu.

I will not deal here with monasteries belonging to other areas of Tibetan culture outside China, such as Ladakh, Spiti or Bhutan.

However, when I speak here of Tibet, I do not use the Chinese definition, which encompasses only the Tibetan Autonomous Region (TAR) – that is, only Central and Western Tibet – but Tibet as a cultural and ethnic entity that includes the traditional Eastern provinces of Khams and Amdo. In contemporary Chinese administrative terms, this means including monasteries that are now in the TAR, Qinghai, Gansu, Sichuan and Yunnan. This "cultural Tibet" covers an area of roughly 2.5 million square kilometres – that is, as large as the whole of Western Europe, and one-fourth of China. Over a territory this size, one encounters great ecological diversity which stretches from the desert plains of the west to the forested alpine area of the east, from the deep gorges of the south-east to the undulated pasture lands of the north-east. This diversity has had a profound impact on the materials and techniques of construction.

* Tibetan words are spelt without the plural form

The Buddhist Monastery, EFEO, 2003, p. 283-304

As for the architectural styles, they have been influenced by the neighbouring cultures of India and China, although the Tibetans rapidly developed an architectural vocabulary of their own, to the point of being in turn copied by the Chinese and the Mongols (Chayet 1985).

Another point that I would like to mention from the beginning and which is undoubtedly linked to the low population density and harsh conditions, is that in Tibet, monks did not go out in the morning and beg as they do in South-East Asia. In fact, the opposite occurred, as lay people brought them foodstuffs periodically, in a particular pattern to which I will return, as it influenced the layout of the monasteries. The only monks who begged were those who went on pilgrimage.

Finally, it should be understood that this paper is just meant to serve as a framework for comparative purposes and further studies, as it is impossible, in the space provided here, to accurately survey all aspects of Buddhist monasteries in Tibet.

1. History

Buddhism in its Mahāyāna Tantric form was introduced in Tibet in the 7th and 8th centuries but was initially probably confined to a small section of the society, which included part of the aristocracy. In the Tibetan tradition, the impetus was provided by Santaraksita, a monk who was later assisted by Padmasambhava, a Tantrist from Swat. They came to Tibet at the invitation of King Khri srong lde btsan (r. 755-797), and contributed to the construction of bSam yas (Samye), the first monastery in Central Tibet, in 775.[1] The life of Padmasambhava – known in the Tibetan world as Guru Rinpoche, "the Precious master", and about whose life little is known historically – has taken on epic dimensions. He is credited with amazing feats and especially the subjugation of local deities. His disciples were later known as the rNying ma pa, the "Ancients", and constituted the first religious school of Tibetan Buddhism.

ph. 1 opposite page

In the late 8th and the early 9th centuries, successive edicts of kings Khri srong lde btsan and Ral pa can are landmarks in the history of Buddhism in Tibet. Buddhism became the state religion, supported by the royal family; temples and monasteries were to be maintained; lands and tenant farmers were given to the monasteries, which were also exempted of taxes; and each monk would be supported by seven households (Shakabpa 1984: 38-50). This legal basis followed the Indian model. Three identical lists of thirty "dharma colleges" established in the reign of King Ral pa can (817-841), throughout the Tibetan empire, are found in historical sources (Uebach 1990: 394-395). When the royal dynasty ended in 842, due partly to a political conflict between the tenants of the indigenous religion and those of Buddhism, Tibet entered a century-long "dark age" about which very little is known.

The process that is now called "the second diffusion of Buddhism" started in the second half of the 10th century and resulted partly from the efforts of the kings of Western Tibet who descended from the royal dynasty. While a few Indian masters came to Tibet, the most notable being Atisha who died in Tibet in 1054, Tibetans

1. In fact there are very few references to bSam yas (Samye) prior the 12th century, and the Tang Records do not mention the monastery. The site of bSam yas seems to have been known by the name Brag dmar which is attested to as early as 695 in the Dunhuang manuscripts. On this problem, see the excellent article of Anne Chayet (1988: 19-29).

1 – *bSam yas (Samye) monastery, reconstructed, Central Tibet* (photo F. Pommaret, 1994)

travelled to India to obtain teachings and Sanskrit texts, and translations of them were made on a large scale. At the same time, disciples of monks who had kept Buddhism alive in Amdo, in north-east Tibet, came back to Central Tibet and revived monasticism in this region. The 11th century was a decisive period in the history of Buddhism in Tibet as it saw the emergence of four religious schools: the rNying ma pa, the bKa' gdam pa, the bKa' brgyud pa, the Sa skya pa. Initially, these schools were centred around the charismatic personality of a religious person who attracted disciples, and the building of large monasteries began. In the 12th and 13th centuries, offshoots of the main schools appeared, with powerful personalities – disciples of the main founder – and monasteries multiplied. At the end of the 14th century, the last religious school, the dGe lugs pa, emerged with its founder Tsong kha pa, who was a reformer and imposed a discipline based on the return to the strict rule of the Vinaya. The dGe lugs pa absorbed the bKa' gdams pa and in the 17th century, it became the most powerful school in Tibet, as in 1642, the 5th Dalai Lama became the political leader of Tibet. From the 11th century, each school, each offshoot tried to conquer new territories not only religiously but also economically, as monks depended on laymen to survive. In fact, many monasteries became important centres of economic power, owning land and cattle, and engaging in long-distance trade. They also vied for favours from powerful laymen and lords who were viewed as potential "patrons" (*sbyin bdag*), including Chinese and Mongol leaders. This consequently led to struggles for supremacy among the religious schools, sometimes leading to violent confrontations, followed by severe reprisals from the victorious school.

Not all the religious population of Tibet followed monasticism. A large part was made up of wandering yogis and village priests who were often married and did not live in monasteries. Even high lamas could be married and, in this case, would reside outside monasteries. Celibacy was not a condition of entry into a religious life but it was compulsory for anyone wanting to take the vows of a monk and live in a monastery. The dGe lugs pa school, which insisted on celibacy, was composed only of monks and had the largest monasteries.

As for Bon, which is considered by many scholars to be the indigenous religion of Tibet, it was considerably modified during the second diffusion of Buddhism and became what Western academics call "the organized Bon". It took on many external aspects of Buddhism in Tibet, especially the monastic organization.

This survey, albeit schematic, is nevertheless necessary to understand the religious and historical context in which monasteries developed in Tibet.

2. General location and density of monasteries in Tibet

2.1 Ancient monasteries

No complete scientific survey of monasteries in Tibet was done before 1950 and while we know all the important historical monasteries through texts (biographies, histories of religious schools, secondary sources by Westerners), it is really impossible to accurately give a figure of the number of monasteries in Tibet prior to the Chinese invasion. However, a census carried out in 1663 at the time of the 5th Dalai Lama, lists 1,800 monasteries just in the territory controlled by the Lhasa government; the largely independent principalities of Khams and Amdo were therefore excluded (Meyer and Jest 1987: 60).

It is estimated that 2,600 monasteries (some sources give a figure as high as 6,000), having a population of 110,000 clerics, were destroyed between 1950 and 1976, the latter date marking the end of the Cultural Revolution. However, this is a rough estimation and may also include "temples" (*lha khang* or *gtsug lag khang*) which have only one or two caretakers. A monastery is called a *dgon pa* and it includes, in addition to at least one temple, living quarters for monks, and a kitchen.

Since the mid-1980s, the most famous monasteries of Tibet, including the most ancient, bSam yas, are being restored – often in a way that would not please an archeologist or a heritage architect – either with the help of the Chinese government, which sees in them potential tourist attractions, or by the people themselves, and even with money and craftsmanship from outside Tibet as in the case of bSam yas.

The building of monasteries has to follow certain rules, and the landscape, or at least the perception of it, plays an enormously important role:

> For building, one should seek a place that has the following: a tall mountain behind and many hills in front, two rivers converging in front from right to left, a central valley of rocks and meadows resembling heaps of grain, and a lower part which is like two hands crossed at the wrists. The good characteristics called the four 'earth pillars' are a wide expanse in the east, a heap in the south, a rounded bulge in the west and in the north a mountain like a draped curtain. The Four Guardians are (the four great animals): in the east a whitish path or rock is the tiger, and in this direction there must be ravines cutting across the lower part of the valley. By the river of the southern direction, there must be verdure, which is the turquoise-dragon, and here it is necessary that the water does not plummet into a cavern. Red earth or rock in the west is the bird, and here the path must not be fraught with snags or pitfalls. A bearded rock in the north is the tortoise, and in this direction at the stream's source, the water must not be obstructed by seething soiled water. If these four protectors are all present, the land is perfectly endowed. (Thubten Legshay Gyatsho 1979: 29)

Buddhist monasteries in Tibet

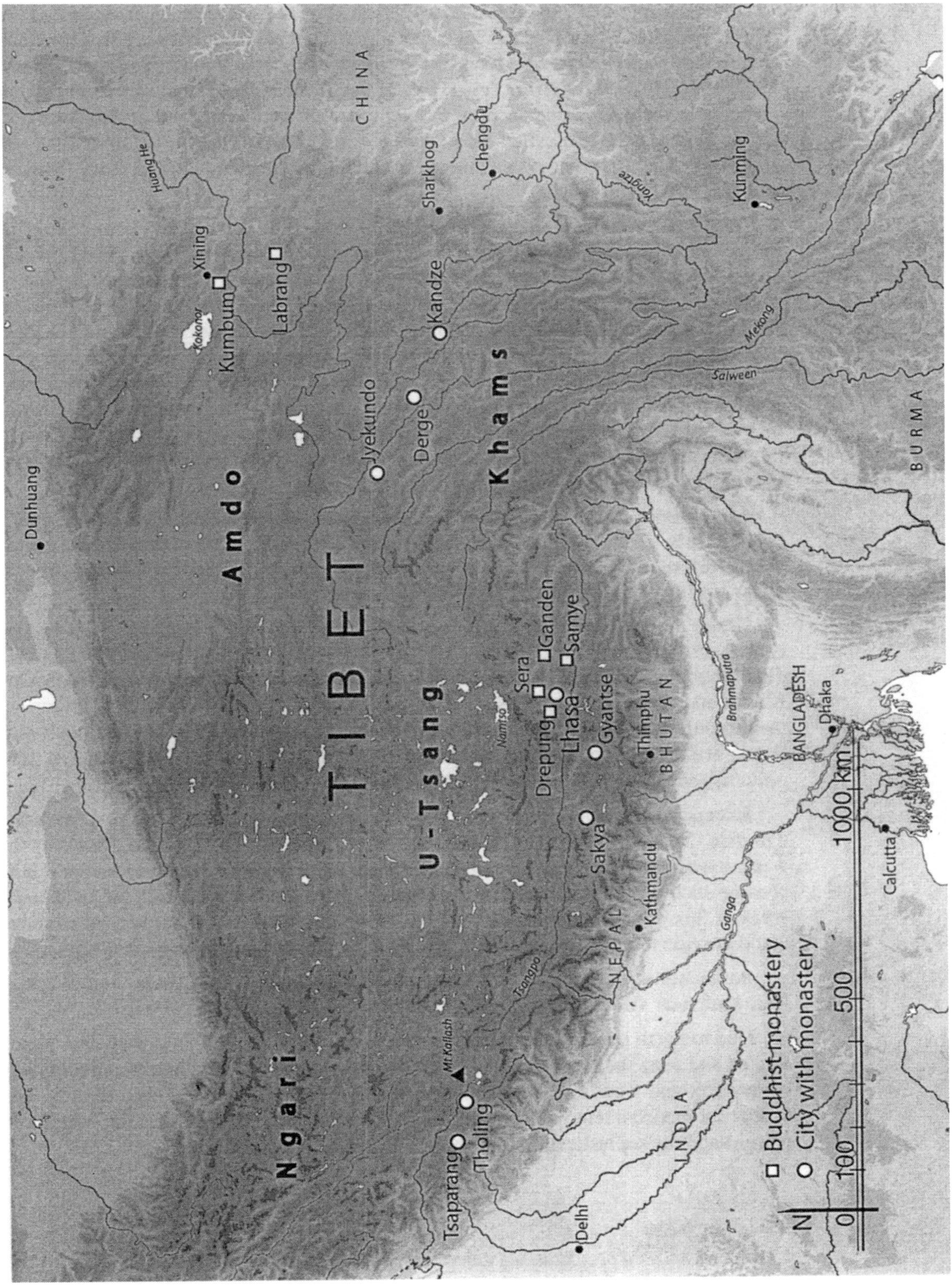

The influence of Chinese geomancy which was introduced in Tibet, according to Tibetan tradition, as early as the 7th century, is discernible here; but we also know that architectural prescriptions were found in the Tibetan texts of the Vinaya (De Rossi Filibeck 1987: 104-110), and the *bsTan 'gyur*, part of the Tibetan Canon, includes architectural precepts in the *bZo rig pa* section. Prescriptions on geomancy and architecture are also included in the text called the *Ri chos mtshams kyi zhal gdams las sa dphyad rin chen kun 'dus* compiled by a lama from Ladakh in the early 20th century (Meyer and Jest 1987: 166 n. 8).

The perfect site was an ideal which could seldom be achieved. When looking at the layout of many monasteries, it is evident that these strict criteria could not be applied. But it is also true that the landscape was sublimated and idealized so that it fits some of them. The oldest monasteries of Tibet (7th-10th century) were built on flat land, without any defensive planning, because there was at that time no obvious threat: bSam yas (Samye) and Tho ling (996), for example, are in a plain near the river. This location was still favoured from the 11th to the 13th century as in the example of Zhva lu (Shalu) in Central Tibet. From the 14th century onwards, with inter-school conflicts and the threat of foreign invasions (Mongol, Manchu/Chinese), monasteries took more defensive positions, almost always located on the side of a mountain with a commanding view of the landscape.

Monasteries were often built in isolated places or places associated with a saint, believed to be conducive to meditation and study. The presence of caves in the mountain was therefore sought after but the most important criterion remained the availability of water (spring or river), crucial in a high-altitude country.

When monasteries were under prestigious patronage, they could be built in the capital of the principality, such as Tsa pa rang (Tsaparang) in Western Tibet or the dPal 'khor chos sde of rGyal rtse (Gyantse), or the monasteries of sDe dge (Derge) in Khams and sKye dgu mdo (Jyekundo) in Amdo; and of course the Potala in Lhasa, at the same time monastery, palace and seat of the government. I will not deal with the Potala here because of its complex structure, of which only part was a monastery; for reference see the excellent article by Fernand Meyer (1987: 14-33).

pho. 2 opposite page

Except when monasteries were in towns such as rGyal rtse (Gyantse) or sKye dgu mdo (Jyekundo), which were important trade marts, the proximity of a trade route was not a decisive factor in establishing a monastery. However, because some of them became such powerful socio-economic entities, they could be a bonus for trade and create a flux around their settlement, as well as the possibility of shelter which they could provide to travellers, traders or not, in such a sparsely populated environment.

Some monasteries were in very remote areas far from any settlement, while some were built near villages.

Due to harsh ecological conditions, materials used for building monasteries were limited and were the same throughout Tibet: stone, earth (unbaked bricks and rammed earth/pisé), and wood.[2] However, there were noticeable differences according to the ecological environment, which influenced the availability of resources, the wealth of patrons and the sophistication of techniques.

2. For an overall view of construction techniques, *cf.* Meyer and Jest 1987: 146-167.

Stone was always considered to be the "noble" material and was preferred to earth. Except in Western Tibet where unbaked bricks were common, temple walls were always built in stone, while less important buildings could be made of bricks or rammed earth. Earth, with a high content of clay if possible, could usually be found near the construction site and bricks were made on the spot. Walls of rammed earth (pisé) were rare for monasteries and reserved for annexes such as toilets or kitchen, and for vernacular architecture. Stone was taken from the river bed or from rocks on the side of a nearby mountain, but quarries were apparently not used. The stonework was excellent and walls were made of layers of dressed stones alternating with flat ones. Between each layer of blocks, a mortar made of clay mixed with sand was used. This bonding agent was weak and, given the risk of earthquakes, walls had deep, thick foundations, and were given a batter which gave some lightness to an otherwise heavy architecture. The truncated-pyramid-shaped buildings seem to be a natural continuation of the mountain.

Wood, which was plentiful in Eastern Tibet, was used there in a way that would have been considered lavish in Central and Western Tibet where wood had to be brought from south-east Tibet, or even Bhutan, Sikkim and Kinnaur. The most frequently used species were poplar, willow and, if available, cypress and juniper. In Eastern Tibet (Khams), the upper part of a monastery was often made of small logs, and the wooden structure above the windows very elaborate.

Most monastery roofs were flat, but in humid regions like the south-east (Kongpo) or eastern parts of Tibet, they were slanted and covered with wooden shingles or tiles.

The building season was more or less from June to September, the rest of the year being too cold and the ground frozen. The season also depended on the agricultural year, as the work force was very limited. Construction work had therefore to be done after sowing and before harvest.

2 – *sKye dgu mdo (Jyekundo) monastery, reconstructed, Eastern Tibet* (photo F. Pommaret, 1997)

Specialized craftsmen were employed in the construction and the decoration of monasteries. The most important was the carpenter (*shing bzo wa*) who also acted as architect. All the assembling and preparation of materials were done at the site, and craftsmen could live for months or years in temporary shelters, as is still done in Bhutan.

The actual construction work could be carried out on a voluntary basis by the people of the region who thus earned merit, or by people doing the compulsory labour due to their lord, or, as a last resort, by recruiting unskilled labourers paid in kind on a daily basis.

2.2 Present situation

The situation in Tibet today is unique, due to the political circumstances, and is completely geared towards reconstruction. From the mid-1980s until 1997, there was great activity in the reconstruction of monasteries that had been destroyed, but this is no longer encouraged by the Chinese government which thinks that it diverts too much of the work force, money and resources from more "productive" occupations. The largest monasteries were partially rebuilt with contributions from the Chinese government. Others were rebuilt with contributions from the people and Tibetans living abroad. Although traditional materials and techniques are still used, one finds the occasional drastic departure from the traditional architecture, as in dKar mdzes (Kandze) in Khams where a new building has been built with the blue smoked windows and white tiles that are so popular in China.

3. The monastery layout

In Tibet, perhaps more than anywhere else, the monastery layout was closely linked to the particular socio-religious organisation of the society, to the low population density and to the environment.

It is quite impossible, when dealing with Tibet, to speak in terms of the two broad classes of monasteries as defined by P. Pichard in his guidelines. Monasteries were at the same time "planned" and "organic". The core of the monastery was usually planned, but then over the centuries, buildings were added, often in a haphazard manner. This came about through the expansion of the number of monks, the diversification of the monastery's activities and the donations of "patrons"; a patron could be a wealthy lord, a religious figure or the community living in the proximity of the monastery.

The early monasteries definitely followed a symmetrical plan which is still recognizable today and which was based, according to Tibetan tradition, on the Buddhist monasteries in Northern India, Nalenda, Odantapuri or Vikramasila, themselves based on the mandala pattern. As mentioned above, early monasteries were built on flat land which made a proper layout possible. The monastery consisted of a central temple, surrounded by a courtyard (*khyams ra*), with or without porticos, and onto which monks' cells opened.

However, bSam yas monastery presents particularities which have been studied by Chayet (1988: 19-29), who questions even the Indian model so readily accepted. She notes the close resemblance of the plan to that for the construction for the ancient *mdos* ritual, to ancient *bon po* architectural concepts (Karmay 1987: 96-98), and to ancient Chinese monuments and tombs (Chayet 1988: 27-28; 1990: 114). Chayet concludes, nevertheless, that the mandala layout favoured by Tibetan tradition did not contradict any pre-existing concept and form, and was a powerful means of Buddhisation (1988: 26-27).

3 – *dGa' ldan monastery, Central Tibet, reconstructed* (photo F. Pommaret, 1994)

While a few monasteries built after the 11th century kept a symmetrical plan as a core, most of them grew organically, taking the terrain into account, and a plan is often difficult to recognize in the maze of buildings added over the centuries. The layout of the main chapel, in particular, shifted from a centred mandala-like plan to a rectangular layout with an entrance portico. And the symbolic layout of the whole monastery, which was centred and symmetrical, became based on the height of the buildings or their location on the side of the mountain. The terrain was used in establishing a hierarchy among the buildings, and the Tibetans developed an exceptional ability to integrate architecture into the landscape (Vergara 1987: 361). One of the earliest examples of this was probably the "northern religious complex" (Chos sde byang) of the Sa skya (Sakya) monastery. Built from 1073, the complex has been totally destroyed.

The expansion of a monastery over the centuries depended on its wealth, its prestige and the generosity of its "patrons" – either clerics or laymen – and significant differences among monasteries existed, in terms of size. Donations for new buildings were closely linked to the religious prestige of the monastery or its sacredness, because donations to places having special religious significance brought more merit to the donors.

The expansion of monasteries was also linked to their activity as religious educational centres: the more students, the more buildings needed to accommodate them. A new building could be constructed by the family of a monk, if the family was wealthy, or by the monastery itself.

The most extreme cases of organic expansion are illustrated by the large monasteries of the dGe lugs pa school in Central Tibet, 'Bras spung (Drepung), dGa' ldan, *ph. 3 above* Se ra (Sera), and in Amdo, in north-east Tibet, sKu 'bum (Kumbum), Bla brang (Blabrang), which had an elaborate but not really planned layout. The number of monks could reach 10,000. These monasteries were divided into colleges, themselves divided into "houses" (*khams tshan*) where monks from the same regional origin lived and studied in a separate building. For example, the largest of the four colleges in 'Bras spung was composed of twenty-three "houses". Each college had its own administrative buildings, storerooms, kitchens, etc. (Ngawang Dakpa 1997: 207-208). These monasteries were real towns and their size is not representative of the majority of monasteries in Tibet, but they illustrate the level of complexity that the architectural layout could reach.

To feed the monks – but also for elaborate rituals which involved many offerings of foodstuffs – large store-rooms were needed to stock supplies and the store-keeper's post was one of the most important. Tibet was a country where fresh products were rarely available and where the diet was basically tea, butter, salt, dried meat and barley flour. Because the population was so sparse, donations of food were not available on a daily basis. Most monasteries had some land or cattle which were leased to laymen on a share-cropping basis. Payment in kind was made to the monastery once or twice a year, and products were entered in a register before being put in storage. Store-rooms were also needed if the monastery was involved in long-distance trade and organized yearly caravans to important trade marts on the border with China. This was the case for the largest monasteries of Central and Eastern Tibet.

All these remarks still do not tell much about the reality of the basic layout of a monastery in Tibet. I do not think it is possible to give a blueprint for a layout of monasteries in Tibet except to say that they had separate buildings delimited, or not, by an enclosure; the main temple building was either in the centre or at the end of the compound if the monastery was built on flat land, and was the highest building if it was located on the side or the top of a mountain. The opening of the main chapel traditionally faced the east, as in India, but from the 15th century temples also opened to the south, as in China, such as the White Temple (Lha khang dkar po) of Tsa pa rang in Western Tibet, or the main temple of the dPal 'khor chos sde in rGyal rtse.

However, basic elements existed and they were combined differently in each monastery according to the factors already mentioned.

Temple building

This can be single- or multi-storied, containing one or several chapels. These chapels, also called "temples" (*lha khang*), can be situated on different levels, and/or at the same level as the main chapel (often called *gtsug lag khang*) but surrounding it. The temple is usually square or rectangular, but cruciform temples also existed (bSam yas, the temple of Ye shes 'od in Tho ling). The example of the ancient vihāra of Paharpur in Bangladesh comes to mind in this context but, again, the cruciform layout was known in Tibet, as tombs and watch towers prove. Ideally the temple opens to the East, or to the South.

ph. 4 page 294

In the oldest temples, a circumambulation path was built inside the temple and circled the main chapel.

There might be several temple buildings in the monastery compound, each dedicated to a different deity and their sizes vary. The library is generally not a separate building except in very large monasteries such as Sa skya (Sakya), but is inside one of the temples, built either along the side-walls, or in a special room at the back of the main altar. The temple also houses the dance costumes and masks; depending on the size of the monastery, these can also be kept in a store-room on the side of the temple building.

A small room on the side of the building can be devoted to the caretaker.

Courtyard

ph. 5 page 294

This is usually found in front of the temple, enclosed by a wall. It can have a portico.

Assembly hall

ph. 6 page 295

The largest temple often doubles as the assembly hall.

Monks' cells

These can be located around the courtyard in the classical Indian layout. More often, they are situated in small houses of one, two or three storeys, often with an indoor kitchen, outside the temple compound. These houses can be free-standing or attached to each other, forming small streets. *ph. 7 page 295*

High lamas' residence

The abbot (*mkhan po*) lives in a house or in rooms near the temple. The head of the monastery (*dgon bdag*), hereditary or reincarnated (*sprul sku*) can live in rooms above the temple, or in a house (*bla brang*), the size of which depends on the wealth of the lineage and of the monastery.

Kitchen

This is in a separate building, close to the temple, ideally opening to the west where the fire deity lives.

Storerooms

Ideally, these are oriented towards the north where the god of wealth resides.

Toilets

These are common toilets, of the drop-pit type. They are in a separate building on the edge of the monastery compound. They are emptied regularly and the waste is used as manure in the fields, if there are any. Ideally, they are oriented to the south, towards the mouth of the God of Dead.

*Stūpa (*mchod rten*)*

There might be several stūpas in the monastery compound, usually on the edge, or at the top of the enclosure wall itself. Their location depends on a number of geomantic and astrological factors. According to their shape, they have different meanings and refer to the eight important events of the Buddha's life. The complete row of eight stūpas is often found. In bSam yas, four stupa were built at the four cardinal points. It is rare to find a stūpa in the middle of the temple courtyard.

Stūpas can also be located inside the temple, their size ranging from twenty centimetres to several metres high, especially in the case of *sKu gdung mchod rten*, which are mortuary memorials for high lamas.

Outside the monastery and several hundred metres from it, a stūpa called *rTa bab mchod rten* is usually erected. The name means "the stūpa where one must dismount from the horse" out of religious reverence.

*Prayer wheel house (*Mani chos 'khor*)*

This is built at the entrance of the monastery, or on the side of the temple courtyard. It can also be built outside the monastery compound on a creek, with the prayer wheel turned by water power. This latter is very common in Eastern Tibet, but rare in Central and Western Tibet.

Enclosure

The whole compound was usually enclosed by a wall or houses forming an enclosure, but with the growth of the monastery, this enclosure could finally find itself in the middle of the monastery, and houses built much beyond its limit. Small prayer wheels could be inserted in the walls.

While these represent basic elements, there can be almost infinite variation in the layout, depending on the size of the monastery. We could conclude in contradictory terms by saying that most monasteries are centred but not symmetrical, compact but sprawling.

It should also be added that in the grasslands of north-east Tibet, where a semi-nomadic population lives, some monasteries are made of tents, the largest being the temples, which are not dismantled.

4 – *Tho ling monastery, Western Tibet, Ye shes 'od 's temple*
(photo F. Pommaret, 1999)

5 – *sMin grol ling monastery, Central Tibet, courtyard and temples, reconstructed*
(photo F. Pommaret, 1999)

'Bras spung monastery – 6
Central Tibet,
the main assembly hall,
partly reconstructed
(photo F. Pommaret, 1986)

rDzogs chen monastery – 7
Eastern Tibet,
monks' cells,
reconstructed
(photo F. Pommaret, 1986)

4. The elements of the monastery

Three of the most interesting features of Tibetan monasteries are the functional polyvalence of the temples, the strict spatial separation for the learning process, and the places of meditation.[3]

4.1 Religious functions

The temples are, of course, the main spaces for religious functions, but individual rooms also serve as private prayer spaces, as every one of them would have a simple altar.

A temple is a symbolic rendition of the three aspects of the Buddha: the Body, symbolized by statues and paintings; the Speech, by the books; and the Mind, by the stūpa.

According to the type of rituals and to which deity they are dedicated, different and specialized chapels can be used. For example, the *mGon khang* is devoted to the cult of the fierce protective deities.

Rituals involving the whole monk community, as well as the religious assemblies twice or three times a day, are held in the largest temple, which is often called the "Assembly hall" (*tshogs chen, 'du khang*). This hall is also used for ordination, community confession and examinations.

There is no fixed or precise day or time for the lay community to attend rituals. The lay community never assembles as a whole with the monk community in the temple, except for the annual monastery festival, and for exceptional teachings and blessings given by a visiting high lama. These activities generally take place not inside the temple but in the courtyard, in front of the temple.

A special wall or building above the monastery, or the wall of the highest temple, is used in certain places to hang, once a year at the monastery festival time, a huge embroidered or appliqué *thang ka* for all to see and worship.

In order to gain merit, a person or family can offer tea or butter for the entire monk community on a precise day, or ask for a precise recitation in return for offerings in kind, or silver and gold, depending on their status.

If the monastery is not too far away from settlements, the most religious lay people, often the elders, will visit it on the auspicious days: that is, the 1st, 8th, 15th and 28th days of the lunar month, as well as on Buddhist festival days. This would also be the occasion to bring food supplies to monks belonging to their family.

People will prostrate, touch the statues with their head to obtain blessings, and offer incense and butter-lamps to the temple, but this would be done on an *ad hoc* basis and not in any formal way involving the monk community, except the temple caretaker. If a lay man wants to meet a monk, he usually goes to his cell; if a woman wants to meet a monk, she would have him called outside. Meetings never take place inside the temple.

If the monastery is not large, costumes for religious dances are kept in boxes inside the temple, and the masks and hats are hung on the rafters of the ceiling. In the same way, painted scrolls called *thang ka*, are kept in boxes in the temple and only taken out

---

3. I would like to thank Samten Karmay for the details he gave me on monasteries.

for ceremonies. However, if the monastery could afford it, a special room, often built on the side of the temple, is devoted to the storage of these religious items. Tailoring, embroidery and appliqué work are done by specialized monks inside one of the temples or in the costume storeroom.

If a monk wishes, he can meditate in his cell, but inside the monastery compound there is no room for common meditation practice, no meditation paths or gardens like in Japan. As for the temple, it is not used as a place for individual meditation.

Individual long-term (3 years, 3 months and 3 days) meditation places have always been separate from the main monastery. These retreats are made in caves and hermitages high up on the mountain, well above the monastery. Meditators are totally isolated from the community and never come out during the period of their retreat. Their food supply is brought to them and left outside the cave or cell.

However, while there are no meditation paths, the monastery is surrounded by a circumambulation path (*skor lam*), marked by constructions: prayer-walls, cairns with *mantras* written on the stones, prayer-flags, stūpas, rocks with low-relief sculpture, stones marked with the imprint of a saint. This path is the symbolic religious enclosure of the monastery and is used at all times of the day by both monks and lay people.

The local deity could be housed either in a small separate building or in a chapel on the side of the main temple.

4.2 *Reliquary, commemorative and funerary functions*

Trees with a special symbolic meaning are sometimes found in monasteries and surrounded by elaborate fencing. These might be the "Bodhi tree" – pipal (*ficus religiosa*) – if the climate allows its growth, trees which have grown from the travelling staff of a high lama, trees upon whose leaves syllables have appeared miraculously. The preferred species are cypress or juniper, well suited to the climate, but never poplar or willow, maybe considered too common for such an exalted symbolism.

Because of the shortage of wood, dead bodies are usually exposed to vultures in special places called "charnel grounds" (*dur khrod*), usually up on the mountain or in remote locations. Dead bodies are associated with the notion of "pollution" (*grib*) but some charnel grounds can be situated close to the monastery. Death rituals are performed in individual houses and the body then carried to the charnel ground for sky burial.

Certain charnel grounds are considered more holy than others. They are considered the equivalent of the cremation grounds of ancient India, and people will travel considerable distances to bring their dead to such places. The charnel ground on a ridge above 'Bri gung mthil monastery in Central Tibet, or the Tirthapuri cremation ground in Western Tibet are very famous.

Stūpas are erected as commemorative monuments for the deeds of the Buddha, as seen above, but also as votive monuments to bring merit to a person, alive or dead. In these cases, they would be outside the temples. When placed inside a temple, stūpas are often funerary monuments, called *sku gdung mchod rten* and contain either the ashes or the mummy of a high lama/reincarnation of the monastery (high lamas are not exposed, but either cremated or embalmed). The most famous stūpas of this type are the gilded stūpas, several metres high, containing the embalmed remains of eight Dalai Lamas in funerary chapels of the Potala.

4.3 Educational functions

The assembly hall is used as a general classroom for the younger monks. It must be understood that at least half the monks never go beyond reading and writing. So higher classes are held for small groups or individuals in the teachers' private quarters, which are much larger than the ordinary cell. The time actually spent in "a class" is quite short and, once they have obtained the explanation, the monks have to memorize the texts by themselves. Memorization is the root of the education system, with the learning process left much to the monk himself. When learning their texts, monks study in their cells, outside the buildings in the sun or under porticos protected from the wind. Places for individual study are left to the preference of the students. Monks study basic daily rituals by attending their celebration. Debate plays an important role in the Sa skya, dGe lugs pa and Bon po traditions and takes place in the garden/courtyard; the latter is also used as an open-air study room.

Monks who are not suited to higher studies, are encouraged to take up other "professions" (painting, music, rituals, tailoring, administration, accounting, cooking, copying and printing), and then their apprenticeship takes the form of on-the-job training with the relevant master. There is no need of classrooms for them.

Books are kept in the temple's library, or, in very large monasteries, in proper library buildings; a monk can keep private books in his room. Students – who also have their own books – can borrow books from the library or from their teacher, who has his own personal library.

A number of monasteries used to contain printing houses. The large ones that produced prestigious editions of the Buddhist Canon, were only a few such as sDe dge in Khams, Co ne and sKu 'bum in Amdo, sNar thang and Zhol below the Potala in Central Tibet. However many middle-size monasteries also had printing houses for local needs: books, prayer-flags, charms.

Printing in the monastery used the xylographic process and this involved not only a skilled monastic work force, but also impressive storage space. It was really a cottage-industry for the monastery. Paper and wood had to be brought from considerable distance, ink had to be manufactured, wood-blocks engraved, in addition to the printing work itself.

Today the situation is different, with offset and computer-assisted facilities which are used to print religious books even in the monasteries, although some of them continue to use the xylographic process which is thought to give more religious value to a book.

4.4 Community functions

If the monastery is large and its activities diversified, separate rooms and even buildings are devoted to administration and accounting.

There is neither bell nor drum tower. Monks are called for the assembly by a monk blowing a conch-shell or beating a gong, or even like in 'Bras spung by a boy with a fine voice shouting a long, shrill sound that can be heard from a distance. He does this about five times at a few-minutes intervals, from the roof of the main building.

As mentioned before, there can be a large prayer-wheel in a separate building. Small prayer-wheels are also disposed in rows around the outside wall of the temples or monastery enclosure.

A tall flag-pole with a long prayer-flag is usually erected in the centre of the front courtyard of the main temple. The printed cloth is changed once a year during a ceremony that involves the cleric and lay communities.

A compulsory construction found either standing free, or on a roof, is the fumigation stove (*bsang thab*). Fumigation rituals, using odoriferous plants and coniferous branches, are performed every morning for the local deities, and also during rituals.

4.5 Accommodation

Residences of the abbot and high lama

In Tibet, a monastery may have a reincarnation lineage but the *sprul sku* is generally not the abbot of the monastery, a position held by a senior and learned monk. The abbot's role is to supervise the administration and ensure the continuity of religious studies. He is the guardian of the monastery's intellectual and religious affiliation to a particular religious school.

Both the *sprul sku* and the abbot have residences in the monastery. The size of the residence depends on the wealth and prestige of the monastery – rooms above the temple or large separate buildings in the compound of the monastery. The living quarters of the most important monks are called by the honorific term for room, *gzims chun* or *gzims khang*. However, the head of the monastery (*dgon bdag*), hereditary or incarnated lama, may live in a large residence which is called bla brang.

The *bla brang*, a multi-storeyed building could contain – in addition to the living quarters *gzims chung* – a kitchen and a chapel, the lama's administrative offices, storerooms and servants' quarters. In Sa skya or certain monasteries in Khams, where reincarnations can be married, women also live in the house. However, they do not go into parts of the complex reserved for monks.

Monks' accommodation

This can vary. Dormitories do not exist. The common pattern is individual or shared (double) rooms. Depending on the monk's level in the hierarchy and his personal wealth, he could have the equivalent of a small flat with two rooms and a kitchen, or a small house to himself. Young novices usually stay with cleric relatives and do housework for them in return for shelter and basic tuition.

Refectory or dining-room do not exist. Monks assemble in the temple three times a day at the time of the prayers, and food and tea from the common kitchen is distributed. Each monk has his own cup and bag for roasted flour. However, many monks have their own food supply which supplements the monastery fare, and they cook in their own kitchen. A young novice from an impoverished family faces difficult times until he can perform rituals for laymen, in return for which he will get payment in kind. Tibetan monks usually eat in the evening.

Visitors' shelters

In the Tibetan world, not every monastery has a special building devoted to the accommodation of visitors or pilgrims. However, some of them have a guesthouse built outside the monastery's compound.

If there is no guest-house, men stay in the rooms of their cleric relatives. Women cannot spend the night in the monastery, but stay in the reincarnation's house if he is married, outside in people's houses and tents if there are any, or with nuns if there is a nunnery nearby. In the Bon po community of Shar khog (Zung chu) in south-east Amdo, lay people had a house built in the monastery for their cleric relatives and it was the custom for women to stay there.[4]

Kitchen

This is a separate building with several earthen stoves, fuelled by animal dung, or wood in some regions. The fuel supply is kept in big piles outside the kitchen.

Without chimney, just an opening in the ceiling, it is a dark and smoky place. Walls and ceiling are covered with soot, which is scraped off at intervals for the preparation of ink. The bare minimum of kitchen utensils – knives, cleavers, teapots, butter-tea churns, ladles and huge caldrons – are kept on wooden shelves and on the floor.

Storerooms

These are also in separate buildings and are used for food (tea, butter, cheese, dried meat, dried vegetables) and non-food items (wool, textiles, leather, felt, porcelain, wax for seals, paper, silver, gold, wood).

Hygiene and sanitary facilities

There are no washing facilities. When the weather is good, monks take a bath in the nearby river and wash their clothes quite often in summer; but in winter this is hardly possible due to the icy weather. Monks send their novices to fetch water from the spring or the river, which means breaking the ice if they are frozen, and keep some water in a container.

The common toilets are located in a long building at the edge of the monastery. Wooden beams render the exercise quite perilous. However, the important monks usually have a private toilet attached to their house.

Water supply

This is problematic. Given the geological conditions, wells are unknown, and water has to be constantly fetched from a spring or a stream outside the monastery.

It is well-known that there was no water-supply in the Potala and that endless lines of people carried water up to the complex.

4.6 Other functions

Garden/Debating arena

The *chos grwa* or debating arena is the equivalent of a garden. Philosophical debate is an essential part of the learned monk's life and takes place every day. The courtyard, enclosed by a wall and often a portico, is planted with trees – willows or poplars – and flowers; the ground is covered with gravel or pebbles, and it is a preferred meeting-place. A large college, like sGo mang in 'Bras spung, may even have two debating arenas, one for summer and one for winter. These gardens are also used for studying, resting, pilgrimage (as the one in Se ra monastery, built near the cave where Tshong kha pa came to understand the meaning of vacuity). But they are not places of meditation.

ph. 8 opposite page

Medical house

In Tibet, monks are the recipients and holders of medical knowledge and many medicinal pills are manufactured on the precinct of the monastery. Learned and skilled monks are trained and employed for this task. The raw material – that is herbs and

4. Personal communication, Samtem Karmay, September 1999.

minerals – are either collected in the summer during long outings in the mountains above the monastery, or imported from the south-east regions of Tibet and Bhutan. Medicinal components are kept in storerooms near the manufacturing unit.

Stables

Monks ride horses to travel to the monastery's estates, individual houses or other monasteries. In large monasteries, horses are kept in stables outside the monastery precinct. In smaller monasteries, they were usually kept in the precinct of the *bla brang*, residence of the highest monastic authority.

8 – *'Bras spung monastery, Central Tibet, monks debating in the garden (*chos grwa*)* (photo F. Pommaret, 1986)

Monasteries in Tibet have been characterised by a great flexibility in layout and by an organic growth, especially from the 11th century. They have always taken into account the configuration of the landscape in order to utilize it to its utmost, and to express a hierarchy in the monastery buildings. Functionality was given pre-eminence over a centred, symmetric layout. From a concentric pattern of buildings, the layout shifted to their juxtaposition. Buildings became modules.

To conclude, I would like to say a word about architectural style. There is a close similarity between vernacular and monastic architectural styles in Tibet. Temples are often recognizable only by roof ornaments and the reddish frieze of butt-ended twigs below the roof. As for the rest of the buildings, they are stylistically no different from noble and village houses. Like the vernacular, monastic architecture has been dependent on the ecological conditions of the region and there is no specific unified monastic style of architecture throughout Tibet.

SELECTED BIBLIOGRAPHY IN WESTERN LANGUAGES

This does not include either Ladakh, Sikkim, Bhutan and Northern Nepal, or articles on specific temples and/or wall-paintings.

BÉGUIN, Gilles
1997 – "Les grands monuments de Lhasa d'après les peintures d'architecture du Musée Guimet", *Lhasa: Lieu du divin*, F. Pommaret éd., Genève, Olizane, p. 75-86.

BUFFETRILLE, Katia
1989 – "La restauration du monastère tibétain de bSam yas: un exemple de la continuité dans la relation chapelain-donateur au Tibet?", *Journal Asiatique*, T. CCLXXVII, 1989, n° 3-4, p. 363-413.

CHAYET, Anne
1985 – *Les temples de Jehol et leurs modèles tibétains*, Paris, Éditions Recherche sur les civilisations.
1988 – "Le monastère de bSam yas: sources architecturales", *Arts Asiatiques*, T. XLIII, 1988, p. 19-29.
1990 – "Contribution aux recherches sur les états successifs du monastère de bSam yas", *Tibet: civilisation et société*, F. Meyer éd., Paris, Fondation Singer-Polignac, p.109-119.
1994 – *Manuel d'Art et d'archéologie du Tibet*, Paris, Éditions Picard.
1997 – "Le Potala, symbole du pouvoir des Dalaï-lama", *Lhasa: Lieu du divin,* F. Pommaret éd., Genève, Olizane, p. 59-74.

DAKPA, Ngawang
1997 – "Les Heures et les jours d'un grand monastère: Drepung", *Lhasa: Lieu du divin*, F. Pommaret éd., Genève, Olizane, p. 203-216.

DENWOOD, Philip
1971 – "Forts and castles. An aspect of Tibetan architecture", *Shambala occasional papers of the Institute of Tibetan Studies*, Tring, p. 7-17.
1980 – "Introduction to Tibetan architecture", *Tibet news review*, vol. 1, n° 2, p. 3-12.
1994 – " Sacred Architecture of Tibetan Buddhism: the Indwelling image", *Orientations*, June 1994, p. 42-47.

HELLER, Amy
1999 – *Tibetan Art*, Milano, Jaca Book/Antique Collectors'club.

KARMAY, Samten
1987 – "L'organisation de l'espace selon un texte tibétain du XIIe siècle", *Demeures des Hommes, Sanctuaires des dieux*, Vergata, Paola et Béguin, Gilles (éds.), Paris/Roma, RMN/Universita di Roma "La Sapienza", p. 96-98.

KLIMBURG-SALTER, Deborah
1997 – *Tabo: a lamp for the kingdom*, New York/Milano, Thames & Hudson/ Skira.

KVAERNE, Per
1984 – "Tibet: The rise and fall of a monastic tradition", *The World of Buddhism,* H. Bechert and R. Gombrich (eds.), London, Thames & Hudson, p. 231-270.

LO BUE, Erberto and RICCA, Franco
1990 – *Gyantse revisited*, Firenze/Torino, Casa editrice de Lettre & CESMEO.

LUCZANITS, Christian
1996 – "A note on Tholing monastery", *Orientations*, vol.27, n°6, June 1996, p. 76-77.

MÉMET, Sébastien
1988 – "Le monastère de bSam yas: Essai de restitution", *Arts Asiatiques*, T. XLIII,p. 30-32.

MEYER, Fernand
1987 – "The Potala palace of the Dalai Lamas in Lhasa", *Orientations*, vol. 18, n° 7, July 1987, p.14-23.

MEYER, Fernand et JEST, Corneille
1987 – "Architecture: fonctions techniques, sociales, symboliques et religieuses", *Demeures des Hommes, Sanctuaires des dieux*, Vergata, Paola et Béguin, Gilles (éds.), Paris/Roma, RMN/Universita di Roma "La Sapienza", p. 52-68.
1987 – "Milieux , Matériaux et Techniques", *Demeures des Hommes, Sanctuaires des dieux*, Vergata, Paola et Béguin, Gilles (éds.), Paris/Roma, RMN/Universita di Roma "La Sapienza", p. 146-167.

NAKANE, Chie
1982 – *Labrang, a study in the field by Li an-che*, Tokyo, Institute of Oriental Culture, the University of Tokyo.

NIETUPSKI, Paul
1999 – *Labrang: a Buddhist monastery at the crossroads of four civilizations*, Ithaca/New York, Snow Lion.

POMMARET, Françoise (éd.)
1997 – *Lhasa: Lieu du divin*, Genève, Olizane.

RICCA, Franco
1999 – *Il templo oracolare di Nechung*, Alessandria, Eds Del Orso.

ROSSI FILIBECK, Elena de
1987 – "Quelques illustrations concernant les prescriptions architecturales dans les textes tibétains du Vinaya", *Demeures des Hommes, Sanctuaires des dieux*, Vergata, Paola et Béguin, Gilles (éds.), Paris/Roma, RMN/Universita di Roma "La Sapienza", p. 104-110.

SHAKABPA, Tsepon
1984 – *Tibet: a political history*, New York, Potala publications.

STEIN, Rolf
1957 – "L'habitat, le monde et le corps humain en Extrême-Orient et en Haute Asie", *Journal asiatique*, CCXLV, 1, p. 37-74.
1957 – "Architecture et pensée religieuse en Extrême-Orient", *Arts asiatiques*, T. IV, n° 3, p.163-186.
1981 – *La Civilisation tibétaine*, Paris, l'Asiathèque.
1987 – *Le Monde en petit*, Paris, Flammarion.

THUBTEN, Legshay Gyatsho
1979 – *Gateway to the temple*, translated by David Jackson, Kathmandu, Ratna Pustak Bhandar.

TUCCI, Giuseppe
1988 – *Indo-Tibetica*, English edition, 7 vols., New-Delhi, Aditya Prakashan.
1973 – *Tibet*, Paris, Archeologia Mundi, Nagel.

UEBACH, Helga
1990 – "On Dharma-colleges and their teachers in the ninth century Empire", *Indo-sino-tibetica: studi in onore di Luciano Petech*, P. Daffina (ed.), Roma, Ismeo, p. 393-418.

VERGATA, Paola
1987 – "Tibet occidental (Ngari) du XVe au XXe siècle", *Demeures des Hommes, Sanctuaires des dieux*, Vergata, Paola et Béguin, Gilles (éds.), Paris/Roma, RMN/Universita di Roma, "La Sapienza", p. 360-367.

VERGATA, Paola et BÉGUIN, Gilles (éds.)
1987 – *Demeures des Hommes, Sanctuaires des dieux*, Paris/Roma, RMN/ Universita di Roma, "La Sapienza" (bilingual edition: Italian and French).

VITALI, Roberto.
1990 – *Early Temples of Central Tibet*, London, Serindia.
1996 – *The Kingdoms of Gu.ge Pu.hrang according to mNga'.ris rgyal.rabs*, Dharamsala, Tholing Committee.
1999 – *Records of Tho ling: a literary and visual reconstruction of the "mother" monastery in Gu ge*, Dharamsala, High Asia, Amnye Machen Institute.

Information on daily life and curriculum in monasteries can be found in most of the biographies written by Tibetans in exile and which have been published in the West since the mid-1980s.

CD-Rom

FOURNIER, Lionel et JOUDET, Gérard
1999 – *Tibet: de la sagesse à l'oubli*, Paris, Bernard Coulon Expressions, (Mac/PC).

This CD contains architectural and iconographic documentation on 75 monasteries in Tibet.

THE PHYSICAL BUDDHIST MONASTERY IN CHINA

Isabelle Charleux and Vincent Goossaert

Research on Chinese Buddhism is a field that has accumulated a huge literature in Chinese, Japanese, and to a lesser degree, in Western languages. It is traditionally dominated by intellectuals seeking within Buddhism a pure spiritual tradition of speculative thinking, and is usually rather anticlerical in its outlook – albeit Japanese Buddhology is still dominated by clerics-scholars. The literature is therefore largely focused on the study of the textual traditions, such as translations and commentaries of Sanskrit scriptures and the writing of Chinese apocrypha, hagiographies and mystical works such as Chan anthologies. The well-established tradition of scholarship on Chinese Buddhist art likewise focuses on ancient sculpture (and to a much lesser degree, painting), whose masterworks have long since been plundered and found their way in various museums around the world: they are mostly studied with no reference to their physical context.

However, the organisation of monasteries has also begun to be studied seriously this century. The sources for such research exist in abundance: besides their scriptural and poetic production, monks and nuns of the past have left us with a large number of historiographical works; hundreds of monastery gazetteers from the 16th to the 20th centuries exist and have been recently reprinted; stone inscriptions, the most important source for the social history of religious institutions in China, can be found by the tens of thousands. Monastic gazetteers and stone inscriptions both provide many maps of monastic compounds. Last but not least, the monasteries themselves are there to be studied. Although most were destroyed on the mainland during the 20th century, a fair number have been partially restored, and have reopened gradually since 1978. They can be studied both for their architectural value and for the monastic life that is trying to reaffirm itself in the old or new buildings. In Taiwan, Hong Kong, and in the many

The Buddhist Monastery, EFEO, 2003, p. 305-350

countries with a sizeable ethnic-Chinese community, including Thailand, Malaysia and the United States, new Buddhist monasteries are appearing, and deserve attention. The oldest Buddhist buildings now extant only date from the 8th century, but older sites, such as the very numerous painted and/or sculpted caves attest to Chinese Buddhist monumental art of the earlier periods. Archaeological work has found abundant evidence of Buddhist architecture in the semi-desertic areas of the Silk road; in China proper, parts of monasteries, notably stūpas, have been excavated and older artefacts been found underground. Finally, many written descriptions of the oldest monasteries are available in literary and historical records.

The Chinese Buddhist monastery would seem too large a topic for a book, not to mention an article such as this. We will not even attempt to summarise the existing secondary literature here, but will only draw on a limited number of seminal reference works as well as our own perusal of the primary sources and fieldwork. From this, we will attempt to sketch the historical formation of the monastery in its physical and spatial dimensions, and in relation to its use by the monastic community. This survey is basically intended for non-China specialists with a comparative interest.[1]

The reference works just alluded to were written during the middle of the 20th century. Extensive studies on the organisation of Chinese Buddhist monasteries were conducted in the 1950's by the diplomat-turned-historian Holmes Welch (1921-1981), in the framework of his larger endeavour to describe modern Chinese Buddhism.[2] Although he could not visit the mainland monasteries, he interviewed more than a hundred monks exiled in Taiwan and Hong-Kong. From 1929 to 1933, Johannes Prip-Moller (1889-1943), a Dane working in North China as a consulting architect, visited hundreds of monasteries in Central China and drew their plans to understand the function and location of the different buildings.[3] Contemporary scholarship inevitably draws on their foundation works, while also taking advantage of rare historical sources now available and enlarging the geographical scope of their enquiry.

At the same time, the study of the evolution of the architectural layout of the monastery was made possible by the identification and detailed study of the earliest Buddhist halls by the architect Liang Sicheng in the 1930's.[4] Although Liang and other scholars such as Liu Dunzhen who inaugurated the field of architectural history in China were not interested in religion in itself, the most ancient buildings they studied were mostly temples and monasteries. However, with the exception of Prip-Moller's outstanding work, architectural studies on Chinese monasteries in any language have so far mainly focused on the carpentry and its evolution from ancient China to Ming (1368-1644) and Qing (1644-1911) times. This type of research does not address religious architecture as such, but studies architectural techniques that happen to be

---

1. For this reason as well, almost all references are in Western languages.

2. Welch 1967; 1968; 1972. Welch's as well as Prip-Moller's work discussed below are used throughout the present paper and are not referred to systematically.

3. Many other Westerners including Heinrich Hackmann, John Blofeld and Ernst Boerschmann visited Chinese Buddhist monasteries in the first half of the 20th century and published detailed descriptions. Japanese scholars also published extensive fieldwork reports.

4. After having studied Liao and Jin dynasty monasteries, Liang Sicheng's more spectacular "discovery" was the Tang dynasty Foguang si [23] in 1937. Within nine years, he studied more than 2,000 buildings in fifteen provinces: Ecke 1936-37; Liang Ssu-Cheng and Fairbank (ed.) 1984. The number in brackets refers to the list of cited monasteries in the annex and on the map.

found in religious settings. Even recent detailed monographs, usually published as a result of a restoration program, are written in this perspective.[5] In such circumstances, very few authors have addressed the monastic layout as a whole and the variations of the buildings' functions in space and in time.

In contrast with the established tradition, the present survey will rather proceed from characterising the Buddhist monastery as distinct from other buildings. We will first describe the monastery as an institution, then sketch the characteristics and historical development of its layout, and eventually discuss individual buildings. Our discussion is focused on the late imperial and modern period (1368-1950) and mostly refers to existing buildings.

See Annex: map and list p. 341-43

1. The place of the Buddhist monastery in the Chinese religious landscape

A major fact that distinguishes the Chinese Buddhist monastery from its counterparts in most other countries is that it is firmly embedded into a much larger system of religious institutions (Goossaert 2000a). Among the many kinds of temples that graced China's cities and countryside, were the shrines for the official cult of the state, Buddhist and Taoist monasteries, temples for various deities, including local saints, past heroes, saint patrons of the corporations and regional associations, schools and academies (that worked as Confucian monasteries). All shared basic architectural features and were used in a rather similar fashion: a caretaker took charge of everyday upkeep, the place opened on holidays, usually the main deity's birthday, for a festival featuring rituals by the religious specialists, devotees coming to burn incense and attractions, such as theatre shows and a market. The day-to-day running of the place was supported mainly by landed endowments, but any major repair work or enlargement was funded by a subscription among the public or a poll tax on all inhabitants.

Some temples had been founded by clerics, or been given to them, and were run as the private patrimony of the cleric in charge. A few others were owned and managed by the state, or by the Saṅgha, but by far the largest part was the property of and run by rather small, localised social groups: inclusive village or neighbourhood associations, clans or corporations. Many were too poor to support a professional caretaker, but in the largest ones, it was usually considered desirable to have a resident cleric. Eligible clerics included Buddhist monks and nuns, and Taoists also of both sexes; many temples also had a medium. This was chosen regardless of the nature of the temple: Buddhist monks lived in lineage halls and temples devoted to all kinds of divinities. In such places, monks and nuns were only employees, and could be fired if they misbehaved. They enjoyed however customary rights; they could till part of the temple land (if any) for their own consumption, and use the donation money as they wished. They also gained a living from the liturgical services, mostly funerals, offered to the neighbours and members of the temple community. The position was also hereditary, which means, for unmarried clerics like the Chinese Buddhists, that one could choose a successor, usually taken in as a novice during his/her teens. From the clerical perspective, such places were thus called "hereditary temples".

5. The Wenwu Press in Beijing has published during the last fifteen years some twenty comprehensive and richly documented monographs on Chinese or Tibetan monasteries.

None of this fits with the canonical definition of a Buddhist monastery, which is the common property of the Saṅgha and is ruled by the sole Buddhist canonical law. Moreover, in temples, the main icon was that of the local god or ancestor, and most did not even have a Buddha image or a stūpa. Monasteries, organised around Buddha images, with a large congregation abiding by the monastic rules, practising meditation and having a library, also existed. Actually, both kinds of establishments — the hereditary temples and the monasteries — were intimately dependent on each other. The canonical ordination was split into two stages: when entering a hereditary temple, and thus leaving the family, the novice was tonsured and received a religious name that integrated him/her in the spiritual lineage of his/her master. Very often, the temple could only provide for a single monk with one or two novices. Many clerics also went on endless pilgrimages throughout the country as a vocation. Temples had no regular program of meditation and study, no code of rule, but the master nonetheless tutored the novice in reading the scriptures. If the novice later went to a monastery and enrolled in an ordination class (not all novices had the opportunity or will to ever do this), he would receive there a sound training in the rules, deportment and liturgy and the full precepts of the *Prātimokṣa*. The few large monasteries organising ordination platforms, which were very costly endeavours, were thus maintaining the standards of self-control and purity that justified the Buddhist clergy as a whole.

Welch has shown that during the early 20th century the large monasteries accounted for about 5% of the Saṅgha, the remaining 95% being itinerant or resident cleric in temples. The same can be said for the smaller Taoist Quanzhen (celibate) clergy, and the figure can also be considered to be valid for earlier periods, at least since the beginning of the Ming dynasty (1368). There was thus a vertical hierarchy between the elite clerics living in large communities, and the "clerical proletariat" of hereditary temples.

China also enjoys the distinction of having a sizeable female clergy. Buddhist nuns have existed from the onset of the Buddhist arrival in China, but till now they have to contend with a lower position. There is no very large nunnery but smaller ones are found everywhere. Specific laws were adopted (but not systematically enforced) to prevent young females from entering the clergy. Many widows, prevented from or unwilling to remarry, became nuns.

Buddhist monks and nuns freely co-operated with their Taoist counterparts; although there has been confrontations between the two religions in Chinese history, mostly between the 6th and 13th centuries, the vision of systematic antagonism is more a projection of Christian ways of thought upon China than a Chinese reality. In modern China, both clergies had extremely similar conditions, and their destiny was indissolubly linked. Buddhists and Taoists helped each other, and many rituals necessitated their co-celebration. Chinese Buddhists, moreover, had to relate to the monks of the Tibeto-Mongol clergy. Ever since the emperors of the Mongol Yuan (1277-1367) dynasty patronised Tibetan Buddhism, and particularly after the 17th century, a fair number of monks, indiscriminately called "lama" by the Chinese, have been present in China proper, working as chaplains to the Ming and Qing courts, or for local Chinese, Manchu and Mongol believers. They had their own monasteries in China proper, which are not discussed here. Their influence on Chinese Buddhism extended to spiritual practice and liturgy, but also to art and architecture.

A definition of the Chinese Buddhist monastery

The large monasteries are usually named *si* or *yuan*, both originally meaning a bureaucratic office. *An*, hermitage, is mostly used for small convents (especially for nuns), but may be used for any Buddhist community. As these terms have no precise legal value, they may be used in place of each other. Names are no sure indication of the status of an establishment; the original name of a place remains in use even when the clerics in charge are replaced with laymen or clerics of another confession.

The Buddhist monastery under discussion here is restricted to the larger establishments run as the collective property of the Chinese Saṅgha and opened to all monks. They are qualified as "universal" or "ecumenical", *shifang*.[6] They housed an average of 100 (and up to 500) monks, some in almost permanent residence and some staying for a few months en route for other famous pilgrimage and formation centres. The prestige of these places stayed with the discipline they maintained, the teaching or meditation training available to all ordained monks willing to enrol, and to the personal charisma of the elected abbot. Monasteries often controlled branch temples and hermitages for elderly monks and ascetics. Such Buddhist monasteries rank among the largest religious complexes in China; only a few central urban temples (although on a smaller acreage) and a dozen official temples dedicated to the most sacred mountains and rivers can compare in terms of number and size of buildings.

Despite differences in size, monasteries and temples were not strictly separate categories: a flourishing temple could be turned into a monastery when its cleric in charge enacted the rules and regular liturgy proper to the monastic status. Conversely, it happened regularly that an abbot seized for himself the monastery's property and ran the place as his own hereditary temple. The monastery status was not permanent, and it did not depend on the identity of the founder – the person who initiated the fund-raising for the construction and who could be an emperor, an official, a layman, or a cleric. Furthermore, this distinction was customary and, albeit used by law-enforcing agents, was not really incorporated either in civil or Buddhist law. This gave rise to many particular situations lying in between monastery and temple and combining elements of both: for instance, some ecumenical monasteries training novices functioned as hybrid institutions, like Yongquan si [62] (Welch 1967:138-141, and Appendix V).

From the perspective of the layout, the basic distinction is rather clear-cut: monasteries have large conventual quarters arranged around halls for communal practice whereas temples are made up almost entirely of halls devoted to deities, and retain only marginal space for clerical accommodation. Buddhist chapels built for the private or diplomatic use of the emperors were located in the Palace or near outer imperial residences. Although they deserve great attention due to their lofty architecture and artistic contents, they belong to the temple category and thus do not fall in the purview of the present survey.

During the modern period, the large model monasteries were mainly located in lower Yangzi valley: one may mention Jinshan [46] and the nearby Gaomin si [47] for meditation practices, Lingyan shan [3] for Buddha recitation, and Huiju si [45] for ordination. [46] *fig. 8 p. 347*

6. The distinction between hereditary temples and *shifang* monasteries, referring primarily to the fact that any eminent monk was qualified to become abbot of the latter, appeared during the late Tang. During the Song, *shifang* monasteries could accept novices, but not any more in the modern period, when, outside ordination classes, only ordained monks could take residence.

Although this small region had long been China's most densely populated and most culturally and economically active, its quasi-monopoly on the major monasteries is not merely the result of the concentration of people and money. The situation dates back to the Southern Song dynasty (1126-1279), when the large Chan monastery as an institution found its final form. The state then actively promoted a group of very large elite Chan monasteries, the "Five mountains and ten monasteries", who benefited from special protection and patronage. All but one of these 15 were located near the capital, in the area between modern Nanjing in the North and Ningbo in the South, and, indeed, several of them were still listed among the model monasteries of the early 20th century.

Monasteries, the state and the laity during the modern period

The imperial state never maintained a comprehensive roll of all temples on its territory and the first law-mandated survey dates from 1928 – and even then it was properly conducted only in a few places. Laws, decreed dynasty after dynasty, submitted the construction of monasteries or temples to a formal authorisation, but these laws were not well respected. Large monasteries, however, needed the magistrate's support (if only for protecting their landed endowments from encroachment, and also for fiscal advantages) and courted official recognition. The imperial state had few quarrels with the orderly large monasteries and were more suspicious of the itinerant clergy and those actively engaged in society. For these reasons, large monasteries often obtained recognition from the central government, materialised as a name plaque (a horizontal wooden board suspended above the monastery's gate, sometimes calligraphied by the emperor himself) that gave a monastery prestige and some security. Monasteries were usually rather secure, with the exception of the few large-scale persecutions during the 1st millennium, and much more localised actions of militant anticlerical magistrates in modern times, who seized monasteries and turned them into schools or Confucian shrines. The large monasteries with a long history were normally treated as treasures and, in case of need, were well protected by local magistrates.

Benign protection did not mean active involvement. The state was a major monastery builder during the 4th-10th centuries, but ceased to fill this role afterwards. Almost none of the large monasteries that can be visited today is properly speaking a state- or imperial monastery. Imperial personal favour, as opposed to state actions, could include occasional grants for repair works; others were designated for holding regular prayer services for the living emperor or for his predecessors. Even then, monasteries living off imperial generosity were exceptional. Most of them were supported by endowments contributed by local gentry and merchants. Moreover, the late imperial state took very little interest in Buddhist affairs, and did not try to regulate art, liturgy or doctrine. The Saṅgha administration (Senglu si), theoretically in charge of the administrative control of the whole clergy, was completely powerless; monasteries were thus totally independent in their mundane and religious activity – as long as they did not stray into criminal or political ventures, which they very rarely did. Abbots even enjoyed the customary right to try monks and nuns who were guilty of minor offences.

What sort of social space was the monastery in such conditions? Whereas temples built by lay communities really belonged to the bourgeois who held all their public functions there, *shifang* monasteries were ordinarily closed to the public. Rich donors were always welcome and entertained in the guest department: Chinese gentry enjoyed coming to the monasteries for their atmosphere and gardens, and for interacting with the elite monks; they often set up together lay associations for funding pious activities such as releasing live animals, chanting scriptures, or conferral of the lay five vows (Brook 1993). For ordinary devotees, the monastery only opened its doors, literally, once or twice a year, for a major festival. Only at pilgrimage sites lay visitors could stay for the night, but even then, they would stay in separate convents, not inside the main monastery. By contrast, many temples doubled as inns for lay travellers.

The monastery was clearly not a public space (in sense of state-managed or open to all). The monastery was "public" only for all ordained clerics, who could come and stay there at their free will. The absence of a tradition of debates, however, and the highly hierarchical monastic organisation precluded monasteries from turning into contested places. Whereas Tang (618-907) and Song (960-1279)-times monasteries had a leading role in local political and economic life (initiating large infrastructure projects such as land reclaiming and irrigation), the modern monasteries limited their involvement in local society. Their public functions had been taken over partly by lineages and charitable foundations and partly by temples.

Schools

During the formative period of Chinese Buddhism, especially in the 6th-8th centuries, several schools or "sects" – a particularly unfortunate term often encountered in English language literature – developed different doctrines and practices. The Tiantai had the deepest influence on the doctrine, while the Pure Land school placed the emphasis on devotional practices aimed at rebirth in Amitābha's Western Paradise. The esoteric school spread during the Tang period but disappeared as a separate school by the 9th century, being assimilated in common liturgical practice. The Chan school (Meditation, skt. Dhyāna, jap. Zen) emphasised the search for enlightenment by intuitive comprehension. Moreover, the standard organisation (including the layout of the monastery, the liturgical program and the set of rules – superimposed upon the *Vinaya*) of the largest monasteries that formed during the 10th-11th centuries is traditionally described as "Chan" (Foulk 1993).

Since the 10th century, large monasteries are sometimes designated as "doctrinal", "Vinaya" or "meditative". This classification actually refers to the lineage of the abbot, and in communal practice it meant little more than a specialisation of some monasteries in Tiantai doctrinal studies, in the observance of rules (and therefore ordinations) or in Chan collective meditation. A state-led effort at imposing a sort of hierarchy among Chan (and later also "doctrinal") monasteries did not outlive its initiator, the Song dynasty. In modern times, monasteries can definitely not be classified by a particular school any more. There are no different orders, as monks travel from one monastery to the next: rules and liturgy are broadly similar in all monasteries, and differences are proper to each individual monastery. This stands in marked contrast to the Japanese situation where different schools maintain different liturgies. In China, a strong tendency to synthesis has gradually managed to combine originally divergent practices such as those of Pure Land and Chan, beginning as early as the 10th century, and with particular effect after the 16th century. As a result, monasteries have undergone a trend towards standardisation in building style and organisation.

What remains of the "schools" of Chinese Buddhism is lineages: founded by prestigious monks, lineages were transmitted automatically from master to disciple at the tonsure ceremony, and implied the choice of the novice's religious name according to the lineage's generation chart. Belonging to such and such lineage did not imply any doctrinal and otherwise singularity. Monks could have different masters belonging to different lineages, and monasteries could change their "affiliation" with a new abbot. In the Republican period, the majority of the monasteries belonged (i.e. their abbot belonged) to one of many Chan lineages, but ordinations centres normally belonged to the Vinaya lineage. Those who gave the preference to Chan operated a Meditation hall, but also maintained a hall for reciting Buddha's name (a Pure Land practice), and welcomed masters who gave lectures on Tiantai, Avatamsaka or Dharmalaksana doctrine. The joint practice of Chan and Pure Land could even be seen in the same hall, mixing sitting meditation and circumambulation while reciting aloud Buddha's name.

Buddhist monasteries, far from sectarian, were also opened to some interactions and mutual borrowing with the other two institutionalised religions, Confucianism and Taoism. Elements of rites, rules and gods were borrowed from and by Taoist institutions. Popular gods like Wenchang, the kitchen god, and Guandi were included in the Buddhist pantheon protectors. Many Buddhist monasteries were turned into Taoist institutions and reciprocally.

A quantitative note

Statistics on the number of monasteries and monks are based on literary sources, censuses organised at different periods, compiled by local officials, and on registers of ordination certificates.[7] Naturally, they cannot be accepted as entirely accurate, and it is often difficult to ascertain exactly what was accounted for (ordained monks or all persons living as clerics? monasteries or all kinds of temples?). Moreover, figures for the earlier periods are mere national aggregates and do not provide detailed break-ups. It is estimated that the Buddhist clergy may have represented up to 1% of the total population at its peak during Tang times (Gernet 1995:3-14); by the late imperial period, it was about 0,3 to 0,5% (Goossaert 2000b).

The numbers for monasteries are not more precise. Historical sources document only the most prominent monasteries while smaller ones are often not mentioned at all. Local gazetteers[8] contain a special section listing temples and monasteries, but with very little information: at best the location, the date of construction and main dates of restoration and destruction, the name of the founder, the lands they owned, and the famous statues, works of art and stone inscriptions. Most of the time however, it is difficult to make, from such sources, the difference between a small temple and a large monastery, and a complete reconstruction or restoration from a redecoration. Authors who have worked on such data have been able to evidence differences in time and space (a greater concentration of monasteries in some regions, and periods of intense construction, for instance) but no absolute numbers (Yang 1961, Eberhard 1964). The known historical trends suggest that the number of clerics in residence per monastery declined in the long term, correlatively with the average size of monastic landholdings. For instance, historians suggest that whereas a large number of very affluent monasteries controlled a large part of areas such as Fujian, Guangdong and Southern Zhejiang provinces land up to the 13th century, hereafter their dominance declined and in modern days, only a few large monasteries remained in these areas.

7. Most figures from the standard historical sources are quoted by Ch'en 1973. No attempt to a more imaginative use of other sources (epigraphy, notably) has yet been made.

8. This kind of source exist from the 11th century onwards, but becomes very numerous after the 15th.

China in 1900, at the beginning of the large-scale destruction that continued all along the 20th century, had about a million temples; maybe 10% to 20% had a resident clergy, Buddhist or Taoist, and this temple clergy (without counting the Taoists living at home) numbered between 500,000 to one million (Goossaert 2000a: 100). For the 1930's, Welch gave estimations of the size of the Saṅgha and the number of monasteries and nunneries, based on various surveys by the Chinese Buddhist Association and others (Welch 1967: 411-20). He reaches a total of 738,000 monks and nuns, of which 513,000 monks and 225,000 nuns (excluding the Tibeto-Mongol clergy). Nuns thus represented about one third of the Saṅgha at the beginning of the century. In contemporary Taiwan, this proportion has dramatically increased, and most Buddhist clerics, including the best-educated and the more engaged in the modernisation of the Buddhist institutions, happen to be nuns. This clergy lived in 257,096 Buddhist establishments, of which 98,400 had monks in residence, and 134,500 had nuns (24,196 having laymen and laywomen). Of course, the huge majority of those were temples, not monasteries. The monasteries were about 300, of which 200 housed an average of 50-75 monks, and the 100 largest housed an average of 130 monks each.[9] By comparison, Quanzhen Taoists were only about 20,000, and had about 25 large monasteries.

2. The monastery layout

2.1 Building a monastery

Location and environment

There is no canonical prescription on the location of a monastery, and it happened frequently that a monastery was moved from one place to another, either because the original location was seized by local authorities for urban development, or because the new location was more auspicious or larger. The choice of an auspicious site is an essential stage of the founding of a monastery. A *kanyu* [10] (geomancy, siting) practitioner analyses the physical characteristics of the ground and the surrounding landscape, secures the good influences and compensates the evil ones. Ideal characteristics include a protective mountain ridge on the northern side. A monastery or, more often, a stūpa could be erected especially to conjure up bad geomantic characteristics. Stūpas are often built alone to ensure the prosperity of a place.

The idealised Chinese monastery (as well as any temple) is constructed as a mountain (Goossaert 2000a: 122-131). Its main gate is called *shanmen*, "gate of the mountain"; its roofs are compared to mountain peaks; its foundation is called *kaishan*, "open the mountain". Literary sources often describe a monastery as located in mountainous areas, even when they lay on flat land, in view of a distant mountain.

Mountains were indeed a location of choice for a rural monastery, especially those of the Chan school who were looking for a congenial environment to retreat. Monasteries occupy the most picturesque mountain-sides (incorporating caves), hill-slopes or islands of the big rivers. Sacred mountains, many of which already had shrines before the

9. Welch (1967) has collected figures on 98 monasteries with an estimated population of 13,100 monks. By extrapolation from more documented provinces like Jiangsu, he concludes that large public monasteries gathered 25,000 monks, about 5% of the monks.

10. Traditionally called *kanyu* or *dili*, now popularly called *fengshui*: Smith 1991, chap. 4.

advent of Buddhism, were covered with temples and monasteries. In such cases, the large monastery is located at the mountain's foot, while the many (sometimes hundreds) of smaller temples uphill cater to pilgrims, smaller clerical communities or ascetics. The Four sacred Buddhist mountains, each regarded as the abode of a specific bodhisattva, as well as hundreds of other mountain sites attract devout pilgrims. Some have Buddhist and Taoist communities of fairly equivalent sizes; others were almost completely taken over by the Saṅgha. Wherever Buddhism took foot, it transformed the landscape with stūpas, giant rock-carved statues and architectural feats such as the hanging monastery of Hengshan [28], which in turn contributed to attracting visitors.

Many large Buddhist monasteries are located in town, especially when they are built by noblemen, high officers, member of the imperial family and eunuchs.[11] Although after the Song period the proportion of urban monasteries was on a downward trend,[12] major modern cities, even those that developed during the 19th century like Shanghai, usually had one major monastery. The most ancient institutions are still found in the heart of the city, while more recent ones are located in the suburbs. Furthermore, inner-city monasteries may have stūpas and cemeteries out of town, and these different parts may be visually and topographically connected.[13]

Whatever their location, monasteries, like temples, usually face south, the traditional orientation of ancient Chinese architecture, except when the topography does not permit it. For instance, the main hall of the Tang dynasty Foguang si [23] faces west because of the configuration of the ground.

Building materials and resources

Building materials are baked bricks or timber for the walls, timber for the framing and stone for the basement, the staircases, the terraces and the courts pavement. Forests were quite abundant in ancient China, and timber as building material was easier to process compared to stone, yet the reliance on complex wooden carpentry characterised monumental Buddhist buildings along with imperial architecture, as opposed to common vernacular buildings. More or less standardised and prefabricated ways of construction appeared during the Tang and matured by the Ming. During the Ming dynasty, timber became more expensive due to intensive deforestation. Some monasteries had their own forests, managed both as nature sanctuaries and as a reserve for future timber needs, but in most construction projects, timber was a major expenditure item. The gigantic timbers and stones were often hauled from great distances at huge expenses. Rich monasteries like the Lingyin si [54] and the Puji si [60] even imported timber from Oregon, USA, during the early 20th century (Reichelt 1927: 245).

Due to the pre-eminence of wood, Chinese architecture is short-lived and buildings were burnt and razed to the ground with distressing easiness during the waves of destruction. Most of the monasteries built during the first millennium were destroyed by the 845 anti-Buddhist persecutions, and the antireligious movements of the Republic and the Cultural Revolution also laid waste to a huge quantity of buildings. Each war

11. In and around Beijing, eunuchs of the Ming dynasty (when they wielded huge resources) were major patrons of Buddhist and Taoist monasteries.

12. Eberhard 1964: 293-94 attempts to evaluate the decline of the proportion of urban monasteries in Southern China.

13. Steinhardt 1994: 9 discusses the case of the of the Dule si [19].

has taken its toll, and, even in times of peace and tolerance, neglect condemned buildings in the short term. Last but not least, accidental fires causing a whole monastery to go up in flames is a sadly common occurrence in historical sources.

Later rebuilding are considered by the Buddhists as replicas of the early architecture, with the same value as the original ones. The permanence of the monastic institution was thought to lay more with the official name-plaque and the lineage than with any physical building. Moreover, preserved monasteries were continuously repaired, restored, enlarged by lay donations and by the monks' initiatives. Depending on the available funding, minor repairs occur every five or ten years, but as wooden architectures seldom last more than two generations (60 years), restoration often means reconstruction.[14] Restoring as radically as possible (and more than necessary) is a standard way for patrons to mark their personal imprint on a site. This is true of both local pious associations and emperors. Under Qianlong's reign (1736-1796) large-scale campaigns of restoration of religious buildings with imperial money were undertaken, especially in Beijing.[15] Such restorations are documented by laudatory inscriptions, but no archives or other historical documents detailing what exactly was done exists any more. Restorations entailed renaming halls and shifting statues between them. For these reasons, it is often difficult to distinguish the original state and layout of the monastery, and to trace in detail their evolution in time.

The earliest preserved Chinese architectures are brick and stone stūpas, cave temples, the stone pillar bases of wooden buildings and two halls dating back to the 9th century: the main halls of Foguang si [23] and Nanchan si [22] in mount Wutai. [22] *fig. 1 p. 344* Around 30 buildings date back from the 9th to the 13th century (most of them are part of Buddhist monasteries), plus 60 masonry stūpas of the Five Dynasties and Song. Our knowledge of early monasteries must be gained indirectly, mostly from written sources,[16] painted representations and from buildings preserved in Japan. The first Japanese monasteries were strongly inspired by temples now lost in China: some go back to the 7th century; twenty-two remain from the period of Tang influence, culminating in the 8th century complex at Tôdaiji in Nara. *See Japan p. 417*

Buddhist monasteries in China started a monumental tradition that seems to have been unprecedented in China's ancient architectural history. The growth of the Buddhist institution can be measured by the size and material of its buildings, horizontally and vertically, from a small thatch shrine to huge precincts, and also by an increase in the statues height and the number of stūpa storeys (from three, in the 4th century, to five, nine and then twelve in the 6th century). The stūpa of the Yongning si [33] for example, built from 516 on, was said to be visible at a distance of 50 km from the capital. The extant Fogong si wooden stūpa [24], built under the Liao dynasty, is 67 m high and visible on a clear day from a distance of 30 km (Soper 1971: 389; Steinhardt 1994). [24] *fig. 4 p. 345*

In spite of this, and with the exception of rock-cut shrines and stūpas, Buddhism did not bring any alien architectural technique in China. The origins of the Chinese Buddhist monastic architecture can be found among Chinese traditional secular layouts and wooden buildings. This can be explained in part by the fact that devout princes and

---

14. Welch 1968: 87-98 and Brook 1993:157sq describe the monastic "cycles" of restoration and decay, and discuss the cost of restorations.

15. The Qianlong emperor, as a "restorer", was actually responsible for the loss of much old architecture.

16. For instance, Soper 1939-40 on the descriptions of Japanese travellers.

officials gave their great mansions to the clergy in order to convert them into monasteries. This tradition of transforming houses into temples or monasteries (of any confession) have been maintained all along Chinese history. Under such circumstances, there can be no fundamental architectural difference between a Buddhist monastery, a Taoist monastery, a Confucianist temple or a palace: most buildings are polyvalent, serving secular or religious needs according to their contents. During the reformation movements of the end of the empire, most religious institutions have been forcibly laicised and Buddhist monasteries have been turned into administrative offices (schools, barracks) or housing estates. The fact that carpenters and artisans (including painters) worked equally for religious or lay projects also contributed to this technical lack of differentiation.

2.2 History of the formation of the monastery

The phase of adaptation, 1st-6th century

Buddhism penetrated into China under the Eastern Han dynasty (AD 25-220): missionaries from the various Central Asian states, coming along trade routes, brought icons and scriptures, built sanctuaries and converted local people. The earliest Chinese Buddhist architectures (from the 1st to the 3rd century) were clearly dominated by the stūpa, when they were not reduced to a stūpa-temple. The first mention of a Buddhist temple in historical records is the Baima si [32], an administrative office converted into a monastery in 67 to store Buddhist scriptures carried from the West.[17] Other early sources all insist on the central role of relics or other devotional objects: a noted example is the Buddha shrine, resembling a stūpa, composed of "nine tiers of bronze disks raised above a two-storey pavilion", with covered galleries large enough to accommodate 3,000 people, erected about 190, by an official in Jiangsu (Ch'en 1964: 40-41; Soper 1971: 386). Other monasteries claim to date to a Han foundation, like the Baoguang si [66] and the Wutai shan [4] complex. It was not before the 4th century, however, that Buddhist constructions took place on a large scale.

During the first centuries of our era, Buddhism slowly adapted to Chinese conditions.[18] Beginning around 400, its growth accelerated and a fever for Buddhist constructions seemed to engulf the whole of China. The building activity was supported by all levels of society: imperial favours went to huge projects in their capitals; the nobility adopted patronage of monasteries as a confirmation of their status, while local congregations of devotees formed around the more charismatic monks. The spread of the Dharma was not impeded, and actually perhaps furthered by the volatile political situation (and frequent human disasters) during the four centuries after the collapse of the Han dynasty in the 3rd century. In the North, the Northern Wei dynasty (386-634) of proto-turkish origin proclaimed Buddhism as a state religion in the 5th century and undertook extensive programs of construction of monasteries and high stūpas in their capitals.[19] Southern dynasties engaged in similar activities, but there remain very little material traces.

During that period, the stūpa was the first building encountered upon entering the central courtyard after the storied gates, lined up on the central axis with the main devotional building (the Buddha hall) behind, and, closing off the courtyard at the rear,

---

17. The Baima si still exists, although its present state dates from a much later period. Its name refers to the white horse that is supposed to have carried the scriptures from the West.

18. The classical study on this point is Zürcher 1959.

19. A classical source is a mid-6th century description of the capital, the *Luoyang qielan ji*, translated

the Dharma hall (*fatang*, a place for teaching and debating). The abbot's quarters were located close to the Dharma hall. The monasteries of Eastern Turkestan may have been the source of this layout (Soper 1971: 392), which is also attested in Japanese and Korean monasteries of that period (e.g. the 7th century Hôryûji). One example is the Yongning si [33] (burnt in 534), whose above-mentioned huge stūpa with gold bells and lacquered doors was the apex of the monastery. The monastery had a thousand cells for monks, many trees and bamboo groves in the courtyards; images and sūtras presented by foreign countries were kept there. The description insists on the similarity of the complex with halls of the imperial palace (Soper 1971: 389).

See Japan p. 425

Although none of these monasteries subsist, the period unmitigated taste for monumentality[20] is still evident today in rock-cut sanctuaries: although hundreds of such sanctuaries have been excavated down to the modern period, the largest sites date from the 5th to 7th centuries. The two most famous caves are Yungang [5] and Longmen [6]. Some of them housed a colossal Buddha image, often Maitreya. Some cave sites, such as Dunhuang [8] (mostly known for the treasures of manuscripts and wall paintings discovered a century ago), featured living quarters for travelling monks, and thus echoed the Indian and central Asian tradition of cave monasteries. The largest Chinese cave sites, however, were purely shrines, excavated to serve as symbols of the permanence of the Dharma or to fulfil personal wishes: they were not at all monasteries. The destination of yet other caves found all over China is not altogether clear: they might have been meditation cells for ascetic clerics, or parts of real monasteries completed by wooden structures that have long since disappeared.

The period of development, 6th-11th century

With the return of a unique central political control all over China in 589, Buddhist assimilation into Chinese culture was confirmed. The Sui (589-618) and the beginning of the Tang witnessed a continued frenzy of construction. The Tang emperors gradually raised the notion of the equality and peaceful coexistence (without syncretism) of the Three religions (Confucianism, Buddhism and Taoism) as a state dogma; this was to remain until the fall of the empire in 1911. Confucianism began to regain control of state rituals that it had shared with Buddhism and Taoism; Buddhist monasteries would henceforth be used ever less for state purposes, and therefore obtain less from state coffers. Meanwhile, individual emperors could still affirm separately their own religious convictions. Some, acting as a *cakravartin* ruler or a bodhisattva's incarnation, built out of their own (big) purse monasteries and stūpas.

On the other hand, the heated debates about the "foreign" religion continued, as the state began to limit the extraordinary fiscal privileges and autonomy of the Saṅgha, and to impose a minimal form of administrative control over it. Even though, the Saṅgha was considered by some as a state within the state, and a scapegoat of choice. The spirit of grandeur of the monasteries and their drain on public coffers went against the Confucian ideal of austerity. The 845 campaign of persecution, caused by xenophobic and economic concerns, exceeded all earlier anti-Buddhist movements, such as those in 446 and 574-577 in North China. All over China large monasteries and centres were destroyed, monks and nuns were defrocked, metal images were melted into coins. Although this persecution was of short duration, it looms large in Buddhist historiography in China. Beyond its immediate consequences, it would seem that it coincided

20. Gernet (1995) discusses the medieval drive to ever larger, costlier monasteries as a sign of prestige.

with a turning point in the history of the Buddhist institution: from then on, it would depend less on imperial patronage and sumptuous monuments, and more on a network of small and medium size temples and oratories serving local communities and feeding (in human and financial resources) the secluded monasteries.

As the earliest extant halls date from the very end of this period, our knowledge of the great Tang monasteries is still drawn from literary descriptions, archaeological finds and Japanese contemporary examples such as the Tôdaiji of Nara. This evidence suggests that during the 7th-8th centuries, the stūpa of the large monasteries was often duplicated and the pair was placed outside the central enclosure, in front and to either side of the main building, the Buddha hall. The importance of the stūpa, shifted away from the central axis, was reduced to the advantage of the Buddha hall: it even became unnecessary. The design of the Buddha hall was modelled on the emperor's throne hall, with the Buddha images facing south, forming a chancel surrounded by a corridor. Behind the Buddha hall, either within the precinct or outside, lied the Dharma hall, the third main element of the monastery. The monks' quarters were at the rear or lateral side. The new two-stūpas symmetrical arrangement was probably more in accordance with the Chinese "order", but it must have been limited by its very high cost to a few large monasteries. In the 8th century, the Fayuan si [9] had two wooden stūpas that were rebuilt in bricks after their destruction by fire.[21]

[9] *fig. 2 p. 344*

After the middle of the 9th century, the Dharma hall lost its pre-eminence on the central axis, being moved to a lateral axis, along with the abbot's quarters. At the same time, monasteries reverted to a single-stūpa plan, it being either located behind the Buddha hall or relegated to one side. Its role was further reduced in the monasteries of the Chan and Pure land schools that placed less emphasis upon the veneration of relics. Stūpas continued to be erected during the second millennium, but mostly outside monastic compounds. Late Tang monasteries, in contrast to their predecessors, favoured horizontal expansion, and preferred few, large and spacious elements. It was about that time, as far as we can ascertain, that the two or three-storied massive *ge* or *lou* pavilions came into fashion (Soper 1971: 401). A late 9th century example is the three-storey Guanyin ge[22] of Fayuan si [9]; the oldest extant ones include those at Longxing si [18] and Dule si [19]. Such pavilions have remained ever since in fashion, usually located at the rear of the main axis.

[18] *fig. 3 p. 345*

The most momentous change that occurred during that period was the gradual advent of the Chan school, which emphasised the discipline of collective meditation. Meditation was practised early in China but collective halls, although mentioned in Vinaya and Chinese texts, do not seem to have played a major role before the Chan school. Monks also meditated in their cells or retreated to huts or caves in the surroundings of a monastery (Prip-Moller 1937: 68-71). The first Chan monks certainly lived in regular monasteries or were itinerant; they began to build their own modest communities by the late 8th or 9th century, and the "Chan monastery" had gradually matured by the 10th century. According to the oldest sources, that have a strong hagiographic and iconoclast flavour, the early Chan monasteries dispensed with worship, and thus with Buddha halls and stūpas. In reality, documented monasteries did have both a Buddha hall and a Dharma hall, and the liturgical program was far from cursory. A few later

21. Nothing was left of the monastery from this period. Its plan has been reconstructed by Fu Xinnian (1998:264-67) from literary descriptions and stone inscriptions, and recalls that of Tôdaiji.

22. Guanyin is the Chinese personality of Avalokiteßvara, and we use his/her Chinese name here.

reformers tried to revert to this ideal plan without a Buddha hall, such as the very eminent Zhuhong (1535-1615). His monastery had only a Meditation hall and a Dharma hall on the central axis (Yü Chün-fang 1981: 22, 215-26). The exemple does not seem to have been followed elsewhere."

In any case, the monastery according to Chan ideology was centred on the Monks' hall (*sengtang*)[23] or Meditation hall (*chantang*), its spiritual and material heart. Whereas in earlier monasteries monks lived in individual cells arranged in rows, they were now to share a huge single open hall, sitting in collective meditation, eating, and reclining to sleep. The largest monasteries were to also build separate halls for itinerant monks. The abbot's quarters, at the rearmost position of the central axis, connected with the Business office saw its position enhanced. As the Chan abbot is the living incarnation of the Dharma, his residence is also a place for teaching and communal functions.

Another novel aspect of the Chan monastery was that it was a closed space. Although it is difficult to determine to which extant the great pre-Tang and Tang monasteries were open, it would seem that the Chan monastery insisted on a strict separation from the outside world: the high enclosure wall (found in most religious complexes) had only one gate, guarded by a gatekeeper, and only monks and persons on business could get in.

However radical the Chan "revolution" appears in its own hagiography, the Chan ideal actually swiftly extended to the whole Saṅgha. By the 11th century, all major monasteries, whether or not formally Chan, had adopted broadly this organisational model, both in terms of rules and physical layout: notably, they had a Monks' hall.[24] The "Chan monastery" is actually not a separate model, but a stage in the global evolution of the Chinese monastery. The shift of patronage from lavish imperial or aristocratic projects towards a more localised funding also contributed to the success of the self-contained monastery promoted by Chan ideology. As a result, from the mid-Song dynasty onwards, the standard monastery plan had reached a modern form. Although many of the major monasteries of the modern period can claim a name plaque granted as far back as the 5th or 6th century, it was during the Song that they were rebuilt in a way similar to their present aspect. The physical arrangement of the Song monasteries was transmitted to Japan during the 13th century (Collcutt 1981). Japanese Chan monasteries took great pains to conform to the plan and style of their models, and precise maps of the latter, drawn by Japanese travellers, have been kept in monastic libraries.

The early modern period, 11th-14th century

The advent of the modern monastery, naturally, was not a sudden or uniform evolution. Older fixtures were still found, such as a four-storey gate-tower and the twin stūpas in front of the main courtyard of the Xiangguo si [34], the major monastery of the Northern Song capital. It also featured two courtyards dedicated to the practice of Meditation and to the study of Vinaya.[25] The Longxing si [18] is the only extant establishment that still gives an idea of its original Song layout. The long and narrow compound comprises from the Gatehouse, Bell and Drum towers, a central [18] *fig. 3 p. 345*

23. This term may also be translated as Saṅgha's Hall, which highlights its being, with the Buddha hall and Dharma hall, the third of the halls housing the "Three jewels".

24. Beginning in the 10th century, the abbacy of some monasteries was officially reserved to members of Chan lineages: Foulk 1993, that also discusses the layout of 13th century Lingyin si [54].

25. The division of a monastery in several communities dedicated to separate schools or lineages, although contrary to the Chan model, is occasionally found all along the 2nd millennium.

hall (in ruins), and a square hall with porticoes projecting on the four sides. In the rear courtyard, two lateral two-storey pavilions face each other: a Sūtra library on the west and a Maitreya pavilion on the east. The northern element on the axis houses a colossal statue of seventy-two arms-Guanyin, towering above the rest of the precinct. Chongfu si's [27] layout (1143) emphasises the cult of the Western paradise with a large Amitābha hall and a Guanyin hall on the central axis, behind a small Buddha Śākyamuni hall.

While the Song dynasty witnessed the birth of the modern monastery, most ancient surviving buildings were actually built by the Song's rivals, the "alien" dynasties in the North: the Liao (907-1125) and Jin dynasty (1115-1234) (Steinhardt 1994, 1997). Liao and Jin monasteries have large and massive buildings and favoured multilevel pavilions; they are reinterpretations of Tang rather than Song prototypes. The Chan as practice flourished under these dynasties, and Chan lineages were granted official pre-eminence after 1075; meditation halls were erected within the precincts of many large monasteries. Liao and Jin monasteries, however, did not conform closely to the model of the Song monasteries that embodied Chan ideals. The numerous Liao and Jin masonry stūpas, which rise alone today, usually stood on the main axis of their temple, behind the main [24] *fig. 4 p. 345* hall or sometimes in front. Fogong si's [24] octagonal five-storey stūpa, the unique wooden survivor of its kind of the Liao dynasty, lied in the exact centre of its monastery.

[26] *fig. 5 p. 346* The main surviving Liao monasteries are Huayan si [25], Shanhua si [26], and Fengguo si [21]. According to an inscription, Fengguo si (11th century) comprised on its central axis a Gatehouse, a Guanyin ge, the large Buddha hall (9x5 bays) and the rear Dharma hall (9 bays wide). The Buddha hall houses seven colossal images (the seven Buddhas of the past) in a row against the rear wall. Huayan si is divided between an Upper monastery centred on a large Buddha hall (9x5 bays), and a Lower one on the south, whose Library (completed in 1038) seems to be the original foundation. Shanhua si features a Gatehouse, a hall of the Three Holy Ones (12th century), the main hall (7x5 bays, 11th century), and a pair of small two-storey pavilions dedicated to Mañjuśrī and Samantabhadra.

Meanwhile, interest in and patronage of Tibetan Buddhism began during the Xia (1032-1227) and the Mongol Yuan dynasties, persisted throughout the Ming and, to an even larger extent, the Qing dynasty. Under the Yuan, a few Tibeto-Mongol monasteries were built, mostly in Beijing, and in relation to the court's cults. They used a distinctive national style, introducing foreign elements such as the Tibetan form of the stūpa.[26] This style had a limited influence on religious architecture in the country at large. The "alien" regimes thus did not hamper the self-contained development of native Buddhist architecture, while introducing Tibetan Buddhism as a separate religious presence.

The Ming and Qing periods

Traditional historiography (Chinese, Japanese and Western) consider the modern period to be that of the decline of the Buddhist faith, material and intellectual culture in China (*mofa*, the "latter days of the Law").[27] Meanwhile, the number of Buddhist establishments, especially chapels for family rites, and Guanyin temples, has never stopped growing. Although the proportion of large monasteries among all Buddhist sites may be on a downward trend, these elite institutions have never failed their role of educating the hundreds of thousands of novices that had visited them, upholding an

26. The most famous example is the Baita of Miaoying si [10].

27. Ch'en 1964:390-98 is a classic if extreme example.

extremely rich clerical culture. Welch argues astutely that as modern monasteries are less entwined in political and economic affairs than their predecessors of the Tang period, their spiritual life must indeed have improved in the meantime.

Under the Ming emperors Buddhism and Taoism continued their cohabitation, albeit with less support from the state. The strongly anticlerical policies of the first Ming emperor, who tried to regroup all monasteries to a limited number of approved establishments, were quickly abandoned, but the mistrust between Saṅgha and mandarins remained. With the exception of some sites personally favoured by individual emperors, monasteries had to rely ever more on local gentry, rich landowners and some merchants, although the latter tended ever more towards patronising the large urban temples instead. However, with the great commercial expansion of the 16th century, local gentry patronage and devotion helped a large movement of monastery restoration and enlargement (Brook 1993). The well-documented Ming monasteries of the southern capital (Nanjing) were already confirming to the modern layout (He Xiaorong 2000: 155-75). It is also during the Ming period that the sectarian movements of lay Buddhist inspiration emerged as a major religious actor on the Chinese scene, but they never developed large physical institutions, and monasteries felt little effect from this quarter.

The Manchu Qing dynasty broadly maintained the Ming policy of religious status quo, while the inner court favoured some Tibeto-Mongol monasteries, partly out of faith and partly for political reasons. It introduced a style characterised with heavy external decoration, relying on glazed tiles, but this was mostly used in monasteries of the Tibeto-Mongol tradition. Otherwise, the monasteries of the Ming and Qing period may be said to have exhibited a noted "classicism", and both style and layout were fairly constant during that long period. This classical style clearly originated with the Song models, but buildings were somewhat less monumental. Notably, the large Monks' hall has been replaced by the smaller Meditation hall and Wandering monks' hall. Whether the downsizing reflects a decline in available funding, or a trend towards clerical modesty and smaller communities is a matter of conjecture.

The Chinese monasteries prospered up to the 19th century when the great economic depression imperilled their financial base. The Taiping civil war (1851-1868) caused the destruction of hundreds of monasteries in the all-important lower Yangzi valley area. It was a sign of their vitality that the greatest part managed to be rebuilt within a few years. Other dangers were approaching: radical anticlerical movements, that first had brief political power in 1898, called for the nationalisation of all temples and monasteries, and their conversion into schools and other public buildings. Although temples suffered even more than monasteries, most of the latter had to resist downright confiscation, and often accept seizure of part of their buildings and lands. Many active abbots were successful at maintaining their rights and some managed to undergo restoration works (Welch 1968). The Nanjing regime (1928-1937), although not favourable to Buddhism, somehow calmed down the situation. The war waged by Japanese invasion caused again a new wave of destruction.

The Peoples' Republic, founded in 1949, nationalised what was still standing,[28] and allowed only a few monks to stay in the monasteries. During the iconoclast Cultural Revolution, many monasteries were destroyed; preserved architectures have been emptied of their statues, paintings, liturgical implements and written documents. Even when

28. According to Welch 1972:150, some 230,000 monasteries and temples still had monks and nuns in residence before 1949.

ancient buildings were preserved, dormitories, kitchen, and bathhouses were squatted or razed down, hence now there are very few complete ancient monasteries left over. Since 1978, when a new constitution allowed for the partial authorisation of religious activities, the government has slowly restored the most famous and ancient monasteries; a few have been entrusted to the National Buddhist Association, while the others were turned into museums.

Among the sites that benefited from this policy are a number of Tibeto-Mongol monasteries, with the object of winning the favour of minorities, as well as lonely stūpas and disaffected buildings preserved for their historical or architectural interest, not for supporting Buddhism as a living religion. Others were rebuilt for political and diplomatic reasons or even built from nothing. The policy of conservation aims at promoting tourism against cult. Active monasteries remain strictly controlled by the State.[29] Meanwhile, recent but affluent Taiwanese and Hong Kong monasteries are flourishing and often contribute to the revival of the mainland Buddhist institutions. In Taiwan, no monastery properly speaking has ever existed. However, charismatic monks since the 1970's have founded large communities, whose organization and physical layout differ in several ways from the traditional model discussed here.

Due to the disappearance of schools as distinct organisations after the Ming, monasteries came to be built or, more often, rebuilt along a standardised style and layout. Relatively few new monasteries were founded, however, and most modern large monasteries preserve ancient idiosyncrasies. This standard layout and the many variations in the location of the various elements are described in some detail in the following chapter.

3. The elements of the monastery

The monastery, in its minimum form during the modern period, consists of the main hall housing the Buddha images, the abbot's quarters and the monks' quarters.[30] Beside this basic structure, monasteries featured a large array of buildings related to the material and spiritual needs of the monastic community and lay patrons. A monastery housing hundreds of monks was a small city with a complex management. During the early 20th century, this management was spread between four "bureaucratic" departments, each in charge of a number of buildings: the Meditation hall, the Guest department, the Business office and the Sacristy (Welch 1967: 8-9).

This management was somewhat less centralised compared with the Song model monastery, where all monks (except itinerant clerics or unordained novices) lived in the communal Monks' hall. In modern monasteries, only those engaged in a meditation season stayed in the Meditation hall (the smaller heir of the Monks' hall), the others living in the buildings where they worked, worshipped or studied. This accounts for the spread of the monastery on the lateral axes, in ways that differed in each monastery – which did not change very much the layout of the central axis.

29. Monasteries are managed by an elected "Democratic management committee", under the direction of the local branch of the National Buddhist Association, which is subordinate to the Religious Affairs Bureau under the direct leadership of the State Council.

30. A standard canonical definition of the monastery lists the "seven-halls plan of the Saṅghârâma": the Shanmen, the Tianwang dian, the Bell and Drum towers, the two lateral halls and the Buddha hall. This definition omits the conventual buildings.

Ming and Qing monasteries have a regular elongated plan. The main devotional halls, each with one or several statues and an altar featuring ritual vessels, are symmetrically arranged on a central longitudinal axis. Gradation of importance, from south to north, separates the guardian deities who did not reach enlightenment in the front halls, from the highest Buddhas and Bodhisattvas in the rear halls. The buildings commonly built on the central axis are the Gatehouse, the hall of the Guardian Kings, and the Buddha hall. The rearmost element of the central axis can be the Dharma hall with the Library on the second floor, the abbot's quarters with a garden, a multi-level building housing a colossal statue or the chapel of a Patriarch. While the general layout is not distinctive, the images of the various Buddhas, Bodhisattvas and deities and their location in the various halls are proper to each monastery. Through gates, corridors and lateral buildings, access is available to the communal halls and offices on the sides.

All the major buildings face south just like ordinary dwellings and offices. North China layouts avoid prominent or towering groups of structures and prefer a spreading over expansive precincts, with galleries and walls connecting and encircling single buildings, hence forming a series of courtyards. During the Song to the Ming period, long covered galleries, often decorated with murals, were common, but they are rarely seen nowadays. In Central and South China, and generally in mountain monasteries, plans tend to be more compact, with more multi-level buildings.[31] Side buildings form one long row under one roof and with one continuous colonnade in front. The rear and side parts of the monastery can be shaped as a reverse U being inaccessible to public – e.g. Pilu si [43] (Prip-Moller 1937: fig. 89). The unconventional layout of Huiju si [45] is justified by the comparison to the shape of a lotus flower. More often, the variations in the layouts depend on the topography, the geomantical situation, or the individual tastes of abbots or patrons.

With the exception of a few specific buildings (the Meditation hall, the Five hundred *arhat* hall, the stūpa), most elements conform to the conventional style common to all Chinese religious buildings. The traditional wooden pavilion (*dian*) has an oblong plan, with a peristyle or an enclosed porch on the front or rear. Its structure with non-bearing walls allowing free openings could easily be enlarged. The overhanging eaves serve to moderate bright light as well as heavy rains. Doors and windows are concentrated on the façade. The most elaborated halls could be decorated with carved wood, stuccoes, ornamental bracketing, paintings, and covered with glazed tiles (since the Song dynasty). The Library, Bell and Drum towers, abbot's quarters and shrines built to shelter monumental images could be two storey pavilions (*louge*). The different styles of *dian* and *louge* are characterised by the structural features of framing, the complex bracketing, the ptofile of the roof, the columns height, and the proportions. A few examples of vaulted pavilions, called Wuliang dian, "beamless hall", were built during the 15th and 16th centuries. However, their exterior form completely imitates the traditional timber building. This kind of hall is well-suited for a Library, like at the Linggu si [41].

The presentation of the different buildings below proceeds by function, which only partially overlaps the topological differentiation axis by axis. The first section addresses halls for worship. As these were the only parts of the monastery that could be accessed by laity, there were usually on the main axis. Then come the places where monks lived and practised spiritual exercise, by definition off-limits to visitors and located on either

31. Mountain monasteries feature high terraces. On Emei shan [3] layouts, see Prip-Moller 1937:91 and fig. 112.

side of the main axis. The third part is devoted to buildings of educational vocation. The last sections are concerned with functions relevant to communal life: death and memorials, economic life of the monastery, reception of guests, food and hygiene, gardens.

3.1 Halls for worship: The front part of the monastery

3.1.1 The entrance and the first courtyards

Three elements that characterise any monumental architecture may precede the main Gatehouse of a large monastery. Firstly, a large wooden or masonry archway covered with tiles (*pailou* or *paifang*), located before the Gatehouse, functions as a visual signal, symbolising the passage from the profane realm to the sacred world of the monastic compound. Secondly, in front of the entrance hall, and of every main hall sit two stone or bronze lions, male and female, keeper of treasures. Their adoption in Chinese architecture is linked to Buddhism, since the lion is the symbol of the Buddha's loud voice. Thirdly, screen-walls (*zhaobi* or *yingbi*) in front of the Gatehouse save the entrance from prying eyes and keep the good fortune inside, against evil spirits. Other screen-walls with protective images can be erected in order to rectify geomantical defects.

The monastic compound is surrounded by a 2 to 3 m high rectangular wall.[32] The Gatehouse (*shanmen*), at the south of the compound, is a wooden pavilion edged by lateral screen-walls. Above the Gatehouse is written the name of the monastery on a name plaque, with the official title given by the emperor if such is the case; similarly, above the door of every hall is hanged a sign bearing its name. The name plaque, as well as other horizontal boards carrying short speculative expressions, and couple of vertical boards carrying distichs, all composed and calligraphed by eminent persons, featured among a monastery treasures.

The Gatehouse opens by one or three doors,[33] in which case the central one is reserved to the emperor or for exceptional festivities. Sometimes the Gatehouse features statues of guardian deities posted there to frighten enemies of Buddhism and ill-disposed persons: the two generals Heng and Ha, naked giants armed with clubs,[34] two Vajra-bearers (who often had a separate hall during the Ming), or the Four Guardian Kings when they do not have a separate hall (Prip-Moller 1937: 16-20, fig. 16 sq).

A paved way, sometimes slightly elevated, indicates the main central axis. The Bell and Drum towers are symmetrically arranged in the first courtyard or in the Buddha hall's courtyard. The bell and drum express the exorcist function of percussion, but, together with smaller gongs located in each building, play a part in a very complex system of sounds guiding the monks' daily life. The bell (*yang*, celestial)[35] is beaten on the morning to call the monks; the drum (*yin*, earthly), in the evening, signifying the end of the day's work. The musical signals are especially important in the Chan liturgy,

---

32. Although monasteries may serve as centres of local self-defence organisations, none are known to be really fortified.

33. For symbolical reasons, the gatehouse is also called *sanmen*, "three gates", whether there is actually one or three gates.

34. Heng and Ha may also have a separate shrine, like in Biyun si [16], on the central axis.

35. Some monks even lived inside the Bell tower, striking the bell night and day for the benefit of souls suffering in hell: Welch 1967:321. Bells themselves were cast in bronze, or in iron when bronze was unaffordable. Ceremonial or monumental bells were inscribed with whole sutras. Bells offered by patrons were inscribed with their names.

and their use is described in much detail in the various Chan rules compiled through the centuries. The twin towers are identical, with a square plan and an open storey revealing the instrument. They also serve as watch-towers. Their presence may date from the early monastic layouts, and there are Tang dynasty examples.[36] The two pavilions were originally kept at the rear, behind the Buddha hall and in line with, or in front of the Dharma hall; they were later moved to a front courtyard; in Song dynasty Lingyan si [38], they are in front of the Buddha hall. If the Bell tower is more important and can stand alone (like in Linggu si [41], Ayuwang si [58]), neither is indispensable: the instruments can be placed inside the main hall. They are more frequently seen in North China monasteries.

A pond full of fishes and tortoises (*fangsheng chi*, "pond for the release of leaving creatures") is often seen in the first courtyard, in front of the main gate or in the surrounding gardens. Its function is to protect life: devout people practise the *fangsheng*, releasing fishes in the pond in order to gain merits.[37] Pairs of poles (*chuanggan*) in front of the Gatehouse or of the Buddha hall are used to hang banners, lanterns or vases during the festivals. They are made of wood or stone, carved with a coiling dragon and stand on a pedestal. Of all these elements, the Fangsheng chi is rather (but not exclusively) characteristic of Buddhist monasteries, while the others are seen in the other Chinese religious compounds.

The hall of the Guardian kings (Tianwang dian) is usually the next building closing the first courtyard. It may date back to the 8th century, when the group of four *lokapāla* (Tianwang, celestial kings), guardians of the cardinal directions, assumed a separate identity and iconography. According to Prip-Moller, the Tianwang dian has become a mandatory hall during the Qing period. The four statues are placed along the east and west walls, facing each other by pair. From the Ming dynasty onwards, a statue of Maitreya as a fat monk[38] is found in the middle, on the main altar, facing south and standing against a light partition wall. As in most of the halls on the central axis, the hall of the Guardian kings has a secondary altar facing north at the back of the main altar, and a door piercing the northern wall. The back altar is dedicated to the celestial general Weituo,[39] who faces the Buddha hall to protect the Saṅgha. When there is another hall between the hall of the Guardian kings and the Buddha hall, such as a shrine to Guanyin, Weituo may be present twice or only in this second shrine.

*3.1.2 The Buddha hall (*Fo dian*), or Big hall (*Da dian*), or Hall of the Great Hero (*Daxiongbao dian*)*

Ever since the stūpa has ceased to be the centre of devotion in the Buddhist monastery, the so-called Big hall has remained the central building. This rather colloquial name refers to it being the largest (albeit not necessarily tallest) building in the compound. Also called Buddha hall or Hall of the Great Hero (an epithet of Śākyamuni), it houses a big seated image of Śākyamuni or three statues of Buddhas on lotus thrones. These three may be Bhaishajyaguru, Śākyamuni and Amitābha, a triad especially

36. Prip-Moller 1937:7-8, 10, 207. In Shentong si [39] the two towers are apart, on another axis.

37. De Groot 1893:110-26. Cattle, pigs, and other livestock rescued by devout Buddhist were also kept in stables behind the monastery, to be fed by those who saved them.

38. This monk, Budai, who appeared during the Song, is considered as the Nirmânakâya (body of change) of Maitreya, and is located with deities who have not reached buddhahood.

39. While the Four heavenly kings are common to the *Mahāyāna* tradition, Weituo seems to be a purely Chinese innovation.

favoured by the Chan tradition, or the Buddhas of the past (Dīpankara), present (Śākyamuni) and future (Maitreya). In certain localities, the patron deity of a monastery (like the four main Bodhisattvas on their holy mountain) or the funerary monument of a monk[40] can replace the Buddha in this hall of honour, which therefore will be called by another name.

The usual dimensions of the Big hall are five bays in façade by three or four bays deep, or seven bays by six. Before the Tang period, the Buddha hall was one or two-storey while the rear hall was single-storey, but later on, the last major hall of the axis became the highest, and almost all modern *Da dian* are single-storey.

The Buddha hall was not originally designed for accommodating large numbers of people: during the Tang period the colossal icons placed on platforms and the altar occupied two-third of the surface area, a proportion that constantly declined afterwards. In the earliest shrines, the images symmetrically faced the four directions, recalling the stūpa allowing for ritual circumambulation. From the Tang period onwards, the icons stand on platforms and face south, and the Buddha hall came to resemble imperial audience halls. The roof is supported by columns placed in rows, the central bay being the widest, so as to leave a free space in the central section for the main altar and images. The central images are backed by a partition, with or without a back altar; behind, one bay is left for circumambulation, or more often off-limits to worshippers.

In addition to the central images, statues of the 18 *arhat*, alternatively or along with the 24 *deva* (including the Guardian Kings, Weituo, Brahmā, Indra and purely Chinese deities like Guandi) may be placed on platforms along the side walls. Prip-Moller reckons that in Tang and Song layouts, two protectors of the Dharma, Weituo and Vaishravana, were probably seen at the right and left hand side of the entering visitor.[41] The rear altar behind the partition is usually dedicated to Guanyin, Amitābha, or to the trinity of the Western Paradise (Amitābha, Guanyin and Mahāsthāmaprāpta). Images of Mañjuśrī and Samantabhadra, or Kshitigarbha or Guandi are placed against the rear wall, at each side of the back door, or on the main central platform to the right and left of Śākyamuni (Prip-Moller 1937: 48-52).

On the altar are displayed the five offerings (one incense burner[42] in the middle, two candlesticks and two flower vases), as well as lamps. Round cushions used by the monks during services lie in rows across the floor and square kneeling cushions for devotees face the altar. Musical and liturgical instruments are placed on strands, canopies and silk banners hang from the ceiling. The major function of the Buddha hall is to provide the stage for morning and evening services, performed by all the monks, except the kitchen staff, and most of the other major rites are also held there. Outside of the offices, laymen visiting the monastery kneel, pray and honour the Buddha images and offer them fruit and incense.

---

40. In the Zhenjue si [61] built around the funerary monument of the monk Zhiyi, the Śākyamuni image is moved to the hall of the Celestial kings. In Qixia shan [42], the *Da dian* is dedicated to Vairocana according to the wish of a donor. Prip-Moller 1937:2-3, 40 sq. In two earlier examples, Longxing si's [18] Main hall is dedicated to the Chan's Sixth Patriarch, and Chongfu si's [27] small *Daxiongbao dian* precedes a large Amitābha hall which thus became the Main hall.

41. Like in Sheng'en si [52]: Prip-Moller 1937:33.

42. The incense burner is a fundamental element of any Chinese religious institution.

3.1.3 Other halls for worship

Besides the main devotional hall necessitated by the regular liturgy, any number of halls may be built according to the wishes of the clergy and the laity. They stand on the main axis when they are part of the original design; those added thanks to the generosity of a latter-day devotee have their own lateral courtyard. Mentioned here are only the most oft-encountered types.

Up to the 11th century, the northernmost building used to be a multi-level pavilion housing a monumental image of Maitreya (Foguang si [23]) or Guanyin (Fayuan si [9], Longxing si [18]), Fengguo si [21], Chongfu si [27]). It could also be a Hall of Vairocana (*Pilu dian*, like in Upper Guangsheng si [29], Yuan dynasty) or a Thousand or Ten thousand Buddhas hall (*Qianfo dian, Wanfo dian*), when the monastery could afford to have so many statues cast (in Yongtai si [37], Lingyan si [38]).[43] More frequently the Ten thousand Buddhas hall doubles as a Library, as part of a two-storey building. Buddhist caves covered with thousand Buddhas at Yungang [5], Longmen [6], Tianlong shan [7], etc. show that this iconography dates back to the 5th century.

[9] *fig. 2 p. 344*
[18] *fig. 3 p. 345*

Secondary shrines located on the central axis are dedicated to various Buddhas and Bodhisattvas. Classical examples include a Guanyin Hall, Bhaishajyaguru Hall, or paired lateral halls facing each other such as those of Mañjuśrī and Samantabhadra or Kshitigarbha[44] and Guanyin (e.g. Upper Guangsheng si [29], Shanhua si [26]). The 16 *qielan shen*, guardian deities, had in earlier times a separate lateral shrine facing the Ancestors' hall near the Gatehouse (in the Upper Guangsheng si [29]) or in a rear courtyard; this is still attested during the Ming. By modern times, the function of protecting the monastery has been taken over by Weituo.[45]

[26] *fig. 5 p. 346*

The 500 *arhat* are frequently present as bas relief images, rubbings of original steles or, exceptionally, statues in the Buddha hall.[46] In a dozen documented sites, they enjoy a separate building, the Five hundred *arhat*'s hall (*Wubai luohan tang*). That of Xiangguo si [34], built in 1077, seems to be the oldest example.[47] This hall is a rare case of an original creation in both construction and content. It must be large enough to accommodate the 500 life-size statues; it is a huge square structure lightened by four open light wells, hence the name *Tianzi tang* (hall with the shape of character *tian*). In the middle section stand altars dedicated to Maitreya, Weituo, Guanyin, Śākyamuni... Secluded from the rest of the monastic compound, it is connected to the central axis by passages, so that laymen may visit it without entering the residential part of the compound.

Other shrines are dedicated to minor deities of the Buddhist pantheon, and the saints of Chinese popular religion, like Guandi and Niangniang. No building is dedicated to the representation of hells, which are found in popular temples.

---

43. One exception is Chongfu si [27] (12th century) where the Ten thousand Buddhas hall is the second pavilion after the *Tianwang dian*.

44. Kshitigarbha halls (*Dizang dian*) were often dedicated to rituals for the salvation of suffering souls.

45. Weituo can have a separate hall on the central axis, and another one in the Meditation hall's courtyard. His image is found in several other halls: the Hall of the Guardian kings, the Business office, the Library, the hall of the 500 *arhat*.

46. Sets of 500 statues are found in Pude si [44], Huating si [70] and Qiongzhu si [69].

47. This hall was destroyed, and a new one has been recently built. Other examples include Lingyin si [54] (destroyed), Hualin si [68], Biyun si [16], Tianning si [48], Hualin si [63], Baoguang si [66], Jiechuang si [49], Guiyuan si [65]: Prip-Moller 1937:104-21. These halls act today as important tourist attractions.

3.2 Meditation, recitation and ordination: the monks' activities and accommodation

As mentioned before, an important part of the Chan reform was that the individual cells of the early monasteries, none of which being extant, have given place to communal halls. There lays one of the major differences between temples and monasteries: clerics in residence in temples had their own (very modest) rooms, whereas life in a monastery entailed strict community. Whereas Song model monasteries had all monks living in a single huge Monks' hall (Collcutt 1981: 206-15), modern monasteries feature several, smaller halls. Monks living together in a hall share the same task, either in self-cultivation (meditation, reciting Buddha's name) or in managing monastic duties. Welch gives the capacity of the halls of the largest monastery in the Republican period, the Tianning si [48], which housed a total of 800 monks and 200 lay workmen: it had a large Meditation hall (for 130 monks), a Buddha recitation hall (35 monks), a scripture chamber (50 monks), a seminary (150 monks), a hall for monks who were blind or otherwise disabled (45 monks), a sanatorium (20 monks) separate from the infirmary, halls for the aged, and a wandering monks hall (60 monks: Welch 1967: 234).

3.2.1 Meditation hall, Chan tang

The Meditation hall was the heart of a large monastery, "the flower which other departments served as stalk, leaves and roots".[48] To oversimplify, primacy was given to this hall in Chan oriented monasteries, while Pure Land oriented ones gave primacy to the Buddha recitation hall. In reality, both kinds of halls could probably be found in most of the large modern monasteries.[49] It is now impossible to ascertain how many monasteries had these halls, which have usually been destroyed with the rest of the conventual parts of monasteries during the 20th century. The few preserved Meditation halls are not documented by learned publications and are still off-limits to visitors.

In monasteries that organised ordination such as Huiju si [45], the Meditation hall could also be used for the training and instruction of novices. In most monasteries, however, it was the prerogative of ordained monks who had registered at the beginning of each 6-month season to stay there and practise meditation according to the strict round-the-clock schedule. Not all monks living in a monastery enrolled, either because they had specific duties, or because the harsh regime was beyond their force. The most illustrious monastery in China for meditation before 1949 was Jinshan [46]. A few large monasteries as Qixia shan [42] had no meditation hall.

Meditation halls were characterised by their seclusion and were located on the rear of the central axis (separated by walls from the front part), or more often on a side axis. They functioned somehow as a monastery within the monastery. Jinshan's Meditation hall was located in an isolated compound, with a Weituo hall, the Ancestors' hall and toilet facilities. In the same compound there was sometimes an infirmary, a small kitchen and living quarters for the attached staff. It was a two-storey building with the ordination platform on the second floor. Thus, the search for enlightenment and the most sacred rites – ancestral worship and ordination – were performed in this courtyard.

48. This section closely follows Welch 1967:47-88 and Prip-Moller 1937:75-79.

49. Prip-Moller 1937:146 suggests that the Buddha recitation hall is another name of the Meditation hall in Pure Land oriented monasteries, while Welch 1967:89-104 shows clearly that the two halls had a comparable layout but different functions.

A – *Baoguang si [66] Monks sitting in the Meditation hall*

(Prip-Moller 1937: ph. 93, p. 71)

Jinshan's Meditation hall measured about 18 by 30 m and housed a hundred participants. The room had an image of Bodhidharma[50] on a central dais, with an empty space around for circumambulation. Two steps of wooden platforms for sitting and sleeping respectively, separated by curtains, ran along the walls.[51] Above the monks' heads were shelves with baskets containing their personal belongings, monks were placed according to rank and seniority. A special seat for the abbot was located at the rear of the hall. An architectural peculiarity of this hall was the absence of columns between the platforms to facilitate circumambulation: columns were grouped together as closely as possible in the very centre, surrounding the altar. On the floor, marks directed the monks during the circumambulation. The monks alternatively sit to meditate

50. In other monasteries, Bhaishajyaguru, Śākyamuni (with Maitreya behind), or less frequently Guanyin, Maitreya, Kshitigarbha or Vairocana was enthroned on the altar. Prip-Moller 1937: 73-74. In Song Monks' halls, this place was occupied by Mañjuśrī.

51. This layout was supposedly fixed in the 8th century by the Chan master Huaihai. In Hualin si [68], the hall proper and the sleeping quarters are two separate rooms, which seems to be very unusual. Prip-Moller 1937: 69, 73-75.

and walked in two circles, while receiving explanations. A large bell and a board, suspended along the front wall, marked the daily schedule from 3 am to 10 p.m. In Jinshan, they had seven to nine hours of meditation a day, three meals, three teas and two naps. There was also one to seven even more intense meditation weeks a year.

Some monasteries had two separate Meditation halls for beginners (with a stricter program), and for the older monks, who meditated more freely in small cubicles. Other Meditation halls had benches and tables and looked more like a classroom.[52]

3.2.2 The Buddha recitation hall, Nianfo tang

The cult of Amitābha and his Pure Land, their painted and sculpted representations, and the organisation of groups vowing to be collectively reborn there have become ever more widespread since the 6th century. The appearance of a new type of building, the Buddha recitation hall, cannot be dated and only few descriptions exist. Monks and laymen recited Amitābha's name up to nine hours per day. Along with the monks searching for enlightenment in the Meditation hall, they belonged to the elite of the monastery.

In the Republican period, the model for this practice was Lingyan si [51]. Its Buddha recitation hall, rebuilt in 1933, housed a hundred participants (for 200 to 400 monks in the whole monastery). Schedule and rules were inspired by Jinshan's Meditation hall, with alternation of sitting-plus-chanting and walking-plus-reciting, but discipline was less severe. The large layout was also copied on the Meditation hall with a central altar dedicated to the trinity of the Western Paradise, and benches. Above the recitation hall was the Library.

The Buddha recitation hall of Fayu si [59] is a peculiar case as it was split between two places. The room called Nianfo tang was located on the second floor above the Ancestors hall, with dormitories on either side, no sitting bench along the walls but desks to study the scriptures. 24 monks lived there, studying upstairs but going downstairs to recite the Buddha's name (Boerschmann 1911: 30). In most monasteries, the recitation hall was probably much smaller and the organisation simpler and informal. It was a place for relative relaxation – even retirement – for elderly monks trying to have a vision of the Paradise before dying (Welch 1967:89-102).

3.2.3 Ordinations

Ordination was a highly complex ritual requiring experience and a costly endeavour; it was thus only organised in some of the largest monasteries.[53] The especially renowned Huiju si [45] ordained every year 600 to 800 persons through two ceremonies, but ordinary monasteries only hold ordination once per generation. Separate ordinations were conferred to monks, nuns, lay brothers and lay sisters taking the Five vows. Ordinands stayed in, and were supported by the monastery during a period of normally 53 days when they studied the monastic vows and proper deportment. At the end of this period was the ordination ritual itself.

Whereas the training and the ordination ritual were fairly standardised, the necessary physical structure varied quite a lot. In contrast to the Theravāda tradition, ordination does not necessarily call for a specific building. Ordination-related structures may be as modest as a temporary makeshift platform (an elevated terrace is necessary for

---

52. Like the Fayu si [59], Boerschmann 1911:136-37; the Zhaoqing si [55], Prip-Moller 1937:70.

53. Welch 1967:285-96; de Groot 1893:127-30; Prip-Moller 1937:92-98. Ordinations could only take place in monasteries, not in nunneries.

B – *Huiju si [45]*
Rehearsal
of ordination ceremonies
in front of the main hall

(Prip-Moller 1937: ph. 307, p. 303)

ordination rituals), or a permanent room with a platform. Conversely, they may be as extensive as a secluded compound comprising several structures: an Ordination hall, an open-air stone or wooden platform in a courtyard,[54] halls for novices, separate halls for nuns, a kitchen, covered passages, toilets, and a garden. The halls for novices (six at the Huiju si) had a similar plan to that of the Meditation hall, and served as classroom plus sleeping quarters during the training that preceded ordination. The plan of an Ordination hall is close to that of a Meditation hall housing 60-70 persons, with sleeping platforms along the side walls. In former days the ordination compound was located outside the precinct, later on the central axis[55] or more frequently on a side axis, not far from the Ancestors' hall and the Meditation hall (Prip-Moller 1937: 89-90). The Refectory or the Dharma hall, because of their size, could also be temporarily turned into an Ordination hall.

54. Old stone platforms were attested at Zhaoqing si [55] (978), Kaiyuan si [50] and Xianlin si [56] (12th century): Prip-Moller 1937:344-48.

55. In Longxing si [18]: behind the Buddha hall; in Wenshu yuan [67]: ordination platform between the Buddha hall and the Dharma hall; in Gulin si [40]: behind the Dharma hall; in Baoguang si [66]: the rearmost part of the Dharma hall.

3.2.4 Ceremonies for monks and laity, rituals and sermons

Lay disciples, usually patrons, could participate in recitation of Amitābha's name in the Buddha recitation hall. Thousands of laymen and laywomen took lay vows during ordination ceremonies. However, no regular sermons and teaching for the laymen and very few public initiations were given. There was no place in monasteries for the laity to assemble because this function had been gradually assumed by temples since the Song. Buddhist lay associations for spiritual practice and good deeds were usually based in a monastery, but, by the end of the 19th and 20th century, new lay associations had their own buildings and entertained ever fewer connections with monasteries (some even had tough anticlerical stances). The festivals were the only occasion when large number of laypersons could enter the monastic compound. Temporary altars were raised just for the time of a festival or a prayer against drought, flood or other calamities. The main ceremonies were in honour of the dead (see below).

3.3 For educational functions

*3.3.1 The Dharma hall (*Fa tang*), or Lecture hall (*Jiangtang*)*

This essential component of the early Chinese monastery was a one or two-storied building (often with the Library upstairs) located at the rear of the central axis, behind the Buddha hall. It remained secondary to the Buddha hall, however, except maybe in the Song period. The rear Dharma hall of Fengguo si [21] (11th century) was intended to hold one thousand monks. The model Song monasteries also had very large Dharma halls, possibly as large as the Buddha hall, where the abbot engaged daily the whole community in debates, and conducted many of the communal rituals (Collcutt 1981: 194-97). Later, probably during the Ming dynasty, as group debates lost their importance and the performance of some rituals was moved to other buildings, the Dharma hall was often relocated in one of the side groups, as well as the abbot's quarters, and its role declined.

As it befits a place for lecturing and studying, Dharma halls usually provide a spacious floor area, only limited by a platform bearing a small altar, behind which the abbot's chair and insignia (stick and staff) were placed. The altar displayed an image of the trinity of the Western Paradise, of Vairocana or Maitreya. In summer time, lectures on sacred texts were usually delivered by the abbot or by a specialist invited from another monastery with his disciples.[56] The place could be the Dharma hall or any room in the monastery that could fit the number of persons. The abbot also transmitted the *dharma* to his successor in the Dharma hall (Welch 1967: 156; 310-15; Prip-Moller 1937: 83-84; de Groot 1893: 132-42).

In the monasteries which organised an Uposatha, it usually took place in the Dharma hall, or in the Refectory. Twice a month, monks gathered to read the 250 Prātimokṣa rules and the 58 vows of the *Fanwang jing*; they could confess their sins before the assembly. This ceremony requires a specific building in Theravāda monasticism: in China, the term Prātimokṣa hall is encountered in texts, but it was usually not a special hall. The Song dynasty Xiangguo si [34] and Yuan dynasty Guangsheng si [29], had a Vinaya hall (*Lü tang*) for this purpose, as a lateral building facing the Meditation hall. This feature seems to have disappeared by modern times, except in Huiju si [45].

56. Chan tradition preferring wordless teaching, there were no lectures at Jinshan.

Beside the Dharma hall, there was traditionally no specific classroom for young monks, who had already received a basic training in their hereditary temples. After 1905, however, and under outside pressure, seminaries or school for monks on a western pedagogical model were founded in monasteries as Tianning si [48], or Wenshu yuan [67]; classrooms were in the Meditation unit (Prip-Moller 1937: 139-46).

3.3.2 Library, Zangjing lou

Monasteries were reputed both as centers of learning and as treasure-troves for scholars. Any major monastery had a library, containing both Buddhist canonical works and the more mundane literature of the monks-poets and historiographers. Throughout Chinese history, the compilation of Buddhist Canons was an imperial privilege, and with a few exceptions, ancient complete canons possessed by monasteries were imperial grants. Ornate libraries had to be built to decently house such gifts.

One of the oldest preserved library is the pavilion of the Lower Huayan si [25] (11th century), with images in the middle allowing circumambulation. Two-storey sūtra cupboards run round the walls. The library could be a lateral hall on the central axis, as in Zhihua si [11]. More frequently in Ming and Qing times, it was located on the second floor of one of the buildings north of the Buddha hall: either a Dharma hall, or less frequently the Meditation hall or the Buddha recitation hall.

The Buddhist scriptures, along with the wood blocks from which they were printed, were kept in wooden cases. The library also contained tables and chairs, and a big altar in the centre with the trinity of the Western Paradise, the thousand arms Guanyin or Vairocana. In front of the hall, a platform was used once a year to clean and dry the sūtras in the sun. Since the Qing dynasty, the Library frequently merged with the Thousand or Ten thousand Buddha's hall: small Buddha images cover the hall. Art objects of special interest or value were also kept in the library (Prip-Moller 1937: 52-67; de Groot 1893: 142-43).

Revolving wooden bookcases imitating an eight-sided reduced architecture, are a device invented in the 8th century; their style was closely related to stūpas and stone *dhāranī*-pillars, and the representation of celestial palaces on their upper parts recalled pictorial representation of the Western paradise (Loveday 2000). A famous early example is in the Longxing si [18]. The cost of such an artful library was beyond the reach of the smaller monasteries, but they were common during the Song dynasty. They rarefied during the following centuries, and iconographically similar but stationary bookcases became more common, such as in Zhihua si [11].

[18] *fig. 3 p. 345*

Modern monasteries do not usually have a reading room separate from the library, but plans of Song monasteries show the existence of a large hall, adjacent to the Monks' hall and modelled on it, but fitted with desks and skylights. The Liuyun si [53] had a *Yuejing lou* (scripture perusal chamber) where old monks "read" the Buddhist scriptures, just glancing at each page of the Tripitaka. Some monasteries had specialised halls devoted to the study or recitation of a single text, in order to cope with popular demand. At Tianning si [48], young monks recited the Diamond Sūtra in a *Jing lou* (scripture chamber) modelled on a Meditation hall with sleeping platforms and a central altar.

Some monasteries had a printing office, such as Tianning si and Huiju si [45] during the Republican period (Welch 1968: 98 sq.; de Groot 1893: 142-43). Monasteries routinely printed documents for internal use (such as rules or ordination documents.). Printing was not, however, a major activity of modern monasteries, and the Buddhist literature that flowed in Chinese society was produced by private printing shops or lay charitable foundations.

3.4 For reliquary, commemorative or funerary functions

3.4.1 Stūpas

The Chinese stūpa or pagoda has developed into a multiple-use structure: it is a commemorative, funerary, reliquary (for ashes or mummy of an eminent monk, of Buddha etc.), and/or votive monument, but also a multi-storey building that can be entered and contains images of Buddhas for worship (a shrine), a watchtower, or a library (masonry stūpas having the advantage of being fire-proof). All of them are called *ta* in Chinese and refer, even tenuously, to Indian origins. Stūpas' sizes range from a small reliquary sheltered in a special hall to a huge towering building from seven to fifteen storeys: it is the latter, usually hollow buildings, that will be discussed here; the more modest funerary stūpa will be addressed in a following paragraph.

Stūpas, as we have seen, were a focus of devotion in early Chinese monasteries. They could be erected independently from a monastery, marking an uninhabited holy site, or located at a precise spot where it may tame the unfavourable forces of the ground. Today, many stūpas stand alone because the wooden monastery has entirely disappeared around. Stūpas' fame depend on both the sanctity of what they enshrine, and their height and architectural prowess that they exhibit. Four Chinese monasteries were supposed to contain relics of the Buddha. Among them, the Famen si [31] kept its treasure in a crypt, sealed in 874. It was excavated in 1987, and was found to contain four Buddha's relics in encased boxes along with texts. The famous stūpa of Ayuwang si [58] was deemed to contain one of the 84,000 relics scattered by king Ashoka that had flown miraculously there.

The Chinese stūpa shows little resemblance with the Indian one. Built with Chinese traditional techniques, it is influenced by early Chinese architecture: watch-towers (dating at least of the Han dynasty, 206 BC-AD 220) and multi-storey wooden pavilions, including elevated towers for the cult of Taoist immortals, also attested during the Han. Stūpas can nonetheless also be considered as inheriting from the Indian *shikara*, the Kushāna multi-storey tower topped by golden disks, and the brick towers of Turkestan. For this reason, it was, and can still be, conceived as the most "alien" element in the precinct. Stūpas can be built of wood, stone or brick masonry. Brick and stone stūpas are often built in imitation of wooden buildings, with overhanging eaves imitating roof tiles. The central pillar running up the core of the stūpa symbolises the Sumeru mountain of the Indian cosmology.

The oldest preserved Chinese examples are rock-cut stūpas of the Yungang caves [5]. These multi-tiered square towers are located in the middle of the caves like a central pillar. According to literary descriptions, wooden stūpas of the 5th-7th centuries could reach 100 m high, but, exposed to fires, hurricanes and lightning, they have not survived up to the 20th century. Japan has been fortunate to preserve two 7th century wooden stūpas based on the Yungang and Longmen [6] types. Cubic, single-storey types surmounted by a small dome are closer to Indian models (Shentong si [39], 544). Most of the extant Tang period stūpas are square structures of brick masonry, from the simple cube to the multi-storey tower often accessible by interior stairs: Dayan ta [30], and the stūpas of Yunju si [17] (both early 8th century). Another type is modelled on the Indian Gupta *shikara*, like the dodecagonal Songyue si stūpa [35], built around 523.

Octagonal ground plans are attested during the 7th century and became widespread especially after the 10th century (stūpa of Qixia shan [42]). The Liao decorated their stūpas with the Four buddhas of the cardinal directions and the Four Bodhisattvas of esoteric Buddhism. Hexagonal plans are common starting from the Song period onwards (stūpa of Tianning si [13]).

The model of a main stūpa surrounded by four minor ones standing on a platform appears during the 8th century in Yunju si [17]. It refers to the five divisions of the Buddhist pantheon (cardinal points plus zenith). During the Ming and Qing dynasties, this type becomes more common and explicitly echoes the temple of the Mahābodhi in Bodhgaya: examples are found at Zhenjue si [14] and Biyun si [16]. Tibetan-style stūpas mentioned above were also built by the Mongol rulers of the Yuan empire, and later again by Manchu emperors (Baita of Qionghuadao [12]). [16] *fig. 6 p. 346*

3.4.2 Funerary buildings

The Chinese have always buried their dead. Cremation, brought by Buddhists, was slowly adopted, and many monks of the early period were buried. It gained currency, though, and by the Song, cremation was fairly common even for laymen. It sharply regressed after the Yuan. In modern times, monks are usually cremated, but laymen very rarely – until communist laws imposed it (at least in cities). During the cremation of eminent monks, it was common, as in other Buddhist countries, to find relics (*sharīra*) among the ashes; this would prompt the erection of an embellished stūpa as well as an inscription.

A cremation oven was located at some distance of the monastery, outside the walled compound. In modern times, the corpses were burnt in a jar;[57] then the ashes were stored in urns and placed in a Colombarium. The Colombarium could be one or several stūpas with inaccessible subterranean chambers for the ashes, located at the extremity of the precinct or on a hill slope above it. Abbots, monks, nuns, wandering monks, devout laymen and laysisters were placed in separate chambers or in separate stūpas. Funerary stūpas have been widespread since the 11-12th centuries, and could be grouped in "forests" (*ta lin*), forming a sort of monastic cemetery in a separate lateral courtyard. These forests include different styles of stūpas, from the simple cubic monuments to multi-storey stūpas and late Tibetan-style stūpa. Modest stūpas have a short square inscription mentioning the name and dates of the deceased; large ones have a full epitaph, similar in composition to the tomb inscriptions of eminent laypersons, fitted into the stūpa body. The most famous stūpa forests include those of Shaolin si [36] and Tanzhe si [15].

The Colombarium could also be a building with individual urns placed on shelves, with an altar dedicated to Kshitigarbha. It was then located on a lateral axis, in a corner or in the garden. The embalmed and gilded mummy of a high monk could be honoured as a most sacred image in a special funerary hall, like that of the Chan's Sixth Patriarch (died 713) preserved for centuries in the Nanhua si [64], or in any hall like the Buddha hall. Temples, and more rarely monasteries, also had a warehouse to store coffins waiting to be buried elsewhere on an auspicious day.[58] Laymen could buy land to bury their dead near a monastery and some monasteries were famous for the geomantical quality of their site.

---

57. Great wooden pyres were used for self-immolation, but not (due to the cost of wood) for cremation unless the monk was very eminent and his cremation was a public ceremony.

58. Welch 1967:204, 340; Prip-Moller 1937:163-79. Many temples lived off funerary rituals, but monasteries, as they did not provide such parochial services, had much less to do with the death of laypersons.

3.4.3 Buildings for keeping soul tablets

Funerary services and worship are never performed in front of the urn or stūpa, but in front of the soul tablet of the deceased, which represents him. The soul tablets of former abbots were kept and worshipped in the Ancestors' hall (*Zu(shi) tang*), one of the most sacred halls of the whole monastery. The altar, beside the soul tablets, sometimes featured painted scrolls of the deceased abbots and images or scrolls of the Six Chan Patriarchs. Its location was not fixed: it could be a lateral pavilion in the rear part of the central axis, near the last big hall (in Fayu si [59]) or near the entrance hall (in Jiechuang si [49], balanced by the Guardians' hall, Qielan dian). In Baoguang si [66], a major establishment of the Linji lineage, the Ancestors' hall was in the rearmost courtyard, balanced by a memorial hall for Linji patriarchs. It could also be placed in the lateral groups, close to the ordination platform or the Meditation hall (Prip-Moller 1937: 94-97; Welch 1967: 48, 101, 341). An additional shrine could be dedicated to one Patriarch (Shaolin si [36], 1125).

Tablets of worthy and titled monks as well as generous patrons could be placed in the hall of Merit (Gongde tang); tablets of menial officers, in the hall of Service (*Gonghang tang*). As for ordinary monks, their individual and collective tablets were kept in the hall of Rebirth (*Wangsheng tang*, also called *Shuilu tang*, or Nirvāna hall, *Niepan tang*), presided by Amitābha.[59] All these memorial halls were of a rather limited size, since the rituals performed there did not require the whole community's assembly: offerings were made on the 1st and 15th of every lunar month by a number of monks assigned to this task. Longevity halls (*Yanshou tang*) kept tablets during a person's lifetime; the merit of prayers recited here was transferred to lengthen a person's life. It was presided by Bhaishajyaguru, the Buddha of Medicine and Longevity. In small communities, all the tablets could be found in the Buddha hall, those of the dead in the west and those of the living in the east.

By modern times, some monasteries such as Gaomin si [47] refused to perform any sort of funerary services for laymen, so as to concentrate on meditation and study. Most, however, did not totally decline to act for the welfare of the suffering souls of former lay believers. During the Hungry Ghosts festival (mid of the 7th month), and on other occasions, because of either patrons' demand or a major disaster, the monks would hold a large ritual for the salvation of suffering souls, and part of the monastery's ground would be open for lay patrons and onlookers. The major Buddhist version of this ritual since the Song is the Shuilu zhai (Penance [for beings living] on earth and in water). Organised along a program lasting several days, the very complex procedure necessitates several altars functioning simultaneously, set up in the various halls and courtyards. The paper soul tablets of the deceased, which are burnt on the 7th day of the ritual, are installed on a temporary altar of Rebirth or in the hall of Rebirth. The Shuilu festival can also be performed in the Ancestors' hall or in the library. Huge paper objects, like boats or houses, are burnt in a courtyard and painting scrolls are hung in the hall. Although this is not necessary, some monasteries have erected a hall destined to become the main altar of such rituals. A famous example, noted for the remarkable 15th century murals depicting the pantheon of deities taking part in the ritual, is at the Pilu si [20].

---

59. Between the death and the presumed reincarnation, the tablets were exposed for 49 days on an altar in the Buddha hall with offerings, before being moved to the Ancestors' hall, the hall of Merit or the hall of Rebirth (Welch 1967: 99).

3.5 The management of the monastery

3.5.1 The abbot's quarters, Fangzhang

The abbot's quarters were very spacious, sometimes luxurious, and housed the abbot's apartment (bedroom, room for study, dining hall), the Sacristy,[60] a private kitchen, an altar, guest rooms, offices, toilets and a garden.[61] This residence was usually located close to the Dharma hall. The oldest known location of the abbot's quarters was in the rearmost part of the central axis, behind the Buddha hall or the Dharma hall: it was a two-storied residential complex with the library upstairs (Lingyin si [54] and Tiantong si [57]). It was later moved to one of the lateral axis, along with the Dharma hall (Linggu si [41], rebuilt in 1659).

Retired abbots were also granted with a comfortable apartment with reception rooms, a shrine, garden, rooms for guests and servants. An usual arrangement since the Ming dynasty was the abbot's quarters at the eastern side of the Dharma hall and the retired abbots' apartments at the west.[62] Other high-ranking monks also enjoyed the privilege of private apartments at their retirement. In Jinshan [46], there were 20 to 30 apartments, some being grouped together in a building. Some ex-abbots retired to a small separate temple.

As explained above, ordinary monks lived together in halls according to their function. Individual cells were found only in temples and the smallest, less strict monasteries. Servants (unordained novices in ancient times, but seemingly not after the Yuan; lay artisans and menial workers) had their own quarters. The monks on duty in the various halls and departments of the monastery had sleeping and living rooms adjacent to their office or hall.

Isolation was not planned for in the framework of monastic life. Chinese Buddhism has a strong eremitic tradition, however: some monks enclosed themselves for months or years in a separate unit (with sleeping room, altar, kitchen, vegetable garden) that could be located in a remote corner of the monastery's ground, but more often at some distance of the precinct (Prip-Moller 1937:150-52, 186-87). The door was sealed and food, provided by the active monks, was passed inside through a wicket.

3.5.2 The Guest department, Ke tang

The Guest department was in charge of both religious and lay guests.[63] It was therefore usually divided in two sections, and was found on a side axis close to the Gatehouse, or even inside of it. It offered free accommodation to monks according to their status, such as a private room for a respected cleric (high-ranking visitors and personal guests stayed in the abbot's quarters) or a place in the Wandering monks hall for ordinary

---

60. *Yibo liao,* the apartment and office of the Yibo, the abbot's personal assistant and his representative, often in charge of finances.

61. Welch 1967:145. In large public monasteries, all the monks had a rank and duties and held an office for six months only, except the abbot. About the abbot, the precentor and other offices, see Welch 1967: 37-46, and chap. VI.

62. Prip-Moller 1937:80-82, fig. 165. In modern Buddhist protocol, the western side is more honorific than the eastern side. The Chinese directional preferences have a complex history and also show regional differences: McDermott 1999:330, n. 120.

63. The guest department was also in charge of internal housekeeping and supervised the Refectory, the kitchens etc. (Welch 1967: 10-25).

ordained monks (Chinese Buddhist, Tibeto-Mongol and Taoist).[64] This was granted after the arriving monk had proved his status to the Guest prefect by showing him his written credentials and his mastery of the elaborate rites governing a request for residence. Monks of dubious credentials, "wild (ascetic) monks" and vagabonds were turned down, as well as nuns (except in monasteries where they were ordained during the ordination period)[65].

The Wandering monks hall (*Yunshui tang*) was built like other dormitories accommodating clerics, but as its inhabitants changed constantly, it was not ruled by the same discipline. In theory, monks staying up to three days lived there, and those staying longer had to take residence in a regular hall, if room was available. In any case, they had to respect the monastery's own rules and attend daily services. The largest Wandering monks halls could have a capacity of more than one hundred persons. They comprised an altar and the regular platforms for sleeping and eating; toilet facilities and sometimes a garden were attached.

Patrons on visit were also received in the Guest department and discussed with the Guest prefect, a crucial post on which a good part of the monastery's immediate reputation and resources depended. Laymen were not supposed to stay at night, except on large pilgrimage sites which had a guesthouse (dormitories for the poor pilgrims, and luxurious suites for those who could afford it) and a separate dining room for laymen (like Tanzhe si [15], Putuo shan [1] monasteries). In such cases, the guesthouse was separate from the monastery proper.

3.5.3 Other offices, commercial and welfare activities

The religious administration or Business office (*Ku fang*) was located on a side axis. It collected the rents of the farmlands owned by the monastery, bought the food supplies and altar furniture, received the donations, and stored goods. Other administrative offices, together with the officer's apartment, were located in the abbot's quarters. Their altar could bear an image of Caishen, the patron deity of merchants. The Infirmary (*Ruyi liao*), halls for disabled and old monks could be located in the rear part of the central axis. Workshops for carpenters, painters etc., tailor's shop, farm buildings, granary, buildings to stock timber, limestone fabric, brick kilns, stables were relegated in the outskirts of the monastery.

The shops catering to pilgrims, selling incense and other goods, although sometimes owned by the monastery, were not managed by monks. Monasteries until the Yuan ran a large range of businesses: water-powered mills, oil presses, hostels, pawnshops (also mortgaging lands), safe-deposit vaults etc. These businesses occupied an important part of the outer ridges of the monastic complex. They declined dramatically by the Ming. As these activities have not left durable architectures, they should not be discussed here.[66]

---

64. Temples may accommodate wandering clerics if the abbot wished, but they did not have to, and often did not. The right of any ordained cleric for free accommodation was a major difference between monasteries and temples.

65. This was not so in some Song large monasteries, which had both monks and nuns quarters (Foulk 1993:183).

66. The major reference work concerning economic activities of the monasteries during the high period remains Gernet 1995.

Ancient monasteries also established and administrated hospitals, dispensaries, feeding stations, havens for the aged, bathhouses and rest-houses for pilgrims, and sponsored roads, bridges, wells and tree-planting. Many of these welfare activities were organised by lay associations in monasteries rather than by the monks themselves. One of the main anticlerical attacks of the modern period is precisely that the clergy itself had no interest in charity. For that reason, some monasteries opened schools, orphanages, clinics, and sanatoriums during the Republican period.

3.6 Communal functions, hygiene and monastic environment

3.6.1 Refectory, dining-room, kitchen, storeroom

The Big kitchen (*Daliao*) and a small contiguous storeroom were located either in the southern part (Tanzhe si [15]) or in the northern part (Song plans of Chan monasteries) of a side axis. It was close to the Refectory but also connected with a vegetable garden and open land. It consisted of one big hall or a group of halls containing stoves, huge iron cauldrons, tables for chopping vegetables, room with water boilers for the preparation of tea, room to store fuel, jars, rice, room to make bean-curd. An image of the popular Kitchen God was found, as in every Chinese kitchen. Bamboo or wooden pipes could carry water from mountain streams. A smaller kitchen was used for preparing special dishes served to the dignitaries and guests. The abbot had his own kitchen to prepare dinner, especially when he received guests.

Close to the kitchen was a mill, and not far away, a vegetable garden. The garden and farmlands employed lay workmen. Monks were supposed to work in the fields according to Chan rules, but it has always been exceptional in large monasteries. Monks had no individual kitchen and ate their simple fare of cereals and vegetables together in the Refectory (*Zhai tang*). It was a long and narrow side building facing the central court, accessible from all quarters, and was sometimes located on the ground floor of a two-storey hall, with a scripture chamber upstairs. In the middle of the rear wall lies the abbot's table and chair, and a small image of Maitreya placed on a small platform. Outside the hall, a small carved seven-sided pillar was erected to offer rice to the hungry ghosts. Because it was very large, the Refectory could be used for other purposes: Prātimokṣa recitation, ordination... Kitchen staff and servants could have a special refectory. The uncanonical informal dinner, called "tea", "hot water" or "medicine", was taken in the monks' own quarters. The residents of the Meditation hall ate dinner in the same hall.

3.6.2 Sanitary facilities, water supplies, wells

Bathing and washing of clothes were done four times a month in winter, and daily during the hot season. The bathroom consisted of a room for taking off shoes and robes, a room with fire pot used for complete undressing, baths, toilets, a stone reservoir for water, a stokers pit for the heating of bath water, and the attendant's room.[67] Latrines were two-storey buildings with an open-air pit on the outskirts of the premises, near the back yards. Separate units as the Meditation hall, and the Wandering monks hall had their own toilets.

---

67. Welch 1967:18, 115-16. See the layout of the bathroom at Baoguang si [66], Prip-Moller 1937:125, fig. 155, 230. Collcutt 1981:201-06 details Song-times bathrooms and toilets and notes the importance in the eyes of Japanese monks acclimating the Chan monastery in Japan to have the physical organisation of these buildings right.

3.6.3 Inscriptions, trees and garden

Sometimes sheltered by hexagonal pavilions (*beiting*) in the main courtyard, the stone inscription is a necessary element of the monastery and for us a precious document on its history. Stelae are so important and so numerous than they must be considered as an integral part of its architecture. Poems of emperors or famous scholars, drawings of Buddhas or *arhat* are also recorded in stone: the monastery was a museum of painting and calligraphy that was visited by the gentry.

Ancient descriptions show that monasteries were extensively planted with flowers and rare plants. With the deforestation of China beginning in the 16th century, trees mainly found protection within or around religious institutions. When old, trees are regarded as objects of veneration. In the modern period, a separate courtyard was dedicated to an elaborate garden, secluded from the secular world. It is usually the rearmost part of the central layout. Like its secular counterparts, it is ornamented with "false mountains", small pavilions, ponds, and sometimes a representation of Amitābha's paradise. As mentioned above, monasteries also worked as sanctuaries for animal life through sanctuary ponds and stables.

Through the nearly two thousand years of its history, the Chinese Buddhist monastery has exhibited considerable resilience and continuity. The outward-looking, economically and socially active monasteries of the high period (5th-9th century) have gradually turned into the closed, less monumental "Chan-model" institution. The former was usually the locus of lay communities' religious life, while the latter was more aloof, and very quiet when compared to village or urban temples. The modern physical monastery is nonetheless the direct heir of the ancient one. This is only partially an effect of the distinctiveness of Buddhist building style. Throughout its long history, Chinese Buddhism has maintained a measure of stylistic uniqueness through the stūpa family of buildings (extending to smaller monuments such as stone pillars engraved with texts and wooden bookcases), and, to a lesser extent, through communal halls and the monumentality of statues. Most architectural and decorative elements of the Buddhist monastery, however, would not strike anyone as uniquely Buddhist.

The resilience of the physical monastery is best explained by the conservatism of the Saṅgha as a social institution. This was not effected by an unification imposed by a centralised Church: monasteries were free to develop as they wished, and normative texts, in matters of architecture and physical organisation, were not supported by any enforcing procedure. On the other hand, the model monasteries were highly effective in diffusing their layout, style and protocol through networks fed by ordination graduates and dignitaries. These networks extended over the whole of China. Despite the size of the country and variety of local conditions, modern monasteries are remarkably homogenous. Besides the presence of famous ancient monuments or scenery associated with classical poetry, the peculiarities that distinguished every singular monastery are rarely readily apparent to the lay visitor. Many rituals may be shifted, according to time and location, from one building to another, and devotional halls may be consecrated to another deity or Buddha without its external aspect changing in the least.

More than a strict ordering of buildings, the homogeneity of monasteries layouts derives from the universal observance of basic principles. The first one is common residence and meal in each of the several secluded worlds: the Meditation hall, the abbot's quarters, the *Ke tang*, the Wandering monks hall, and the Ordination compound. Secondly, the symmetry and yet hierarchical lateralisation dictates both the place of the buildings and the ranking of monks in any circumstance. Even moves (ritual processions, walking between halls, but also devotees' visits) are prescribed in relation to other persons' and building's positions. This finely tuned ordering of the position and routes of the clerics and laymen in the monastic space is certainly what characterises best the Chinese Buddhist monasteries, both among other Chinese buildings and non-Chinese Buddhist institutions.

ANNEX

1 – List of monasteries quoted in the text and located on the map

Name, locality. Date or period of foundation and major reconstruction.
Preserved buildings (date of their last reconstruction).

The four sacred mountains
1. Putuo shan 普陀山
2. Jiuhua shan 九華山
3. Emei shan 峨眉山
4. Wutai shan 五臺山

Caves
5. Yungang 雲崗
6. Longmen 龍門
7. Tianlong shan 天龍山
8. Dunhuang 敦煌

Beijing and Hebei
9. Fayuan si 法源寺, Beijing. 696, 755, 882, 1438. Preserved (Ming-Qing)
10. Miaoying si 妙應寺, Beijing. 1096, 1271. Pagoda (1271), temple (Ming-Qing)
11. Zhihua si 智化寺, Beijing. 1444
12. Baita 白塔 of Qionghua dao 瓊華島, Beijing.
13. Tianning si 天寧寺, Beijing. Northern Wei, Sui... Pagoda (11-12th c.)
14. Zhenjue si 真覺寺 (Da zhengjue si 大正覺寺), Beijing. 1403-24. Pagoda (1473)
15. Tanzhe si 潭柘寺, West of Beijing. 3-4th c., 12th c., 1457. Preserved (Ming-Qing)
16. Biyun si 碧雲寺, West of Beijing. 1331, 16-17th c. Pagoda (1748), temple (Ming-Qing)
17. Yunju si 雲居寺, Fangshan. Early 8th c. Pagoda
18. Longxing si 龍興寺, Zhengding. 586, 971. Moni dian (1052), Cishi ge (971)
19. Dule si 獨樂寺, Jixian. 984. Shanmen, Guanyin ge (10th c.)
20. Pilu si 毘盧寺, Shijia zhuang

Liaoning
21. Fengguo si 奉國寺, Yixian. 1019, Liao, Jin. Temple (11th c.)

Shanxi

22. Nanchan si 南禪寺, mount Wutai. Before 782. Main hall (before 782)
23. Foguang si 佛光寺, mount Wutai. End of 5th century. Temple (857)
24. Fogong si 佛宮寺, Yingxian. 1056. Wooden pagoda (1056)
25. Huayan si 華嚴寺, Datong. Liao (1038), Jin. Temple (11-12th c.)
26. Shanhua si 善化寺, Datong. Tang, Liao, Jin. Temple (11-12th c.)
27. Chongfu si 崇福寺, Near Datong. 665, 1150. Temple (1143)
28. Xuankong si 懸空寺, Heng shan. Wei, Jin, Yuan... Temple (Ming)
29. Guangsheng si 廣勝寺, Hongdong. 147-149, Yuan... Temple (Yuan-Ming)

Shaanxi

30. Ci'en si 慈恩寺, Xi'an. 652
31. Famen si 法門寺, Fufeng. Tang?. Ming pagoda, crypt

Henan

32. Baima si 白馬寺, Luoyang. 67
33. Yongning si 永寧寺, Luoyang. 516
34. Xiangguo si 相國寺, Kaifeng. Tang. Temple, Qing
35. Songyue si 崧嶽寺, mount Song. Pagoda, 523
36. Shaolin si 少林寺, mount Song. 1125. Temple, Song-Qing
37. Yongtai si 永泰寺, mount Song.

Shandong

38. Lingyan si 靈巖寺, Changqing. 354, Song. Pagoda (1044)
39. Shentong si 神通寺, Licheng. 2 pagodas, 6-12th c.

Jiangsu

40. Gulin si 古林寺, Nanjing
41. Linggu si 靈谷寺, near Nanjing. 6th c., Tang... Temple (1659)
42. Qixia shan/si 棲霞山/寺, near Nanjing. 489, 601. Song pagoda, temple (modern)
43. Pilu si 毘盧寺, near Nanjing
44. Pude si 普德寺, near Nanjing
45. Huiju si 慧居寺 or Baohua shan 寶華山, Jurong. 1605
46. Jinshan 金山 or Jiangtian si 江天寺, Zhenjiang. Tang, Song...Temple (Qing)
47. Gaomin si 高旻寺, Yangzhou
48. Tianning si 天寧寺, Changzhou
49. Jiechuang si 戒幢寺, Suzhou. Ming, 1892
50. Kaiyuan si 開元寺, Suzhou. 925, 1618... Wuliang dian (1618)
51. Lingyan si 靈巖寺, Suzhou. Burnt in the 19th c., rebuilt in the 20th
52. Sheng'en si 聖恩寺, Dengwei shan, near Suzhou. Song dynasty layout

Shanghai, Zhejiang

53. Liuyun si 留雲寺, Shanghai.
54. Lingyin si 靈隱寺, Hangzhou. 4th c., 10th c. Pagoda (late 10th c.), temple (19th c.)
55. Zhaoqing si 照慶寺, Hangzhou. 947- 978. Destroyed
56. Xianlin si 僊林寺, Hangzhou. 12th c.
57. Tiantong si 天童寺, near Ningbo. 759, 14th c... Song dynasty layout, Qing
58. Ayuwang si 阿育王寺, near Ningbo. 405, 522... Ming dynasty
59. Fayu si 法雨寺, Putuo shan. Destroyed in 1880, rebuilt, fl. 20th c.
60. Puji si 普濟寺, Putuo shan.
61. Zhenjue si 眞覺寺, Tiantai shan.

Guangdong, Fujian

62. Yongquan si 湧泉寺, Gu shan, Fuzhou. 10th c.
63. Hualin si 華林寺, Guangzhou.
64. Nanhua si 南華寺, near Shaoguan.

Hubei, Sichuan, Yunnan

65. Guiyuan si 歸元寺, Hanyang.
66. Baoguang si 寶光寺, Xindu. Eastern Han, 881, 1670.
67. Wenshu yuan 文殊院, Chengdu.
68. Hualin si 華林寺, Chongqing.
69. Qiongzhu si 筇竹寺, Kunming. 638, 15th c.
70. Huating si 華亭寺, Kunming, western hills.

2 – Location of the monasteries

Numbers refer to the list

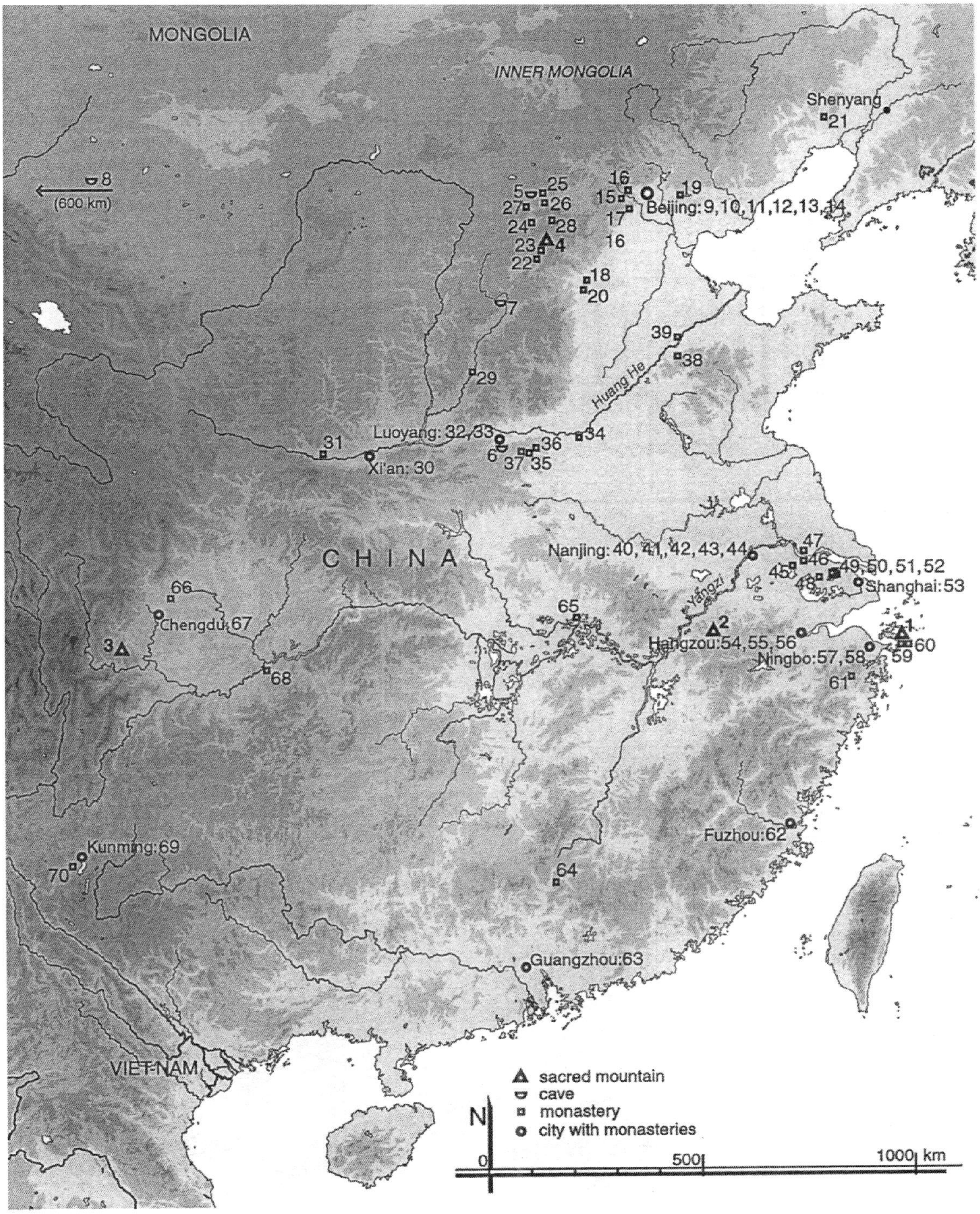

3 – Figures

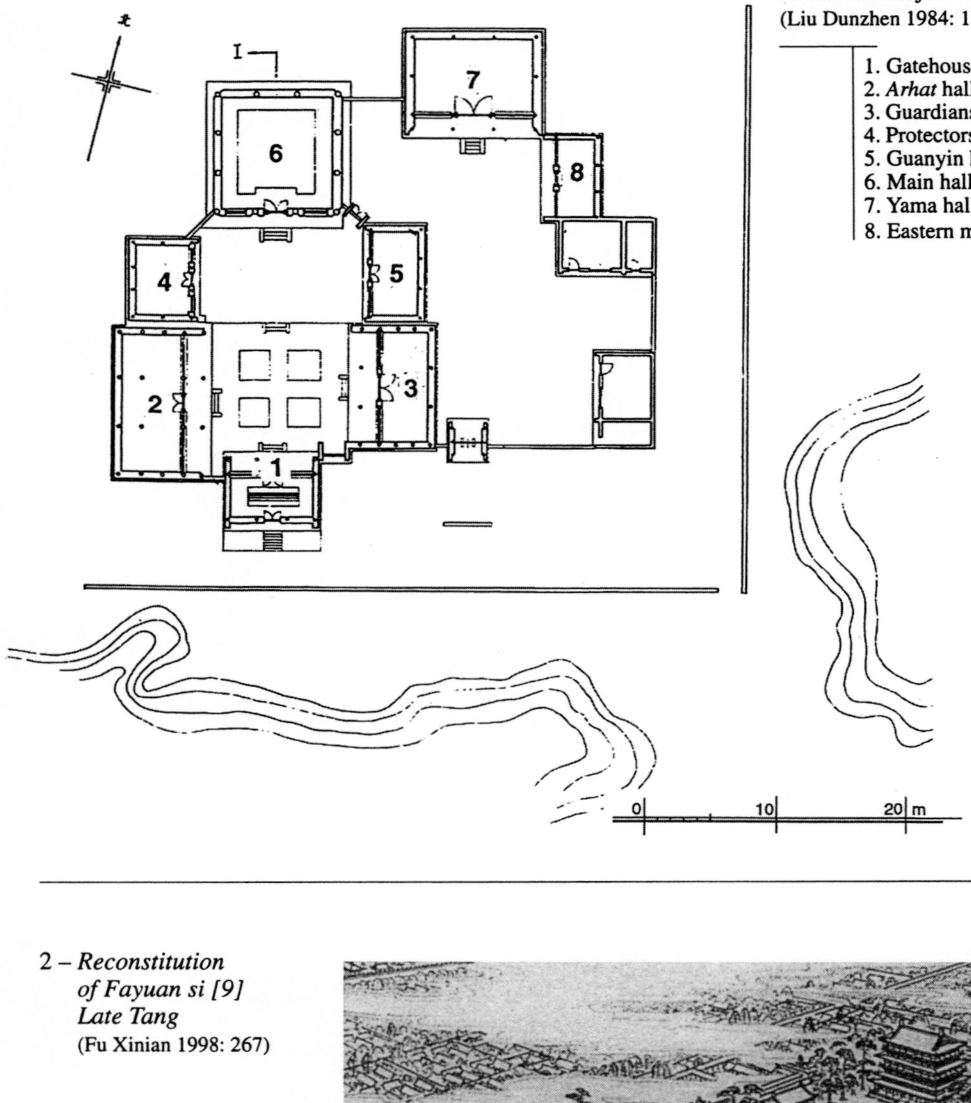

1 – *Layout of the Nanchan si [22]*
Main hall: before 782
(Liu Dunzhen 1984: 132)

1. Gatehouse
2. *Arhat* hall
3. Guardians' hall
4. Protectors' hall
5. Guanyin hall
6. Main hall
7. Yama hall
8. Eastern meditation hall

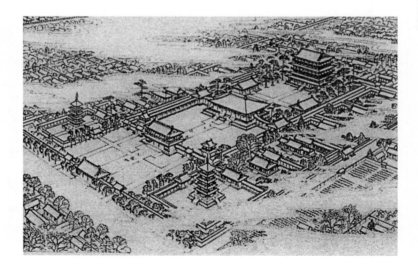

2 – *Reconstitution of Fayuan si [9]*
Late Tang
(Fu Xinian 1998: 267)

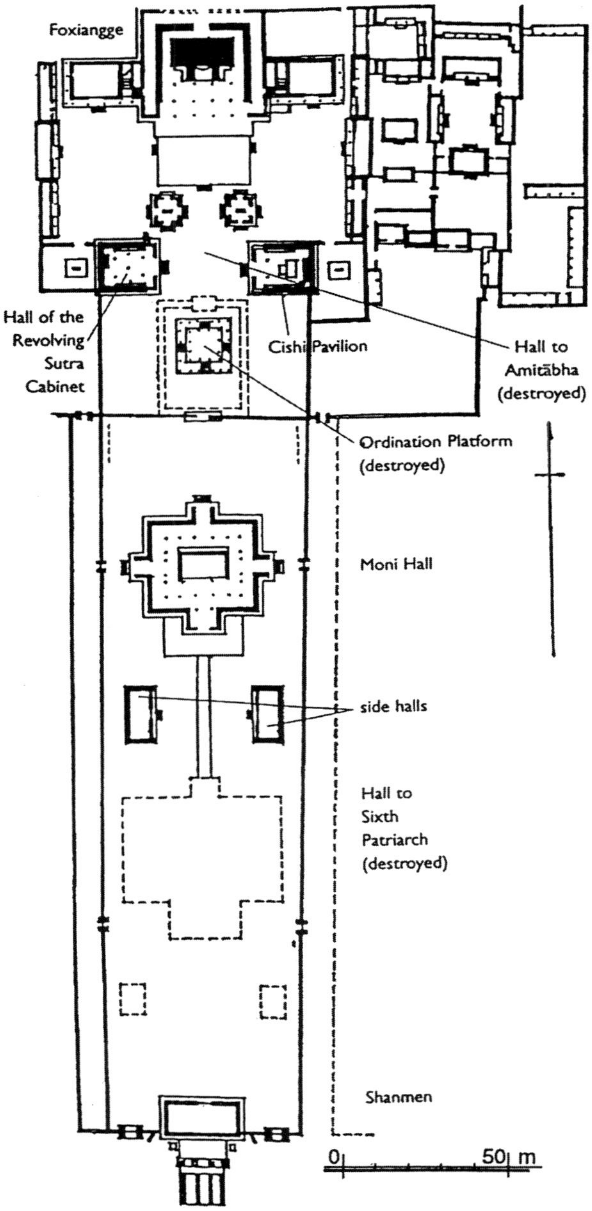

3 – *Layout of Longxing si [18] Song layout (971, 1052)*
(Steinhardt 1997: 193)

4 – *Layout of Fogon si [24] and its wooden stūpa, 1056, reconstructed plan*
(Liu Dunzhen 1984: 215)

1. remains of the Gatehouse
2. Drum tower
3. Bell tower
4. Śākyamuni stūpa
5. Main hall

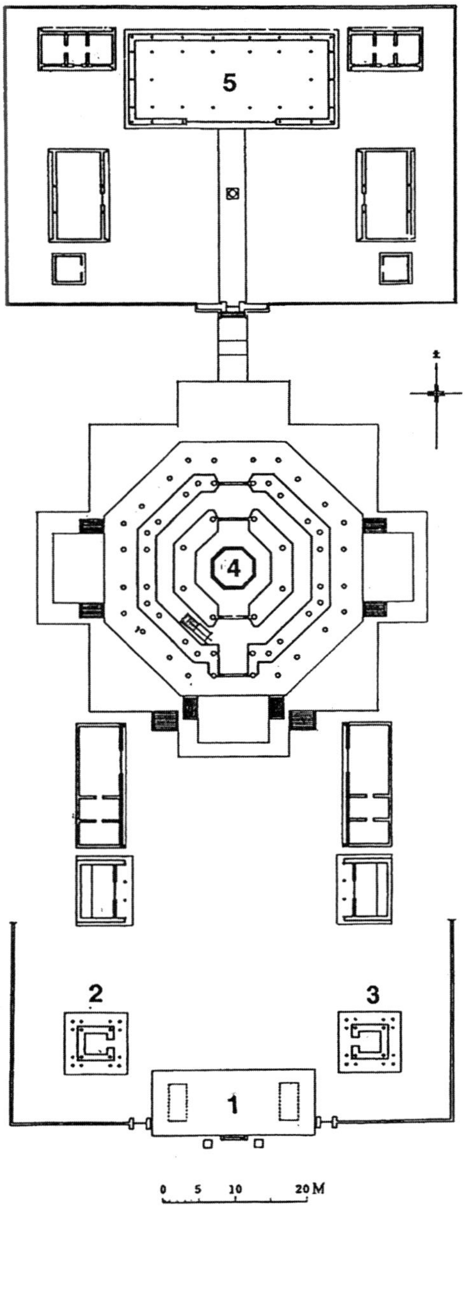

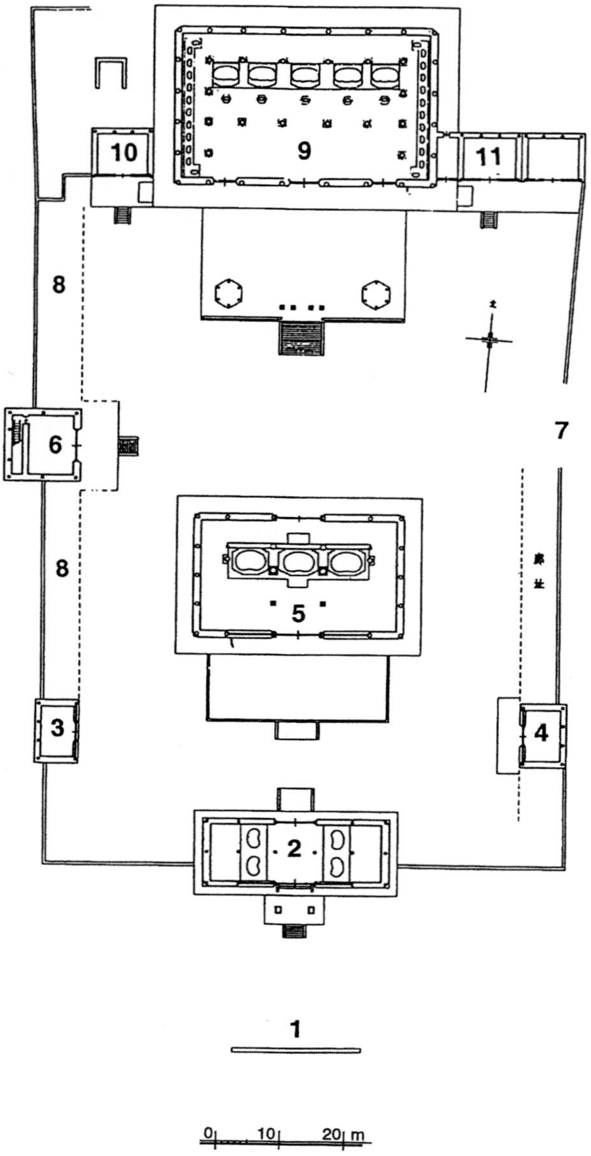

5 – *Layout of Shanhua si [26]*
11-12th century
(Liu Dunzhen 1984: 212)

1. Screen wall
2. Gatehouse
3. West side-hall
4. East side-hall
5. Three Holy ones pavilion
6. Samantabhadra pavilion
7. Mañjuśrī pavilion (destroyed)
8. Galleries
9. Main hall
10. Guanyin hall
11. Kshitigarbha hall

6 – *Layout of Biyun si [16]*
16-17th century
(Fu Xinian 1998: 423)

1. Gatehouse
2. Heng and Ha hall
3. Drum tower
4. Bell tower
5. Hall of the Guardian kings
6. Jade emperor hall
7. Guanyin hall
8. Main hall
9. Steles
10. Marble stūpa
11. 500 *arhat* hall

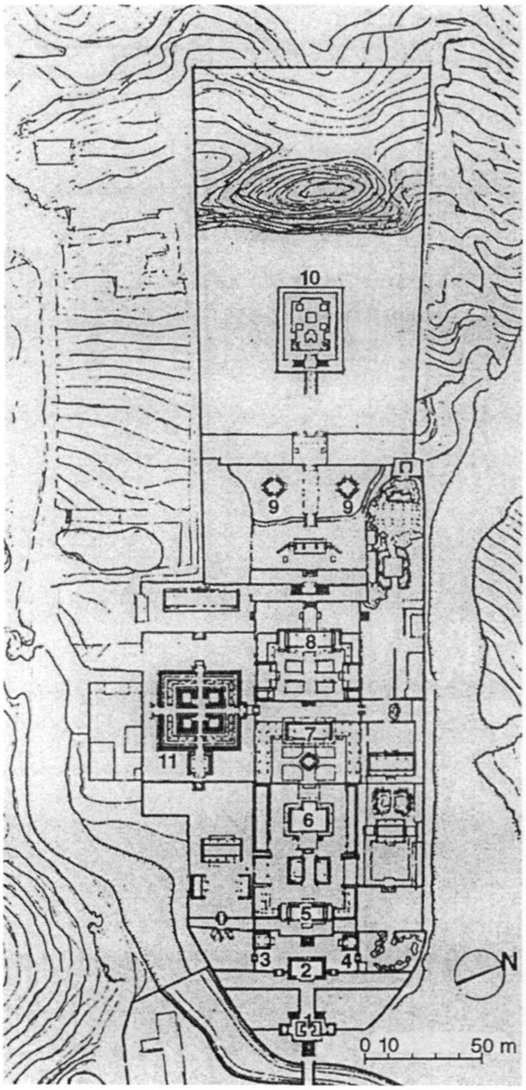

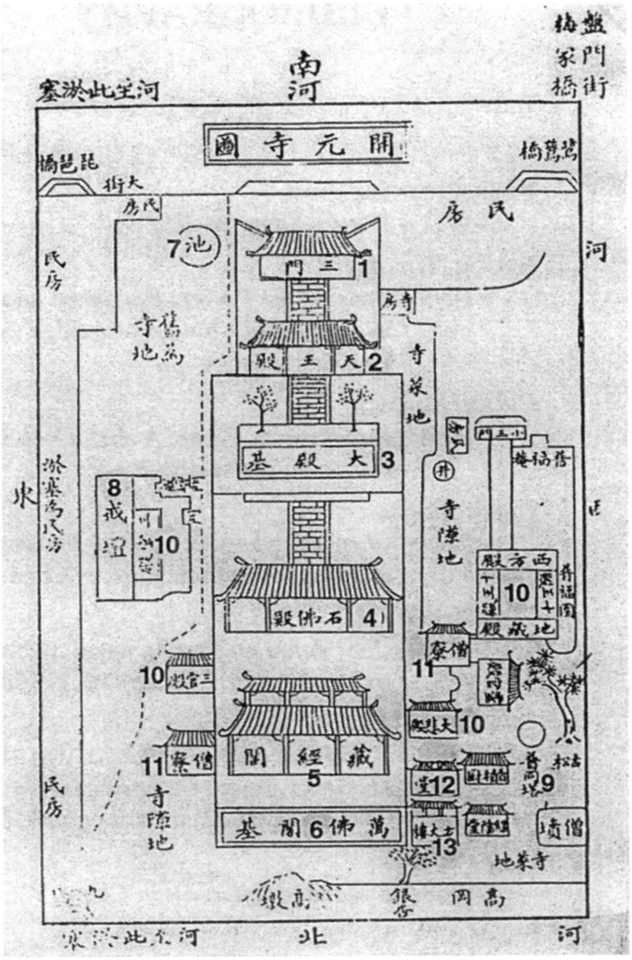

7 – *Layout of Kaiyuan si [50], from the monastery's gazetteer*
(Kaiyuan si zhi, *1922 edition)*

This illustration is typical of the plans found in traditionnal monastic gazetteers.

1. Gatehouse
2. Hall of the Guardian kings
3. Main hall (destroyed)
4. Hall of the stone Buddha
5. Library
6. Pavilion of the ten thousand Buddhas (destroyed)
7. Pond
8. ordination platform
9. Monastic cemetery and monks' colombarium
10. Hall to various Buddhas and deities
11. Monastic offices
12. Dharma hall
13. Abbot's quarters

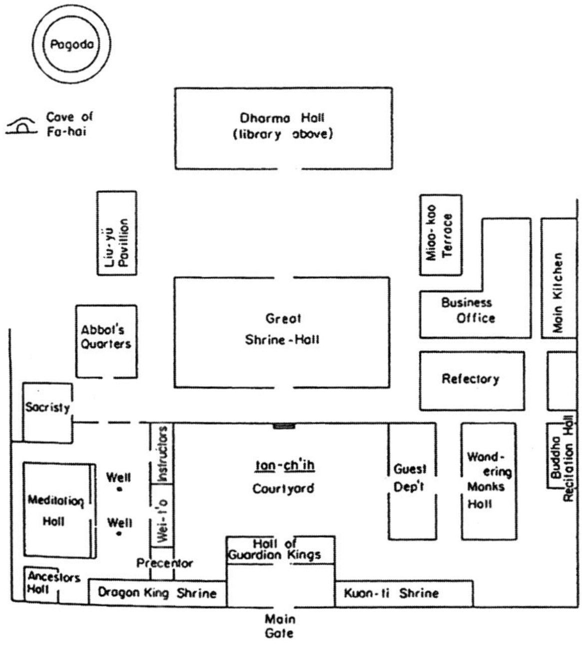

8 – *General arrangement of the courtyards at Jinshan si [46] Early 20th century*
(Welch 1967: 9)

BIBLIOGRAPHY

BOERSCHMANN, Ernst
1911 – *P'u-t'o Shan*, Berlin.

BROOK, Timothy
1993 – *Praying for Power: Buddhism and the Formation of Gentry Society in Late-Ming China*, Cambridge (Mass.) and London, Harvard University Press.

CH'EN, Kenneth
1964 – *Buddhism in China. A Historical Survey*, Princeton (New Jersey), Princeton University Press.

CHEN Mingda
1998 – *Chen Mingda gujianzhu yu diaosu shilun* [Historical essays on ancient architecture and sculpture by Chen Mingda], Beijing, Wenwu chubanshe.

CHAI Zejun
1999 – *Chai Zejun gu jianzhu wenji* [Collection of articles on ancient architecture by Chai Zejun], Beijing, Wenwu chubanshe.

COLLCUTT, Martin
1981 – *Five Mountains. The Rinzai Zen Monastic Institution in Medieval Japan*, Cambridge, Harvard University Press (Harvard East Asian Monograph, 85).

DAIJO Tokiwa
1938 – *Buddhist Monument in China*, V. 5, Tokyo.

EBERHARD, Wolfram
1964 – "Temple Building Activities in Medieval and Modern China, an Experimental Study", *Monumenta Serica* 23, p. 264-318.

ECKE, Gustav
1936-1937 – "The Institute for Research in Chinese Architecture", *Monumenta Serica* II, p. 448-474, summary of the fieldwork, list and bibliography of monuments rediscovered and studied by the Institute for Research in Chinese Architecture (Zhongguo yingzao xueshe).

FOULK, T. Griffith
1993 – "Myth, Ritual, and monastic Practice in Sung Ch'an Buddhism", *Religion and Society in Tang and Sung China*, Patricia Ebrey and Peter Gregory (eds), Honolulu, University of Hawaii Press, p. 147-208.

FU-CH'ÜAN, Lawrence
1982 – *Taiwanese Buddhism and Buddhist Temples*, Taipei, Pacific Cultural Foundation.

FU Xinian
1998 – *Fu Xinian jianzhu shilun wenji* [Collection of articles on the history of architecture by Fu Xinian], Beijing, Wenwu chubanshe.

GERNET, Jacques
1995 – *Buddhism in Chinese Society. An Economic History from the fifth to the tenth centuries*, Franciscus Verellen (trans.), New York, Columbia University Press [French original edition 1956].

GOOSSAERT, Vincent
2000a – *Dans les temples de la Chine*, Paris, Albin Michel.
2000b – "Counting the Monks. The 1736-39 Census of the Chinese Clergy", *Late Imperial China*, p. 21-2.

DE GROOT, J. J. M.
1893 – *Le Code du Mahāyāna en Chine. Son influence sur la vie monacale et sur le monde laïque*, Amsterdam, Johannes Müller.

HACKMANN, Heinrich
1902 – "Buddhist monastery life in China", *East of Asia Magazine* 1(3) (September), p. 239-261.

HE Xiaorong,
2000 – *Mingdai Nanjing siyuan yanjiu* [Buddhist Monasteries in Nanjing during the Ming], Beijing, Zhongguo shehui kexue chubanshe

ITÔ Chûta
1936 –*Tôyô kenchiku no kenkyû* [Studies in Far Eastern Architecture], Tôkyô.

LIANG Ssu-Cheng (Liang Sicheng) and FAIRBANK, Wilma
1984 – *A Pictorial History of Chinese Architecture: a Study of the Development of its Structural System and the Evolution of its Type*, Cambridge, The Massachussetts Institute of Technology (reprint 1991).

LIU Dunzhen
1984 – *Zhongguo gudai jianzhu shi* [History of ancient Chinese architecture], Beijing, Zhongguo jianzhu gongye chubanshe (reprint 1997).

LOVEDAY, Helen
2000 – "La bibliothèque tournante en Chine: quelques remarques sur son rôle et son évolution", *T'oung Pao* LXXXVI, p. 225-79.

MCDERMOTT, Joseph
1999 – "Emperor, élites and commoners: the community pact ritual of the late Ming", *State and court ritual in China*, Joseph McDermott (ed.), Cambridge, Cambridge University Press, p. 299-351.

NAQUIN, Susan
1998 – "Sites, saints, and sights at the Tanzhe Monastery", *Cahiers d'Extrême-Asie* 10, p. 183-211.

PIRAZZOLI T'SERSTEVENS, Michèle
1970 – *Chine*, Fribourg, Office du Livre (Architecture universelle).

PRIP-MOLLER, Johannes
1937 – *Chinese Buddhist Monasteries: their Plan and its Function as a Setting for Buddhist Monastic Life*, Copenhaguen and London (reprint Hong-Kong, Hong-Kong University Press, 1967).

REICHELT, Karl Ludvig
1927 – *Truth and Tradition in Chinese Buddhism*, Shanghai, Commercial Press.

SIRÉN, Oswald
1930 – *Histoire des arts anciens de la Chine*, vol. IV, *L'architecture*, Paris et Brussels, Van Oest.

SMITH, Richard J.
1991 – *Fortune-Tellers and Philosophers: Divination in Traditional Chinese Society*, Boulder (Colorado), San Francisco and Oxford, Westview Press.

SOPER, Alexander
1939-1940 – "Contribution to the Study of Sculpture and Architecture, III: Japanese Evidence for the History of the Architecture and Iconography of Chinese Buddhism", *Monumenta Serica* 4, p. 638-679.
1971 – "Architecture", *The Art and Architecture of China*, Laurence Sickman and Alexander Soper, p. 361-471, New Haven, London, Yale University Press (Pelican History of Art).

STEINHARDT, Nancy S.
1994 – "Liao: An architectural Tradition in the Making", *Artibus Asiae* 54 (1-2), 5-39.
1997 – *Liao Architecture*, Honolulu, University of Hawaii Press.

TANAKA Tôyôzô
1933 – "Archaic Type of Buddhist Temples", *Bijutsu kenkyû* 16.

WANG Yi-t'ung (trad.)
1984 – *A Record of Buddhist Monasteries in Lo-yang, by Yang Hsüan-chih*, Princeton, Princeton University Press.

WELCH, Holmes
1967 – *The Practice of Chinese Buddhism, 1900-1950*, Cambridge (Mass.), Harvard University Press.
1968 – *The Buddhist Revival in China*, Cambridge (Mass.), Harvard University Press.
1972 – *Buddhism under Mao*, Cambridge (Mass.), Harvard University Press.

YANG, C. K.
1961 – *Religion in Chinese Society. A Study of contemporary social functions of religion and some of their historical factors*, Berkeley, the University of California Press.

YÜ Chün-fang
1981 – *The Renewal of Buddhism in China. Chu-hung and the Late Ming Synthesis*, New York, Columbia University Press.

ZONG Yuangzhao (Ed.)
1986 – *History and Development of Chinese Architecture*, comp. by the Institute of the History of Natural Sciences (Chinese Academy of Sciences), trans. from Chinese, Beijing, China Academy of Sciences.

ZÜRCHER, Erik
1959 – *The Buddhist conquest of China*, Leiden, Brill, (2 vols.).

BUDDHIST MONASTERIES *IN SOUTHERN MONGOLIA*

Isabelle Charleux

From the end of the 16th century onwards, Tibetan Buddhism flourished among Southern Mongols, bringing revolutionary changes to their nomadic society. With the support of Mongol kings and, later, the Manchu emperors, the Gelugpa (*dGe-lugs-pa*) Buddhist institution expanded all over the country, while local religious life organised itself around Buddhist monasteries. Although Tibetan Buddhism was first introduced among the Mongols during the 13th century, it failed then to take hold in Mongols' hearts and very few monasteries were founded. Almost nothing of the present physical heritage of Mongol Buddhism dates from this period. Therefore, I will focus on the historical background and the architectural aspects of the Southern Mongolian monasteries from the 16th to the 20th century. Inner or Southern Mongolia[1] is today an "autonomous region" of the People's Republic of China, and has been largely settled by Han Chinese since the mid 19th century. Due to border modifications that occurred repeatedly during the 20th century, former Mongol territories now belong to other provinces of China (especially Liaoning), and thus are included in this survey.

This study is mainly based on fieldwork undertaken between 1993 and 1999, which allowed me to visit more than thirty monasteries. The data gathered on the field along with the historical documentation were exposed in detail in my dissertation thesis (Charleux 1998).

1. The former Outer Mongolia was part of the Qing empire from 1691 to 1911. Thereafter under the sway of the former Soviet Union, Mongolia is now a sovereign nation. Qalqa Mongols form the majority of its population.

The Buddhist Monastery, EFEO, 2003, p. 351-390

In Mongolia, as in Tibet, the frontiers between a monastery and a temple are blurred. Should we call by the same name small "temples"[2] kept by one or two monks, "monasteries" inhabited by ten monks yet attracting hundreds of them during festivals, and large permanent communities of over 500 monks? Mongolian monasteries and temples were called by different names, each with a precise original meaning:

- *süme*: sedentary monastery or temple sheltering a statue, without monks' dwelling;[3]
- *juu*: "image", then "temple", from the Tibetan *jo-bo*, the famous statue of Śākyamuni in Lhasa;[4]
- *küriye*: ring, enclosure, encampment, a nomadic monastery with a yurt or a wooden temple surrounded by monks' dwellings;
- *keyid*: hermitage.[5]

The oldest constructions were temples built to shelter an image of Buddha, while the first monastic communities lived in yurts (felt tents). Later on, *juu*, *süme* and *keyid* often became monasteries and *küriye* settled. Hermitages seem to have either completely disappeared or merged with the monasteries. Eventually, probably after the 17th century, all these appellations came to designate any kind of religious buildings, from small local temples to large monasteries (Pozdneev 1978 [1887]: 25; Miller 1959: 11-14). Nunneries never existed in Southern Mongolia – although old women sometimes took monastic vows, while staying at home.[6]

The main difference between a shrine, a temple and a monastery is thus a difference of size – size of the monastic communities and physical size of the architectural complex. Within a period of four centuries, many temples became monasteries and, during the present revival, old monasteries were revived as small temples. The adaptation to a local as to a large scale is one of the original characteristics of the Tibeto-Mongol institution.

2. We also use the term "temple" to designate a place of worship inside a monastery, often dedicated to particular deities or bodhisattvas.

3. *Süme* is also the official term for a Mongol monastery in Qing documents.

4. Transcribed *zhao* in Chinese.

5. *Küriye* and *keyid* are seldom used in Southern Mongolia.

6. In 1636 the Manchu emperor Abahai prohibited women to become nuns. There were a few exceptions among the Tümed, and nowadays in Northern Mongolia.

Buddhist monasteries in Southern Mongolia up to the 15th century

1. Introduction of Buddhism in the country

Mahāyāna Buddhism was initially introduced in the territory of Southern Mongolia during the Northern Wei (Toba) dynasty (386-534). The nomadic people who occupied this area later on, like the Kitan and the Jürchen, were also converted to Mahāyāna Buddhism; they used Buddhism as a state religion in order to unify their heterogeneous empire, to protect and legitimate their dynasty (Sinor 1990; Kessler *et al.* 1993). Large monasteries of the Kitan, who founded the Liao dynasty (916-1125), could be found in every city of their empire, such as Fengzhou (near Kökeqota), Qingzhou, and their five capital cities.[7] The main remaining sites are located in Chifeng district and in Liaoning province. Kitan Buddhist architecture was mainly of Chinese style and techniques. Except a few cave temples, seven to thirteen storeys Chinese-style pagodas are the only remains of their numerous foundations that dotted the whole Mongolia.[8] The Kitan cave monasteries of Γilubar juu [30][9] and Qianzhao miao, located near their upper capital (Shangjing, Baγarin banner) became under the Qing dynasty (1644-1911) important monasteries and pilgrimage sites.

The Jürchen, who founded the Jin dynasty (1115-1234), reoccupied and restored many Liao Buddhist sites. Several Jin pagodas have been preserved. In the Western part of the territory, the Tangγud founded the Xia empire (1032-1227) whose nobility was first converted to Mahāyāna, and then, in the 12th century, to Tibetan Buddhism. They built monasteries, invited Tibetan lamas at their court, exchanged *sūtras* and paintings with the Mahāyānist Song, Liao and Jin people. Their Buddhist vestiges in Inner Mongolia include ruins of monasteries, Tibetan style stūpas in Qaraqota city in present Alashan Ejin region, and Chinese style square pagodas (Linrothe 1995 and 1998; *Sulla via della seta* 1993).

2. Buddhist monasteries under the Yuan dynasty: 12th-14th c.

Tibetan Buddhism (often referred to as "Lamaism") was first introduced among the Mongols during the 13th century.[10] The descendants of Γengis qan who founded a universal empire met with different religions: Nestorianism, Buddhism, Taoism, Islam. Those who conquered China (and called themselves the Yuan dynasty, 1277-1368) adopted Buddhism as a state religion, seeing a political advantage in an alliance with the flourishing culture of Tibet. The emperors, especially Qubilai (r. 1260-1294), ordered the conversion of the Yuan empire to Tibetan Buddhism, patronised constructions, translations and debates. Several Sakyapa (*Sa-skya-pa*) lamas contracted with the Mongol rulers a *yon-mchod* (donator-lama) relationship, like 'Phags-pa, who served as Qubilai's spiritual adviser. In this personal relationship, the lama recognised the Qan as an incarnation of a Bodhisattva and a universal emperor (*cakravartin*); in exchange the Qan gave him titles, honours, protection and patronage. The motivations for the

7. The only complete study in a Western language is Steinhardt 1997.

8. Such as Wanbuhuayanjing ta of Daming monastery (Fengzhou, near Kökeqota), three pagodas in the Central capital (Dading, west of Ningcheng), South and North pagoda of Shangjing, Baita of Qingzhou.

9. The number in brackets refers to the list of cited monasteries in table 3 and on the map p. 362-364.

10. On the general history of Tibetan Buddhism in Mongolia, Heissig 1973 [1970].

Qan's interest and patronage were not only religious: he expected his rule to be legitimated as he was identified as Great Qan, ruler of all the Mongol domains. Lamas were appointed to high offices and monasteries were built with state funds.

The influence of Karmapa (*ka-rma-pa*) and Sakyapa lamas at the Yuan court affected essentially the Mongol nobility. Tibetan Buddhism remained mainly a urban religion organised around the imperial monasteries of Northern China, and very few monasteries were founded in Southern Mongolia. Shamanism was still the religion of the majority of the Mongols, while the Chinese were mostly unaffected by this policy.

Almost nothing remains of the architecture of these few Yuan foundations, except some Tibetan-style stūpas. They probably mixed different styles, mainly Chinese and Tibetan, but also imported ones. Qubilai recruited a Muslim architect to help him plan his capital city, Dadu/Beijing/Dadu. Later he employed other foreigners, including the Nepalese sculptor and architect Anige, to build monasteries in Dadu. The Yuan emperors wanted to be perceived as the rulers of a universal empire by using multiethnic styles of architecture. However, the excavations of Shangdu (or Kaiping), their summer capital, revealed that the architectures were mainly Chinese.

Some Yuan monasteries are known by archaeological vestiges in the territory of Southern Mongolia, such as the Sakyapa monasteries in and around Shangdu (the largest were Huayan si and Qianyuan si),[11] and the Longxing si. Isolated pagodas are still standing in Yingchang (Kesigten banner) and Kailu cities. The Longquan si [24] is the only one that was still in activity under the Qing dynasty, but nothing of the Yuan buildings has remained.

Of these nomadic people who once occupied the territory of Southern Mongolia up to the 16th century, very few Buddhist remains are left, and nowadays all are deserted. More have been preserved in China proper because they were restored by the following dynasties up to the Qing. Most of their Buddhist monuments were located in settled urban agglomerations, ruins of which still dot the countryside. A few archaeological sites are documented by Russian and Japanese expeditions of the late 19th and early 20th century, and by recent Chinese excavations.

History of Buddhism in Southern Mongolia from the 15th century onwards

1. The Dark Age, 1368-16th c.

After the fall of the Yuan dynasty in 1368, most of the Mongols returned to nomadic life in their homeland. During this "Dark Age", virtually nothing is known of Buddhism in Mongolia: it seems to have retreated when faced with the resurgence of Shamanism (Serruys 1963 and 1966; Jagchid 1972; Charleux 1998: 15-24). However, the speed and the strength of the revival of Buddhism during the 16th century can only be explained by the fact that it still coexisted with Shamanistic practices during this period. Moreover, Southern Mongols had diplomatic, commercial or bellicose relations with the surrounding Buddhist tribes of Gansu, Turkestan and Amdo (A-mdo, especially the Kukunor area) who certainly influenced their Buddhist renaissance. There were probably nomadic monasteries adapted to the pastoral life, too small to be recorded in the historical sources.

11. Shangdu was imagined as a maṇḍala, surrounded by eight monasteries at the cardinal plus intermediary points. The place is also known as "a hundred and eight monasteries". According to Delege 1998: 61, there were 167 monasteries in and around Shangdu, yet no archaeological evidence confirms their existence.

Indeed, the recently discovered Baiyanyao caves show a rare case of the continuity of a Buddhist presence from the Northern Wei (386-534) up to the Ming period, 1368-1644 (Charleux 1998: 18).

During the 15th century, the Western Mongols, who founded the Oyirad khanship, adopted Buddhism in order to legitimise their power. Their monasteries were probably also moveable, nothing having been left after the fall of their kingdom.

2. The Mongolian renaissance of the 16th c.

Tibetan Buddhism was officially re-introduced at the end of the 16th century by Altan qan (1507-1582), a descendant of Gengis qan and leader of numerous military campaigns. During the early period of this cultural "renaissance" (1566-1634), unreformed schools of Tibetan Buddhism (Sakyapa, Nyingmapa (*rNying-ma-pa*), Karmapa) were in competition with the growing Gelugpa school founded by Tsong-kha-pa (1357-1419).[12] Monks from Amdo, Gansu, Central Tibet but also from China competed to convert the Qan.

Altan's Tümed tribe lived in the rich plain situated in the northeast corner of the loop of the Yellow River. Buddhist predication there was part of a larger socio-economic change: the construction of towns, palaces and houses preceded the foundation of temples by Altan qan. From 1546-1550 onwards, the Tümed Mongols used the manpower of 50,000 to 100,000 Chinese immigrants and prisoners (perhaps as numerous as the Tümed themselves) who developed agriculture and contributed their technical and architectural skills. Altan qan first constructed in the mid-16th century a palace and a town commonly referred to as Yeke bayising.[13] In 1572, the year following the Sino-Mongol peace treaty re-establishing border relations, Altan qan founded a new capital, Kökeqota (Hohhot, "the Blue City", Ch. Huhehaote).[14] The establishment of these urban centres offered new opportunities for craftsmen, thus inspiring a renaissance of the arts and architecture. The acceleration of the settling process among the Tümed encouraged the foundation of fixed religious centres.

From 1572 to 1577, the Mongols repeatedly asked the Chinese court for religious texts, images and other worship items, as well as for monks and carpenters. The propagation of Buddhism in Mongolia initially came from Amdo and China, which explains the numerous Chinese features of the Buddhist monastery in Mongolia.[15] Kökeqota was then inhabited by Mongols and Chinese who seemed to cohabit peacefully,[16] contributing to the foundation of the same temples and monasteries. The Blue City quickly became the economic, cultural and religious capital of Mongolia, redistributing the Chinese products from the market-towns of the Great Wall to the other tribes, who, save the Ordos, refused to sign any treaty with the Chinese. The commercial relations between the tribes contributed to the rapid diffusion of Buddhism.

---

12. "The Virtuous", also called "Yellow hats" or "Yellow religion" in China, in Mongolia and in Western countries because of the colour of their hats. Compared to the "Red hats" or unreformed schools, the Gelugpas insist on strict monastic discipline, on celibacy and on the "gradual way" of the spiritual formation.

13. Litt. "The Big house". *Bayising* first refers to the houses of Chinese settlers in contrast to the Mongolian yurt.

14. Kökeqota is now the capital city of Inner Mongolia. On its history: Hyer 1982; Charleux 1998.

15. At first, for several reasons, the Tümed did not directly address their demands to Central Tibet, as one may have expected. No official relation with Tibet was established before 1577.

16. In the end of the 16th century the Chinese immigrants suddenly disappeared from the records: some of them returned to China or died during the outbreaks of smallpox epidemics; perhaps others stayed in Southern Mongolia and became mongolised.

The Tümed and their allies, the Ordos and Qaracin tribes eventually gave pre-eminence to the Gelugpa school in 1578, when they met its hierarch, bSod-nams rgya-mstho (1543-1588), at the Kukunor lake. Altan qan gave him the title of Dalai Lama. He was in turn recognised as a reincarnation of Qubilai qan, reinstating the interdependent relationship between Mongolian kings and Tibetan lamas.[17] The adoption of Tibetan Buddhism had mutual political advantages for the Tümed and for the Gelugpas. Altan qan, acting as a *cakravartin* king, assumed a legitimacy based not only on inheritance but also on reincarnation. He hoped to unify again the Mongol tribes in a confederation based on this universal and organised religion, which had attracted the settled Tümed nobility by its sophisticated rituals, doctrine, and literature. For his part, the Dalai Lama hoped to find in these new allies a strong military support that could allow the Gelugpas to consolidate their influence and to conquer the whole of Tibet.

From this time onwards, the Tibeto-Mongol relations intensified while the Sino-Mongol relations were limited to economic exchanges. The Mongol princes all wanted to visit the holy city of Lhasa and to meet the Dalai Lama, in order to either reinforce the relation or to establish a concurrent relation. The trip of the Dalai Lama to Mongolia in 1586-87 expanded the young faith, provoking a huge wave of conversions and foundations of monasteries. Within the next few decades, ordinary Mongols became Buddhist, either voluntarily or under pressure. The Tibeto-Mongol connection became even stronger when the Fourth Dalai Lama Yon-tan rgya-mtsho (1589-1617), the reincarnation of bSod-nams rgya-mtsho, was recognised in the person of a great-grandson of Altan qan.

The mobile monasteries that followed Altan qan in his military campaigns progressively settled: a small temple was probably founded in Kökeqota around 1572. In 1575 Altan qan founded the Mayidari-yin juu (temple of Maitreya) [3] (Charleux 1998: 44-48, 68-71; Charleux 1999), maybe on the site of his former palace, and the Yeke juu, "Big Temple" [1], a few years later, the first two of a large princely monasteries that survive today.

3. The early 17th c. and the elimination of the unreformed schools

The first foundations were made by members of the gengisqanid nobility; then followed "spontaneous" communities formed at the end of the 16th century around monks and hermits arriving from Tibet or from within Mongolia. Missionaries from Central and Eastern Tibet, but also from Chinese Tibeto-Mongol centres and members of the Mongolian nobility such as Neyici toyin (1557-1653) extended their activity all over Mongolia. They converted princes, established congregations and acted as ambassadors mediating the internal disputes between the various tribes. The missionary struggle against Shamanistic practices was especially tough in the Eastern part of Southern Mongolia.[18] Buddhist missionaries also obtained favours from the rising Manchu dynasty, who gave them money, *shabinar*[19] and land to establish monasteries.

17. Altan qan enacted new Buddhist laws for Mongolia, including the prohibition of human sacrifices and *ongγod* (Shamanistic figurines) worshipping, and the conferment of status and privileges for monks.

18. Heissig 1953. Shamanism was never completely eliminated, and Buddhism had to accommodate with several Shamanistic practices.

19. "Disciples", laymen given by a prince to a monastery.

The history of foundations reflects the irresistible progression of the Gelugpa "orthodoxy". The reasons why the Tümed Mongols chose the Gelugpa school rather than an unreformed one remain unclear. They probably gave their preference to this young school because the Karmapas were too close to Beijing, while the Sakyapas were politically feeble and lacking missionary ardour. Other princes like Ligdan qan (1592-1634), descendant of the elder son of Gengis qan, hence the legitimate emperor of all Mongols, "Qan of qan-s", patronised the unreformed orders. The Gelugpa school gained the support of the Manchu dynasty and then the religious monopoly over all Mongolia after the defeat of Ligdan qan, who failed to reunite the fragmented tribes.[20] The monasteries of the unreformed orders, with a very few exceptions, were probably converted into Gelugpa ones, although the sources are silent on this subject.

4. The heydays of the Manchu period: 1636-1840

By 1636, all the Mongol princes had negotiated alliances with the Manchus or had become their subjects following military defeat. Seduced by the Manchu support of Tibetan Buddhism, they recognised the emperor as their legitimate ruler.[21] Their cavalry significantly increased the military might of the Manchus who conquered China, taking the mandate of Heaven from the fallen Ming dynasty in 1644. At the same time, in 1642, the Western Mongol Gusri qan conquered Central Tibet for the Fifth Dalai Lama (1617-1682). The centralisation of the political and spiritual powers in Beijing and, in a lesser degree, in Lhasa established a new deal that challenged the previous independence of the Mongolian Buddhist centres.

The Manchu emperors of the new Qing dynasty became in the 17th century the masters of a vast empire including Mongolia, China, Tibet and Eastern Turkestan. It was by that time that a distinction was introduced between the Southern or Inner Mongols, who were by now Qing subjects, within the borders of the Qing empire, and the Northern Qalqa or Outer Mongols, who were outside that border. By 1691 the Qalqa Mongols were so pressured by their enemies, the Western Mongol Jungars, that they called the Manchus for help and submitted to their rule.

After the Manchu conquest of China in 1644, the situation became stable in Southern Mongolia. The Qing established new political and institutional structures to control the society. The traditional economy was transformed by the creation of banners with a fixed territory, hence restricting the mobility of the nomads. Gengisqanid princes were appointed rulers of these banners and thus officials of the empire, subordinate to the Lifan yuan (Court of Colonial Affairs) in Beijing. The Qing tried to isolate Mongolia from China and from Tibet, prohibiting the Chinese to settle there.

Early on, the Qing encouraged and patronised Buddhist foundations in order to maintain peace among the Mongols, and especially to solve the conflict between the Qalqas and the Jungars. According to the Kangxi emperor (1662-1722), who hoped that the pacific message of Buddhist doctrine could prevent the Mongols to rebel, "building only one temple is equivalent to feeding a hundred thousand soldiers in Mongolia". The Qing

20. Ligdan qan attempted to restore the glory of the Mongol empire by terrorising other tribes to submit to his harsh rule, causing the majority of his subjects to finally join the Manchus.

21. The Manchu emperor proclaimed himself as Qan of qan-s, Yuan emperors' true heir because he appropriated Qubilai's imperial seal and the sacred image of Mahākāla carved under the Yuan dynasty, then transmitted to Ligdan qan. Moreover, he presented himself as an incarnation of the Bodhisattva Mañjuśrī, spiritually equal to the Dalai and to the Panchen Lama.

established the lCang-skya qutuγtu, a reincarnation discovered in Amdo, as the spiritual leader of Inner Mongolian Buddhism, to counterweight the Boγdo gegen of Outer Mongolia. In order to facilitate the control of the Buddhist institution, they made Beijing into one of the major centres of Inner Mongolian Buddhism. Imperial foundations in Beijing, Jehol and in Mongolia proper (especially in Dolonnor/Doluγan naγur), marked important political events. All these "imperial monasteries" were characterised by a monumental and syncretic architecture devised to impress the Mongols.

These few prestigious constructions did not overshadow the numerous private foundations that testify of the faith of the people. Although their political role was limited to a banner or a district, the academic and spiritual renown of monasteries founded by lamas or Mongol princes crossed the borders. All over the country, small communities developed into large "academic" monasteries,[22] with colleges for the study of the doctrine, esotericism, Kālacakra (including astrology, mathematics and divination), and medicine, that attracted the most learned Mongols. Because academic studies were expensive, rules were strict and examinations difficult, and only about 1% of the monastic population entered colleges. The monks had to travel to famous monasteries of Southern Mongolia (Badγar coyiling süme for instance), then to Kumbum, Labrang or Beijing and finally to Lhasa to pass the higher degrees.

In other words, by that time, a three-fold categorisation among Mongolian Buddhist places had become clear. It distinguished:

1 – "Imperial monasteries": four monasteries founded by the Qing emperor and twenty "imperialised" old monasteries of Kökeqota.[23] All are located in banners directly administrated by the Lifan yuan (because of the elimination of local Mongol nobility who rebelled against the Qing). The emperor took the place of the Mongol prince in the role of the donator.

2 – Monasteries founded by a monk or offered by a layman to a famous monk. The monk became the abbot and his reincarnation, found after his death, guaranteed a long-date reputation for the monastery.

3 – "Banner monasteries": local monasteries, founded by and belonging to a prince or a lay community. Some of them attracted famous lamas and became large academic monasteries. The modern chief-towns formed around such banner monasteries.

The monastic institution expanded its influence to become the dominant force in the culture and the economy of Mongolia. Monasteries were not only spiritual centres of learning but also played an important role in finance, trade and patronage of arts. Moreover, the management of their flocks and herds provided a livelihood for many dependent people called *shabinar*. They promoted changes in the traditional Mongol society and in the physical appearance of the country, counterbalancing the impact of sinisation.[24]

---

22. Monasteries are classified by Nagao Gajin 1991 [1947] into "academic" and "ritualistic". The first ones place their major emphasis on learning, the second ones, on worship and rituals.

23. For all these imperial monasteries, the Lifan yuan enacted an ordinance fixing the status and income of the monastery, appointed its administrators, gave an official title to the monastery and ordination certificates to a quota of monks. When monastic communities were created *ex nihilo*, every banner was ordered to send monks and money to support them. Besides the imperial monasteries, other large monasteries received an official title with a wooden board.

24. For the economic, institutional and socio-political aspects of Mongol Buddhism, Miller 1959.

Every family aspired to have at least one child accepted into the monkhood. Quotas of monks imposed by the Qing to the largest monasteries[25] were not respected, therefore the vast majority of monks was "unofficial". Among them, some[26] lived permanently in the monastery and depended on it. However, the majority of them were just novices; they worked as herders or farmers most of the time, coming to the monastery only to attend the festivals. Others were wandering monks, beggars, bards or pilgrims. Hence, by the middle of the 19th century, between 30% and 65% of the male population of the banners had taken monastic vows, and the largest congregations gathered several thousands of monks.

Monks were often travelling to Tibet and China (especially Beijing and mount Wutai) for scholarly, diplomatic or pilgrimage purposes. High ranking lamas occupied a privileged position, all the more so since the lay nobility did not, like in Tibet, counter-balance them. The clerical hierarchy was equated with the civil one in the Manchu administrative system, the highest rank being the *qutuγtu* (reincarnated monks). There were in the 19th century 157 reincarnations recognised by the Lifan yuan in Inner Mongolia. Exempted from taxation and corvée labour, they accumulated considerable property, wealth and labour force, exploiting an important population of *shabinar*. The most learned ones were translators of Buddhist texts, writers, painters, sculptors and architects.

5. The end of the Qing dynasty: 1840-1911

When the ideological and economic conjuncture was turned upside down after 1840 because of the Chinese internal crisis and recession, the Buddhist church lost the support of the court. The ban on Chinese immigration was lifted, and colonisation began at a rapid pace. As a result of one hundred fifty years of immigration, the population of Inner Mongolia is now overwhelmingly Chinese, Mongols representing only 16%. Moreover, during the many upheavals of this troubled period, many monasteries were abandoned, destroyed or squatted. From 1862 to 1877 the Chinese Muslims' rebellion destroyed most of the monasteries in Ordos and Alashan. The imperial monasteries rapidly declined, but independent monasteries continued to prosper until the beginning of the 20th century. Paradoxically this period witnessed an efflorescence in literature and arts, as shown by the bronze workshops of Dolonnor for instance.

In the beginning of the 20th century, there were about 1,340 monasteries and temples[27] in an area with less than two million inhabitants, and an average of twenty monasteries per banner. Compared to the population, monasteries were more numerous *Table I p. 360* in pastoral regions of Ordos, Ulagan cabu, Caqar and Sili-yin γoul, and less numerous in agricultural regions of the north-east. The density of religious buildings was higher in the Tümed and Ordos regions, probably because their construction began as soon as the 16th century. The apparent disparities between different areas can also be explained *Table II p. 360* by the heterogeneity of sources and by the concentration of monks in the largest monasteries in the beginning of the 20th century, forsaking smaller ones. In the 1930's

25. The official monks received from the Lifan yuan an ordination certificate and a prebend. They were exempted from military service, taxation and corvée labour.

26. Initiation degrees are exactly the same as in Tibet. A fully ordained monk is a *gelong*, from Tibetan *dge-slong*. Gelugpa monks are not supposed to marry.

27. According to estimations based on Mongolian, Chinese and Japanese sources. Charleux 1998: 218-222. The figures of Table 1 are global estimations.

and 1940's, the only two large academic monasteries in activity were Badɣar coyiling süme [4] and Bandida gegen süme [18]. At the end of the Qing dynasty, about 5% of the monasteries had more than 500 monks,[28] a concentration which was comparable to that of Tibet and Northern Mongolia. These larger and more documented monasteries tend to conceal the number and dispersion of small local monasteries in Southern Mongolia.

Table III p. 362

Table I

Number of monasteries compared to population and area at the begining of the 20th century

Leagues	Population 1911 census	Surface km2	Number of. monasteries	Density of popu.lation	Density of mon. for 1000 km2	Nb. of mon. for1000 inhab.
Tümed of Kökeqota	56 337	20 000	41	2,82	2,05	0,73
Ordos (Yeke juu)	66 096	100 000	274	0,66	2,74	4,15
Ulaɣan cabu	52 550	110 000	118	0,48	1,07	2,25
Alashan	24 942	270 000	24	0,09	0,09	0,96
Caqar	42 211	75 000	92	0,56	1,23	2,18
Sili-yin ɣoul	54 297	105 000	130	0,52	1,24	2,39
Josutu	237 195	30 000	282	7,91	9,40	1,19
Juu uda	274 633	90 000	107	3,05	1,19	0,39
Jerim	561 909	120 000	197	4,68	1,64	0,35
Barɣa	60 933	250 000	42	0,24	0,17	0,69
Yeke mingɣan	4110	?	34	-	-	8,27
Buteha	59 282	?	-	-	-	-
Southern Mongolia	1 494 495	1 170 000	1341	1,28	1,15	0,90

Table II

Maximum number of monks per monastery in Southern Mongolia at the end of theQing dynasty

The number of monasteries counting less than 500 monks is the substraction of the two previous columns from the first one

Number of monasteries	Total nb. of monasteries	> 1000 monks Nb. mon.	% total	500-1000 monks Nb. mon.	% total	< 500 monks Nb. mon.	% total
Tümed of Kökeqota	41	3	7,3%	1	2,4%	37	90,2%
Ordos (Yeke juu)	274	2	0,7%	7	2,5%	265	96,7%
Ulaɣan cabu	118	3	2,5%	3	2,5%	112	94,9%
Alashan	24	4	16,6%	2	8,3%	18	75%
Caqar	92	3	3,3%	1	1,1%	88	95,6%
Sili-yin ɣoul	130	2	1,5%	5	3,8%	123	94,6%
Josutu	282	3	1,1%	8	2,8%	271	96,1%
Juu uda	107	1	0,9%	13	12,1%	93	96,1%
Jerim	197	3	1,5%	3	1,5%	191	97%
Barɣa	42	0	-	1	2,4%	41	97,6%
Yekemingɣan	34	-		-		34	100%
Southern Mongolia	1 341	24	1,8%	44	3,3%	1 273	94,9%

28. For descriptions of the largest monasteries: Qiao Ji 1994; Delege 1998.

6. Present situation

Most of the monasteries have been destroyed at the beginning of the century and during the iconoclast Cultural Revolution (Charleux 2001). Preserved architectures were emptied of their statues, paintings and sacred books; the monks' dwellings and lateral monastic buildings were destroyed. Since the partial authorisation of religious activities at the end of the seventies, between one and three monasteries were reopened and re-occupied by a few monks in every banner or county under public or private initiative. The Buddhist revival was strong in the eighties and has become more cautious in the last decade. The more intense manifestations of religious life are seen during the great annual festivals, which attract many Mongolian, but also Han Buddhists. Pilgrimages, cult to local gods and *oboγa* (cairns, pronounced *ovoo*) became popular again. *figure 5 p. 372*

The revived Buddhist institution, subordinate to the Chinese National Buddhist Association, remains strictly controlled by the state, and very few people are allowed to become a monk. Some young monks receive a basic religious education in Buddhist schools of Inner Mongolia, Kumbum (sKu-'bum, in Amdo) or Beijing.[29] The monastic communities are very small compared to the situation at the turn of the century. The largest monasteries (housing from 500 to 2,000 monks before) have nowadays 30 to 40 monks plus some unofficial monks[30]. The People's Republic did not recognise new reincarnation in Inner Mongolia, but the Dalai Lama recently recognised the reincarnation of the lCang-skya qutuγtu, who lives in India.

Even when in activity, monasteries are considered as museums under the administration of the Bureau of "Cultural Heritage". In 1995, 74 reopened monasteries received national or provincial protection. Twenty-seven of them had been partially rebuilt after having been severely damaged or razed to the ground. In the eighties, the authorities invested fifteen million yuan in reconstruction and restoration of the main historic and scenic monasteries. But official protection does not mean conservation, except when a quick profit can be expected from tourism. There is no sustained policy and punctual restorations often go with the sinisation and/or folklorisation of the monastery (building of Chinese pavilions, stone inscriptions, shops and even Disneyland-like attractions).

Today, probably a hundred monasteries are in activity, some of them waiting for official recognition. Scattered data on some banners suggest that many non-official small monasteries have been locally reconstructed without reporting to the authorities. Today's active monasteries are located in the historical Kökeqota region, in villages and in remote places inhabited by Mongol nomads and farmers who support them.[31] In rural areas where Chinese are more numerous than Mongols, or where Mongols are sinicised (the southern part of Inner Mongolia), there is no rebuilding. Mongol monasteries previously situated in remote areas, far from urban centres are now integrated in Chinese villages or settlements, in towns or in industrial areas. Today's largest Inner Mongolian towns are mainly inhabited by Chinese people.[32] The old capital city Kökeqota still has two active monasteries, but the "new" big towns – Baotou (Bogutu), Jining, Chifeng, Hailar – and smaller county seats – Xilinhot (Sili-yin qota), Dongsheng, Bayanhot (Bayan qota), Wulanhot (Ulaγan qota), Balinzuoqi, Balinyouqi (Baγarin Left and Right banners) etc. – have no monastery at all, or an old monastery turned into a museum.

30. Among the 31 monasteries I visited, 20 of them were active. One claimed to have 100 monks, two had 40 monks, three had 30 monks, one had 20 monks, 13 had between one to 15 monks.

31. Nine out of twenty are in remote areas, six in small villages and five in towns.

32. Mongols represent only 5% of the population of Kökeqota city. The Chinese there have a few Buddhist (and Taoist) temples but I do not know of any Chinese monastery.

Modern monasteries have to be economically self-sufficient, so they engage in the service industry and exploit their "relics". Yet they cannot revive the old economic relationship with the laymen. The Buddhist revival (survival?) is now threatened by the generation gap within the clergy, the superficial training of young monks, the folklorisation of the sites, and the impoverishment of rural Mongols. On the other hand, spontaneous rebuilding of a monastery by young monks trained in Kumbum shows instances of a genuine, popular revival.

General location and density of the monasteries

Table III *This table gives the common names of the monasteries, their location (town, tribe or banner, with their early 20th century definition), the main dates of their fondation and the present state of preservation. Chinese names ending by* si *(monastery) are titles given by theLifan yuan. Twenty-six "large" but poorly documented monasteries are not listed here.*

Abbreviations – W.P.: Well preserved; P.P.: Partly preserved; D.: Destroyed; R.: Rebuilt

Tümed of Kökeqota

1. Yeke juu (Dazhao 大召, Hongci si 弘慈寺, Wuliang si 無量寺), Kökeqota, 1579-1580, W.P
2. Siregetü juu ("Xilitu zhao", Yanshou si 延壽寺), Kökeqota, 1585 — 1616, W.P
3. Mayidari-yin süme ("Meidai zhao" 美岱召, Lingjue si 靈覺寺, Shouling si 壽靈寺), east of Baotou, 1575 — 1606, W.P

Ulaγan cabu league

4. Badγar coyiling süme (Udan juu, "Wudang zhao", Guangjue si 廣覺寺), north-east of Baotou, 1727-1749, W.P
5. Mergen juu (Guangfa si 廣法寺), west of Baotou, 1677 or 1702, P.P
6. Köndenen juu (Faxi si 法喜寺), Baotou district, 1713 or 1729, P.P
7. Beyile-yin süme (Bailing miao, Guangfu si 廣福寺), Darqan wang, 1703, rebuilt in 1925, P.P
8. Sira mören süme (Xilamulun miao, Puhe si 普和寺), Dörben keüked, 1758, P.P
9. Bayan shanda-yin süme ("Shanda" miao), Urad, Rear banner, 1738, D, R

Ordos : Yeke juu league

10. Jungγar juu (Baotang si 寶堂寺), Jungγar, 1623 — 1920-1922, W.P
11. Üüsin juu (Γanjuur nom-un süme), Üüsin, 1713 — 1764, P.P

Alashan banners

12. Aγui-yin süme ("Agui" miao, Chongcheng si 崇乘寺), Left banner, 1798, D, R
13. Baraγun keyid (Helanshan nansi, Guangzong si 廣宗寺), Left banner, 1756-1757, D, R
14. Jegün keyid (Helanshan beisi, Fuyin si 福因寺), Left banner, 1804, D, R
15. Yamun süme (Yanfu si 延福寺), Bayanqota, 1733, W.P

Caqar banners (these banners are now divided between Sili-yin γoul league and Hebei)

16. Köke süme (Huizong si 彙宗寺), Dolonnor, 1691-1711, D
17. Sira süme (Shanyin si 善因寺), Dolonnor, 1727-1731, D

Sili-yin γoul league

18. Bandida gegen süme (Beizi miao 貝子廟, Chongshan si 崇善寺), Sili-yin qota (Abaγanar), 1729, P.P
19. Caγan oboγa süme, Sünid, Left banner, 1714, P.P
20. Blama-yin küriye ("Lama kulun miao"), Üjümücin, Right banner, Qing, ?

continued page 364

Map of the largest monasteries of Southern Mongolia

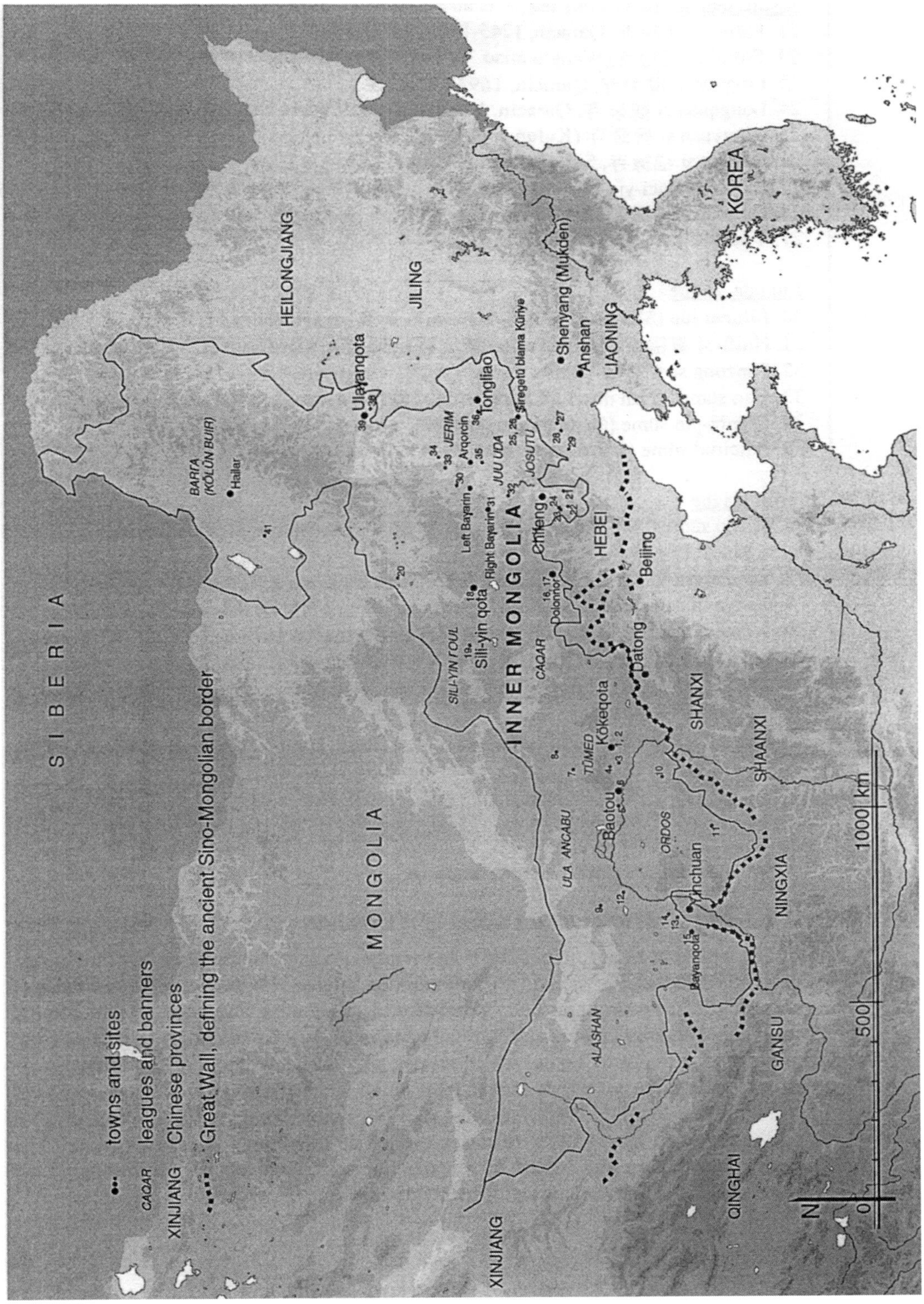

Table III continued

Josutu league (part of this league is now included in Liaoning province)
21. Falun si 法輪寺, Qaracin, 1745-1803, P.P
22. Fuhui si 福會寺(Wangfu miao 王府廟), Qaracin, Kangxi reign, P.P
23. Lingyue si 靈悅寺, Qaracin, 1692-1711, P.P
24. Longquan si 龍泉寺, Qaracin, Yuan — Qing, P.P
25. Xingyuan si 興源寺 (Kulun si 庫倫寺), Siregetü blama küriye, end of Ming or 1649, P.P
26. Fuyuan si 福緣寺, Siregetü blama küriye, 1733-1742, W.P
27. Caγan diyanci-yin keyid ("Folama" miao, Ruiying si 瑞應寺), East Tümed, 1640-1650, P.P
28. Huining si 惠寧寺, East Tümed, 1738-1757, W. P
29. Youshun si 佑順寺, East Tümed, 1698-1707, W. P

Juu uda league
30. Γilubar juu (Shanfu si 善福寺), Baγarin, Left banner, about 1770, P.P
31. Huifu si 薈福寺(Dongda miao 東大廟), Baγarin, Right banner, 1706, W. P
32. Fanzong si 梵宗寺 (Beida miao 北大廟), Ongniγud, 1743-1755, P.P
33. Qan süme ("Han miao", Cheng'en si 誠恩寺), Arqorcin, 1674, P.P
34. Gembi-yin süme (Guang'en si 廣恩寺), Arqorcin, 1816, D,R
35. Balcirud süme (Baoshan si 寶善寺), Arqorcin, 1665 or 1689, P.P

Jerim league
36. Morin süme ("Moli miao", Jining si 集寧寺), Darqan wang, Shunzhi reign or 1679, 1801, 1826, P.P
37. Shongqoru-yin süme (Shuangfu si 雙福寺), Boγu wang, 1680, P.P
38. Gegen miao (Fantong si 梵通寺), Jasaγtu wang, 1740, D, R?
39. Wangye miao 王爺廟(Puhui si 普慧寺), Ulaγanqota, 1619 or 1691, D, R?
40. Bayan qosiγun keyid (Xiafu si 遐福寺), Tüsiyetü wang, 1813, D, R?

Barγa banners (Kölün buir)
41. Γanjuur süme (Shouning si 壽寧寺), New Barγa, Left banner, 1781-1784, D
42. Baraγun süme (Xi miao 西廟), Left banner, 1887, D, R.

1. The monastery and its environment

1.1 The ideal and actual siting of a monastery

fig. 1 opposite page

The choice of an auspicious site is an essential stage of the founding of a monastery. For Southern Mongols, there is no contradiction between Chinese and Tibetan rules of geomancy,[33] the two systems being considered as equivalent. The work requires a monk astrologer, who uses Tibetan and Mongol handbooks — the latter being translated from the Chinese. A famous Chinese *fengshui* specialist can be invited too. The astrologer is further consulted to tell where to search for building materials and to solve problems of "pollution" by building stūpas to tame evil forces, by changing the orientation of a building or even by deciding to move the whole monastery to another place. The construction is then punctuated by a series of rituals such as the propitiation of the deities of the soil and the consecration ceremony.

33. Indeed, as early as the 7th century Tibetan geomancy was influenced by Chinese geomancy.

1 – *Sira mören süme [8]*
Mural painting depicting the ideal features of a site

(photo I. Charleux)

Rules of geomancy are so strict that the choice of a site presenting the ideal characteristics can last several years. The location of mountains and cliffs, the view of the site, the direction of flow of the nearby rivers, the location of wells, wooded areas, auspicious or inauspicious signs must all be interpreted on a symbolical level. For instance a mountain looking like a bell or a site compared to an eight-petals lotus are excellent omens. Besides the Daqing,[34] Helan and Kinggan (Xing'an) ranges, Southern Mongolia is not a mountainous country, so the founders have to content themselves with hillocks, sand dunes or artificial terraces. The geomancer adapts the ideal rules to the characteristics of the landscape and manages to compensate a defect of the ground by another advantage, or by the edification of a stūpa. These geomantical rules match up with more practical considerations to determine the site of a nomadic camp. A northern elevation protects the camp as the monastery from the northern and north-western winds, while the presence of water — a river, a well or a spring — remains the most important criterium of selection for a site in this continental country.

Provided the geomantical constraints were satisfied, a monastery was free to settle almost wherever it wanted. The agreement of the banner prince was easy to obtain, the Vinaya rules were flexible and the only decree issued by the Qing on this subject aimed at protecting the surrounding fields that could be damaged by the construction.

Table II page 360
fig. 2 opposite page

Among the sixty eight monasteries housing more than 500 monks in the early 20th century,[35] four were built in pre-existent cities, Kökeqota and Bayanqota. Eighteen "banner monasteries" founded by the banner prince were built within six kilometres from his residence. In a city or in the steppe, a temple could not be built contiguous to the back side (northern wall) of a palace or residence: it was usually built on the south, east or west side. Most of them are now located within cities or in the suburb of the city that was formed around it. Eighteen other monasteries are far from the banner centre and urban centre, yet eleven out of these eighteen are close to old travel routes (for trade or nomadisation), like Bayan shanda-yin süme [9]. Therefore, it is often difficult to know if the initial desire was isolation. Seven are found in "dramatic spots" in the mountains, like Aγui-yin süme [12] in Helan shan.

As a general rule, a more contemplative or academic monastery searched for an isolated site, off the tracks, in a curved valley at the end of a narrow gorge, with a nice view on the plain. But as the basic criteria for selecting a site — the proximity of water and wooded areas — were the same as for the settlement of a camp, a monastery was never very far away from human beings. Even when isolated in the mountains, it received donations from laymen and possessed herds grazing in the plain. The examples of Badγar coyiling süme [4] and Aγui-yin süme [12] show that the apparent isolation of a monastery was not a bridle to its economic development.

Monasteries founded by members of the nobility were often situated near their residence. Every banner had a "banner monastery" close to the camp or to the settled residence of the prince. The population density in Inner Mongolia was very low (0,3 to 1,3 inhabitant per km^2 in the early 20th century), and until the 19th century, there were only a few urban centres, such as Kökeqota, Bayanqota, Dolonnor, plus Manchu garrisons where Chinese and Manchu soldiers had their own temples, and a few Chinese

34. Many monasteries were built at the foothill of Daqing mountain (Yin range), facing the Yellow River: Mayidari-yin juu [3], Köndenen juu [6], Mergen juu [5] etc.

35. Small and medium-size monasteries are not documented. As we have already stressed, the majority of the monks was herders or farmers and came to the monastery only to attend the festivals.

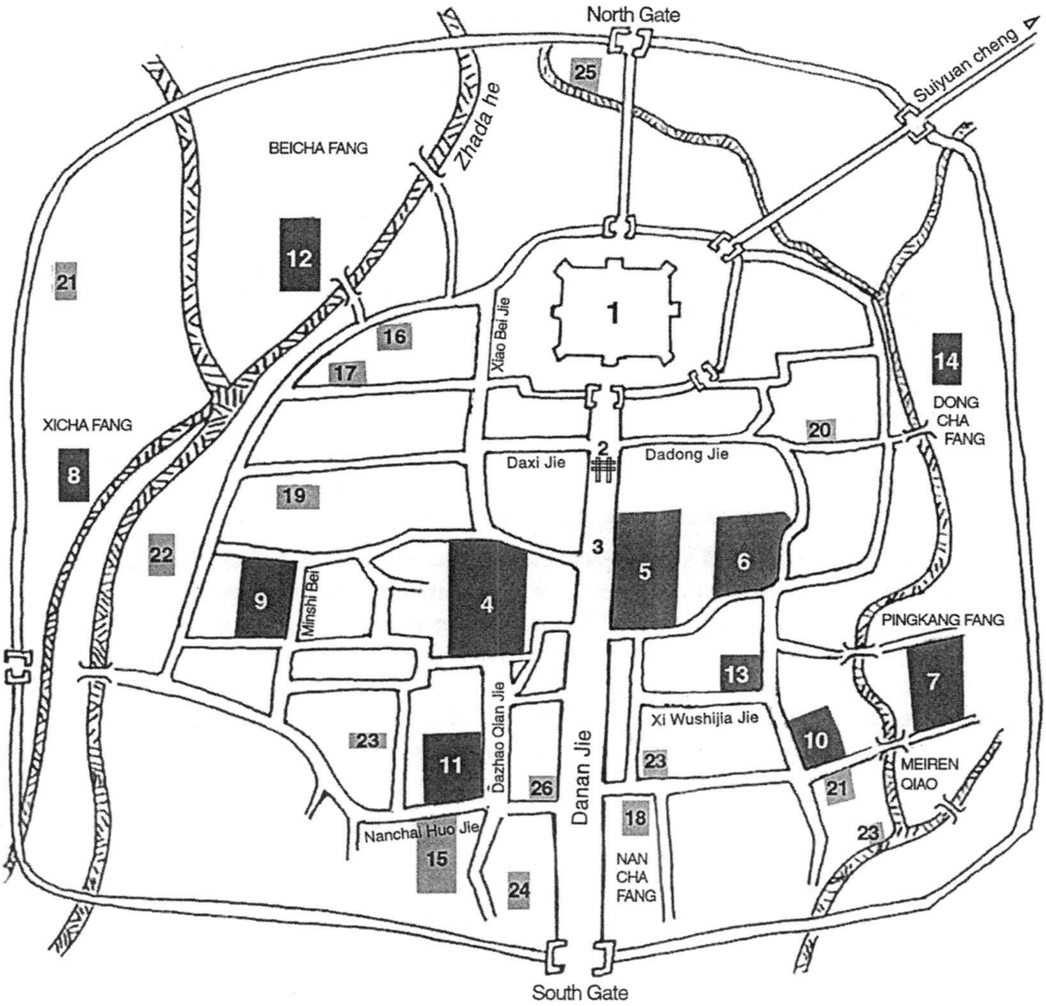

2 – *Kökeqota at the end of the 19th century*
(Guihua cheng ting zhi)

1. Fortress-yamen
2. *Pailou*, Dashizi
3. Danan street

Mongol monasteries

4. Yeke juu (Wuliang si)
5. Siregetü juu (Yanshou si)
6. Baɣa juu (Chongfu si)
7. Tabun suburɣan-u süme (Cideng si)
8. Pungsuɣ juu (Chongshou si)
9. Emci-yin juu (Longshou si)
10. Corji-yin juu (Yansi si), Yanfu si
11. Rabji-yin juu (Hongqing si)
12. Qosiɣun-u süme / juu (Taiping zhao)
13. Guangfu si
14. Ɣaran juu

Chinese temples

15. Guanyin miao
16. Shiwang miao
17. Wen miao
18. Guandi miao
19. Sanguan miao
20. Lüzu miao
21. Longwang miao
22. Jisheng miao
23. Wudao miao (3 temples)
24. Menggu wen miao
25. Chenghuang miao
26. Caishen miao

settlements. "Ritualistic" monasteries, more dependent on liturgical services and related donations than "academic ones" settled near travel routes and thus often assumed a prominent role in trade. The attraction of Mongol and Chinese tradesmen to the monastery fairs as well as the location along trade routes led to the growth of trade centres around the main monasteries. As they required supplies even outside the fairs, food and crafts, villages and towns developed around the religious centres. Monasteries thus both followed and fostered a slow but steady trend of sedentarisation and urbanisation over the whole period 16th to 20th century.

1.2 Mountain caves and occupancy of ancient sites

Mountain caves were essential to the Mongol and Tibetan religious tradition. Moreover troglodytical dwelling was common in Inner Mongolia. Originally the dwellings of ascetics, caves became sanctuaries protected by an architecture and were later integrated into a monastery. About 50 monasteries were named *aγui*, "cave". In the Nyingmapa monastery of Aγui-yin süme [12], the five caves where Padmasabhava, according to the legend, meditated in 774, are up to the present time an important pilgrimage site. Like Tibetan "womb-caves", they contain sacred sources, circumambulation corridors around statues, and narrow initiatory passages.

Monasteries turned the old Shamanistic natural sites (mountain graveyards, natural caves, rocks, woods) into reserves where it was prohibited to hunt, pasture, cut trees, build, ride horse and cultivate land. Tibetan Buddhism superimposed a new sacred geography upon the old Shamanistic and Buddhist one and took possession of ancient sites. Two monasteries were founded around well preserved Kitan caves containing Buddhist sculptures: the Qianzhao miao and the Γilubar juu [30]. The three caves of Γilubar juu still contain images of Buddha and Bodhisattvas. An assembly hall was built during the Qing dynasty to protect their entrance.

A few Buddhist monasteries took possession of ancient historical sites in order to re-use their building materials, like Darqan agula-yin süme near the ruins of the Yuan city of Yingchang (Kesigten banner, Juu uda). However, except for the Kitan caves previously mentioned, a new monastery was never built directly on an old site, to avoid to take away the ruins and clear the ground, and out of fear that the ruins may be inhabited by a *deus loci*. This can explain why the old Kitan pagodas were not restored and included in new monasteries.

1.3 The relation between the realised structures and locally available resources

Most of the Mongolian monasteries, as well as the earlier Kitan and Tangγud ones, used local building materials and resources. These are, like in North China, baked bricks for the walls, timber for the framing and stone for the basement, the staircases, the terraces and the courtyards' pavement.

Wood

Conifers (pines, cypress, larches, cedars), mountain poplars, oaks, and also white birches, elms, and willows were commonly used. Monasteries were usually situated near protected wooden areas; in addition, monks planted trees within the fence or near the monastery to supply for their needs. Southern Mongolia was rich in forests before the 18th century, but none of the monasteries that have subsisted is entirely built of timber, which was common in Northern Mongolia. Scarcity of wood due to wood-collecting for fuel,[36] extensive agriculture of Chinese settlers and exportation of timber to China has been a major problem since the 18th century. Decrees issued by the Qing to forbid tree-cutting proved to be useless. Except for the more forested areas of the north-east, Southern Mongolia imported large quantities of timber from Northern Mongolia.

Tibetan architecture is well adapted to deserted areas like Ordos and Alashan, where wood is scarce and timber-consuming Chinese roofs are seldom seen. Chinese roofs often appear to be a luxury decorative item placed up on a Tibetan flat roof. For reasons of prestige, wealthy monasteries used to import high quality timber and stone from thousands of kilometres away.

Bricks

Bricks – a building material well fit to the region and the climate – have been baked in Southern Mongolia since the first millennium. Glazed bricks and tiles were imported from Datong. Bricks and stones were sometimes taken from ruined or partially ruined architectures, such as old cities or the Great wall.

Stone

Very few monasteries were entirely built in stone. They are located in mountainous regions, mainly in the Western part of the country (Yin, Helan mountains), such as Baraγun and Jegün keyid [13, 14], Gembi-yin süme [34], or Badγar coyiling süme [4].

Itinerant Chinese and Mongolian carpenters were employed in the construction and directed local workmanship. When and how they were employed and where they came from are still open issues, which need addressing before we may fully understand the foreign influences and trends. These anonymous carpenters had the difficult task to combine Chinese and Tibetan construction techniques, which were fundamentally opposed.

The monastery layout – 16th to 20th century

The minimum monastery consists of the assembly hall or *coγcin* containing the main statues and altar, located at the northern side, and the monks' dwellings. To this central nucleus can be added many elements according to the development of the community. As in Tibet and China, monasteries are continuously repaired, restored, enlarged by lay donations and by the monks' initiatives. They reached their maximum size under Qianlong reign (1736-1796). Therefore, it is often difficult to distinguish the original state and layout of the monastery.

Like Tibetan monasteries, larger Southern Mongolian monasteries are real towns built on an area of one or two hundred thousand square meters. The hierarchy between the different buildings is immediately perceptible because of their situation, height, size, roofing and decoration. The main assembly halls and temples (the highest and the more decorated buildings) lie in the middle or on the northern side of the compound, and face south, except when the configuration of the ground does not permit it. They are surrounded by colleges' minor assembly halls, the reincarnations' residences and their storehouses, stūpas and minor temples, monks' dwellings, kitchen and miscellaneous buildings. Layouts can be divided into five basic categories: the *küriye* or circular layout of itinerant monasteries, the Chinese symmetrical arrangement, the "scatter-shot" arrangement, the mixed arrangement and the fortified monasteries.

36. The main fuels used for building (baking bricks) and living (heating, cooking) were wood, charcoal, and coal after the discovery of mines in the Daqing mountains in the 19th century.

1. Mobile monastery in yurts

During the 16th and 17th centuries, except for the Tümed and a few tribes already settled and partly living on agriculture, the great majority of Mongols were nomads and lived in felt tents. In Alashan, Western Mongolia (and Qalqa Mongolia up to the 18th century), monasteries in yurts followed the nomadic way of life of the lay community, and nomadised with their herds.[37] Even the great kings (Qan) had no fixed religious centre. All Inner Mongolian banners used to build fixed monasteries since the end of the 17th, but small nomadic monasteries-in-yurts still existed in the Ordos and Ulagan cabu leagues, and were widespread in Alashan banners at the beginning of 20th century. Among settled Mongols, the presence of monasteries in yurts can be explained by a lack of finance.

The monastery-in-yurts followed the *küriye* (litt. "ring") layout of princes' encampments, with minor temple-yurts and monks' yurts arranged in circle around the central yurt for assembly. The mobile Γanjuur süme [41] settled in 1781-84, adopting a "mixed layout" reminiscent of the circular arrangement. Wooden structures that could be dismantled are not attested, unlike in Northern Mongolia.

figure 4 opposite page

2. Symmetrical Chinese style layout

The necessity of building a sedentary monastery appeared when big Buddhist statues had to be sheltered. The earliest monasteries showed a preponderance of Chinese style layout and structure, because in the 16th century the Tümed employed Chinese carpenters. Later on, all the imperial monasteries and Kökeqota's imperialised monasteries also followed the Chinese style layout. Generally, the majority of the sedentary monasteries adopted a symmetrical layout, especially among the Tümed tribe and in Eastern Mongolia. This layout is adapted to cities and steppe areas, but is also often seen in mountainous regions. Asymmetrical elements in a general symmetrical layout may be explained by the historical development, the topography and the geomantical situation.[38]

figure 4 opposite page

figure 3 opposite page

figure 3 opposite page

In this layout, the monastic compound is surrounded by a rectangular wall defining its extent. Ranging from 1,7 to 2,5 m in height, the enclosure wall has no defensive purposes. The main halls are symmetrically arranged on the central axis with gradation of importance from south to north. The buildings and courtyards commonly built on the central axis are: the entrance gate (with one or three doors); the first courtyard leading out to the hall of the Four guardian kings (*lokapāla*) that can be crossed to enter the second courtyard; the Central assembly hall with lateral temples for a particular deity; and, at the northern side of the compound, the Chinese style two storied abbot's dwelling. Miscellaneous Chinese elements can be added, like an archway (*pailou*) in front of the entrance gate, Bell and Drum towers symmetrically arranged in the first courtyard, screen-walls in front of entrances. Other ordinary Chinese elements are stone lions and incense-burners. Stone inscriptions recording the foundation and restorations are found in imperial monasteries and recently repaired ones. None of these Chinese elements is absolutely necessary. Moreover, many elements of Chinese Buddhist monasteries are absent, such as the ordination platform, the bathroom, or the garden. Monks' dwellings and minor buildings are arranged in two or three lateral private axis, to the east and west.

---

37. Documentation on mobile monasteries is restricted to a few descriptions in Chinese sources, in 19th-20th centuries travelogues, and some photographs.

38. In Siregetü juu [2] for instance (fig. 4), the first historical axis was the western one; in the 17th century the founder added two axis to the east and the central one became the main axis (Charleux 2000).

3 – *Siregetü juu [2]*
Main courtyard,
Central assembly hall
and stone inscriptions
under pavilions
(photo I. Charleux)

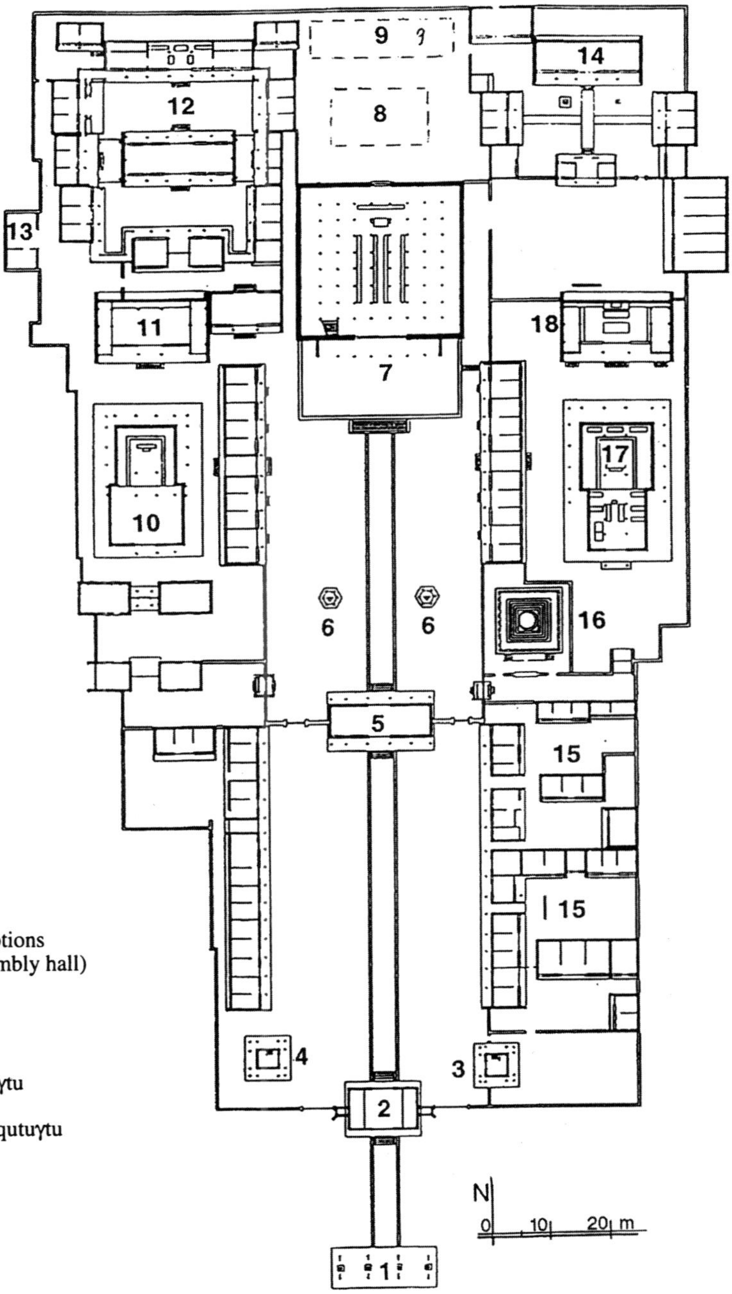

4 – *Layout of Siregetü juu [2]*
(Kökeqota)
(Liu Dunzhen 1997 [1984]: 381)

1. *Pailou*
2. Entrance gate (*shanmen*)
3. Drum tower
4. Bell tower
5. Shrine (*fodian*)
6. Pavilions for stone inscriptions
7. *Γoul coγcin* (Central assembly hall)
8. Main shrine (destroyed)
9. *Jiujian lou* (destroyed)
10. Western temple
11. Western shrine
12. *Labrang* of Siregetü qutuγtu
13. Stables
14. *Labrang* of Darqan corji qutuγtu
15. Monks' dwellings
16. Stūpa
17. Eastern temple
18. Eastern shrine

5 – *Siregetü juu [2]*
Festival gathering Mongolian lamas, Chinesse Buddhist monks and lay believers, summer 1995
(photo I. Charleux)

The western axis is considered as superior to the eastern one and the richest lamas used to live in the north-west corner. Courtyards are large, the buildings forming only about 15% of the total surface area. Entrance gate, temples, storehouses and dwellings are Chinese pavilions (*dian*) covered by a Chinese sloping roof. The adaptation of the Chinese layout are the same as in the Tibeto-Mongol monasteries of China (Yonghe gong, mount Wutai). The only Tibetan or Sino-Tibetan architectures are the Central assembly hall, lying in the centre of the main courtyard, the college halls and the stūpas.

3. The "scatter-shot" layout

fig. 6 opposite page The scatter-shot layout is comparable to the layout of the Gelugpa monasteries in Tibet: it usually can be explained by the landscape's features and by the growth of the monastery over the centuries. Followed by a quarter of the main fixed monasteries, it is common in mountains and hills of Western Inner Mongolia (Qaraγuna mountains, Helan mountains), and also in the steppe (Ulaγan cabu, Ordos, Sili-yin γoul, Arqorcin and Baγarin banners in Juu uda). This apparently unplanned, "organic", layout is characterised by the absence of enclosure wall, of entrance gate, of axis, and of symmetry. It is organised in conformity with the terrain, favouring narrow mountain passes, deep gorges and defiles opening into a large circle at the foot of a high peak. Buildings are scattered up and down a mountain or hill slope in step-like style. Assembly halls can stand side by side on an east-west line or along a ridge (Badγar coyiling süme [4], Baraγun keyid [13]). The most important halls face approximately south while minor ones can open east or west according to the terrain. As in Tibet, the Central assembly hall, main temples and *fig. 6 opposite page* residences of reincarnated monks are located higher on the slope and the monks' quarters spread out in various directions around the main buildings. The buildings are built mostly in Tibetan or Sino-Tibetan style flat-roofed square or oblong structures *fig. 7 opposite page* with thick outer walls. Large temples have two to four storeys, with each succeeding storey being built back from the edge of the last, so that the result presents a step-like appearance. The walls made of brick or stone are whitewashed with limestone. Ornamentation is given to the more important temples and halls: red attic friezes bearing decorated brass mirrors, wooden decorations carved into beams, capitals and columns, porch, window frames with a cornice at the top, plates of glazed ceramic on the wall, animal figures and symbolic ornaments on the roof... Decorative Chinese roofs (covered with tiles), symbols of prestige, can be added atop flat roofs.

7 – Badγar coyiling süme [4] (Urad, Ulaγan cabu league)
(photo I. Charleux)

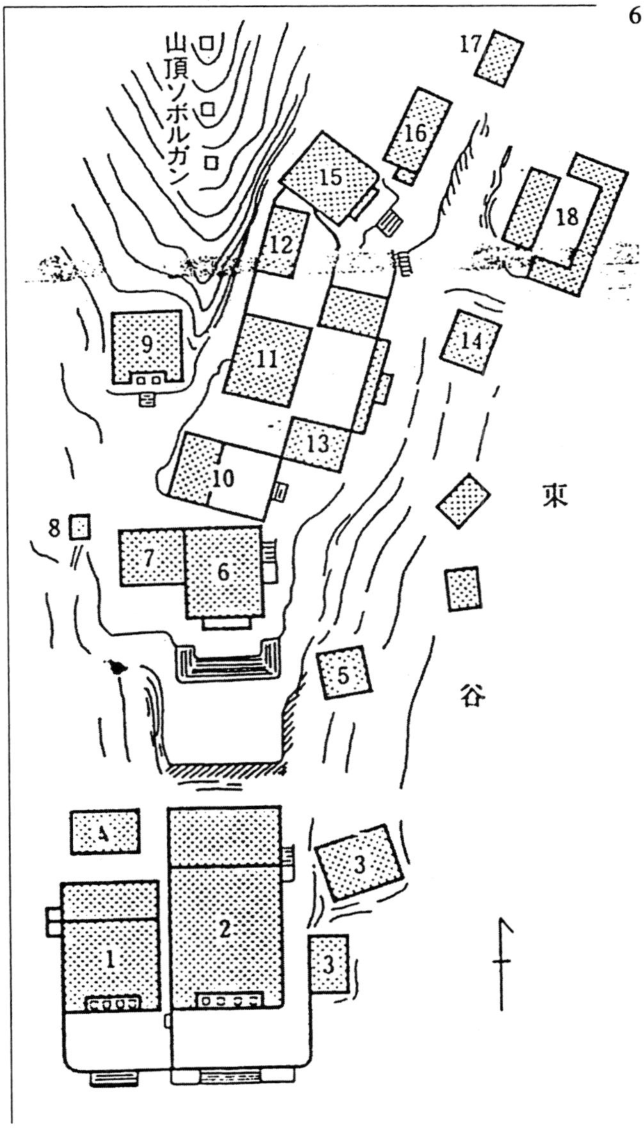

6 – *Layout of Badγar coyiling süme [4] (Urad, Ulagan cabu league)*
(Nagao Gajin, 1991 [1947]: fig. 2 p. 137)

1. Coyiling duγang (college of Doctrine)
2. Coγcin duγang (Central assembly hall)
3. Main *shang* (treasury) and kitchen
4. *Shang* "sanishito"
5. Dungqor qutuγtu's *shang* (treasury)
6. Dungqor duγang (college of Kālacakra)
7. Doγsid duγang (*mgon-khang*)
8. Tsongkhapa's shrine
9. Lam-rim duγang
10. Janggia qutuγtu's *labrang*
11. Dungqor qutuγtu's *labrang*
12. Γanjurbar qutuγtu's *labrang*
13. *Shang* "rapuran"
14. *Shang* of *suburγa* (stūpa)
15. Aγui duγang (college of esotericism)
16. Hall of funerary stūpas
17. *Shang* "sepuchi"
18. *Shang* gegen

4. The mixed layout

Some monasteries combine the symmetrical and the scatter-shot layout. The main temples are enclosed in independent courtyards but we do not find central and lateral axis with successive courtyards. Moreover the typically miscellaneous Chinese buildings like Bell and Drum towers or archway are lacking. This layout can sometimes be explained by the growth of the monastery, the first foundation being enclosed by a wall, which later finds itself located in the middle of the monastery. The mixed layout is also seen in Kumbum and in other monasteries of Eastern Tibet. It is common to find in the same compound Tibetan style temples, Chinese and mixed-style architectures.

5. Fortified monasteries

The necessity of fortification was a main criterion for only two known foundations *fig. 8 below* of the 16th century (Mayidari-yin juu [3] and Huayan si). It became unnecessary in Southern Mongolia under the *pax manjurica* of the Qing dynasty.[39] The walls, covered with stone and bricks, are typical of Chinese fortifications that could also be seen in Amdo monasteries such as Honghua si (15th century). These religious compounds seem to be a survival of Central Asian square fortified monasteries of the 9th to the 11th century like those of Turfân, Qocho and Duldur-âqur. Their inner arrangement follows the "mixed layout".

This schematisation must not conceal the great diversity of layouts. Moreover, because of the bad state of preservation of minor buildings and enclosure walls, it is sometimes difficult to know what was the original complete layout of a monastery.

8 – *Layout of Mayidari-yin juu [3]*
(Jin Shen 1984: p. 137)

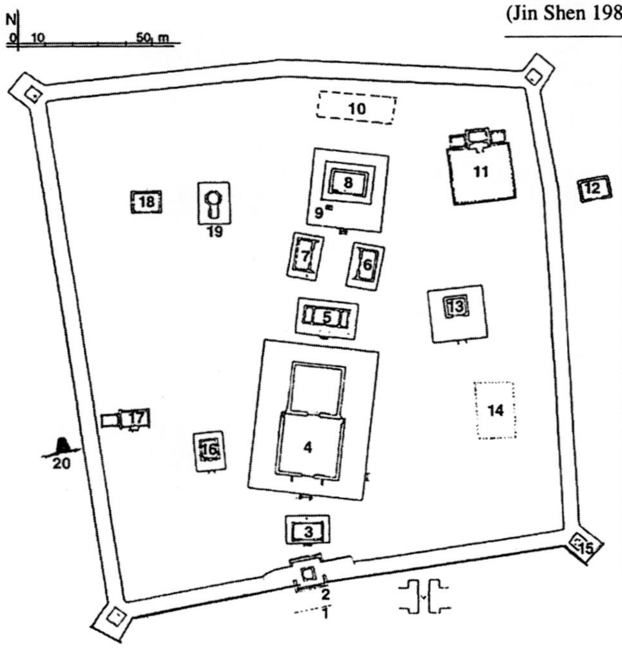

1. *Zhaobi* (screen-wall, destroyed)
2. Taihe gate
3. Hall of the Four guardian kings (destroyed)
4. *Γoul coγcin* (Central assembly hall)
5. Baima tianshen miao (destroyed)
6. Temple of Avalokiteśvara
7. Temple of 18 *arhat*
8. *Liuli dian* (Hall with green glazed tiles): main shrine
9. Stūpa (destroyed)
10. Gongye fu (residence)
11. Temple of the Dalai Lama
12. Eastern hall of 10,000 Buddhas
13. Temple of the Empress (with funerary stūpa inside)
14. Dajiwa dian (destroyed)
15. Pavilions at the four corners
16. gNas-shung süme (temple of Pe-har)
17. *Qutuγtu*'s residence
18. Western hall of 10,000 Buddhas
19. Octagonal temple
20. Cross section of the wall

39. It was not the case of Northern and Western Mongolia until the late 18th century because of the wars between the Jungars and the Qing dynasty. Hence, other examples of fortified monasteries are known in Qalqa Mongolia (Erdeni juu, Caγan bayising) and in Western Mongolia (Ablai keyid of the Qoshuud).

The elements of the monastery[40]

The various monastic buildings (or yurts) had the same functions as in monasteries of Central and Eastern Tibet, and the inner arrangement did not differ from that of a Tibetan monastery, even in yurt-monasteries. However, the architecture freely adapts to various situations and needs. Buildings' layouts have a square or rectangular shape, sometimes with a porch and a small apse or *cella* at the back.

1. For religious functions

1.1 Monks assembly and rituals: the Central assembly hall

The Central assembly hall (*γoul coγcin*[41]) is the most important edifice of a monastery. It was used for daily services carried out by the monks, as well as for ordinations, teaching, examinations, and confessions. Laymen were not supposed to attend the rituals – except when they asked for private prayers in exchange for offerings –, but could observe them from outside, standing under the porch or indoors. When the *cella* is at the back side of the assembly hall, with no door opening on the outside, laymen were sometimes allowed to enter during ceremonies to make their devotions to the Buddha images: they then walked along the walls, knelt, prayed, placed their offerings on the altars, and went out without stopping, so as to not disturb the assembly.

The building opens on a courtyard used for open-air rituals, debates and gatherings, where one or two poles are erected for hanging prayer-banners. A large *thang-ka* could be suspended between the two poles during the festivals. The hall has a south-facing entrance with a portico and a large hypostyled hall. Its size should be proportional to that of the whole monastic community, who was supposed to daily gather inside. During the Qianlong period, as communities increased in size, many assembly halls were enlarged or rebuilt. The largest have 64 columns, a square shape (8 x 8 columns, about 700 m^2), and could house 500 monks. Bays are regular in measure except in the 16th century temples of Kökeqota (Yeke juu [1], Mayidari-yin juu [3]), characterised by "missing" columns and irregular bays, according to Chinese Ming architecture. Because of its large size, the hall receives light from a skylight. Assembly halls all follow the same basic inner arrangement which does not differ from a Tibetan assembly hall, with many paintings, banners, seats for the monks according to their rank,[42] cupboards containing small images, offerings and sometimes secondary shrines with statues. The musical and liturgical instruments used during the services, the costumes and masks for the masked dances are stored in a room near the entrance.

fig. 1 p. 365 and 3 p. 371

40. Our presentation of the organisation of the monastery is mainly based on our fieldwork observations, completed by old photographs (*Nei Menggu gu jianzhu* 1959), 19th and 20th century travelogues (Pozdneev 1977, 1978), records and studies done by the Japanese during the Manchukuo (Nagao Gajin 1987, 1991), and modern studies (Su Bai 1994). The massive destruction of purely monastic buildings such as monks' quarters and offices does not allow us to draw a complete survey of these elements.

41. From Mongol *γoul*, "central" and Tibetan *tshogs-chen*, "assembly hall".

42. The monks' seats are on the right and left side of the central aisle; the seats of the reincarnated monk and of the important monks are close to the altar, on the west side and facing right (or east). The central seat near the altar and facing south is reserved for the highest ranking monk who is likely to visit the monastery, such as the Dalai Lama, the Panchen Lama, and occasionally the reincarnated lamas.

1.2 Cult for monks and laymen: the main shrine (ɣoul süme)

At the north of the Central assembly hall lies the main shrine or *cella*, that houses altars and offerings in front of the images of Buddha and deities, paintings, plus a library of sutras. Canopies and silk banners hang from the ceiling. The main statues, along the north wall and facing south, are the Three Buddhas of the Past, Present and Future, with four Bodhisattvas and a *dharmapāla* on each side (along the eastern and western walls). The back wall has no opening. On the altar are displayed incense-burners, oil-lamps, the eight auspicious symbols and food offerings. Cushions for prostration are displayed in front of the altar. A Chinese style incense-burner or a fumigation stove is often seen outside.

Like in Tibetan monasteries, there is a clear separation between assembly halls for rituals and chapels for the cult. The architecture of the Central assembly hall and the main shrine, either combined in one building or in two separate buildings, illustrates the "conflict" between rituals and devotion. As this relation is the more original architectural feature of Mongolian monasteries, it deserves a special attention.

fig. 9 opposite page

Nine types are divided up as follows into two categories

A. The assembly hall and the shrine in the same building

fig. 10 and 11 p. 378

In Tibetan style and in some Sino-Tibetan style architectures , the main shrine is the rear part of the large *gTsug-lag-khang*, a building comprising the assembly hall and the shrine on the ground level, chapels and rooms on the second and third floors. The skylight of the assembly hall opens on the inner courtyard of the first floor, and the back shrine, with a very high ceiling, receives light from a window opening on the flat roof of the first floor. The *gTsug-lag-khang* adopts different layouts and sizes:

1 – The small square temple with no inner division. Images are placed along the back wall (the shrine) and a few monks can sit and pray in front of the images (the assembly room); there is no other shrine. It can be the main hall of small monasteries or a minor hall of large monasteries. The elevation is Chinese, Tibetan or Sino-Tibetan.

fig. 10, 11, p. 378 and 12 p. 379

figure 13 p. 379

2 – The Tibetan style gTsug-lag-khang, with a rectangular shape composed of a square assembly hall and a main shrine at the back, in a separate room. The elevation is Tibetan or Sino-Tibetan. The growing Tibetan influence on Mongol architecture coincides with the rise of the Manchu dynasty (1644), and the establishment of the Dalai Lama's rule in Tibet. The pure Central Tibetan style is rarely seen in Mongolia, though: buildings are made of bricks and have Chinese roofs upon the flat roof. They are smaller, more decorated and more symmetrical than their Tibetan models.

fig. 14 p. 379 and 15 p. 380

3 – The Kökeqota-style *gTsug-lag-khang*. The elevation of the whole building is Sino-Tibetan, covered by a succession of three Chinese roofs: the first one covers a room on the first floor above the porch; the second one, larger, covers the skylight of the assembly hall surrounded by a flat roof; and the third one, higher, is above the high ceiling of the back shrine. The back shrine is a quadrilateral apse on the northern side of the assembly hall, surrounded by a peristyle on the east, north and west side for outer circumambulation, which recalls the circular corridor found in ancient Indo-Tibetan layouts. Two doors at the north-east and north-west corners of the assembly hall open on the peristyle. After the 16th century, the circumambulation seems to have been abandoned, the two doors being closed. The tripartite facade is inspired by contemporary Gelugpa models with a projecting central part surmounted

9 – *Typology of assembly halls and shrines*

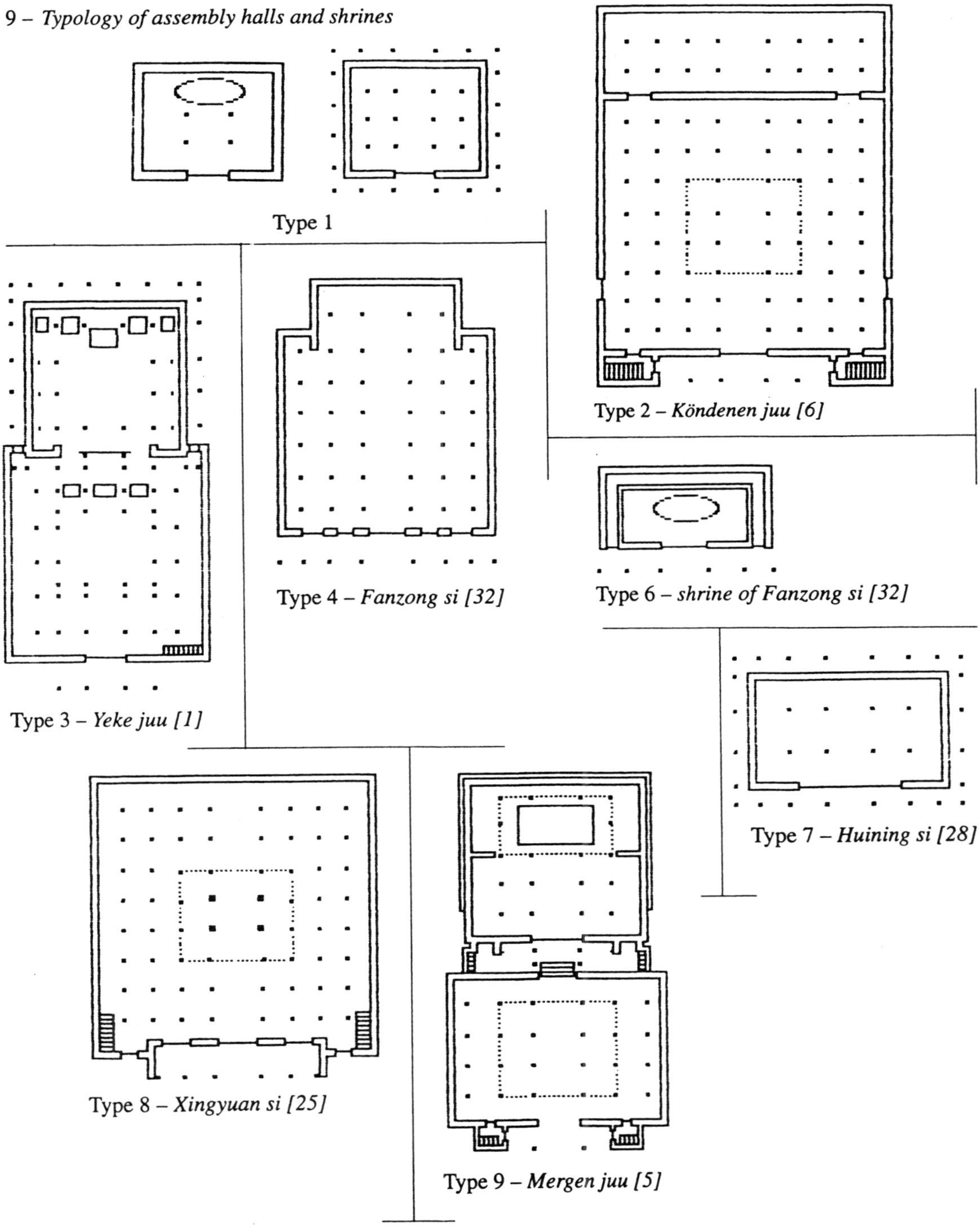

by a veranda and rectangles with metal disk recalling the vegetable frieze. The building technique and materials are entirely Chinese. This original building appears as soon as 1575 and was never exported out of the Tümed banners. Although inspired from the Tibetan *gTsug-lag-khang*, it has no direct Tibetan antecedent. The general layout of the monastery follows the Chinese arrangement or the fortified one. *fig. 16 p. 380*

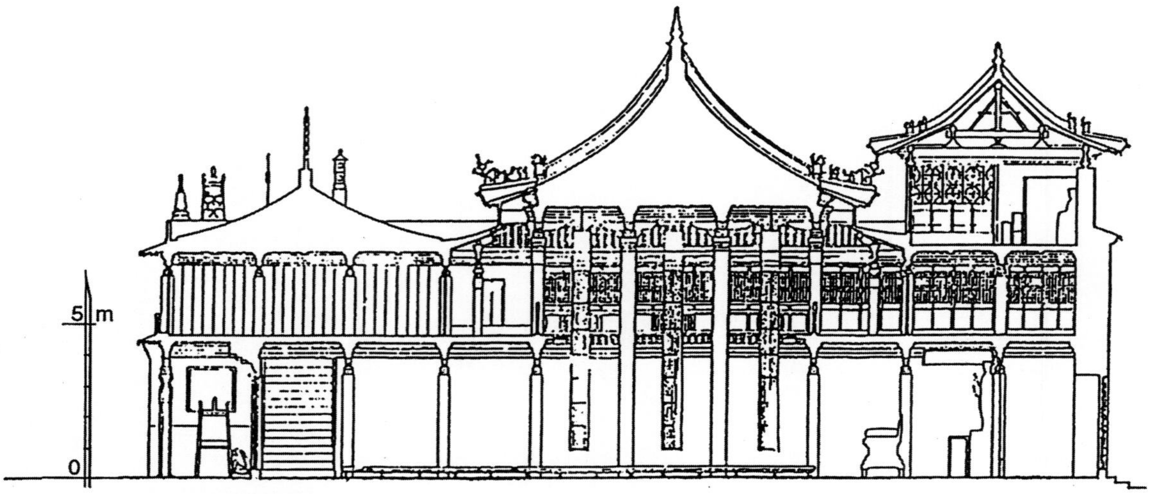

10 – Siregetü juu [2], Kökeqota,
cross section of the assembly hall (Type 2)
(From Liu Dunzhen 1991 [1984])

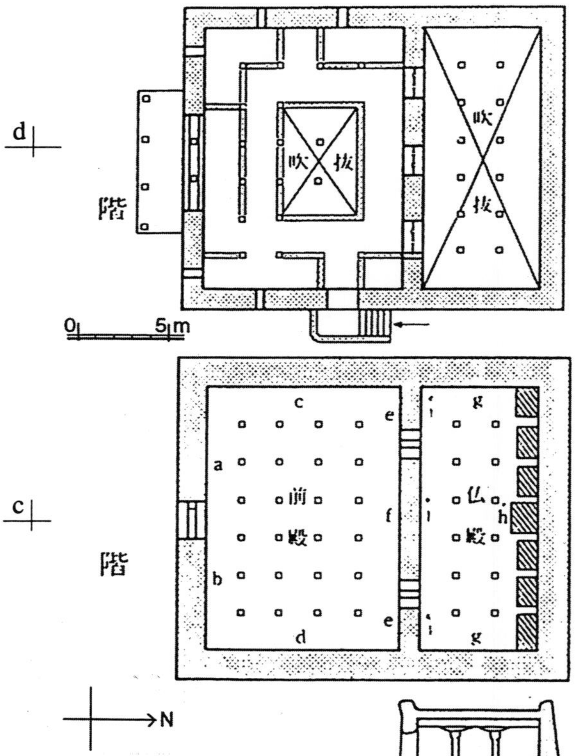

11 – Badɣar coyiling süme [4],
Dungqor dugang (Type 2)
(From Nagao Gajin 1991 [1987] p. 221)

a. Elevation
b. Cross section
c. Ground-floor plan
d. First-storey plan

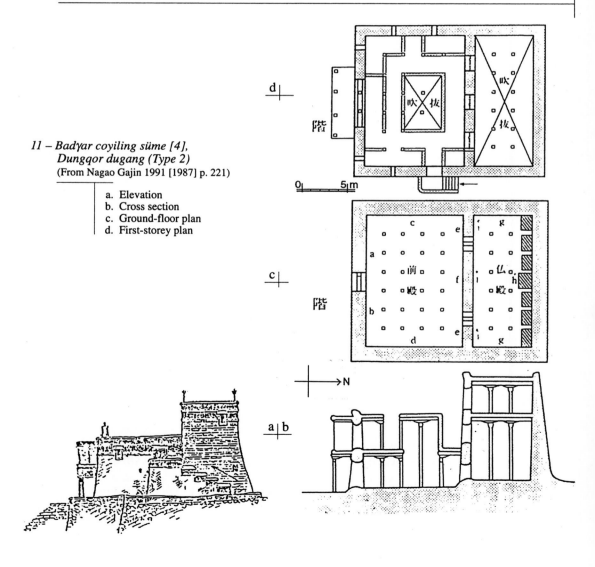

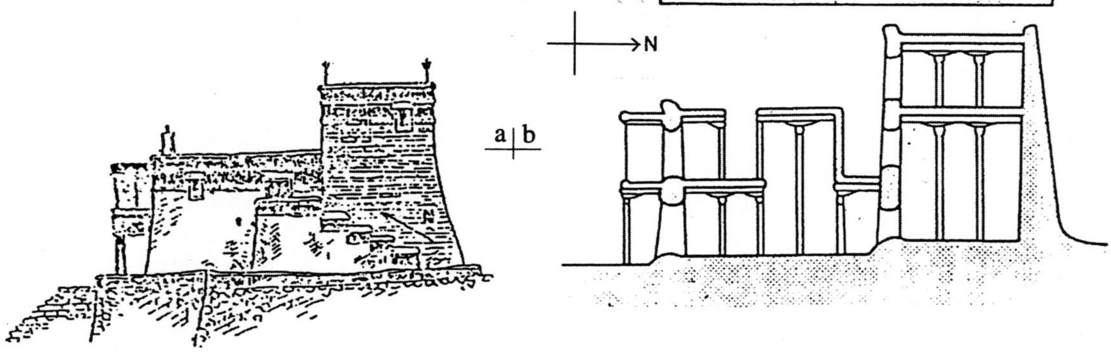

12 – Mergen juu [5], (Type 2)
(photo I. Charleux)

13 – Sira mören juu [8], (Type 2)
Puhui si, summer residence of the 6th Siregetü qutuγutu (photo I. Charleux)

14 – Beyile-yin süme [7], (Type 3)
Vue from above

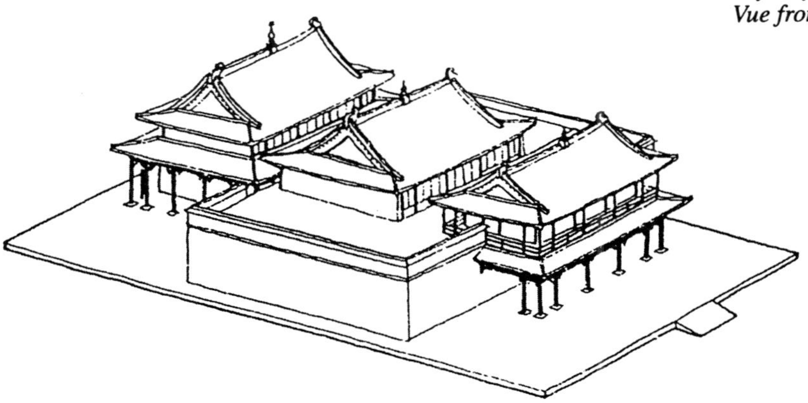

内蒙古百霊廟大經堂

15 – Mayidari-yin juu [3] central assembly hall from west (Type 3)
(photo I. Charleux)

16 – Yeke juu [1], front vue (Type 3)
(photo I. Charleux)

17 – Fanzong si [2] front vue (Type 4)
(photo I. Charleux)

4 – The square assembly hall with a smaller square shrine at the back. Although the layout is close to type 3, the elevation is completely different. The assembly hall is covered by a high Chinese roof with a skylight on the false second storey and the back shrine is covered by a lower Chinese roof. There can be a second larger separate Chinese style shrine (type 6, 7) in the back courtyard. This type is found in Josutu and Juu uda leagues (Fanzong si [32], Fuhui si [22]). *figure 17 opposite page*

Compared to the assembly hall, the main shrine of type 3 is larger than in other monasteries, because Kökeqota monasteries are "ritualistic" temples founded by the nobility with an emphasis on devotion. In type 4, the back shrine is small but there is a larger separate shrine behind, which is much more practical to ease the flow of the numerous visitors. On the contrary, the Tibetan style academic monastery of type 2 emphasises the assembly hall to the detriment of the shrine.

B. The assembly hall and the independent shrine

The main shrine can also be a separate Chinese style building placed in a courtyard located north of the assembly hall, which often has a door on the north side.

5 – Mobile "monastery-in-yurts". According to old photographs and descriptions, in mobile temples two different yurts were used for the assembly hall and for the shrine.

6 – The small shrine with an inner corridor to circumambulate main images. It exists in Fanzong si, in several cave temples and probably in two other temples now destroyed. These corridors are surviving examples of ancient types of buildings in Amdo and Central Tibet. The elevation is entirely Chinese with the entrance on the larger side (*dian*).

7 – The rectangular Chinese style separate shrine sometimes surrounded by a peristyle. The elevation is entirely Chinese (*dian*). It is found behind assembly halls of type 4, 8, 9 and sometimes behind assembly-hall-in a yurt.

8 – The large square assembly hall with no inner division and a Chinese, Tibetan or Sino-Tibetan symmetrical elevation around a central skylight. It often has a door opening in the northern wall to go to the separate shrine (1 or 3).

9 – Other types of *gTsug-lag-khang*. In Mergen juu [5] and Junggar juu [10], the courtyard between the assembly hall and the shrine is a small impluvium giving some light to the shrine. The shrine of Mergen juu is built to shelter a huge image of Maitreya. The elevation is Tibetan, Chinese or Sino-Tibetan.

*1.3 Other assembly halls (*duγang, *< Tibetan* 'du-khang*)*

In academic monasteries, the monks can study medicine, doctrine and Vinaya, esotericism, and/or Kālacakra in colleges (*rasang* or *dacang*, from Tibetan *grwa-tsaṇg*). Some monasteries are specialised in one of these four subjects but large academic monasteries have an important college of doctrine and sometimes two or three other colleges. These have an independent organisation and treasury. During the services, the monks recite sutras and learn specific rituals in their college assembly hall (of type 2, 5), which has a small shrine along the rear wall with the main images (Tsong-kha-pa for the college of doctrine, Kālacakra for the college of Kālacakra). Laymen cannot attend these specific rituals. In the 19th century, 19 monasteries of more than 500 monks were academic.[43]

43. For the course of studies in Badγar coyiling süme [4] –21 years for the college of doctrine–, Nagao Gajin 1987 [1947] and 1991 [1947].

1.4 Cult for monks and laity: other shrines

Besides the main shrine, any number of chapels (*lha-khang*) may be built according to the wishes of clergy and laity. These can be single buildings around the Central assembly hall or rooms located at the upper storeys of a Tibetan or Sino-Tibetan style assembly hall. The higher the place the deity occupies in the very large Tibeto-Mongol pantheon, the "higher" his shrine will be located — on the second floor of the assembly hall, on the northern part of the symmetrical compound or higher on the hill. For instance, the chapel of Maitreya is "higher" than that of the lokapāla. The most common shrines are consecrated to Maitreya, Avalokiteśvara, Tārā, Tsong-kha-pa and the 18 *arhat*. The shrine of the wrathful tantric deities – the *yi-dam* and dharmapāla – called *mgon-khang*, is often located at the southern or western side of the assembly hall. In Chinese style monasteries of Eastern Mongolia, small shrines in the north of the compound are dedicated to Chinese deities such as Guandi (martial god identified with Gesar) and Niangniang (child-giving goddess). In the 19th and 20th centuries, it was common to build high constructions sheltering a monumental statue of Maitreya or Avalokiteśvara (4 to 15 m high). Local mountain deities are sometimes found in small individual chapels or included in the *mgon-khang*. The inner arrangement is the same as in the main shrine. Monks and laymen make their private devotions; laymen can also pay some monks to perform a special service. Therefore, there is often some place and seats in front of the altar, like a small assembly hall, so that a few monks can sit and pray.

Other cultual elements include stūpas (see 2.1.) and prayer-wheels. Even when there is no enclosure wall, stūpas, cairns, prayer flags, prayer-wheels, painted and carved rocks delimited a cirumambulation path which is often difficult to find today because of the massive destruction of these elements. Prayer-wheels, that could be housed in small pavilions or surround shrines and assembly halls, have been removed during the Cultural Revolution.

1.5 Meditation, ordinations and debates: the monks' activities

The nature, organisation and buildings housing the monks' activities were the same as in Tibet. The Tibeto-Mongol monastery has no special building for ordinations: these ceremonies were performed in the Central assembly hall. Debates between monks, an ordinary and ritualised exercise of Tibeto-Mongol Buddhism, took place in a specific courtyard enclosed by walls and planted with trees. When there was no such delimited area, debates were organised on the paved ground or on the platform in front of the Central assembly hall or in front of the college of doctrine. The monks practised meditation and prayers in their own dwelling. There was no specific building for collective meditation like in China, and the assembly hall was not used as a meditation place. For individual long-term meditation, monks locked themselves in cells or caves depending on their monastery. Ideally, these were located high up in the mountain, above the main temples.

1.6 Ceremonies for the laity: festivals, rituals, and initiations

The laymen often came to the monastery twice a month (the 1st and 15th days of the moon month) and for the festivals (New Year festival with a procession of Maitreya, Buddha's Birthday etc) that also attracted many Chinese traders. During the festivals, the laymen of the whole countryside gathered to give offerings to the monks, to buy Chinese items in exchange for cattle and wool, and to participate in the *naadam* games. The monks performed various rituals such as processions round the enclosure wall and public masked dances. Some monasteries had a special platform in front of the assembly hall or even in front of the main gateway (in the Köke süme and Sira süme [16, 17]) for the masked dances, but these were usually performed in front of the Central assembly hall.

At any time, the lay donators were welcomed in a reception room or yurt, located near the main halls. Noblemen could receive special initiations in their residence, but there were no public sermons and teaching for the laymen, and very few public initiations were given (the most famous one was the Kālacakra initiations given by the Panchen Lama in the 1930's).

2. For reliquary, commemorative or funerary functions:

2.1 Stūpas

As in Tibet, the stūpa (Mong. *suburgan*) can be a commemorative, funerary, reliquary and/or votive monument. It cannot be entered, and its size ranges from a small reliquary sheltered in a special hall to a monumental building. The location and number of outside stūpas is not fixed: there can be one on a lateral axis, two twin stūpas in front of a temple or assembly hall, a "forest of stūpas" in a lateral courtyard, the complete set of the eight canonical stūpas corresponding to the eight important events of Buddha's life (Mahāvaitya), stūpas above the compound wall of a monastery, above the main gate of a compound, or stūpas lined up on the ridge of a mountain. Small stūpas placed on an altar or in a special building often have a funerary or a reliquary function.

The Mongol stūpa is modelled on the contemporary Tibetan one and borrows elements from contemporary and older models, like the Xia stūpas of Qaraqota or Yuan and Qing dynasties stūpas of Beijing. It is externally adorned with a small niche containing a Buddha image, tiles around the top of the *anda* and glazed ceramic. Some atypical ones are the stūpa of Köndenen juu [6], close to Chinese votive columns; the stūpa of Hanbai miao with its quasi-spherical *anda*; the huge stūpa of Bayan shanda-yin süme [9] with a peristyle; the big stūpa of Üüsin juu [11] with a decreasing octagonal base *fig. 18 below*

18 – Stūpa of Sirigetü juu [2]
(photo I. Charleux)

19 – Tabun suburγa (Wuta si) of Kökeqota
(photo I. Charleux)

and twenty-five niches around its *anda*. The one exception far from Tibetan models, is the Tabun suburγa (Ch. *Wuta*, "Five stūpas") of Kökeqota, which takes the Ming dynasty stūpa of Dajue si (Beijing) as a model.[44] The only examples of Chinese style tower stūpas date from the Kitan Liao dynasty.

fig. 19 above

2.2 *Funerary building*

Stūpas containing the ashes or the mummy of the dead reincarnated monks were set in a funerary hall. During the initial period of the Buddhist renaissance, several Mongol members of the nobility were cremated after their death and their ashes were preserved in a stūpa set in the temple they founded (Mayidari-yin juu [3]). The cremation was not a local tradition – corpses were abandoned to animals of prey or buried in the mountain; because of opposition to habits and popular belief it was soon abandoned for laymen.

44. "Stūpa sarira of the diamond throne" type, imitating in Chinese style the temple of the Mahābodhi in Bodhgayā.

2.3 Oboγa *(cairns)*

One of the most original characteristics of Mongolian monasteries is the presence of *oboγas*. Although basically opposed, the stūpa, "support" (Tib. *rten*) of Buddha's mind, and the Shamanistic *oboγa*, support of a local god, share common characteristics. The first meaning of a "stūpa" is a pile of stones and earth above a tomb. Buddhist monks took over for their own purpose the *oboγa* worship and even wrote prayers for *oboγa* rituals. Laymen can offer to build an *oboγa* to fulfil a wish, and it is common to find 13 or 108 *oboγa* representing the Buddhist cosmology (mount Sumeru surrounded by the four continents and the eight minor continents). Other *oboγas* are found on mountain passes and summits above and around a monastery, and often side by side with a stūpa, on the ridge of a mountain, close to the compound. *Oboγas* can be surrounded by stūpas or surround a stūpa to protect it and subdue the *deus loci*. In Blama-yin küriye [20], an *oboγa* is even located on the central axis of the Chinese style layout.

3. For educational functions: library, classroom and printing workshop

Buddhist scriptures were stored on shelves in assembly halls and in shrines. Some Chinese-influenced monasteries had a library in a distinct building, indifferently situated north or south of the Central assembly hall. In the monasteries of Kökeqota, the Jiujian lou ("two-storied building of nine bays large"), located at the northern part of the compound, has a library on the second floor. The hollow Tabun suburγa pagoda was used as a library. Monks also possessed books they kept in their dwelling.

There was no specific classroom for young monks: they studied prayers, Tibetan language in the Central assembly hall and studied rituals by attending celebrations. They also learnt by heart and recited private lessons in their dwelling or in their master's dwelling. Students learnt rituals in their college assembly hall and debated in a courtyard. The majority of the monks was assigned to simple tasks or worked as apprentice with the relevant master. No education was given to laymen in the monasteries. Many young noblemen were trained as novices in a monastery and quitted before pronouncing monk's vows.

Some of the largest monasteries had a printing office (located on a lateral axis in symmetrical layouts). None has subsisted. They did not supply books for all Southern Mongolia: books were mainly produced and bought in Beijing or in Tibet. Beijing printed liturgical books in Tibetan, but also in Mongolian.

4. Offices and treasuries

In symmetrical layouts, the religious administration was located on a side axis. Monasteries with an official title had a *tamaγa-yin γajar* (*yinwu chu* in Chinese), "place where the seals [(given by the Lifan yuan) are kept]". None has subsisted.

The treasuries (*shang* or *jisa*) were essential economic components of a monastery. They stored food and all kind of donations (monk's clothes, carpets, silk, silver), products for trade, religious implements, books and other goods. The treasury of the assembly hall was the public treasury of the whole monastery, while individual ones were attached to particular colleges, to specific religious services and to the reincarnation(s) living in the monastery. They were located close to their unit, usually on its northern side (where the god of wealth resides). There were twenty-two treasuries in Dolonnor [16, 17], and fourteen at Bandida gegen süme [18]. Very few have been preserved.

Larger monasteries also had workshops for carpenters and painters, buildings to stock timber, fabric limestone, brick kilns, medical house, stables...

5. For accommodation

5.1 Residence of the reincarnations

As in Tibetan monasteries, the *labrang* (from Tibetan *bla-brang*) was an important residential complex for the reincarnation. Often located in an enclosed courtyard, it included a chapel (on the ground floor), an apartment (on the second floor), a kitchen, a reception room for high-ranking visitors and an office in the main building, a storehouse, quarters for the servants and sometimes a library in other buildings. During the summer, the reincarnated lama could live in a yurt inside the courtyard. In symmetrical layouts, the *labrang* was a Chinese style compound lying at the northern part of a lateral axis. In Tibetan style monasteries, it was a courtyard similar to those of Kumbum or Labrang in Amdo.[45] Every reincarnated monk had his own *labrang*: in Badgar coyiling süme [4] for instance, there were three *labrang* for the three reincarnations (although two of them resided elsewhere most of the time).

5.2 The abbot's residence

The abbot (*kambo*, from Tibetan *mkhan-po*), who was the effective ruler of the monastery, lived close to the Central assembly hall. In symmetrical layouts, his residence was the northernmost building of the central axis. In Kökeqota monasteries the abbot lived in the Jiujian lou, which also comprised a library on the second floor.

fig. 4 page 371

5.3 Monks' quarters

Ordinary monks' dwellings were simple mud-brick huts or/and yurts, with an area around 10-12 m^2 (3 bays). There were a bed heated by a *kang*, an altar for individual daily prayers plus a small kitchen. The roof was flat or slightly inclined and covered with clay and straw. A monk might have a small compound with a hut used for storage and study, coupled with a yurt for living quarters. Fortunate monks had a brick house with a sloping roof covered with tiles, north of the compound. Lamas lived with their disciples and with their servants. In Tibetan style monasteries like Badγar coyiling süme [4], the dwellings were big cubic houses of two or three storeys, in brick or stone covered with limestone. Monks dwellings were located around the main temples; they could form small streets when attached to each other. In the symmetrical layouts they were arranged in the private lateral axis, and often out of the compound too. There were no dormitories like in Chinese monasteries.

fig. 20 opposite page

High-ranking visitors (rich donators, important monks and reincarnations) stayed in a reincarnation's residence or in a yurt. Other visitors were accommodated in monks' dwellings, laymen yurts or houses, or brought their own tent for festivals.

The kitchen and a small contiguous storeroom were located either near the assembly hall or in the southern part of the monastery. It was specialised in the preparation of milk tea and food for the services. Monks had a small kitchen in their room to prepare independent meals; they ate meat and took food after noon. There was no refectory or dining room.

Monasteries settled close to rivers or wells. There were usually no toilets or sanitary facilities. Monks normally relieved themselves by squatting anywhere they like (in order not to soil their long robes). Perhaps there were Chinese style toilets in urban monasteries, but none has been preserved. Some Chinese style monasteries had a pond or a garden (without the Chinese Buddhist religious background).

45. Perhaps the reincarnated lama could also live on the first on second floor of the Central assembly hall, as in Tibetan monasteries.

20 – Badgar coyiling süme [4]
Monks' dwellings
(photo G. Béguin)

6. Inscriptions, trees

Chinese style stone inscriptions in Mongolian, Chinese and Tibetan were made for the first foundations of the 16th century but this practice was soon abandoned by Mongols. Later, the Qing emperors offered stone inscriptions sheltered in Chinese pavilions in the main courtyard, to commemorate the foundation and restoration of the imperial and imperialised monasteries. The official title received by the largest monasteries was calligraphed (sometimes by the emperor himself) in four languages (Mongol, Chinese, Tibetan and Manchu) on a horizontal wooden board suspended above the monastery's gate. In Chinese style monasteries, every major building can bear a name written on a wooden board.

From ten to several hundred metres outside the monastery, a stone tablet notified it was compulsory to dismount from one's horse.

Many trees located in the courtyards were considered as sacred. People making vows used to tie red ribbons to the boughs, which is a Shamanistic practice. Pipals cannot grow in Mongolia (there is one in a temple-greenhouse in Ivolginsk datsan, Buriatia).

The Mongolian Buddhist architecture has a relatively short history when compared to other Buddhist countries. Our very limited knowledge of the Mongol secular or religious building traditions before the 16th century makes it difficult to find the local roots of the Mongol monastic architecture. In any case, from the 16th century onwards, the mixture of various influences borrowed from China and Tibet led to typical Mongol features, such as the adaptation of a Tibetan multilevel structure with local materials and Chinese techniques, the creation of a framework and a sloping roof adapted to the large square structures of the assembly halls, a peculiar taste for external decoration with glazed tiles and brass objects as well as some iconographical specificities. The role of the unreformed schools of Tibetan Buddhism, which were influent until the mid-17th century, may explain some original features like the inner corridor for circumambulation around the shrine, that seem to contradict a certain uniformisation of Gelugpa architecture. The result in the physical aspects of these buildings is often a large heterogeneity of styles and techniques, ranging from almost pure Tibetan styles to various Sino-Tibetan styles and imitations of Chinese styles. Some are very original and prove to be unique technical and aesthetic achievements which later served as models for Northern Mongolian temples and Sino-Manchu monasteries of Jehol and Beijing. Several structures organised around the central skylight pavilion are reminiscent of mandala-based temples of India and of the First propagation of Buddhism in Tibet like bSam-yas, bringing to light a typical Mongolian taste for symmetry.

BIBLIOGRAPHY

ANONYM
1959 – *Nei Menggu gu jianzhu* [Ancient architectures of Inner Mongolia], Beijing, Wenwu chubanshe.

CHARLEUX, Isabelle
1998 – *Histoire et architecture des temples et monastères lamaïques de Mongolie méridionale*, Ph.D. Dissertation, Sorbonne University, Paris, unpublished.
1999 – "La Peinture des donateurs du temple de Maitreya en Mongolie méridionale", *Arts Asiatiques* 54, Paris, p. 85-102.
2000 – "Un Exemple d'architecture mongole: le Siregetü juu de Kökeqota", *Histoire de l'Art* 46, p. 91-110.
2001 – "The Reconstruction of Buddhist Monasteries in the Chinese Autonomous Region of Inner Mongolia: Between Sanctuary and Museum", *Proceedings of the International Conference "Revival of Buddhism in Mongolia after 1990"* (Warsaw, 24-28th November 1999), forthcoming.

DELEGE
1998 – *Nei Menggu lamajiao shi* [History of "Lamaism" in Inner Mongolia], Kökeqota, Nei Menggu renmin chubanshe.

HEISSIG, Walther
1953 – "A Mongolian Source to the Lamaist Suppression of Shamanism in the 17th century", *Anthropos* 48, Vienne and Fribourg, 1-2: p. 1-29 and 3-4: p. 493-536.
1961 – *Erdeni-yin erike: Mongolische Chronik der lamaistischen Klosterbauten der Mongolei*, trans. and commentary of the Mongolian chronicle written by Isibaldan in 1835, Copenhague, Ejnar Munksgaard (Monumenta linguarum Asiae majoris, Series nova, II).
1973 [1970] – "Les Religions de la Mongolie", *Les Religions du Tibet et de la Mongolie*, Giuseppe Tucci and Walther Heissig, trans. from German by R. Sailley, Paris, Payot [Stuttgart].

HYER, Paul
1982 – "An historical Sketch of Köke-Khota city capital of Inner Mongolia", *Central Asiatic Journal* 26 (1-2), Wiesbaden, p. 56-77.

JAGCHID, Sechin
1972 – "Buddhism in Mongolia after the Collapse of the Yuan Dynasty", *Traditions religieuses et para-religieuses des peuples altaïques*, Strasbourg, PUF (reed. in *Essays in Mongolian Studies*, Utah (USA), Brigham Young University, 1988).
1988 – *Essays in Mongolian Studies*, Utah (USA), Brigham Young University.

JAGCHID, Sechin and HYER, Paul
1978 – *Mongolia's Culture and Society*, Boulder (Colorado), Westview Press, Folkestone (UK), Dawson.

KESSLER, Adam T. et al.
1993 – *Empires beyond the Great Wall, The Heritage of Genghis Khan*, Los Angeles, Natural History Museum of Los Angeles County.

LINROTHE, Rob
1998 – "Xia Renzong and the Patronage of Tangut Buddhist Art: The Stūpa and Ushnīshavijayā Cult", *Journal of Sung-Yuan Studies* 28, p. 91-121.
1995 – "Peripherical Visions on recent Finds on Tangut Buddhist art", *Monumenta Serica* 43, p. 232-262.

LIU Dunzhen
1997 [1984] – *Zhongguo gudai jianzhu shi* [History of ancient Chinese Architecture], Beijing, Zhongguo jianzhu gongye chubanshe.

MILLER, Robert James
1959 – *Monasteries and Culture Change in Inner Mongolia*, Wiesbaden, Otto Harrassowitz (Asiatische Forschungen, 2).

NAGAO Gajin
1980 – "The Architectural Tradition in Buddhist Monasticism", *Studies in History of Buddhism* (Papers presented at the International Conference of the History of Buddhism at the University of Wisconsin, Madison, August 19-21, 1976), Delhi, B. R. Publishing Corporation, p. 189-208.
1987 [1947] – *Môko ramabyô ki* [Notes on Mongol "lamaist" monasteries], Kyôto, Chûkô bunko.
1991 [1947] – *Môko gakumon ji* [Academic monasteries in Mongolia], Kyôto, Chûkô bunko.

POZDNEEV, Aleksei M.
1977 [1896-1898] – *Mongolia and the Mongols*, vol. II, trans. from Russian by W. Dougherty, Bloomington: Mouton & Co. [St. Petersbourg].
1978 [1887] – *Religion and Ritual in Society: Lamaist Buddhism in late 19th in Mongolia*, trans. from Russian by Alo Raun and Linda Raun, Bloomington: The Mongolia Society [St. Petersbourg] (The Mongolia Society Occasional Papers, 10).

QIAO Ji, Coyiji
1994 – *Nei Menggu simiao* [Temples and monasteries of Inner Mongolia], Kökeqota, Nei Menggu renmin chubanshe.

SERRUYS, Henry
1963 – "Early Lamaism in Mongolia", *Oriens Extremus* 10 (2), Wiesbaden, October, p. 181-218.
1966, "Additional Notes on the Origin of Lamaism in Mongolia", *Oriens Extremus*, 12 (2), Wiesbaden, p. 165-173.

SINOR, Denis (ed.)
1990 – *The Cambridge History of Early Inner Asia*, Cambridge, New-York, Cambridge University Press.

STEINHARDT, Nancy S.
1997 – *Liao Architecture*, Honolulu, University of Hawai'i Press.

SU Bai
1994 – "Huhehaote ji qi fujin ji zuo zhaomiao diantang buju de chubu tantao" [Survey of the layout of several monastic buildings of Kökeqota and of its surroundings],*Wenwu* , Beijing, p. 53-61.

Sulla via della seta. L'Impero perduto: Arte buddhista da Khara Khoto (X-XIII secolo)
1993 – Milan, Fondazione Thyssen-Bornemisza / Electa.

YANG Jizeng (ed)
1997 – *Nei Menggu lamajiao jili* [Chronicle of "Lamaism" in Inner Mongolia], Kökeqota, Nei Menggu wenshi shudian (Nei Menggu wenshi ziliao, 45).

BUDDHIST MONASTERIES IN KOREA

Kim Dong-uk

Currently, almost half the population of South Korea professes some kind of religion. Among them, Buddhists amount more than 45%, followed by the Protestants and the Catholics. In Korean history, Buddhism became the main religion in the fourth century AD, and flourished for one thousand years. In the fifteenth century, Buddhism faced harsh repression from the government. It continued about five hundred years. During these hard periods, monasteries in the urban areas vanished almost completely. Only the monasteries in remote mountainous areas survived. They were places for the monks' self-training in Zen Buddhism. In spite of the political suppression, Buddhism was popular among peasants and women, the lower classes of the society, and the monasteries were maintained partially by only the few supporters and monks. During these periods, Buddhist believers, peasants or women, had to take long and painful walks to visit their favourite monasteries. It was only at the end of the nineteenth century that the political repression ended officially. From this time on, Buddhism gradually regained its power.

Korea, located on a peninsula at the eastern end of the Chinese landmass, has suffered from continuous invasions by its northern neighbours, always resulting in hazardous plundering and burning down of Buddhist monasteries. The invasion of Japanese armies at the end of the sixteenth century also brought about another immense disaster. This is the main reason why very few historic Buddhist monasteries remain in Korea in spite of their long and proud history.

Most of the existing Buddhist monasteries were built or rebuilt after the seventeenth century. Only a handful of buildings built before the sixteenth century are still extant in North and South Korea. Archaeologists' efforts provided some information on their aspects, but the present political situation, with North and South Korea divided since 1945, has disrupted the exchanges of mutual knowledge, and I cannot get any reliable sources about the present situation of Buddhist monasteries of the Democratic People's Republic of Korea.

Hence, this article only deals with the sources limited to the southern part of the Korean Peninsula.

The Buddhist Monastery, EFEO, 2003, p. 391-410

1 – A brief history and chronology

Buddhism was introduced to Korea around the fourth century AD, when the Korean Peninsula was divided into three kingdoms, Koguryŏ, Paekche, and Silla. Koguryŏ, the northern kingdom, was visited by a Chinese monk in the year AD 372, and a dozen years later, neighbouring Paekche was host to an Indian missionary who had come also by way of China. Silla was not exposed to Buddhist influence until about AD 528, and openly preaching Buddhism had been allowed there since the martyrdom of the saintly monk Ichadon.

In each of the three kingdoms, the royal houses took the principal initiative in the acceptance of Buddhism. Buddhism was seen to be well suited as a spiritual prop in support of the new governing structure centred on the authority of the throne. Many temples and monasteries were constructed and numbers of believers were converted. So deeply rooted did Buddhism become in Paekche and Koguryŏ, that by the sixth century priests, scriptures, and religious artisans and artefacts were being sent to Japan, forming the basis of the early Buddhist culture there.

After the peninsula was unified as a single nation under Silla in AD 668, Buddhism was embraced as the state religion, although the governmental system was already being run along Confucian lines, with no conflict between the two. Buddhism was the dominant system of thought in United Silla. As the religion was revered and professed alike by all the people, from the king to the populace at large, Buddhism played a vital role in Silla society. The many monks who returned to Silla after studying in China brought back the doctrines of the various Buddhist sects that had proliferated under the Tang dynasty. In this way, five major doctrinal sects became established in Silla: the Nirvāṇa school, the Vinaya, the Buddha-nature, the Avatamsaka and the Dharmalaksana. The great popularity of Pure Land Buddhism, principally among the common people, is another striking feature of the history of Buddhism in the United Silla period.

Royal patronage during this golden age produced a magnificent flowering of Buddhist arts and architecture. However, the fragmentation of the kingdom after less than 200 years did not harm the dominant position of the Buddhist, and the succeeding Koryŏ Dynasty (936-1392) that came to power in AD 936 was even more enthusiastic in its support of the imported doctrines. The new trend in Buddhism in the late Silla period was the popularity of Zen (in Korean, *Sŏn*) as the religion of the local gentry.

In the eleventh century, the golden age of the Koryŏ dynasty, the new Tien-tai doctrine dominated the circles of Buddhism and showed eager efforts to unify the conflict between the Textual and the Zen Schools. The efforts ended in vain in 1170, when military forces took political control and favoured Zen Buddhism.

During the Koryŏ period, monks became politicians and courtiers. In the thirteenth century, the Mongols invaded Korea. The entire country was conquered and ravaged except for the island of Kanghwa, in the estuary of the Han River, where the king and the court took refuge. The reaction of the court was to implore divine assistance by undertaking the immense project of carving the entire bulk of Buddhist scriptures onto wooden blocks for printing. This is the so-called *Tripiṭaka Koreana*, still extant today and on display at Haein-sa. Nevertheless, this act of piety did not result in the defeat of the Mongols, who made Korea a vassal state.

It was quite natural that Buddhists were to share some of the blame for the national disaster, since power had been in their hands. From that period may be dated a definite and rapid decline in Korean Buddhism. After General Yi Song-gye staged a revolt and had himself proclaimed king in 1392, his policy was anti-Buddhist. Although the new king, his family, and most of his successors were devout believers in Buddhism, every possible influence of the religion was removed from the government. The vast wealth and land holdings of temples were seized.

Throughout the history of Chosŏn (1392-1910), Buddhism seemed to revive whenever the politically powerful members of the royal family were Buddhists. However, efforts for Buddhist revival met with strong opposition from Confucian scholars and officials. Buddhist monks organized armies of monks to help defend the country during the Japanese invasions of Korea between 1592 and 1598, winning a number of decisive victories. Despite such contributions to the national defence, official oppression of Buddhism continued until the last years of the Chosŏn period. Buddhist monks were ranked the lowest social class and were not allowed inside the capital. The severe oppression drove the temples into remote mountainous areas, making Buddhism a monastic religion rather than a religion for laymen. This historic background accounts for the fact that today the major Buddhist temples are in deep mountainous areas.

During this political repression, Buddhism tended to incline strongly towards the Zen school. Most temples had internally various doctrines like Hua-Yen or Pure Land belief, but Zen Buddhism impregnated almost all the monasteries.

Confucianism was the state cult or national religion during that entire era. In an effort to prune and control Buddhism, several kings forcibly reformed and consolidated the various sects. When the Japanese took over and colonized Korea in 1910, there were several attempts to infiltrate Korean Buddhist sects or amalgamate them with Japanese Buddhist sects. Those attempts by and large failed, and may even have resulted in a revival of interest in native Buddhism on the part of Koreans.

Marriage was allowed to Japanese monks, while the entire Korean Buddhist tradition had been one of clerical celibacy. Under the Japanese influence, some Korean monks adopted the custom of marrying, and, after the liberation in 1945, there were bitter legal battles for many years over the legitimacy of ownership of certain temple properties between the married and celibate sects. The celibates eventually won.

Buddhism has the largest number of followers among all Korean religions. The 1995 survey recorded 39 Buddhist sects and 11,561 temples with more than 11 million followers in Korea. Chogyejong is the largest of the sects. Buddhism in Korea is currently undergoing a sort of renaissance stemming from a conscious attempt to adapt to the changes of industrialization, an increased interest among Koreans in traditional thought and stricter standards for monks. Buddhist orders have set up urban centres for the propagation of the faith. The *Tripiṭaka Koreana* is being translated into modern Korean and digitalized on CD-rom. Foreign monks are receiving training in Korean monasteries, and temples are being built in foreign countries.

Brief chronology of Buddhism in Korea

372 Beginning of Buddhism in Korea: Monk Sundo of the Earlier Chin state comes to Koguryŏ with Buddha image and Sutras

375 The two first temples of Korea built in Koguryŏ

384 Monk Malananta brings Buddhism to Paekche from the Eastern Chin state

394 Monk Mukhoja introduces Buddhism to the people of the northern province of Silla

527 After the martyrdom of Ichadon, the King of Silla authorizes Buddhism

534 Nine monks of Paekche sent to Japan

643 Monk Chajang becomes the chief abbot of the State, the leader of the sect of Vinaya
671 Monk Uisang returns from Tang China with the Hua-yen doctrine
821 Monk Toui comes back from Tang China after studying Zen Buddhism
918 Ten monasteries built at Kaesŏng, the capital of the Koryŏ dynasty
958 The government service examination for monks begins
989 The complete collection of Buddhist *sūtras* is brought in from Sung China
1067 Hungwang-sa, the largest monastery of the Dynasty, completed
1086 The Korean Tien-tai sect initiated by Uichŏn
1097 First carving of the *Tripiṭaka* on woodblocks
1106 The memorial service of the one hundredth day after the king's death is held in the court of the Palace
1205 The Chogyejong, a sect of Korean Zen school, established
1232 The Mongol army invades the peninsula
1236 New carving of the *Tripiṭaka Koreana* starts at the refuge, Kanghwa Island
1251 The *Tripiṭaka Koreana* is completed on woodblocks
1391 Bureaucrats appeal to the king to reject Buddhism
1392 Establishment of the Chosŏn Dynasty
1406 King Taejong orders to restrict the number of Buddhist monasteries
1424 The existing seven sects of Buddhism are merged into two, the Contemplative (Zen) and the Textual (Kyo) school
1451 The monks are banned from entering the capital
1458 The Storage Hall of *Tripiṭaka Koreana* at Haein-sa built with governmental aid
1503 The examination of the monks to be selected for administrative position is abolished
1566 The repression of Buddhism is tightened after the death of the Queen Dowager Munjong
1592 The Japanese army invades the peninsula
1592 Troops of Buddhist monks cause severe blows to the Japanese army
1623 Monk Kaksong directs the construction of the Namhansan Fortress
1790 Yongju-sa, guardian temple for the tomb of the king Chŏngjo, established with governmental aid
1897 The ban on monks entering the capital is revoked
1910 Korea becomes a Japanese colony
1911 Thirty-one head monasteries are selected
1941 Chogyejong, a unified sect of Buddhism, established
1945 Korea liberated from the Japanese colonialism
1950 Korean War starts. Many monasteries are burnt down during the three years of war

1953 Government officials order married monks to leave the monasteries

1970 Taekojong, a sect of married monks, is established

1975 The birthday of Buddha, April 8th of the lunar calendar, becomes a national holiday

2 – General location and density of monasteries in the country

2.1 The location of the ancient monasteries

As Buddhism was welcomed by the royal houses of the Three Kingdoms, dozens of temples and monasteries of early period were built in the capitals of each kingdom; Pyongyang of Koguryŏ, Puyŏ of Paekche, and Kyŏngju of Silla. Among the numerous Buddhist monasteries, Paekche's Wanghung-sa ("Temple of the King ascendant"), and Silla's Hwangnyong-sa ("Temple of the Illustrious Dragon"), both dedicated to the dissemination of the doctrine of State protection, were built on the grandest scale.

No visual remains exist except some structures made of stone, like stone pagodas (stūpas). Through archaeological excavations, numerous temple sites were partially revealed. The following sites can be considered to represent the main layouts:

- the site of Keumgang-sa (Pyongyang):
  one wooden stūpa with three image halls;
- the site of Chongneung-sa (Pyongyang):
  the largest monastic complex ever known in Koguryŏ, the protecting temple of the first king;
- the site of Keumgang-sa (Puyŏ):
  one wooden stūpa with one image hall;
- the site of Chongrim-sa (Puyŏ):
  one stone stūpa with one image hall;
- the site of Neung-sa (Puyŏ):
  protecting the royal tomb, where a renowned gilt bronze vessel was found;
- the site of Hwangnyong-sa (Kyŏngju):
  its complete layout reveals the largest monastery ever known in Silla.

When the Korean Peninsula was unified by Silla in the seventh century, Buddhism spread nationwide. One source indicates that eight or nine of every ten Silla people professed Buddhism. Various Buddhist doctrines were introduced, among them, the Avatamasaka (Hwaŏm: Chinese Hua-yen) and Pure Land Buddhism were widely accepted. Under these new doctrines, monasteries spread into the remote rural areas apart from the capital.

At the beginning of the ninth century, a new trend in Buddhism was the popularity of *Sŏn* (Zen). The Zen, or Contemplative School, tended to locate their teaching centres in remote mountains, away from cities and even villages. The Zen faith gradually started to spread more widely, leading to the establishment of the so-called Nine Mountain Sects of Zen. The great popularity of Zen is explained by the warm reception it received from the powerful gentry families in the countryside. Most of the nine sects of the Zen school had close ties with the local gentry.

Buddhism's impact on everyday life was of great significance for Koryŏ society, from the 10th to the 14th century. The Koryŏ aristocracy regarded Buddhism not merely as an otherworldly religion but as a faith that would influence the fortunes of the state and individuals in the contemporary world. Numerous monasteries were built in the capital as well as in remote rural cities. Renowned mountains were filled with numerous monasteries and monks. The Hungwang-sa temple, extending over 2,800 kan (about 9,270 square metres) of floor space and completed after twelve years of construction in 1067, is perhaps the most notable example of a temple built with the objective of ensuring dynastic well-being. The proliferation of temples in Koryŏ – there were as many as seventy in Kaesŏng, the capital, alone – itself conveys a clear picture of Koryŏ as a thoroughly Buddhist state.

Monasteries expanded their landholdings through donations from the royal house and aristocracy, through demands to the peasants, and by outright seizure. Because these lands enjoyed the special privilege of tax exemption, Buddhist establishments grew ever more powerful economically. They also increased their riches through commerce, wine making, and livestock raising.

Often, monasteries were built in commercial areas or along traffic routes. The Han river, which flows across the middle of the Korean peninsula, played the main role in water traffic and many monasteries were located along its banks. The Silrŭk-sa at Yŏju was one of the dominant examples, and its famous seven storeyed brick stūpa must have been a good landmark for the people on the boats.

The Chosŏn dynasty was established in 1392 by an aristocratic group who had strong belief in Confucianism. Buddhism could not but wither in a society where Confucianism was paramount. The first king instituted a registration system to prevent the monk population from increasing and banned any founding of new monasteries. The third king inaugurated a severe repression on Buddhism, leaving only 242 monasteries throughout the whole country, at the same time confiscating their lands and slaves. This was a blow of such magnitude for Buddhism that it could never recover, though a few monasteries remained in the urban areas.

The repressive policy on Buddhism did not remove all monasteries, but those in the cities and on the traffic routes disappeared. Only few of them could avoid the disaster by searching for new functions. In Yŏju the Silrŭk-sa survived by voluntarily taking up the burden of protecting and managing the royal tomb nearby. Only the monasteries secluded in the mountains could survive. They were maintained by monks' own labour and supported by peasants and a limited number of women of the royal families. Buddhist believers and pilgrims, women and peasants mostly, had to travel a long way to visit those holy places up in the mountains.

2.2 Present situation

In the 1995 census, the number of officially registered monasteries amounts to 11,561 and 26,037 monks were recorded in about 39 Buddhist sects. The number of Buddhist devotees was estimated as 10,231,000, which is 23% of the whole population (44,608,000). The Buddhist believers took the largest number among those who answered as having a religion, followed by 8,700,000 Protestants, and 3,240,000 Catholics.

It is quite difficult to find Buddhist monasteries in the urban areas except for new temples, which serve as preaching centres, or small house-like temples. Still now, almost all monasteries are found on far away mountains. Believers who want to reach the nearest monastery have to take at least more than a one hour's ride. Sometimes they have to climb the mountain to visit their favourite monks. When a Buddhist festival is

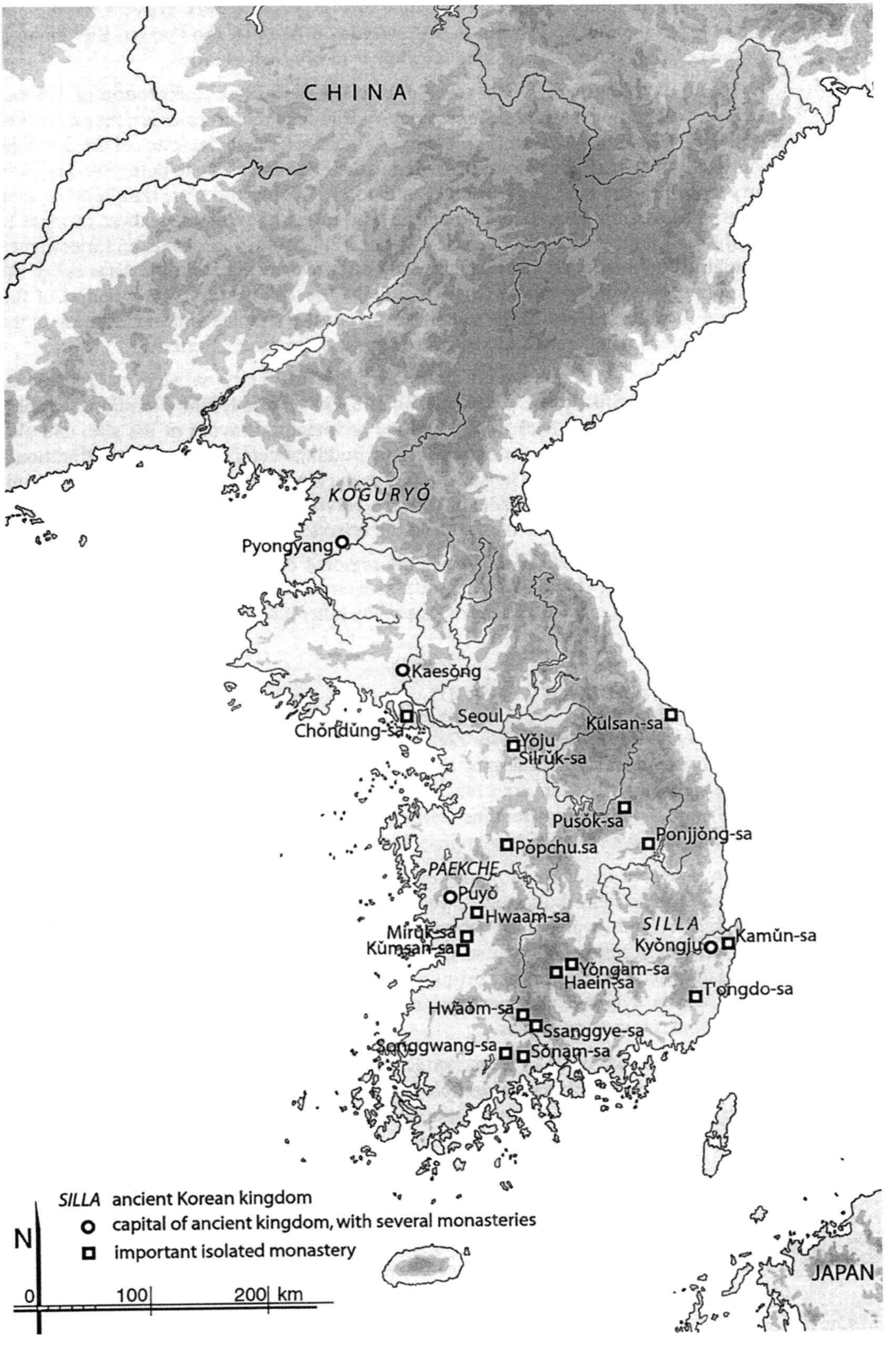
CHINA
KOGURYŎ
Pyongyang
Kaesŏng
Seoul
Chŏndŭng-sa
Kŭlsan-sa
Yŏju
Silrŭk-sa
Pusŏk-sa
Pŏpchu.sa
Ponjjŏng-sa
PAEKCHE
Puyŏ
Hwaam-sa
SILLA
Mirŭk-sa
Kŭmsan-sa
Kyŏngju
Kamŭn-sa
Yŏngam-sa
Haein-sa
T'ongdo-sa
Hwaŏm-sa
Ssanggye-sa
Songgwang-sa
Sŏnam-sa
SILLA ancient Korean kingdom
capital of ancient kingdom, with several monasteries
important isolated monastery
N
0
100
200 km
JAPAN

held, like the birthday of Śākyamuni, hundreds of people gather to every temple and monastery in the mountains. But in the everyday urban life, the trace of Buddhism is seldom noticed, and a monk asking for alms is rarely seen in cities.

Those characteristics seem to be due to the historical background of Korean Buddhism. It could be said that contemporary Buddhist monasteries are the product of the historic transition from the 17th century. At that time, the social status of the Buddhist monks was to be partially recovered, owing to their dominant role to defeat the Japanese army invading the peninsula in 1592 and 1597. During the war, hundreds of men gathered to the monkhood, and when the war ended, they devoted their strength to rebuild their temples and monasteries. In the 17th century, peasants and merchants, originally Buddhist, who had earned wealth after recovering from the disasters of the war, supported willingly these reconstructions. The 18h century was a period of full blossom for the recovery of the temples. Most of the temples and monasteries in the mountain areas which remain today were rebuilt during these periods.

At present, 841 temples and monasteries are officially enlisted as "traditional temples" by the Ministry of Culture and Tourism. The criteria for the "traditional temple" status are the historical background and the architectural layout of the site, and also some intangible assets like the occurrence of Buddhist ceremonies. These "traditional temples" are selected among those built before the nineteenth century, generally rebuilt in the seventeenth or the eighteenth century. Having conserved the traditional architectural model is also a decisive factor in the selection.

The map, on opposite page, shows the regional distribution of these "traditional temples". We can easily note that the south-western areas have a large number of them, while they are rare in the central provinces. The latter also applies to large cities with a dense population.

3 – The monastery layout

Buddhism had been integrated by Zen thought in Korean monasteries throughout the whole Chosŏn dynasty, submerging the various doctrines and schools developed since the Koryŏ dynasty. These doctrinal changes affected the layout of the monastery. Magnificent and glittering Buddhist ceremonies were significantly reduced, while the whole complex was arranged to emphasize the function of meditation.

The layout of the Korean monasteries had been established under the influence of China. The ancient monasteries were directly built on the Chinese model. From the eighth or ninth century, the monasteries began to bring out native architectural characteristics in spite of continuous Chinese influence. It could be said that the Korean monasteries accomplished their originality in the fifteenth century, at the beginning of the Chosŏn dynasty. The mountain monasteries for self-training and meditation are the most relevant examples.

There were two types of monasteries: the first type combined a symbolic feature like a stūpa with one or several temple halls; in its earliest examples, built in urban areas by order of the ancient kings, the layout and architectural elements were influenced by that of China. In the second and later type, buildings were arranged around courtyards in monasteries built by donations of bureaucrats and nobles from the ninth or tenth century. Since the monasteries began to spread to the remote mountains, the second type was adopted widely throughout the country with various forms of courtyards and buildings arranged in harmony with the shapes of valleys, directions of sunrise, locations of streams, etc. The theory of geomancy played a great role in the shaping of these mountain monasteries.

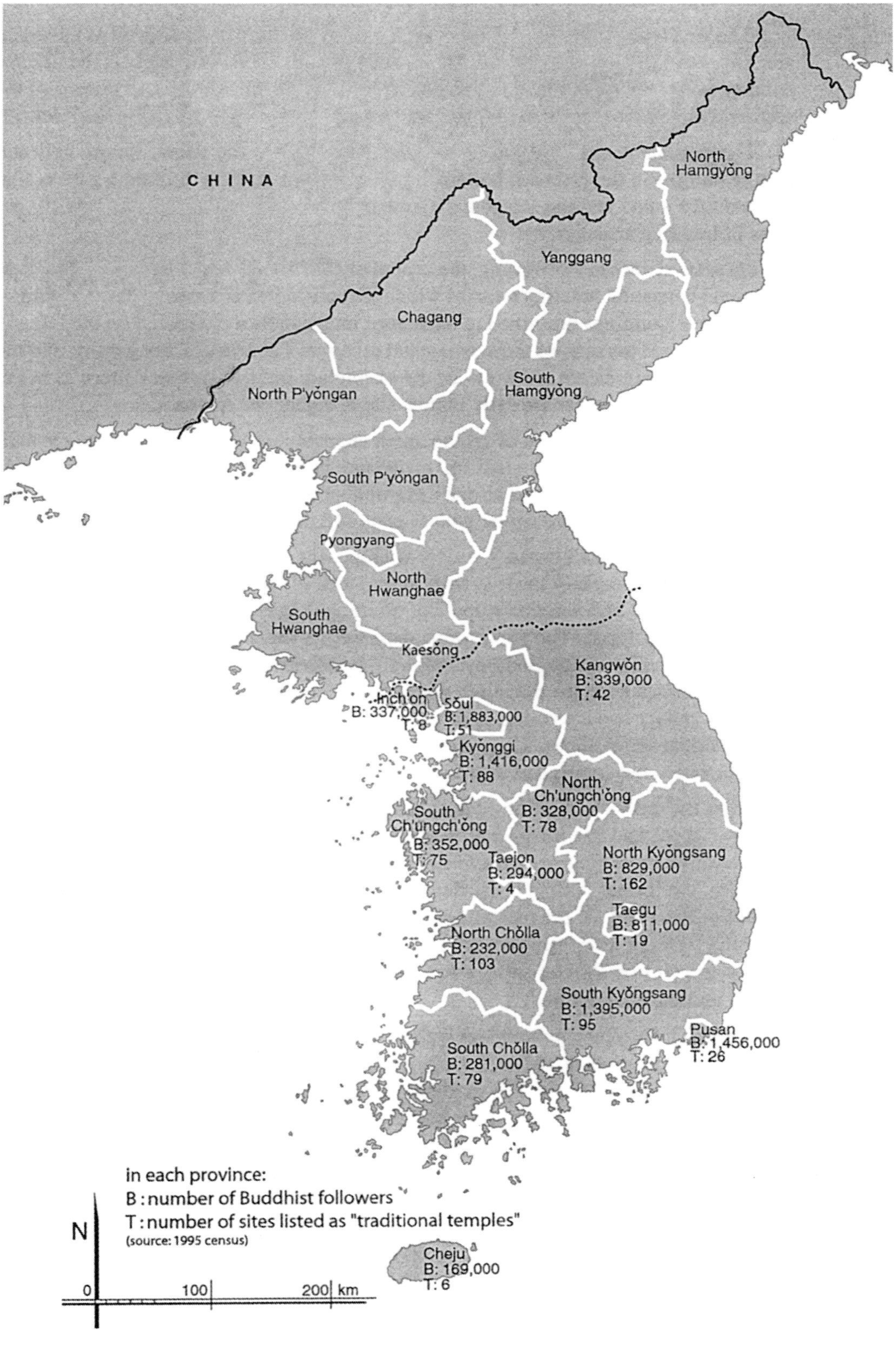
CHINA
North Hamgyŏng
Yanggang
Chagang
South Hamgyŏng
North P'yŏngan
South P'yŏngan
Pyongyang
North Hwanghae
South Hwanghae
Kaesŏng
Kangwŏn
B: 339,000
T: 42
Inch'on
B: 337,000
T: 8
Sŏul
B: 1,883,000
T: 51
Kyŏnggi
B: 1,416,000
T: 88
North Ch'ungch'ŏng
B: 328,000
T: 78
South Ch'ungch'ŏng
B: 352,000
T: 75
Taejon
B: 294,000
T: 4
North Kyŏngsang
B: 829,000
T: 162
Taegu
B: 811,000
T: 19
North Chŏlla
B: 232,000
T: 103
South Kyŏngsang
B: 1,395,000
T: 95
Pusan
B: 1,456,000
T: 26
South Chŏlla
B: 281,000
T: 79
in each province:
B : number of Buddhist followers
T : number of sites listed as "traditional temples"
(source: 1995 census)
N
Cheju
B: 169,000
T: 6
0
100
200 km

3.1 The first type: the ancient urban monastery

The first type was built in the capitals of the ancient kingdoms as well as the urban areas of the Koryŏ dynasty. These monasteries were destroyed completely in the Chosŏn dynasty, with a few exceptions. Owing to the efforts of the archaeologist, dozens of the ancient temple sites were exposed, among which several sites showed the whole layout.

These ancient monasteries had a symmetrical plan, the stūpa, image hall and lecture hall being the essential buildings. A rectangular corridor formed a gallery that enclosed the stūpa and the image hall. Archaeologists have revealed a couple of patterns of building arrangement.

On several sites in Pyŏngyang, the capital of the Koguryŏ kingdom, archaeologists excavated octagonal building remains which are considered as bases of wooden stūpas. Two or three buildings presumed to have been image halls were placed on the left and right sides, or at the rear, of these octagonal remains. The site of Chongam-ri, and the site of Chongnung-sa are known to be the exemplary ones. A similar pattern as in the Chongam-ri was found at the early temple site of Japan, the Asukadera.

In Puyŏ, another pattern of arrangement appears, one stūpa with one image hall. The gate, the stūpa, the image hall and the lecture hall stood in a straight line one after another. The site of Kunsu-ri is an early example of this pattern, constructed by the end of the sixth century. A rectangular gallery enclosed the stūpa and the image hall.

In the early seventh century, a new attempt was to build stūpas of stone, as we could see in an example of the five-story stone stūpa in Chongrim-sa temple, following the general shape of a wooden stūpa, but omitting details of woodwork incompatible with the new material. The stone stūpa deserves its reputation of a creative Korean achievement in East Asian Buddhist culture. The Mirŭk-sa temple, 60 km south of the Puyŏ city, shows a unique planning, where three rectangular galleries are juxtaposed. The main gallery had a wooden stūpa at its centre, while the galleries on right and left sides had both stone stūpas. These stone stūpas soon spread into other areas, including Kyŏngju where the details had been simplified even more

After the unification of the peninsula by the Silla Kingdom, a new layout appears with two stūpas and one image hall, seemingly under the influence of the Tang China. The site of Sachonwang-sa (built in 679) and the site of Kamŭn-sa (682) are typical examples, the former with two wooden stūpas, the latter with two stone stūpas. At the site of Sachonwang-sa, the two wooden stūpas stood in front of the image hall while the belfry and the *sūtra* tower were at the left and the right side, behind the image hall. At the site of Kamŭn-sa, the two enormous three-storey stone stūpas are the biggest and the best defined.

fig. 1 opposite page
fig. 2 opposite page

In the eighth century, monasteries with more than one enclosure had become popular, which reflected various Buddhist doctrines and faith. Bulkuk-sa of Kyŏngju is regarded as a representative of them. The precinct of Bulkuk-sa consisted of more than three enclosures; each had their own image hall. Skilful rubble masonry and stone pagoda of the Bulkuk-sa temple showed refined stone workmanship of the eighth century. The Hungwang-sa temple at Kaesŏng, capital of the Koryŏ Dynasty, built in the eleventh century with royal supports, was made up of five or more enclosures. It is known to have had the most grandiose scale in the period. The main enclosure, with two stūpas and one image hall, was located at the centre of the site. The other surrounding enclosures took various forms that reflected their different functions.

1 – *The site of Kamŭn-sa* (ph. Kim Dong-uk)

2 – *The three-storey stone stūpas at Kamŭn-sa* (ph. Kim Dong-uk)

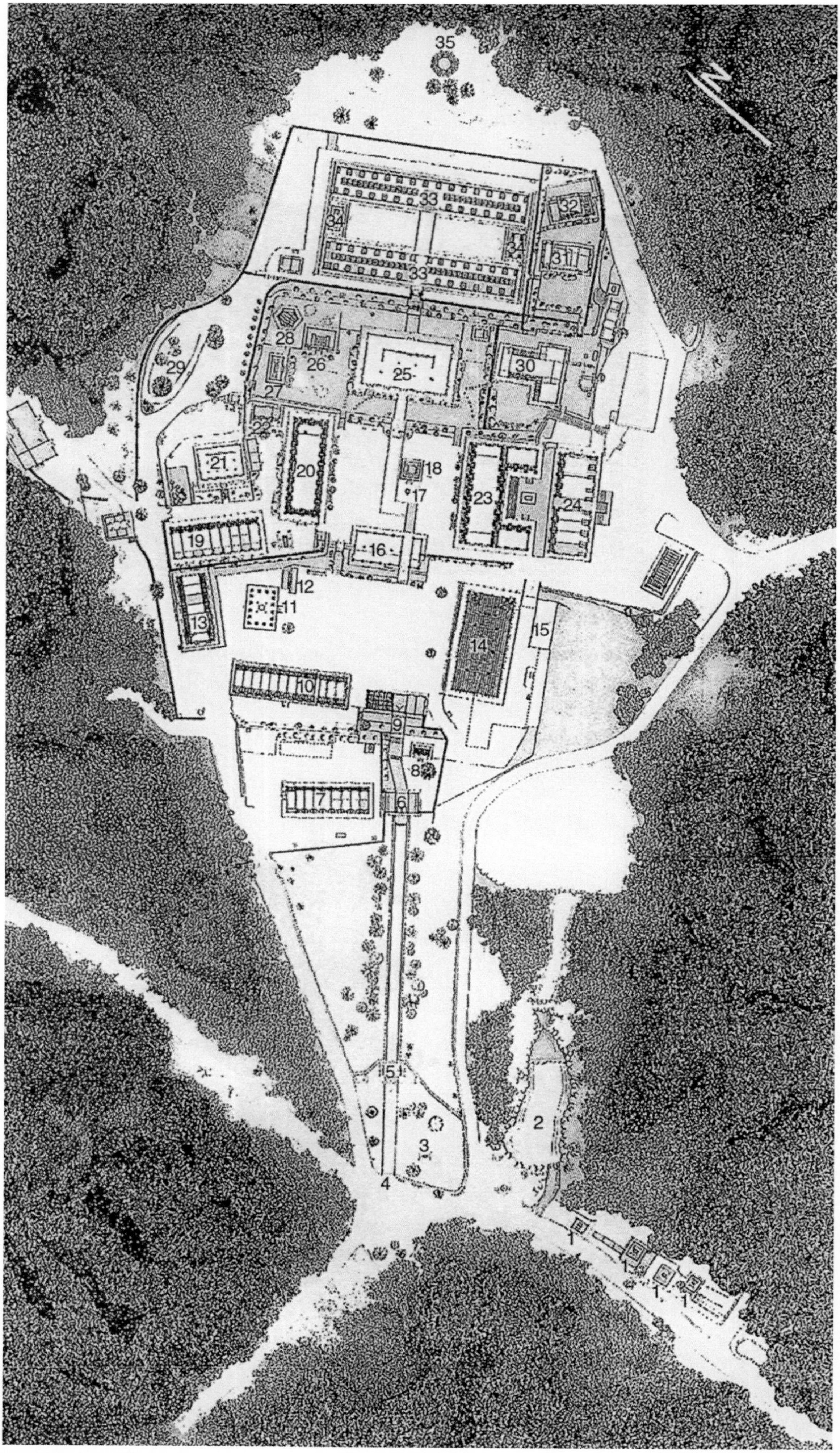
N
35
33
34
32
31
33
28
26
25
30
29
27
22
21
20
18
17
23
24
19
16
12
11
13
14
15
10
9
8
7
6
5
2
3
4
1
1
1
1

3.2 The second type: the mountain monastery with courtyard

The second type of monastery, which spread nationwide from the ninth and tenth centuries, under the Koryŏ and Chosŏn dynasties, is found mostly in mountainous areas.

It is hard to find any regulated principles for their layout, which seemed to be decided according to the terrain and the surrounding circumstances in order to achieve a good harmony with the natural setting. Most mountain monasteries are planned around one or several courtyards.

The monastery compound is usually demarcated by a single-pillar gate at the front entrance. At a short distance from this first gate stands the gate of the four Heavenly Kings, marking the entrance to the temple precinct proper. Soon after this second gate, a large pavilion obstructs the inner view. A narrow passage under the pavilion leads to a courtyard surrounded by buildings on its four sides. Small scale monasteries have only one courtyard, while large monasteries have several courtyards established at different levels.

The layout of the Haein-sa in South Kyŏngsang province is a proper example of these large scale monasteries. Though Haein-sa was established in the ninth century, its present layout basically dates from the fifteenth century, when the hall of *Tripiṭaka Koreana* was built with governmental aid. *fig. 3 opposite page*

The monastery, which presides today over a network of 75 affiliated monasteries and 16 hermitages, is located on the mid-slopes of the magnificent Mt. Kaya. At the head of a 4-kilometre long valley where a verdant tunnel of old pines and numerous deciduous trees meets rugged cliffs and wild streams, several stone monuments indicate the approach to the sacred world. The precincts, with their numerous buildings, show a certain regularity. Dominant buildings are placed on an alignment across the whole site, divided into several areas according to their function. Three consecutive gates, a main pavilion, a main image hall and the storage hall are located on the central axis, moving aside to the left. Buildings for the monks' worship and training are placed to the left side of the axis, dining rooms and dormitories for monks at the right side.

3 – *Site plan of Haein-sa*

1. Stone monuments
2. Pond
3. Two stone banner pillars
4. Land marks
5. *Ilju* gate
6. *Ponghwangmum* (gate of Heavenly King)
7. *Myongwoltang* (guest room)
8. *Kuksadan* (platform for land deity)
9. *Haet'almun* gate (gate of Salvation)
10. *Saundang* (office)
11. *Pŏmjonggak* (belfry)
12. Stone water-tank
13. *Ch'ŏnghwadang* (guest room)
14. *Pulgyohoegwan* (meeting hall)
15. Refectory
16. *Kugwangru* (pavilion)
17. Stone podium for lamp
18. Three-storey stūpa
19. *Yosach'ae* (monks' quarters)
20. *Kunghyŏndang* (lecture room)
21. *Kyŏnghakwon* (lecture hall)
22. *Samsogul* (library)
23. *Kwanŭmjŏn* (hall of Avalokiteśvara)
24. *Taemunchae* (Great Gate building)
25. *Taejŏkkwangjŏn* (hall of Silence and Light)
26. *Myŏngbujŏn* (hall of the Underworld)
27. *Ungjinjŏn* (hall of Arhats)
28. Hall of self awareness
29. Platform for scholars
30. *Sŏnyŏltang* (superior's quarters)
31. *T'oesŏltang* (elderly monk's quarters)
32. *Chosajŏn* (hall for portraits of monks)
33. *Sudarajang*, *Pŏppojŏn* (hall of *Tripiṭaka koreana*)
34. Storage of woodblocks prints
35. Stūpa

4 – *The depository halls for the* Tripiṭaka Koreana *woodblocks at Haein-sa*
(ph. Kim Dong-uk)

The whole complex is divided into five or six terraces rising gradually with the natural slope. On the first terrace are the gate of Heavenly Kings at the southern centre and a guesthouse on the left, a platform with the shrine of the land deity on the right. The second terrace consists of the gate of emancipation at the centre, office and belfry, reception room on the right, large dining room for laity on the right side. Passing under the Kugwangru pavilion, we reach the third terrace. A stone stūpa stands at the centre of the terrace with two large lecture halls and the library on the left, while two large dormitories for monks are on the right side. The fourth terrace is used for worship, with the main image hall, the Hall of Great Silence and Light, Taejŏkkwangjŏn, placed at the centre. The hall of Underworld, the hall of Arhats and the hall of Self-Awareness are placed on the left side, and the superior's quarters on the right side. The storage hall of *Tripiṭaka Koreana* is in the centre of the sixth terrace, at the highest level, with the hall for portraits of successive high monks and the elderly monks' quarters on the right.

fig. 4 above

Through these various types of buildings arranged in a limited area, we can see a clear planning structure in the layout of Haein-sa, which had been conserved from the fifteenth century to the present day. Quite a number of large monasteries in famous mountains show a layout based on similar principles, for instance the T'ongdo-sa in South Kyŏngsang province, the Sonam-sa in South Chŏlla province or the Pŏpchu-sa in North Ch'ungchŏng province.

Small monasteries of a typical layout are found in the mountains near rural villages. They were generally rebuilt after the seventeenth century. Their dominant feature is the central courtyard framed by four buildings: the image hall on the rear side, the lecture hall on the left side, the monk's quarters on the right side and the pavilion on the front side. This layout can be found all over the country.

fig. 5 opposite page

fig. 6 and 7 opposite page

Hwaam-sa in South Chŏlla province, completely rebuilt in the seventeenth century, is located at the end of a narrow stream walled by cliffs and forests, eight kilometres from the closest village. As a pavilion stands in front of the precincts, without any passage, one has to pass on its side to enter the courtyard surrounded by the image and lecture halls, the monks' quarters and the pavilion. A tiny building enshrining the mountain deity stands at the rear side of the image hall, reflecting the native belief. A number of monasteries in the mountains have similar layout, with some variations in accordance with the surroundings.

On a steep site, entering the courtyard is allowed only by ascending narrow stairs under the pavilion. This gives an impression of gradual increase of vista.

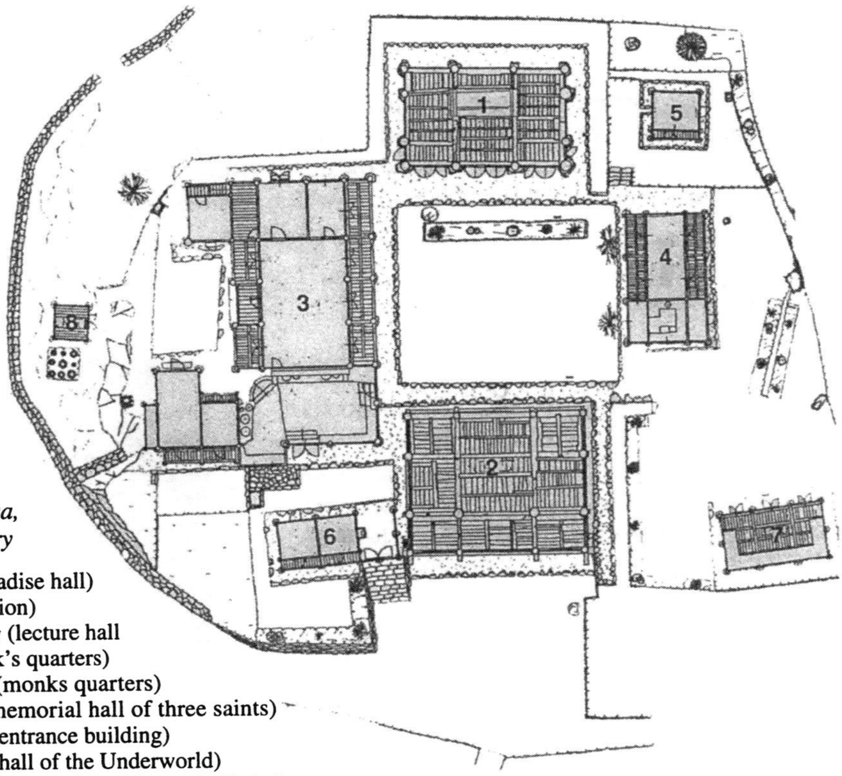

5 – Site plan of Hwaam-sa, a mountain monastery

1. *Kŭkrajŏn* (Paradise hall)
2. *Uhwaru* (pavilion)
3. *Chŏkmukdang* (lecture hall and head monk's quarters)
4. *Bulmyŏngam* (monks quarters)
5. *Chŏlyŏngje* (memorial hall of three saints)
6. *Munganchae* (entrance building)
7. *Myŏngbujŏn* (hall of the Underworld)
8. *Sansingak* (pavilion of the Mountain Deity)

6 – The image and lecture halls at Hwaam-sa
(ph. Kim Dong-uk)

7 – The courtyard at Hwaam-sa
(ph. Kim Dong-uk)

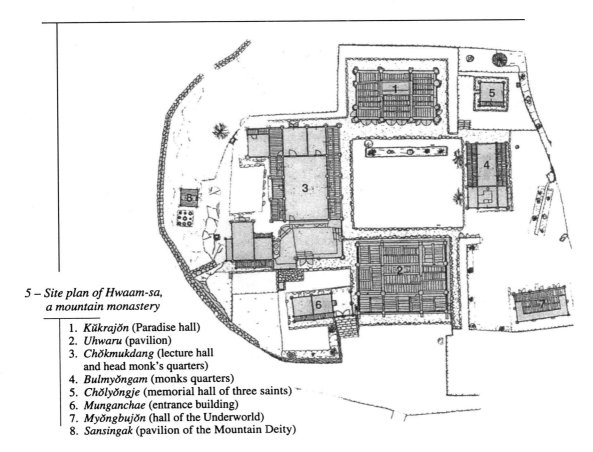

Some monasteries had two juxtaposed courtyards, like Pongjŏng-sa in North Kyŏngsang province. One courtyard is surrounded by the image hall of Śākyamuni, the monks' quarters, the lecture hall and the pavilion, the other by the hall of Amitābha, the superior's quarters and the lecture hall, which separates the two courtyards.

These small monasteries were built with the monks' self-sufficient efforts. It can be said that those unique layouts around one or two courtyards reflect the timeless experiences of long mountain lives.

3.3 The Buddhist grotto

Though Buddhist caves were not popular in Korea, some monks used natural caves as worship or training places between the seventh and the eighth centuries. Among them, the unique Sŏkkuram is an artificial cave hollowed out of solid rock in the eighth century, some 750 meters above sea level on the top of Mount Toham, near Kyŏngju. It consists of a main rotunda, a corridor and an antechamber. In the centre of the main rotunda, the great Buddha image is surrounded by Bodhisattvas, arhats and ancient Indian gods carved in high relief on the circular wall. These elegant and majestic images are said to epitomize the aesthetic concepts of the Korean Buddhist sculpture, and the entirely artificial cave is a witness of the high level of technical development in stone structures in the eighth century.

8 – *The great Buddha image of the Sŏkkuram cave* (ph. Kim Dong-uk)

4 – The elements of the monastery

4.1 The religious function

The image hall and the lecture hall are the main buildings for religious functions. According to various sūtras, the image hall enshrines different Buddha images, Śākyamuni, Vairocana, Amitābha or Maitreya being the most popular. The lecture hall is usually devoted to the practice of Zen meditation, with twenty or thirty monks sitting together side by side, facing the walls without the slightest movement. Neither are any books nor scriptures placed in the room. The practitioners had to face white walls. The lecture hall is also used as a place for meals, the monks facing each other while eating.

fig. 9 opposite page

The basic structure of the Buddhist buildings originates from Chinese building methods. On a platform made of hardened clay, wooden columns and beams form the frame of the building under a curved roof covered by tiles. From outside, some buildings seem to have two or three storeys, but their interior forms a single space. Besides the extensive use of wood, stone or brick had been used for some structures such as platforms or stūpas. In the early years, the Buddhist buildings of Korea were mere imitations of Chinese models, but as natural circumstances and technical backgrounds differed, building forms and structural methods changed progressively.

fig. 10 opposite page

Buddhist Monasteries in Korea

9 – *Meditation at the Songgwang-sa*
(ph. Kim Dong-uk)

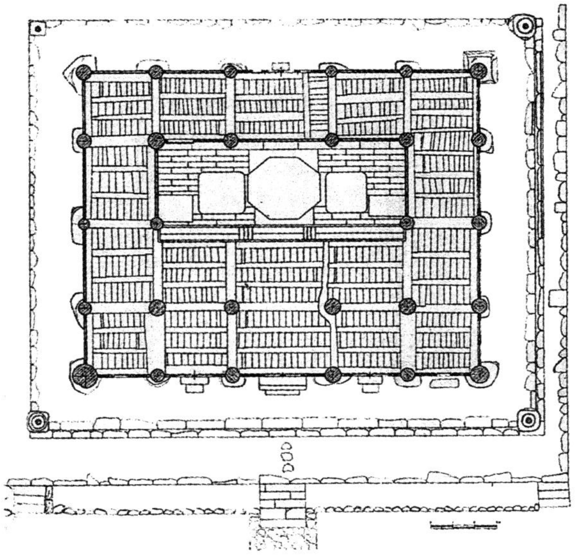

10 – *Plan, elevation and section of the Mirukjŏn hall at Kŭmsan-sa*

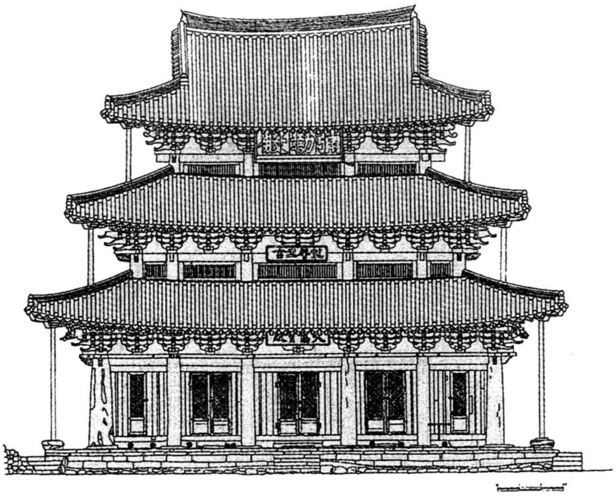

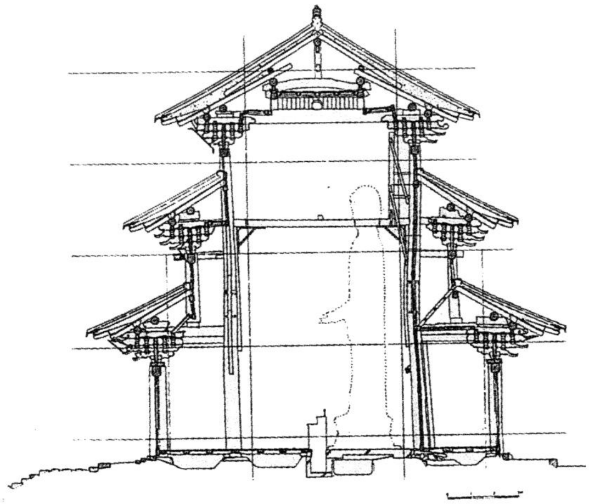

The most evident change affected the structure of the floors. In the ancient era, the floor of the image hall was made of bricks, but wood replaced it not later than the fourteenth century. It suggests that the posture of saluting changed from standing up into sitting on the floor. The use of *ondol*, a unique floor heating system in Korea, for the lecture hall and the monks' quarters could be mentioned as an another innovation. In Korea, where the average temperature of winter often goes down under zero degree Celsius, a suitable heating system in the living quarters is necessary, and the *ondol* device, delivering hot air through tunnels under the floor, seemed to be the proper solution.

The image halls have been used for monks' daily worship and the various rituals with lay followers. Usually, one image hall enshrines one Buddhist image or deity. But since the Chosŏn period, when the sects of Buddhism were integrated, some halls enshrines several images or deities, of different characters, under the same roof.

fig. 11 below

The Daeungjon, the hall of Śākyamuni at the Ssanggye-sa, provides a typical shape for enshrining a single Buddhist image. The building was reconstructed in 1621, up on Mount Chiri in the South Kyŏngsang province. Standing on a stone foundation, the hipped and gabled roof, the round columns, the bracketing and the ornate eaves show all the characteristics of an image hall of the seventeenth century. There is a Śākyamuni triad on the altar in the middle of the hall, placed rearward so as to get enough worshiping space in front of the altar. A portrait of Buddha surrounded by heavenly gods was hung behind it and an image of a heavenly palace was set up above. Those portraits and images symbolized the hall as the heavenly world of Buddha.

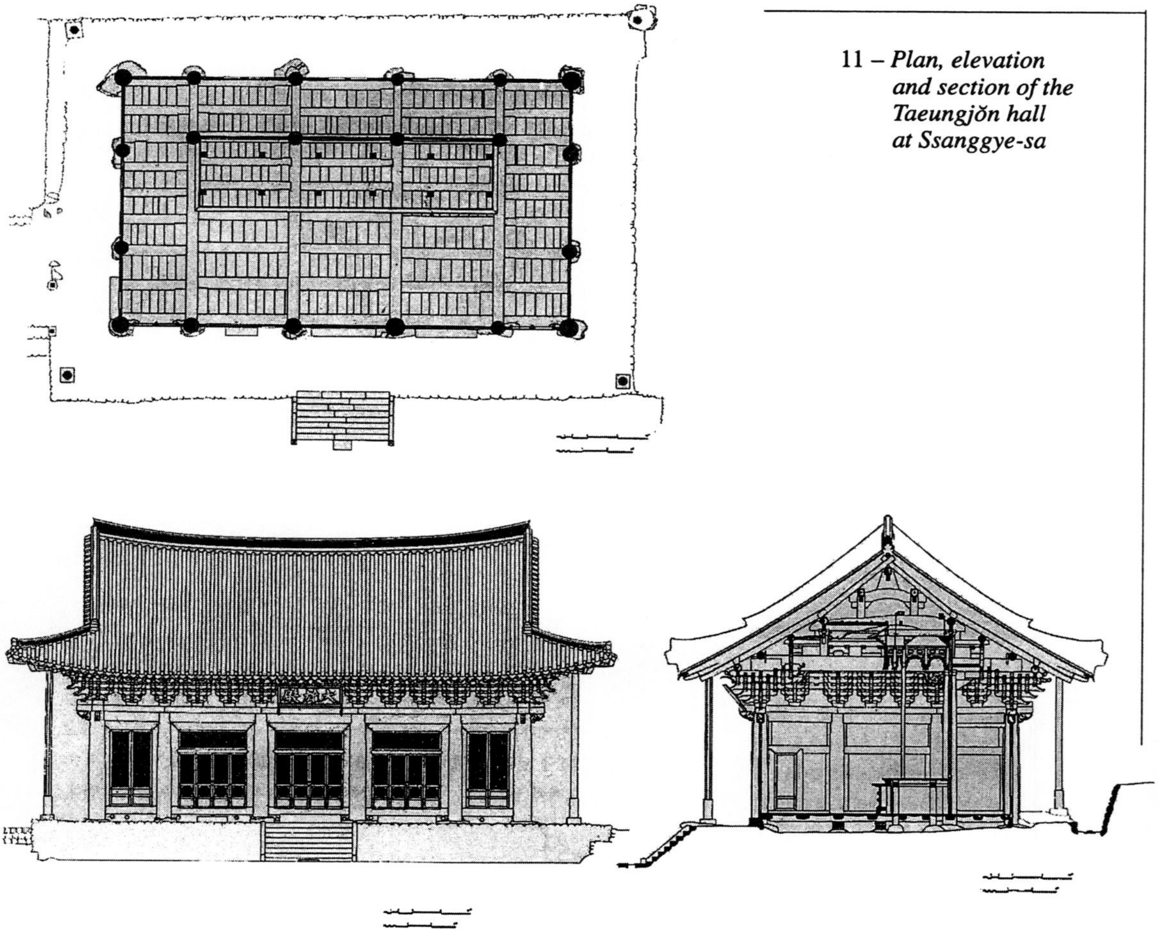

11 – *Plan, elevation and section of the Taeungjŏn hall at Ssanggye-sa*

The Daejŏkkwangjŏn, the hall of Great Silence and Light at the Kŭmsan-sa temple in the North Chŏlla province, constructed in the middle of the seventeenth century, is supported by eight pillars across the front and the back, and eventually took a great width. Inside the hall, there is a wide altar on which are five Buddhas, six Bodhisatvas and numerous arhats. Behind the altar is a mural painting of Avalokiteśvara and a Kumara. This hall symbolizes the integrated faith of various Buddhist sects, a characteristic of Buddhism under the Chosŏn Dynasty.

4.2 The reliquary function

In Korea, the faith in *sarira* (relics of the Buddha) was very popular in the ancient times. Many *sarira* stūpas and exceedingly refined *sarira* caskets stemmed from the ancient eras. During recent repairs of ancient stone stūpas, unexpectedly beautiful *sarira* caskets were found. In addition, sūtras sometimes found in stūpas are regarded as relics like *sariras*.

12 – *The* sarira *casket found in the three-storey stūpa of Bulkuk-sa in Kyŏngju*
(ph. Kim Dong-uk)

The *sarira* casket of the three-storey stūpa at the Bulkuk-sa and at Songri-sa in Kyŏngju, and that of the five-storey stūpa at the Wanggungri of Puyŏ, are famous. The *sarira* casket of the Bulkuk-sa, discovered when repairing the stūpa in 1966, consists of a bronze outer box in which was placed an oval silver bowl with a lid. In the bowl was the *sarira* in a bottle of green glass, small glass beads and a bronze mirror. A roll of paper on which a *dharani* is written was also discovered in the bowl. All these relics are supposed to have been encased before the ninth century. *fig. 12 above*

Stūpas of monks are an outcome of Zen Buddhism, where elder monks can be worshiped. After the demise of a respected monk, his disciples erect a stūpa to cherish his memory, usually made of stone in the shape of a bell. Almost every monastery in Korea has a group of monks' stūpas in one corner.

4.3 The community function

A bell or a drum are placed near the lecture hall to announce the beginning of the daily tasks. Only large monasteries have a separate belfry or a drum tower in their precincts. There seems to be no typical type or location for them. Generally the bell and the drum are placed in a pavilion. In mountain monasteries, pavilions serve as observatory, belfry or drum tower, as well as places for small-scale ceremonies with the participation of laymen, and resting places for visitors and monks. Being such multi-purpose spaces, these pavilions are placed at the centre of the monastery near the courtyard.

4.4 The accommodation function

During the Chosŏn period, monks' quarters had a strong resemblance to ordinary people's houses. They were made of wood and clay, and had a single story with an *ondol* floor and wooden flooring. Small private rooms attached side by side and large kitchens were the only elements not found in ordinary houses. Recently, ordinary houses have been changed into westernised living places, but monastic quarters maintain the style of the Chosŏn Dynasty firmly: like for their clothes, the monks have kept the old and traditional mode for their living quarters.

The toilet is called *hae-u-so*, which means a place to solve every worry. The structure used to be simple and the partition walls of each cell are not high enough to cover other's eyes. But they seemed to provide some relaxation from the tensions of the training. Toilets were located over a slope where the outflow dropped far down and was collected to be used as fertilizer.

SELECTED BIBLIOGRAPHY

BUSWELL, Francis
1992 – *The Zen Monastic Experience*, Princeton University Press, XVI + 264 p.

MACOIN, Robert E. Jr.
1998 – *Pavillons et monast res de la Cor e ancienne*, Paris, Findakly, 230 p., drawings, photographs, index, bibliography.

PAK, Youngsook
1989 – "Excavations of Buddhist Temple Sites in Korea since 1960", *The Buddhist Heritage*, Tring (U.K.), Institute of Buddhist Studies, p. 157-178.

SON, Chu-hwan (ed.)
1994 – *Korean Cultural Heritage*, vol. 1: *Fine Arts, Painting, Handicraft, Architecture,* Koreana, the Korea Foundation, Seoul, 299 p., maps, drawings, photographs, index.

THE FORMATION AND EVOLUTION OF BUDDHIST MONASTERIES IN JAPAN

Hiraoka Jōkai

Excerpts from a conference
at the Collège de France, Paris 1981
Translated from Japanese
by Frédéric Girard

The Introduction of Buddhism to Japan

Some fifteen centuries have elapsed since Buddhist religion and culture, born in India, were first introduced to Japan from Korea. This event is traditionally dated 552 AD in ancient texts – that is, according to the Japanese system, the thirteenth regnal year of Emperor Kinmei. However, recent critical research tends to consider 538 AD, the third regnal year of Emperor Senka, as a more probable date.

Śākyamuni or Prince Sidhārta, the historical Buddha who first revealed the Law, lived from 564 to 486 BC according to some Sino-Japanese traditions. After 258 BC, King Aśoka undertook to spread the new religion all over India. It seems that around 100 BC, Buddhists divided into two main branches, the Mahāsaṃghikas (the "Majoritarians", in Japanese the *Daishubu*) who later evolved as the Superior Vehicle (Mahāyāna) and the Theravādas (the "Ancients", in Japanese the *Jezabu*), who kept the Vehicle called "Inferior" by Mahāyānists.

From Punjab, Buddhism spread to the Pamir plateau and then to East Asia along the Silk Road, arriving in China by 67 AD (the tenth year of the Yongping Era during the reign of Emperor Ming, that is, 554 years after the supposed date of Buddha's nirvāṇa). From China, Buddhism entered the Korean peninsula, firstly to the Koguryō Kingdom in 372 AD, and twelve years later to its neighbouring Kingdom of Paekche. As Paekche had good relations with Japan, its king Syong-Myong asked military assistance from it against an expected invasion from the rival Korean kingdom of Silla. In making his request for this aid, the king sent to the Japanese emperor a small statue of Buddha Śākyamuni and several Buddhist texts (*sūtras* and *śāstras*), all of which had not yet been known in Japan and so aroused deep interest.

The Formation and Evolution of the Japanese Buddhist Monasteries.

Once this foreign religion introduced to Japan, its monasteries took a wide variety of shapes, depending on the ways the Japanese people integrated Buddhist concepts and culture into their own civilisation.

The evolution of the monasteries can be seen to have undergone several distinct stages:

A – Private temples: private residences transformed into shrines.

B – Large monasteries, where prayers were conducted for the sovereign.

C – Monasteries where prayers were conducted for the State, and scholastic Buddhism.

D – Monasteries where prayers were conducted for members of the aristocracy, during the first phase of patriarchal Buddhism.

E – Structure and organisation of Japanese monasteries.

F – Monasteries built for warriors and the people, in the second phase of patriarchal Buddhism.

A – Private temples: private residences transformed into shrines

The leading local families, as well as the members of the imperial family with important status in society, used to venerate a Buddhist image, to which they prayed for the prosperity of their family and their immediate offspring. This statue was installed in their residence, sometimes in a small pavilion called "hall of the favoured Buddha" or "hall of the tutelary Buddha", but in most cases in just a room of the house. Later, temples were erected on the site of this cult, as for instance the Asukadera (or Hōkōji) built by the Soga Family who adopted and supported the new religion since its arrival in Japan. The aim was to perpetuate the happiness of the family members (father, mother and brothers) and to ensure the ancestors' salvation. As such temples were known in China from the introduction of Buddhism there, they were the models for their Japanese counterparts, which are sometimes called "private residences transformed into shrines".

When Prince Shōtoku, the first, and well known, advocate of the propagation of Buddhism in Japan, decided to build the Hōryuji, a monastery adjacent to his own palace on the site of the present Wakakusa, for the recovery of his ill father, Emperor Yōmei (?-587), he used the best experts in temple construction, architects, masters craftsmen and sculptors, well trained in their original Paekche Kingdom and able to transfer their continental style to Japan. The Hōryuji is a masterpiece, the most representative of these private monasteries.

fig. 1 p. 414

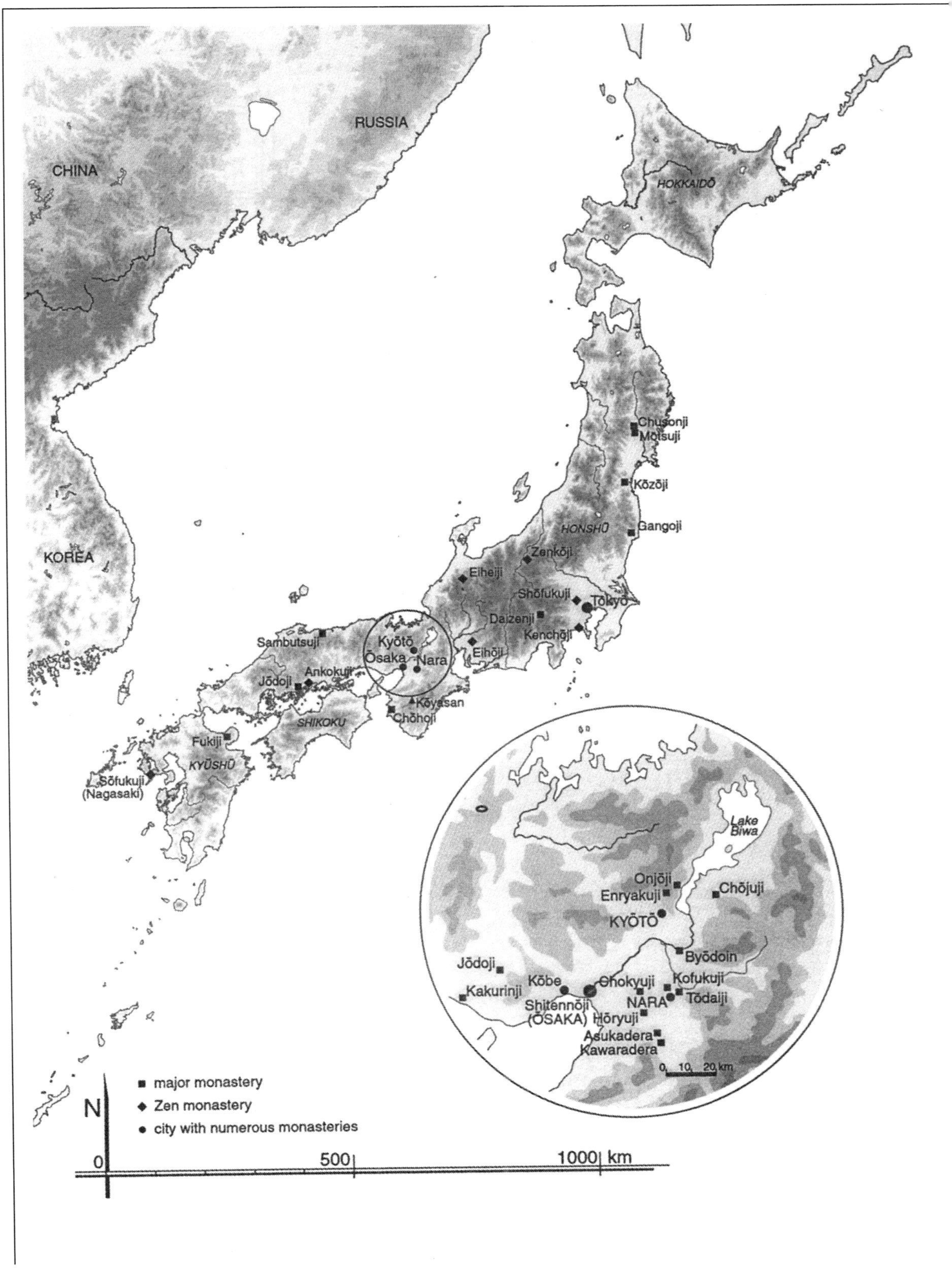
RUSSIA
CHINA
KOREA
HOKKAIDŌ
HONSHŪ
SHIKOKU
KYŪSHŪ
Chusonji
Motsuji
Kōzōji
Gangoji
Zenkōji
Eiheiji
Shōfukuji
Tōkyō
Daizenji
Kenchōji
Eihōji
Kyōtō
Ōsaka
Nara
Sambutsuji
Ankokuji
Jōdoji
Kōyasan
Chōhoji
Fukiji
Sōfukuji
(Nagasaki)
Lake Biwa
Onjōji
Enryakuji
Chōjuji
KYŌTŌ
Byōdoin
Jōdoji
Kōbe
Ghokyuji
Kofukuji
Kakurinji
Shitennōji
(ŌSAKA)
NARA
Tōdaiji
Hōryuji
Asukadera
Kawaradera
0 10 20 km
major monastery
Zen monastery
city with numerous monasteries
N
0
500
1000 km

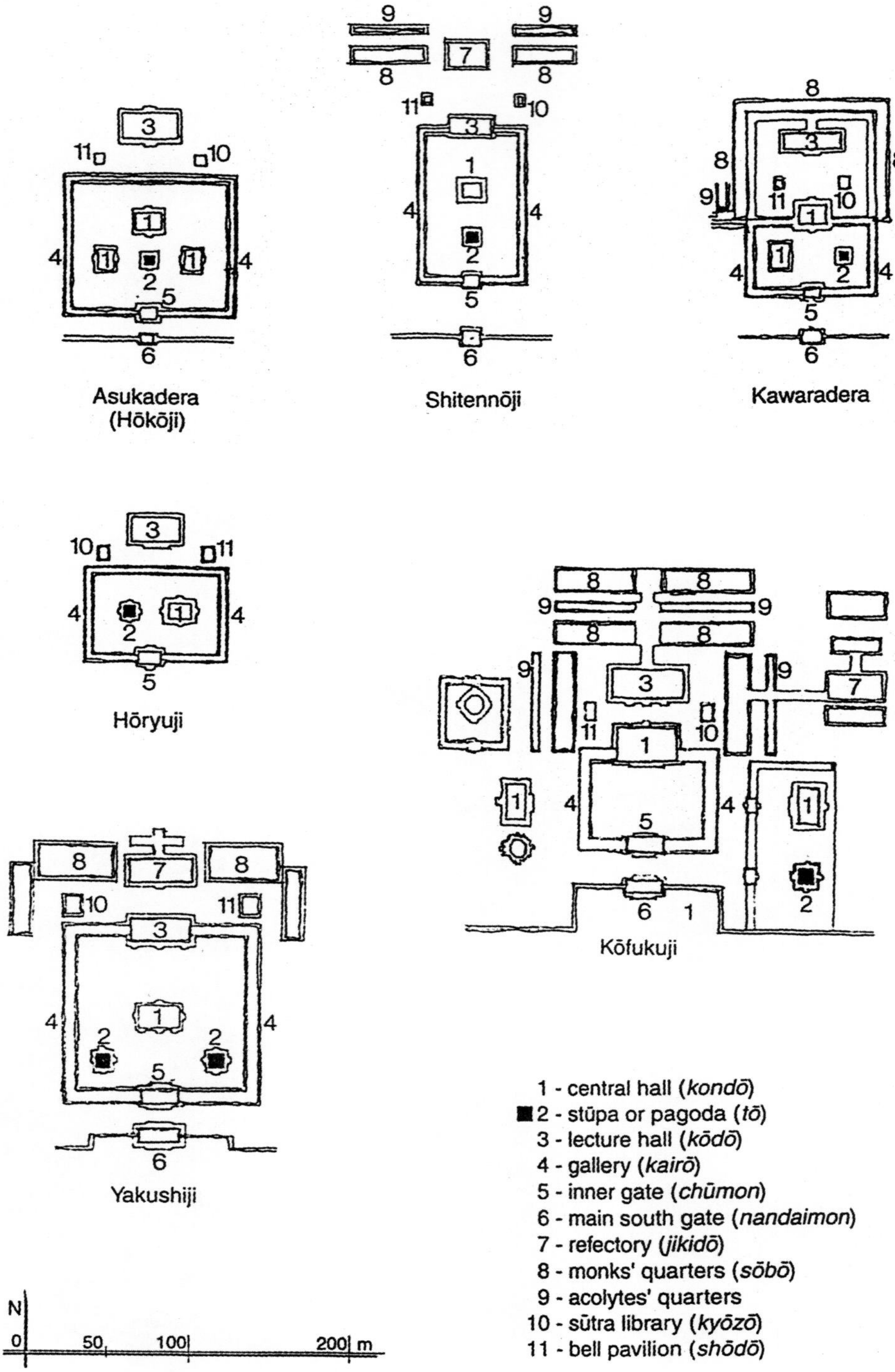

1 – *Monasteries around Nara city*

The respective number and location of *stūpas* (pagodas) and main halls was experimented in various ways:
one pagoda between two halls at the Asukadera (or Hōkōji, ~ 596);
one central pagoda in front of the hall at the Shitennōji (~ 600);
one pagoda side by side with the hall at the Kawadera (~ 650) and at the Hōryūji (~ 607, rebuilt ~ 670);
then two symmetrically placed pagodas at the Yakushiji (~ 695);
and a single one, in a lateral courtyard, at the Kōfukuji (~715).

(after Nishi and Hozumi)

During this last phase of the introduction of Buddhism, temples were used to enable one to perform the filial duties to one's father and mother as well as to secure one's afterlife happiness. Prince Shōtoku's active dedication for Buddhism, however, was also enhanced by his deep respect for Chinese culture, dating from the Han period (second century BC to second century AD), which had previously been introduced by Korean immigrants, but could only be fully understood through Buddhism.

B – Large monasteries, where prayers were conducted for the sovereign

The Emperor himself could personally found monasteries, as did Jomei (592-641) near his palace in 639 (his 11th regnal year). They are called *ōtera*, "great monasteries", and are architectural complexes on a large scale, built for the present and future well-being of the Emperor and for the peaceful rest of deceased sovereigns. A new institution, the "Office for the Construction of Buddhist Monasteries" was officially set up at that time.

see Annex 1 p. 432

Monks and students who had been to China and witnessed the foundation of the Tang dynasty played an important role in the establishment of a new legal policy in 646 on the Chinese model; they were the most active agents of the new state organization centred on the Emperor.

Built on imperial orders, temples like the Kudara no ōtera, or the Takechi no ōtera set up by Emperor Tenmu (r.672-686), as well as the Yakushiji founded by Empress Jitō (r. 686-697), were called "great state monasteries" and were under the state control.

C – Monasteries where prayers were conducted for the State and the scholastic Buddhism (Nara period, 710-793)

1 – The formation of provincial monasteries

The monasteries founded in the provinces during the Nara period were built near the provincial government agencies, under the care of the sovereign who made use of all the country resources.

Following the reforms of the Taika era (645-646), the country had been divided into 66 provinces, each one subdivided into districts. On the basis of concepts drawn from a Buddhist text, the *Sūtra of the most excellent, metal-radiant king*, monasteries were erected in each province to pray for prosperity, bountiful rice crops and the avoidance of natural disasters and epidemics, primarily smallpox. This *sūtra* explains how, when a king reveres and propagates it, the four royal Gods (*Shitennō*, Caturdevarajā) who protect the Law come to his country to preserve it from distress, illness or foreign invasion, and to maintain peace. Accordingly, Emperor Shōmu ordered two monasteries to be built in each province, one for monks (*kokobunji*, or by their full name: "monastery devoted to protect the country under the four royal Gods of the *Most excellent, metal-radiant king Sūtra*") and one for nuns (*kokubunniji*, or "monastery devoted to destroy faults under the *Lotus Sūtra*"). The number of monks in a *kokubunji* was set at twenty, that of nuns in a *kokubunniji* at ten. The provincial governors, appointed by the Emperor, were in charge of the construction, maintenance, and administration of these monasteries.

With this monastic network, the Emperor intended to use Buddhist values to develop the provinces and to enhance the national culture, but his major aim was to put an end to a series of disastrous events which had distressed the country since 737, such as droughts, large earthquakes and smallpox epidemics. Other factors, vital to the imperial family, were also involved: when the sole heir apparent to the throne, Prince Motoi no ō, died suddenly at the age of two, the Emperor ordered the building of numerous monasteries where praying for the prince should be performed. Other provincial monasteries were founded hastily in 740 to pray for the suppression of a rebellion in Kyūshū by Fujiwara no Hirotsugu.

2 – The founding of the Tōdaiji.

In 743, Emperor Shōmu decided to erect a giant statue of Buddha Vairocana, "[the Buddha] who enlightens all directions". Originally, he intended to have it installed near his Shigaraki Palace, in Omi province and at some distance from Nara. But, as the work could not proceed as he wanted, he decided for a new site, at the foot of the mountains east of the capital Heijōkyō (close to the present site of Nara). Casting the bronze statue took six years (only the eighth attempt was successful), and its dedication occurred in 752, on the ninth day of the fourth month, with the ceremonial "eye-opening" of the Giant Buddha, called Daibutsu.

fig. 2 opposite page

A wide monastic complex, the Tōdaiji, was then built around the statue (then the highest bronze statue in the world), using the latest technical skills from the continent. Four people were in fact instrumental in founding the Tōdaiji, first of all Emperor Shōmu; then the monastic abbot Rōben (689-773) who introduced the Emperor to the philosophical doctrine and practical implications of Floral Ornamentation (*Kegon*); then again, Gyōki (668-749) who, totally devoted to improving the life of the people, travelled incessantly all over Japan to build roads and bridges, and to collect donations for the Daibutsu (unfortunately, he died at 73 before the statue could be consecrated); and at least Bodhisena (704-760), the first Indian monk to reach Japan after crossing China, who performed as the master of ceremony at the dedication of the Giant Buddha.

fig. 3 opposite page

The Tōdaiji was the most important Buddhist centre during the Nara period. A special office was set up in the monastery to copy Buddhist texts, brought from China by monks like Genbō (d. 746), and to send the copies to numerous other monasteries. Originally written in Sanskrit, these texts copied in Japan from their Chinese translations were the sources of Buddhist studies, exegeses and practices. As a result, a foreign religion and culture were accepted, appreciated and assimilated by the Japanese people in a surprisingly short time. Together with its giant statue and the great timber hall above it, the Tōdaiji manifests the prosperity and expansion of Buddhist culture during the Nara period, as well as the political will of the central government. At the same time, when the silk road was an active link between China and Europe, some technical achievements of the Roman Oriental Empire such as glass objects or musical instruments could reach Japan through its embassies to Chang'an, the Tang capital.

3 – The Scholastic Buddhism of the Nara period.

From the embassies of Japanese monks to China, a considerable understanding of contemporary Buddhist studies could reach Japan, and the prevalent scholastic trends of the continent were adopted. The main Chinese schools of thought were introduced into Japan, sometimes through Korea, and Nara Buddhism was organized around six main schools:

1 – the gnoseological school, studying the signs of things (*Hossōshū*);
2 – the school based on the Abhidharmakośa (*Kushashū*);
3 – the school studying the Satyasiddhiśāstra (*Jōjitsushū*);
4 – the school of the middle path, based on the "three treatises (*Sanronshū*);
5 – the school studying the Floral Ornamentation Sūtra (*Kegonshū*);
6 – the school of *vinaya*, the disciplinary rules (*Risshū*).

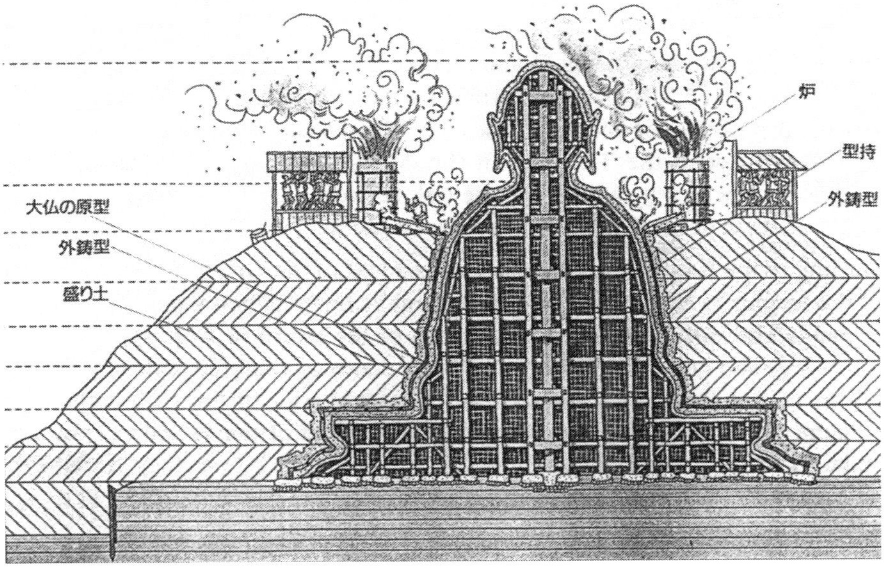

2 – *Tentative reconstruction*
of the casting of the giant bronze statue of Buddha Vairocana (746-752),
around which was built the Tōdaiji (after *National Treasures of Japan* 02/15, 1998)

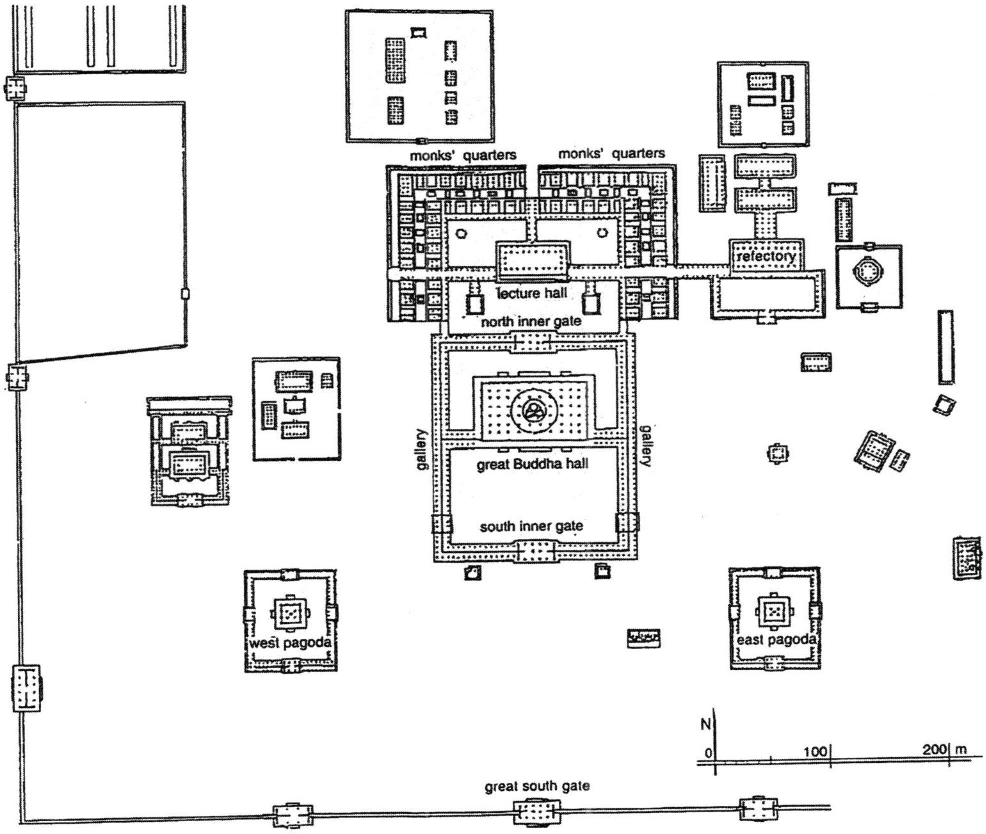

3 – *Plan of the Tōdaiji, the largest monastery of the Nara period, founded ~752* (after Hiraoka Jōkai)

This order follows the one commonly used to teach the Buddhist doctrines: firstly, the doctrines about aspects of being (1 and 2), then the doctrines concerning the negative aspects of reality (3 and 4), the doctrines on the universal presence of being (5), and finally the practical rules and their bases (6). When he understood these doctrines, the novice was to read the Treatise on the Act of faith in the Upper Vehicle (*Dachengqixinlun*), which by explaining the link between the Buddha and the human thought, gives access to the *Floral Ornamentation Sūtra.*

According to the Kegon school, this *sūtra* is a text of the Great Vehicle supposed to reveal the teachings of the Buddha Śākyamuni as he preached them just after his enlightenment. The *sūtra* exposes a conception of the world in which the Buddha, conscious beings and individual thought are three states of a unique reality. There are two versions of this text, one translated in the first quarter of the fifth century by Buddhabhadra, in 60 rolls, the other translated at the end of the seventh century by Śikṣānanda, in 80 rolls.

During the Nara period, small-scale study groups were formed under learned scholars to develop the doctrines of several schools, as was done in China where large state monasteries like the Daxingssi or the Daciensi specialized in the deeper study of specific doctrines. Originally, however, teaching was not limited to a single topic, and similarly in Japan, the novice could be introduced to the teaching of the six schools in the Tōdaiji or in the Daianji of Nara. This was the case up to, and during, the Heian period, and the same freedom from sectarianism can be seen in the Shingon school, founded by Kūkai (774-835) who recommended that a monk first study the Hossō and Sanron doctrines. In this way, the Nara Buddhism gained a strong scholastic character, the sacred texts being copied and deeply studied in great monasteries much as it is done in the research centres and universities of today.

For common people during the Nara period, to enter a monastic order was possible only through a formal ordination, which consisted of accepting the disciplinary rules (*jukai*), pronouncing the ten vows implying a commitment to the Buddhist way, and receiving the permission of a master. However, some people were also entering monastic life outside of any official control, as "privately ordained monks". To end this practice, regarded as dangerous, Emperor Shōmu decided to set up an ordination stage in the Tōdaiji, where formal ordinations followed an uniform and orthodox ritual. This change required the presence of learned monks, well acquainted with the disciplinary code, to give the Mahāyanist sacrament called the "Bodhisattva ordination", and the Emperor sent two monks from the Kōfukuji, Yōei and Fushiō, to China. They went by boat in 733, and met there the famous Ganjin (Jianzhen, 688-763) in the Damingsi monastery at Yangzhou. At their request, Ganjin agreed to go to Japan, but had to make five attempts to cross the East China Sea, from 743 to 753 when, already blind, he finally reached the Satsuma coast. Hearing the good news, former Emperor Shōmu and Empress Kōmyō, (both having abdicated) were ordained by Ganjin in front of the hall of the Great Buddha. Under the novice (*shami*, skt. *śrāmaṇera*) name of Shōman, Emperor Shōmu ordered the construction of an ordination stage in the Tōdaiji, appointed Ganjin to administer it, and decreed that anybody wanted to become a monk should be ordained at the Tōdaiji stage during an official ceremony to be held every year in the third month.

D – Monasteries where prayers were conducted for members of the aristocracy during the first phase of patriarchal Buddhism

1 – Saichō (767-822) and the Enryakuji.

In 794 the capital was moved north of Nara, on the site of present Kyōtō, and was called Heiankyō, the City of Peace. A new type of monastery appeared then in the centre of a mountainous area where monks could practice asceticism away from the great monastic foundations of the Nara region. This move was also a reaction to cases of clerical interference in politics at the end of the Nara period, for instance the Dōkyō affair. In 804, Saichō, together with Kōkai, accompanied an embassy to China, where he received instruction on Tendai teachings by Daosui in the Guoqingsi Monastery, founded by Zhiyi (538-597) on Mount Tiantai. Upon his return, Saichō was eager to found a school devoted to doctrines inspired by the *Lotus Sūtra*, on which Prince Shōtoku had composed a commentary, the *Hokke gisho*. He saw in this new school a way to circumvent what he considered the excessively abstruse character of Nara Buddhism. With the support of Emperor Kanmu (736-806), Saichō developed in 806 the Ichijō shikan-in, a small hermitage on Mount Hiei, into a monastic complex of pavilions and stūpas, which grew steadily under the name of Hieizanji. One year after the death of Saichō, an imperial decree gave it the name of Enryakuji, "Monastery founded in the Enryaku era", in the first known instance of the later practice of giving a monastery the name of an era.

In the Enryakuji, Saichō taught a practice including four exercises of mental concentration (*shishu zanmai*) : *fig. 4 p. 420*

1 – the permanently seated concentration (*jōza zanmai*), in which the adherent unifies his thought and follows exclusively the seated *dhyāna*;

2 – the permanently wandering concentration (*jōgyō zanmai*), in which the adherent peregrinates through the mountains around Mount Hiei, applying his thought exclusively to the Amida Buddha;

3 – the alternately wandering and seating concentration (*hangyō hanza zanmai*), in which the adherent alternates between both exercises, repenting his faults according to a ritual of the *Lotus Sūtra*.

4 – the neither wandering nor seating concentration (*higyō hiza zanmai*), in which, wherever he happens to be, the adherent should apply his thought to the way of the Buddha and keep faith in the Buddhist path.

Any monk joining the Hieizan community had to practice these exercises on at least 208 days a year.

Saichō supported his teaching with the Mohe zhiguan (*Great treatise of peace and introspection*), a method of meditation both theoretical and practical, which he read and commented on to his disciples. When dealing with the monastic discipline, the first reference of Saichō was the ten great precepts exposed in the *Sūtra of the Net of Brahmā*. But in addition he composed a set of rules for the Enryakuji monks, and a treatise on discipline in which he strongly criticizes the insufficiently strict practice of the Nara clergy and of the monks attached to the Kōfukuji and to the Tōdaiji.

The candidate entering the community to study Tendai doctrines could not come down from the mountains during the twelve years of his practice, and of course women were strictly forbidden to come near the monasteries. It was only after these twelve years

4 – *Plan of the Enryakuji (~ 806 and after), on Mount Hiei, near Kyoto* (after Nakagawa)

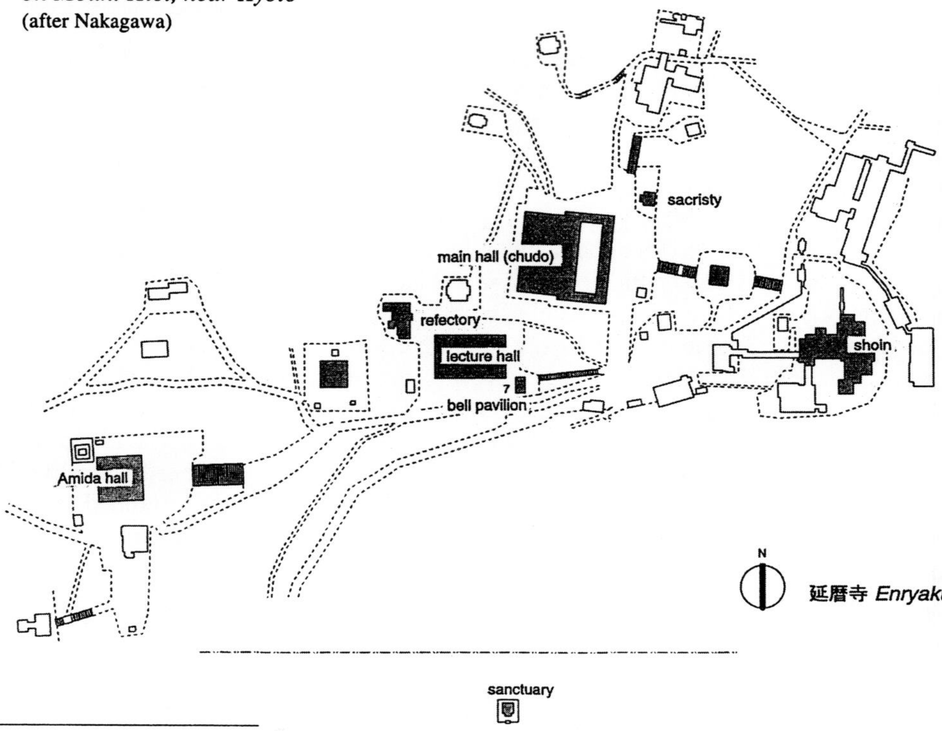

of "mountain reclusion" that the candidate was allowed to receive the annual ordination, then to proceed to provincial monasteries, in the vicinity of which he should build pavilions, administratively separated from, but affiliated to, the main centre of the school.

Several halls in the Hieinzanji, like the Konponchūdo (main hall), the Jōgyō zanmaidō (hall of the permanent doctrine) or the Hokkedō (hall of the *Lotus Sūtra*), were centres for this mountain asceticism.

This type of Buddhism, in which doctrinal and practical achievements were conceived by a single man acting as the patriarch of his sect, can be called "patriarchal Buddhism" (*soshi bukkyō*). Quite different from the Chinese Buddhists' abstruse quest for philosophical concepts, Japanese were eager to find an actual Buddhist practice consistent with doctrinal theory, and through this practice, to look for the means to lead the greatest number of people to salvation. On this point, Saichō and Kūkai were in total agreement. With the imperial family as well as the Fujiwara nobility actively supporting their activities, the two schools of Tendai and Shingon were extremely influential in the aristocratic society of the Heian period, and conferred a distinctive character to the Buddhism of their time.

2 – Kūkai (774-835) and the monasteries of the Shingon school.

Kūkai was introduced to the esoteric Shingon doctrines by Huiguo (746-805) in the Qinglongsi at Chang'an (Xi'an), in China. These doctrines, previously transmitted by the Tripiṭaka masters Śubhakarasīṃha (d. 735) and Amoghavajra (705-774), teach that beings and things are naturally pure, as shown by the "three mysteries": the body, the word, and the thought. They are called mysteries to express the unavoidable opacity of the genuine Buddhist teachings for beings like humans, whose faculty for understanding is clouded by suffering and error. It is only through sustained ascetic practices that one can penetrate the "mysterious" word of Buddha, and doing so, rise to Buddhahood.

Kūkai established the Shingon school in Japan on the basis of two texts, the *Mahāvairocana Sūtra* and the *Sūtra of the diamond summum*, and of two world circular representations, the *kongōkai mandara* (skt: *vajradhādumaṇdala*) and the *taizōkai mandara* (skt: *garbha[dhātu]maṇdala*). Under the doctrinal achievements of Kūkai the Shingon school flourished in Japan to a degree never attained in China.

On his return from China, Kūkai settled first in the Takaozanji monastery (later known as the Jingoji), at the foot of Mount Takao near Kyoto, and started practicing the ointment ritual (*kanjō*, skt. *abhiṣeka*) which Huiguo had taught him. After joining in these rituals, Saichō left after some disagreement, without completing his training in esotericism.

As Kūkai was from the Saeki family (from Sanuki in Shikoku Island), a member of which, Saeki no Imaebisu (719-790), had directed the building of the Tōdaiji, his family connection enabled him to extend his influence on the Nara clergy (according to some sources, he even became the Superior of the Tōdaiji). In contrast with Saichō, Kūkai was able to keep good relations with the Nara monasteries, inducing several of them, like the Shitennōji, the Hōryūji and even the Tōdaiji, to draw closer to the Shingon school. Later in 819, Kūkai established the Kongōbuji Monastery on Mount Kōya, where he "entered in mental concentration" at his death. Another important monastery built in 796, the Tōji, was entrusted to Kūkai in 823 by Emperor Saga (786-842), and in 825 it was given the name of Kyōō gokokuji, "Monastery for the teaching of the prince and the protection of the country". The Tōji was the centre of the Shingon school in the capital: only there could monks of the Kūkai lineage learn the doctrine, transmitted from master to disciple, practice asceticism and receive the ordination ointment. Other monasteries were restricted to followers of the Shingon school, such as Daigoji established in 877, the Daikakuji built in 876 and the Ninnaji in 885, all being votive monasteries (*goganji*). The Ninnaji was founded by Emperor Uda (867-931) after his entry into the order in 899: an emperor who abdicates is called *jōkō*, and *hōō* if he settles in a monastery to become a monk and follow the Buddhist path. It happened however that the monk-emperor persisted using his political power, sometimes more effectively than his reigning successor: this type of reign is called *insei*, "government by the retired emperor". As seen in the monasteries founded by Emperors Ennyū (959-991) and Goshujaku (1009-1045), the purpose of a monastery might be to ensure a long and healthy life to the emperor, and to keep his ashes after his death in a special temple called *bodaiji*, built near the monastery.

see Annex 1 p. 432

The monasteries of this time were built on the model of large aristocratic residences, following a style called *shinden-zukuri*, whereby the centre of the compound was a garden in which was dug a large pond with an island in the middle, and monastic buildings were located around the pond. The main hall (*kondō*) housed a statue of Mahāvairocana, and the hall devoted to Bhaiṣajyaguru (*yakushidō*) seven statues of this Buddha. Members of the nobility came here to pray to avoid illness and obtain a long life. In another hall were placed the statues of the five "great kings of wisdom" (*godaidō*): Fudō myōō (skt Acala vidyārāja), Gosanze myōō (skt: Trailokyavijaya vidyārāja), Gundari myōō (skt: Kuṇḍali vidyārāja), Daiitoku myōō (skt: Yamāntaka vidyārāja) and Kongō yasha myōō (skt: Vajrayakṣa vidyārāja). An esoteric ritual of igneous purification was conducted there as a protection against the vengeance (*tatari*) of malevolent spirits, by burning wooden tablets in a special brasier. There was also a hall to the Amida Buddha (*Amidadō*), with his seven statues, in which people prayed to be reborn in his heaven. Affluent families patronized the building of such monasteries, where they requested high monks from the Shingon and Tendai schools to perform esoteric rituals. As long as Saichō was alive, the Tendai school was not inclined to esotericism, but became subject to it later, with Ennin and Enchin, who initiated an esoteric trend in the Tendai school, called *Tendai mikkyō* (or *Taimitsu* for short), and propagated it from the Onjōji Monastery, near the city of Ôtsu. From that time, the Tendai school has been divided between the "mountain branch" (*sanmon*, Hieizan) and the "monastery branch" (*jimon*, Onjōji).

3 – Votive monasteries of Heian aristocratic families

During the Heian period, and more precisely between 915 and 1086, the Fujiwara families of the northern branch (*hokke*) became more powerful than the Emperor, by profiting from the blood relationship they had with him. When the heir to the throne, the son of the emperor and of a Fujiwara woman, was still a small child, the Emperor was forced to abdicate and allow a member of the Fujiwara to become regent (*sesshō*) and the effective ruler. Even when the new emperor reached adulthood, the regent as grand chancellor (*kanpaku*) retained the greater power.

At the basis of such events was the fact that Japan, an island country, had a homogeneous population, never subjected to foreign invasion or immigration. (It should be noted that this rise to power of the Fujiwaras came after the decision to cease sending embassies to China in 894.) It can then be understood that, from the end of the Heian period to the Kamakura period, with political and economic power passing from the aristocracy to the military, the emperor and the aristocrats had much less political leadership. Here is one of the historical contrasts between Japan and Europe.

After Fujiwara no Fuhito (659-720) had built the Kōfukuji in Nara for the prosperity of his family, the Kasuga jinja became the Fujiwara family shrine, and the Kōfukuji became the family monastery (*ujidera*). Managed by the head of the family, the Kōfukuji grew in importance. Later, Fujiwara no Tadahira (880-949), as head of the house and minister, had another monastery, the Hōshōji, built in Kyoto for the family wealth. It later was used to pray for his happiness after his death. In these family monasteries of the Fujiwaras, esoteric rituals were performed and unction given to the laity. Besides the attainment of a long and powerful life for the family members, the main aim for founding a monastery was usually to be reborn, immediately after death, in the Pure Land of Amida.

fig. 5 opposite page
In the Hōjōji, built by Fujirawa no Michinaga (966-1027) at the apex of the Fujiwara family power, the buildings had a different configuration from the Nara period monasteries. The Byōdōin, erected by one of his sons, had a similar layout with a pond in the middle of the central garden. On an island in the central pond of the Hōjōji, flutes and kotoes were played, and a gilded statue of Mahāvairocana was erected in the main hall. Michinaga also built a hall for Bhaiṣajyaguru (*yakushidō*), with seven statues of this Buddha, to pray for the healing of his eye illness, and two other halls, for Amida with nine statues and for the five kings of wisdom. The Hōjōji then was a faithful replica in our world of the Pure Land. The six "excellent monasteries", a series of monasteries with the character *shō* (excellence) in their name were erected side by side in the Higashiyama quarter of Kyoto by successive emperors between 1077 and 1155: the
fig. 6 opposite page
Hosshōji, the Sonshōji, the Saishōji, the Enshōji, the Jōshōji and another Enshōji. At that time, Kyoto as a whole was a capital of Buddhism and deserved to be called the Pure

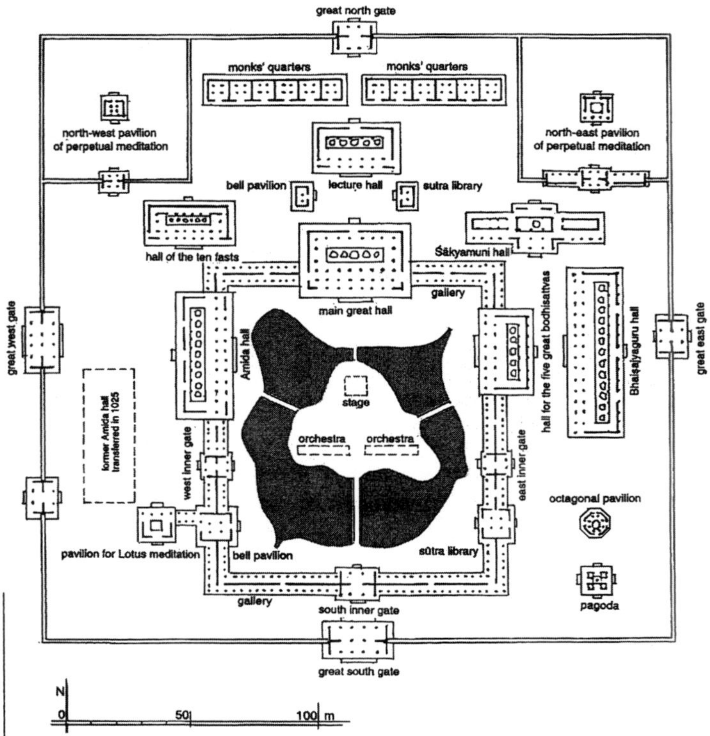

5 – *Plan of the Hōjōji*
Built in Heian (Kyoto)
by Regent Michinaga in 1022
and destroyed by fire in 1058

(after Shimizu)

6 – *Plan of the Hosshōji*
Built in Heian (Kyoto)
by Emperor Shirakawa
in 1077-83

(after Soper)

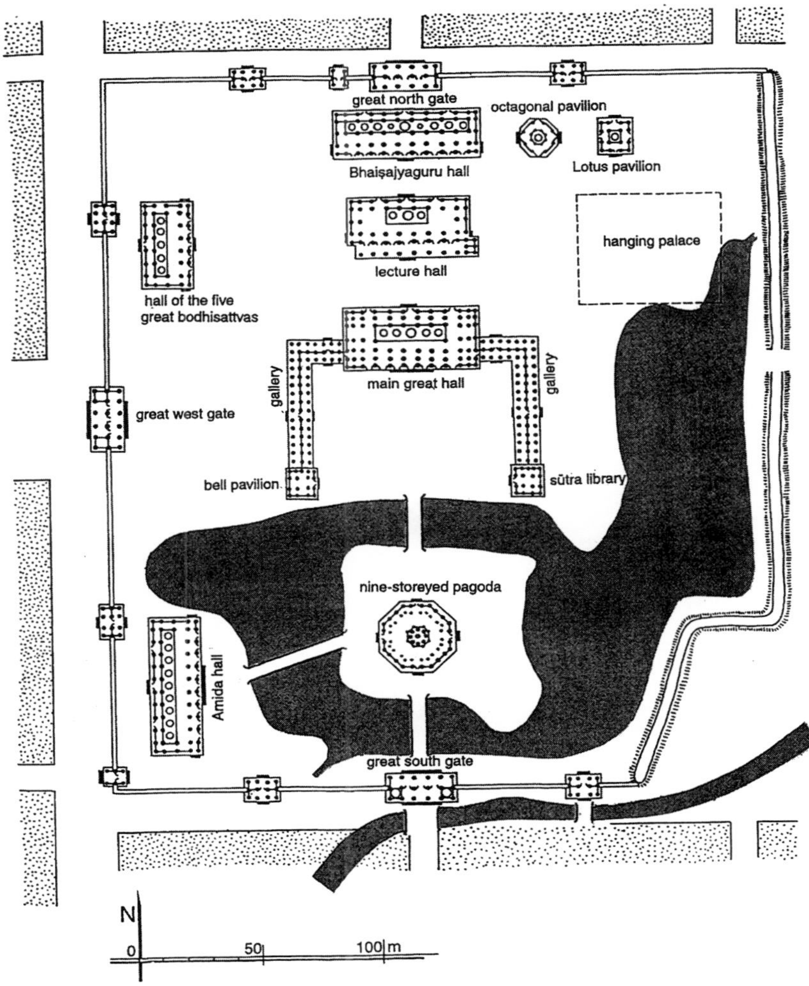

Land of the Buddha, with the emperor and several families competing to build their own magnificent monasteries, lavishly decorated and painted with representations of the Sukhvatī heaven on their walls. But at the end of the Heian period, civil wars raged from 1156 to 1185 between the Taira and Minamoto families. Kyoto became a true hell, as all the monasteries built by the Heian aristocracy were reduced to ashes (most of the monastery plans illustrating the present text are tentative reconstructions from archaeological excavations and textual records).

E – Layout and organization of Japanese monasteries.

Japanese Buddhism had from its origins integrated a pantheon of local deities, already attested in the Heian period, and monasteries were usually devoted not to a single, specific, Buddha, but to several gods of the pantheon mentioned in canonical texts.

Theoretically, monasteries reflect the seven-pavilion structure of the *saṃghārāma:*

fig. 7 below
fig. 8 opposite

1 – the central hall, *kondō*, in which is the most venerated image. Alternatively called *butsuden* (pavilion of the main Buddha) or *taiyūden* (pavilion of the great hero);

fig. 9
opposite page

2 – the stūpa or pagoda, *tō*, a reliquary;

3 – the lecture hall, *kōdō*, where canonical texts are read and explained (called *kondō* in Zen monasteries);

4 – the gallery, *kairō*, surrounding the central courtyard;

7 – *The main hall (*kondō*)*
in the Tōdaiji (ph. C. Pottier)

8 – *Section of the main hall (*kondō*)*
in the Hōryūji
(after Soper)

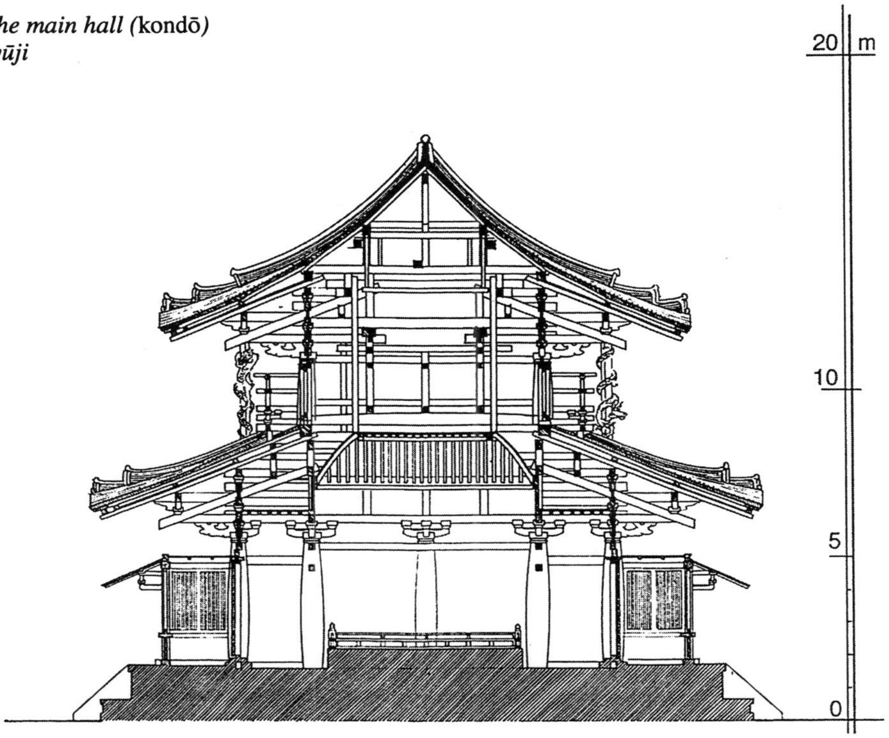

9 – *The five-storeyed*
pagoda in the Hōryūji
(after Nishi and Hozumi)

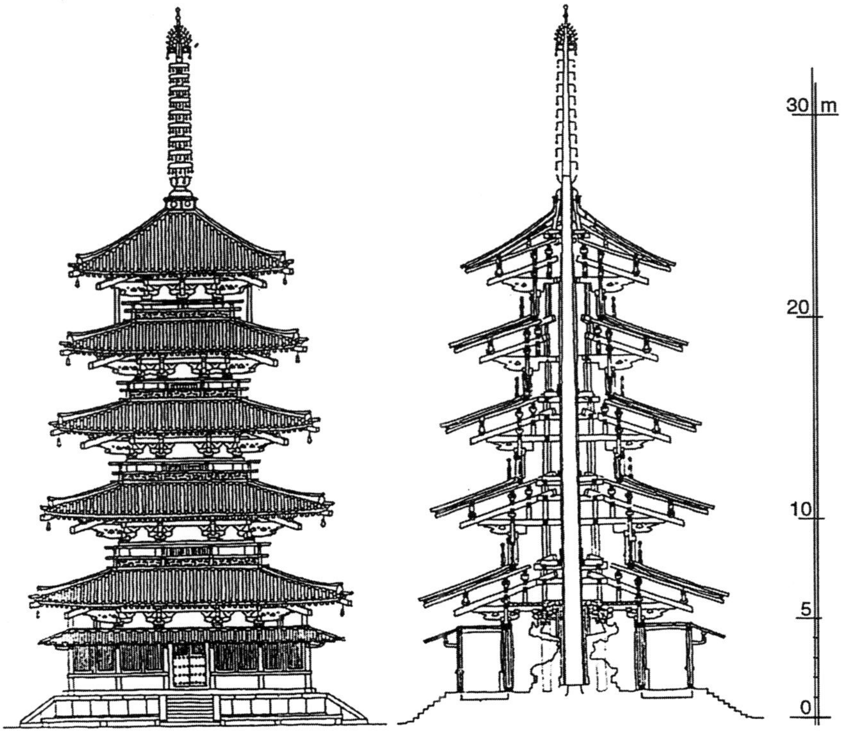

5 – the south middle gate, *chūmon*, giving access
to the gallery and the courtyard;

6 – the library, *kyōzō*, where the canonical scriptures (*sūtra*) are kept;

7 – the bell tower, *shōrō*, and the gong, *korō*, for the Zen school

Other elements can be added:

the ordination stage, *kaidan-in*;
the pavilion of the founder, *kaisandō*;
the monks' quarters, *sōbō*; *fig. 10 below*
the refectory, *jikidō*;
the toilets, *tōshi*;
the bathhouse, *yokushi, yokushitsu, yokudō* or *saijō*.

10 – *Monks' quarters in the Gangōji, 8th century, and in the Gankōji, 13th century*
(after Nakagawa)

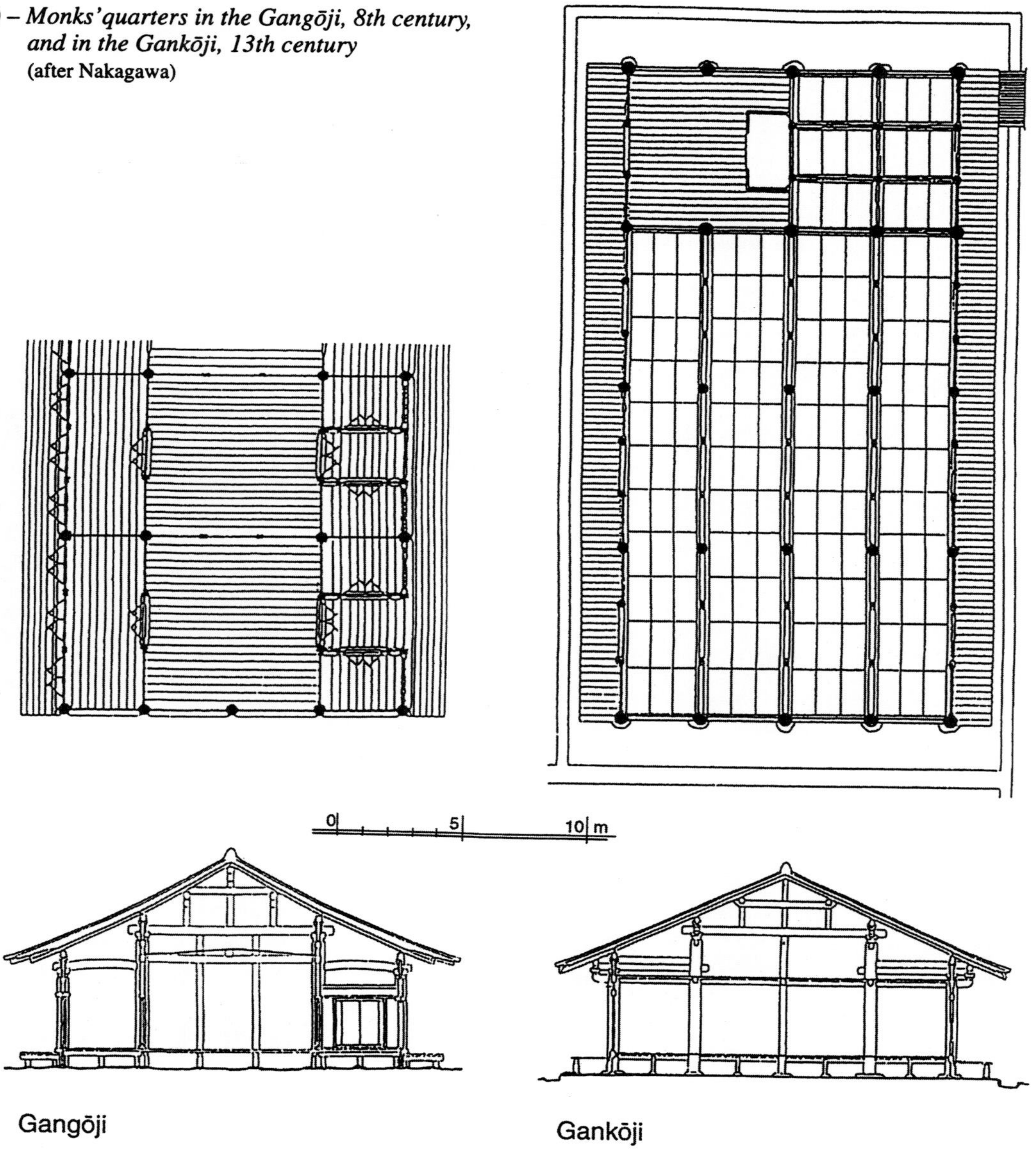

In the Shingon school usually, monasteries include a five-storeyed stūpa (*gojūnotō*), a central hall, a lecture hall, a bell, a library, the main and middle gates.

Tendai monasteries have generally a western circular stūpa (*saitō*), a central hall (*konponchudō*), a lecture hall, an ordination stage, a pavilion for perpetual practice (*jōgyōdō*) and a Mañjuśrī tower (*monjurō*).

In the Kamakura period, Zen monasteries were built on the Chinese Zen model, with a main gate (*sanmon*, short for *sangedatsumon*, gate of the three savings), a preaching hall (*hattō*), a hall for the main Buddha (*butsuden*), a pavilion for the seated meditation (*zendō*), and the cell of the superior (*hōjō*). In accordance with the Zen doctrines of non-reliance to the letter and of non-textual teaching, there is no library. In the Jōdo and Nichiren schools, preaching and textual commenting were performed in the main hall. These monasteries, where public lectures were conducted, became the most common type in the Edo period, and in villages, their main hall was commonly used as a meeting hall. Though the killing of living creatures and their interment were formally banned in monasteries, it became more and more usual to perform funeral ceremonies there.

The regular orientation of monastic buildings was towards the south; the main gate of the whole complex also faced south and was called the great southern gate (*nandaimon*).

Similarly, the hall of the main Buddha (*butsuden*) was in most cases open towards the south, so that at midday its gilded Buddha statue was brightly shining. As a rule, nobody was allowed to enter the central hall except during religious services. On the east side, the rising sun was considered as manifesting Mahāvairocana, and the setting sun on the west, Amitābha. Pavilions devoted to Avalokiteṣvara (*kannondō*), the bodhisattva leading to the Pure Land of Sukhāvatī, were erected on steep, cliff-like locations, as if the bodhisattva was revering the setting sun from his belvedere.

The ancient monastic community was divided into three organizational levels: intendants (*bettō*), monks proper, i.e. the learned monks who devote themselves to textual and doctrinal studies (*gakuryo*) and lived in the monastery rows of cells (*sōbō*), and monks of lower status (*dōshū* or *dōchu*).

1 – The intendant

The intendant was the administrator of the monastery, appointed by imperial decree. His function was introduced during the Nara period, but his title differed from one monastery to the other: *bettō* in the Tōdaiji and the Kōfukuji, *Tendai zasu* (Superior of the Tendai) in the Enryakuji, or *chōja* at the Tōji. In command of the monastery at the highest level, is main duties were to ensure the discipline of monks and nuns, control their promotions and inform the government when monks were unfrocked or died. It was also his task to see that the life of the monastery could proceed peacefully, and he was responsible for the management and upkeep of the monastery as well as of its estates, often of a very large size, the products of which were used to construct, maintain and repair the monastic buildings.

Intendants were appointed for four years, after being nominated by a council of learned monks. Later, young members of aristocratic families entered the monastery and were frequently appointed as intendants. As most of the intendants came from the imperial family or from the aristocracy, access to this position was practically impossible for a member of the lower clergy.

The regulations for intendants' appointment are based on those stipulated in 927 during the Engi era. They required intendants to live permanently in the monastery and to have entered the monastic community under a decree of the court. To become the intendant of the Tōdaiji, one was also required to have assisted, at the invitation of the emperor, at the three annual conferences on doctrinal issues, the Yuimae in the Kōfukuji, the Saishōe in the Yakushiji and the Misaie at the imperial court, and to have received the highest monastic distinction, the Seal of the Law (*hōin gon daisōzu*).

The intendant had three directors (*sangō* i.e. the three reins) under him.They were appointed monks: the dean (*jōza*) was in charge of general administration, the second (*jishu* or *teraju*) managed the properties, and the third (*tsuina*) kept control of rituals and discipline.

2 – The learned monks

The learned monks (*gakuryo*), respecting the monastic discipline and devoted exclusively to doctrinal studies, formed collectively the main body of the clergy. During religious services and doctrinal seminars (*ronji*) organized in monasteries, they were regularly invited to be readers, discussants (*kōji*) and examiners (*monja*). Still today, these seminars are organized in the Tōdaiji according to this medieval tradition. In renowned monasteries like the Tōdaiji and the Kōfukuji, most of the monks came from aristocracy and were expected to lead the community. The learned monks, to whom the court awarded monastic distinctions, at the same time had a high proficiency in Buddhist doctrines and held a leading administrative position. The same situation existed in the Shingon school, where it was also required to have been anointed as Transmitter of the Law.

3 – The lower clergy

The lower clergy was composed of ordinary monks (*shu*) attached to certain halls (*dō*), where they had to place flowers in front of the altar and, more generally, to make all necessary arrangements for the various religious ceremonies. To enter monastic life, they had to be ordained in the Nara Kaidan-in, and to change their lay name to a religious one. They were not invited to the conferences organized by the court and the noble families; however some of them practiced asceticism regularly, for instance at Hieizan during thousand days.

4 – The warrior monks

It is wrong to see the warrior monks as forming a distinct group inside a monastery. Strictly speaking, there were no specifically armed groups permanently residing in great monasteries like the Tōdaiji, the Enryakuji, the Onjōji, the Kōkufuji or the Kōyasan. It was only in times of trouble – when warriors or rebels invaded a monastic domain – or during conflicts amongst these large monasteries, that armed forces were levied from the monastic community. Carrying revered symbols such as the tree dedicated to the Kasuka deity (at the Kōkufuji) or the Hachiman palanquin (at the Tōdaiji) they marched on the capital, Kyoto, and complained to the high authorities against some detrimental and illicit decision. Under the leadership of higher monks, these armed forces consisted on the one hand of monks of all status, and on the other of local laymen living in the monastic domain.

In 1180, Taira no Shigehira (1156-1185) led an attack against Nara, resulting in the burning of the city, as a response to the alliance of the Tōdaiji, Kōkufuji and Onjōji monasteries with the Minamoto troops. The Nara monasteries levied theses armed forces to support either the Minamoto or the emperor, according to the changing circumstances.

Again at the end of the Heian period, the Tōdaiji, the Enryakuji and the Onjōji entered repeatedly into violent conflicts caused by the desire of the Enryakuji to erect its own ordination stand. And the retired emperor Gotoba (1180-1219), as well as Emperor Godaigo (1288-1339) were willing to use these armed monastic troops to overthrow the Kamakura Bakufu.

F – Monasteries built for warriors and the people, in the second phase of patriarchal Buddhism

From 1150 to 1185, the end of the Heian period was marked by thirty-six years of civil wars which are among the worst that Japan has ever known. They raged all over the country, and numerous monasteries were totally destroyed in Kyoto, including the Tōdaiji and the Kōfukuji which were burnt to ashes.

While shifting the seat of his new military government to Kamakura, Minamoto no Yorimoto (1123-1160) undertook to restore these monasteries and, in order to pray for the spirits of the battlefield dead, carried out repairs on the Daibutsu in Nara with the assistance of Chōgen (alias Shunjō, 1120-1206) and went from Kantō to assist in the ceremony set up by Emperor Gotoba to celebrate the completion of these works. For his part, Eisai (or Yōsai, 1141-1215), the founder of the Kenninji in Kyoto, had transmitted from China the Rinzai branch of the Zen school (he had also sent tea seeds to Myōe (1173-1232) who was living in the Kōzanji monastery near Kyoto; here can be seen the origin of the Japanese tea ceremony).

Myōe had studied at the Tōdaiji before founding the Kōzanji, where he professed the unity of the Kegon and esotericism doctrines. He expressed some of his concepts in his *Diary of dreams* (*Muki*) and had an extremely active life, even planning a pilgrimage to the Buddhist sites of India.

Dōgen (1200-1253) introduced the Sōtō teachings, which he had studied at Mount Tiantong in Zhejiang province in China under Changao Jujing (1162-1227).

Willing to answer to the aspirations of the people and to put an end to the ravages of the civil wars, Hōnen embraced the concept of reincarnation in Amida Pure Land, and exposed his thought in his *Compendium on the Commemoration of [Amida] Buddha by Selecting the Fundamental Vow*. His best-known disciple, Shinran (1173-1262) wrote a treatise on teaching, practice, faith and fulfilment, on the possible salvation of faulty people through invocation to Amida.

During the Kamakura period, Buddhist monasteries were built in all regions of Japan, no longer by the nobility but as votive temples to pray for the fortunate ending of warriors' fights, and also, as their death was frequent, as places for the funerary cult (*bodaiji*). These monasteries were located near the residence of their warrior-patron, who adopted the ideas of the Zen schools where they could connect their martial art of swordsmanship with the techniques of mental concentration. The main hall (*hondō*) became a preaching room for the benefit of warriors, who practised the seated concentration (*zazen*) in a specific Dhyāna hall (*zendō*). Zen schools and their monasteries benefitted abundantly from the warriors' donations, primarily in Kamakura where new large monasteries like the Kenchōji and the Enkakuji were built with the support of the Hōjō family. *fig. 11 p. 430*

With Buddhism distancing itself gradually from esotericism, new devotional practices appeared in which faith was directed towards a single Buddha, Amida, in the schools of the Hōnen Pure Land and Shinran. The faithful believed that by reciting the invocative formula "Namo Amida Butsu" (Veneration to Buddha Amida), they could escape the suffering of this world and gain access to the Western Heaven. Concurrently,

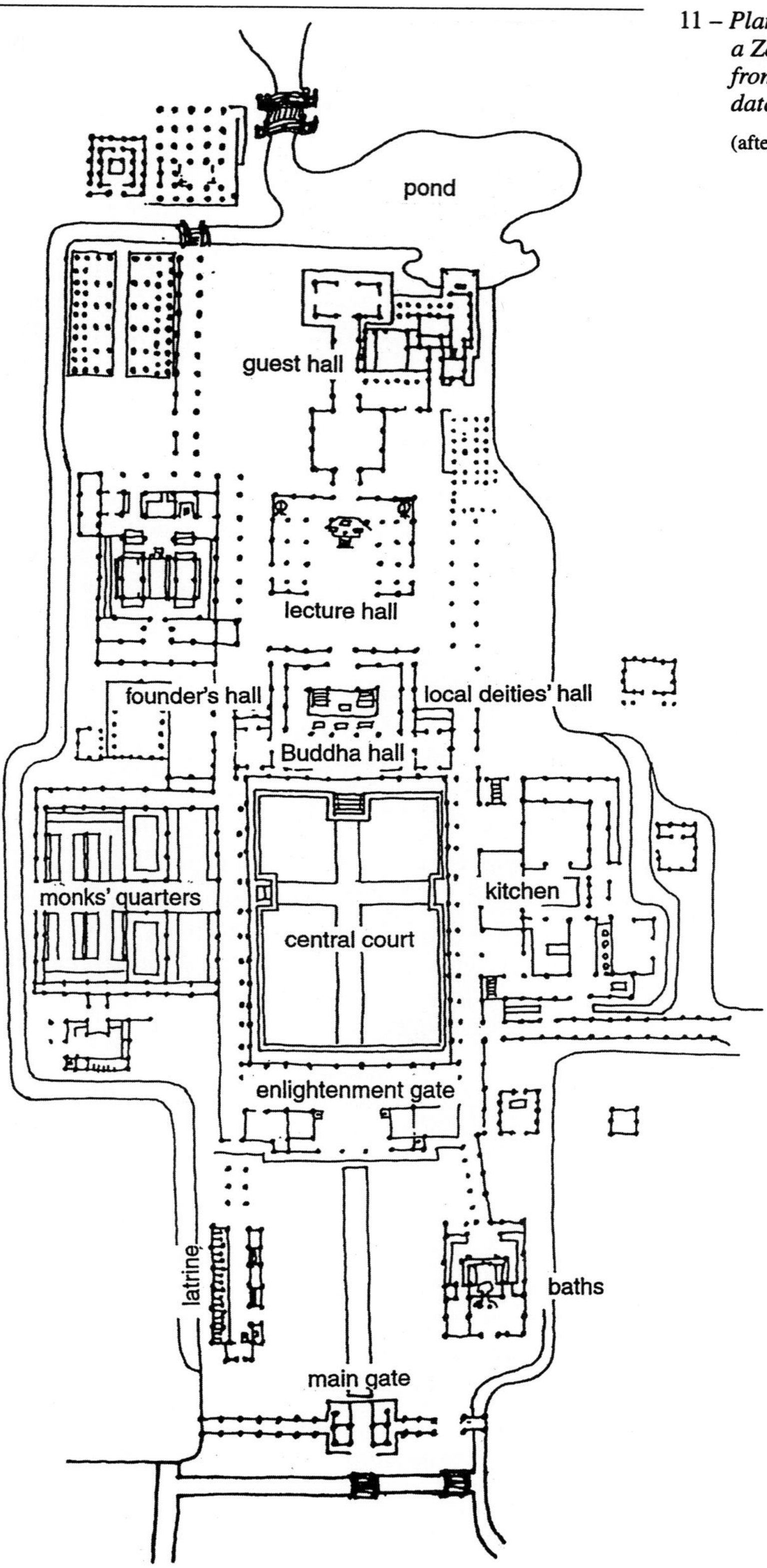

11 – *Plan of the Kenchōji, a Zen monastery, from a drawing dated 1331*

(after Nishi and Hozumi)

Nichiren (1222-1282) was teaching that, instead of reading the whole *Lotus Sūtra*, it sufficed to recite its title formula "Namu Myōhōrengekyō" (Veneration to the *Lotus Sūtra*) to save all beings of this world. These new schools, originating in the Tendai sect, had little use for Chinese texts and were eager to find a Japanese expression of Buddhism. In the preaching hall of monasteries, all texts were translated or read in Japanese (in fact, Nichiren preached in public spaces). Buddhism became simpler and spread amongst the lower social strata. Strengthened by new schools and communities organized by devotees for commemorating the Buddha Amida, patriarchal Buddhism entered a second stage. Large amounts of funds were collected in monasteries affiliated to the Ikkō and Nichiren schools, and concurrently with an expansion of currency circulation during the Muromachi period, the Ikkō school blossomed and impressive temples appeared, such as the Ishiyama Honganji (on the site of the present Osaka castle).

During the Edo period, strict controls were enforced on monasteries to limit the expanse of their domains and their annual income. The Edo government appointed an inspector of Buddhist monasteries and Shinto shrines, and the Bakufu issued a set of rules (*shoji hatto*) for each school that strengthened its control.

Previously, within the framework of the isolation policy adopted by Tokugawa Iemitsu (1604-1651) in 1639, which put an end to the preaching of Christianity by Iberian missionaries to Japan, Buddhist monasteries were used to record the lay population. In order to identify Christian converts, every subject was required to be inscribed in household registers kept in specific monasteries.

The Edo government ordered the feudal lords to turn their family monasteries (affiliated to the Rinzai, Sōtō or Jōdo school) into votive monasteries or into personal shrines for their ancestors' cult, to affiliate their vassals' temples to the Sōtō school; it also ordered those of the people to affiliate with other schools such as the Pure Land. In the cities of the feudal lords, monasteries were clustered in a special, monastic quarter (*teramachi*) under the lord's administration. With the shōgun government confiscating all the lands of monasteries and replacing them with an annual monetary pension, the wide monastic domains created in the Heian period disappeared. This pension allotment was maintained up to the early Meiji reforms, when it was finally abolished.

From the Heian period, syncretistic tendencies between native Japanese creeds and Buddhism resulted in Buddhist monasteries being attached to Shintō shrines (*jingūji*), where Japanese deities were considered as partial and fleeting manifestations of Buddhist figures, and were integrated in the Buddhist pantheon.

The interdiction of Buddhism in the Meiji era dissociated the two cults. Buddhist temples built as annex to the Shinto shrines disappeared and Buddhist monasteries had to survive on their own. Today, most of the major monasteries survive mostly as popular tourist sites, and other temples (like the Pure Land ones) specialize in funerary services and are often managed merely as cemeteries.

Still, Buddhism persists as a strong latent force at the root of Japanese beliefs and culture. From the Edo period, when public schools (*teragoya*) were set up inside monasteries, the role of Buddhism in popular teaching was significant. There, warriors and monks taught writing and arithmetic to the children of commoners, who thereby became familiar with Chinese characters. The present Japan rate of literacy, one of the highest in the world, comes certainly from the educational activity of Buddhist monasteries.

⁕⁕⁕
⁕

Annex 1

Some of the great monasteries bearing the name of *ōtera*. A more complete list may be found in H. Durt, under *Daiji*, *Hōbōgirin*, fasc. 6, pp. 704-711.

686 (Shuchō, 1):
Daikan daiji (Otsukasa no ōtera, later Daianji), Kawaradera (alias Gūfukuji), Asukadera (alias Hōkōji).

Before 690 (Jitō, 1):
Daikan daiji, Asukadera, Kawaradera, Toyoradera, Sakatadera.

703 (Taihō, 3, 1st month, 5th day):
Daianji, Yakushiji, Gangōji, Gūfukuji (Kawaradera).

735 (Tenpyō, 7, 5th month, 24th day):
Daianji, Yakushiji, Gangōji, Kōfukuji.

745 (Tenpyō, 17, 5th month, 4th day):
Daianji, Yakushiji, Gangōji, Kōfukuji.

749 (Tenpyō shōhō, 1, 5th intercalary month, 20th day):
Tōdaiji, Hōryuji, Gūfukuji, Shitennōji, Sōfukuji, Kayama Yakushiji, Kenkōji, Hokkeji.

Annex 2

Examples of emperors or important noblemen from Kyoto (col. 1) with their votive monastery (col. 2), the date of its dedication (col. 3) and the time elapsed after their enthronment or their nomination to a high position (col. 4).

Emperor Uda	Ninnaji	885.8.17	2 years after enthronment
Emperor Ennyū	Ennyūji	983.3.22	15 years after enthronment
Emperor Ichijō	Enkyōji	998.1.22	25 years after enthronment
Fujiwara no Michinaga	Hōjōji	1022.7.14	6 years after being *sesshō* and 6 years after becoming monk
Fujiwara no Yorinaga	Byōdōin	1052.3.28	35 years after being *sesshō* and *kanpaku*
Emperor Shirakawa	Hōshōji	1077.12.18	5 years after enthronment
Emperor Horikawa	Sonshōji	1102.7.21	16 years after enthronment
Emperor Toba	Saishōji	1118.12.17	21 years after enthronment
Taikenmon.in	Enshōji	1128.3.13	4 years after his *nyoin* title
Emperor Sūtoku	Jōshōji	1139.10.26	17 years after enthronment
EmperorKonoe	Enshōji	1149.3.20	8 years after enthronment

BIBLIOGRAPHY

FORTE, Antonino
1988 – "Mingtang and Buddhist Utopias in the History of the Astronomical Clock, the Tower, Statue and Armillary Sphere Constructed by Empress Wu", *Ismeo 59 - Pefeo 145.*

FUKUYAMA Toshio
1943 – *Nihon kenshiku-shi no kenkyū* [studies on Japanese architecture].

FUKUYAMA Toshio
1944 – *Narachō no jiin* [temples and monasteries of Nara period].

HIRAOKA Jōkai
1977 – " Tōdaiji" [the Tōdaiji Monastery], *Rekishi shinsho* 6, Kyōikusha, Tokyo.
1981 – *Nihon jiinsh i no kenkyū* [Studies on Buddhist Monasteries in Japan], Yoshikawa kōbunkan, Tokyo.

HIRAOKA Myōkai
1935 – "Tōdaiji-shi" [history of Tōdaiji monastery], *Kegonshū Tōdaiji*, Nara (2nd. ed. 1938).

ISHIDA Mosaku
1966 – " Tōdaiji to kokubunji" [Tōdaiji and provincial monasteries], *Nihon rekishi shinsho*, Shibundō, Tokyo (2nd. ed. 1973).

GADJIN Nagao
1980 – "The Architectural Tradition in Buddhist Monasticism", *Studies in the History of Buddhism* (Papers presented at the International Conference on the History of Buddhism at the University of Wisconsin, Madison, August 19-21, 1976), New Delhi, B.R. Publishing Corporation.

OOKA Minoru
1967 – "Nanto shichi daiji no kenkyū" [studies on the seven great monasteries of Nara], *Chūō kōron bijutsu shuppan*, Tokyo.
1973 – *Temples of Nara and their Art, Heibonsha Survey of Japanese Art, vol. 7*, New York and Tokyo, Weatherhill/Heibonsha.

NISHI, Kazuo; HOZUMI, Kazuo
1985 – *What is Japanese Architecture?*, Tokyo, Kodansha International, 144 p., maps, drawings, bibliography, index (paperback edition 1998)

PAINE, Robert Treat; SOPER, Alexander
1958 – *The Art and Architecture of Japan*, New Haven and London, Yale University Press (reprint 1981), 521 p., maps, drawings, photographs, bibliography, index, glossary.

SOPER, Alexander
1942 – *The Evolution of Buddhist Architecture in Japan*, New York, Hacker Art Books (reprinted 1978).

RÉSUMÉS

Pierre Pichard (p. 17)

LES MONASTÈRES BOUDDHIQUES INDIENS

Apparu en Inde au IVe siècle avant n. è., le bouddhisme en disparaît au douzième siècle. Aujourd'hui désertés, les monastères bouddhiques de l'Inde se présentent comme des sites archéologiques en général réduits à la base de leurs murs, à l'exception des régions himalayennes (Ladakh, Sikkhim) où le bouddhisme est encore vivant.

Les monastères constituent le plus souvent des fondations satellites autour d'un stūpa (Taxila, Sanchi), ou alternent avec des halls abritant des stupas (*caitya-gṛha*) dans les sites excavés (Karla, Nasik, Ajanta).

Dans la configuration courante du quartier monastique, une cour ou un hall central sensiblement carré est entouré de cellules sur trois ou quatre côtés, dans les monastères construits aussi bien que dans ceux excavés dans une falaise. À partir du Ve siècle, ce modèle intègre un temple axial qui abrite une statue du Bouddha, au centre de la rangée de cellules qui fait face à l'entrée.

Dans les cas extrêmes, l'inclusion du sanctuaire dans le monastère peut aller jusqu'à marquer le centre de la cour par un stūpa (Nagarjunakonda 38) ou un temple (Paharpur).

Ashley de Vos (p. 38)

LA TRADITION ARCHITECTURALE
DU MONASTÈRE BOUDDHIQUE À SRI LANKA

Au troisième siècle avant n. è., le roi de Lanka offre une partie de ses jardins à la communauté bouddhique pour y construire son premier monastère. Dans la capitale, Anuradhapura, vont ensuite s'élever de gigantesques stūpa entourés de monastères.

Trois types principaux émergent: le *pañcāyatana*, un quinconce de cinq bâtiments, enclos d'un mur, constitue une unité collégiale dans un ensemble monastique plus étendu; le *pabbata vihāra*, formé d'une double enceinte où quatre bâtiments rituels sont implantés dans la cour centrale (mais en évitant visiblement d'occuper son centre exact), et les cellules monastiques dans la cour périphérique; et le *padhānaghara pariveṇa*, situé hors des villes.

Aujourd'hui, les monastères sri lankais groupent généralement un stūpa, un temple (*vihāra*), un hall dordination ou salle capitulaire (*uposathāgāra*), l'arbre de la bodhi (*bodhighara*), une salle de prédication (*dharmasālā*), une bibliothèque et l'habitation des moines (*pansala*) et du supérieur.

Pierre Pichard (p. 59)

ANCIENS MONASTÈRES BIRMANS

Sur plus de 500 monastères identifiés à Pagan, capitale du premier royaume birman de 1044 à 1287, deux seulement suivent fidèlement le modèle indien (cellules autour d'une cour et temple face à l'entrée). La plupart des autres sont construits, aux XIIIe et XIVe siècles, selon le modèle inédit d'un édifice mixte, constitué d'un bâtiment de brique sensiblement cubique, réservé aux moines, précédé d'un hall ouvert sur piliers de bois pour la prédication et les réunions. Les monastères de ce type peuvent être des fondations isolées ou se grouper autour de grands stūpa, et aussi former les éléments multiples de grands complexes monastiques dont le plan rappelle celui des *pabbata vihāra* de Sri Lanka. Jusqu'au XIXe siècle (Amarapura, Mandalay), le monastère évolue selon une composition linéaire, où les édifices s'alignent sur une longue plate-forme de bois flanquée de perrons de maçonnerie.

François Robinne (p. 75)

LES MONASTÈRES VILLAGEOIS DE BIRMANIE CONTEMPORAINE.

Cette étude sur les monastères bouddhiques de Birmanie est basée sur les enquêtes ethnographiques menées ces dix dernières années en milieu rural. Elle porte plus spécifiquement sur trois monastères localisés dans les régions de Birmanie centrale et de l'État Shan, deux régions ayant en commun d'avoir été marquées par la double influence birmane et thaïe. En dépit des transformations successives qu'ils ont pu subir au cours de ces dernières décennies, les monastères en bois considérés ont par ailleurs en commun d'avoir été construits à la fin du XIXe siècle. À l'analyse des principales caractéristiques architecturales abordée dans un premier temps fait suite un rapide survol de la dimension sociale du monastère dans son rapport aux réseaux villageois.

Pierre Pichard (p. 93)

LE MONASTÈRE THAÏ

Le monastère siamois groupe plusieurs bâtiments, correspondant à des fonctions distinctes, sur un vaste espace délimité par une clôture percée de portails. Les plus anciens dont le plan reste lisible ont été construits à Sukhothai, Sri Sachanalai et Khamphaeng Phet à partir du XIIIe siècle. Seules les parties maçonnées (plate-formes et piliers) subsistent. Le hall d'assemblée (*wihan*) est généralement aligné avec un grand stūpa, tandis que le hall d'ordination (*ubosot*), plus petit, se trouve désaxé ou plus éloigné. Cette disposition perdure dans les monastères royaux d'Ayutthaya (XIV-XVIIIes siècles) où le stūpa reste l'élément dominant, mais sous la forme spécifique du *prang* dont la forme sinspire de la tour des temples khmers, au centre d'une cour entourée d'une galerie couverte. Après la fondation de Bangkok (1782) l'*ubosot* tend à devenir le bâtiment principal et la division entre le *buddhavasa* (l'espace du culte) et le *sanghavasa* (le quartier monastique) est souvent clairement marquée. Des compositions moins strictes et de tradition régionale ont été préservées hors de la capitale, en particulier dans le Nord et le Nord-Est de la Thaïlande.

On trouve aujourd'hui (1997) 30 377 monastères, inégalement répartis sur le territoire national, qui abritent quelque 270 000 moines.

Thada Sutthitham (p. 119)

L'ARCHITECTURE DES MONASTÈRES
DU NORD-EST DE LA THAÏLANDE

Deux types de monastères, du point de vue des rapports entre la communauté des moines (*saṅgha*) et de la société, se distinguent dans le Nord-Est de la Thaïlande: les monastères de village, étroitement liés à la vie des communautés locales, et les monastères dits "de forêt" théoriquement installés en dehors des établissements humains dans le but de s'isoler des activités séculaires.

Les monastères de village ont suivi l'expansion du peuplement lao dans l'actuel Nord-Est de la Thaïlande (Isan). À chaque nouveau village était adjoint un premier monastère construit sur un terrain assez vaste dont l'usage ou l'accès (zone publique, bâtiments, verger) n'était jamais restreint.

L'architecture des monastères d'Isan, bien qu'étroitement liée à celle des monastères bouddhiques du Centre et du Nord de la Thaïlande, possède des caractères particuliers bien évidents sur certains types de structures. On notera, par exemple, les stūpa ou *phra that*, les halls d'ordination ou *sim* et les bâtiments réservés à la prédication ou *ho chek* dont l'aspect original (plan, décoration, usage) les distinguent clairement des bâtiments correspondants dans le reste du pays.

Wiroj Srisuro (p. 131)

LES HALLS D'ORDINATION DU NORD-EST DE LA THAÏLANDE

Dans la région du Nord-Est (Isan) le *sim* (appelé *ubosot* dans le centre de la Thaïlande) est le second bâtiment du monastère après le reliquaire (*thāt*). Ce nom, qui désigne le hall d'ordination, trouve son origine dans l'établissement des limites (*sīmā*) définissant l'espace où peuvent être validés les actes officiels de la communauté. Construits au XIXe siècle, les *sim* étudiés sont de petits halls exclusivement réservés aux moines et leur entrée est interdite aux femmes.

La typologie distingue deux types principaux de *sim* dans l'Isan: les *sim* "ouverts" (sur piliers, sans porte mais avec un mur derrière l'image du Bouddha) et les *sim* "fermés" (par quatre murs, de bois ou de maçonnerie). Dans chaque catégorie, les *sim* (avec ou sans galerie) peuvent refléter un style purement régional, soit s'inspirer de styles "importés" où l'influence laotienne, vietnamienne ou européenne reste visible sous son interprétation locale.

François Lagirarde (p. 149)

UNE FORME DISTINCTIVE DE DÉVOTION
DANS LES MONASTÈRES THAÏS: LE CULTE DU MOINE VENTRIPOTENT

Dans les monastères theravādin d'Asie du Sud-Est, la dévotion des moines et des laïques se tourne avant tout vers les images du Bouddha, vers ses reliques ou les symboles liés à sa biographie. Les monastères relevant historiquement du bouddhisme thaï abritent régulièrement des statues de disciples, de "Grands Auditeurs" (*Mahāsāvaka*) ou de saints non-contemporains du Bouddha dont le culte est laissé libre, voire soigneusement organisé. Parmi ces disciples, le moine bedonnant, souvent obèse, appelé Sangkachai ou Kaccāyana, occupe à l'évidence la première place.

Si ce "Moine Ventripotent", connu des Môns puis des Birmans de Pagan, a disparu de Birmanie depuis plusieurs siècles, son image continue d'être révérée en pays thaï et son installation est possible dans tous les bâtiments monastiques. Lorsqu'une statue du Moine est d'une importance particulière (valeur intrinsèque ou volume gigantesque) un *wihan* spécial peut éventuellement lui être octroyé.

Un tel soin pour ce personnage original, inconnu de la tradition du Mahāvihāra de Sri Lanka, met probablement en évidence la force de résistance de certains aspects du bouddhisme des Môns établi au premier millénaire sur l'actuel territoire des civilisations thaïe et lao.

Louis Gabaude (p. 169)

UN PHÉNOMÈNE NOUVEAU
DANS LES MONASTÈRES THAÏS: LE STŪPA-MUSÉE

Au cours de leur histoire, les bouddhistes ont créé divers types de monuments et de bâtiments soit pour leur rappeler le Bouddha et les saints, soit pour abriter la communauté monastique, soit pour fournir à la communauté des laïcs des lieux de rassemblement et de culte. Dans la plupart des cas, un monastère thaï remplit toutes ces fonctions.

De nos jours, un nouveau type de bâtiment apparaît en Thaïlande qui résulte du culte des bonzes célèbres considérés comme "saints" ou "arahants". Il est souvent appelé "cetiya-musée". Conjuguant la forme d'un stūpa avec la fonction d'un musée, il expose les objets personnels du saint, ses livres, les amulettes qu'il a pu produire, et surtout, chaque fois que cela est possible, la preuve matérielle de sa sainteté: ses ossements cristallisés.

Michel Lorrillard (p. 187)

LES PREMIERS MONASTÈRES BOUDDHIQUES DU LAOS: DONNÉES MANUSCRITES ET ÉPIGRAPHIQUES

En l'absence de réels vestiges architecturaux, les seules sources qui nous renseignent sur les plus anciens monastères lao sont les chroniques historiques et les inscriptions. Les secondes attestent la présence au XVIe siècle d'un certain nombre d'édifices bouddhiques sur les bords immédiats du Mékong, entre Luang Prabang et Vientiane. Les premières, qu'il faudra considérer avec plus de prudence, évoquent des fondations religieuses dès la seconde moitié du XIVe siècle.

Les textes montrent l'importance originelle du stūpa et de l'arbre de la bodhi pour la délimitation de l'espace sacré. Ils mettent également en évidence le rapport étroit entre l'autorité royale et les monastères, et donc la fonction politique de ces derniers. Destinées à garantir les avantages accordés à ces fondations, les sources nous livrent en outre un grand nombre de données utiles pour une histoire économique du bouddhisme lao.

Christophe Pottier (p. 199)

L'*ĀŚRAMA* BOUDDHIQUE DE YAŚOVARMAN À ANGKOR

Les inscriptions du Xe siècle K290, K209 et K 701 donnent les règlements de trois fondations monastiques d'Angkor. George Cœdès pensait quelles étaient respectivement dédiées au Bouddha, à Śiva et à Viṣṇu, mais la stèle K290 n'avait pas été trouvée à son emplacement originel. L'analyse spatiale de la périphérie du baray oriental et les possibilités offertes par la télédétection ont maintenant permis d'identifier plus clairement les caractéristiques communes de ces sites monastiques, et de conclure qu'en fait quatre d'entre eux étaient implantés autour du baray, dédiés au Bouddha (Prasat Ong Mong 394 et stèle K290), à Brahmā (Prasat Prei 720 et stèle K209), à Viṣṇu (Prasat Kâmnâp 747 et stèle K701) et à Śiva (Prasat Kâmnâp CP175). Il apparaît en outre que le monastère śivaïte occupa originellement un autre site, sur la rive sud du baray comme les trois autres, mais aurait été déplacé sur la rive nord à la suite de la construction, soixante ans plus tard, du temple de Pre Rup.

Olivier de Bernon (p. 209)

ORGANISATION ET SYMBOLIQUE DES MONASTÈRES DU CAMBODGE

Il n'existe, pour les bouddhistes du Cambodge, comme pour tous ceux qui sont adeptes du bouddhisme theravāda, qu'un seul type de lieu de culte consacré: le *vatt*, ou plus proprement *vatt ārām* "lieu de l'exultation".

Le vatt est d'abord un lieu habité par au moins un moine (*bhikkhu*) ; c'est un espace orienté et défini dans un système de "limites" (*sīmā*) au sein desquelles la vie communautaire s'organise et surtout, hors desquelles l'accomplissement des rituels les plus importants n'est pas valide; c'est, enfin, un ensemble de bâtiments caractéristiques, que les bouddhistes khmers parcourent et pénètrent rituellement, en fonctions de représentations issues principalement des métaphores obstétricales habituelles du bouddhisme indochinois.

Min Bahadur Shakya (p. 219)

UN MONASTÈRE BOUDDHIQUE NEWAR,
LE HIRAṆYAVARṆA MAHĀVIHĀRA.

Toute proche de Kathmandu et bornée par quatre stūpa cardinaux, Patan (Lalitpur) serait la plus ancienne cité bouddhique du Népal. Le bouddhisme, attesté par des inscriptions dès le Ve siècle, aurait connu un âge d'or autour du Xe siècle. Cependant, sous l'influence des doctrines tantriques mahāyāna, les moines abandonnèrent progressivement le célibat entre le XIIe et le XVe siècle. Nombre de monastères bouddhiques furent construits à cette époque, tenus par des lignages de prêtres bouddhiques héréditaires (*śākya* et *vajrācārya*). Patan abrite aujourd'hui plus de 160 monastères (*bahā* et *bahī*), construits sur un modèle commun: une cour carrée entourée de bâtiments généralement sur deux niveaux, avec le sanctuaire principal face à l'entrée. Dans le Hiraṇyavarṇa Mahāvihāra, l'un des *bahā* les plus fameux, ce sanctuaire principal est dédié au Bouddha Śākyamuni, et plusieurs chapelles autour de la cour abritent les images du panthéon tantrique.

Corneille Jest (p. 245)

DU MONASTÈRE BOUDDHIQUE AU TEMPLE DE VILLAGE
AU DOLPO (NORD-OUEST DU NÉPAL): UNE APPROCHE HISTORIQUE.

La région de Dolpo, bien que située sur le versant méridional de la haute chaîne himalayenne, fait partie intégrante de l'aire de culture tibétaine. L'histoire de l'expansion du Bouddhisme à partir du XIIe siècle à Dolpo et sa pratique actuelle permettent de présenter les principes qui ont fixé les règles de fondation, de construction et de maintenance des monastères, temples et autres lieux de culte. Ainsi le complexe monastique de Yangtsher-Margom comprend le monastère proprement dit, des ermitages, lieux de méditation, mis en valeur dans un site exceptionnel considéré comme sacré.

Dolpo est devenu aujourd'hui un conservatoire de la tradition religieuse bouddhiste et dans le domaine de la conservation une référence pour des études comparatives. En effet il y a une prise de conscience de l'importance de la conservation des éléments tangibles comme les temples et les monastères, les membres des communautés devenant leurs gardiens vigilants.

Karma Wangchuk (p. 265)

DZONG ET *GOMPA* AU BHOUTAN

Bien que certains indices pourraient impliquer une date plus ancienne, l'établissement du bouddhisme au Bhoutan est attribué à la venue depuis le Tibet, au VIIIe siècle, du fondateur de l'école Nyingmapa, Padmasabhava (Guru Rinpoche).

Au XVIIe siècle, le Zhabdrung Ngawang Namgyal (1594-1651) fonde une chaîne de grands monastères fortifiés, les *dzong*, qui dominent les principales vallées du Bhoutan et en constituent le centre religieux et administratif.

Plus de 2000 *dzong* et *gompa* (monastères villageois) existent au Bhoutan. Dans leur forme actuelle, ils ne datent en général que des XVIIe et XVIIIe siècles mais leur fondation peut être beaucoup plus ancienne. D'autre part ils ont souvent été plusieurs fois modifiés ou agrandis, ou reconstruits après des incendies.

La plupart des monastères sont implantés sur des hauteurs, face à la vallée et souvent à une rivière sacrée. Une ou plusieurs cours intérieures sont utilisées pour les grandes cérémonies et les danses rituelles. L'édifice principal est une tour, l'*utse*, qui peut contenir plusieurs sanctuaires superposés dans ses étages. Les autres fonctions se répartissent autour des cours: hall d'assemblée et d'enseignement, bureaux, logements monastiques, cuisine et réserves.

La configuration générale du monastère dépend étroitement du terrain, souvent très accidenté.

Françoise Pommaret (p. 283)

LES MONASTÈRES BOUDDHIQUES DU TIBET

Introduit de l'Inde au Tibet aux VIIe et VIIIe siècles, le bouddhisme du Mahāyāna a connu une seconde diffusion dans la seconde moitié du Xe siècle avec la fondation des quatre grandes écoles religieuses. À la fin du XIVe siècle, l'école réformée des *dGe lugs pa* affirme sa domination lorsque le cinquième Dalai Lama devient le chef politique du pays.

Sous l'influence initiale de l'Inde et de la Chine, le Tibet a développé sa propre tradition architecturale, qui a influencé à son tour la Chine et la Mongolie.

L'architecture des monastères dépend étroitement de leur situation en terrain plat ou pentu, de l'altitude et du climat local, des matériaux disponibles. Certains sont isolés dans la montagne, d'autres au milieu des agglomérations, et leur implantation est définie en accord avec une géomancie dérivée des principes chinois, bien que le site idéal soit généralement impossible à trouver.

Le plan du monastère est à la fois systématique et organique, en général initialement régi par un *maṇḍala* puis modifié et agrandi au cours des siècles. De grands monastères d'enseignement comme Drepung ou Sera regroupent plusieurs collèges, eux-mêmes constitués de plusieurs bâtiments.

Les éléments importants du monastère sont le temple, sur un ou plusieurs étages, le hall d'assemblée (qui sert aussi de salle d'enseignement), souvent des stūpa, une bibliothèque et parfois un atelier d'impression des xylographies, et le quartier monastique, soit disposé autour d'une cour soit constitué d'habitations séparées. Peuvent s'y ajouter divers services comme les cuisines et les écuries, parfois une herboristerie et un atelier pour la fabrication de médicaments. Le tout est entouré d'un mur d'enceinte.

Isabelle Charleux et Vincent Goossaert (p. 305)

LE MONASTÈRE BOUDDHIQUE CHINOIS: INSTITUTION ET ARCHITECTURE.

Le monastère bouddhique s'est implanté en Chine depuis les débuts de notre ère en s'adaptant à un paysage où coexistent plusieurs formes d'institutions religieuses, consacrées au culte (temples) où à une communauté cléricale (taoïste, confucéenne). Dans ce contexte, le monastère bouddhique partage de nombreux éléments avec les autres institutions religieuses, tant dans le langage architectural que dans la décoration et l'art, tout en préservant des traits caractéristiques liés au mode de vie et aux exigences liturgiques du Saṅgha. L'histoire du monastère bouddhique chinois doit donc se comprendre dans une perspective de comparaison au sein d'un paysage religieux varié et d'analyse des spécificités du monastère bouddhique dans son plan et dans la diversité de ses bâtiments. Pour ce faire, on peut élaborer sur les analyses classiques de J. Prip-Moller et autres historiens de l'architecture et du bouddhisme, en prenant en compte l'état actuel des monastères restaurés et remis en fonctionnement ainsi que de diverses sources historiques qui permettent d'esquisser une évolution sur le long terme de l'organisation physique du monastère.

Isabelle Charleux (p. 351)

MONASTÈRES BOUDDHIQUES DE MONGOLIE INTÉRIEURE

Le bouddhisme Mahāyāna fut connu en Mongolie dès les IVe et Ve siècles, et au XIIIe siècle par ses écoles tibétaines, mais les constructions de ces époques n'ont pas survécu et les monastères ici décrits datent du XVIe au XXe siècle. En effet, le XVIe siècle a connu une véritable renaissance bouddhique, influencée par le Tibet et la Chine.

Au début du XXe siècle, on comptait 1340 monastères (dont 68 abritaient plus de 500 moines) en Mongolie intérieure. Depuis, la plupart ont été détruits et environ une centaine sont aujourd'hui de nouveau en activité.

L'implantation des monastères suit les règles des géomancies tibétaine et chinoise. On peut distinguer trois types de plans:

- Le monastère circulaire, sur le principe des campements de yourtes. Il s'applique plus particulièrement aux monastères nomades.
- Le monastère symétrique, sur le modèle chinois, avec ses halls principaux alignés sur l'axe d'une enceinte rectangulaire.
- Le monastère dispersé, qui dissémine ses bâtiments selon la configuration du terrain.

Les bâtiments principaux s'implantent en général au centre du côté nord et s'ouvrent au sud sur les cours. Une typologie est possible à partir de l'articulation du hall d'assemblée central et du sanctuaire principal, qui peuvent être réunis dans un bâtiment commun aussi bien que former deux édifices distincts. Les autres éléments du monastère comprennent des halls secondaires, des stūpa commémoratifs, les bureaux et services, le trésor et les résidences des moines.

Kim Dong-uk (p. 391)

LES MONASTÈRES BOUDDHIQUES EN CORÉE

Venu de Chine vers le IVe siècle, le bouddhisme a été religion d'État de la Corée du VIIe au XIIIe siècle, mais a été soumis à une répression intense après 1392. L'entrée des villes fut interdite aux moines (jusqu'en 1897) et les monastères bouddhiques ne subsistèrent que dans les régions écartées et montagneuses.

On compte aujourd'hui (1995) quelque 26 000 moines dans 11 561 monastères, et 23% de la population de Corée du Sud se déclare bouddhique.

Selon le modèle chinois, la composition spatiale des premiers monastères urbains, mis au jour par les fouilles archéologiques, était axée sur l'alignement du stūpa, du hall de la statue principale et du hall d'enseignement, dans une ou plusieurs enceintes.

Les monastères encore actifs, construits ou reconstruits depuis le XVIIe siècle, sont implantés dans les régions de montagne. Les plus grands s'organisent autour d'une succession de cours ménagées sur la pente ascendante, sur lesquelles s'ouvrent les halls principaux, tandis que des monastères plus modestes regroupent les mêmes éléments (halls, sanctuaires et quartier monastique) autour d'une cour unique.

Hiraoka Jōkai (p. 411)

FORMATION ET ÉVOLUTION DU MONASTÈRE BOUDDHIQUE AU JAPON

Le bouddhisme a été introduit au Japon depuis la Corée en 552, voire en 538. Aux premiers monastères, aménagés dans des résidences privées offertes par des familles de la noblesse ou de la cour, succédèrent de grands monastères où l'on priait pour la santé et le bonheur de l'empereur. Au VIIIe siècle, l'empereur Shōmu ordonna la construction de deux monastères bouddhiques, l'un pour les moines et l'autre pour les nonnes, dans chacune des 66 provinces du pays. Il fit aussi fondre de 743 à 752, près de sa capitale Nara, une gigantesque statue du Bouddha Vairocana, autour de laquelle se développa l'un des plus célèbres monastères japonais, le Tōdaiji. Les plans d'ensemble organisent dans la symétrie un nombre variable de halls et de stūpa, tandis qu'aux Xe et XIe siècles les halls majeurs s'aligneront entre un étang artificiel central et le quartier monastique, situé au fond de l'enceinte des grands monastères construits autour de Kyōtō, la nouvelle capitale.

Aux développements doctrinaux des différentes écoles bouddhiques (Shingon, Terre Pure, Zen) correspondent des types particuliers de monastère, qui restent composés d'éléments traditionnels: le hall central (*kondō*) qui abrite la statue principale, ouvert sur une cour en général entourée d'une galerie couverte (*kairō*); le stūpa (*tō*) sous la forme d'une tour à ossature de bois (pagode); le hall de prédication (*kōdō*); la bibliothèque (*kyōzō*); le quartier monastique (*sōbō*) avec le réfectoire et les installations de bains.

Le monastère était dirigé par un intendant assisté de trois directeurs, et sa communauté se divisait entre moines lettrés et bas clergé.
